AIRLIFT DOCTRINE

by

CHARLES E. MILLER, LT COL, USAF
Research Fellow
Airpower Research Institute

Air University Press
Maxwell Air Force Base, Alabama 36112-5532

March 1988

Library of Congress Cataloging-in-Publication Data

Miller, Charles E. (Charles Edward), 1948—
   Airlift Doctrine.

   "March 1988."
   Includes bibliographies.
   1. Airlift, Military—United States—History.
I. Title
UC333.M55   1988   358.4'4'0973   88-6293

              ISBN   1-58566-019-1

DISCLAIMER

This study represents the views of the author and does not necessarily reflect the official opinion of the Air University Center for Aerospace Doctrine, Research and Education (AUCADRE) or the Department of the Air Force. This publication has been reviewed by security and policy review authorities and is cleared for public release.

For sale by the Superintendent of Documents
US Government Printing Office
Washington DC 20402

To Phyllis Mae Miller

1925-1984

Contents

Chapter		Page
	DISCLAIMER	ii
	FOREWORD	vii
	ABOUT THE AUTHOR	ix
	INTRODUCTION	xi
1	THE PRE-WORLD WAR II ERA	1
	The Air Power Debate	1
	Air Transportation Ideas	9
	A New Air Transport Organization	13
	The Woodring Program	17
	Prewar Doctrine	19
	Prelude to World War II	21
	Notes	22
2	WORLDWIDE AIRLIFT IN THE WAR YEARS	27
	The Air Corps Ferrying Command	27
	June 1942	32
	The Air Transport Command	35
	Army Air Force Regulation 20-44	65
	The Nexus of Policy and Doctrine	67
	White and Green: Doctrinal Hallmarks	72
	The Strategic Airlift Heritage of World War II	73
	Notes	74
3	TROOP CARRIER AND THEATER AIRLIFT IN WORLD WAR II	79
	Origins of Troop Carrier Aviation	79
	The Mediterranean and European Campaigns	80
	Troop Carrier Operations in the Pacific	122
	Troop Carrier Aviation in the China-Burma-India Theater	139
	The Troop Carrier Heritage of World War II	151
	Notes	154
4	AIRLIFT IN THE POSTWAR ERA	161
	The Fiscal Context	162
	Postwar Airlift Consolidation Efforts	164
	Airlift in Support of the Korean War	194

Chapter		Page
	Troop Carrier Issues	205
	"Official" Doctrine	217
	Jet Transport Aircraft	221
	New Tactical Airlifts	224
	The Airlift Heritage of the Postwar Era	225
	Notes	226
5	THE TURBULENT YEARS	235
	The Airlift Policy Context	235
	The Congressional Context	242
	The Presidential Context	272
	The Airlift Heritage of the Turbulent Years	290
	Notes	291
6	THE VIETNAM ERA	299
	The Doctrinal Context	299
	Overwater Airlift	308
	Tactical Airlift in Vietnam	311
	Airlift Support of Ground Operations	317
	Strategic Airlift Support of SEA	326
	Estes on Airlift	343
	Airlift Consolidation	347
	The Doctrinal Context at the End	353
	The Airlift Doctrinal Heritage of the Vietnam Era	357
	Notes	358
7	THE MODERN AIRLIFT ERA	365
	The Mobility Triad	365
	The Congressionally Mandated Mobility Study	371
	A View from the Top	373
	A View from Inside	377
	The Doctrine Debate	383
	Official Airlift Doctrine	413
	The Airlift Doctrinal Heritage of the Modern Era	415
	Notes	416
8	IDEAS AND CONCEPTS	421
	Airlift at Risk	423
	Airlift Doctrine and National Strategy	424
	Some Thoughts on the Future of Airlift Doctrine	434

FOREWORD

Airlift is the movement of goods and people to where they are needed, when they are needed there. Since the 1920s there has been an evolving awareness and articulation of how to best organize, train, and equip airlift forces for that mission. The worldwide orientation of American foreign policy, the numerous threats to free world interests, and the speed and complexity of modern warfare have combined with political and resource constraints to produce today's airlift doctrine and force structure. Colonel Miller's study traces these many interrelationships to discover what critical airlift decisions were made, why they were made, and what they may mean in the future.

This is not a history of military airlift but rather an investigation of ideas and concepts as they have evolved and have been applied to warfighting. Airlift is the backbone of deterrence. A properly structured and equipped airlift force is critical to the successful execution of the national military strategy. How we think about airlift and how we translate those thoughts into a meaningful expression of how to develop, deploy, and employ airlift forces is vital to the national defense. Colonel Miller's study is a definitive step in that important process.

JOHN C. FRYER, JR.
Brigadier General, USAF
Commander
Center for Aerospace Doctrine,
Research, and Education

ABOUT THE AUTHOR

Lt Col Charles E. Miller

Lt Col Charles E. Miller was born at Lakehurst Naval Air Station, New Jersey. He attended college at West Virginia University, Morgantown, West Virginia, where he received his commission through AFROTC in 1970. He also attended graduate school at West Virginia University where he received his MA in rhetoric and public address in 1971. He came on active duty with the United States Air Force at Keesler Air Force Base, Mississippi, and then served as executive officer to the inspector general of the Aerospace Rescue and Recovery Service at Scott Air Force Base, Illinois. In 1973 he was assigned to Norton Air Force Base, California, where he was aide to the commander, 63d Military Airlift Wing, until 1975. He was next assigned as aide and executive officer to the commander, United States Air Forces Azores, Lajes Field, Azores. From 1976 until 1980, Colonel Miller was instructor, course director, assistant professor, and director of forensics in the Department of English at the United States Air Force Academy. In 1980 he was assigned to Headquarters Military Airlift Command, first as an action officer in the Policy and Doctrine Division, and then as chief of the Plans Integration Branch of the PPBS Division. In 1983 he was selected as the CINCMAC-sponsored visiting research fellow at the Airpower Research Institute, Maxwell Air Force Base, Alabama. He is currently assigned to the War and Mobilization Division, Headquarters United States Air Force, as an action officer. Colonel Miller, his wife Carolyn, and his daughters Kathleen and Amanda, currently live in Alexandria, Virginia.

INTRODUCTION

Unit histories, official reports, studies, and correspondence; articles in professional journals, and a modest level of personal experience bear out the fact that airlift doctrine has evolved. Discovering this evolution is only one step, albeit an important one. Knowing why a particular pronouncement was made is sometimes of equal importance. The changing of ideas can be traced and patterns do emerge. National military strategy, economics, politics, Air Force doctrine, and technical advancements all have an impact on the airlift decision recommenders and makers.

Airlift history can be filed into convenient time blocks: the pre-World War II era, World War II, the postwar period, the 1955 to 1965 era (which I call the turbulent years), the Vietnam experience, and the modern airlift era. There are overlaps in these divisions, but they do offer a degree of organization and continuity. Each also has a benchmark that serves as a measure of where airlift thinking stood—that defines the prominent themes of the period. In the pre-World War II era, for example, military air transportation emerged as an important, but tertiary service for the combat air arm. There was a growing, but slow recognition of its contributions to mobility and logistics matters, but primarily as they supported air power. World War II saw the invention, implementation, and refinement of both strategic air transportation and troop carrier aviation. The functions were separated by doctrine and practice—at least on the surface. However, even in those formative years there were overlaps in capabilities and missions. Both types of airlift suffered in the postwar era from resource poverty and were still officially separated. Between 1955 and 1965, they remained officially separate, with tactical airlift organizationally buried and Military Air Transport Service (MATS) threatened with execution. Only a radical change in national military strategy "saved" each mission. The Vietnam experience saw them once again, in the jargon of the day, interfaced, with capabilities and shortfalls put to severe tests. Following Vietnam, civilian and high-level military considerations caused these two functions to be consolidated and what appears to be permanently elevated to a level of national importance. The advent of the C-17/C-5/747 debate, coupled with the Congressionally Mandated Mobility Study, and the resulting Airlift Master Plan, placed airlift doctrine at a watershed. How to think about airlift is again an important public question.

As Col Dennis Drew, director for research, Air University Center for Aerospace Doctrine, Research, and Education, so aptly points out, "the word doctrine conjures up confusion and consternation." His offer of the definition of military doctrine as "what is officially believed and taught about the best way to conduct military affairs" is clear, concise, and functional. It implies a thought process—a comparing of alternatives, perhaps thorough discussion and debate. Its use of "officially believed" can be easily interpreted to include all organizational levels. And, the word taught opens up a significant source of ideas. The definition also makes it obvious that the *process* of arriving at the official doctrine is a valuable and legitimate area for study.

What is officially believed is reflected not only in "doctrinal documents" but also in policy decisions, budgets, and plans for the future. Doctrine does not necessarily have to be the result of a long, drawn out period of contemplation. It can be a hasty reaction to a tactical situation that turns out to be a good idea whose time has come. It can be the application of common sense or the result of a detailed economic analysis. It can even be devastatingly wrong. It still comes out doctrine. Doctrine making occurs at all levels of an organization, from the small unit battlefield leader who finds through trial and error that a particular way of doing things always seems to work out, to the President making strategic decisions. This study primarily concentrates on doctrine above unit-level tactics but, when necessary, will trace a "low-level" issue as it works its way upward. Colonel Drew's definition is so useful because of its very broadness.

CHAPTER 1

The Pre-World War II Era

The Air Force recently announced that the history of the Military Airlift Command (MAC) officially hearkens back to the creation of the Air Corps Ferrying Command in May of 1941.[1] However, important ideas and events concerning air transportation can be traced further back than that. In 1941 Gen Henry H. Arnold wrote in *Winged Warfare* of the importance of air transport:

> Any nation in building an air force cannot think of its fighting planes alone. This air transport service for troops, supplies, ambulances and medical service, and for the transport of artillery and heavy equipment is a necessary adjunct to the maintenance of any efficient fighting force in the field. The speed and range of modern air forces makes it imperative that they be self-sustaining. The speed of the modern mechanized forces makes it distinctly advisable that at least a portion of their supply columns and agencies travel through the air.[2]

General Arnold was speaking from almost 20 years of collective experience and thinking about air transportation.

Air power leaders in the 1920s were primarily concerned with defining air power as an entity in and of itself—with the debates focused on the fundamental questions of a separate air arm and issues of bombardment, pursuit, observation, and attack aviation. Air transport was not used as an example in these arguments. The intimate linkage that we see today between airlift and ground forces would not have been a particularly persuasive argument for air power enthusiasts in the 1920s.[3]

This is not to say that there was no action concerning air transport. There were 88 types of transport aircraft purchased or tested by 1930, and military air transports were in constant demand by the Air Service (as it was called until 1926). However, "there was no real theory of use. The concept of aerial transport as an element of the Air Service's tactical function had not been thought out to the point where it could be defined in terms of a definite policy with clear-cut objectives."[4] What did and did not occur concerning air transportation in the 1920s and 1930s has to be viewed in the broader context of many other air power happenings.

The Air Power Debate

At the end of the First World War, "the Air Service had to face the sober realities of life in the peacetime US Army. The wartime machinery of expansion had to be thrown into reverse."[5] With these few words the noted Air Force historian Alfred

Courtesy Air Force Art Collection

Figure 1. Randolph Advertising Art (no artist noted).

Goldberg started his story of the cancellation of 13,000 aircraft orders, demobilization of nearly 200,000 airmen, and the liquidation of nearly 90 percent of the existing aircraft industry.[6] In 1920 the Congress provided only one-third of the funds necessary to man the Air Service at levels approved by the General Staff causing a 50-percent cut in overall strength. The director of the Air Service provided a succinct description of the situation: "Not a dollar is available for the purchase of new aircraft."[7]

All, however, was not bad news, at least for the air power moderates. In the same year Congress also made the Air Service a combatant arm of the Army. This was very much in keeping with the desires of Gen John Pershing. "An air force, acting independently, can of its own account neither win a war at the present time nor, so far as we can tell, at any time in the future" wrote General Pershing in January of 1920.[8] Instead he stressed that it was an essential combat branch and should be an integral part of the Army during peace and war.

The Lassiter Board

The concept of a General Headquarters (GHQ) Air Force combat force evolved during the early 1920s. In his annual report of the chief of the Air Service in 1922, Maj Gen Mason Patrick noted that

> in a properly balanced air service, 20 percent of the total strength should be made up of observation units and the remaining 80 percent devoted to "air force" or combat aviation. In the present organization . . . this ratio has been departed from to such an extent that 38 percent of the total strength is "air service."[9]

He suggested an additional organization with more combat units. In a letter from the War Department's adjutant general, Col H. H. Tebbetts expressed an appreciation of the "growing importance of aviation with the National Defense" and asked for a study of the measures necessary "to place the peace establishment of the Air Service upon a basis adequate to meet the approved wartime expansion."[10] General Patrick answered that "all air force troops, that is, attack, bombardment, and pursuit aviation, should be concentrated in a pool in GHQ Reserve," instead of parceled out to Army field commanders.[11] Included in his proposed organization were 18 service squadrons totaling 36 planes with transport type missions.[12] He presented the same proposal to a board of general staff officers headed by Maj Gen William Lassiter in March of 1923, calling for the expenditure of some $25 million per year for 10 years to meet the force goals envisioned.[13] The Lassiter Board's report acknowledged that the peacetime organization of the Air Service bore no relation to its wartime mission and that experiences gained since 1920 called for a review of organizational issues as well.[14] It concurred with the $25 million calculation, but modified the Patrick GHQ proposal. Instead of assigning all combat aircraft to a reserve, it continued the practice of assigning portions directly to the field armies. It did, however, allow for the assignment of

> Air Force bombardment and pursuit aviation . . . directly under General Headquarters for assignment to special and strategical missions . . . in connection with the operation of the ground troops or entirely independent of them. This force should be organized into large units, insuring great mobility and independence of action.[15]

In April 1923 the Secretary of War approved in principle a program for increasing the strength of the Air Service, but as of June 1924, the program had not been forwarded to Congress. Even though the War Department approved GHQ recommendations of the Lassiter Board, the chief of the Air Service was forced to write to the adjutant general that "the Air Service is today practically demobilized and unable to play its part in any national emergency."[16]

The Air Corps Act

The year 1926 served as a milestone of sorts for air power, for it saw the continued, albeit incremental, recognition of the special advantages offered by the airplane. In response to recommendations by a board headed by Dwight Morrow, which reported to President Coolidge, the Air Corps Act of 1926 changed the name of the Air Service to the Air Corps, created an assistant secretary of war for air, authorized air sections within the War Department, and initiated the delayed five-year expansion program for the Air Corps. "Viewed in retrospect, the Air Corps Act of 1926 was only one of several pieces of legislation which manifested a belief within Congress that the pioneering years of aviation were ending."[17] In spite of the fact that hardly any of his personal recommendations for the legislation were adopted, General Patrick called the Act "a long step in the right direction."[18]

In preparation for submission of the five-year plan, the G-3 Division of the General Staff originally used wording to the effect that 2,200 airplanes, *not including* those on order, would be authorized. At submission that wording was changed to reflect 2,200 airplanes *including* those on order. In the resulting Air Corps Act of 1926, Congress authorized 1,800 aircraft "provided that the necessary replacement of airplanes shall not exceed approximately 400 annually."[19]

A five-year plan *proposed* by the Air Corps called for a total of 3,530 airplanes and asked the War Department to sponsor changes to the Air Corps Act in support of the new number. The grand total was arrived at by consideration of such factors as obsolescence of the current fleet, crashes, metal fatigue, natural deterioration (corrosion), and the need for a 50-percent reserve, as practiced by the Navy. Of the 3,530, 158 were to be cargo airplanes, mostly assigned to the GHQ units.[20] Considering that as of 30 June 1929, there were 31 cargo planes on hand and 10 on order but undelivered, that particular segment of the expansion was significant. The Air Corps also predicted that the following year one-half of the cargo fleet would be obsolete and would have to be replaced. Due to funding delays, the five-year program did not start until 1927, with a goal of 800 serviceable aircraft.[21]

None of the numbers matched up with the supposed requirement for cargo planes submitted to the War Department in mid-1929. The Army chief of staff had created a Survey of Preparedness Committee to document known military requirements. The critical question for the Air Corps was "the requirement in airplanes of every type for a force of 2 Field Armies of approximately 1,000,000 men."[22] Maj Gen James Fechet, chief of the Air Corps, provided an answer that included 171 cargo planes to support the air power associated with such an organization.[23] All the numbers were for naught, however, because by November 1929 General Fechet was forced to tell the adjutant general that "as chief of the Air Corps I cannot carry out the statutory requirements of the five-year program unless adequate funds are provided."[24] Noting that the program was about $50 million behind schedule as of its third increment and that it was beyond the realm of probability that such funds would be forthcoming, General Fechet recommended that "the size of the Air Corps be scaled down so that the tactical units may be fully equipped and maintained."[25]

The Drum Board

In October 1933, a War Department board headed by Maj Gen Hugh Drum, after a thorough review of the defensive plans of the Army, validated the idea of a GHQ Air Force. The board recognized the flexibility of such a force in its ability to concentrate power in any area of the United States.[26] However, the board also noted that every branch of the Army was well below required strength and said emphatically that "the War Department should take no action and Congress should make no appropriation towards carrying out the recommendations contained herein for any increase of the Air Corps' 1,800 serviceable airplanes which will be at the expense of the other arms and branches of the military establishment."[27] They recognized the need for 2,320 airplanes, but the War Department directed the chief of the Air Corps to prepare a plan "in which the procurement objective and the reorganization of the Air Corps may be coordinated and effected progressively."[28] The board report and the War Department directive both noted that the 2,320 planes seemed an attainable goal within the parameters described. The number of cargo planes authorized by the War Department was 105, regardless of what total Air Corps size was achieved.[29] The Drum Board allowed 120 and the chief of the Air Corps wanted between 200 and 250. Maj Gen Benjamin Foulois also wanted a total force of over 4,400 planes.[30]

The Baker Board

In April 1934, the secretary of war appointed former Secretary of War Newton Baker to head a board that was to survey the Army Air Corps as an agency of national defense, to study the proper relationship between Army aviation and civil aviation, and to point out the lessons learned from flying the mail.[31] In 25 days the board heard 105 witnesses and took over 4,000 pages of testimony. The Baker Board made several observations and recommendations that were critical to air transportation. Literally its first major point was that "the most striking development in the commercial field is the progress made in scheduled airline transport and the impetus given to the consequent improvement in aircraft and aircraft accessories and facilities."[32] It cited great increases in general flying and airmail mileage and significant improvements in safety records. Almost in passing, the Army Air Corps was also noted as having made substantial progress, with many of the improvements in commercial aviation "pioneered, and in certain instances developed, by the Army Air Corps."[33] The board, however, was enamored with civil aviation, especially air transport:

> One of the most important recent developments in civil aviation is the production of the high speed, long range, large capacity passenger and cargo air transport. This type of airplane with certain structural changes in its design can be so constructed as to be adapted for military use. There are other types of commercial airplanes now being built which without material modification may be used for some military purposes. The development along the lines indicated creates a new and heretofore unexpected source of production in the event of emergency.[34]

The emerging civil aviation industry was clearly important to the national defense:

> There should be a very close liaison between civil and military aviation but the control of the two systems, civil and military, must be separate and distinct. . . . The granting of government subsidies to provide for the conversion of commercial airplanes to military airplanes is undesirable. The use of commercial airplanes as a reserve of transport and cargo is desirable.[35]

The board also recommended this close liaison "in order to familiarize the Air Corps with the latest developments in use in commercial air transport."[36] Although subsidizing the commercial lines to convert their cargo planes was not desirable, "the Army Air Corps should whenever possible use converted commercial air transport of acceptable performance for cargo and transport airplanes."[37] The commercial planes were preferred because the "latest technical developments are adopted much more rapidly in commercial air transport than in military types of airplanes. In general, it seems desirable that cargo and transport airplanes procured by the Air Corps be developed from types in use in commercial service and in production, instead of specially developed types that would not be available in large quantities in the event of an emergency."[38]

The Baker Board recommended what the earlier Drum Board had also suggested, that is

> a General Headquarters Air Force comprising all air combat units and auxiliaries thereto organized and trained as a homogeneous unit capable of operating in close cooperation with the ground forces or independent thereof, and coming under the direct control of the Commander in Chief in war and the Chief of Staff in peace.[39]

They wanted the chief of the Air Corps to lead the business side of the Air Corps—the procurement and supply functions. He did not have to be, in fact should not be, a flying officer. The principle of basing air units at strategic locations in peacetime was not necessary because of the flexibility of the air component. "With adequate landing fields in readiness, the great mobility of the Air Corps permits its rapid concentration in any critical area."[40]

The board urged immediate organization of the GHQ Air Force "commanded by a leader with suitable general officers' rank who has had broad experience as an airplane pilot," also noting that his "headquarters should be with his troops, away from Washington."[41] The board set the minimum number of airplanes necessary to meet peacetime requirements at 2,320, with modification of this number allowed by subsequent War Department studies.[42] Since an "adequate aircraft industry" was in the national interest because of the need to build aircraft in "the first few and vitally important months of a war," the board suggested that a normal annual replacement of the recommended force structure for the Air Corps (plus the Navy) would ensure a healthy production base.[43]

Maj Walter Frank, chief of the Air Corps Plans Division, told the Baker Board that the Air Corps had been prepared "to show the advantage to the operation of the Air Corps of the establishment of aerial transport facilities for supplying Air Corps units in time of war in the theater of operations."[44] No action had been taken, he reported, because the Air Corps was limited to 1,800 airplanes and "even 1,800 will not give [us] an Air Force that meets the minimum requirements for the air defense of the United States. Therefore, the Air Corps did not feel justified in diverting any additional number of that 1,800 from combat to supply planes."[45]

Maj Gen Benjamin Foulois, chief of the Air Corps, took strong exception to the Baker Board's conclusions concerning using existing commercial transport planes. His arguments in November of 1934, although ultimately rejected on economic grounds, were right on the mark:

> While the desirability of utilizing standard commercial transports for military cargo- and passenger-carrying is thoroughly recognized by this office, the following facts must be borne in mind:
>
> a. Commercial transports are built primarily for high speed passenger-carrying with every attention paid to the comfort of the passengers.
>
> b. Commercial transports operate from large landing fields located near large centers of population and, hence, can afford to have high landing speeds and run considerable distances before taking off. They are not designed to get in and out of small fields with heavy loads.
>
> c. Commercial transports are not designed to carry heavy concentrated loads of bulky articles which require large openings in the fuselage for loading and unloading purposes.
>
> d. Commercial transports have achieved extremely high speed at the cost of reduced load-carrying capacity, small fuselages and very large and powerful power plants.
>
> e. The military cargo airplane does not require extremely high speed and, consequently, does not need large powerful expensive power plants.
>
> f. The military cargo airplane should be designed primarily to carry heavy and bulky loads of freight with the comfort of the passengers distinctly a secondary matter.
>
> g. The military cargo airplane to be of real value to air units under service conditions must be capable of getting into and out of small fields which, in time of peace, would be considered only as emergency fields. This requirement called for low landing speeds, quick take-offs and the ability to clear obstacles safely, immediately after leaving the ground, during both daylight and night flights.
>
> h. The comparison between the commercial transport and the military cargo airplane is practically identical with that between the passenger automobile and the cargo-carrying truck. While it is true that the passenger automobile can carry a certain amount of freight, true economy demands the use of a cargo truck for such purposes.

AIRLIFT DOCTRINE

> i. Commercial airplane manufacturers are not specializing in the development of cargo-carrying airplanes as such, so that if a cargo airplane is desired by the Army Air Corps it must be developed under government supervision and with government funds, primarily as a cargo airplane, with the capability of conversion for passenger-carrying or air ambulance work as secondary considerations.
>
> j. The cost per pound mile of carrying cargo will be immeasurably higher in the case of a converted high speed passenger transport than in an airplane designed originally as a medium speed freight carrier.[46]

The boards of the 1920s and 1930s (and there were many more than covered here) were pointed to one purpose, after all the chaff is cleared away, to discuss the question of a separate air arm. Some of them were mere rubber stamps for the prevailing thoughts of senior Army leaders. Others were honest brokers. The fruitful expression of the theories of air power was an incremental process and the debates took place in the relative open. The public was more than aware of the emergence of aviation as an effective military and civilian tool. The advocates of air power had ample opportunity to express their ideas. It is understandable that not all the ideas were well developed or well expressed. Those who called for a separate air arm were right—just ahead of their times. They had to exist in an era of budgetary limitations, isolationist sentiments, and organizational inertia. Actually, a good argument can be made that given these severe restraints, they were quite successful. Some, however, were impatient to the point of evangelistic indignation. With the benefit of hindsight, we can see establishment compromises and recognition of the special features of air power, as they became evident. After all, the Air Service did become a combat arm, a separate GHQ "striking force" was organized, and considerable sums of money were spent on airplanes and airmen.

Ideas about air transportation were not in the forefront. Combat was the issue; concerns about support issues came later. As the extreme mobility and flexibility of the airplane became more obvious, so too the importance of transportation became an issue. The airplane pilots always used their machines to haul spare parts, mechanics, and blankets. As the GHQ concept grew, the logisticians rose in importance. Enthusiasts could not argue that air power is an essential element of defending the nation, especially when limited to the bounds of the continent, if they could not deploy and supply air forces in a manner that allowed air power flexibility to be effective. The GHQ idea was absolutely essential to the development of air transport thinking. As the world view of the strategists grew, the importance of the airplane as a deployer and resupplier also grew.

Even the recognition of the transporter as important to air power was limited. The concept of deploying, in the modern sense, a large army was technologically limited. They just did not have the airplanes with lift capability to consider moving a reasonably sized portion of that 1,000,000-man army any distance. To be sure, the planners thought about using the civil airlines, but trains and trucks were what were available within the continental limits of their thinking, and ships were the way to get overseas. Capable, long-range airplanes were a thing of the future. Even the long-range bombers of the visionaries were not the carriers of the huge tonnages needed to move an army.

Air Transportation Ideas

There was evidence of the future value of air transport in the 1920s. In 1921, for example, when the General Staff circulated a questionnaire concerning future trends of aerial warfare, the Air Service Engineering Division's response "suggested that in the event of war, ground attack airplanes would be efficiently reinforced by airborne troops landed behind the enemy's line. If the terrain were such that it is impossible for the craft to land, small detachments could drop by parachute."[47] The division also noted that airborne troops could be used to capture such notorious bandits as Pancho Villa. Critically, the Engineering Division also proposed that the government establish an air transportation program in peacetime. "This could be accomplished through either the agency of subsidized commercial lines or an aerial transport system similar to that for troop transports on water."[48] The 1923 Army Field Services Regulation recognized that the transportation system in a theater or operation could include rail, road, water, and air. Air employment was to be "ordinarily limited to emergency transport of mail, ammunition, staff officers, carriers, and possibly small detachments."[49]

The Air Service Tactical School at Langley Field joined the discussions in its 1924-25 academic offerings maintaining "that the maneuverability of an Air Service Unit was limited to that of its ground components despite the fact that its flying equipment and personnel were transported great distances within a short time."[50] Interestingly, one of the early papers prepared at the Army War College concerning air transportation was a polemic against the bomber, concluding that airplanes were good for nothing except transportation.[51]

The early maneuvers of the Air Service/Air Corps give some indication that those operators were learning their air transport lessons. The 1925 maneuvers, held at Mitchell Field, New York, and Langley Field, Virginia, were under the command of Brig Gen James Fechet. His staff included Maj Carl Spaatz, Capt Ira Eaker, and Maj Henry H. ("Hap") Arnold. The first major conclusion of the 1925 maneuver staff was that "air transports are essential for the movement of an Air Force. The defense of our coastline by an air force depends to a large extent on the mobility of the forces engaged."[52] The exercise was so designed as to leave doubt as to the exact location of the enemy attack until the last possible movement and "the change of base of the air brigade to meet this change in the enemy's plans could be accomplished only with the assistance of air transports."[53]

The 1927 maneuvers planned for the air corps units to concentrate at San Antonio, Texas. This time their function was to support the ground operations of a

AIRLIFT DOCTRINE

maneuvering army. General Fechet made it clear that Air Corps successes in this maneuver were limited:

> Our concentration, I believe, demonstrated the ability of the Air Corps to move large distances and operate for a short period of time with comparatively few enlisted men and those such as can be transported by aerial transport. However, I think we should realize also that the units we had here, had available, facilities, transportation and supplies which we did not bring with us by air [sic]. Conditions for air operations here were almost ideal and would not necessarily be obtained in actual operations.[54]

Maj Gen Mason Patrick, chief of the Air Corps, said that Fechet was "right in reference to supplies, which brings up the question of transports. We are working on that particular problem now. Spare parts and men must be transported by air and kept up with land troops, at least in time to serve our purpose."[55] Lt Col C. C. Culver, commandant of the Air Corps Tactical School (ACTS), suggested that one way to deal with emerging air transport problems was to test them out in the next maneuvers, recommending that the 1928 maneuvers demonstrate that "it is practicable to supply Air Corps troops by air."[56]

The 1928 maneuvers, between Virginia Beach and Langley Field, fulfilled the Culver recommendation, with 14 bombers carrying 73,721 pounds of equipment and personnel. All but 8,000 pounds was delivered between seven in the morning and noon of the first day. The group airdrome officer reported the remaining 8,000 pounds could easily have been carried by three that afternoon but the cargo was gasoline not needed immediately and "it was desired to allow officers and men to have their usual Wednesday half holiday."[57]

The report of the ACTS supply officer for the Virginia Beach maneuvers said that there were two unit moves of 30 miles each without interruption to operations. "Except that air transport was utilized in all cases the supply was entirely normal." The report also suggested that either a platform be built to carry six passengers in the bomb bays of their bombers or that at least one transport to each few bombers be used in any move.[58] The reporting officer, Maj H. H. C. Richards, thought there should be a minimum of assigned transports.

> Provision of a large number of transports would simplify the transportation problem [and permit] carrying a large advance and rear personnel echelon economically. It would make the economical transportation of bulky freight easier. On the other hand, it is an extra type and, by, so much, complicates the supply problem.
>
> The transports which may be idle cannot be used for bombers in an emergency.
>
> In the future, air transport squadrons will probably be equipped with types of planes no longer suitable for use on the front.

> War plans (made during peace) should be based on the use of bombers for transports. A few transports (in the proportion of 1 transport to 4 bombers) should be provided. If it be possible to furnish additional transports the plans as drawn will be, by so much, easier of execution.[59]

His conclusion was that "movement of Air Corps units by air is entirely practicable and, if not the normal means of changing stations, will be much used in future wars."[60] It interrupted operations less than either rail or truck movement and overcame congested roads. Supply of attack units by air would be difficult due to the need to carry large numbers of bombs, but supply of advanced airdromes "can quite readily be accomplished by air."[61]

An Air Materiel Command historical study claims that the beginning of air transport shipments of supplies for the Air Service began in June 1922 when the Air Service devised a model airways "to maintain a regular schedule for aerial transportation of government officials and express."[62] The assistant executive of the Office of the Chief of the Air Corps, H. R. Harmon, said the model airways was devised "mainly to show the American public what can be done with the airplane as a carrier and to advertise American aviation and secondly, to obtain certain statistics pertaining to flying over given distances."[63] In its first eight and one-half months of operation, the airways carried over 11,000 pounds of freight. The system began by serving Bolling, McCook, Langley, and Mitchell Fields and, by the end of 1923, had added Fairfield, Selfridge, and Chanute Fields and a western division for service to Kelly, Brooks, San Antonio, and Scott Fields.[64] By August of 1925, Maj A. W. Robins, commanding officer at the Fairfield Air Depot was able to report that "the Airway at present is taxed to its fullest capacity, both in passenger reservations and in increased cargo."[65] He recommended the purchase of "ten Douglas airplanes of a new type especially designed for cargo carrying" to replace the small, open-cockpit DeHavillands that had little capacity for stowing bulky packages. The experimental model airways was a success but was dissolved when the Air Corps was created in 1926.

The ACTS report received support from the commander of the 2d Bombardment Group, Maj Hugh J. Knerr, who claimed the Air Corps must develop cargo planes to achieve independence. He believed the 1928 maneuvers had demonstrated that "air units could be self-sustaining."[66]

The Knerr proposal, maneuver reports, and model airways experience convinced the Materiel Division, which recommended the activation of one or more air transport squadrons at designated depots to obtain test data. Their proposal not only allowed the gathering of operational experience, it also provided for the capability to transport supply items and a pool of transport aircraft for the ubiquitous "miscellaneous purposes."[67] The chief of the Air Corps directed the inauguration of a transport supply service within each of the four depot control areas, with two aircraft per depot.

Knerr's arguments reflected a fairly sophisticated degree of thinking concerning the needs of the military in future wars. He said that the peacetime function of the Field Service Section of the Materiel Division was "largely one of data compilation and financial estimation," whereas he proposed "to enlarge these functions to include the development of services and methods that will stand up under the transition to, and demands of, war conditions."[68] This appears to be a very apt expression of the "think war" attitude of later years. He continued this line by arguing that in order to prepare for its wartime mission, such a service must "be employed in the routine accomplishment of peacetime requirements. Only by practical everyday employment of these services and methods can we keep them up to date."[69] Knerr did not invent the concept of preparing for war by practicing in peace, but he may have been the first to apply it to air transportation. His theory of air logistics was relatively straightforward: use the inherent speed of air transport to resupply units from the rear, where the risks of loss are much less.[70] Tying this to air power was a simple enough process; he said that every unbiased study concluded that the success of a war plan depended on the success of the air force assigned to the problem. The next logical step was that the success of the air force was "in turn a direct consequence of the functioning of the logistical elements of the air force itself, as distinct from the G-4 function of the ground forces."[71]

He rolled the whole concept together rather neatly arguing that

> in order to obtain the maximum/mobility for an air force in active operation, it is obvious that the transportation item is the controlling factor. If an air force is tied down to railheads and its service of supply dependent upon motor transportation, its mobility is that of the flat car and the truck. The ideal situation is one wherein the air force is maintained and accomplishes all of its transportation by air.[72]

Forecasting some vital concerns of the 1980s, Major Knerr also justified air transportation development in terms of the realities of the battlefield.

> A very great misconception exists within the Air Corps as to how it is going to function under field conditions. Too great dependence is being placed upon airdrome facilities such as one encounters on a transcontinental flight. We should boldly face the fact that there are going to be no facilities, no airdromes, no gas trucks, no lights, nothing but the bare hands of the ships' crews. . . . To exist within striking distance of our enemy, we must build up a system of supply that will work under conditions of extreme dispersion.[73]

Like countless planners who came after him, he attempted to quantify the airlift requirement, calculating that "the number required is not relatively great. For example, in order to mobilize and maintain in active operation the Air Force required by a Field Army of 1 million men, 1 transport wing of 5 squadrons with a total of 235 airplanes is required."[74] His claim that these 235 transports of 3,000-pound payloads were going to deploy a 9,000-man, 1,600-airplane force and supply "every ration, every round of ammunition, every bomb, every gallon of fuel, and oil" and evacuate the wounded and clean up salvage may be somewhat "soft."[75] A critique of Major Knerr's proposal by an Army War College captain in 1932 missed the essence of the proposal but made an interesting observation for his times:

> Of course, it may happen that the commander of our field forces will not appreciate the capabilities of our air force and that he may fail to make proper provisions for its supply. But it is my opinion that under such a commander the situation of our ground forces soon would be so grave that Major Knerr's fleet of cargo airplanes also would be taken from our air force and placed in the service of our ground troops.[76]

The Army War College during this time actively engaged in the many debates concerning air power and offered a course on *Motor and Air Transportation in the Theater of Operations*. The student seminar for the 1932-33 class provided some insightful observations about air transportation of the times by noting that "no authoritative regulations exist for the organization, control, and operation of air transport in the theater of operation" but that "air transport in major warfare should be used when practicable for supply of air combat units, for evacuation, and for emergency troop movements."[77] The students recommended that the "control of all airplanes in a theater of operations be centralized in the commander of the theater."[78] They enclosed a historical annex to their report as evidence, presumably, of the desirability of their recommendations. The annex referred to the parachuting of personnel and machine guns at Brooks Field, aerial resupply of the Pershing expedition in Mexico, extensive use of air transportation by the Marine Corps in Nicaragua, and several examples of foreign air transport operations.[79]

A New Air Transport Organization

When the transport supply program began in January 1932, it suffered the defect of decentralization. The aircraft were used primarily to improve the supply systems of the individual air depot districts rather than to provide the nucleus from which "a highly efficient logistic mechanism could be developed in a national emergency."[80] As Dr Robert Futrell observes, "not many Air Corps leaders had as yet grasped the roles and missions of air transport aviation."[81] By October of 1932, the faults of the system apparently were becoming obvious. Lt Col Albert Sneed, commander of the Fairfield Air Depot, "presented the beginning of a true concept of airpower."[82] In essence, he urged that Air Corps officers had too limited a view of air power—they thought only in terms of destruction. "There was a larger area of action," he said, "the field of transportation."[83] He sought to broaden the listeners' horizons with the point that they should not think of air transportation as only supporting the needs of the air force, but "those of the other services as well." Air transportation should move to its "logical destiny" by expansion "to a position of equality with rail and motor transport." It could not do so, Colonel Sneed maintained, as long as the existing supply machinery lacked centralized control.[84] At the same Engineering Supply Conference, Major Knerr suggested the establishment of a transport group, headquartered at Wright Field, that would serve as a peacetime skeleton for a wartime expansion. Concomitantly, he wanted an independent squadron formed at each of the four depots, distinct from the services squadrons of the tactical groups. Again, the chief of the Air Corps responded positively, directing on 11 November 1932 the establishment of the "1st Air Transport Group (Provisional) and four (provisional) transport squadrons, one each at the Sacramento, San Antonio, Fairfield, and Middletown Air Depots."[85] The headquarters group was to function in a "manner similar to that contemplated in war." With the existence of such an organization, "the transportation problems of maneuvers, concentrations, and extraordinary cargo were solved. It was anticipated, however, that by far the largest part of employment would be that involved in the depots serving their respective control areas."[86] A critical organizational (read doctrinal) position had been established—centralized control of air transportation.

The creation of the aerial supply system focused attention on the fact that a suitable cargo airplane was not available. The depots had to rely on the Bellanca Y1C-14 to carry bulky items, and it had limited capability and poor loading qualities. The 1932 appropriation allowed for the purchase of four Bellanca Y1C-27 transports, but they too had severe shortcomings in loadability, especially of engines. The need for a specifically designed transport aircraft became so apparent that the chief of the Materiel Division appointed a board to draw up specifications. The results, approved by the chief of the Air Corps, called for simple design, rugged construction, low cost, and economical maintenance.

By March of 1933, the Materiel Division was ready to let a contract when Brig Gen Oscar Westover, chief of the Air Corps, lowered the payload and upped the speed requirements for such an airplane. He told the Materiel Division to look to modifying a commercially available transport primarily with an eye to carrying maintenance people for the tactical units. General Westover said that if such a plane did not exist, then the Materiel Division should modify the requirements to one that did. Brig Gen H. C. Pratt, chief of the Materiel Division, disagreed. Practicality and economics argued against such an approach. Modifying existing airplanes always led to unacceptable compromises. Noting that the tactical unit needed their mechanics in place with the new high-speed pursuit, attack, and observation aircraft (not two or three days later), General Westover said his idea was best. General Pratt said that the mobility of the Air Corps was the reason for cargo transports, with supplies the critical factor. Civil aircraft were not available that could operate over the rough terrain expected. Any properly trained pilot could do the maintenance chores Westover was concerned about. Since the troop transport proposed was only a small part of the total requirement and because the high-speed troop carrier was twice as expensive as the cargo plane, economics led to an obvious conclusion. In spite of the serious shortage of procurement and research monies, however, the chief of Air Corps persisted in developing two different types of airplanes.[87]

The Materiel Division also wanted to make its transportation organization something more than provisional. The essence of the argument revolved around fully manning and equipping the squadrons as "real" squadrons rather than as units with two aircrafts. The provisional squadrons were able to deliver only a part of the tactical demands, and scheduled operations at depots were totally disrupted by emergencies such as the airmail operations. The establishment

> of a full strength squadron at each depot would, during an emergency or tactical maneuvers, permit the detachment of transport airplanes (and) provide complete, effective mobility for the tactical unit and practically eliminate ground transportation.[88]

What General Pratt wanted was enough resources to do the job; apparently the way to that goal was thought to be an institutionalized "regular" group and squadrons.[89]

In 1935 the squadrons were fully designated, but the group was abolished. No new resources were forthcoming. There were not enough airplanes or people to go around. The Materiel Division argued, to no avail, that it could at least man the group from within its own assets thus preserving an important concept—centralization. The chief of the Air Corps said that he was satisfied with the support the Materiel Divisions provided to the GHQ units. Besides, the new logistics air manual from the tactical school proposed that the command problem could be solved by assigning such aircraft to a central reserve under the GHQ, which would allocate them as needed; and that idea was approved. The resource issue was essentially unanswered. For normal operations between depots, the Materiel Division was the controlling agency, and the system worked.[90]

April of 1936 saw another attempt by the Materiel Division to put the transport house in order. Some especially important points emerged from that effort. Brig Gen A. W. Robins, the new division chief, first noted that the success of the GHQ Air Force depended on its successful supply, and that in its movement into any concentration area "the maximum use will be made of any air transports that are in service throughout the Air Corps."[91] After tracing the history of assignment of a few airplanes to each depot and to the GHQ, General Robins made an argument that would be heard for many years to come in somewhat different circumstances:

> The permanent assignment of cargo transports to tactical units for cargo-carrying purposes is believed uneconomical and incorrect in principle. All cargo airplanes, regardless of type, should be concentrated in our depots, available on call for whatever purpose the tactical units may require of them, when tactical units are called into the field for training, maneuvers, field service, or other purposes, returning to the depots immediately when the necessary purpose had been accomplished. . . . This transport service properly organized and set up in each of our depots would be available on call to serve the needs of the field in their control area. Likewise, the entire group would be available to serve the needs of the GHQ Air Force or any part of it, on call. As all cargo planes are capable of carrying either cargo or personnel, they could meet any demand made on them.[92]

AIRLIFT DOCTRINE

This argument very much has the ring of a centralized control of air transport resources, allocated for requirements as they arise—a system similar to what exists today. The argument also is the special application of a grander air power position: do not fritter away the unique capabilities of air power by assigning it to tactical units when you can maximize flexibility by assignment to a central organization.

By September 1936 General Arnold was to note that "apparently most of the General Staff sections do not seem to understand the motive behind or the results obtained by the use of cargo transports in time of peace." He directed that a recent staff study concerning the subject be reviewed, put in shape, and kept on file for information.[93]

The staff study took the form of a report on air transport operations from 1 November 1932 to 30 June 1933, as detailed records were available concerning this feasibility testing period.[94] The study pointed out that the lack of an effective air supply system during the airmail crisis caused the delay or cancellation of missions; that supply costs were saved by not having to have high stock levels when quick delivery means are available; that even express ground transportation is comparatively slow; and that the mobility of GHQ forces is dependent to a marked degree on air transportation, with the concept of the central pool highlighted. The missions of the air transport cargo service included scheduled supply, special supply, emergency supply, passenger carriage, emergency repairs to downed airplanes, salvage of wrecked airplanes, tactical operations, and mercy missions. The transportation service routinely requested return loads, normally consisting of repairable engines and parts for depot overhaul, to make the operation as efficient as possible. The study reported that had it not been for the existence of the air transport service, it would have been necessary to curtail Air Corps flying operations during the last three months of fiscal year 1933: they almost ran out of rail transportation funds and relied heavily on air transportation. Almost as an afterthought, the report also invited attention to the "recent demonstration in Russia where great quantities of machine guns and field pieces were successfully transported by aircraft and dropped by parachutes (also 1,800 men)."[95] It suggested that one of the reasons for continuing an air transportation service in peace was that it could provide "training and development which can be rapidly expanded in an emergency, as well as augment the movement of personnel and supplies of tactical units in peace maneuvers."[96]

In December of 1936 General Arnold again entered the fray, attempting to justify the procurement of additional transport aircraft. He deplored the scarcity of transports and argued that an effective air transport system would be especially valuable in making it possible to operate the Air Corps on a minimum budget "since it provided for the rapid shuttling of concentrated supplies thus keeping the total [supply] requirement to a minimum."[97] The number of transport airplanes needed was set at 149: 63 to GHQ; 50 to Materiel Division; 36 to air bases.[98] He also raised the GHQ Air Force needs as a justification for more aircraft. The inherent necessity for high mobility of the GHQ forces demanded an effective air transport system, and peacetime maneuvers were prima facie evidence of that point. The movement of people was equally important. General Arnold relied on the recent experiences of the Italian air force in Ethiopia as proving the feasibility of his position. He noted that, in 21 days of conflict, the Italian aviation unit had dropped 385 tons of materiel to the combat troops. He concluded:

> It is axiomatic that the development of any facility must have an ultimate objective of war employment. . . . Secondary uses function as means of training and improvement of material and organization preparatory to the emergency use. The tremendous import of having available the facilities and experience of transport service for mobilization and experienced means of flow of supplies to consuming units cannot be overemphasized.[99]

Despite General Arnold's interest in the matter, air transport made limited progress, and this only in the Materiel Division's cargo service.

The Materiel Division had been allowed to proceed with the development of an interdepot air service under the direct control of the chief of the Field Service Section, and this led to an improved Air Corps-wide supply system. Perhaps because of this success, or simply because of the logic of needing an effective management structure, a headquarters (the 10th Air Transport Group) and headquarters squadron for the command of the transport squadrons of the depots was finally activated in June 1937.[100]

In August of that year the Materiel Division attempted to consolidate the assignment of all C-33 cargo airplanes away from the GHQ into the new organization. The position has the ring of many future exchanges on the issue:

> Their assignment of the transportation squadron of the 10th Transport Group, makes them available on call for the GHQ Air Force in any maneuver, concentration or movement of personnel and, in a like manner, available for missions originating in the Office Chief of Air Corps, permitting the Materiel Division, while not on any of the above missions, to utilize them to the their maximum capacity.[101]

The Air Corps chief of supply ended that initiative by noting that removal of the C-33s from the jurisdiction of the GHQ "even if its requests for transportation are extended highest priority" would lessen the flexibility of the GHQ because it would not have direct control of operating personnel.[102]

The Woodring Program

New Secretary of War Harry Woodring said in August 1937 that he saw no rationale "for buying any transports due to their high price."[103] He directed that only 36 be purchased in 1938 and none in 1939. The money saved was to be used to buy new bombers; transport requirements would be met by converting old bombers.

Consequently, in fiscal 1938 the 10th Transport Group had 32 new C-39 aircraft; only 3 C-39s went to the GHQ. There were no transports ordered in fiscal 1939 for anyone. The Air Corps proposed to purchase 121 transports between fiscal years 1940 and 1945, but that number was overcome by events.[104]

Woodring's bomber conversion concept was unworkable as illustrated by the Materiel Division's attempt to convert a damaged B-18 to test the idea. General Robins' test report was devastating. The conversion would hold only a few types of aircraft engines; there was no emergency exit from the aircraft; costs per airplane were $50,000 to $75,000 (more than the cost of a new cargo plane); weight and balance were out of kilter; and the structural integrity of the airplane was in question. General Robins concluded that "the efficient movement of supplies in time of emergency will demand an airplane designed for this purpose and the regular procurement of transport airplanes . . . is strongly recommended."[105] The Woodring Program remained unchanged. In June 1939, the Air Corps had 2,080 planes on hand; 75 were transports. They had 1,115 undelivered; 21 were transports.[106] "Because of the myopic Woodring Program, the Air Corps would be woefully lacking in air transportation when the United States entered World War II."[107]

The larger meaning of the Woodring Program was more staggering in its realities. At the end of July 1938, the secretary directed the Air Corps to confine its fiscal 1940 program to light, medium, and attack bombers—on the eve of Munich the Air Corps was limited to the 40 B-17s already ordered.[108]

The chief of the Air Corps, General Westover, urgently recommended the reconsideration of the bomber decision; declaring that the Air Corps program "constituted a comprehensive objective arrived at after exhaustive studies on the subject of the War Department General Staff as well as the Air Corps, and should not be changed unless subsequent and comprehensive studies have determined modifications are necessary on account of new strategic considerations."[109] He also apparently was willing to compromise on the bomber issue somewhat—noting that if not allowed to procure a different aircraft (a long-range bomber), at least experimentation and development should not be limited. General Westover's closing is particularly interesting: in order to "efficiently and effectively discharge his duties and responsibilities as Chief of the Air Corps" he once again specifically recommended reestablishment of the previous program.[110]

The War Department's answer reaffirmed the B-17 decision per se, but did allow for development of an airplane "to provide suitable future replacements for the standard B-17 type of airplane now in service."[111] Other portions of the War Department letter were less promising. The adjutant general lectured the chief of the Air Corps that the rapid development of aviation did not overcome the concept that the infantry division "continues to be the basic combat element by which battles are won, the enemy field forces destroyed, and captured territory held."[112] The requirements of the Air Corps were no more important than the requirements of the other combat branches of the Army. The Air Corps was to plan on using the maximum trained personnel in the Reserves and civil aviation in times of emergency, rather than maintain a higher state of readiness than the other arms. Personnel requirements would not grow and force structure should be studied (again) with an eye to reducing serviceable aircraft numbers.[113] Given the Woodring limits, only 19 transports were to be procured in FY 1941.[114]

The Czechoslovakia crisis showed the importance of air power, and if Secretary Woodring did not recognize the threat, President Roosevelt did. He asked the War Department for a program that would produce 10,000 airplanes. General Arnold argued for a balanced program that included training and basing. After presentation to Congress in January of 1939 this equated to 5,500 airplanes. Industrial limitations further reduced this to 3,251 planes in two years.[115]

Prewar Doctrine

There emerged from the 1920s and 1930s a doctrine of military air transportation, in practice if not anywhere else. The tenets of that unpublished doctrine may be loosely stated as follows:

• The primary and overriding role of military air transportation is to support the air forces. As such, it belongs to the air forces and will be controlled by them.

• Military air transportation is vital to the flexibility and mobility of GHQ air forces. Some degree of air transportation should be organic to that force, and other air transportation assets will be called upon to augment that fighting force when required, at the expense of other missions.

• Military air transportation is also important as a logistics tool for the entire air force. It offers an economic and very reliable way to distribute supplies and to avoid certain stock level costs.

• All of the advantages of military air transportation notwithstanding, it is less important than the development, acquisition, and operation of combat forces. As the infantry is called the queen of battle, so too combat aviation may be called the queen of the air forces.

• Civil air transportation is relatively plentiful and becoming more so with time. Although civil air transportation airplanes are not perfectly designed for military purposes, they are sufficiently so that the air forces will rely on mobilizing them in wartime, at the expense of building an organic capability in peacetime.

There were, of course, arguments about this doctrine. But these arguments were not in the forefront of the "thinking" that was going on about air power, at least not in the public's eye and probably not in the eyes of many air power enthusiasts. Given the severe cramping that such a doctrine must of necessity lead to, it is

AIRLIFT DOCTRINE

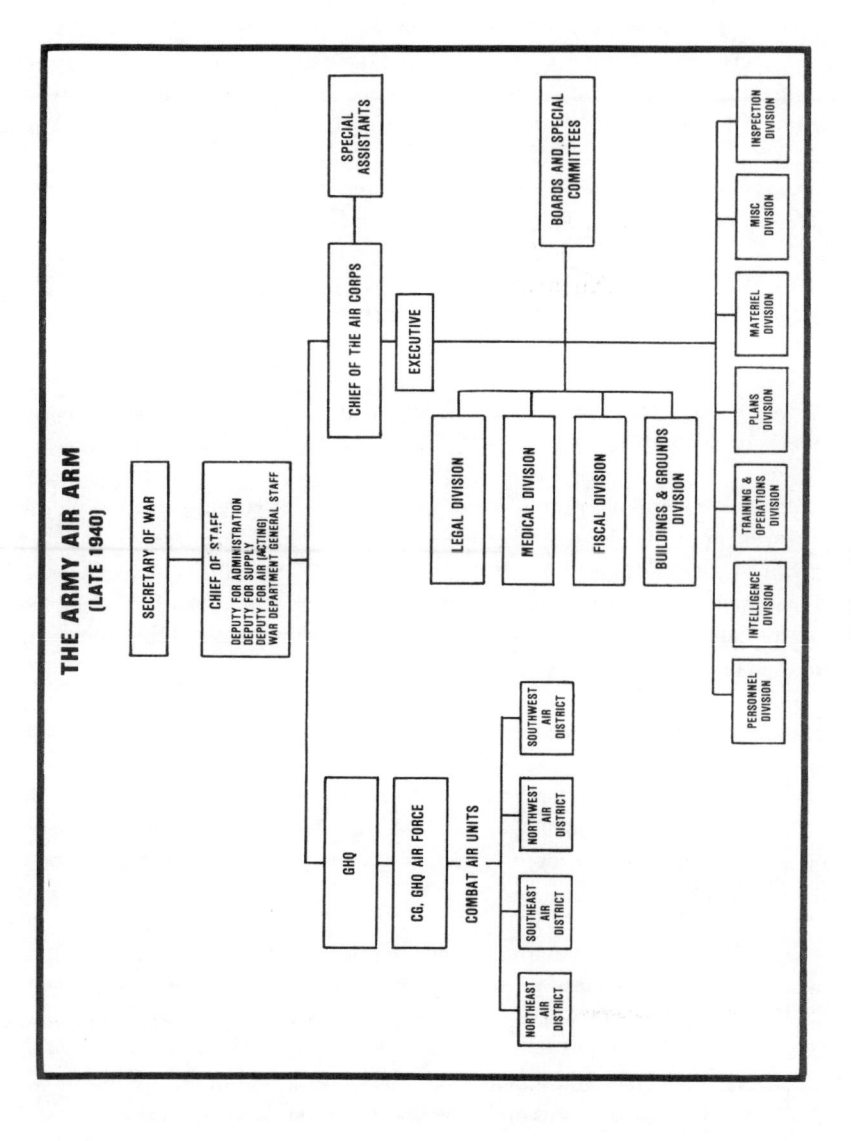

Figure 2

nothing less than astounding that the tremendous strides of World War II were possible. Clearly men of vision—like Knerr and Arnold—were ready to fill the gaps when the situation demanded it.

Because of the ill-thought-out Woodring Program, the Air Corps had to concentrate on building its combat strength. However, the augmentation program called for new depots to support the expanding Air Corps and three new transport squadrons were activated in October 1939. By efficient use of existing assets, the 10th Transport Group now owned 44 C-39s and by August 1940 had opened a weekly logistics run to the Panama air depots.[116]

Prelude to World War II

With the success of the Nazi blitzkreig, isolationist positions were eroding in late 1939 and early 1940. "Hemispheric defense," with money not a controlling factor, became the watchword of War Department planning. The Army's First Aviation Objective—based on defending the Americas (not defeating the Nazis)—called for 54 combat groups (4,006 aircraft) and 6 transportation groups (252 aircraft).[117]

After the fall of France in the summer of 1940, substantial orders for transport aircraft were an integral part of the expansion program. In September of that year, the Air Corps ordered 545 C-47s and 200 newly designed and much more capable two-engined C-46s. In May of 1941, an additional 256 C-46s were ordered, followed in June by 100 C-53s, the militarized version of the DC-3. That same month the Air Corps also took over the orders for 61 four-engined C-54s, originally destined for civilian airlines. The following September they ordered 50 more C-53s and 70 more C-47s. All of these airplanes were originally designed as civilian passenger transports. Until virtually the end of the war, the Air Corps depended on converted passenger planes and converted bombers. None of the newly ordered planes had been delivered at the time of the Pearl Harbor attack.[118]

To manage this growing force properly the Materiel Division recommended the creation of a transport wing, providing a definite military chain of command for the three groups assigned to the division, and the three groups awaiting permanent stations and assignment to the Combat Air Command (the GHQ's new name). The chief of the Air Corps recommended the establishment of the 50th Transport Wing Headquarters and Headquarters Squadron at Wright Field. The adjutant general directed the creation of the wing in January 1941, "under the control of the chief of the Air Corps."[119] The newly created wing faced so much demand for transportation services that, in its first six months of existence, it carried more cargo than all the civil airplanes combined, with scheduled services including deliveries to the Panama Canal Zone.[120] It could be argued that "the 50th Transport Wing might well have developed into the worldwide agency that ATC later became. Instead, the Air Command had its origin in the Air Corps Ferrying Command."[121]

NOTES

1. Col Richard Binford, deputy director, Manpower and Organization, deputy chief of staff, Manpower and Personnel, Headquarters USAF, to commander in chief, Military Airlift Command, letter, subject: Organization Action Affecting Military Airlift Command, 13 May 1982.

2. Maj Gen H. H. Arnold and Col Ira C. Eaker, *Winged Warfare* (New York: Harper and Brothers, 1941), 14.

3. I found the following particularly good reading to help understand the early air power debates: Robert Frank Futrell, *Ideas, Concepts, Doctrine: A History of Basic Thinking in the United States Air Force 1902–1964* (Maxwell AFB, Ala.: Air University, 1974); John F. Shiner, *Foulois and the US Army Air Corps 1931–1935* (Washington, D.C.: Office of Air Force History, 1983); and Alfred F. Hurley, *Billy Mitchell: Crusader for Air Power* (New York: Franklin Watts, 1964).

4. Genevieve Brown, Historical Division, Air Technical Service Command, historical study, *Development of Transport Airplanes and Air Transport Equipment*, April 1946, 19.

5. Alfred Goldberg, ed., *A History of the United States Air Force, 1907–1957* (Princeton, N.J.: D. Van Norstrand Co., 1957), 29.

6. Ibid.

7. Ibid.

8. Futrell, *Ideas, Concepts, Doctrine*, 20.

9. Maj Gen Mason Patrick, chief of Air Service, statement to the War Department committee, 17 March 1923, in *Report of Committee of Officers Appointed by the Secretary of War* [Lassiter Board], 22 March 1923, appendix II, 3. Hereafter cited as *Report of the Lassiter Board*.

10. H. H. Tebbetts, adjutant general, War Department, to chief of the Air Service, letter, subject: Preparation of a Project for the Peace Establishment of the Air Service, 18 December 1922, in *Report of the Lassiter Board*, appendix I, 2.

11. Maj Gen Mason Patrick, chief of Air Service, to the adjutant general of the Army, letter, subject: 1st Indorsement Preparation of a Project for the Peace Establishment of the Air Service, 19 January 1923, in *Report of the Lassiter Board*, appendix I, 2.

12. Maj Gen Mason Patrick, chief of Air Service, to the adjutant general of the Army, letter, subject: 3rd Indorsement Preparation of a Project for the Peace Establishment of the Air Service, 7 February 1923, in *Report of the Lassiter Board*, appendix I, 5.

13. Ibid., 9–10.

14. *Report of the Lassiter Board*, 3.

15. Ibid., 6.

16. Maj Gen Mason Patrick, chief of Air Service, to the adjutant general, War Department, letter, subject: Air Service Legislation, 9 June 1924.

17. Futrell, *Ideas, Concepts, Doctrine*, 29.

18. Ibid.

19. Maj Gen Mason Patrick, chief of the Air Corps, to the adjutant general, War Department, letter, subject: Necessity for an Increase in the Number of Planes Allowed the Air Corps by the Act of July 2, 1926, 30 November 1927.

20. Ibid.; Brig Gen Benjamin Foulois, acting chief of the Air Corps, to adjutant general, War Department, letter, subject: Airplanes Necessary to Equip the Air Corps, 14 November 1928.

21. Futrell, *Ideas, Concepts, Doctrine*, 39; Memorandum, Brig Gen W. E. Gilmore, chief, Training and Operations Division, to chief of the Air Corps, subject: Comparison of Air Corps Personnel and Materiel Requirements, 6 September 1929.

22. Memorandum, Col S. D. Embrick, chairman, Coordinating Committee, War Department, to president, Air Corps Five-Year Program Board appointed by A.G. 580 (1-30-29) Off., dated 26

February 1929, subject: Data Required by Survey of Preparedness (Instructions of the Chief of Staff, 1-28-29), 20 May 1929.

23. Maj Gen James Fechet, chief of the Air Corps, to the adjutant general, War Department, letter, subject: Requirement in Airplanes of Every Type for a Force of Two Field Armies of Approximately 1,000,000 Men, 26 May 1929.

24. Maj Gen James Fechet, chief of the Air Corps, to the adjutant general, War Department, letter, subject: Abandonment of the Five-Year Air Corps Program, 5 November 1929

25. Ibid.

26. Robert Frank Futrell, USAF Historical Studies: No. 23, *Development of Aeromedical Evacuation in the United States Air Force 1909–1960* (Maxwell AFB, Ala.: Aerospace Studies Institute, 1961), 10. In addition to being an excellent source concerning early air transport history, this study is the authoritative work on aeromedical evacuation history.

27. Robert Collins, adjutant general, War Department, to the chief of the Air Corps, letter, subject: Report of Special Committee of the General Council on the Employment of the Army Air Corps, 30 January 1934.

28. Ibid.

29. Ibid.

30. Futrell, *Development of Aeromedical Evacuation*, 10; Memorandum, Maj Gen Benjamin Foulois, chief of the Air Corps, to assist chief of staff G-4, subject: Air Corps Program, 2 February 1934.

31. Final Report on War Department Special Committee in Army Air Corps [Baker Board], 18 July 1934, 2–3.

32. Ibid., 5–6.

33. Ibid., 7.

34. Ibid.

35. Ibid., 59.

36. Ibid., 75.

37. Ibid.

38. Ibid., 60.

39. Ibid., 29.

40. Ibid., 30.

41. Ibid., 67.

42. Ibid.

43. Ibid.

44. Transcript of the shorthand report of proceedings, transactions and testimony, before the Special Committee on Army Air Corps [Baker Board], morning, 21 May 1934, testimony of Maj Walter Frank, chief of Air Corps Plans Division, 2796.

45. Ibid.; for a discussion of intra-Air Corps jockeying for the few air transport aircraft available see Futrell, *Development of Aeromedical Evacuation*, 10.

46. Maj Gen Benjamin Foulois, chief of the Air Corps, to the adjutant general, War Department, letter, subject: 1st Indorsement Recommendation of Special Committee, Air Corps (item 28, pp. 31 and 73, and item 41, p. 75), 30 November 1934.

47. Brown, *Development of Transport Airplanes*, 20.

48. Ibid., 21.

49. Ibid., 21–22.

50. Ibid., 21.

51. Maj Hugh Knerr, Air Force Logistics and the Cargo Transport with comments by Capt P. S. Seaton, 30 March 1932, a summary, with extensive quotations of Knerr's and Seaton's papers by an unknown author.

52. Air Force Maneuvers, October 1925, an unsigned report.

53. Ibid.

54. Brig Gen James E. Fechet, commander, Army Air Corps, report, "Critique of Air and Ground Maneuvers, San Antonio, Texas, May 15–19, 1927," ca. 1927, unedited stenographic remarks.
55. Dorothy Bruce, Air Materiel Command Historical Study No. 262, *The Evolution of the Storage System of the Air Technical Service Command Part I, 1918–1940* (Wright Field, Ohio: Air Materiel Command), 127.
56. Lt Col C. C. Culver, commandant, Air Corps Tactical School, to chief of Air Corps, letter, 16 July 1927.
57. 2Lt William Wolfinbarger, group airdrome officer, Report of Group Airdrome Officer Covering the Transportation of Supplies and Personnel of the ACTS to Virginia Beach and Return to Langley Field, Virginia, 23 April 1920.
58. Maj H. H. C. Richards, supply officer, 1st Provisional Squadron, Air Corps Tactical School, Report of Supply Officer, Virginia Beach Maneuvers, 18–20 May 1928, n.d., 1.
59. Ibid., 9.
60. Ibid., 12.
61. Ibid.
62. Bruce, *The Evolution of the Storage System*, 126.
63. Ibid.
64. Ibid.
65. Ibid., 127.
66. Brown, *Development of Transport Airplanes*, 31.
67. Ibid., 32–33.
68. Knerr, *Logistics and Cargo Transport*, 1.
69. Ibid.
70. Ibid., 1–2.
71. Ibid.
72. Bruce, *Evolution of the Storage System*, 128.
73. Knerr, *Logistics and Cargo Transport*, 2.
74. Ibid., 4.
75. Ibid.
76. Ibid., 5.
77. Ibid.
78. Ibid., 6.
79. Ibid., 8.
80. Brown, *Development of Air Transports*, 49.
81. Futrell, *Development of Aeromedical Evaluation*, 9.
82. Ibid., 10.
83. Brown, *Development of Air Transports*, 49.
84. Ibid., 49–50.
85. Futrell, *Development of Aeromedical Evacuation*, 10.
86. Brown, *Development of Air Transports*, 51.
87. Ibid., 55–63.
88. Lt Col H. C. Pratt, office of chief of division, Materiel Division, to chief of Air Corps, letter, subject: Recommendations for Organizing Transport Squadrons, Change in Supply System, 20 July 1934.
89. Memorandum, Maj Hugh Knerr, chief, Field Service Section, Materiel Division, to executive, Materiel Division, 28 September 1934.
90. Brown, *Development of Air Transports*, 102–104.
91. Brig Gen A. W. Robins, chief of Materiel Division, to chief of the Air Corps, letter, subject: Development of the Transport Group and Squadrons, 22 April 1936.
92. Ibid.

93. Maj Gen H. H. Arnold to Col Rush Lincoln, chief, Plans Division, routing and record sheet, subject: Cargo Transports, 2 September 1936.

94. Draft memorandum, Col Rush Lincoln, chief, Plans Division, to chief of the Air Corps, subject: Cargo Transports, 14 September 1936.

95. Ibid.

96. Ibid.

97. Brown, *Development of Air Transports*, 86.

98. Col Frank Lackland, chief, Field Service Section, to chief, Materiel Division Liaison Section, letter, subject: Transport Aircraft, 30 March 1937.

99. Brown, *Development of Air Transports*, 37.

100. Ibid., 103–4.

101. Brig Gen A. W. Robins, chief of Materiel Division, to chief of the Air Corps, letter, subject: Assignment of C-33 Transport Airplanes to Transport Organizations, 19 August 1937.

102. Supply, J.B.J., to Plans, routing and record sheet, subject: Assignment of C-33 Transport Airplanes to Transport Organizations, 21 August 1937.

103. Futrell, *Development of Aeromedical Evacuation*, 12.

104. Maj Gen Oscar Westover, chief of the Air Corps, to the Secretary of War, letter, subject: Five-Year Airplane Replacement Program, 18 November 1937; Col Rush Lincoln, chief, Plans Section, to executive, unknown organization, letter, subject: C-33 for Transport Squadron at Chanute Field, 30 September 1938.

105. Brig Gen A. W. Robins, chief of Materiel Division, to chief of the Air Corps, letter, subject: Policy on Future Procurements of Transports, 31 August 1938.

106. Brown, *Development of Air Transports*, 105.

107. Futrell, *Development of Aeromedical Evacuation*, 12.

108. E. R. Householder, adjutant general, War Department, to chief of the Air Corps, letter, subject: Aircraft Programs, 29 July 1938.

109. Maj Gen Oscar Westover, chief of the Air Corps, to adjutant general, War Department, letter, subject: Air Corps Program and Directive, 31 August 1939.

110. Ibid.

111. E. R. Householder, adjutant general, War Department, to chief of the Air Corps, letter, subject: 1st Indorsement Air Corps Program and Directive, 5 October 1938.

112. Ibid.

113. Ibid.

114. Office of the Chief of the Air Corps to chief, Materiel Division, letter, subject: 1st Indorsement Policy and Future Procurements of Transports, 18 April 1939.

115. Goldberg, *History of USAF*, 43–44.

116. Futrell, *Development of Aeromedical Evacuation*, 18; W.F.V., Materiel Division, to Plans Division, routing and record sheet, subject: Establishment of Transport Wing, 6 November 1940; chief of the Air Corps to the adjutant general, War Department, draft letter, subject: Transport Wing Headquarters, 6 November 1940.

117. Futrell, *Ideas, Concepts, Doctrine*, 55.

118. W. F. Craven and J. L. Cate, eds., *The Army Air Forces in World War II*, vol. 7, *Services Around the World* (Chicago: University of Chicago Press, 1958), 5.

119. Chief of the Air Corps to adjutant general, War Department, letter, 6 November 1940; R. E. Fraile, adjutant general, War Department, to commanding general, Fifth Corps Area, letter, subject: Constitution and Organization of 50th Transport Wing, 8 January 1941.

120. Craven and Cate, *The Army Air Forces in World War II*, 7:4.

121. Ibid.

CHAPTER 2

Worldwide Airlift in the War Years

A new era opened in the development of air transportation when President Franklin D. Roosevelt approved the sale of bombers to the British. Initially, American civilian pilots flew the bombers from production plants in California to Montreal, where British civilians took over for the rest of the flight. In November 1940, a Canadian civil agency under contract with the British government began ferrying American-built bombers across the North Atlantic to Scotland, a distance of approximately 2,100 miles.[1]

Under the pressures of wartime needs, the British Ministry of Aircraft Production could not provide the requisite number of military crews when they took over the second leg of the trip, without actually withdrawing pilots from combat. The manufacturers also were experiencing difficulties in recruiting a sufficient number of crews for the initial ferrying to Canada.

The Air Corps Ferrying Command

With the Lend-Lease Act a reality in March of 1941, Gen H. H. Arnold recommended that the Air Corps do the ferrying from California to Canada. This not only freed up British pilots, it also gave Air Corps crews a greatly needed opportunity to fly first-line, modern aircraft and improve their general flying skills.[2] The need for flying hour experience was very high on General Arnold's list of priorities. There was a critical shortage of modern aircraft for the Air Corps, in large part caused by the diversion of much prewar production to the British and other potential allies. Multiengine aircraft in particular were not available for training. American military crews needed training "in navigation, weather and radio flying that a coast-to-coast ferrying service would give them—and on the latest, hottest equipment."[3]

Announcing approval of General Arnold's idea in a letter to Secretary of War Henry L. Stimson on 28 May 1941, President Roosevelt said:

> I wish you would take full responsibility for delivering planes, other than PBYs [patrol bombers], that are to be flown to England to the point of ultimate takeoff. I want the Army to make sure that these planes are delivered speedily.[4]

AIRLIFT DOCTRINE

The next day, the Army Air Corps (AAC) directed Col Robert Olds to create such a ferrying service. On 5 June 1941, the AAC confirmed these verbal orders by establishing the Air Corps Ferrying Command (ACFC) retroactive to 29 May, under the direct jurisdiction of the chief of Air Corps. The mission statement was fairly broad: "Move aircraft by air from factories to such terminals as may be directed by the chief of Air Corps," and "maintain such ferrying service as may be required to meet specific situations."[5] Memoranda from that period indicate that the Air Corps Maintenance Command would assume the responsibilities after the ferrying system was well established and working, but the ACFC history indicates "there is reason to believe that Colonel Olds' force of character and his clear conception of his Command's mission were important factors in preserving it as an independent organization."[6] By October of that year, the Air Corps Maintenance Command had "the responsibility of operating all bases, stations, and other facilities created to meet the requirements of the Air Corps Ferrying Command," while the original mission of the ferrying command was reaffirmed.[7]

Between 6 June and 7 December of 1941, "approximately 1,350 aircraft were ferried to points of transfer, nearly all by pilots of the Air Corps."[8] In the summer of 1941, the ACFC opened the "Arnold Line" service between Washington, D.C., and Scotland via Montreal and Newfoundland. Flying six round-trips a month until forced to close the route due to bad weather, the ACFC carried diplomatic mail and VIPs in the bomb bays of modified B-24s. The command also sponsored north-route survey flights and the establishment of weather and communication capabilities.[9] In the same period the United States took steps to open a South Atlantic route joining the United States to Africa and the Middle East.

Establishing the Routes

As part of the lend-lease program, Britain requested 50 transport aircraft for its strategically important air line of communication between England and the Middle East. The British used the route to ferry fighters and they needed the transports to return pilots and carry critical supplies. Only 20 aircraft were available. The Air Corps could find no experienced military or civilian crews that were not already engaged in the North Atlantic route, so it turned the job over to Pan American Airways, primarily because of Pan American's extensive experience in developing commercial airlines in Latin America. Atlantic Airways, a Pan American subsidiary, found the crews and the British provided the navigators. The first flight left Miami on 21 June 1941. The crews were arrested upon arrival in Belem, Brazil, for neutrality violations (a problem apparently solved three days later).[10]

On 26 June General Arnold hosted a planning meeting with British and Pan American officials to establish a contract ferrying operation in anticipation of a steadily increasing flow of lend-lease bombers along the South Atlantic route. Pan

American agreed to establish both a ferrying and air transport operation along this route, then across Africa to Khartoum. Through three subsidiaries, Pan American was responsible for recruiting crews and maintenance personnel, establishing training programs, setting up bases, and administering the entire system. By the time the Army Air Forces (AAF) militarized the personnel and facilities of this route at the end of 1942, Pan American crews had delivered some 464 planes.[11]

Figure 3

Concurrent with the South Atlantic civil air program, a military ferrying and transport service developed. German successes in Europe, the Soviet Union, and North Africa created extensive pressures to keep open the lend-lease lines to both Britain and the Soviet Union via the Middle East. A Washington-to-Cairo military route opened on 14 November 1941. Maj Curtis LeMay served as copilot of the 26,000-mile round-trip survey of that route.[12]

In order for US military crews to deliver aircraft overseas, it was necessary to expand the Air Corps Ferrying Command's 3 October mission statement. That document, signed by President Roosevelt, authorized the command to deliver lend-lease aircraft to "any territory subject to the jurisdiction of the United States, to any territory within the Western Hemisphere, the Netherlands East Indies, and Australia."[13] President Roosevelt responded to the new request with a blank check on 24 November, authorizing deliveries "to such other places and in such manner

AIRLIFT DOCTRINE

as may be necessary to carry out the lend-lease program."[14] The ACFC now had a truly global mission. By 7 December, the command was deeply involved in surveying and equipping routes to Alaska, Australia, Africa, India, and Great Britain. Actual deliveries across many of these routes were small at first but

> measures taken by the United States in the immediate prewar period for development of the South Atlantic route proved to be more important as preparation for the impending war than for the ferrying and transport work actually accomplished. Only a handful of planes, ferried and transport, moved over the route prior to Pearl Harbor. But thanks to the work of the Air Corps Ferrying Command and the Pan American organization, and to the courage and resourcefulness of the pioneer crews who flew the route, the United States had made a substantial start toward the development of a vital line of communications when, after 7 December, aircraft and supplies for its own forces joined the increasing flow of lend-lease goods to the Middle East, to India, China, and the Southwest Pacific.[15]

The importance of both the concept and the reality of the air line of communication were firmly in the minds of those making the critical decisions. The Washington meeting in December 1941 between the American and British war planners set as its first goal to secure "important areas of war production," and second "to provide the security of the principle sea routes and seven main air routes over which men and supplies could be moved to the battle fronts."[16] The air routes were started; the complexities of devising and maintaining such an undertaking were already underway. The entry into the Second World War increased the pace and scope of what the ferrying command was already doing.

John D. Carter, an early Air Transport Command (ATC) historian, makes a fairly substantial argument that the concept of air transportation was not a foremost consideration during these early days.

> In 1941, in fact, the concept of air transport as one of the principal channels of supply for the military forces in the field had not been fully grasped. Probably no one then foresaw that a network of long-range transport routes, supporting the daily movement of hundreds of tons of supplies and thousands of passengers, would spread over the world and that daily flights to such remote areas as the Aleutians, Australia, the Philippines, India, and China would become commonplace. Indeed, a limited view of the role of long-range air transportation in the war persisted for some months after the United States became an active belligerent. Not until the late spring and summer of 1942, when large backlogs of supplies awaiting air shipment to the front began to build up at ports of embarkation and when it became clear that almost unlimited demands would be made in the future for air cargo space for the rapid movement of urgently needed materials and personnel, did the idea of air transport as a major instrument of logistics begin to take shape.[17]

Although the core of his argument is most probably correct, there is some evidence that thinking on a grander scale was occurring. Lt Col Oliver LaFarge, the primary historian of the Air Transport Command, notes that what conscious planning there was for developing long-range air transportation originated in the Army Air Forces. In the first half of 1941 there was a continuing interchange of views and suggestions within the then Office of the Chief of the Air Corps concerning overseas ferrying, development of possible routes, and transport services. All this was conceived of on what would look like a very small scale in 1945; nonetheless, when the Presidential directive of May 28, 1941, opened the way to establishment of the Air Corps Ferrying Command, from the Air Corps point of view it was a green light to put plans into execution, rather than the proposal of a new idea.[18]

Colonel Olds apparently also had a very strong hand in the expansion of his command's mission. He recommended that the president expand the command's authority to include the delivery of aircraft and the provision of such facilities as staging fields, weather and communications stations, air traffic control points, and installation and transfer points "where necessary in the interest of our own strategic defense."[19] President Roosevelt gave him that authority.

Early Organizational Issues

Nonetheless, at the beginning of the war, the War Department had scarcely any long-range transports available: 4 Boeing Clippers, 5 Stratoliners (on contract), and 11 converted B-24s. The commercial airlines had 406 multiengine transports, but all except a handful were twin engine. However, because of their reservoir of trained personnel and facilities and their invaluable operating experience, "it was immediately obvious that the emergency war needs for air transportation could not be met without recourse to the services of the civil airlines."[20] When President Roosevelt signed the executive order on 13 December directing the secretary of war to take possession of any portion of any civil aviation system required in the war effort, a plan in existence since 1936 allowed for the immediate harnessing of those assets. Contracts were quickly let with Pan American Airways, Transcontinental, and Western Air, Inc., providing for aircraft ferrying and air transport services over numerous worldwide routes. Eventually every major civil air carrier provided some type of contract service.[21]

As a temporary expedient to overcome the overlap of ACFC and Air Service Command (ASC) missions, a series of meetings held on 20 and 21 March 1942 convinced General Arnold to assign to the Air Service Command responsibility for transporting "such aviation technical supplies as facilities permit to units or bases in the Western Hemisphere including Iceland, Greenland, Trinidad, and the Caribbean area on the East, and Alaska on the West." On the other hand, the Ferrying Command was to "operate, either directly or by contract, all transport lines extending beyond the Western Hemisphere," gradually militarizing all its personnel outside the United States. It was given total charge of all ferrying operations, regardless of geography. Critically, the Air Service Command was given the responsibility of "building up transport squadrons capable of carrying out missions with airborne infantry, glider troops and parachute troops."[22]

The Air Corps Ferrying Command's mission statement, which separated troop carrier units from the ferrying and transport service end of the business, was the codification of a long-standing reality. One part of air transport—the GHQ Air Force—was associated with tactical transport. Another part—the Materiel Division—was associated with scheduled air logistics. The logistics planes were called upon to augment the tactical mission during deployments and maneuvers. There came to be a clear distinction, at least organizationally, between air transport for support combat forces and a logistical mission meant to implement worldwide strategy.[23]

June 1942

June 1942 was a vital month in the history of air transport. The adjutant general of the War Department issued an immediate action directive to the commanding generals of every major Army unit worldwide, clarifying the nonavailability of Ferrying Command assets for theater use. John Carter provides an excellent background for why this action was necessary:

> A long-range air supply system, conducted on the basis of predetermined and established schedules and operating into or through a number of theaters and independent commands exercising military jurisdiction along overseas air routes, had to be reasonably free from control by local commanders. A transport or ferried airplane flying from the West Coast to Australia in 1942 passed through the territory of four principal commands before reaching its destination; and over the North Atlantic a plane flying from the United States to Great Britain might traverse the jurisdictional area of as many as five separate theater or base commands. In the early months of the war, the theater commanders, whose powers, traditionally, were almost without limits within the established boundaries of their own commands, frequently diverted scheduled transport aircraft and crews operating under the control of the Ferrying Command to their own immediate tactical needs. In other instances, ferrying crews, upon completion of deliveries to a theater, were held for a time by local authorities instead of being returned promptly to the United States. While such practices might have been justified in emergencies, if carried too far they would have led inevitably to a complete breakdown of the developing system of strategic air supply. The theater commanders were, in short, adopting a policy contrary to their own long-range interests.[24]

Recognizing that theater prerogatives must of necessity modify the "operational activities" of ACFC assets to "conform with the existing combat situation," the War Department nevertheless directed the theater commanders to "make every effort to minimize interference with the efficient operations" of the Ferrying Command. When the theaters did have to appropriate Ferrying Command crews and assets during a "specific emergency," they were to report immediately to the

War Department, by the most expeditious means of communication, the action taken and the necessity for such action. The rationale for this independence was that the Ferrying Command was a "War Department service agency engaged in the delivery of high priority personnel and materiel" to ultimate destinations specified and prioritized by the War Department, with the commanding general Army Air Corps acting as agent for the War Department.[25] The concept has endured to this day.

June also saw the issuing of a "Memorandum Concerning War Aviation Transport Services" by L. W. Pogue, chairman of the Civil Aeronautics Agency. The memorandum severely criticized the state of the air transport system. The March clarification of the division of responsibility between the Air Corps Ferrying Command and the Air Service Command turned out to be an incomplete staff action that created a situation General Arnold came to describe as substantial duplication and confusing dual responsibility. The problem revolved around civil air contracts. When the March directive was issued, the Air Service Command was

> completing the necessary arrangements with the commercial airlines for an air freight service between its depots and the various sub-depots and bases. This service was to operate on a regular schedule basis, using aircraft to be furnished by the airlines and converted for cargo carrying. The maximum use of the new service was urged, in order to free the equipment of the 50th Transport Wing for tactical operations with the parachute troops, airborne infantry, the air transportation of GFE [ground forces equipment?] and supplies, and depot-to-depot operations.[26]

The divided responsibility in letting contracts for domestic and offshore areas and for issuing directives caused duplication and overlap. The Pogue memorandum put the confusion in a broader context. He initially observed:

> This is the first war in which the transportation for the Army and Navy of any substantial amount of material and personnel by air has been undertaken. . . . It is now clear that in this worldwide war the speed and mobility of aircraft as a transportation medium has rendered the entire world to one theater of operations so far as vital supply lines by aircraft are concerned.[27]

Unfortunately, said Pogue, "there has been a very sporadic and somewhat uncoordinated growth of war air transport services within the Army and Navy, all carrying war material and personnel."[28] He foresaw a very destructive tendency of these uncoordinated demands:

> In view of all the demands being made upon the airlines, either the flow of key and technical personnel into the Army and Navy will have to stop soon and an effective control established over conflicting demands upon the airlines, or the airline organizations will collapse and they will not be able to do the enormous job ahead of them for any command of the Army or for the Navy; and as a result the nation's best interest will be jeopardized.[29]

Pogue pointed to organizational jealousies, parallel routes, and wasted resources and warned of a breakdown. His recommended solutions were made obvious by his statement of the problem:

> The sound solution is to place all war air transport operations, except for limited operations where the compelling necessity therefore is clear, such, for example, as those in the immediate vicinity of combat, in the hands of one command which will herein be referred to as "War Transport Command," independent of both the Army and Navy, responsible directly to the commander in chief.[30]

Oliver LaFarge observed that "recognizing, presumably that there was little hope of obtaining a single, independent agency of this sort, the memorandum then recommended the establishment of a single 'Air Force Transport Command' to handle all air transportation for the Army."[31] Specifically, Pogue said

> the alternative solution is to unify in a similar way all of the air transport services now being conducted . . . within the Army so that there will be but one centralized Army demand upon this limited facility of our nation. All that has been said above in favor of unifying control over war air transport applies here in a more limited way. It would constitute a great step forward if the air transport services of the Army could be consolidated and placed under one command, provided all other commands and branches of the Army were required to present their demands for services of the airline organizations to such a unified Air Force Transport Command and to abide by its decisions.[32]

General Arnold issued his own memo on 12 June on the same subject:

> The existing division of responsibility for air transport operations of the Army Air Forces must be reconsidered for the accomplishment of the following purposes:
>
> (a) To permit the most efficient utilization of aircraft, facilities and personnel by the elimination of dual responsibility and duplication of services.
> (b) To provide transport operations by military personnel, rather than by civilians under contract, on routes that enter combat areas or areas likely to become combat areas.
> (c) Reorganize the air transport services of the two commands so that the Army Air Forces may plan for and prepare to meet the growing demands of the Army for general air transport services.[33]

His suggested course of action was to limit the Air Service Command to continental US operations and give the Ferrying Command responsibility for the rest of the world. The chief of the Air Staff, Maj Gen M. F. Harmon, passed General Arnold's memo and Pogue's study to his assistant, directing him to head up a board and solve the problem.[34] General Arnold made up his mind before the board could report, and on 20 June 1942 directed the creation of the Air Transport Command (ATC).

The Air Transport Command

AAF General Order Number 8 put Arnold's decision into effect. The overriding purpose of the new command was to "assure the effective utilization of air transport facilities of the Army Air Forces." It was responsible for ferrying all aircraft within and outside the United States, the air transportation of people, materiel, and mail for all War Department agencies (except for troop carrier operations); and the control, operation, and maintenance of bases on its air routes. The intratheater transportation of materiel was to be accomplished by attaching troop carrier units to the theater Air Service commands. The command was also admonished to "utilize to the fullest extent possible the services, facilities, and personnel of the civil air carriers."[35] These orders directed no really new function "but the command now had a clear mandate to develop its air transport activities to the fullest extent possible and to extend its control of air traffic along all routes leading from the United States to the several battle fronts."[36]

More than any other command during World War II, the Air Transport Command represented the worldwide nature of the war. It started with the five wings established to administer and control the routes of the Ferrying Command: the Caribbean, South Atlantic, Africa-Middle East, North Atlantic, and South Pacific Wings. Between October 1942 and January 1943, four more were added: the Alaska, the India-China, the Pacific (with a subordinate West Coast unit), and the European Wings. It also had a domestic wing that continued ferrying within the United States.[37]

As the war progressed, the command grew both in absolute numbers and in the quality of its services. It started operations with 11,000 people and nearly 1,000 transports. When the war ended, ATC had over 200,000 people and some 3,700 airplanes. At the peak of ferrying operations, it delivered 108,000 aircraft in 1944.[38] Its growth was recognized through the redesignation of its wings as divisions in 1944 and through the creation of numerous subordinate units. The majority of cargo was carried by military aircraft and crews. In 1942, civilians carried some 87 percent of the cargo; by 1945 that became 22 percent. The war average for civilian ton-miles was 33 percent. By 1945, the ATC and contract carriers had carried some four million passengers and had flown 2.7 billion miles. Long-range cargo aircraft showed marked development and improvement throughout the conflict. By 1 May 1945, ATC had 598 four-engine transports and 553 C-46s.[39]

A substantial part of the story of ATC in World War II was one of expansion. Patterns of how best to run this air trucking company emerged, patterns that set the tone and provided the doctrine of intertheater and intratheater airlift for many years to come. The first had to do with centralized control.

AIRLIFT DOCTRINE

Figure 4. Maj Gen Harold George, commander of Air Transport Command, from April 1942 through September 1946.

Centralized Control

In July 1942, the first commander of ATC, Brig Gen Harold George, suggested that General Arnold issue a memorandum laying out the principle that the "operation of air transport services by the Army Air Forces is one of its *primary* functions and responsibilities." General George explained that the AAF needed the memo because "many branches of the services as yet fail to realize the logistical requirements for transportation by air in the present conflict."[40] The AAF was more than willing to oblige. Calling an efficient air transport system a primary function of the AAF, the letter noted that "the value of air transportation for the rapid movement of men and materials within the United States and between the United States and foreign theaters cannot be overemphasized. Without air transportation, our coasts are separated by days instead of hours and our far-flung forces are months instead of days distant."[41]

The ideal shaping the development of ATC was that of a strategic air transport system. Centralized control in conformity with the highest considerations of national strategy was the underlying theme. This concept brooked no interference from the theater commanders. If the point was valid for the Air Corps Ferrying

Command it was doubly so for ATC. Apparently the theaters either did not read or they ignored the previously discussed adjutant general's letter concerning the independence of the ferrying command. Or perhaps, as suggested by an ATC historian, the original directive had not proven effective because it was relatively weak.[42]

By August of 1942, General George felt compelled to report that there had been frequent and serious interruptions in scheduled operations based on the erroneous assumption by other commands that "transport operations that traverse their areas are under their complete control."[43] In the face of the shortage of aircraft, the only way to get the fullest possible use from the planes available was to stick to predetermined schedules, violated only due to weather, mechanical failure, security, "or other reasons of extreme urgency."[44] Arguing that the problem could only get worse as the volume of operations expanded, he asked for a new, stronger War Department letter. He got what he wanted. In fact, the Air Staff strengthened a proposed draft to ensure that it emphatically showed that the commanding general (CG), the AAF, and not the theater, was the controlling agent.[45]

The new directive appeared on 21 September 1942. It was, in fact, quite strong:

> The Air Transport Command, Army Air Forces, is the War Department agency for the transportation by air of personnel, materiel, and mail. Aircraft and crews engaged in the operation of air transportation and ferrying services will not be diverted from such operation by commanders concerned except in cases requiring that such operations be delayed until security will permit resumption of operations.[46]

This new rule allowed interference only to protect the ATC operations themselves. No reporting by exception—just don't do it. The principle was a vital one and it survives to this day. Theater commanders continued to violate it until the end of the war, but to a lesser extent.[47]

The South Atlantic Route

The oldest route and the most important theater route for 1942 ran from Florida to South America, across the South Atlantic, through Africa, and on to the Middle East. ATC ran this route with three wings—the Caribbean, the South Atlantic, and the Africa-Middle East (following the invasion of North Africa, ATC divided the Africa-Middle East Wing into the North Africa and Central Africa Wings). The Caribbean Wing served primarily as the manager of the continental US aerial port system. Airplanes were handed off to the control of the South Atlantic Wing—a 5,000-mile route extending from Trinidad to the African coast, via five major bases in South America. The bases were spaced to allow shorter range aircraft (including fighters) emergency landing and overnight stop locations. Within this system, Ascension Island achieved great strategic importance. Located almost exactly

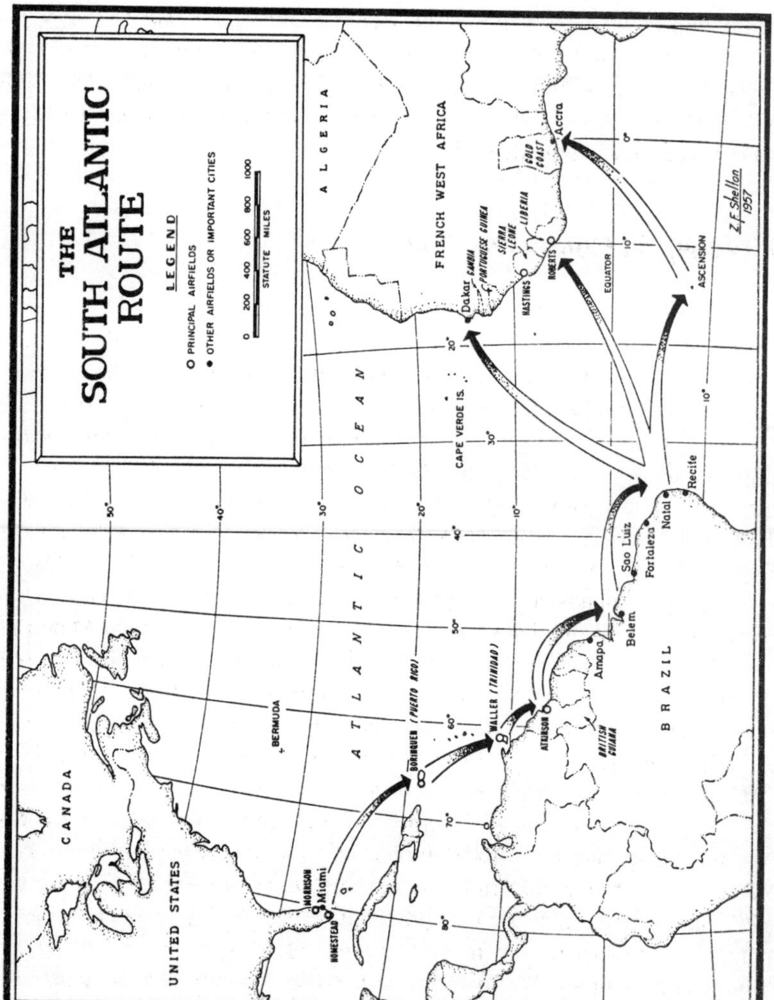
THE
SOUTH ATLANTIC
ROUTE
LEGEND
O PRINCIPAL AIRFIELDS
● OTHER AIRFIELDS OR IMPORTANT CITIES
0 200 400 600 800 1000
STATUTE MILES
CANADA
UNITED STATES
HOMESTEAD
MORRISON
Miami
BERMUDA
BORINQUEN (PUERTO RICO)
WALLER (TRINIDAD)
ATKINSON
BRITISH GUIANA
ATLANTIC OCEAN
Amapa
Belem
Sao Luiz
Fortaleza
Natal
Recife
BRAZIL
CAPE VERDE IS.
ALGERIA
FRENCH WEST AFRICA
Dakar
GAMBIA
PORTUGUESE GUINEA
SIERRA LEONE
HASTINGS
ROBERTS
LIBERIA
GOLD COAST
Accra
ASCENSION
EQUATOR
Z.F. Shellon
1957

Figure 5

halfway between Brazil and Africa, Ascension Island was an easy stopping point for twin-engine airplanes. Prior to its opening, the 1,900-mile direct flight was possible only with the expensive and time-consuming addition of extra gas tanks. Even many four-engine aircraft that could have easily made the longer flight used the island base due to the increased cargo loads made possible by lighter fuel loads.[48]

One of the unique features of the South Atlantic and Africa-Middle East Wings was that the wing commanders were also theater commanders, as the ATC operations in those areas were the primary military mission and activity. The theater commands were the United States Army Forces in South America and the United States Army Forces in Central Africa.[49]

An Air Transport Control System

After Rommel's victories in the Middle East in May and June of 1942, the United States committed extensive air forces to that area. Maj Gen Lewis Brereton was ordered to the area with the bombers and some transports of the Tenth Air Force, which became the Middle East Air Force and later the Ninth Air Force. This command was extremely reliant on air transport as the sea lines of communication were long and dangerous. The route to the theater was already saturated and backlogged with supplies for forces in Egypt, the USSR, India, and China. At the end of June, the cargo awaiting shipment in Florida was 53 tons, while along the route another 40 tons awaited transshipment on larger aircraft. When General Brereton's supply demands hit the system, the total went to a 138 and 88 tons respectively. By August, the backlog reached a staggering 250 tons at Miami and 325 tons in the system. General George called for more transports, warning quite correctly that "grave issues" depended on an efficient transport system to the Middle East. The ultimate cause of the backlog was, indeed, a shortage of airplanes and could only right itself slowly with the eventual delivery of airplanes on order.[50]

Another cause of the backlog was how to make the most efficient use of existing resources. Part of the issue was the training of people in the intricacies of handling air cargo—preparing cargo for air shipment and loading airplanes properly. As experience grew with the air transport system, large amounts of cargo were repackaged, having arrived at the port prepared for rail or sea shipment in heavy, bulky containers. The experts also found that much planning had to go into deciding just what was important enough to be air shipped and, within that category, what the priorities of movement were.[51]

The prioritization process proved to be a critical step in the air system. When the backlogs at Miami were exceeding the capability even to store the volume of materiel involved, upwards of 75 percent of the cargo was arriving at the aerial port without a priority classification. The backlogs were such that some materiel

AIRLIFT DOCTRINE

actually could have gotten to its destination faster by sealift. The War Department had banned the practice of shipping without a priority in November of 1942, but it was not until July of 1943 that it was brought under control.[52]

The November order also had given ATC full authority to control air cargo movements and thereby get a handle on volume, but the basic problem of what was air eligible was much more complex. As the prioritization program evolved, ATC originally set priorities that had to depend on information from the theaters, which had an understandable tendency to exaggerate their claims to get highest priority. However, experience proved that "as a rule" the individual theater commanders were best qualified to determine relative urgency of cargo and personnel assigned to them. By August of 1943, a reasonable system evolved whereby the theaters were given a monthly quota of available airlift, and allowed to work out their own priorities within that allocation of capability. The War Department, with ATC assistance, derived the allocation based on strategic needs and system capabilities. It also provided the theaters a three-month projection to aid in their planning. The AAF assigned ATC officers experienced in priority work to the theaters to provide assistance. This priority system could work only if ATC had good data on how much the airlift system could handle.[53]

The Priorities and Traffic Division of ATC formulated a transportation control system that went far toward solving the problem. Established in June 1943, the program was to "provide Air Transport Command Headquarters with a clear understanding of the traffic capacities of its routes" and it limited the "loading of traffic at originating terminals to that which can be moved through to destination without delay."[54] The system was a fairly sophisticated project that devised route transportation standards, defined operating factors based on flying hours, and divided capability between channel traffic, all of which computed together showed the headquarters what a particular route or route segment was capable of handling for a given time period. April of 1944 saw a War Department order to the theaters establishing local priority boards that set priorities for all incoming, outgoing, and intratheater air shipments.[55]

The development and maturation of the transportation control system was one of the unheralded but vital accomplishments of the air transportation system. It

> brought order and efficiency into the movement of cargo, mail, and passengers along the foreign routes of the command, thereby permitting the general staff and theater commanders to make the most economical use of strategic air supply in the conduct of military operations. Considerable difficulties were experienced, of course, but constant improvement was achieved by insistence upon reasonably accurate estimates of weight and arrival time at ports of embarkation, by improved daily reports of backlogs and traffic movement, by thorough checks on undue delays, and spot checks on actual transit times.[56]

The eventual system was not without its faults. The War Department agency setting quotas for the theaters was the Operations Division (OPD), which had to balance its decisions between the grand strategy of the war and the immediate tactical needs of the theaters. Some theaters were better at making their needs understood and sometimes received materiel by air that could have gone more justifiably by sea; others, by necessity, received an insufficient cut of the pie. Col Ray Ireland, chief of the Priorities and Traffic Division (ATC), suggested that one way to ultimately overcome this problem was to

> place the Air Transport Command and the Naval Air Transport Service, either as a unified organization or as separate units, under a single high agency. This agency would have complete control over all allocations of air transport space as well as priorities, and in order to carry out its responsibilities, would have representatives of its own in every theater.[57]

Colonel Ireland's idea, in a modified form, would be tried in 1948.

North Africa and the Mediterranean

The evolution of the ATC program in support of the US operations in North Africa and the Mediterranean also offered some important ideas on how to best run the air road in the future. ATC support for the Allied invasion of North Africa—Torch—began on 10 October 1942 with the creation of a select planning group that was sworn to highest secrecy while working on its "day-and-night, black coffee job."[58] The apparent strategic considerations involved using existing ATC facilities and routes to and in North Africa as jumping off points for ferrying and transport operations. Because of the distances involved, A-20s and B-25s were the shortest range aircraft considered. The planners did not consider using Gibraltar because of overcrowding and susceptibility to attack. A direct route across the Atlantic was out of the question because the Azores and Cape Verde Islands were not yet available due to Portuguese neutrality. Four-engine, long-range airplanes would use the northern route, through England, if they were required. The eventual plan called for the bombers to begin arriving on D plus 6 through D plus 60, staging at Miami and stopping at Ascension Island. Aircraft were dispatched to the theater on call after reception fields became available. The first flight of A-20s departed Miami on 8 November, flown by ATC ferrying crews. Later flights of B-26s were flown by their own crews, with ATC providing en route support, briefings, and follow-up transportation of additional crewmembers.[59]

By January 1943, the system had developed to the point that ATC planes brought cargo and personnel as far as Marrakech, where troop carrier planes picked up the loads and distributed them throughout the theater. As the fighting moved eastward, ATC extended its routes. By May of that year, theater air transport activities were so extensive as to create a single controlling agency—the Mediterranean Air Transport Service (MATS). It controlled some squadrons of the 51st Troop Carrier Wing, British civil and militarily transports, and similar French forces. Questions

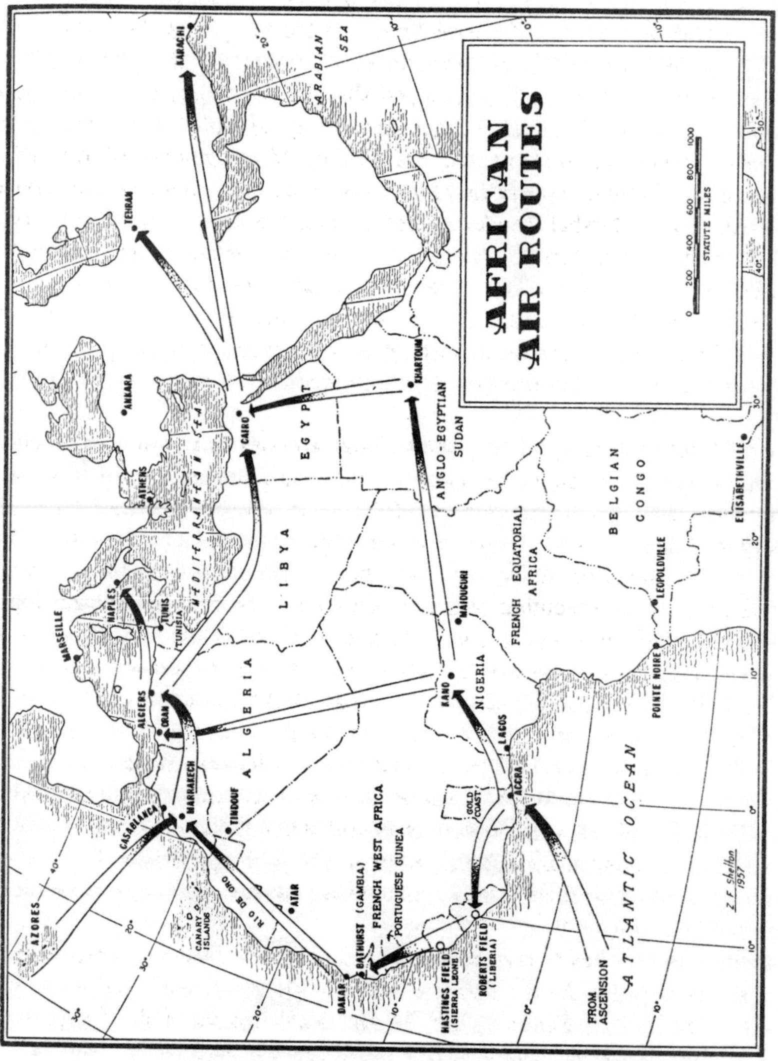

AIRLIFT DOCTRINE

Figure 6

of control of ATC forces naturally arose.[60] In fact, Air Chief Marshal Sir Arthur Tedder noted in a telegram to General Arnold in mid-May of 1943 that "problems created by the increased use of air transport operating within this theater and the Middle East necessitate immediate reorganization [including] the coordination of all transport services."[61]

Brig Gen Cyrus Smith, ATC chief of staff, attended a conference with Air Chief Marshal Tedder in late May. General Smith started the proceedings with a clear discussion of the February War Department memorandum that exempted ATC operations from theater control but stopped short of demanding complete freedom of action. Air Chief Marshal Tedder apparently accepted the more general limitations. General Smith also noted that ATC could and would perform "local" (as opposed to "through") operations for the use and benefit of the theater serviced. He and Air Chief Marshal Tedder agreed that in the case of the local services provided to the North African theater, ATC would operate in accordance with theater-established priorities and schedules, based upon the operating limits of ATC. General Smith also limited the services provided to those jointly arrived at. Both agreed removing aircraft from through services would happen only in the case of grave emergencies. The through operations were more important than the local ones.[62]

General Smith's agreement to provide local services reflected a more general ATC policy to take over duties from troop carrier and cargo units when asked by the theater concerned.[63] As the strength of ATC grew in terms of airplanes and people, generally, the theaters were maturing and expanding as well. For example, at the time of the invasions of Sicily and Italy, troop carriers were intensely involved either training for or executing airborne operations; meeting intratheater logistic requirements came up a poor second. By late 1943 ATC and MATS agreed that ATC would take over considerable portions of the air transport services in North Africa and later extended such services into Italy. MATS would essentially act as a priority maker and requirements collector.[64] As the Allies pushed the Germans back, ATC operations moved forward, with responsibilities divided appropriately among its wings. Eventually, ATC set up its own station units and detachments at bases in Sicily, Sardinia, and southern Italy and at points "along the West Coast of Italy reaching the combat zone in the northern half of the peninsula. Following the invasion of southern France, these intratheater-theater lines were extended to Corsica and Marseilles."[65]

In addition to services to the theater per se, ATC was also very interested in an operation across North Africa that "would provide the missing link in a shorter route from the United States to the Middle East and the CBI [China-Burma-India]."[66] The North African Theater of Operations, US Army (NATOUSA) apparently wanted to delay the operation. The ATC liaison officer in Algiers reported that on 18 April 1943 he had learned in a meeting with Maj Gen Carl Spaatz and Air Chief Marshal Arthur Tedder that NATOUSA was strongly opposed to the extended service and that General Spaatz had said action should be taken to prevent airlines, not under the control of the theater, from extending operations at the present time. General George apparently thought that the resistance came from the British:

> Of late, when any question about air transport is discussed with the British the question of the "airlines" usually arises. The British at this time are seemingly very "postwar conscious" on this point. It appears that the British fear that the American airlines will continue their present contract operations as civil operations after the war is over, over the routes where they are now operating.[67]

Gen Dwight D. Eisenhower had already denied contract operators in-theater operating rights except for a Trans World Airlines (TWA) service from Marrakech to Britain, apparently because too many such operations would irritate the British, thus being harmful to combat operations.[68] Since ATC planned to make the run to Cairo and eastward a purely military operation, Smith was able to turn all objections. By the end of 1943, the route was operational and on its way to becoming the primary way to the Middle East and India.[69]

The European Wing

The development of ATC operations into and within Europe also followed the course of the war. The decision to execute the first major US operation in Africa and the problems caused by weather on the North Atlantic route early in the war played heavily in the process. As noted earlier, the North Atlantic route developed in support of the delivery of aircraft under the lend-lease program in 1940 and 1941. A stepping-stone system of bases in Newfoundland, Labrador, Greenland, and Iceland made possible the delivery of short-range fighters to Britain. Developing the Great Circle route took advantage of the shortened distance between California and England offered by the northern flying.[70]

Part of this process included extended discussions with the British concerning a completely Americanized airway, including reception airfields in the United Kingdom. All concerned reached agreement in December of 1942. The US Army Air Corps, through ATC, was to establish communication services and flight procedures along the entire route. ATC assigned control officers to the en route bases for exercising command control and accepted joint tenancy with the British at four bases in Scotland and England—along with the designation of four alternate bases. ATC created a European Wing as its agent, and by May 1943, ATC's control of its aircraft and activities over the North Atlantic was virtually complete.[71]

The northern route actually reopened in April of 1943, with weather conditions better than the previous year. ATC added Dow Field in Maine and Meeks Field near Keflavik, Iceland, to the route to prevent system saturation. Throughout 1943

AIRLIFT IN THE WAR YEARS

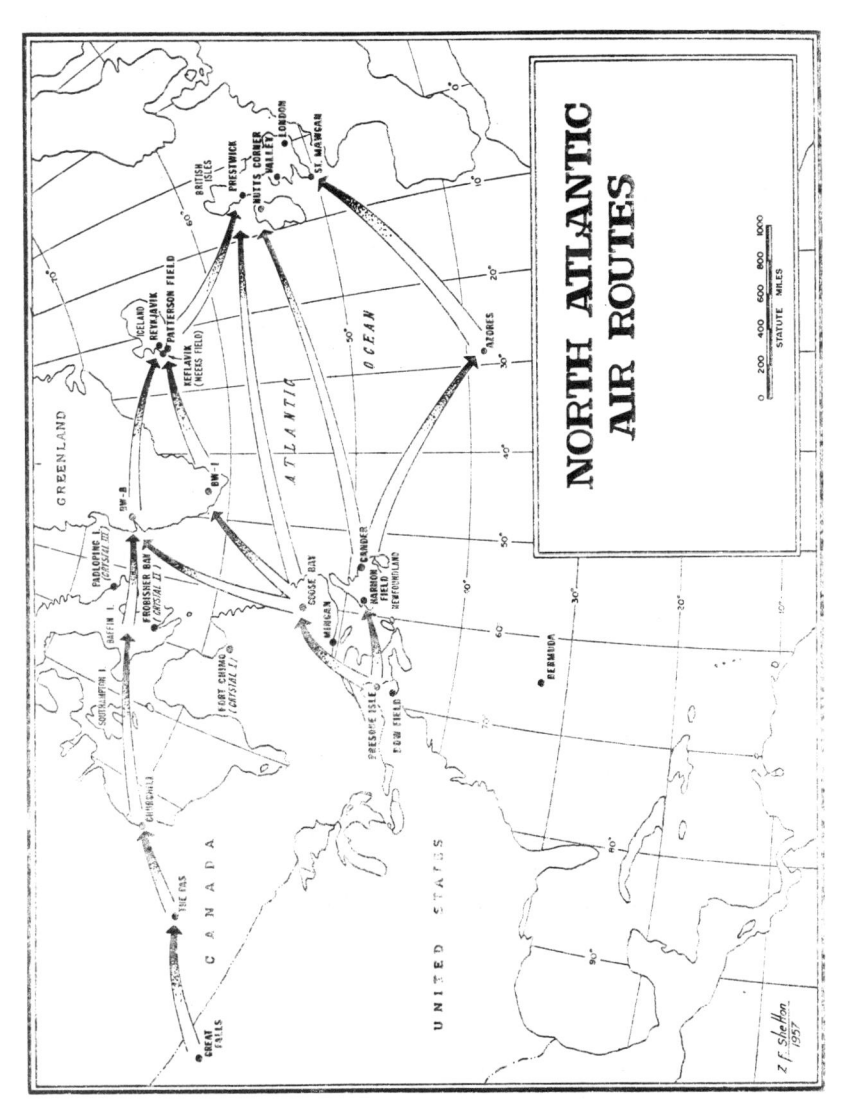

Figure 7

traffic across the route was primarily in support of the buildup for the bomber offensive against Germany. Over 3,000 bombers crossed the North Atlantic in 1943 with less than 700 traveling the longer southern route.[72]

With the increased tempo of the war in Europe, it was obvious that ATC could not continue to abandon the northern route during the winter months. ATC took steps to improve the weather forecasting along the track, including augmenting the B-25s of the 30th Weather Reconnaissance Squadron with C-54s to fly between stations collecting up-to-date information. This filling of information voids and the establishment of operating standards allowed for the firm planning of winter operations. Three hundred or so bombers crossed the route in the winter months of 1943 and 1944. Because of westbound wind limitations, ATC developed a round-robin system for C-54s in the winter of 1943. When Lajes Field, Azores, became available in December of 1943, all transports flying between the United States, Great Britain, and North Africa began using it on return trips. Between January 1944 and July of that year, tonnages over the route increased from 350 to 1,900 per month.[73]

The Allied landings in Normandy in June of 1944 opened another phase in ATC operations in Europe. As the Allies advanced into France so too did ATC. At the end of August 1944, four days after the last Germans left Paris, ATC aircraft started landing at Orly Field, and by early October regularly scheduled services between New York and Paris were a reality. After December, the theater allowed contract carriers to operate on that route. Cargoes into Europe also reflected the normal demands of war, with an emergency delivery of mortar ammunition in December in support of the Battle of the Bulge. By late winter 1944–45, a guaranteed, scheduled flight service existed between Washington and Paris, with passengers actually making reservations they could count on.[74]

The European Wing continued the ATC policy of providing intratheater services when possible. Until late in 1943 the ATC crews had delivered cargo and passengers and ferried planes to England, where Ferry and Transport Service of the VIII Air Service Command accepted responsibility through its subordinate organization, the 27th Air Transport Group. The European Wing suggested and finally gained approval for an intra-England shuttle for delivery of aircraft direct to users and for carrying passengers and cargo between its bases in England. That concept simply extended to the continent upon Allied success there.[75]

By mid-1944 the president, the secretaries of state and war, and General Arnold were all greatly interested in Air Transport Command operations in Europe. The president wanted to ensure that the United States provided the liberated areas with full relief and rehabilitation, the initial burden for shipping obviously falling on the Army.[76] The secretary of war directed General Arnold to make military air transportation available to those working on the relief and rehabilitation programs "on a basis subordinate to all of our purely military requirements." He also directed that ATC not carry military traffic if it could be handled by the civil airlines, and that the carriage of relief-oriented traffic only be viewed as an interim measure until the civil airlines could operate over the routes involved.[77] General Arnold sent General Smith, ATC chief of staff, to discuss the matter with General Spaatz, then commanding general of the US Strategic Air Forces in Europe, on the same day he received the secretary's letter. In a short letter to General Spaatz, General Arnold said that

> the services provided by the Air Transport Command should be of such character as to reflect credit upon the Army and upon American air transport operations from the point of view of efficiency and should compare favorably with service provided by any of the other nations, in both facilities and convenience.[78]

If it sounds like a rather low-key response to a major policy statement by the president and secretary of war, it is because Generals Arnold and Spaatz had already agreed, almost four months previous, on how to run airlift in Europe. ATC, General Spaatz, and General Arnold all saw eye-to-eye on how to run the show. ATC would run regular services into London (and other cities) with high-urgency cargo, mail, and passengers bound for England. The Ferrying and Transport Groups of the XII Air Service Command (ASC) would distribute the goods. The ASC would also call on IX Troop Carrier Command for augmentation when needed. Responsibility for transportation between England and the continent would initially be the responsibility of troop carrier units. ATC would establish trunk lines into Europe as ports of entry became available. Likewise, ASC would start continental operations in support of AAF requirements when bases became available. As the theater matured ATC would expand its system of trunk lines throughout Europe and meet requirements of US ground forces and civil agencies. ASC also would create a feeder system, limited to AAF support. Troop carrier forces were to be primarily responsible for combat operations, augmenting ASC when possible. This system, designed in the midst of the execution of the invasion of Europe, fairly describes what became reality.[79]

The contributions of the North Atlantic route and the European Wing were vital to the success of the war effort. In all, nearly 14,000 planes were ferried across the route after 1942. Equally important was the development of a reliable strategic transportation system. During the last five months of the war in Europe more than 10,000 tons of cargo moved over the route per month.[80]

China-Burma-India: The Hump

The air transportation of materiel, personnel, and gasoline between India and China—known as flying the Hump—may be the most famous of ATC's World War II air transport operations. In order to best understand the contributions of the Air

AIRLIFT DOCTRINE

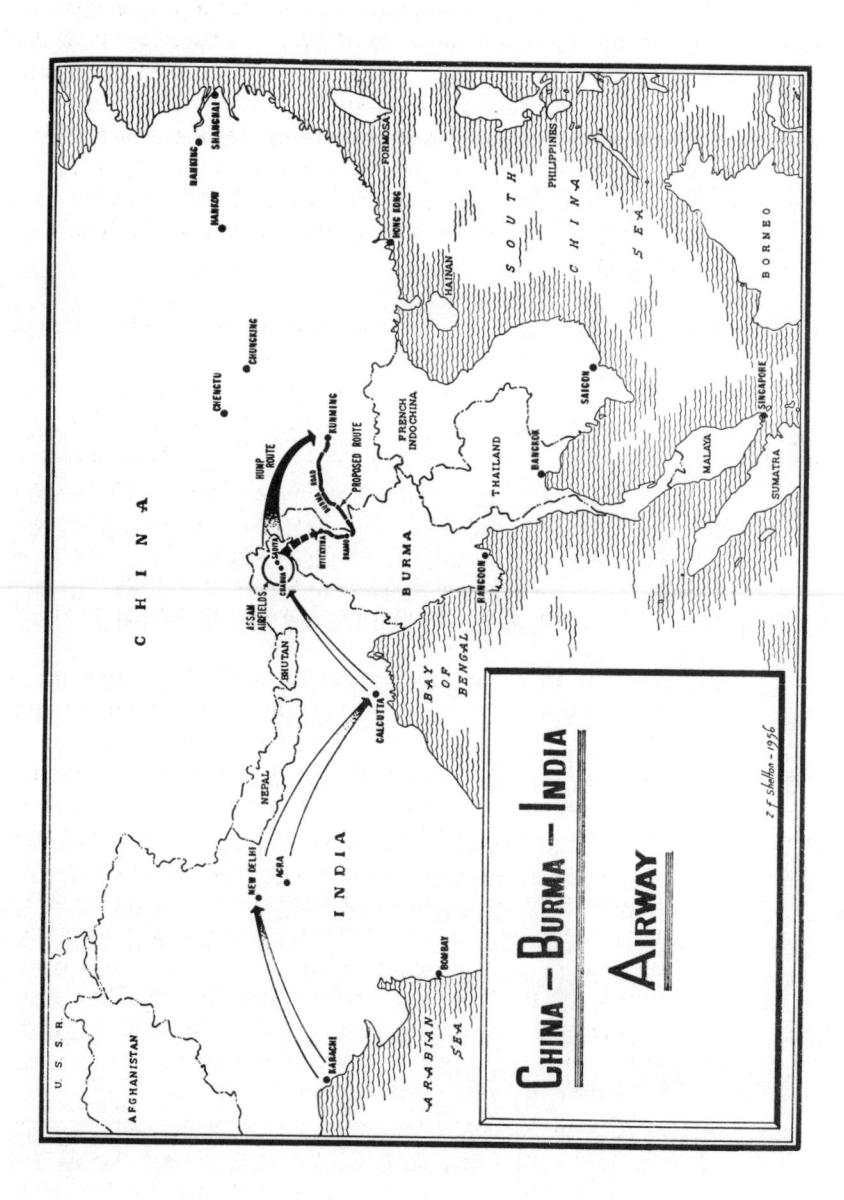

Figure 8. Major airlift routes in the China-Burma-India theater.

Transport Command to this vital operation, it is necessary to explore its beginnings under the Tenth Air Force.

The continuation of China as an active participant in the war was a basic tenet of Allied policy and strategy. It had President Roosevelt's personal attention. But keeping the Chinese supplied was particularly tough because China sat at the end of the longest supply line of war. In February 1942 the Japanese captured Singapore. After a quick Malay Peninsula campaign, Rangoon fell in late March. This cut off the Burma Road, the last remaining land line of communication to China. The rapid Japanese advances in Indochina and Burma sealed off China, except for air transportation. On 21 March, President Roosevelt directed the initiation of the Assam-Burma-China ferry route, which became the mission of the Tenth Air Force's 1st Ferrying Group.[81]

Under the Tenth Air Force. General Arnold wrote to the president in early February that the airdrome facilities in the CBI were not sufficient for a large number of transport aircraft and that it would be "very wasteful and perhaps disastrous if they were sent in without facilities." General Arnold noted that plans called for the eventual assignment of 50 to 75 airplanes to the intratheater transport service.[82] President Roosevelt authorized the secretary of war to requisition a minimum of 25 transport airplanes from the civil airlines for use in the airlift.[83] General Brereton, commander of the Tenth Air Force, believed that the shortage of operating airdromes both in India/Burma and China, combined with a very slow construction program (caused by the monsoon season), would limit the system to 25 transport aircraft for at least eight months.[84]

Initial plans by the Tenth Air Force called for the use of Myitkyina airdrome in Burma as a main operating location for the service into China. Using Myitkyina as a terminus, the Tenth Air Force thought they could move up to 7,500 tons per month into China. These plans included 75 aircraft to the Tenth Air Force and 25 to the China National Aviation Corporation (CNAC). Pan American Airways owned 45 percent of CNAC and the government of China owned 55 percent. CNAC had been involved in numerous hazardous operations in the Chinese-Japanese war prior to American entry. The Japanese, however, captured Myitkyina on 8 May 1942. The loss of this important airfield left a 550-mile flight path across mountains at least 16,000 feet high, through some of the worst weather faced in the Second World War. It took 40 to 50 days for the supplies to arrive in India by sea. Then it was another 1,500 miles via primitive railroads to Assam. But the materiel had to be airlifted because "every vehicle, every gallon of fuel, every weapon, every round of ammunition" which made it to China got there by air.[85]

The operations of the Tenth Air Force's airlift to China were originally planned and executed by Brig Gen Earl Nigel, General Brereton's chief of staff and immediate successor. ATC's early role was to ferry transport aircraft to the Tenth. By November 1942, ATC had delivered 15 aircraft to CNAC and 63 to the 1st

Ferrying Group. In June, General Brereton had taken all the bombers and 13 of the transports of the Tenth Air Force for an emergency reinforcement of the Middle East.[86] Eight transports were returned within six weeks, but an additional 15 had been destroyed by enemy action or lost in service, leaving only 43 actually on hand to cover both the trans-India shuttle and the Hump airlift. The airlift fell far short of any reasonable goal because of poor weather, poor training for aircrews, poor maintenance due to a scarcity of spares, a small number of aircraft, and diversion to other operations. Between May and November, the group had carried 2,200 total tons, showing a gradual increase each month, slowly approaching an 800-ton total a month. Apparently that was not enough.[87]

In July, Gen Joseph W. Stilwell, in command in China, proposed that CNAC be taken over by the Army under a military contract. General Arnold was apparently more impressed with CNAC's operations, and he counterproposed that it be put in charge of the entire operation. General Stilwell convinced General Arnold that civilian control of a military operation was not a good idea and also offered an effective insight into how best to run the operation. He argued for maximum use of existing and planned facilities, a higher crew ratio per transport airplane, and control of the civilian operation by the military to ensure the most efficient operation possible. He also called for delivery of all 100 planes originally planned for and the return of all the transporters General Brereton took. Five days later Gen George C. Marshall approved Stilwell's plan. Even the Chinese cooperated.[88]

In September of 1942, China Defense Supplies, Inc., sent a report by Frank Sinclair to ATC concerning his recent trip to China and conditions on the India-China ferry. The importance of the study, beyond its information value, was that it served as the basis for a subsequent ATC initiative to take over the Hump operation.[89] The cover letter to the study put the issue in its proper context:

> Mr Lauchlin Currie, who has recently returned from China where he went as the President's personal representative, says that no single factor has done more to buck up the Chinese morale than the presence of the American Air Force. This Force must be kept going and its effectiveness must be increased. This means the transport in increasing quantities of gasoline, bombs, ammunition and spare(s) from India to China.[90]

The Sinclair study details how not to run an airlift. He observed numerous critical difficulties in the operation:

- A general defeatist attitude by the Tenth Air Force over the likelihood of carrying 10,000 tons per month to China.
- Practically no spare engines.
- No available engine overhaul bases.
- Poor ground facilities for handling aircraft.
- Lack of spare parts.
- Lack of an effective training program for Hump pilots.

- A poor communications system.
- Lack of accurate weather forecasting.
- Poor living conditions.[91]

Little wonder that the 1st Ferrying Group was not living up to expectations. Sinclair was almost vehement in his belief that 10,000 tons was a proven possibility "if approximately 125 aircraft are assigned to this specific project and this project only."[92]

On October 1942, a much more balanced, evenhanded report came to General Arnold from then Col Cyrus Smith, ATC chief of staff. Colonel Smith took no fact-finding trip to China or India, but he certainly had his facts together and his analysis was devastating. The Tenth Air Force and CNAC delivered 85 tons in July 1942; even if original planning estimates were overoptimistic by 50 percent, that number should still have been 2,700 tons. Colonel Smith knew the cause of the problem and laid it on the doorstep of the Tenth Air Force, not the 1st Ferrying Group:

> Perhaps the factor which has contributed most to the lack of effectiveness in achieving the objective of the group, i.e., the transportation of materiel to China, has been the lack of singleness of purpose. . . . Often other urgent tasks in the theater were for the moment considered to be more important than the transportation of materiel to China. . . . At no time did the India-China operation have the full benefit of the personnel, aircraft and materiel which were sent to that theater for the purpose of transporting materiel to China. . . . No measure is going to be sufficient to insure substantially increased performance unless that measure includes a very narrow definition of duty, a singleness of purpose and a definite order to get one job, and only one job, done.[93]

Colonel Smith argued that transferring the mission to ATC would provide that singleness of purpose, if divorced from theater control, but made important caveats that other improvements were, indeed, also needed:

> The transfer of this function to the Air Transport Command would not, of course, in itself cure all of the ills which have plagued this operation. Even if the responsibility should be transferred to Air Transport, there would still remain the job of increasing the effectiveness of communications, bettering the weather reporting and forecasting, materially improving the maintenance of aircraft and engines, and, perhaps, the furnishing of a type of aircraft better suited to the peculiarities of the high terrain operation.[94]

Colonel Smith volunteered ATC to the task only on this basis.

ATC Takes Over. Eight days later, General Marshall notified General Stilwell that as of 1 December 1942, ATC would assume the India-China transport operation. In February 1943, General Arnold set the Hump tonnage objective at 4,000 tons per month.[95] ATC did not meet that objective until August. In the interim, there was slow but steady progress in the monthly rates. This progress was

AIRLIFT DOCTRINE

FLYING THE HUMP

Figure 9

Figure 10

AIRLIFT IN THE WAR YEARS

Figure 12. "Supply Line in China" by Loren R. Fisher.

AIRLIFT DOCTRINE

made possible by the addition of more aircraft, the replacement of less-capable airplanes with ones of larger capacity, the completion of departure airdromes, an increase in crew ratio, and a general improvement in wing operations.[96]

Although improving, ATC operations were not a model of efficiency. For example, in June 1943 the ATC India-China Wing (ICW) had 146 aircraft and delivered 2,219 tons of cargo. CNAC had 20 DC-3s and moved 761 tons. In September, ATC, with 225 planes, flew 5,198 tons; CNAC, with only 23 planes, flew 1,134 tons. ATC responded to criticisms and inefficiency by noting that it needed time to overcome the mistakes it inherited from the old ferrying group—especially the lack of a true independence from theater control and the need for inviolability of its spares and equipment.[97]

Brig Gen Clayton Bissell, commander of the Tenth Air Force, wanted to fold ATC into the operations of the theater commander. General Bissell's opinion ran counter to the way General Arnold envisioned ATC operations, but it did serve to highlight the organizational mess in his theater:

> The construction of fields in Assam was planned by Americans and accomplished by Indian labor under British supervision, using materials supplied by the British. . . . Flying of cargo ships into China was done by the ICW, troop carrier units, and CNAC. . . . But the responsibility for moving freight into Assam from Calcutta was British. . . . The Air Transport Command did not control loading and unloading of aircraft, a function of SOS and theater troops. ICW policies were determined in Washington, but priorities on its freight were controlled by a theater board which sat in New Delhi, hundreds of miles from Assam. Chennault's force, whose very existence depended upon the air supply line, had no representative on the priorities board.[98]

Reorganization of the theater helped solve some of the problems, while better leadership and management dealt with others. ATC got better at doing the job.

However, the 4,000-ton objective was not enough to properly support American forces in China. In March and April of 1942 Brig Gen Claire Chennault, Fourteenth Air Force commander, was so short of fuel and other vital supplies that he had to suspend combat operations. In May, President Roosevelt ordered ATC to deliver 7,000 tons in July and 10,000 tons per month starting September. The results were 3,451 and 5,125 respectively. In December ATC reached and sustained the 10,000-ton goal.[99]

During its assignment to the theater, the India-China Wing violated a fundamental principle of its founding by participating in operations other than supplying China by air. ATC had criticized the Tenth Air Force for this very practice "yet after the India-China Wing had been established, it was found that some of them were unavoidable."[100] The threats to the theater, and sometimes to the very existence of operating locations and reception fields for ATC, could not be ignored. These missions, although violating the apparent doctrine of independence, actually pointed out the application of a higher principle of air power—flexibility. In February 1944, ATC planes airdropped 446 tons of food to besieged Indian forces. In March and April, ATC aircraft delivered 2,100 tons of food, fuel, and ammunition to Allied forces defending the Imphal area of Burma. In late April, the India-China Wing flew approximately 18,000 Chinese troops into position for action in North Burma. In May, the wing flew 2,500 combat troops and engineers from southern India into Burma as part of the successful campaign to retake Myitkyina airdrome, materially assisting in the opening of a more direct and safer southerly Hump route. From July through December, ATC was the prime mover of threatened Chinese forces and supplied them as they faced a major Japanese initiative in South China. ATC redeployed and/or evacuated over 32,000 troops and moved over 500 tons of ammunition and equipment.[101]

In mid-1944 pressures grew to significantly increase Hump tonnages. The source was the arrival of the XX Bomber Command in China. A board presided over by Brig Gen William Old suggested that better use of existing resources and more resources would lead to substantial gains. Brig Gen William Tunner, the new commander of the ATC India-China Division, was a bit more specific. He recommended the opening of three new airfields, timely arrivals of already allocated aircraft, and significantly improved and enlarged maintenance services. The AAF and the War Department agreed and acted. By December 1944, deliveries reached almost 32,000 tons.[102] General Tunner brought with him the techniques of big business. He and his staff did not talk of how much tonnage the routes could handle but instead maintained that virtually any amount could be delivered given the facilities and men.

One of General Tunner's major contributions was to institute production line maintenance (PLM) within the India-China Division. PLM took an aircraft through maintenance stations, with experts performing the technical chores in a standardized manner. It replaced a complete mishmash of maintenance organizations and practices. Until its institution, no two bases were alike. Some used a few specialized crews to perform engine changes and periodic inspections, while others relied on the crew chief system to perform almost every maintenance task associated with a given airplane. General Tunner directed PLM whenever and wherever practical and separated maintenance from operations. The wing trained and assigned maintenance specialists; crew chiefs remained, but no longer would these mechanics attempt all the maintenance tasks of a specified aircraft. Each base commander had to appoint a director of aircraft maintenance directly responsible to the base commander. The wing developed standardized manning tables based on number and type of aircraft assigned and the volume of transient traffic. After some experimenting and growing pains, the system worked superbly. Operational-ready rates climbed to 85 percent and inspection downtime dropped 25 percent. By August 1945 the ICW carried 53,000 tons to China. Only the end of the war caused tonnages to decline.[103]

By August of 1945, the ATC India-China Division had over 21,000 men and 367 airlift airplanes. Daily utilization rate for the fleet was 8.8 hours (on the C-54 it

AIRLIFT DOCTRINE

```
           AIRCRAFT IN INDIA — CHINA DIVISION
              DAILY AVERAGE — SEPTEMBER 1944
```

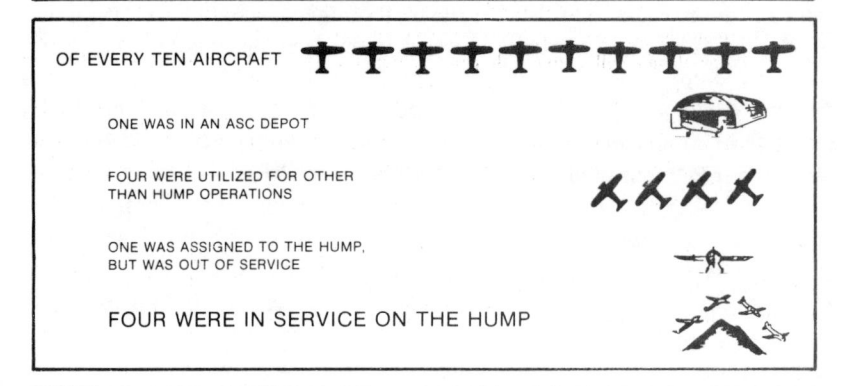

OF EVERY TEN AIRCRAFT

ONE WAS IN AN ASC DEPOT

FOUR WERE UTILIZED FOR OTHER
THAN HUMP OPERATIONS

ONE WAS ASSIGNED TO THE HUMP,
BUT WAS OUT OF SERVICE

FOUR WERE IN SERVICE ON THE HUMP

TOTAL PLANES ASSIGNED TO ICHD (Daily Average)	372	
Less: Planes in Hands of ASC Depots		34
Planes Assigned to Other than Hump Operations		151*
Total Planes Not Available for Hump Assignment	185	
Planes Assigned to Hump Operations	187	
Less: Planes Out of Service	42	
PLANES IN SERVICE ON HUMP	145	

*Total of 151 planes consisted of 9 C-87s, 13 C-46s, 108 DC-3s, and 21 miscellaneous.

Figure 13

reached 10.8). Between December 1942 and the peak month of August 1945, the unit had moved 721,700 tons—76 percent in its last year of operation. Not to be lost in these numbers is the fact that although Hump tonnage was a critical measure of merit for the division, the ferrying of 4,671 aircraft to the China-Burma-India theater was a tribute to the entire ATC route organization and a vital contribution to the war effort. Also vital was ATC's flexibility, demonstrated by the movement of seven entire Chinese divisions in the last year of the war. Considering the political and strategic importance placed on ATC operations in support of the CBI theater and the stationing of American bomber forces there, Brig Gen Joseph Smith's statement that not once were the operations of the XX Bomber Command curtailed because of a lack of supplies must have been particularly gratifying to ATC and the division.[104]

AIRLIFT IN THE WAR YEARS

A former ATC historian claimed after the war that

> the Air Transport Command's crowded airways to China were the proving ground, if not the birthplace, of mass strategic airlift. Here the AAF demonstrated conclusively that a vast quantity of cargo could be delivered by air, even under the most unfavorable circumstances, if only the men who controlled the aircraft, the terminals, and the needed materiel were willing to pay the price in money and in men. In military and civilian circles alike men were forced to modify their thinking regarding the potential of airlift. The India-China experience made it possible to conceive the Berlin airlift of 1948-49 and to operate it successfully. When the Korean War in 1950 required the emergency delivery of large numbers of men and equipment to the Far East, the precedents and the techniques for doing so were at hand.[105]

Since General Tunner was in charge of all three airlift operations (at one time or another), it is difficult to debate the claim, even if it is stated in somewhat grand terms. The real doctrinal heritage of the Hump, and other CBI operations, was that a properly supported and managed airlift could achieve results never dreamed of before World War II. The Hump experience demonstrated airlift flexibility and capability. What must not be forgotten is that the Hump itself was only the end of a long, and often tenuous, supply line. The entire logistics system had to function for the Hump airlift operation to be successful. And the combat forces had to provide relatively secure operating areas and some degree of air superiority for airlift to provide its vital services.

Across the Pacific

That there was a route across the South Pacific available in January of 1942 was a tribute to the foresight of the Army Air Corps. The trans-Pacific route used from mid-1941 until December to ferry heavy bombers to the Philippines via Hawaii was nullified by the Japanese capture of Wake Island. The alternate route from Miami via South America, across North Africa, and onward via Singapore and the Netherlands East Indies was operating on borrowed time. The War Department had supported the trans-Pacific route but opposed the development of the South Pacific one, noting on 21 February 1941 that it saw no need for Army bombers in the Orient. The rationale for the statement was that the United States should not take any action in the Pacific that would offend the Japanese or appear unduly aggressive. Maj Gen George Brett, then assistant chief of the Air Corps, disagreed. Noting the threat from Japanese bases in the Marshalls, Marianas, and Carolines, he recommended the development of facilities at Canton, Jarvis, and Johnston Islands as the first step in building a route to Australia. Growing Japanese aggressiveness and the strength of General Brett's argument caused the War Department to reverse itself. In August of 1941 it informed the Ferrying Command of the "necessity for funds to develop long-range land-plane facilities in the South Pacific." The

AIRLIFT DOCTRINE

Ferrying Command made arrangements for lend-lease funds, General Arnold kept the Navy informed, and the Department of State started arrangements for landing and operating rights. The AAF provided the funds to the commander of the Hawaii Department, who faced a deadline of 15 January 1942 for initial operations.[106]

Although this was the longest overall overwater route of the war—its longest stretch was between California and Hawaii, some 2,400 miles—it could be used easily by four-engine aircraft and also by two-engine planes large enough to carry extra gas tanks. Three B-17s piloted by their own crews departed Hawaii on 3 January 1942 en route to Java, marking the first direct ferry movement to the Southwest Pacific over the route. They used Palmyra Island instead of Christmas Island, which was opened a week later. The Pacific sector of the Ferrying Command simultaneously opened at Hamilton Field, California. The first aircraft ferried by the command—an LB-30 transport—left Hamilton Field on 11 March. The first bombers under the control of the Ferry Command left on 27 March. As early as 28 January it had became clear that the Navy could not guarantee the return flight of ferrying crews; thus, in April, ACFC initiated a contract with Consolidated Aircraft Corporation for service between the West Coast and Australia to overcome this bottleneck. By April 1942 ACFC developed an alternate route from Hawaii through other, more closely spaced islands, allowing for easier movement of twin-engine planes as well as transport operations, perhaps decongesting the main route as well.[107]

By the time the Ferrying Command became the Air Transport Command, 182 aircraft had crossed the Pacific to Australia, some flown by combat crews, some by the Royal Air Force (RAF), some by civil crews of Consolidated Aircraft, but most by Pacific sector military crews. The Ferrying Command cleared all of them from Hamilton Field.[108]

It took five months for a cargo ship to make the round-trip from California to Australia, through Japanese-patrolled waters. The official AAF history for the period summed up the contribution of the early South Pacific ferry route as "the lifeline of the Air Forces in Australia, for without it there could have been no heavy bomber replacements, no rush deliveries of desperately needed supplies, and no speedy transportation of urgently needed personnel."[109]

When ATC inherited the route, it created the South Pacific Wing as its agent. At the beginning of this operation, the wing controlled nothing beyond its headquarters at Hamilton Field. Everything between California and Australia belonged to and was controlled by other commands. At Hickam, the 7th Airways Detachment and the 19th Troop Carrier Squadron supervised and supported ATC operations. All along the island-hopping route other airways detachments handled ferried and transport airplanes on behalf of ATC. At the end of the route—Australia—it took ATC four months to get disentangled from the control of the intratheater air transportation agency, the Directorate of Air Transportation (DAT). The Ferrying Command control officer in Australia had found himself captured by the same

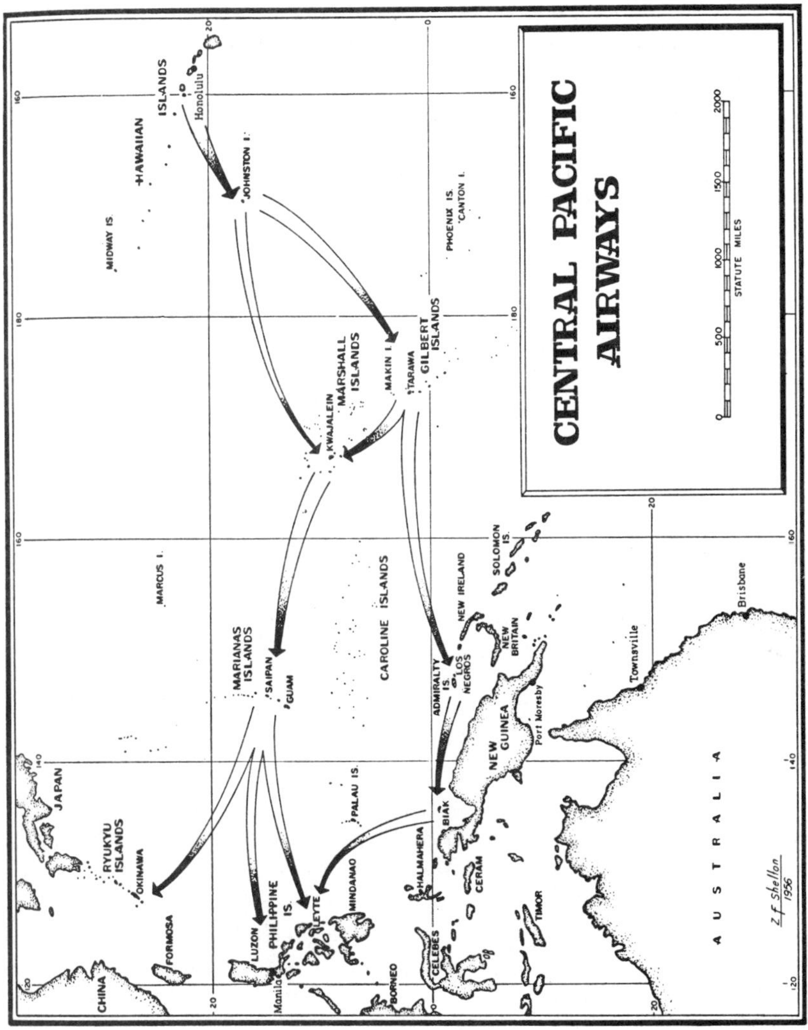

AIRLIFT IN THE WAR YEARS

Figure 14

organization and DAT continued its usurpation of ATC by naming the ATC control officer its own as well. DAT was under the extreme pressure of providing airlift to a theater that had very few resources of its own and grabbed any asset it could get its hands on. After all, there was a war being fought, and early on, there was a large question as to who would win. Nonetheless, DAT overstepped its bounds and interfered with larger strategic issues. DAT ignored the War Department order giving ATC independence from theater control, even to the extent of dictating precise cargo loads for contract aircraft returning to the United States. Maj Gen George Kenney, commander of the Allied Air Forces in the Pacific, unaware of the situation, personally called the ATC control officer to obtain support for the movement of some fighter aircraft "belly tanks" aboard ATC aircraft. The control officer lost no time in informing General Kenney of DAT's interference. Two days later General Kenney called back, reporting that he had ordered DAT to run its internal show and keep its hands off ATC. The problem promptly disappeared.[110]

By the end of 1942, ATC's Pacific operations were, in both General Arnold's and General George's opinions, "very much a barnstorming set-up—without proper organization, standardization, maintenance, or discipline."[111] With the planned increase in operations over the route for 1943, General Arnold directed that ATC have its own people along the Pacific route. The airways detachments immediately fell to ATC. The wing soon thereafter established a headquarters in Hawaii and a full colonel went to Australia as control officer. In May through August 1943, in preparation for the New Guinea offensive, ATC delivered one-half of the passengers and freight and 70 percent of the ferried planes for the entire year. The wing also made several unique contributions to the success of the drives throughout the theater. In June 1943 ATC delivered to Port Moresby two shipments of horizontal stabilizers for the crippled B-24 fleet, using American Airlines C-54As under contract. In August, ATC provided special missions to deliver 36 tons of parachutes for use by the Australians in the upcoming air assault on Nadzab. ATC was also proud of its direct delivery to the Solomon Islands of 11,000 pounds of hand grenades by two C-87s in January 1943. Gen Douglas MacArthur had personally appealed for quick delivery, and ATC managed the whole job in three days—from notification to delivery. Airlift grew from 107 tons in December 1942 to 355 tons 12 months later. Ferrying operations moved 1,575 airplanes.[112]

The end of 1943 also found ATC in the disagreeable position of lagging far behind the advance of the forces it was supporting. Why it was so far behind is a matter of some speculation. As early as November 1942, the ATC Pacific Wing commander had attempted to provide proper support to the theater. Col James M. Gillespie wanted to shift ATC operations northward, delivering men and materiel directly to Port Moresby rather than to Australia. He also suggested that ATC provide intratheater service between Australia and Port Moresby, thus freeing up DAT resources for direct support within the combat zone. He asked ATC for more airplanes and suggested that the American portion of DAT—the 347th Troop

Carrier Group—operate under ATC, which would provide operational efficiency. General Kenney, on the other hand, wanted the troop carrier units to remain under his command for combat service, with ATC providing intratheater and extended intertheater support. Colonel Gillespie's rationale was one heard many years later in somewhat different circumstances:

> Air Transport Command is worldwide in experience and scope. The value of integration of operations under one command from the United States to final destination is apparent. The Air Transport Command is competent and capable to modify and conform its activities to any existing combat situation in any theater of operations.[113]

ATC headquarters squelched the whole package in December 1942, losing sight of the proposal to extend operations northward from Australia and concentrating on the intratheater issues. The headquarters was concerned that (1) taking over the troop carrier intratheater logistics mission would set a precedent for other theaters and (2) that ATC did not have the resources to accomplish the mission regardless of whether it got troop carrier resources.[114]

In March 1943, Col Milton Arnold, executive officer for the ATC G-3, reported to General George on his inspection trip of the Pacific. In that report, Colonel Arnold recommended that both Guadalcanal and Port Moresby become Pacific terminals for ATC operations in the Pacific. His reasoning was simple: "The war in the Pacific is flexible; consequently our service must be flexible if we are to serve this area."[115] He also reported that he had discussed ATC's flexibility with General Kenney, who was most anxious for the northward extension of ATC services. In April, General George took his own inspection trip through the Pacific.

He went on that trip armed with a prediction that ATC resources in the Southwest Pacific Area (SWPA) would increase six times by the end of the year. Headquarters provided these figures to all ATC agencies in the Pacific with orders to use them as a basis for planning throughout the year. General George promised the Pacific commanders that as soon as resources became available ATC would extend both its intratheater services and its intertheater operations—to include moves north. "General George had spoken of several thousand ATC personnel in SWPA, and it was expected that at least 1,200 men would be based at Amberly as a prelude to great ATC developments yet to come."[116]

By December 1943, ATC was providing some intratheater shuttle services, but it had not moved its terminal out of Australia northward with the war. Its final delivery terminal in SWPA was 1,500 miles behind the lines. There was extensive planning but no action. Colonel Arnold's observation from almost a year before remained valid: "Very few supplies carried by air are needed 1,500 miles from the front."[117]

The official ATC history of this period says that the best explanation of this delay was the "lack of a clear comprehension by the Pacific Wing of the ATC's mission in the SWPA."[118] Capt Richard Davis of ATC headquarters reinforced that idea in his report concerning an inspection trip in November and December of 1943:

> The Pacific Wing is not playing with the theater as closely as it should and is not sufficiently responsive to local needs. We are largely overshadowed by the air transport agencies which make us look like a peacetime, postwar commercial air route to Australia, not really involved in the struggle.[119]

Captain Davis provided some measure of why this occurred when he reported that the "Pacific Wing has endeavored to keep in touch with these trends, but the establishment of a strong through route to Australia has largely absorbed its energies and its attention."[120] He placed some of the blame on ATC headquarters as well:

> In retrospect it is evident that the plan tentatively agreed upon last spring . . . of immediately swinging a portion of the Pacific route through Espíritu Santo to Townsville with a view to operating into Guadalcanal and Port Moresby as soon thereafter as practicable, should not have been discarded by this Headquarters.[121]

Three days later, General George sent a memorandum to his chief of staff, Brig Gen Robert Nowland, that laid the issue out clearly. He said:

> It seems to me that the ATC has been very derelict in not pushing its services as close to our advancing units as possible. Our staff should be keeping itself abreast of the mission of the command, and should have observed long ago the fact that we were following a static condition and not keeping abreast of the tactical situation. Please have this entire subject studied at once, and see that we are not "left behind" from now on.[122]

General George also used the memorandum as a vehicle for making sure the ATC staff understood its mission in relation to the theaters:

> For the information of the staff, we should plan to take over from the theaters all intratheater transport operations as early as possible, leaving the theaters to use their transport equipment for employment in the actual combat area. I feel sure that both the Southwest and South Pacific theaters will gladly relinquish that job to us as soon as we are able to take it on . . . although we probably will not have planes with which to start this earlier than May or June, let's begin now to find out from the theater commanders how much of the job they are willing to turn over to us, so that by the time the summer is well along we will be giving to the theaters the service they have a right to expect from us, and which I know General Arnold wants us to handle.[123]

By June 1944 the wing executed a well-coordinated, successful move to begin direct delivery of supplies by air to Nadzab, a major supply base for campaigns in New Guinea. Prior to that, some 80 percent of cargo delivered by ATC was transshipped by the theater's Air Service Command. Thereafter, ATC moved its operations forward as the combat theater moved, the only delay being a common one in the Pacific—lack of promised resources (facilities, housing, and maintenance help, for example). The Pacific area followed the same pattern as other theaters in one respect—it wanted intratheater assistance from ATC as soon as possible. If nothing else, ATC represented additional resources. General Kenney was looking for ways to increase his airlift capability. The air supply of his forces was particularly important due to the distances involved and the lack of a transportation infrastructure in the Pacific. General Kenney had a theater policy of using all theater airlift resources in the most flexible way possible. He used troop carrier units for logistical purposes when needed and called upon the DAT (a logistical organization) for direct support of combat units as required. But these diversions had the effect of disrupting the orderly flow of supplies throughout the area.[124]

In January 1944, General Kenney proposed to General Arnold and General George that ATC assign additional squadrons to the Pacific under General Kenney's control. General George's reply, direct to General Kenney, showed ATC's doctrinal thinking for the war years:

> You desire ATC to assign airplanes and flight crews to you for control by your DAT, with the responsibility of ATC being restricted to maintenance and administration of personnel. Based upon wide experience that the ATC has had in North Africa and India, I personally think that this would not result in efficient air transport operation. I propose that ATC be given a job to do in your theater and that the line of responsibility be clearly delimited geographically. We will fly, of course, such routes and carry such cargo as you direct. I know the ATC can render you an efficient and highly flexible air transport service and, based upon the excellent assistance that ATC has been able to render in intratheater operations in North Africa and India, this will permit you to utilize your troop carrier organizations for tactical operations in the forward areas. This message has been shown to General Arnold.[125]

General George also wired Maj Gen Laurence Kuter, assistant chief of the Air Staff for plans, then on a special mission to the SWPA, noting that General Arnold had been consulted and was in favor of the ATC plan. Col Robert Love, ATC deputy chief of staff, met with General Kenney in an attempt to clear the issue. He reported that General Kenney said that the Australians "were afraid of an ATC air line in Australia." He did agree, however, that there was little chance of SWPA obtaining the additional 200 airplanes ATC would make available for the operation without ATC control. By the end of March, General Kenney relented. His message to General George was a classic statement of how to operate airlift in support of a theater:

> I would like to have you transport our total load over the general route Melbourne to Nadzab. It is not proposed to have DAT assume any command functions over your operating agency. Your operators will be furnished with information depending upon your current handling ability as to where the job is, what the job is, and what the priorities are, but we do not expect to tell them how to do it.[126]

AIRLIFT DOCTRINE

General Kuter added one more concern to the process, one that was to resurface 40 years later in other intratheater airlift initiatives. He wrote to General George that there was a widespread impression that all authority over the operation would remain at ATC headquarters. He recommended that ATC make clear that the final decision over controversial matters would be made in the theater, not at headquarters. General George's reply is well worth extensive quoting:

> When ATC first began operating in foreign theaters, its job for the most part was furnishing of through services while intra-theater transport was relegated to troop carriers and other local air transport organizations. Present trend in many theaters is for ATC to take over both services. . . . No good reason exists why we should change our present method of inter-theater operation, and such services should continue under ATC direction with maximum of support and minimum of interference from theater or air force commanders. Since these commanders help establish the priorities, their interest in the through service is protected. But where ATC operates an intratheater-theater service fuller participation of theater or air force commander in the operation can be permitted for the reason that the service is operated primarily on his behalf. However, in operating such local services we must insist that the ATC retain command of its own operations. We agree that the theater or air force command should lay down the routes we are to follow, and the personnel and materiel we are to carry by means of instructions to the ATC commander. We are also agreeable that we have the right to temporarily abrogate schedules and services to accomplish special missions. To allay the anxiety of theater or air force commanders that the ATC through its Washington headquarters might divert a substantial portion of the aircraft from the theater for more urgent use elsewhere, it is the policy of this Command not to remove aircraft assigned for local theater transportation, unless there is concurrence of theater or air force commander or substitution of aircraft of similar capacity.[127]

Numerous intratheater routes followed, with excellent support by the theater for ATC needs. Combat avoiditis disappeared. The ATC wing actually beat part of the headquarters forces to Leyte. ATC started flying into Quezon airstrip while Japanese forces were still active in Manila City.

Through late 1944 and early 1945, the command expended significant efforts in the top secret buildup of the XXI Bomber Command movement to the Marianas. The movement of the giant bombers differed from other ferrying jobs in that the crews were somewhat better prepared for long-range flights, even though thorough briefings were still very much required. Between October 1944 and September 1945, 1,442 B-29s arrived in Saipan. All told, ATC ferried or controlled the delivery of 8,047 aircraft across the Pacific. Cargo tonnages increased as well, from 494 in December 1943 to 3,483 in July 1945. The command started its Pacific operation with one officer in Australia in 1942; by the end of the war in 1945 it had 41,657 people in the Pacific Division.[128]

ATC also was called upon to participate in the final occupation of Japan—Mission 75. The Far East Air Forces (FEAF) were in operational control of the project, which called for ATC to provide at least 180 C-54s, while FEAF supplied 180 C-47s and 272 C-46s. ATC aircraft from all over the Pacific, the India-China

Division, the North Atlantic Division, and the North Africa Division were all concentrated in the Pacific for the critical mission of Kadena mission at Kadena Air Base. Kadena had originally been built as an advanced base for B-29 operations but was yet unused. ATC had to provide a complete air-base setup in order to operate there. The operation began on 30 August and 13 days later was completed without an accident. The combined airlift forces moved the 11th Airborne Division (Reinforced), the 27th Infantry Division, and advanced elements of three headquarters from Okinawa to Atsugi Field.

> In all, over 23,000 troops, 924 jeeps, 9 disassembled liaison aircraft, 329 other vehicles and pieces of equipment, including tractors, bulldozers, and 6 x 6 trucks, made the flight from Okinawa to Atsugi. In addition, 2,348 barrels of gasoline and oil and rations to the amount of over 900 tons were offloaded at Atsugi. More than seven thousand released prisoners of war and internees of sixteen different nationalities were brought back to Okinawa, on the first or second lap of their repatriation journeys.[129]

Army Air Force Regulation 20-44

As the war progressed, a large number of transport services developed in the individual theaters. Each had its own particular mission and did not necessarily contribute to the whole. Theater air forces and bomber commands attempted to set up additional, dedicated airlift services by requesting assignment of crews and airplanes from ATC or whatever source available. In March 1944, ATC suggested a War Department memorandum that would:

- Discourage the establishment of miscellaneous transport units.
- Advise theater commanders that efficient use of air transport requires their relying on the ATC for air transport from the United States to the theater and between theaters.
- Define or redefine the transport function of Troop Carrier units within the theater, their relationship to theater air service commands and the Transportation Corps.
- Authorize the ATC to undertake such intra-theater services outside of forward areas as may be deemed necessary by the theater.[130]

The Air Staff, too, had several concerns about the Air Transport Command, Troop Carrier Command, and the Air Service Command Transport Service performing similar missions and directed the Army Air Forces Board to undertake a study concerning the "achievement of maximum efficiency in the accomplishment of the various tasks undertaken by the air transport system."[131] This recognition of a "system" was, in and of itself, a doctrinal step forward of rather grand proportions. Admitting that its study suffered from severe time constraints (11 days), the board

AIRLIFT DOCTRINE

nonetheless recommended intertheater airlift continue under ATC; that the theater Air Force commander have a theater air transport command (as a separate unit); and that troop carrier units retain at least 35 percent of their forces on a full-time basis for airborne training, with full assignment three to four weeks prior to airborne operations. The study also found that there was no requirement for assignment of transport aircraft to tactical combat units (except under most unusual circumstances).[132]

The Air Staff directed the AAF Board to undertake further study of the issue, noting that its only exception to the first report was that the delivery of supplies in the theater would rest with the Air Transport Command and that recommendations would be consistent with the delegation of responsibility.[133] The second report responded more to the Air Staff position. It recommended that ATC be responsible for inter- and intratheater delivery of supplies, except for the mission reserved for the troop carrier units. The report additionally recommended limiting the Air Service Command to utility cargo aircraft, and directed ATC to make use of civil air carriers.[134]

The result, in August of that year, was a new AAF regulation (20-44) that replaced the General Orders Number 8 of June 1942. It included a broader statement of ATC's mission, officially recognizing ATC responsibilities for control and operation of aerial ports of embarkation, and full operational control by ATC of tactical or other aircraft "engaged in movements between the United States and theaters of operations" over established routes controlled by ATC. It also granted ATC the authority to provide scheduled intratheater air transport services at the request of the theater commanders and formally directed the Air Transport Command to utilize civil air carriers to the fullest extent possible. To solve the proliferation of air transport services' problem, the new regulation limited the theater air commanders, and consequently the theaters themselves:

> The assignment of cargo transport aircraft to agencies other than the Air Transport Command and Troop Carrier Command (including troop carrier training activities) will be restricted to the utility cargo (UC—) transport types and will be limited to those essential for emergency maintenance and reclamation, emergency delivery of supplies and equipment, staff administrative purposes and maintenance of flying proficiency. The provision of additional air transportation or the operation of any scheduled air transport service is a function of the Air Transport Command.[135]

This particular paragraph was strengthened three months later with the following amendment:

> The assignment of cargo transport aircraft to agencies other than the Air Transport Command and I Troop Carrier Command will be limited to those essential for staff administrative purposes, training, maintenance of flying proficiency, and for local transport services operated for emergency maintenance, reclamation, and emergency delivery of supplies and equipment. In no case will these local services duplicate the services of Air Transport Command, which command is primarily responsible for the

> operation of all military air transport conducted under the jurisdiction of the commanding general, AAF. Prior to the establishment of a scheduled or regular air transport service by a command or air force, other than Air Transport Command and other than I Troop Carrier Command . . . such service will first be requested of the Air Transport Command, through Headquarters, AAF, Traffic Division, Assistant Chief of Air Staff, Materiel and Services, and approved by Headquarters, AAF.[136]

Since the AAF controlled the airplanes available for the creation of specialized air transport services, this policy had the effect of limiting the theaters, and their air forces, to those airlift organizations approved by ATC. This centralized the control of scheduled airlift, except for the airborne functions of the troop carrier forces, in ATC and had a dampening effect on the proliferation of such services.

The fact that an AAF regulation had such a limiting influence on the theaters was something of a doctrinal coup in itself. Originally, it took a War Department circular to literally force theater commanders' attention to the issue and to give sufficient weight to the doctrine/policy to make it stick. By the latter part of the war, the theater air forces were so strongly recognized as "in charge of" air matters, that the AAF could control air transport issues in a way internal to the AAF.

The Nexus of Policy and Doctrine

As early as October of 1942 General Arnold expressed the vital link between military air transportation and civil aviation, one that carried through the war into the postwar era:

> It is necessary, in all of our air transport operations, that we consider the effect of our current and projected activities on US air transport operations, both military and civil, after the war. Whenever practicable, consistent with our war effort, we should take action to insure that our military air transport routes and facilities are establishing and furthering our post-war position in the air transport field.[137]

The results of an AAF study appeared in April 1944 as a War Department policy statement that was to "govern all AAF thinking and planning in respect to Post-War Civil Aviation."[138] The War Department based its policy on a relatively short AAF document that embodied several critical doctrinal concepts. The realities of war had created the awareness that a "powerful air force is a prerequisite of adequate national defense."[139] There was still a heavy reliance on the civil sector: "A strong air transport system together with its aircraft, air bases, and airway facilities—readily adaptable to military use, and the principle non-military support of the peacetime aviation manufacturing industry—is vital to the nation's airpower."[140]

The policy started with the position that "national security is of first importance and the national policy in regard to civil aviation must be in accord with the military

AIRLIFT DOCTRINE

requirements of national defense." It further argued that a "primary essential to a powerful air force is the existence, in time of peace, of several strong aircraft, aircraft engines, and accessory manufacturing companies, together with progressive and competitive engineering and research associated therewith." With these fundamentals as a backdrop, the War Department subscribed to the policy of a "regulated and supervised competition in international commercial aviation." At the national level, the War Department advocated "maximum encouragement to the development of private competitive enterprise in United States international airline operations subject to reasonable regulation." Although the regulatory issue makes for interesting contemporary discussions, the essential ingredient concerning encouragement had particular importance to the implementation of the policy.[141]

By late 1945 the War and Navy Departments had reworded the policy into a more understandable format. Air power shifted from a "prerequisite of adequate national defense" to "an essential element of national security." Subscription to the policy changed to advocacy and the expression improved as well:

> Since national security is best served by the maximum contribution from civil aviation to airpower, the military services advocate:
>
> a. Encouragement to the development of private competitive enterprise, on a sound economic basis, in United States domestic and international air carrier operations, subject to reasonable Federal regulation.
> b. Encouragement to the development of other commercial aviation, enterprises, and private civilian flying, subject to reasonable Federal regulation.
> c. Encouragement to education and training in all phases of aeronautics and the coordination of such education and training, to the extent practicable with the methods and requirements of the military services.[142]

ATC passed the policy along to its divisions noting that they were to provide "every possible assistance" to the civil airlines that operated over routes that coincided with ATC's, because this aided in the maintenance of the "preeminent position of the US air carriers" and the resultant "strengthening of the nation's defense."[143] The policymakers were serious. ATC was to "make available its bases for use by the carriers in establishing their certificated international routes, and to sell fuel, oil, spare parts, supplies, and services to the carriers at ATC foreign bases."[144]

Numerous other pressures played in the decision-making process, especially when the war began to wind down. There were the natural desires from all concerned that American servicemen return to civilian life as soon as possible—demobilization. There were also pressures from the Allies for ATC to stop serving as an agent for the American civil carriers, and the AAF wanted ATC out of the middle of this turmoil. And, the high-level decision makers had already decreed a "progressive reduction of ATC C-54 operations and their release for disposal to the airlines and foreign governments."[145] General Arnold wrote to President Truman in August 1945 that by the following year, ATC would operate only limited through routes worldwide, that theater commanders would assume local intratheater services as soon as possible, that ATC personnel strength would be significantly reduced, and that over 500 C-54s would be declared surplus.[146]

A series of letters between Generals Cyrus Smith, Harold George, H. H. Arnold, and Carl "Tooey" Spaatz reflected this nexus of policy and doctrine. General Smith reported a conversation with General Arnold that concerned the composition and duties of the Air Transport Command, based upon wartime experiences. Here are the key points of that conversation:

- ATC should remain as an AAF command, reporting directly to the Commanding General, AAF.
- ATC should be a self-contained organization, with its own maintenance, communications, and weather system.
- ATC should develop a coast-to-coast airway system, both as a baseline for ferrying operations and as a laboratory for research and development in the air transportation field.
- ATC should develop a military northern route to link Europe and Japan, with tie-ins to southern destinations.
- ATC should be the preeminent airline operator in the world, better than any airline organization; but it should maintain very close coordination with the US airlines, with ATC as *the* point of contact with civil aviation.
- ATC should *plan* to move 36,000 troops and equipment promptly, with civil airlines contributing three fourths of the airlift capability.
- ATC should keep its strength to the minimum consistent with getting the job done.
- The objective of the peacetime ATC is to be an organization that can expand rapidly without bringing in a new organization. All personnel must be trained to be the executives of the future wartime ATC.[147]

The net impact of this policy of supporting the civil airlines reflected a clear doctrinal predisposition. ATC was not only a military instrument; it was also an instrument of national economic policy. The unique interrelationship between military air transport and civil air transport, influential during the prewar era and heavily relied upon during World War II, carried into the postwar period. Foreign concerns that the US government would use ATC as a wedge to assist in the development of international US carriers were well founded.[148] The president, the War Department, and the Department of State were all concerned that the tremendous strides made and advantages gained by ATC in the war, both technical capabilities and of the magnificent international route structure (with all its attendant facilities), would be lost to foreign governments and carriers. "Luckily," ATC could reduce its wartime level of effort, thus also reducing its visibility in the marketplace, and still contribute to the enhancement of American civil air carriers, because the carriers could fill in with their new found capability. This not only allowed a mobilization base for the next war, it was very cheap airlift at a politically and militarily acceptable rate. Doctrinally, this meant that a significant amount of air transport power would reside in the civilian sector, theoretically available when needed. It also meant a continuation of the 20-year trend of relying on airplanes designed for civil airlines rather than military purposes.

General Arnold further summarized his thoughts concerning ATC in a letter to General George in early December 1945. The majority of the letter follows:

> The technique, knowledge of procedure, and experience that has been acquired by the Air Transport Command must never be lost to the AAF. Accordingly, we should have in peace time an Air Transport Command flying service between the United States and our bases in the Azores, Iceland, Greenland, Alaska, Okinawa, and the Philippines—this to insure the personnel we have in the Air Transport Command, and incidentally in our long range bombing units, are competent and capable of flying over any part of the earth's surface, regardless of weather conditions, climate, or geography.
>
> I think we should also establish a model airline independent of the commercial airlines from Washington to Los Angeles. We should utilize the latest gadgets to insure that routine flights, regular and scheduled, are made regardless of weather conditions. We should always be ahead of the commercial airlines in technique of operations and in latest developed gadgets. The airline itself should be as straight as it is possible to make it, whether we hit large or small towns along the route.
>
> The size of the Air Transport Command should be such that, together with its reserve in the airlines themselves, it can pick up and carry one Army Corps to either Alaska or Iceland. With this concept of airpower, the Air Force must, at all times, be ready to utilize civil aviation—personnel, aircraft, and facilities. This, therefore, requires that civil aviation be kept as strong as possible and coordinated with the Air Forces.
>
> From my knowledge of ATC operations and my experience on the JCS and CCS, I, probably more than anyone else, fully appreciate the job the Air Transport Command has done and, because of its world wide activities, the vital necessity for its continuation as a command, not under any of the air forces, and operating independently.[149]

Equally revealing was his letter the next day to General Spaatz as he was preparing to become the commanding general of the Army Air Forces. In the five-page "Dear Tooey" letter, more than in any other official document, General Arnold linked ATC with the fundamental issues facing the postwar Air Force. After reminding General Spaatz of the need to be "constantly alert to obtain and maintain the autonomy of the Air Forces" he stressed that "we must not forget the great difficulty now almost forgotten, of *deploying* and establishing our Air Forces in the areas in which they are to fight. During times of peace, we are apt to retain our combat units and sacrifice the essentials to their successful deployment and immediate operation. We must retain our bases and our means of deployment."[150]

His rationale was a mixture of military utility and an appeal to the shared goal of an autonomous Air Force:

> I have long felt that the Air Transport Command has a unique value which had never been fully appreciated throughout the Air Forces. The contribution which it has made and can make to national security, and to the autonomy of the Air Forces is little understood but of vital importance. As a result of my experience as a member of the United States Joint Chiefs of Staff and the Combined Chiefs of Staff, I firmly believe that an essential component of American airpower is an integrated autonomous single Air Transport Command, reporting *directly* to the Commanding General, Army Air Forces. I believe that it is an essential instrument to the Commanding General, Army Air Forces, in the accomplishment of his mission, in the execution of national aviation policy, and in the fostering and retention of an autonomous Air Force. I believe it offers a means of insuring our capacity to support the immediate worldwide deployment of our Armed Forces; of contributing materially to autonomy of the Air Forces; giving essential unity to the Air Forces command. This latter aspect had been invaluable to me, and will be no less valuable to you. The Air Transport Command is *the* Air Forces and *the* War Department's high speed physical connecting link between headquarters and the field commands.[151]

This strongly emotional passage almost carries the sense of pleading for recognition of the importance of strategic airlift. It also represents a unique expression of the many roles of airlift.

General Arnold also articulated the importance of ATC in its newly recognized diplomatic role:

> American foreign policy is naturally not the primary responsibility of the air forces. However, aviation matters are of growing number and importance in our foreign policy. Since the Air Transport Command will always enjoy free entry into foreign circles, and particularly since that Command will exercise military authority in the territories of several foreign countries, it is mandatory that maximum cooperation and assistance to the State Department for the furtherance of our American objectives be firmly charged to the Air Transport Command as the field agent of the Air Forces and the War Department. This will require understanding and strong support within our own Air Forces Headquarters. It is necessary also that the War Department as a whole be educated to the Air Forces' and the Air Transport Command's greatly broadened responsibilities and functions, and [to] the Air Transport Command's need for support and assistance from the working members of the higher echelons.[152]

Although later operations may be viewed as the first use of air transportation as a diplomatic tool, it is clear that both the policies discussed earlier and General Arnold's articulation of the potential of ATC in such a role presaged what had become, by 1945, a fact of life.

General Arnold also touched on the separation of ATC operations from the control of theater commanders, perhaps providing a hint, beyond military necessity, of why he so strongly supported this principle throughout the war:

Finally, I want to reemphasize a strong personal conviction. In time of war the authority of the theater commander in his area is paramount. This is as it should be, and I have no reason to believe that such will not continue to be the case. The Air Transport Command has always been an exempted agency operating into and through the various theaters. This principle should be retained. These operations have had a great effect on maintaining the unity of overall Air Forces organization, control, and perspective. They have given me an opportunity to keep my fingers on the pulse of Air Force's activities in the various theaters and to observe firsthand the part of the Air Forces is playing in the logistical and tactical support of the combat units. Of equal importance, it gives one an opportunity to preserve a worldwide viewpoint so essential in present military philosophy. I believe it essential that you have such a means at your disposal.[153]

White and Green: Doctrinal Hallmarks

Perhaps the single greatest indicator of the successes of ATC in World War II, and of the trust that the senior leadership had come to place in strategic airlift, was a planned series of redeployments that were to move the majority of men and aircraft from European theater of operations (ETO) to the Pacific theater. The White Project called for the return of 2,825 heavy bombers from Europe and 1,240 from the Mediterranean theater, using all three major Atlantic routes. The planes would include their own crews plus whatever additional personnel and equipment they could carry. ATC provided the entire spectrum of en route services and was in command control of the crews and airplanes while they were in the route system. The project started on 20 May 1945.[154]

Most of the planes from Europe or North Africa had completed the passage by the end of August. During the course of the project, 5,965 aircraft made the westward crossing of the Atlantic (some 4,000 from ETO and more than 1,900 from the Mediterranean theater), all but 521 by the close of August. Most of the 4,182 heavy bombers made the homeward flight in June or July. The passage of two-engine aircraft began in June and was substantially completed during July and August. The last large contingent consisted of 433 Flying Fortresses, which came home in September or October via the South Atlantic airway.[155]

Because of the earlier than expected surrender of the Japanese, no unit that flew to the United States for assignment to the Pacific ever served in the theater.[156] Even though there was a normal amount of staff planning involved in this huge movement, the White Project was "no big deal," an amazing transformation given the fact that the entire strategic airlift concept and route structure had emerged and become a reality in only a scant five years.

Perhaps even more revolutionary, at least from the perspective of a five-year-old organization, was the Green Project—a plan to redeploy some 50,000 passengers a month from Europe to the United States, at the same time as the White Project. The AAF strengthened ATC with an additional 33,000 men and an additional 256 C-47s from the troop carrier units. Planning began at least one month before V-E Day, with ATC submitting its plan on 12 April and receiving War Department approval on 17 April. Changes in the plans, mostly caused by cessation of hostilities in Japan, never fully taxed the capabilities of ATC, but the results were a hallmark of international air transportation:

> Of all the aerial redeployment programs of 1945, the Green Project was the most impressive. It illustrates the capacity of the War Department, and particularly of the mature Air Transport Command, to plan an air transportation operation of tremendous magnitude and to carry it out in a completely effective fashion. At a word from Washington supplies of every kind were procured and transported to the points where they would be needed. Several thousand men were moved by air and water and were put to work again, often at entirely unfamiliar assignments, thousands of miles from their previous duty stations. It is no wonder that the mimeographed Standard Operating Procedures prepared for the project in several of the participating divisions ran to over 75 pages. It was a tremendous demonstration of the mass airlift of manpower, certainly most striking of those marking the end of the war. Within less than five months, over 166,000 passengers—50,514 in a single month—were flown across the Atlantic without a single fatality. Nothing like it had happened before. What its sequel might be—for peace or war—in a day of larger, more efficient air transports, was a challenge which demanded little of the imagination of the men who had had a part in it.[157]

The Strategic Airlift Heritage of World War II

Ideas, concepts, and (to an extent) doctrines about strategic airlift existed in many forms at the end of World War II. In a summary form they said:

• Strategic airlift is a function of airpower that supports the entire defense establishment, not just the air component. Its scope is also broad enough to serve as an agent of diplomatic and economic policies of the nation in its own right.

• Strategic airlift is a vital element of airpower and the national military strategy. Its potential contributions are so important as to justify exemption of these forces from the day-to-day control of the theater commanders and concentration of their control at the highest possible level of strategic decision making.

• Strategic airlift is separate from troop carrier aviation, but has such flexibility as to be available for scheduled airlift services within the theaters upon common agreement of all concerned. In unique circumstances, strategic airlift may perform combat supply by air, both air landing and air dropping, but again only upon agreement of all concerned.

• Strategic airlift will exist in peacetime at a militarily acceptable minimum strength to be prepared for extensive expansion during wartime. Strategic airlift will rely overwhelmingly on civil aviation for its initial wartime capabilities. In peacetime, the Air Force will encourage, to the maximum extent possible, the development and success of national and international US civil aviation.

• Strategic airlift is a complex logistical operation that depends on an extensive system of bases, intensive management by air transportation experts, and a tightly controlled program of user priorities. While aircraft specifically designed for military air transportation may be desirable, they are not required for effective mission accomplishment.

- Strategic airlift can be routinely relied upon to execute extremely demanding missions on a sustained basis, once it is given sufficient resources.[158]

General Arnold, whose vision in the field of air transportation was surpassed by no one, encapsulated the operational success and doctrinal importance of strategic airlift this way in March 1945:

> We have learned and must not forget that from now on air transport is an essential element of airpower, in fact, of all national power. We must have an air transport organization in being capable of tremendous expansion.[159]

NOTES

1. W. F. Craven and J. L. Cate, eds., *The Army Air Forces in World War II*, vol. 1, *Plans & Early Operations January 1939 to August 1942* (Chicago: University of Chicago Press, 1948), 313.
2. Ibid., 314.
3. Administrative History, Ferrying Command, 29 May 1941-30 June 1942, 3.
4. Ibid., 9.
5. The Adjutant General's Office, War Department, to the commanding generals, all armies, GHQ Air Force departments and corps areas et al., letter, subject: Constitution of the Air Corps Ferrying Command, 5 June 1941.
6. History, Ferrying Command, 41 n. 35.
7. Ibid., 45.
8. Craven and Cate, *The Army Air Forces in World War II*, 1:316.
9. Ibid., 317-18.
10. Ibid., 320-22.
11. Ibid., 322-24.
12. Ibid., 325-26.
13. History, Ferrying Command, 58.
14. Ibid., 59.
15. Craven and Cate, *The Army Air Forces in World War II*, 1:328.
16. Ibid., 310-12.
17. Ibid., 350.
18. Lt Col Oliver LaFarge, historical officer, Headquarters Air Transport Command, to Col Francis D. Butler, Office of the Assistant Chief of Staff—5, Headquarters Army Air Forces, letter, 28 September 1945.
19. History, Ferrying Command, 57.
20. Ibid., 64.
21. Craven and Cate, *The Army Air Forces in World War II*, 1:350-52.
22. History, Ferrying Command, 101.
23. Col Samuel Moore, Historical Office, Headquarters Army Air Forces, historical study, *Tactical Employment in the US Army of Transport Aircraft and Gliders in World War II*, ca. 1946, 69.
24. Craven and Cate, *The Army Air Forces in World War II*, 1:364-65.
25. History, Ferrying Command, 120.
26. Ibid., 121.

27. Ibid., 145.
28. Ibid., 146.
29. Ibid., 149–50.
30. Ibid., 155.
31. LaFarge to Butler, 28 September 1945.
32. Ibid., 156–57.
33. History, Ferrying Command, 142–43.
34. Ibid., 144.
35. Ibid., 158–59.
36. W. F. Craven and J. L. Cate, eds., *The Army Air Forces in World War II*, vol. 7, *Services Around the World* (Chicago: University of Chicago Press, 1958), 14.
37. Capt Frank Heck, report, subject: History of the Air Transport Command, 29 May 1941–30 September 1945: A Brief Sketch.
38. Craven and Cate, *The Army Air Forces in World War II*, 7:19.
39. Heck, A Brief Sketch, 8–14.
40. Administrative History, Air Transport Command, June 1942–March 1943, 126.
41. Ibid., 125.
42. LaFarge to Butler, 28 September 1945; History, Air Transport Command, 1942–1943, 136–42.
43. History, Air Transport Command, 1942–1943, 136.
44. Ibid., 137.
45. Ibid.
46. Memorandum No. W 95-18-42, Brig Gen H. B. Lewis, acting adjutant general, War Department, to distribution A, subject: Air Transport Operations, 21 September 1942.
47. See, for example, the following letters. Maj Gen Harold George, commanding general, Air Transport Command, to commanding general, Army Air Forces, letter, subject: Relationship Between the Theaters and the Military Air Transportation Agency, 15 March 1944; Maj Gen H. A. Craig, acting chief of Air Staff, Army Air Forces, to deputy chief of staff, Operations Division, letter, subject: Relationship Between the Theaters and the Military Air Transportation Agency, 7 April 1944; and Lt Col Samuel Gates, chief, Organization and Contract Supervision, Headquarters Air Transport Command, to Col H. R. Naddux, Operations Division, War Department General Staff, letter, subject: Relationship Between the Theaters and the Air Transport Command, 29 April 1944.
48. Craven and Cate, *The Army Air Forces in World War II*, 7:51.
49. Memorandum, Brig Gen C. R. Smith, deputy commander, Air Transport Command, to commanding general, Army Air Forces, subject: Relationship of Air Transport Command to Theaters, 7 August 1943.
50. Craven and Cate, *The Army Air Forces in World War II*, 7:58–59.
51. Ibid., 59–60.
52. Administrative History, Air Transport Command, March 1943–July 1944, 178–79.
53. Craven and Cate, *The Army Air Forces in World War II*, 7:60–61; History, Air Transport Command, 1943–1944, 180-81.
54. History, Air Transport Command, 1943–1944, appendix, 10.
55. Ibid.; Circular No. 180, War Department, subject: Air Transport Command-Capacity Control in Theaters, 4 April 1944.
56. History, Air Transport Command, 1943–1944, 183–84.
57. Ibid., 185–86.
58. Lt Col Oliver LaFarge, historical study, *North Africa—The First Phase*, n.d., 1.
59. Ibid., 6–7.
60. Craven and Cate, *The Army Air Forces in World War II*, 7:76–77, 80-81.
61. Air Chief Marshal Sir Arthur Tedder, air commander in chief, Mediterranean Air Command, to Gen H. H. Arnold, W583, message, 5-15-43, attached to memorandum, Maj Gen Harold George, commanding general, Air Transport Command, to General Hanley, subject: ATC Operations in North African Theater, 20 May 1943.
62. Brig Gen C. R. Smith, chief of staff, Air Transport Command, to Sir Arthur Tedder, letter, 1 June 1943.
63. History, Air Transport Command, 1943–1944, 185-87.
64. Craven and Cate, *The Army Air Forces in World War II*, 7:84.

65. History, Air Transport Command, 1943–1944, 187.
66. Craven and Cate, *The Army Air Forces in World War II*, 7:82.
67. George to Hanley, 20 May 1943.
68. Ibid.
69. Craven and Cate, *The Army Air Forces in World War II*, 7:83–84.
70. Ibid., 92–99.
71. Lt Gen H. H. Arnold, commanding general, Army Air Forces, to commanding general, Eastern theater of operations, letter, subject: Airport for Air Transport Needs in the United Kingdom, 10 August 1942; General Arnold to Maj Gen Carl Spaatz, air officer, European theater of operations, United States Army, message, 30 November 1942; Col Robert Love, deputy chief of staff, Air Transport Command, to commanding general, European theater of operations, letter, subject: Air Transport Command Operations, 2 May 1943; Lt Col John de P. T. Hillis, Headquarters European Wing, Air Transport Command, to Col Robert Love, deputy chief of staff, Air Transport Command, letter, subject: Eighth Air Force Service Command Ferrying and Transport Service, 10 May 1943; memorandum for record, Brig Gen Hugh Knerr, deputy commander, Eighth Air Force Service Command, subject: Conference Report, 6 August 1943.
72. Craven and Cate, *The Army Air Forces in World War II*, 7:98–99.
73. Ibid., 99–102.
74. Ibid., 104–6.
75. George to Hanley, 20 May 1943.
76. President Franklin Roosevelt to the secretary of war, letter, 10 November 1943.
77. Robert Patterson, secretary of war, to Gen H. H. Arnold, commanding general, Army Air Forces, letter, 11 September 1944.
78. Gen H. H. Arnold, commanding general, Army Air Forces, to Lt Gen Carl Spaatz, commanding general, United States Strategic Air Forces, letter, 11 September 1944.
79. General Arnold to General Spaatz, letter, subject: US Military Air Transportation, European Theater, 5 June 1944; General Spaatz to General Arnold, letter, 20 June 1944; Operations Division, War Department, disposition form, subject: Future Development of Military Air Transportation in the European Theater, 16 July 1944; Col Joe Loutzenheiser, chief, Operational Plans Division, Headquarters Army Air Forces, to Post-War Division, Headquarters Army Air Forces, routing and record sheet, subject: Future Development of Military Air Transportation in the European Theater, 24 July 1944.
80. Craven and Cate, *The Army Air Forces in World War II*, 7:113.
81. Ibid., 405–6; Lt Col Oliver LaFarge, *Air Transport to China Under the 10th Air Force April–November 1942*, historical study, n.d., 1-7; Headquarters Army Air Forces, China Theater, *Military Histories*, 31 December 1945, sec. 5, 1; Lt Col Samuel Moore, historian, US Tenth Air Force, *History of the India-China Ferry Under the Tenth Air Force*, ca. 1943, n.p.
82. Memorandum, Lt Gen H. H. Arnold, deputy chief of staff for air, War Department, to President Franklin Roosevelt, subject: Cargo Planes for China, 4 February 1942.
83. LaFarge, *Air Transport to China*, 2.
84. Maj Gen Lewis Brereton, commanding general, Tenth Air Force, to adjutant general, War Department, paraphrased message, 28 March 1942.
85. Craven and Cate, *The Army Air Forces in World War II*, 7:114–17.
86. W. F. Craven and J. L. Cate, *The Army Air Forces in World War II*, vol. 4, *The Pacific: Guadalcanal to Saipan August 1942 to July 1944* (Chicago: University of Chicago Press, 1950), 411.
87. Ibid., 414; see also 7:119; Moore, *History of the India-China Ferry*.
88. LaFarge, *Air Transport to China*, 13–17.
89. Ibid., 33.
90. Whiting Willauer, secretary, China Defense Supplies, Inc., to Col Harold Harris, Plans Division, Headquarters Air Transport Command, letter, 23 September 1942.
91. Frank Sinclair, aviation technical adviser, China Defense Supplies, Inc., Memorandum re Air Transport System, Dinjan-Kuming, China, n.d., 51–52, attached to Willauer to Harris, letter, 23 September 1942.
92. Ibid.
93. Memorandum, Col C. R. Smith, chief of staff, Air Transport Command, to commanding general, Army Air Forces, subject: India-China Ferry Operation, 13 October 1942.
94. Ibid.

95. Craven and Cate, *The Army Air Forces in World War II*, 7:121-22.
96. Ibid., 122–23; Military Analysis Division, The United States Strategic Bombing Survey (USSBS), *The Air Transport Command in the War Against Japan*, December 1946, 12.
97. Craven and Cate, *The Army Air Forces in World War II*, 4:446–47.
98. Ibid., 448.
99. Craven and Cate, *The Army Air Forces in World War II*, 7:125.
100. LaFarge, *Air Transport to China*, 32.
101. Craven and Cate, *The Army Air Forces in World War II*, 7:135-36; India China Wing, Air Transport Command, *Story of Spring Diversion, February to June 1944*, n.d.; USSBS, *Air Transport Command Against Japan*, 11.
102. Brig Gen William Old, to commanding general, Army Air Forces, India-Burma Sector, China-Burma-India Theater, report; subject: Report of Findings of Board Directed to Investigate the Maximum Delivery of Air Cargo to China, 21 June 1944; Maj Gen Harold George, commanding general, Air Transport Command, to commanding general, Army Air Forces, letter, subject: Report of Findings of Board Appointed by Commanding General, India-Burma Sector, China-Burma-India Theater, to Investigate the Maximum Delivery of Air Cargo to China, 8 July 1944.
103. India-China Division, Air Transport Command, *A History of Hump Operations 1 January 1945 to 31 March 1945*, ca. 1945, 199–202; Memorandum, Col R. B. White, chief, Aircraft Maintenance, India-China Division, Air Transport Command, subject: Summary of the Development of Production-Line Maintenance in ICD, 15 May 1945, attached to *A History of Hump Operations*, as appendix 13, 325–26; Craven and Cate, *The Army Air Forces in World War II*, 7:140–47; see also Lt Gen William Tunner, *Over the Hump* (New York: Duell, Sloan, and Pearce, 1964), 93–95, 104, 107–8, 132–33.
104. USSBS, *Air Transport Command Against Japan*, 4–5.
105. Craven and Cate, *The Army Air Forces in World War II*, 7:151.
106. Historical Branch, Intelligence and Security Division, Headquarters Air Transport Command (ATC), historical study, *The Air Transport Command in the Southwest Pacific December 7, 1941-August 1, 1944*, May 1946, 1–9.
107. Ibid., 11–19.
108. Craven and Cate, *The Army Air Forces in World War II*, 7:175.
109. Headquarters ATC, *Air Transport Command in the Southwest Pacific*, 21.
110. Ibid., 35–62.
111. Craven and Cate, *The Army Air Forces in World War II*, 7:179.
112. Headquarters ATC, *Air Transport Command in the Southwest Pacific*, 143–48.
113. Ibid., 85, 86–89.
114. Ibid., 89–90.
115. Ibid., 103.
116. Ibid., 181–82, 103–11.
117. Ibid., 183.
118. Ibid.
119. Ibid., 184.
120. Ibid., 185.
121. Ibid., 186.
122. Ibid., 187.
123. Ibid., 187–88.
124. Ibid., 90–93.
125. Ibid., 284–85.
126. Ibid., 288.
127. Ibid., 290–91.
128. USSBS, *Air Transport Command Against Japan*, 10.
129. Craven and Cate, *The Army Air Forces in World War II*, 7:203.
130. Memorandum, Col James Douglas, Jr., acting chief of staff, Headquarters Air Transport Command, to Colonel Mason, assistant chief of staff, Plans, subject: Air Transport Services in Theaters of Operations, 4 March 1944.
131. Brig Gen H. A. Craig, assistant chief of Air Staff, Operations, Commitments, and Requirements, to executive director, Army Air Forces Board, letter, subject: Staff Study of the Air Transport System, 29 February 1944.

132. Report of the Army Air Forces Board, Project No. (U) 6, subject: Staff Study of the Air Transport System, 10 March 1944.
133. Col William McKee, deputy assistant chief of Air Staff, Operations, Commitments, and Requirements, to executive director, Army Air Forces Board, letter, subject: Staff Study of the Air Transport System, 5 April 1944.
134. Report of the Army Air Forces Board, Project No. (U) 6a, subject: Staff Study of the Air Transport System, 29 April 1944.
135. AAF Regulation No. 20–44, *Responsibilities for Air Transportation*, 17 August 1944.
136. AAF Regulation No. 20–44 A, *Responsibilities for Air Transportation*, 11 November 1944.
137. History, Air Transport Command, 1 August 1945–31 December 1946, 360.
138. Lt Gen Barney Giles, chief of the Air Staff, Headquarters Army Air Forces, to distribution list, letter, subject: Policy of the War Department in Regard to Post-War International Civil Aviation, 23 May 1944.
139. Ibid.
140. Ibid.
141. Ibid.
142. Lt Gen Harold George, commanding general, Air Transport Command, to commanding general, Atlantic Division, Air Transport Command, letter: Air Transport Command Policy with Respect to US Commercial Air Carriers, 14 October 1945.
143. Ibid.
144. Lt Gen Harold George, commanding general, Air Transport Command, to commanding general, Army Air Forces, letter, subject: Assistance to Carriers vs. Demobilization, 17 Dec 1945.
145. Memorandum, Col James Douglas, deputy chief of staff, Headquarters Air Transport Command, to Robert Lovett, assistant secretary of war for air, 24 August 1945.
146. Memorandum, Gen H. H. Arnold, commanding general, Army Air Forces, to President Truman, 24 August 1945; Lt Gen Harold George, commanding general, Air Transport Command, to commanding general, Army Air Forces, letter, subject: Future Scope of ATC Operations, 23 August 1945; Lt Gen Harold George, commanding general, Air Transport Command, to commanding general, Army Air Forces, letter, subject: Orderly Reduction of the Air Transport Command, 23 August 1945.
147. C. R. Smith to Lt Gen Harold George, commanding general, Air Transport Command, 26 November 1945.
148. See memorandum, Robert Lovett, assistant secretary of war for air, to Generals Arnold and Eaker, subject: Development of Plans for Reduction of Air Transport Command Activities, 23 August 1945; Memorandum, Gen Reuben C. Hood, deputy chief of the Air Staff, to Brig Gen Kenneth Royall, special assistant to the secretary of war, subject: Mead Committee Investigation—AAF Overseas Installations, 15 October 1945.
149. General Arnold to Lt Gen Harold George, letter, 5 December 1945.
150. General Arnold to General Spaatz, letter, 6 December 1945.
151. Ibid.
152. Ibid.
153. Ibid.; Memorandum, General Arnold to General Spaatz, subject: Future of the Air Transport Command, 7 January 1946.
154. Craven and Cate, *The Army Air Forces in World War II*, 7:212-15; Lt Gen Harold George, commanding general, Air Transport Command, to Brig Gen Earl Hoag, commanding general, European Division, Air Transport Command, letter, 4 June 1945, with plan booklet entitled *Green Project; Redeployment Projects: Air Transport Command*, an unsigned, undated, but presumably official historical study of the Green Project, White Project, and Purple Project, in Air University Library.
155. Craven and Cate, *The Army Air Forces in World War II*, 7:215.
156. Ibid.
157. Ibid., 216–23.
158. Ibid., 226–27.
159. Gen H. H. Arnold, Third Report of the Commanding General of the Army Air Forces, to the secretary of war, 12 November 1945, 62–63.

CHAPTER 3

Troop Carrier and Theater Airlift in World War II

On 17 October 1918, Gen John J. Pershing, the commander of the Allied Expeditionary Forces, gave Col William "Billy" Mitchell the go-ahead to begin detailed planning for an airborne assault against the German stronghold at Metz, France. Mitchell's concept called for 12,000 parachutists, each with two machine guns, to drop from 1,200 bombers, creating havoc in the enemy's rear and an opening for an Allied advance. The paratroopers were to drop simultaneously and be resupplied by air. Mitchell envisioned close air support for the force until it got dug in. Pershing was skeptical but asked for details of how such a venture would be executed. Mitchell put his new operations officer, Maj Lewis H. Brereton, to work on the project but the armistice stopped his study. The Allies would not test the ideas for many years to come.[1]

Origins of Troop Carrier Aviation

During the years before World War II the American Army experimented with parachute troops and techniques but not in a very serious way. However, the impending war caused a turnabout. Urged on by the Army chief of infantry, the War Department organized an airborne force, the 501st Parachute Company, at Fort Benning, Georgia, in July 1940. Expansion of the unit to a battalion soon followed.[2]

The original concept used B-18s as the drop platform for the parachute forces, but Brig Gen F. L. Martin, commander of the Third Wing of the HQ Air Force, objected that bombers were not designed for such a mission and that transports should be used instead. His argument that commercial transports would be available in wartime was not right on the mark, but several of his ideas closely resembled what later became doctrine. Responding to the contention that bombers could "get through" but that transports could not, Martin pointed out that parachute operations would necessarily require air superiority. Either nighttime darkness or adverse weather could be used to protect transports and preserve the likelihood of surprise, he thought. Plans Division bought his argument in principle but noted that neither transport airplanes nor B-18 bombers would be available.[3]

AIRLIFT DOCTRINE

The resource problem plagued the entire air transportation program:

> Driven by an urgent need for fighters and bombers and influenced by a belief that transports could always be bought off the shelf, the Air Corps placed almost no new orders for such craft in 1939 or in the first half of 1940. In June 1940 this policy was abruptly changed, and by the middle of 1942 no less than 11,082 medium transports were on order. However, it had not been possible to buy thousands of transport planes off the shelf. Exactly five were delivered in the last half of 1940, and at the end of the year the Air Corps had a total of 122 transports, mostly obsolescent. Only 133 more were delivered in 1941.[4]

As noted earlier, troop carrier aviation was separate from the strategic air transportation organization from the beginning. Originally, the only fully organized air transportation unit in the Army Air Corps (AAC) was the 50th Air Transport Wing (ATW), and to it fell the responsibility of supporting Army parachute forces. That unit was also charged with the mission of cargo air transport in the United States on a 24-hour transcontinental schedule, and, in addition, operated regular weekly schedules to bases in Trinidad, Panama, Newfoundland, and Alaska.[5] The 50th provided support to the growing aircraft from their regularly scheduled runs during Army maneuvers. Pilots had no specialized training in this type of flying; the aircraft were not adapted to many of the specialized tasks they were required to perform; and there was a complete absence of the special equipment necessary to support airborne missions.[6] In June 1941, the 50th ATW could not provide 12 airplanes needed for paratroop training, and it had to work hard to support the November 1941 maneuvers with 39 planes for airborne operations. It was in those maneuvers that the Air Corps first dropped more than one company of paratroopers.[7]

In February 1942, the experimental parachute group had grown to four battalions and wanted a transport group assigned to support its training requirements. The Army Air Forces (AAF) agreed to the need but could not spare the planes. In the face of German successes with airborne operations—for example, their May 1941 massed glider, parachute, and airlanding of troops at Crete—the US Army split the 82d Motorized Division to create the 82d and 101st Airborne Divisions. These were trained under the Airborne Command, formed in March 1942. Impetus for the Airborne Command and the forthcoming Troop Carrier Command came from the contemplated airborne division assault portion of Bolero, the buildup for the cross-channel invasion of Europe.[8]

The Mediterranean and European Campaigns

As events in Europe unraveled conventional notions of warfare, the War Department directed the AAF to assign the 50th ATW the primary duty of operational training with ground forces. This was formalized in April 1942 with the creation of the Air Transport Command (ATC). Its mission was to emphasize "the conduct of operations involving the air movement of airborne infantry [and] glider troops, and to make such units available to other elements of the Army Air Forces to meet established requirements, but the primary initial objective will be to meet specified requirements for airborne forces."[9] Air cargo movement within the United States remained with the Air Service Command; outside the Continental United States (CONUS) it was left to the Ferrying Command. "The responsibility for air cargo within the theaters," the War Department memo said, "will be that of the theater commander."[10] Three months later there was another shuffling of names, as well as clarification of some important issues of command control and roles and missions. With the creation of a new Air Transport Command came the redesignation of the old ATC as the Troop Carrier Command (TCC). Subordinate units, designated troop carrier wings, groups, and squadrons within a theater of operations were to be assigned to the air force commander in that theater. Equally important was the notation that troop carrier units could be temporarily attached to the theater air service commands for the transportation of material. On 17 July 1943 Gen H. H. Arnold formally announced the creation of the I TCC, whose job was to train its units and then give them away to the theaters.

In mid-summer 1942, the 2d Battalion of the 503d Parachute Regiment deployed to England to train with the British 1st Airborne Division. With five months' warning, the TCC was able to send two of the directed eight troop carrier groups to England. The 51st Troop Carrier Wing (TCW) landed in England on 1 September 1942 to command the groups assigned directly to the Eighth Air Force. The 64th Troop Carrier Group arrived in late September. The wing and its three groups were the entire troop carrier force throughout the North African campaign.[11]

In addition to deploying these forces to England, the TCC conducted extensive maneuvers in the United States with airborne troops in the autumn of 1942 and the spring and summer of 1943. In those maneuvers they developed their tactics and air skills and demonstrated to all concerned how the US Army could employ airborne forces.[12]

Torch: November 1942

> World War II was to see larger operations than the Anglo-American invasion of Northwest Africa, but none surpassed it in complexity, in daring—and the prominence of the hazard involved—or in the degree of strategic surprise achieved. . . . The TORCH operation, and the lessons learned in Africa, imposed a pattern on the war.[13]

The use of airborne forces was a vital part of the Torch plans for quick seizure of Algeria and the dash to Tunisia. The paratroop task force was to include the 2d Battalion, the 503d US Parachute Infantry, and the 60th Troop Carrier Group (TCG) of the 51st TCW. The 64th TCG was to provide airlift for two parachute groups of the British 3 Paratroop Battalion. On 7 November 1942, Lt Gen Dwight

AIRLIFT DOCTRINE

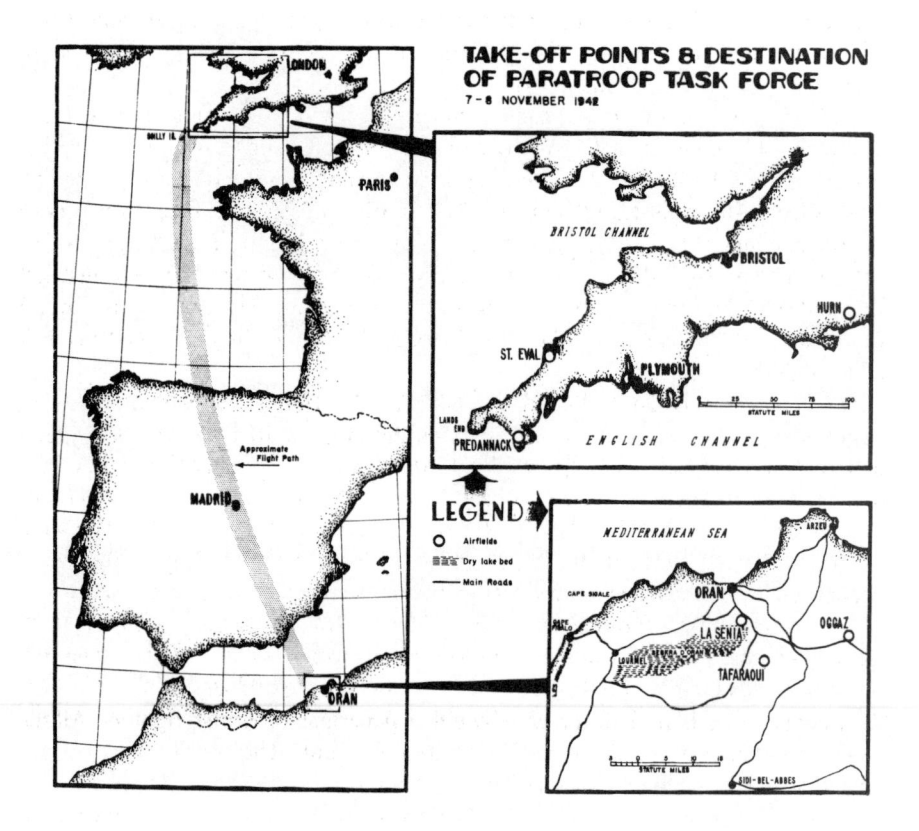

Figure 15

D. Eisenhower gave the signal that La Senia airport, five miles from Oran, would be available for an unopposed landing. The task force departed England for its 1,100-mile trip to Algeria—the longest range air assault of the war.[14]

Considering the operational difficulties of just arriving in the general area of the target, the mission was a good proving ground for how not to conduct an airborne assault. About half the flight route was over Spain, a neutral country somewhat friendly to the enemy. Navigators had only limited celestial navigation training and were unfamiliar with their British equipment. Due to a combination of bad weather, bad piloting, and bad luck, the formation lost contact with its many elements during the flight. The flight was made at night—at 10,000 feet, in the clouds—which made ground references useless. Fourteen of the pilots were assigned planes at the last minute, departing England with minimal rest and briefings. Only one-tenth of the airplanes had adequate charts. The flight failed to receive signals from two clandestine radio beacons near Oran. When they did manage to arrive at La Senia, they came under French antiaircraft fire. Twenty-eight of the C-47s landed in a nearby dry lake bed. Several sticks of troopers jumped upon sighting a column of French tanks—which turned out to be American.[15]

The airborne troop commander, having learned that Tafaraoui military airdrome—17 miles from Oran—was in Allied hands, organized the C-47s and troops on the dry lake for an airlanding at that airport. This flight was greeted by attacks from American-flown Spitfires. The Spitfires missed, but French artillery in the surrounding hills damaged several C-47s after they landed. French fighters also shot or forced down three C-47s in the dry lake area. Of the 39 C-47s that left England on 7 November only 14 were serviceable a day later: 9 were missing, 3 destroyed, and 13 damaged. The next morning French shelling knocked out still another C-47.

On 9 November, 34 C-47s of the 64th TCG left England with 450 British paratroopers. They airlanded at La Senia on the morning of 11 November, after a stopover at Gibraltar, to be greeted by Allied aircraft fire. The next day they dropped their troopers near the port of Bône as part of a British effort to capture it. They returned to Bône the following day with gasoline and antiaircraft guns to help the force fight off German attacks. From 12–15 November the troop carriers were unopposed as they moved paratroopers to two fields near the Tunisian border.

The last major paratroop operation in the North African campaign occurred on 28 November, just south of Tunis. The objective was to take Oudna airport, then link up with the advancing Allied armies. C-47s from both the 60th and 64th TCGs flew the troopers in, escorted all the way by either American or British fighters. All the C-47s returned safely. Few of the paratroopers did. The airport was heavily defended and the planned Allied advance had not materialized.[16]

Airborne operations per se were not the only missions flown by the troop carriers. They were also extensively involved in evacuation of casualties and in resupply of forward combat locations. For example, between the end of November 1942 and mid-February 1943, a daily average of 140 operational transports delivered 5,733 tons of critical cargo and moved nearly 32,000 passengers. When German Gen Erwin Rommel's success at the Kasserine Pass forced the evacuation of Youks-les-Bains, Tebessa, Feriana, and Thelepte on quick notice, the 64th TCG moved personnel and supplies so effectively that the rear bases became operational without interruption of combat operations. When the Allies recaptured the advanced bases, troop carriers played a critical role in flying the combat engineers to restore them and by carrying the restocking supplies. The wing also was occupied with the training of British paratroopers throughout the Middle East. By March 1943 the TCGs had been "taken away" from the theater in preparation for Husky—the airborne invasion of Sicily. The Northwest African Air Forces Troop Carrier Command (NAAF TCC) (Provisional) was activated on 18 March 1943, absorbing the 51st TCW and its 60th, 62d, and 64th TCGs.[17]

Some valuable lessons were learned from Torch, but this first use of airborne troops was a grave risk and produced no positive combat results. Ground troops captured the Tafaraoui airdrome. Landing at Oran would have been disastrous, and landing at a "friendly" La Senia airport would not have saved enough time to justify the risks of the long flight. The better choice than piecemeal application of the airborne forces would have been to use the concentrated airborne force for later operations in a dash for Tunis.[18]

Ladbroke-Husky: July 1943

The final plan approved for the invasion of Sicily included two airborne assaults followed by eight seaborne assaults.[19] The NAAF TCC was to deliver the paratroops and gliders and then transport equipment and supplies to Sicily while evacuating casualties. On 10 July 1943 the final assault on Sicily opened with the first large-scale airborne operations undertaken by the Allies in World War II.[20] One of the airborne assaults, code-named Ladbroke, was to seize the Ponte Grande bridge near Syracuse and assist the advance of the British Eighth Army. The other, Husky 1, was to capture the high ground overlooking the beach exits where the American 1st Division was coming ashore. Gen James Gavin called these assaults the "birthplace of American airborne technique."[21]

Training for the operation began in June. The 51st TCW trained with both the British 1 Airborne Division and the American 82d Airborne Division and was the prime glider organization. The 52d TCW trained exclusively with the 82d. Brig Gen Paul L. Williams, commander of the NAAF TCC, considered the training sufficient, although "the combat units found that there was not enough time to obtain training that would acquaint them with combat operations."[22] The gliders arrived late and were put together at four different seaports, then towed to the assembly fields, giving C-47 crews about half of their training time actually towing gliders. The training (which included replicas of the operational area built in French Morocco) placed great stress on rapid assembly and reorganization, made especially important by the fact that no one had ever attempted a night parachute operation.[23]

Ladbroke included 133 tow planes (105 of which were American C-47s of the 51st TCW) pulling American gliders full of British troopers. The mission was poorly executed but generally successful despite strong winds, visibility problems, and some pilot nervousness caused by flak en route to the drop and landing zones (DZ/LZ). All that, combined with the fact that many British glider pilots had only three weeks training in the American Waco gliders, led to only 12 of 133 gliders landing in the general vicinity of the LZ. Forty-seven went down in the sea, drowning 600 men. The British glider pilots had trained on large landing zones in Britain and could not handle the slower American gliders. The LZs were small and there were many unnecessary crash landings. The 73 paratroops who had made it to

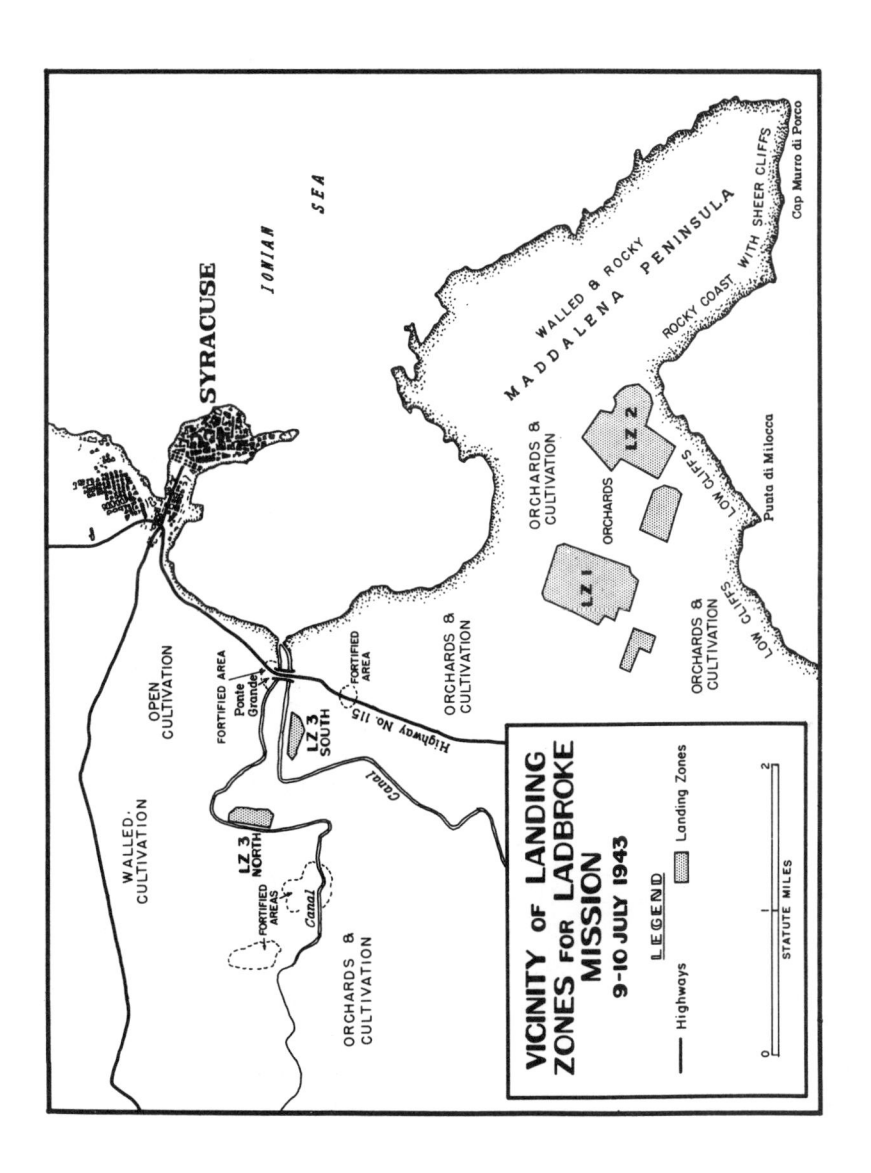

Figure 16

AIRLIFT DOCTRINE

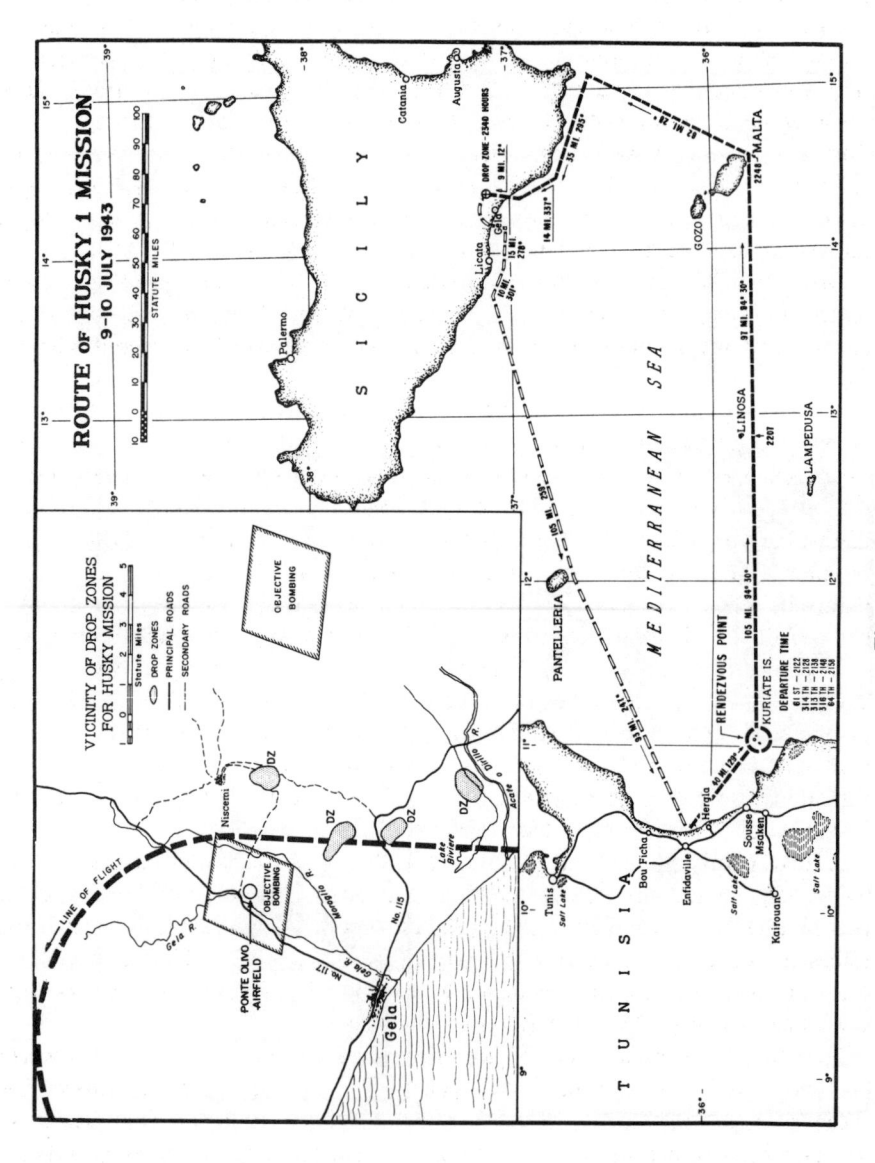

Figure 17

the drop zone were able to hold the bridge until ground troops arrived; those scattered about the countryside attacked what enemy they found and added to the general confusion, contributing to the success of the assault by some measure.[24]

Husky 1 paralleled Ladbroke. There were 226 C-47s carrying 2,700 members of the 82d Airborne Division and 891 parapacks. Like Ladbroke, this operation ran into wind problems, navigational difficulties, fires, and smoke from earlier bombardment obscuring the DZ; and it had to drop in the dark due to late arrival. The paratroopers planned to drop in a 36-minute column. They were scattered, but were close enough to seize the high ground. One group even managed to capture a town. The aggressive troops, along with the enemy's general unpreparedness for an airborne assault, demoralized the Italians, some of whom retreated 10 miles.[25]

Diversions accompanied both operations. B-17s flew radio direction-finding obstruction missions, other aircraft dropped hundreds of dummies to confuse the enemy, and diversionary bombers used incendiaries, which interfered with the Husky 1 accuracy.[26]

The German counterattack did not arise until D plus 1. That night the 52d TCW dropped 2,000 paratroopers from 144 C-47s in an attempt to assist the Allied ground forces. Planned on the very night of execution, the assault faced a severe test. It took a complicated route to Sicily and then flew through a corridor over Allied ships that had not been warned of the impending operation. Worse yet, the Germans had recaptured the drop zone—Gela/Farello airport—ironically, with the 4th German Parachute Regiment. As the formations approached Sicily, they were subjected to heavy Allied antiaircraft fire from naval forces that were soon joined by enemy ground fire. Fire into, over, and out of the drop zone was deadly; it destroyed 23 aircraft (fortunately, most had already dropped their troopers). Half of those that made it back were badly damaged. Ninety-nine aircraft were out of commission the next day. Paratroopers were scattered all over eastern Sicily, and General Eisenhower said their accomplishments were more than offset by their casualties. Even the Allied ground forces had fired on the paratroopers.[27]

A final, poorly planned and coordinated airdrop, code-named Fustian, took place on 13 July. Its mission was to drop British paratroopers to capture the Primasole Bridge, thus giving the British ground forces a good exit into the plains. The British forces succeeded, but only at a high cost to the troop carriers. The safety corridor was not open; friendly fire destroyed 11 C-47s and badly damaged 50. Twenty-seven had to return to base with full or partial loads.[28]

In light of the circumstances, it is surprising that three of the four airborne operations were tactically successful. Gen George S. Patton said that Husky 1 had speeded up the movement of the Seventh Army by 48 hours. Gen Harold L. Alexander noted that the early capture of Syracuse was largely due to the airborne attack, and Gen Bernard L. Montgomery estimated that airborne troops dropped in front of his Eighth Army advanced the timetable by a week. Gen Karl Student, the foremost authority on airborne operations in the German army and commander of their airborne assault on Crete, praised the ultimate results of the Husky operations:

> The Allied airborne operation in Sicily was decisive despite widely scattered drops which must be expected in a night landing. It is my opinion that if it had not been for the Allied airborne forces blocking the Hermann Goering Armored Division from reaching the beachhead, the division would have driven the initial seaborne forces back into the sea. I attribute the entire success of the Allied Sicilian operation to the delaying of German reserves until sufficient forces had been landed by sea to resist the counterattacks by our defending forces (the strength of which had been held in mobile reserve).[29]

This success was at a cost of 42 aircraft lost out of 666 troop carrier sorties flown. The most serious cause for concern was that 25 of these losses were from friendly fire. Equally bad was that 60 percent of the 5,000 troopers droplanded far from the DZs.[30]

Husky: Lessons Learned

Brig Gen Paul Williams' perceptions are enlightening concerning the troop carrier lessons learned from Husky. The XII TCC commander devoted much of his discussions to the naval fire problems. He reported that the Navy's "excuse" for shooting up so many transports was that "the Navy had a lot of merchant ships which they had no control over and they claim that most of the firing on our planes was done from these ships." He did note that the naval forces had suffered three recent "enemy air attacks but implied that this was not much of an excuse, as the enemy very seldom comes in low, as the troop carriers do." Having to avoid the naval concentrations for the very preservation of life caused a great deal of navigational problems because, as General Williams said, "you have got to have simple routes."[31]

Williams also stressed the need for larger landing and drop zones, as a significant amount of equipment was lost or ruined by the crash landings of gliders and parachutists missing their targets. He strongly objected to the diversionary bombings: "They were set on by somebody else. We knew nothing about it." Little wonder he believed that 60 percent of the losses were unnecessary. Even given the relatively uncoordinated operation he was reviewing, General Williams had the vision to observe that "I look to the future to bring large-scale operations of gliders."[32]

Lt Col Charles Billingslea, the official observer for the Fifth Army Airborne Training Center, was also tough in his evaluation of the Husky operation. He said the most important causes of poor drops were:

> a. Training was inadequate, especially along aerial operational lines.

> b. The course was unnecessarily long and complicated with poor cooperation by the Navy small craft.

c. Very few pilots or commanders were flown over the DZs in combat planes to study the terrain before the operation began even though countless flights were made over the area daily.

d. Meteorological data was incomplete. No reports came from ships in the target area.

e. Medium bombers familiar with the terrain of Sicily were not employed as guides in any formations, nor was the radar used or a scout company dropped.

f. Pilots were too dependent on lead ships. They were given only overlays, no air photographs. Insufficient navigators proved costly.

g. Close proximity of American and British formations mixed some units, particularly when their takeoff fields were so close and times of takeoff identical.

h. Flying V of Vs made formation difficult for wing planes.

i. Pilots were not seasoned to operating in flak. Some attempted evasive action on approach to DZ.[33]

Dr John Warren, writing an official US Air Force history of Husky, draws the lessons together well:

> The most striking lesson, and the one which first produced results, seems to be the demonstrated need for beacons and signals set up by pathfinder units to guide a mission to its objective. Evident, too, was the necessity of simple routes, sound navigation, and close formation flying, especially at night. Ladbroke taught the folly of releasing gliders in the dark over water. Husky 2 and Fustian painfully proved the need to avoid any concentration of friendly antiaircraft or else to secure absolute control of its fire.[34]

Avalanche: September 1943

Allied leaders had discussed and refined their post-Husky strategy at both the Trident conference in May 1943 and at the Algiers conference in late May and early June of the same year. They eventually settled on Avalanche—the invasion of Italy on the coastal plains near Salerno—which General Eisenhower formally announced to his commanders on 19 August 1943. (Planning for the operation had been taking place since July.) Avalanche called for the Fifth Army to seize Salerno and the airfield of Montecorvino, then to capture Naples and surrounding airfields. The Fifth Army first considered using airborne forces to capture the passes through which the Germans could reinforce their Salerno garrison. They abandoned that plan due to the harsh mountainous terrain that would have been prohibitive for gliders and difficult for paratroops. As it turned out, the Germans did pass through that area with reinforcements, and Allied control of the passes could have been of great assistance to the troops on the beachhead.[35]

Instead, the airborne forces were to perform Giant I—a paratroop and glider mission to cut and hold the main highways across the Volturno River north of

AIRLIFT DOCTRINE

Figure 18

Naples using 130 Waco gliders and 300 C-47s. Initial planning estimates showed that the airborne forces would be isolated for 4 to 8 days, although later analysis showed it would have been up to 30 days. This called for an aerial resupply provided by 90 to 145 C-47s per day—30 to 45 percent of all C-47s in the theater. Resupply flights would have been unprotected and likely ambushed by the German air forces. Upon review, General Eisenhower ordered the operation both scaled back and dropped with a five-day supply in hand. He later cancelled that mission altogether.[36]

On 22 July 1943, at the first hint of airborne operations in Italy, the XII Troop Carrier Command initiated refresher training in night formation flying, glider training, and paratroop dropping. From that date until the first drop in September, the XII TCC trained intensively with the 82d Airborne Division and moved its own units and the combat echelons of the 82d to forward staging bases, taking great care to incorporate the lessons learned in Operation Husky:

> Combined Troop Carrier—Airborne training exercises were conducted mostly at night, simulating courses, distances, drop zones, landing zones, and objectives as near as possible to those that were to be encountered during the actual AVALANCHE operation. Also during the training period, Troop Carrier Command and 82nd Airborne utilized the newly formed Pathfinder units to the fullest extent.[37]

On the nights of 28 and 31 August they conducted full-scale training exercises, with the Navy marking courses with lights and homing beacons. Routes for the training and actual execution were closely coordinated with the Navy, including a safety lane 14 miles wide. Although the operation they practiced for was significantly modified by later events, the training paid great dividends in flexibility.[38]

The airborne operations in support of Avalanche proved the majority of training and doctrine developed by the troop carrier and airborne commands especially sound. The Avalanche mission finally settled on was to include 247 C-47s and C-53s, plus 157 gliders. Pathfinder crews and paratroopers that preceded the main drop by 15 minutes would light all DZs and LZs. TCC issued its warning order on 1 September for execution on the night of 8–9 September, providing naval and ground units with significant warning time. General Eisenhower cancelled the Avalanche mission on the night of 5–6 September, replacing it with Giant II.[39] He anticipated an armistice with the Italians and had been assured by the secret Italian negotiating team that they would prepare five airfields in Rome to receive troop carrier aircraft and paratroopers and protect the fields against the Germans. The Italians had overestimated their capabilities, and when Brig Gen Maxwell Taylor (commander of the 82d) and Col William Gardnier (A2 for the 51st TCW of the Troop Carrier Command) presented evidence to General Eisenhower, he cancelled Giant II as well.[40]

In the interim, TCC and the 82d had replanned the Avalanche route to incorporate Giant II, recoordinated with the Navy, reloaded the aircraft for the Giant II configuration, relocated the troopers for the new operation, and sealed up 135 troop carriers to ensure operational readiness. They issued their warning order on the night of 6 September planning 93 paratroop missions and 42 airlandings, including the use of Pathfinders. Takeoff was set for 1830. The troops loaded and the gliders hooked up; the cancellation order arrived at 1730.[41]

As noted earlier, Giant I replaced Avalanche's original air assault plan. It in turn officially changed to Giant I (Revised) at 1540 on 13 September. Mission orders followed at 1830. Pathfinder aircraft took off at 2045. Planners made quick

AIRLIFT DOCTRINE

adjustments with Army, Navy, and antiaircraft units. The cause of these extreme measures was a highly successful German counterattack that so threatened the Fifth Army that it needed reinforcements immediately. Lt Gen Mark Clark sent a fighter pilot to make an emergency landing and deliver a map of the proposed drop zone to Gen Matthew Ridgway. General Clark's note said: "I realize the time normally needed to prepare for a drop, but this is an exception. I want you to drop within our lines on the beachhead and I want you to make it tonight."[42] General Ridgway was so concerned about friendly fire that he personally called in the commanders of the Navy and Army units involved and directed that from 2100 until further notice, there would be no antiaircraft fire from American positions. A week-old Pathfinder unit preceded the drop and landed right on the drop zone. The main formation of 90 C-47s and C-53s arrived four minutes ahead of schedule and dropped most of the troops within 200 yards of the DZ. Noted the XII TCC: "Mission accomplished and entirely successful." A force of about 1,300 troops appeared at the battle front within 15 hours of the original request. The success of Giant I (Revised) ensured a sequel.[43]

Giant III, scheduled for the night of 14–15 September, was to drop one battalion near Avellino to destroy railway and highway bridges. The DZ was 15 miles behind enemy lines and offered the most difficult terrain of any airborne operation in the European theater. The Pathfinder team dropped on the wrong spot but set up their equipment anyway—the new DZ was adequate and the first serial was minutes away. On 18 September the XII TCC called this operation entirely successful. They were wrong. One squadron took a wrong turn en route and had to return to the coast to find bearings. Another squadron dropped 10 miles from the DZ. Others dropped 8 to 12 miles from the DZ. Only 15 transports managed to drop within 5 miles of the DZ. The Pathfinder beacons were too weak to be effective in the mountains, and the aircraft were not equipped with Eureka/Rebecca radar units. None of the 40 transports involved received more than a few bullet holes from the enemy and none was hit by friendly fire. Because of the missed DZs and because of jumping from 1,500 to 2,500 feet above the ground (dictated by the mountainous terrain), the paratroops were widely dispersed and never became a meaningful fighting force. They blew up a key bridge, after the battle of Salerno was already won. Nearly 20 percent of the paratroopers became casualties.[44]

Simultaneous with the Avellino jump, Giant IV sent another 130 C-47s and C-53s to reinforce the southern flank of the Fifth Army with 2,100 troopers. The full Pathfinder system worked perfectly; 125 planes delivered their loads, with 123 dropping 1,900 troops within 200 yards of the DZ. Giant V, a 98-glider landing, was indefinitely postponed.[45]

Avalanche: Lessons Learned

The most common thread running throughout the various reports of the Avalanche and Giant operations concerned the importance of the contribution the Pathfinders made to the success of many of the missions. By that time Pathfinder teams of three planes approximately 30 minutes ahead of the main formation were in use. The top navigators in the unit controlled the Pathfinder aircraft to give them the best chance of reaching the right drop zone. Once on the ground, the teams in Italy used krypton lights that could be seen for 30 miles from the air in clear weather and/or, depending on the scene, Ts lighted with gasoline. The teams also refined the use of radars and radios in the Italian invasion.[46]

The 5G and the Eureka were the two primary beacons used. The 5G was a British radio with a 40-mile maximum range that could be rigged to interface with a radio compass installed in the aircraft. The Eureka was a radar beacon that responded to interrogation from the Rebecca mounted in the airplane. All the electronic gear was underpowered, sometimes unreliable, and range-limited by terrain, but it constituted a great improvement over the earlier equipment.[47]

What is not effectively highlighted in the follow-up reports on this series of operations is the amazing flexibility airborne operators displayed during the campaign. All the lessons seemed to focus on tactics and operational doctrine, but the ability of the forces to generate extremely effective, or even mediocre, missions within a matter of hours was really the fundamental lesson learned. It also was a lesson that the airborne operators did not want anyone else to learn. They were committed to the idea of long, detailed preparation, including rehearsals, coupled with intensive training in all tactics for the various kinds of forces involved. They were also committed to the specialness of their forces—forces that should not be wasted performing anything other than demanding air assault missions.

This viewpoint is understandable and, to a certain extent, justified. Fundamental airborne doctrine was in its infancy, facing great pressures to disperse this highly capable fighting force in less-than-most-effective missions. There is very much a parallel to be seen between the air power debate and the period of airborne definition. Air power doctrine argued for a unified force performing a specialized mission, not parcelled out to many commanders who would not necessarily use it to its maximum effectiveness. The airborne commanders were making essentially the same argument, and both groups were concerned with being viewed as a decisive force. Nonetheless, the great resourcefulness and flexibility of airborne forces shone through in Avalanche.

Interim Doctrinal Results

The airborne leaders were relatively satisfied with the performances of their troops during Husky, but the senior leadership of the Army was not. Lt Gen Carl

Spaatz, the mildest critic, wrote to General Arnold that future airborne operations would be successful only if total surprise were achieved, that dropping combat units into prepared enemy positions would incur heavy losses, and that mutual identification training was a must for all future airborne operations.[48] General Eisenhower's reaction was much more negative, "I do not believe in the airborne division," he said.[49] In a memo to Lt Gen Lesley McNair, the commanding general of the US Army Ground Forces, Gen George C. Marshall, the Army chief of staff, recommended restricting airborne operations to battalion size or smaller. On 23 July 1943 General Eisenhower appointed Maj Gen Joseph Swing to see if the airborne concept was valid above the battalion level. General Swing reported in October that the division was the most appropriate size for an airborne unit.[50]

General McNair reserved judgment until completion of the Knollwood maneuvers in North and South Carolina in December 1943. He was concerned as to whether the troop carrier units could navigate for several hours over water to a small drop zone, whether there could be mass drops without excessive casualties, and whether an airborne division could be sustained by airdropped and airlanded supplies. Reportedly, General McNair told General Swing that the future of the airborne program depended on the performance of the six-month-old 11th Airborne Division in the maneuvers.[51]

The umpires judged the airborne phase completely successful. General McNair wrote to the 11th:

> After the Airborne Operations in Africa and Sicily, my staff and I had become convinced of the impracticality of handling large airborne units. I was prepared to recommend to the War Department that airborne divisions be abandoned in our scheme of organization and that the airborne efforts be restricted to parachute units of battalion size or smaller. The successful performance of your division has convinced me that we were wrong, and I shall now recommend that we continue our present schedule of activating, training, and committing airborne divisions.[52]

By early October 1943 the War Department had incorporated the many lessons learned from airborne operations into a new training circular entitled *Employment of Airborne and Troop Carrier Forces*. That document selected five principles so vital as to merit emphasis at the beginning:

> Airborne and troop carrier units are theater of operations forces. Plans for their combined employment must be prepared by the agency having authority to direct the necessary coordinated action of all land, sea, and air forces in the area involved. This responsibility should not be delegated to lower headquarters since positive coordination can be insured only by the one agency in control of all elements.
>
> The coordinating directive must be assigned in ample time to insure its receipt by all agencies concerned, including isolated antiaircraft units and individual naval and other vessels.

> Routes, altitudes, time schedules, and means of identification, both while in the air and on the ground, must be known in advance by all concerned. Procedures must be prescribed which will insure that troop carrier aircraft which are on course, at proper altitudes and on the correct time schedules, are not fired upon by friendly land, sea, or air forces.
>
> Plans should provide for the necessary preparation of troop carrier and airborne units to include training and practice portions and the concentration of these units in the departure areas.
>
> Airborne units should remain under the direct control of the theater commander until they land in the ground combat area when control passes to the officer in command of the area.[53]

It is interesting that the command control issue should receive such a place of importance. Although each of the major reports on Avalanche operations touched on this question, none gave it this level of visibility.

Given the context of the debate over airborne employment, it is surprising that the writers did not also give emphasis to some of the other fundamental issues the circular addressed. For example, they could have selected for special note the paragraph establishing that "airborne troops should be employed in mass," which seems to be a commitment to the airborne *division* concept. Equally important, especially from an air power perspective, was the observation that "air superiority is a fundamental prerequisite for successful airborne operations." The new expression of doctrine was closely followed during Operation Neptune, the airborne invasion of Normandy.[54]

Neptune: June 1944

Airborne operations in support of the Allied invasion of Normandy were aimed at decisive points in order to help secure the initial objectives of the assault. General Marshall wanted to make Overlord essentially an airborne operation, with as many as four airborne divisions delivered well inland from the French coast. He was supporting a plan developed by Brig Gen Fredrick Williams, I TCC commander, and sponsored by General Arnold, which envisioned the airdropping of two divisions to seize and hold an airhead, reinforced by two airlanded divisions. General Marshall wrote to General Eisenhower:

> Up to the present time I have not felt that we have properly exploited airpower as regards its combination with ground troops. We have lacked planes, of course, in which to transport men and supplies, but our most serious deficiency I think has been a piecemeal proposition with each commander grabbing at a piece to assist his particular phase of the operation, very much as they did with tanks and as they tried to do with the airplane itself. It is my opinion that we now possess the means to give a proper application to this phase of airpower in a combined operation.[55]

AIRLIFT DOCTRINE

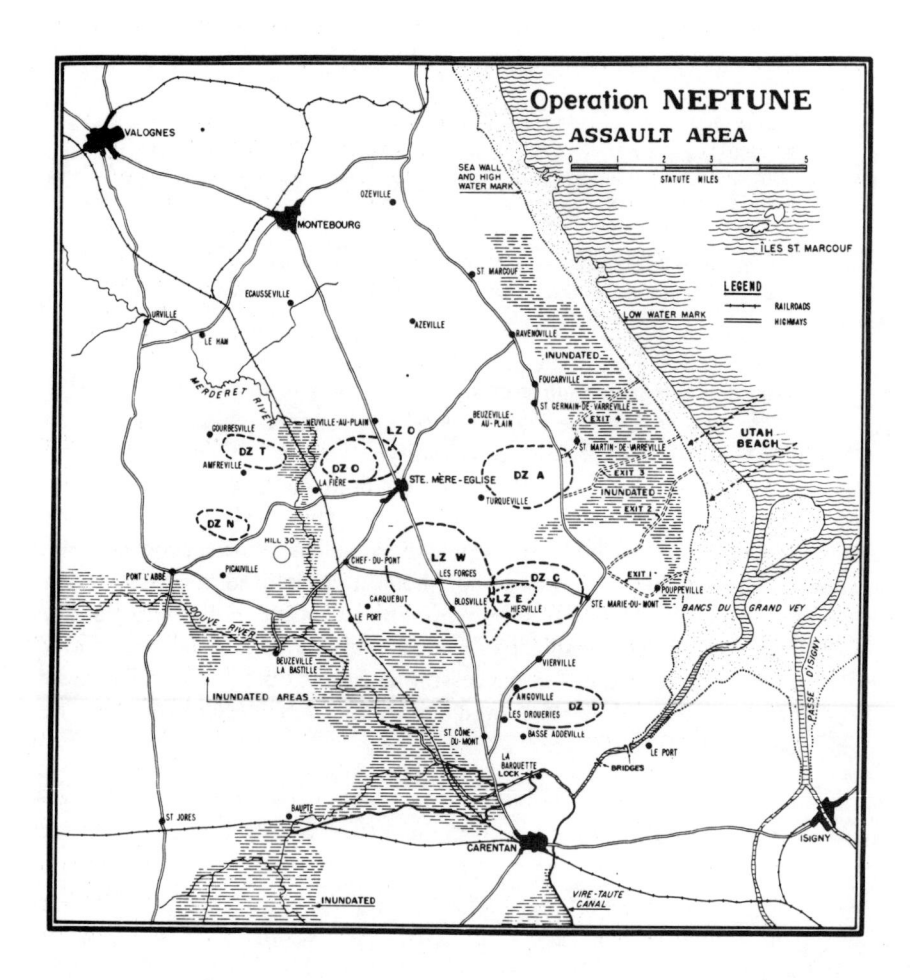

Figure 19

General Eisenhower was not persuaded:

> My initial reaction to the specific proposal is that I agree thoroughly with the conception but disagree with the timing. Mass in vertical envelopment is sound—but since this kind of enveloping force is immobile on the ground, the collaborating force must be strategically and tactically mobile.[56]

His point was that the proper time for a large, strategic, airborne operation in Europe would come *after* the Allies had a firm foothold and control of the water ports. He closed his argument with some astute observations about the necessity for airborne and ground forces needing link-up capability.

> We must never forget . . . the enemy's highly efficient facilities for concentration of ground troops at any particular point. This is especially true in the whole of France and in the Low Countries. Our bombers will delay movement, but I cannot conceive of enough airpower to prohibit movement on the network of roads throughout northwest France. For the past five days there has been good weather in Italy and our reports show an average of 1,000 sorties per day. Yet with only two main roads and a railway on which to concentrate, our reports show a steady stream of traffic by night to the south and southeast from Rome. We must arrange all our operations so that no significant part of our forces can be isolated and defeated in detail. There must exist either the definite capability of both forces to combine tactically, or the probability that each force can operate independently without danger of defeat.[57]

General Eisenhower was correct, not because he supported the doctrine of the day but because the airborne divisions probably would have been decimated. They had no armor, no vehicle bigger than a jeep, and less than half the firepower on an infantry division. Resupply by air of a force that size was still in the experimental stage and rightly viewed with skepticism. There was also significant doubt as to whether troop carrier and bomber aircraft could accomplish the massive aerial resupply in light of weather or enemy actions. "Since in actuality the Allies were unable to break out of their Normandy beachhead for a month and a half after D-day, Eisenhower's fear [for] his airborne forces . . . seems justified by events."[58]

Gen Omar Bradley, commander of the US First Army for the Normandy invasion, reported a critical series of decisions that General Eisenhower had to make concerning the Neptune airdrops and the vital role they played in Allied strategy for the entire invasion. Air Chief Marshal Sir Trafford Leigh-Mallory, commander in chief of the Allied Expeditionary Air Forces for the invasion, proposed that the Allies not airdrop behind the Utah Beach portion of the Normandy site. General Bradley reported that Leigh-Mallory appealed to General Eisenhower for a change in plans.

> Abandon the Utah air drop, he urged, and concentrate the airborne on Caen. To go ahead with the drop as planned, he estimated, would cost us 50 percent casualties among the parachute troops, 70 percent among the gliders. If Leigh-Mallory were right, then Eisenhower would carry those losses on his hands. But on the other hand if he took his air chief's advice, he might jeopardize our landing on Utah Beach. Eisenhower retired alone in his tent to sweat out the decision. Later that evening he announced the attack was to go as planned.[59]

General Eisenhower described his own decision-making process:

> Leigh-Mallory was, of course, earnestly sincere. He was noted for personal courage and was merely giving me, as was his duty, his frank convictions.

It would be difficult to conceive of a more soul-racking problem. If my technical expert was correct, then the planned operation was worse than stubborn folly, because even at the enormous cost predicted we could not gain the principal object of the drop. Moreover, if he was right, it appeared that the attack on Utah Beach was probably hopeless, and this meant that the whole operation suddenly acquired a degree of risk, even foolhardiness, that presaged a gigantic failure, possibly Allied defeat in Europe.

To protect him in case his advice was disregarded, I instructed the air commander to put his recommendations in a letter and informed him he would have my answer within a few hours. I took the problem to no one else. Professional advice and counsel could do no more.

I went to my tent alone and sat down to think. Over and over I reviewed each step, somewhat in the sequence set down here, but more thoroughly and exhaustively. I realized, of course, that if I deliberately disregarded the advice of my technical expert on the subject, and his predictions should prove accurate, then I would carry to my grave the unbearable burden of a conscience justly accusing me of the stupid, blind sacrifice of thousands of the flower of our youth. Outweighing any personal burden, however, was the possibility that if he were right the effect of the disaster would be far more than local: it would be likely to spread to the entire force.

Nevertheless, my review of the matter finally narrowed the critical points to these:

If I should cancel the airborne operation, then I had either to cancel the attack on Utah Beach or I would condemn the assaulting forces there to even greater probability of disaster than was predicted for the airborne divisions.

If I should cancel the Utah attack I would so badly disarrange elaborate plans as to diminish chances for success elsewhere and to make later maintenances perhaps impossible. Moreover, in long and calm consideration of the whole great scheme we had agreed that the Utah attack was an essential factor in prospects for success. To abandon it really meant to abandon a plan in which I had held implicit confidence for more than two years.

Finally, Leigh-Mallory's estimate was just an estimate, nothing more, and our experience in Sicily and Italy did not, by any means, support his degree of pessimism. Bradley, with Ridgway and other airborne commanders, had always supported me and the staff in the matter, and I was encouraged to persist in the belief that Leigh-Mallory was wrong!

I telephoned him that the attack would go as planned and that I would confirm this at once in writing. When, later, the the attack was successful he was the first to call me to voice his delight and to express his regret that he had found it necessary to add to my personal burdens during the final tense days before D-day.[60]

The planning and final execution evolved into a complex series of parachute and glider missions that employed, to a very significant degree, the doctrinal lessons learned in earlier operations.

The original planning had the airborne routes far from naval concentrations, but changes made in German defenses caused a shift that forced the troop carriers over such concentrations. Naval commanders reluctantly agreed to a ban on antiaircraft activity during the scheduled overflight times. Because of the fear of saturating the identification, friend or foe (IFF) system with troop carrier, bomber, and fighter signals, the airlift airplanes and gliders were painted with large white stripes for aiding in identification. The troop carrier command had been considering camouflaging its aircraft, but the need for visual identification was paramount. Because of the need for security, the paratroop missions were to arrive under cover of darkness, with moonlight to aid in formation flying. Thus, 5 June was selected as the perfect night for the operation, with the next two days deemed acceptable.[61]

An extensive system of en route navigation was laid out for successful arrival at the French coast, including lights and radar beacons in the assembly areas and beacons on marker boats across the Channel. The flights across Normandy were to rely on navigation aids in the drop zones set up by Pathfinder units. The Pathfinders, in turn, were to find the drop zones through the use of GEE and SCR-717C radar. GEE was a British radio-position-finding device that relied on triangulation, with a planning error of 400 yards. The radar scanned the terrain and provided a crude but recognizable map of the Normandy coast. The drop zone aids consisted of BUPS, Eureka beacons, lights, panels, and smoke. BUPS was an experimental system similar to the Eureka/Rebecca sets that helped navigators obtain their bearings and distances. Because of technical difficulties, the Eurekas would be activated on a carefully controlled schedule. Each drop zone was also lighted with a 30-by-20-yard T of colored holophane lights, again used on a tightly controlled time schedule. For later daylight missions, the Pathfinders would use fluorescent panels and colored lights, with each drop zone having its own combination of panels and smoke.[62]

In keeping with the preference to practice the actual operation and to train as intensively as possible for as long as practical, a joint training program began on 15 March 1944. The troop carrier and airborne forces worked together closely, arranging training events based on their individual and joint needs. A newly formed organization, the Command Pathfinder School, although limited by the number of SCR-717 sets available, nevertheless intensively trained 24 crews per 60-hour session, beginning in February. The command exercise, Eagle, the nearest thing to a true rehearsal of any American airborne operation in World War II, occurred on the night of 11 May. Except for some serials that got lost in haze, the exercise seemed to confirm the optimism of troop carrier and airborne leaders that the Neptune missions would be exceptionally successful.[63] Dr John Warren makes a particularly strong point of this:

> This optimism was related to neglect of a major variable in the situation, namely the weather. Time and time again in big and little exercises during the past two months, and in several previous missions, wind and low visibility, particularly at night, had scattered troop carrier formations, twisted them off course or spoiled their drops. Yet the halcyon weather in Eagle seems to have pushed all this into the background. The field orders for Eagle had contained full and specific precautions against bad weather. Those for Neptune

were to be notably lacking in such precautions. Even the requirements of security and the need to send the Neptune missions under almost any conditions cannot fully explain neglect.[64]

The Paratroop Operations. The delivery of slightly over 13,000 paratroops of the 82d and 101st Airborne Divisions to six drop zones was a staggering feat. Ten percent landed on their drop zone, between 25 and 30 percent landed within a mile, and between 15 and 20 percent were from one to two miles away. This meant that over 10,000 men were within five miles of their intended zones. Unfortunately, this degree of relative accuracy still left large numbers of troops outside of any effective division control many hours later. This was because it often took the better part of a day to move a mile in Normandy's defended hedgerow country. The far-flung troops performed much valuable but unplanned work and caused considerable communications problems for the Germans, along with meeting their mission goals, but this was in no way due to delivery accuracy.[65]

Several factors caused this inaccuracy. One was a cloud bank extending 10 to 12 miles inland, that caused some Pathfinder errors and even more for 9 of 20 follow-on serials. There was not a procedure for warning others of the cloud bank. No weather plane flew ahead of the drop, even though cloud banks were a common weather factor over Normandy in June. The SCR-717 radar was good for locating the coastline but not for accurately locating drop zones. GEE had about a one-mile margin of error over Normandy and very few planes were equipped with it anyway. The Eureka/Rebecca system had a whole series of problems itself. In some cases the Pathfinder teams turned the system on too late for the first or second serials. Lower operating altitudes over Normandy reduced the range of the system by up to 20 percent and the built-in technical problems often caused the system to show a drop zone about two miles ahead of time. The Eureka/Rebecca also had a tendency to become saturated if more than about 40 sets were used in the same area—triggering the wrong ground receivers and generating false reports. Consequently, the field order for the mission directed stragglers and leaders of straggling elements to use their sets only in emergency.[66]

Many of the errors could have been corrected with the planned lighting of the Ts showing exact drop zone location; but direct enemy action or nearness of the enemy prevented lighting four of the six zones. At a fifth zone, the lights came on too late for two serials, one serial never came in sight of them, and one was too scattered to make a difference. The best drops of the whole effort came on the one zone where lights were used.

The Glider Assault. After much debate during the planning process, the senior leadership decided that follow-up glider missions for Neptune would be relatively small. "Their greatest value lay in the experience they provided in the little-known fields of aerial reinforcement and resupply." A critical concern for safety of the gliders from ground fire led to night operations, much to the objection of the troop carrier and airborne commanders.[67]

The first glider missions on D-day—Chicago—primarily carried artillery. They experienced little weather problems or dispersion, but due to unexpected obstacles and the semidarkness, most of the gliders made crash landings and only 6 of 39 landed on their zone. The subsequent Detroit mission ran into the cloud bank previously discussed and that dispersed the formation. Thirty-seven of 52 gliders reached the vicinity of their LZ. At the other LZ for this mission, 17 of 23 gliders landed on or near their objective. In all cases, safe landings were the exception rather than the rule. On balance, although "hardly more than 50 percent effective," the Chicago and Detroit missions provided the airborne troops with badly needed firepower.[68]

There were two daylight glider missions on D-day; Keokuk with 32 large Horsas, and Elmira with 14 Wacos and 86 Horsas. In Keokuk, 5 gliders landed right on the LZ, and most were within two and one-half miles. As the first Allied tactical glider operation in World War II, "it indicated that gliders, when not exposed to fire at close range, could be landed in daylight without excessive losses."[69] Elmira consisted of two serials aimed at landing zone W. Unknown to the TCC, the Germans were in control of that zone, which had caused the 82d Division to set up its beacon and markers in the vicinity of LZ O. One Pathfinder crewman "had attempted to get word of the situation to IX TCC, first by radio and later by panels laid out for a reconnaissance plane, but the message was not received, and the panels were not observed."[70] The net result was that most gliders were somewhat scattered but fairly close to LZ W. The 82d naturally considered the release inaccurate because few if any troop carriers followed the aids to LZ O. The second echelon of Elmira departed still unaware of the switch of aids to LZ W from LZ O. But, due to the lack of rival beacons, which had been in use for the first echelon, this installment headed directly for the LZ O aids. The gliders came under intense ground fire that was less deadly than apparent and the main body landed quite accurately. All the landing fields for both groups were small and enemy fire was very effective once the gliders landed. Most unloading had to wait until nightfall.[71]

There were two additional daylight glider missions on D plus 1—Galveston and Hackensack—involving a total of 112 Wacos and 38 Horsas. Galveston used LZ E and Hackensack LZ W. In most cases the gliders made reasonably accurate landings and, even though under fire on the ground, most were unloaded in a timely manner. The best overall evaluation said the glider mission

> had gone as well as most experts expected and vastly better than some had predicted. The predawn missions had demonstrated that gliders could deliver artillery to difficult terrain in bad weather and semidarkness and put 40 to 50 percent of it in usable condition within two miles of a given point. The missions on D plus 1 had shown that by day infantry units could be landed within artillery range of an enemy and have 90 percent of their men assembled and ready for action within a couple of hours. While some felt that CHICAGO

and DETROIT proved the feasibility of flying glider missions at night, the general consensus was that landing in daytime or at least about sun-up had proven to be much more accurate and much less subject to accidents and that the vulnerability of gliders to ground fire had been overrated.[72]

Parachute Resupply Missions. There were two parachute resupply missions on D plus 1 of Neptune, one scheduled and one flown for unexplainable reasons. The scheduled one—Freeport—planned to deliver 234 tons with 208 airplanes. Due to terrible departure and en route weather, 51 aircraft turned back and never redeparted England. Their orders were to drop on zone N; the 82d Division operated their beacons on DZ O, due to too much enemy influence at N. Stragglers dropped at O, N, and W. All told, 148 planes delivered 156 tons, of which less than 100 tons were recoverable on the same day. Eventually 140 tons made their way into American hands. Ninety-two airplanes received significant damage from German ground fire.[73]

The Memphis mission was supposed to resupply the 101st Division but the 101st had not called for it, did not expect it, and had no zone markers or beacons set up for it. Obviously, someone had directed the mission because 118 airplanes dropped over 200 tons in the early morning hours of D plus 1. How much got where is something of a mystery, as no documentation from the receiving troops exists. What was documented is that German ground fire damaged 35 troop carriers. The atrocious weather and lack of communications between the airborne commanders and the troop carriers were the two most obvious contributing factors to the relative lack of success of these resupply missions.[74]

Doctrinal Lessons from Neptune

Neptune was critical to the evolution of troop carrier doctrine and to the gradual building of confidence in airborne operations. The success of these missions went far in making airborne concepts a standing consideration in future Allied plans.

> The Normandy airborne landings completely vindicated the Swing Board concept of employing the parachute and glider troops in division size and Eisenhower's insistence on massing them on critical objectives within quick linkup distance of other friendly ground forces. His refusal to consider using the paratroopers as small harassing forces and his equally adamant stand against a deep airborne raid were important factors in the successes of D-day. At the same time, the Allied staffs proved quite capable of planning a large-scale air assault and integrating it into the overall tactical scheme.[75]

The lessons learned from Neptune were many, but the fundamental issues may be highlighted as follows:

• Large-scale, division-size, airborne operations are possible.

- Night airborne operations—parachute and glider—are possible, but daylight operations are much preferred for accuracy.
- Air superiority contributes immeasurably to successful airborne operations.
- Effective communication between the airborne forces in the field and troop carrier forces is a must.
- Bad weather can have a serious impact on an airborne operation.
- Aerial resupply of forces is possible.

An Organization for Theater Airlift in Europe

> On D-Day there were no less than five separate American air transport organizations in the theater: a small naval air transport service; the European Division, AAF Air Transport Command; the IX Troop Carrier Command; the 31st Air Transport Group of the IX AFSC; and the 27th Air Transport Group of ASC, USSTAF. Each was responsible to a different headquarters and was charged with a variety of functions which limited its use in time of emergency.[76]

Prior to D-day, Supreme Headquarters Allied Expeditionary Forces (SHAEF) created the Combined Air Transportation Operations Room (CATOR) to coordinate postinvasion air supply of ground forces other than airborne forces. CATOR's tasks included keeping all concerned informed of the airlift available, allocating aircraft between operational tasks, advising the requesting unit of airlift availability, and allocating scheduled and emergency supply by air missions to the troop carrier and other air transport organizations. It had a detailed and complicated mechanism set up for receiving requests and transmitting them to the airlift units. The important limitation was that CATOR was only a coordinating function, not a command with organic resources. Since its only resources were those allocated by another command, it lacked real authority. In August 1944, CATOR became part of the newly formed First Allied Airborne Army (FAAA).[77]

In December 1943, General Arnold wrote to General Spaatz suggesting that the airborne troops and troop carrier forces in Europe be placed under the Ninth Air Force for command, training, and operations. The British had formed their own similar Headquarters Airborne Troops Command and hinted that they could provide the commander and cadre forces for such an organization. General Eisenhower went a step further and created an airborne command, the First Allied Airborne Army, on 8 August 1944. Lt Gen Lewis H. Brereton, commander of the US Ninth Air Force, became the FAAA's one and only commanding general. The unit formed after the invasion of Normandy because US and British airborne operations there were separate; but future missions, involving multiple divisions of differing nationalities, were clearly in the offing.[78] The mission of the FAAA was deceptively simple:

AIRLIFT DOCTRINE

(1) Supervise the specialized training of the airborne men who will descend on the enemy from the sky.
(2) Prepare plans which are the groundwork of any operation.
(3) Direct and control operations from the marshalling of troops into planes and gliders to the time that they have been dropped behind the enemy lines.
(4) Arrange for and supervise resupply of the troops on the ground with ammunition, weapons, food, clothing and reserve troops.
(5) Provide for the return of airborne troops to their bases once they have been relieved from the battle.[79]

In its first six weeks of existence, the FAAA planned 18 different airborne operations, only to see them cancelled as the ground situation changed rapidly. Late in 1944 it was ordered to plan for an air assault against Berlin to take advantage of possible disintegration of German authority. Those unexecuted operations—Talisman and Eclipse—were to seize airports by use of paratroops and gliders.[80]

In July 1944, over 400 troop carrier planes left England to support operations in the Mediterranean, leaving 870 aircraft for the IX TCC. Until 30 July these forces were more than adequate for the demands placed on them. The airborne divisions were either still in the line or needed extensive refitting and retraining time. However, the breakout at Saint-Lô turned the system into anarchy. Thinking to take advantage of the mobility and power of General Patton's Third Army, General Eisenhower directed the preparations for Transfigure, an airborne operation to trap the retreating German army south of Paris. Planning went so far that the airborne troops and their transports were marshalled and ready on 16 August for launch the next day. However, General Patton's rapid advance overcame the need for the assault. What is important is that the airlift force had to stand down their resupply missions to prepare for the assaults at a time when the entire Allied offensive was gravely suffering from outrunning its ground lines of communication—thus making even a few tons delivered by air worth their weight in gold.[81]

General Eisenhower understood these delicate choices quite thoroughly:

> In late August, with our supply situation growing constantly more desperate, and with all of us eagerly following combat progress in the search for another prospect of cutting off great numbers of the enemy [by airborne assault], the question of the Transport Command employment came up for daily discussion. On the average, allowing for all kinds of weather, our planes could deliver about 2,000 tons a day to the front. While this was only a small percentage of our total deliveries, every ton was so valuable that the decision was a serious one.[82]

The Allied air attack on the transportation infrastructure in France that had so effectively delayed or prohibited German reinforcements from reaching the Normandy beaches also severely handicapped the Allied supply mechanisms in their dash to the German border. General Eisenhower had little choice but to give supply missions precedence over airborne training, which violated the primary mission directives for troop carrier units but fulfilled their ultimate objective of supporting the theater commander. There were provisions for withdrawing the troop carriers for approved air assaults. In reality the battle was moving so fast that most airborne operations may not have had the profound impact some might have thought. In the critical month between the cancellation of Transfigure and the execution of Market, an airborne operation in the Netherlands, the troop carriers delivered about 2,000 tons per day. They were technically capable of at least twice that much.[83]

An extensive study by the IX Troop Carrier Command also concluded that one of the greatest factors in this underutilization of capacity was the absence of suitable destination airfields. Often there were more airplanes available than the strips could handle. The tactical air forces had declared that transports would not use the same fields as the fighters for fear of disrupting tactical operations. The report noted examples of supplies having to be airlanded anywhere from 80 to 120 miles from their destination. The conclusions of the IX Troop Carrier Command study are illuminating:

> It is important to stress here that a plan to use aircraft on large-scale supply movements cannot be successful unless the plan also provides for personnel and equipment to build or repair sufficient airfields, over and above the requirements of the tactical air force, to accommodate the air cargo traffic. With the exception of a limited amount of traffic flown into the Normandy beachhead, the bulk of supplies delivered by aircraft to ground forces have been landed behind the lines and have required considerable motor transportation to move them forward. An air cargo field seventy-five miles closer to the front would mean only an additional hour flying to the airplane but many hours of wear and tear on trucks over highways already heavily congested. The additional wear and tear on pilot and airplane for this short period is almost negligible. Early in the development of an Air Force plan, close coordination and mutual understanding must take place on the Army Group-Air Force-Airborne Army level, to insure adequate loading and unloading terminals to meet the demands of the armies for the airlift. Although it would have been possible to sandwich in a few transport type aircraft, the tactical situation made such operations quite impracticable since one (1) crash landing or stalled transport on the runway would have inactivated all the fighter and fighter-bombers on the station. Another factor which prohibited cargo operations was the nonexistence of parking, unloading, and taxi areas.[84]

In the initial stages, the air supply system responded in spite of, rather than because of, CATOR. General Bradley sent a message to SHAEF headquarters indicating his frustrations:

> Communications from here to others in the intricate organization for air supply is almost impossible. Here is the best we can do. Our request is simple to state: We want the maximum tonnage which can be delivered by air as far forward as possible.[85]

This led the Communication Zone to ask SHAEF for the administrative responsibility for airlift and to put a single Air Force agency in charge of the technical operation.[86] Both General Spaatz and Gen H. J. Knerr strongly resisted the initiative—it encroached on an Air Force responsibility. General Knerr counterproposed to SHAEF that the centralized function (an idea he fully supported) be placed under Air Service Command, an arm of the US Strategic Air Forces (USSTAF). The system he envisioned would have a SHAEF central priority board pass airlift requests, in prioritized order, to the 302d Air Transport Wing for execution. (The 302d was in fact in the process of establishing a control system to operate such a program.) General Knerr made two particularly important doctrinal points. He first stated what has become almost a maxim for airlift:

> In order to be fully effective, it is essential that the operating agency have complete and undivided authority to discharge its responsibility. The plan will not work if the Priority Control attempts to exercise any command authority. Such authority must flow from SHAEF to USSTAF.[87]

His second point reflected a concern for the fundamental issue of who should control theater airlift. "Air transportation is not merely another form of transportation that any logistician can manage," Knerr said. "The highly technical nature of any air operation precludes getting the most out of it except in the hands of air trained personnel."[88] He argued similarly to the commander of the Communication Zone:

> Only a fraction of the potential airlift has been realized, due to conflicting orders, partial loading, duplicated routing, lack of communications, etc. This airlift can be trebled without difficulty through adoption of this proposal largely through elimination of lost time and effort, possible through utilization of standard operating procedures in the hands of trained personnel with both military and commercial airline experience.[89]

SHAEF did not act on General Knerr's proposal, but the commanding general of the Communication Zone, who was clearly acting in good faith rather than trying to assume an Air Force function, immediately offered to improve the situation by placing representatives in the 302d's operations.[90] Generals Spaatz and Knerr were probably reacting to more than just the Communication Zone takeover initiative. On 16 August SHAEF had placed CATOR, along with the IX Troop Carrier Command, under the control of the commanding general of the newly created First Allied Airborne Army.[91]

In some ways the assignment of CATOR made quite a bit of sense. Troop carriers were exempt from CATOR control per se, and only the agency charged with airborne operations would be in the best position to know exactly when and what troop carrier assets would be available to augment CATOR. Since the troop carrier airplanes represented the largest pool of assets, they were critical to both airborne and air supply operations. USSTAF vigorously opposed this assignment of CATOR and a subsequent attempt to put all air cargo hauling under control of the airborne organization. USSTAF argued that only if the theater air commander were responsible for airlift would proper weight be placed on total theater air supply needs (versus airborne requirement and the use of bombers for resupply) and that only the air commander could evaluate combat requirements at forward fields to permit maximum cargo operations. USSTAF Operations suggested that CATOR be placed under USSTAF. The effort was apparently partially successful; CATOR went to FAAA, but other cargo assets stayed with USSTAF.[92]

CATOR was a coordinating agency for the duration of the war in Europe and the theater airlift organization did not take full advantage of its potential. Even with its many limitations, however, CATOR played a potentially vital role. The IX Troop Carrier Command, which knew more about the problems of supply by air than any other command in the European theater, voted to keep a CATOR-like function, and in so doing, stated some critical doctrinal positions:

> The existence of an organization similar to CATOR to perform the functions of analyzing the request, verifying availability of unloading airfields and facilities, locating the supplies, and arranging for their delivery to the carrier airdromes would relieve the carrier of a lot of detail with which he would otherwise be unfamiliar. It is felt that the existence of an organization similar to CATOR, incorporating or working in conjunction with a priorities organization, should be established on the highest possible level. The functions of this organization should be definitely limited to the processing of the request and the assignment of a task to the carrier, but leave the operational control of the aircraft definitely with the carrier concerned. This organization must be a part of the highest headquarters since it must act for the Supreme Commander in allocating carrier aircraft, not committed by the Supreme Commander to airborne training and operations, between the various armies according to their requirements. It must be prepared to ensure cooperation with other services if the armies' needs are sufficiently urgent.[93]

Dragoon: August 1944

The original concept for the invasion of Europe called for an amphibious operation against southern France (Anvil) along with the cross-channel invasion. However, Overlord (the cross-channel invasion) demanded far too many resources for both operations to occur together. A separate operation for August 1944 received final approval in early July. An airborne assault of some type was integral to the invasion, but the details were still unsettled. The options considered, rejected, and finally selected make an interesting study about where the thinking on airborne operations stood shortly after Neptune.

In April 1944, Gen Henry Wilson, supreme Allied commander in the Mediterranean, asked the Combined Chiefs of Staff for enough airplanes to fly an airborne division into southern France, but his request was based more on hopes than specific plans. The only plan available at the time was Anvil, which called for day and night drops on D minus 1 and D plus 1, both aimed at protecting the beachhead. After adjustment, the Allied theater air force called for a daylight mission of 394 aircraft and 30 gliders on D minus 1, with at least three widely

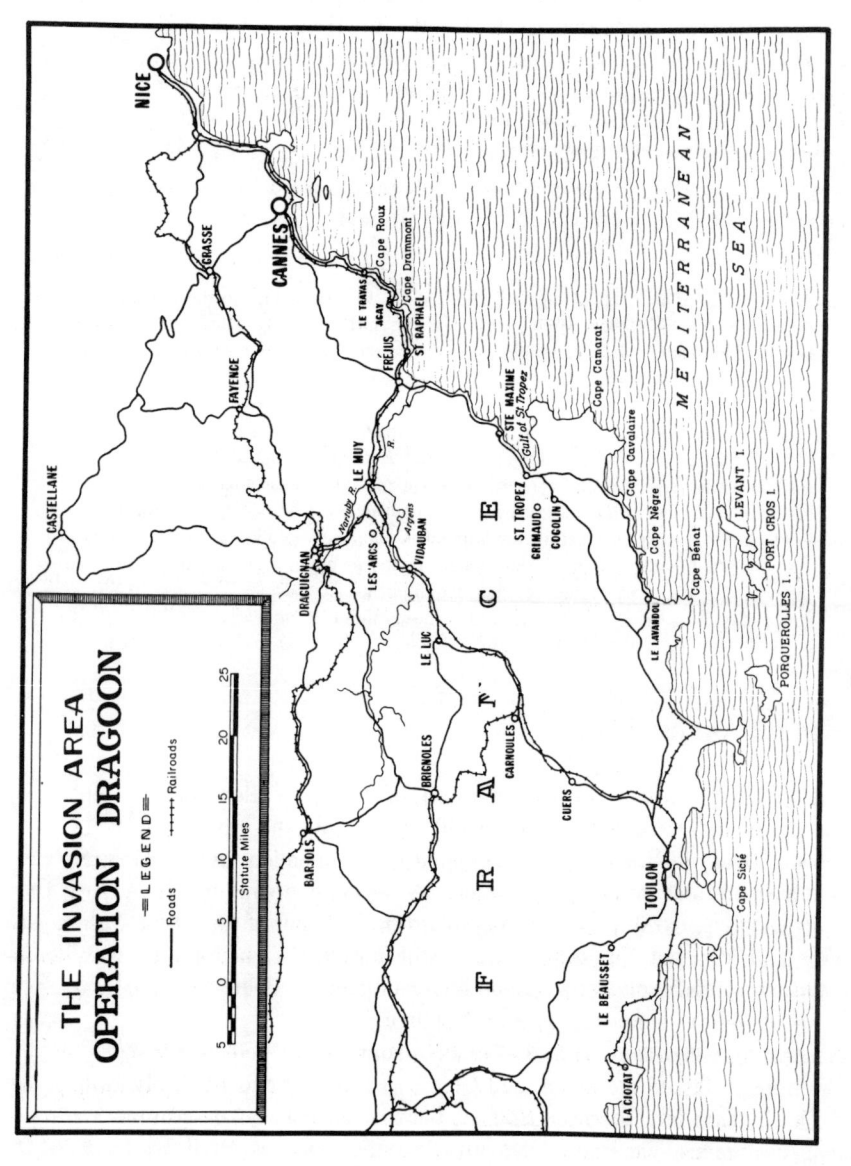

Figure 20

separated drop zone objectives. Lt Gen Ira Eaker, commander of the Mediterranean Allied Air Forces, felt a daylight drop on D minus 1 was too risky and would throw away any opportunity for surprise. Consequently, his command's outline plan offered the morning of D-day as an alternative. The biggest problem with the plan was that it dispersed the airborne forces too widely.[94]

The Air Staff proposed a massive air assault to seize five airfields by a parachute division, followed by the airlanding of three infantry divisions via heavy bombers. The force would maintain a 60-mile perimeter around the airfields and bar a German line of retreat. Resupply needs would require 550 tons per day by C-47s and 70 percent of the bombers of the Fifteenth Air Force for 30 to 60 days. No one in the theater supported the plan. The Fifteenth Air Force did not want to release its bombers. General Eisenhower wanted some of the C-47s for his operations. General Wilson could not spare the three infantry divisions. General Eaker said the target airfields would not physically support the heavy aircraft. The troop carrier commander, Brig Gen Paul Williams, stressed the dangers of antiaircraft batteries to C-47s and bombers on resupply missions. Lt Gen James Gammel, General Wilson's chief of staff, doubted that the force could keep the German artillery out of range. With this kind of support, the plan got nowhere.[95]

Instead, General Williams and Brig Gen Robert Frederick, the airborne commander, hammered out the finally accepted main features of the airborne missions. Their most important tactical change was to concentrate the airborne forces into a tight semicircle near the town of Le Muy. Drop zone/landing zone (DZ/LZ) O was two miles long and from one to one and one-half miles wide, surrounded with several natural landmarks. DZ/LZ A was one and one-half miles long and three-fourths of a mile wide, again surrounded by landmarks. DZ C was a narrow strip over a mile and one-half long, lying between two ridges. It was steep, rocky, and wooded, with only two truly open areas. The planners selected this difficult zone because of its strategic high ground.[96]

General Williams had learned well the importance of daylight airborne operations. Advances in pathfinding abilities convinced him that a dawn drop would work. The logical consequence to this was daylight glider operations as well. The dawn drop would preserve surprise and generally allow a better chance for securing the LZs prior to glider arrivals. The plan also called for air cover en route and close air support just before the drops, with emphasis on attacking antiaircraft emplacements.[97]

In mid-July General Williams assumed command of the Provisional Troop Carrier Air Division (PTCAD). There was some difficulty in obtaining and assembling gliders. This forced PTCAD to direct minimal glider training in order to conserve gliders. Two troop carrier groups had been so tied up in the previous months with providing intratheater airlift logistic services that they were in desperate need of formation flying training. On 7 August PTCAD executed a scaled-down rehearsal primarily aimed at testing and practicing with navigation

AIRLIFT DOCTRINE

aids and familiarizing naval forces with the striped troop carriers and gliders. A final organizational step was the formation of 1st Airborne Task Force.[98]

On 13 August the weathermen predicted fair weather in the object areas, but a day later they warned of fog in the early morning. General Eaker accepted the risk, and PTCAD assumed the responsibility for postponing or recalling missions if instrument flying conditions developed.[99]

The Pathfinders departed at 0100 and ran into heavy fog over their DZs/LZs. The team for DZ C got lost, dropped 10 to 15 miles off target, and did not get to their objectives in time to aid in the drops or glider activities. The team for DZ/LZ A dropped two minutes early and landed three and one-half miles from its target. The team got lost on the ground and was attacked by German patrols. They did arrive at their zone by the afternoon of D-day and were very helpful to later missions. The team for DZ/LZ O landed within 100 yards of its objective.[100]

The first paratroop mission, Albatross, included 396 planes carrying 5,600 troops. They were destined for DZ C. "The drop zone was invisible in the fog; the SCR-717 of the lead ship failed; and no signal was received from the Pathfinder troops who at that moment were wandering in the woods."[101] The crews of the first serial overcame these incredible odds thanks to their careful training at the sand table; the hilltops stuck out of the fog and the crews recognized them. All but a few troopers landed within one-half mile of the DZ. "No other group in the whole course of the war made so accurate a drop under such difficult conditions."[102] The second serial went astray, dropping and badly dispersing their troops 10 miles from DZ A. The rest of the morning serials for DZ A missed and dispersed their paratroops over several miles of countryside. At DZ O, where the Pathfinders were set up and operating, the drops of the first serial were excellent. The Eureka beacons more than proved their worth in the blind-drop situation. The follow-on serials had stragglers who sometimes dropped 20 miles from the DZ. Even with clearing fog, these flights just were not accurate, reducing overall accuracy for DZ A to 60 percent, as compared to 40 percent for DZ C which had no aids whatsoever.[103]

The first serial of the first glider mission for the invasion, Bluebird, had to turn back. The LZs still had significant fog and the C-47s towing the heavy Horsa gliders lacked the fuel to wait for it to clear. The second group, towing the lighter Waco gliders, was able to wait and at 0926 released its 33 gliders over LZ O. The 35 Horsa-towing troop carriers returned to LZ O at 1749 and released without event. Shortly thereafter Canary—41 planes with 736 troops and 10 tons of supplies— made a completely successful drop onto DZ A, where recently arrived Pathfinders had a full set of drop aids in operation. Next came Dove, the mission towing 332 Waco gliders with artillery and 2,250 men. The serials were too tightly spaced both internally and between each other. They were to split between LZs A and O, which were relatively close together (a problem in itself), and the run-in routes edged together. The sky was full of layers of gliders dodging and diving to avoid midair

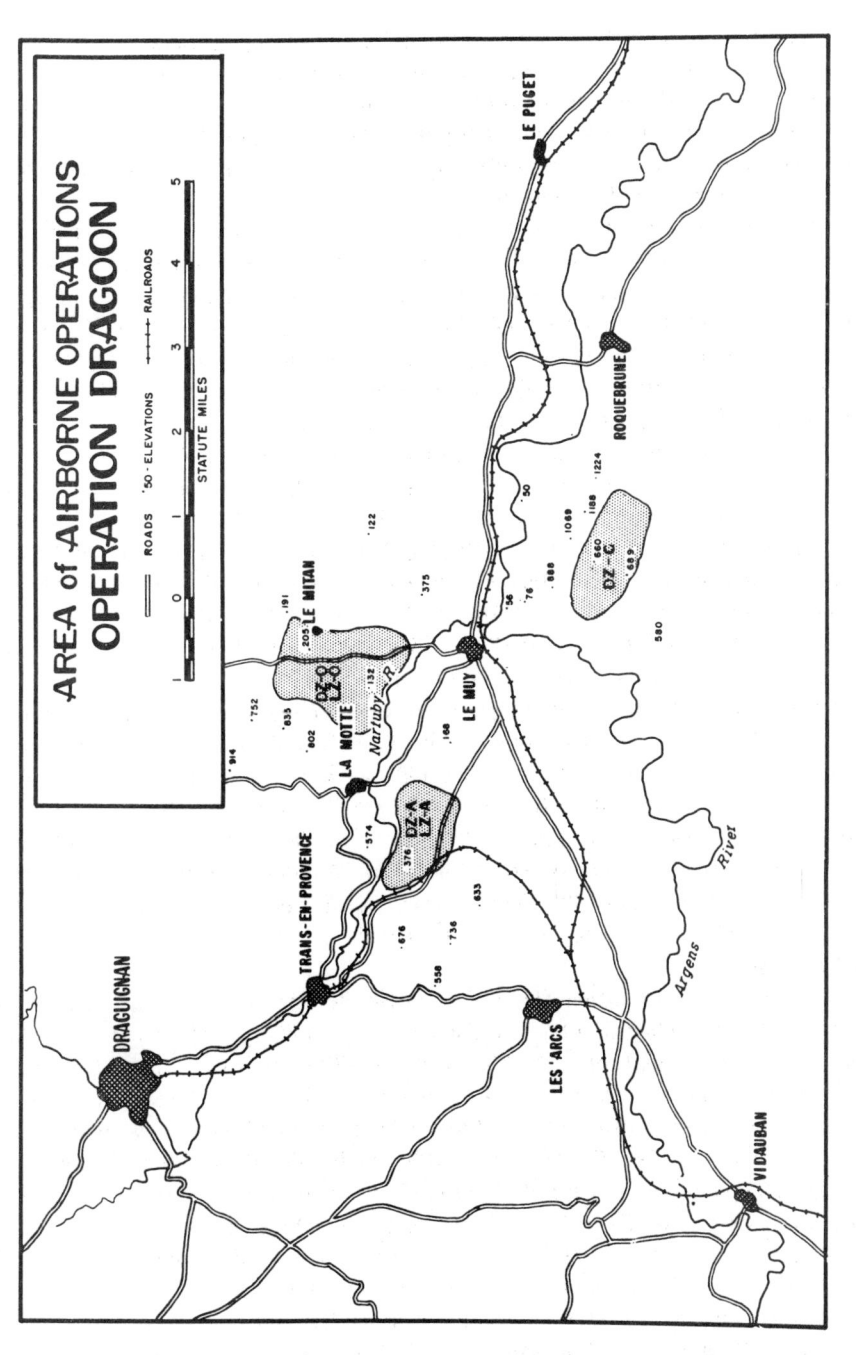

Figure 21

collisions. The LZs were overcrowded, and later serials were preempted by early arrivals. The net result was pilots landing wherever they could, often at dangerously high speeds. Eleven pilots died and 30 were injured, but very little damage was done to the cargoes. The gliders were essentially a total loss.[104]

D plus 1 (16 August) brought Eagle, the daylight automatic resupply mission involving 112 airplanes with 246 tons of supplies, largely ammunition. Part of the load was in externally mounted parapaks and the rest inside, on rollers. Eagle aircraft dropped on DZs A and O, with Eurekas and panels in place and operating. Due to stuck rollers and ill-trained crews, drops took over 2 minutes rather than the planned 30 seconds. Thirty-one parapaks failed to release. Ninety-five percent of the 1,700 bundles landed safely, but only 60 percent were recovered by the desired unit due to mingling on the DZs, dispersion, and lack of collecting personnel.[105]

Dragoon: Lessons Learned

Dragoon indirectly illustrated the importance of air superiority to daylight airborne operations. There was virtually no enemy air action against the paratroop and glider operations either en route or at the targets. Flak was also essentially nonexistent. When in place, turned on, and used, the navigation and drop zone aids proved their worth, especially in prohibitive weather, although they still had room for improvement. Aerial resupply also still needed great improvement, both in technique and conception. All the negative points aside, a hastily assembled and trained troop carrier force did deliver the equivalent of a division over some distance with four missions, in a fairly accurate way. Even lacking an effective enemy resistance, on the ground and in the air, Dragoon proved the potential of daylight airborne assaults. There were to be more major night airborne operations, however.

Neptune and Dragoon together firmly planted the value of airborne operations in the minds of the senior leaders:

> In the minds of most British and American tacticians the Normandy and southern France operations answered all the questions of the validity of parachute and glider operations and proved that airborne was here to stay. The atmosphere in First Allied Airborne Army and in all the planning headquarters changed from a cautious and conservative approach concerning the employment of airborne troops to one of unbridled optimism and audacity. Eisenhower himself called for plans that would emphasize the bold aspect of air assaults, and staffs worked feverishly on a series of plans that, studied now in the light of all that is known of German strengths and dispositions at that time, are amazingly risky.[106]

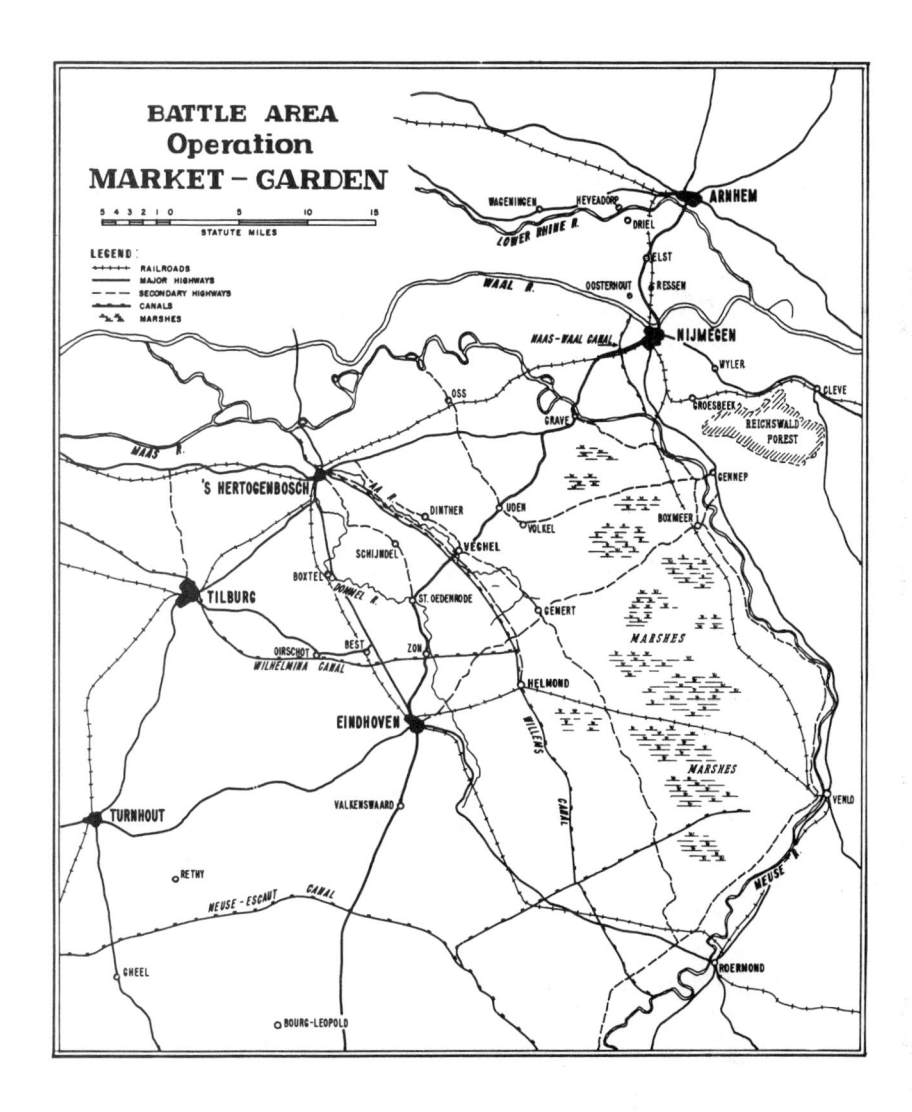

Figure 22

Market-Garden: September 1944

The use of airborne troops was a key factor in the double-pronged plan to move Allied troops, under the command of British Gen Bernard Montgomery, into Germany itself in the fall of 1944. The ground phase of this campaign, to be carried

AIRLIFT DOCTRINE

out by the British Second Army, was code-named Garden; the airborne portion, involving the US 82d and 101st Airborne Divisions, the British 1 Airborne Division, and other elements, was called Market. As described by Gen Omar Bradley, the operation "called for a 60-mile salient to be driven up a side-alley route to the Reich," a route through Belgium and Holland that would outflank Germany's so-called Siegfried defenses.[107] Although it did yield some long-term positional advantages, a variety of factors—faulty intelligence, bad weather, and above all German tenacity—combined to thwart Market-Garden as a means to an early end to the war. The troop carrier part of the operation, however, was a great success.

By mid-August 1944 it was apparent that effective German resistance in France was over. Eisenhower approved Montgomery's strategy of pushing through the Low Countries and across the Rhine River at Arnhem into the plains of northern Germany (Garden) as the most effective way to prosecute the war. To make the strategy work General Montgomery wanted an airborne operation to seize a crossing point on the Rhine along with other water crossings at Eindhoven and Nijmegen (Market).[108]

Market was the largest airborne effort the Allies had mounted and they executed it in daylight. The decision for a daylight mission was an important and logical development in airborne doctrine. The invasion of southern France had occurred with dawn airborne assaults and daylight glider missions, all with negligible losses. The planning predecessors to Market had all been daylight concepts, and the Luftwaffe was not a serious threat. General Brereton, the commander of the First Allied Airborne Army, which would execute the assault, was a highly regarded tactical air expert who judged that the air forces could overcome the flak dangers to a daylight mission. General Montgomery wanted the assault to occur in mid-September, when the moon happened to be dark. The planners knew a night operation so far behind enemy lines, away from effective GEE stations, and with terrain more difficult to decipher with radar than that in Normandy, would be doomed to gross inaccuracies. So Market was a daylight operation.[109]

During the eight major days of the operation, almost 35,000 men either parachuted or rode gliders into a battle. On the first day alone, 16,500 went in. There were almost 5,000 troop carrier missions and more than 2,400 glider missions.[110]

A series of planning factors and events made it almost a foregone conclusion the operation would not succeed. The fundamental issue was that Market was planned as a three-day operation. Even with the huge number of missions planned for the troop carriers, there were not enough resources to make a concentrated drop of forces, equipment, and supplies within a tactically desirable time period. The FAAA was particularly strong in its critique of the Market operation concerning the fundamental need for observance of the principles of mass and timeliness in airborne missions.

> From the moment that airborne troops land, they are faced with three conflicting tasks. These are, first, the accomplishing of the mission assigned to them, a task which becomes progressively more difficult as the enemy recovers from his initial surprise; second, the holding off of the enemy reserves moving up to interfere with their mission; third, the continual protection of some dropping or landing zones if there is to be any operational or administrative build-up by air.
>
> The simultaneous execution of these tasks demands dispersion, which can only be compensated for by concentrating the full effort of large airborne forces upon a small number of tasks, particularly those which no one else can do. Dispersion of airborne troops is just as unsound as is the dispersion of effort of normal ground forces.
>
> Therefore airborne troops must be used in mass and the rate at which they are built up must be extremely rapid.[111]

The airborne forces, instead, had to rely on a series of missions, and that doomed the outcome. General Brereton's personal report to General Arnold was most telling on this point:

> "Don't send a boy to do a man's job," "concentrate the maximum force on the principal objective." This sounds trite, but the ground force planners persist in presenting a multitude of objectives. An all-out effort with everything that can fly must take advantage of the initial surprise by dropping the maximum of supplies and reinforcements before the enemy can muster his air, flak, and ground defenses. All troop drops and landings from the outset must be in combat teams, no matter how small the combat team is.
>
> By this I mean that you cannot count on landing your parachutists today hoping to land their heavy weapons and transport in a landing lift today or tomorrow. Every serial launched must be reasonably capable of sustaining combat, even if a combat team is no larger than a company.[112]

The senior planners did not want to attempt night operations, so the limited daylight of September in Europe, coupled with the distances involved, restricted the IX Troop Carrier Wing to one mission per plane per day. They had just about every plane available but were limited by crew ratio and thus could not simply reload the plane and take off with a fresh crew—they had to wait for crew rest.[113]

The "stretched out" nature of the operation also put the entire air assault at the mercy of the weather and tied up extensive numbers of troops in guarding the drop and landing zones for later arrivals. Because the attack force was operating so far from friendly forces, it had to rely on resupply by air, which only worsened the potential impact of adverse weather. The weather did not cooperate. Reinforcements, in the form of troops, equipment, and ammunition, did not arrive when most critically needed. Bad weather also halted Allied tactical air support at several vital junctures.

Another extremely important factor was the British error of locating their drop and landing zones five to eight miles from their objectives near Arnhem. This ruined any opportunity for quick seizure of bridges and allowed the enemy to bring its forces to bear in a much more effective manner. It also forced the British to divide their forces between achieving objectives and holding zones for later arrivals, compounding an already extended time period for operations. The British were aware of the potential problems, but preferred good drop zones at a distance to bad drop zones close to their objectives. They surmised that the potential zones close to Arnhem were swampy, subject to enemy sweeping fire, and guarded by strong concentrations of flak. Still another contributing factor to the failure of Market was the lack of effective communications. For example, from D-day until D plus 5, the 1 British Airborne Division had very little contact with the outside world.[114]

The final report of the FAAA on Market was strong in suggesting that improved communications could have made a critical difference in the outcome:

> In operation "MARKET" the almost total failure of wireless communication between Airborne Corps Main and 1 British Airborne Division prevented any control of the operations being carried out by that division and the serious situation of the battle on their front was not known until 48 hours too late; consequently no orders could be sent to them in time to influence their action. If communications had been adequate, they might, as an example, have been directed to move west to the area of RENKUM while such movement was still possible; in this area a good bridgehead could have been held over R NEDER RIJN and 30 Corps would have had a good opportunity to cross there comparatively unopposed.
>
> Thus the signal resources of airborne forces are not at present adequate; great opportunities have been lost as a direct result of this and unnecessary casualties have been suffered.[115]

All of these problems paled, however, in light of the fundamental failure—the "extraordinary revival of German fighting capacity brought by General [Walter] Model."[116] General Model replaced Gen Günther von Kluge, who had committed suicide after being unable to stem the Allied breakout from the Normandy beaches. "In one of the enemy's more resourceful demonstrations of generalship, General Model stemmed the rout of the Wehrmacht. He quieted the panic and reorganized the demoralized German forces into effective battle forces."[117] One of his reorganizations was to place two Panzer divisions in the Arnhem area, while Allied intelligence predicted no more than a brigade group. If intelligence had been right about German forces and their state of mind, Market may have been a success. The critical linkup of airborne and advancing ground forces could not occur because the ground forces were faced with a rejuvenated and well-placed enemy concentration of armor, guns, and infantry.

Although the overall mission was not a success, the troop carrier operations were very successful. All ground and airborne troop commanders praised the skill and courage of the troop carrier forces. The vast majority of the troops and gliders made highly accurate drops and landings. The previous combat experience of the troop carrier force, combined with effective Pathfinder assistance, concentrated large numbers of combat forces where they wanted to be. The misses that did occur on three drop zones were caused primarily by the lack of Pathfinders on those zones. Although losses to flak were not staggering, or even significant, the troop carriers on several occasions did encounter heavy fire and continued on their missions even when afire, earning the respect of the combat-seasoned forces they supported.[118]

Market vindicated the decision to fly in daylight. The lesson it taught was that given air superiority and effective flak suppression, daylight operations could succeed. The tactical fighter forces flew 5,200 missions to protect the troop carriers against the German air force and to neutralize flak. Even the official report by the IX Troop Carrier Command paid high tribute to the importance of air superiority in daylight operations:

> The employment of Troop Carrier Forces during daylight hours emerged as a triumphant success after having been previously condemned because of feared effectiveness of enemy air and ground action during daylight hours. Large numbers of supporting aircraft provided superior escort cover and protection from enemy ground installations. These supporting forces deserve much of the credit for the success of Troop Carrier operations and are viewed with great admiration by the combat crews of the IX Troop Carrier Command.[119]

Market was also the initial proving ground for resupply by air of an isolated and very large force. On D plus 1, 252 B-24s of the 2d Bombardment Division took off from England to drop resupplies to the 82d and 101st. Each plane carried about two tons of material in bomb racks, waist compartments, and bomb bays. Ball turrets were removed for pushing out bundles, with a trained dropmaster from the 2d Quartermaster Battalion assigned to each plane as a pusher. They followed by 20 minutes a troop carrier operation and thus were able to use the same zone markers and en route aids, as well as take advantage of the same fighter protection and flak suppression missions. Eighty percent of the supplies destined for the 82d were recovered. At other drop zones accuracy was far less, ranging from 20- to 50-percent recovery. This compared favorably with troop carrier resupply on D plus 2, which yielded a 20-percent recovery rate, a 6-percent recovery by British forces from supplies dropped on the wrong location (due to communication problems) on the same day, and equally dismal rates from other resupply efforts. In fairness, the bombers faced less flak than other missions, but the question has to do not with luck but with reliability of resupply by air in combat conditions.[120] General Brereton's analysis of the importance of all air forces' contributions reveals the extraordinary risk the senior leaders were willing to take in order to seize an opportunity to run to the heart of Germany:

> The success of Airborne operations depends on the proper use of our Air Forces, both Tactical and Strategic. They must make hostile airdromes unusable, attack known and developed flak installations, provide effective fighter screens between hostile air forces and our drop and landing zones, and protect our airborne sky train from hostile

interception. First estimates of probable loss to the airborne lift in Operation MARKET ranged from 25 percent to 30 percent. However, by effective employment of the measures mentioned above, the actual loss to the lift was only 2½ percent.[121]

Varsity: March 1945

The airborne assault across the Rhine—code-named Varsity—was the last major airborne operation in Europe. It was also the exemplification of several critical airborne lessons gained during the war. By early 1945 the Allies had agreed on a three-phase campaign as a final drive to end the war with Germany. The strategic idea was to put pressure along the entire front, not allowing the Germans to concentrate at any given point. General Eisenhower, however, had agreed that a northern assault would be given most emphasis. The Varsity objective was to secure Diersfordter Wald, a wooded area three to five miles east of the Rhine River in the Wesel area. The withdrawing German forces had blown the bridges crossing the Rhine, and General Montgomery planned for an amphibious crossing near Wesel. Airborne forces were to seize the high ground to the east of the river and thus provide artillery protection to the amphibious assault and bridge-building forces. General Montgomery considered the airborne attack so important that he was willing to delay the amphibious assault for five days if bad weather prohibited air operations.[122]

The airborne planners selected 10 DZ/LZs, all very close to their objectives. The operation was to occur in daylight, both to ensure accuracy and to take advantage of air superiority. Critically, eight of the drop zones were within 200 yards of another and all were located in a tight six-by-five-mile concentration. The single most notable feature of the drop was that 17,000 troops along with ammunition and equipment, plus immediate resupply by air, were to arrive within four hours. This incredible concentration of forces was part of General Montgomery's scheme of a massive, overwhelming assault designed to break heretofore stiff resistance.[123]

The airborne forces were to accomplish this feat with 1,264 C-47s, 117 C-46s, and almost 2,000 CG-4a (Waco) gliders. Planners made extensive use of C-47s double-towing the gliders. The C-47, with two additional fuel tanks, could fly the distances involved—which were themselves much shorter than in Market because the planes were based in Paris, not England. The airborne forces also used the multiple-traffic-lane concept developed during Market, in which routes were divided into parallel lanes, with variables of altitudes and speed taken into account, allowing for better concentration of forces. Pathfinders were not used, at least in the sense of earlier drops. Instead, Pathfinders with the first elements were to mark the zones for units arriving later. The planners chose this method because they expected the zones to be too heavily defended for these small units and because they wanted to maintain surprise as long as possible. The surprise element was furthered in that the airborne forces dropped after the amphibious attack started, the reverse of normal practices up to that point in the war.[124]

TROOP CARRIER AND THEATER AIRLIFT

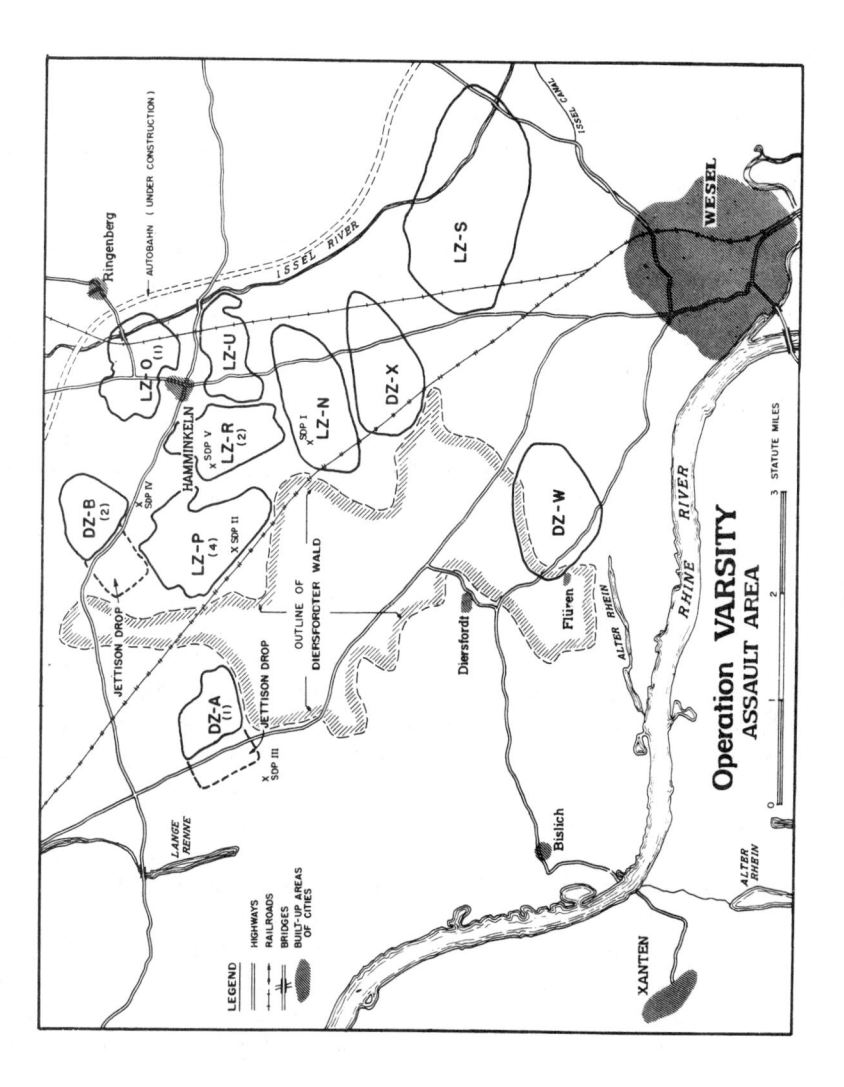

Figure 23

AIRLIFT DOCTRINE

Ever vigilant to the risk of isolating airborne units, and probably still stinging from the lack of a linkup with ground forces in Market, the Varsity planners were extremely concerned with the resupply of the airdropped forces. Because the ground lines of communication (LOC) could not be counted on even if some linkup occurred and because the troop carriers would be busy with the actual drops, the planners decided to use bombers for resupply, much as they had during Market. They requested and received 240 Liberator bombers from England and scheduled 540 tons of supplies for delivery 20 minutes after the last gliders had landed. This closely timed event offered several advantages. First, it got significant stores to the ground troops quickly, freeing them from having to defend drop zones. Second, it allowed the bomber forces to take advantage of the air cover already provided to the troop carriers. The planners also arranged an automatic resupply drop for D plus 1, unless specifically cancelled by the ground forces. This resupply effort was to consist of 680 bomber and troop carrier aircraft with over 1,000 tons of supplies—still only a two-day supply. The planners also arranged for follow-on resupply by request.[125]

Before the last resupply bomber dropped its load, the airborne troops had established contact with the Second Army, and the follow-up resupply for the next day was unnecessary. The heavy, rapid concentration of forces via the airborne assault was a decisive stroke that played a vital part in the breakthrough into the northern German plains.

General Brereton's comprehensive report on Varsity concluded much the same, if in somewhat more formal language:

> The seizing of the designated objectives [by the XVIII Airborne Corps] affected directly, and to a major degree, the quick establishment of the sizable bridgehead and enabled British Second Army to cross the river in force and continue a rapid advance to the north and northeast.
>
> The fact that during D-day the airborne troops took 3,500 prisoners from well-prepared positions within British Second Army area is indicative of the assistance rendered during the initial period of the crossings. These men would have greatly impeded a conventional river assault.
>
> It is concluded that the airborne missions were successfully accomplished and materially aided the ground troops in crossing the Rhine with a minimum of loss.[126]

General Brereton called Varsity a tremendous success. General Eisenhower said it was the "most successful airborne operation we carried out during war."[127] Drop accuracy was superb; massive concentration of forces in an extremely short time was achieved; daylight airborne missions were revalidated; and losses to ground fire were reasonable, especially for the troop carriers.

Figure 24

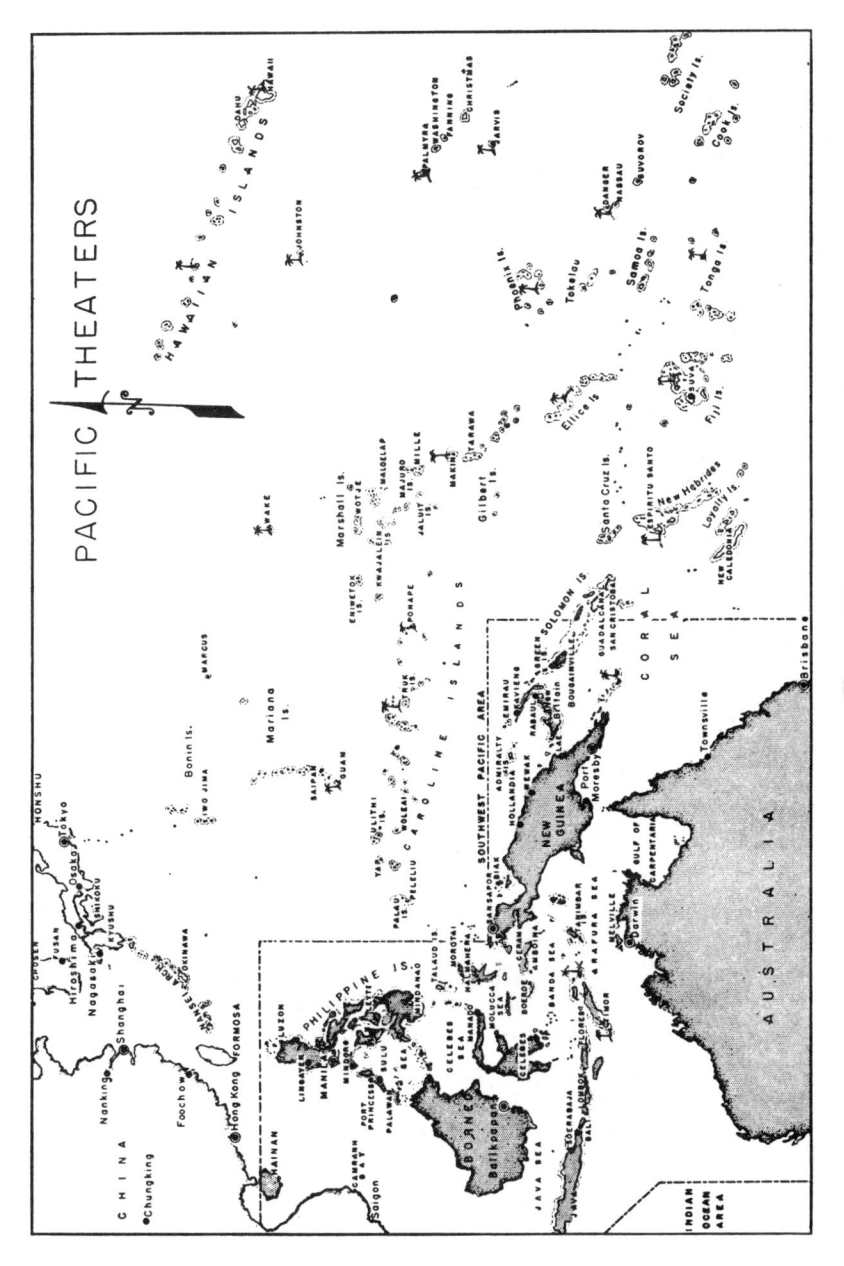

AIRLIFT DOCTRINE

Troop Carrier Operations in the Pacific

The troop carriers in the Pacific theater operated very differently than did those in the Mediterranean and European theaters. The war in the Pacific was different in execution and in geography. In the vast majority of cases, troop carriers were involved in logistical airlift. There were very few paratroop assaults, but the troop carriers became the supply and resupply lifeline of the forces they supported and they provided the mobility that became a hallmark of the ground and tactical air forces in the Pacific. The forces in the Pacific were dependent on aerial logistics to a degree never required in the European theater. This section focuses on the Southwest Pacific Area (SWPA) of the Pacific theater, where the troop carriers were most involved and where we find the most doctrinal harvest.

Since mid-1942 the air headquarters in the Southwest Pacific Area had been the Allied Air Forces, with the Fifth Air Force as the US component. The Thirteenth Air Force became part of this structure with the combining of the SWPA and South Pacific Area commands in mid-1944 under the Far East Air Forces (FEAF). In 1942 the Allied Air Forces air transport organization started out as the Air Transport Command, but the name was soon changed to the Directorate of Air Transportation (DAT) to avoid confusion with the newly created American strategic airlift force.

The original American contribution to DAT was 10 officers and 15 enlisted men of the 7th Bomb Group and the 35th Pursuit Group. Their airlift force consisted of two B-18s and one C-39 that they had flown from the Philippines to Brisbane, Australia. They also managed to "find" five new C-53s aboard the first convoy that had started from the United States for the Philippines but diverted to Australia.[128]

On 28 January 1942 the first formal American transport unit was formed under the Fifth Air Force and ordered to use all US transport airplanes then in Australia and all combat airplanes flyable but unfit for combat. Officially this translated into three B-18s, three B-24s, one C-39, one B-17-C, five C-53s, and three Beechcrafts. During the latter part of January and early February these meager forces flew P-40 mechanics and spare parts to Java and evacuated military and civilian personnel from the Netherlands East Indies.[129]

On 20 February the chief of staff of the AAF in Australia, Maj Gen Julian Barnes, requested activation of two fully recognized transport squadrons built with in-being resources. The outcome was the designation of the 21st and 22d Troop Carrier Squadrons. The squadrons had a motley collection of assets including B-18s, C-53s, DC-2s, DC-3s, DC-5s, DC-39s, C-56s, L-14s, and C-47s.[130] The Australian contribution was equally stark. The Australians had very few transports, and the few DC-2s they had were needed for pilot training. They did manage to form up the 36th Royal Australian Air Force (RAAF) Transport Squadron with some on-loan American planes and DH-84s, -86s, and -89s. (One of the 84s had to be grounded due to termites in the tail section.) By 1944 the Australians were operating seven squadrons of C-47s and C-60s.[131]

Several US Air Transport Command officers visiting SWPA in April of 1943 offered a particularly effective description of DAT and its real function.

> In his capacity as Commanding General of the Allied Air Forces, General Kenney directly commands the Director of Air Transport who runs a truly Allied air transport unit composed in part of troop carrier squadrons, in part of Australian transport squadrons and, in part, of civil airlines under control to the military. There are approximately 66 planes in this unit, which is an administrative unit that directs the underlying airlines, troop carrier squadrons etc., where to run. The underlying units are responsible for maintenance and operational servicing of the planes and furnishing of the flight crews, while the Director of Air Transport handles the loading and unloading, the runs to be made, the grading of priorities, and the paperwork involved in manifests, notification to shippers, etc.[132]

In short, DAT's aircraft, crews, and maintenance personnel remained under virtual control of their real owners—the AAF and RAAF—this very much in parallel with the CATOR system developed in Europe. Nonetheless, it provided a system-oriented perspective to airlift in SWPA and achieved many positive results.

In the rush of establishing the early organization and meeting immediate combat needs, the safest and most efficient loading of the assets available was sometimes ignored. The airplanes were simply loaded and flown, both operations by the seat of the pants. The few loading charts available were ignored and most planes took off overloaded. By April 1942 some semblance of control was taking hold.[133]

The air transports needed a system to properly handle the loading, unloading, manifesting, and dispatching of transport aircraft. It is only through a carefully and tightly managed *system* that the most efficient use of an extremely limited resource is achievable. Overloaded aircraft can crash or suffer undue wear and tear during landings and takeoffs. Poor manifest procedures lead to cargo being mishandled, nonhandled, and lost. An efficient loading and (equally important) unloading system moves cargo quickly to where it is needed. A proper command and control system for dispatch and scheduling is so vital its need is self-evident.

DAT recognized the need and began training station control teams. These teams had a complex job: all members had to have a thorough knowledge of the many kinds of transports, including cargo and gasoline capacities, loadings, and the proper distribution of weight in the aircraft. DAT standardized loading and unloading methods for various types of freight and the manifesting of freight and passengers. Control officers learned to evaluate requests for air transportation, assign priorities, plan the load, and route the airplanes to maintain maximum efficiency. These control teams first were organized under an Airways Control Squadron in June 1943. This disbanded six months later and was replaced by the 1st Air Cargo Control Squadron, with five subordinate teams. The volume and type of cargo handled at individual stations governed team size and composition by individual stations. The teams had direct communication with the airdrome control towers so as to meet the arriving DAT airplanes for off-loading and fuel management.[134]

AIRLIFT DOCTRINE

For all its valiant efforts, DAT's scarce resources did not make it the proper agency for evaluating theater air shipment priorities. GHQ SWPA thus undertook to establish a theater priorities board for all shipments, not just air, under the direction of a cargo regulating officer (CRO). The authorizing letter charged the CRO with assigning priorities to individuals, troops, and organizational equipment; with assigning cargo for water, air, and rail movement; and with coordinating schedules and establishing direct contact with supply, transportation, and similar agencies.[135] Additional regulating officers at the major ports and operating locations could "establish priorities on requests for water and air shipments submitted by commanders of major components in their respective component."[136] Thus, the entire system became unified under theater-wide procedures and cargo movement priority symbols.

On 13 November 1943 the CRO issued a comprehensive set of regulations that provided a strong, centralized control of troop and cargo movements. The theater commander also gave the CRO the responsibility not only for controlling intratheater movements but also for determining the priorities into and out of the theater. Since the War Department circular establishing theater priorities boards was not issued until April 1944, the SWPA actions may be viewed as pioneer work.[137]

The theater also sought some semblance of balance between theater logistics needs and tactical requirements by directing that DAT could divert no more than 60 percent of its capacity to tactical use at any one time. The point here was that at least 40 percent of the airlift capability would be reserved to flying between main bases on relatively routine runs, while up to 60 percent could be used to fly into forward operating bases/areas.[138]

During this initial period the US Army Services of Supply (SOS) was also moving cargo and personnel by chartering flying boats and land-based planes from the Australian civil airlines. Often, the SOS was chartering for the same areas or along the same routes serviced by the DAT. This resulted in an obvious loss of efficiency and often caused important materiel to arrive later than needed because SOS had already booked the space. Despite its obvious seriousness, the problem was not resolved until February of 1943 when, finally in compliance with a War Department circular of July 1942, the SOS ceased its chartering activities.[139]

DAT also took several other steps to increase system efficiency. First, they provided an extensive course to their pilots in instrument flying, requiring at least one-third of flying hours to be "under the hood," even in good weather. Second, they emphasized fuel management techniques so as to improve weight versus fuel load. These rudimentary methods increased average payloads from 5,000 to 6,500 pounds per flight and were especially effective when coupled with airways radio and beacon improvements—which the pilots were more likely to use when properly trained.[140]

The Fifth Air Force activated the 54th TCW on 13 March 1943 in anticipation of growing demands for troop carriers. By September of 1943 the wing was managing 3 troop carrier groups and 14 troop carrier squadrons. The 54th TCW was directly under the Fifth Air Force, on the same organizational level as the fighter and bomber commands. Its official mission was to transport troops, including paratroops, and material to forward areas.

The Directorate of Air Transport disbanded on 3 October 1944, replaced by the 5298th TCW (Provisional). The DAT mission in Australia reverted to the RAAF and many of its intratheater missions were picked up by ATC. On 3 January 1945 the 322d TCW replaced the 5298th, under the operational and administrative control of the Far East Air Forces Services Command (FEAFSC). DAT, the provisional wing, and the 322d TCW, in turn, controlled the 374th TCG, with four troop carrier squadrons. The 322d commander also served as the chief of the Air Cargo Division, FEAFSC, in charge of setting and coordinating general policy matters concerning aircraft loading, routes, and efficient use of FEAFSC aircraft. The wing's mission included night courier services for GHQ SWPA, normal cargo work, and air depot hauling, with the key emphasis in carrying high-priority cargoes destined for Air Corps organizations. The squadrons converted from C-47s to larger capacity C-46s in April 1945.[141]

Consequently, the SWPA theater had two theater airlift systems (the 54th TCW and the 322d TCW), just as in Europe, one to perform traditional troop carrier operations and one to support the needs of the theater US air components. The SWPA Air Evaluation Board reported in April of 1946 that this dual structure was marked by lack of coordination and by duplication and confusion. It suggested raising the TCC to the same organizational level as the FEAFSC, thus allowing the TCC to coordinate efforts of all theater airlift organizations. Despite these problems, "without the air transportation provided by these two Troop Carrier Wings, our northward advance by island stepping stones to Japan would not have been possible."[142] This concise overall evaluation of troop carrier contributions to the war in SWPA provides a useful context for the discussion of actual operations.

- Air transport was the principal means of sustaining the logistical support of initial land and air operations at Darwin, Australia, and in Papua, New Guinea.
- Air transport was essential to the logistical support required in island warfare.
- The employment of troop carrier aviation as air transport greatly aided land and air operations.
- Troop carrier aviation produced far greater effect on the war through its employment as air transport rather than as troop carrier.
- The effort expended on continuous air transport operations prevented troop carrier aviation from training adequately for airborne operations.

AIRLIFT DOCTRINE

- The effectiveness and exceptionally low operational losses of air transport in the initial phase of the war is attributed primarily to the skill and determination of the Troop Carrier pilots and other personnel.
- Fighter escort was effective in preventing troop carrier combat losses.
- The effectiveness of troop carrier aviation contributed to the success of the Allied occupation of Japan.[143]

The lack of transportation infrastructure both in Australia and in the combat areas led Gen Douglas MacArthur to recognize that air transportation was indispensable to his theater. He told the War Department in September of 1942:

> Air transport is the only efficient means of supply because of necessity of convoying against enemy naval activity, absence of docks, unloading and loading facilities, small amounts of shipping available and total lack of road and rail communications in theater of operations.[144]

New Guinea

As the Japanese followed their attack on Pearl Harbor with a rapidly growing list of successes on a southward and eastward drive, Australia became the pivotal point for the Allies, both offensively and defensively. Port Moresby became the focus of Allied attempts to stop the Japanese drive. Located on the southeast corner of New Guinea, its capture by the Japanese would imperil the Allied position in Australia. The port had been the apparent enemy goal in an abortive amphibious invasion in early May 1943, an effort that ended in failure in the Battle of the Coral Sea. The Japanese army drew up its own plans to capture the port via the back door—by capturing Buna on the other side of the Papuan peninsula and crossing the Owen Stanley Mountain Range between the two. It was the task of General MacArthur, who had taken command of the Southwest Pacific Area on 18 April 1942, to stop the Japanese and start the long task of recapturing the many lost bases en route to the Philippines. On 21 July the Japanese landed just north of Buna and started their drive for Port Moresby. An Australian infantry company had already started the long trek over the mountains toward Buna. The scant resources of the 21st and 22d Troop Carrier Squadrons of the Fifth Air Force's Directorate of Air Transport were hard pressed but managed to airlift enough supplies to the greatly outnumbered Australians to allow them to delay the advancing Japanese until 9 August.[145]

By 29 August, the Japanese were less than 30 miles from the critical Port Moresby. The reinforced Australians dug in, held the line, and on 24 September counterattacked. They chased the Japanese far into the mountains and, once on the move, required aerial resupply. A total of 25 tons per day became the normal resupply figure for these troops. The Australians brought their supplies to the departure airfields already prepared for dropping, and recovery rates in the DZs ranged from 60 to 90 percent, depending on the nature of the DZs targeted.[146]

TROOP CARRIER AND THEATER AIRLIFT

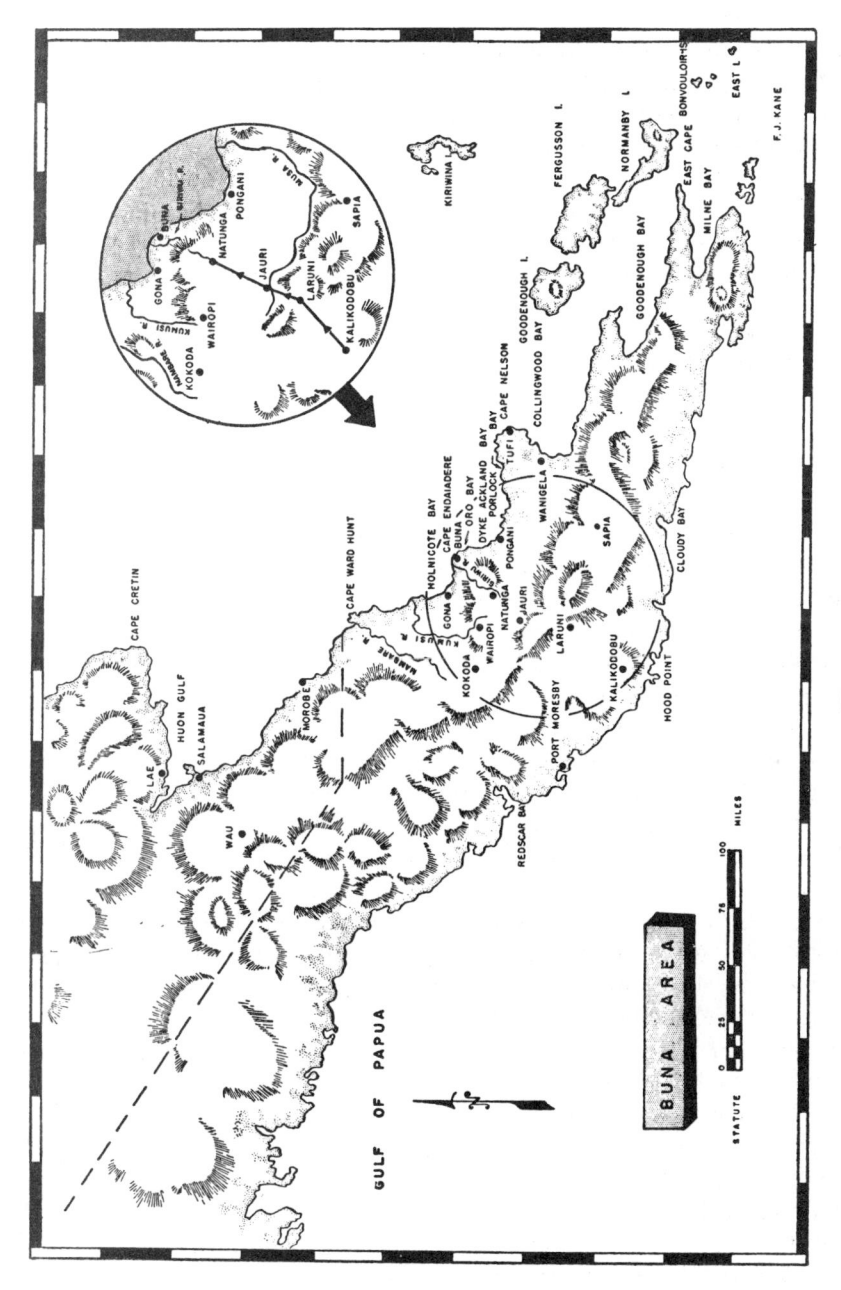

Figure 25

It was at this point that the air transport forces made a genuine contribution to the battle. By 15 September the DAT had airlanded three Australian battalions and, within two weeks, had brought in most of the US 126th and 128th Infantry Regiments in the first real tests of moving entire units by air. With these fresh reinforcements in hand, the combined forces started the drive to retake Buna and force the Japanese out of New Guinea. These Allied efforts depended heavily on air transport.[147]

On 21 September 1942 the 2d Battalion of the US 128th Infantry Regiment moved the 1,400 air miles from Brisbane to Port Moresby. The remaining two battalions moved 700 miles overland between Brisbane and Townsville to then be airlifted to New Guinea. From alert to completion, the move took about 10 days, certainly a well-executed operation considering the lack of expertise of all concerned. On 2 October troop carriers airlifted a provisional Australian battalion from Milne Bay to a forward operating base. On 16 October the 128th deployed forward, and between 6 and 25 November the troop carriers moved the 126th Infantry, plus several Australian artillery batteries, from Port Moresby to the Buna area. Once the troops were in place and engaging the enemy, or at least advancing on its locations, they could only be supplied by air, and by mid-November the troop carrier units were airlanding or airdropping 100 tons of supplies daily.[148]

The supplied and the suppliers both gained rapidly from the operational experiences. At first, the troop carriers dropped all their loads in one pass, spreading material across miles of ground. It was later that they learned to make up to 10 passes to ensure reception and concentration of the supplies. Just about any airplane would do, and the B-26 became a favorite, especially after the carriers learned the proper altitudes for dropping bundles. Both panels and smoke signals marked the drop areas, and the suppliers attached white streamers to their packages to aid in recovery.[149]

By 1 January 1943 the campaign for the Papuan peninsula was nearing its close, but the troop carriers had to fly in the 163d Regiment of the 41st Division from Port Moresby to aid in the offensive. By 22 January organized Japanese resistance in the area ended.[150]

The planned flanking operations up the coast from Milne Bay ran through terrible terrain and there was a distinct shortage of native bearers and shipping. There was still a scarcity of troop carriers but the planners plunged ahead and activated the 374th Troop Carrier Group to provide a structure for the four squadrons that eventually would be available. Even given these limitations the ground forces moved out. They were largely supplied by airdrop—often with only the most fragile items being parachuted. Most supplies were just wrapped in blankets and baling wire and shoved out the airplane door. Severe rains grounded the whole movement at times, but the ground commanders were so impressed as to continue relying on both supply and unit deployments by air.

By late December the pressures applied by the Allied air and naval forces caused the enemy to give up trying to reinforce its garrison at Buna. The Japanese shifted their efforts northwestward to Lae and landed over 4,000 troops, who immediately moved on the small forward Australian garrison at Wau. On 29 January the Australians repulsed a sharp attack and called for help. In two days the troop carriers brought in supplies and 2,000 reinforcements. At times the airfield was so congested that the troop carriers had to circle while the Australians drove the Japanese far enough back into the jungle for the planes to land. That force of Australians who originally occupied Wau had been placed there by troop carrier forces in April of 1942 to harass the Japanese and were supplied by air with a little over one and one-half tons per day.[151]

The consolidation of the Allied position in southeast New Guinea and support of air forces attacking Japanese shipping occupied the troop carrier forces well into the summer of 1943. In March and April alone they supplied a daily average lift of over 300 tons. Maj Gen George Kenney, the commander of both the Allied Air Forces and the US Fifth Air Force, had been promised three and one-half troop carrier groups, and he had plans for every single airplane, and more.[152]

General Kenney's next major operation for the troop carriers involved the seizure of Lae. The Australians at Wau had to be supplied continuously by air, especially when they took advantage of an opportunity to seize the high ground commanding Japanese supply lines. Plans called for an American force to land at Nassau Bay. The force landed and then moved slowly inland to join up with the Australians, fed and in no small part equipped by air.[153]

An important plus in this push was the timely arrival of American troop carrier forces. During the first week of July four new squadrons began arriving at Port Moresby, soon' followed by two more squadrons. But in July 1943, General Kenney pointed out to General Arnold the incredible strain placed on troop carrier units, especially in light of the policies that replacements for troop carrier personnel would be limited to 7.5 percent and that any increase in the one-for-one crew-to-airplane ratio would have to be worked out in-house:

> In the case of troop carriers, I figure I can get five hundred hours of New Guinea operation out of them. It is asking a lot, for the figures show that between weather and Nips a man lives longer in a P-39 than he does in a C-47 flying the troop carrier supply runs in New Guinea. . . . The replacement rate per month for troop carriers should be twenty five percent. The troop carrier group working between Australia and New Guinea is averaging over one hundred hours per month per crew. The great part of their haul is over the 750-mile over water hop from Townsville to Moresby on schedule—which they keep regardless of weather. I don't know how much of the grind they can take but with a replacement rate of seven and one half percent I cannot think of sending them home before fifteen hundred hours.[154]

By mid-August the Allies were ready to inaugurate their air offensive against Lae, which was greatly facilitated by the development and rehabilitation of an old

AIRLIFT DOCTRINE

airstrip at Tsili Tsili. That base would serve as an all-weather interim forward base for fighters that would provide escort for bombers attacking Lae and air cover for later amphibious operations. The troop carrier C-47s flew a company of airborne engineers into Tsili Tsili with their miniature bulldozers, graders, and carryalls. At the end of 20 days, half of which saw weather interruptions, the base could handle up to 150 C-47s per day. By the end of July the troop carriers moved in an Australian infantry battalion and an American automatic weapons battery, and by mid-August Tsili Tsili was a fully equipped and functioning Allied fighter base.[155]

The plan was to seize Lae by a shore-to-shore amphibious troop movement, coupled with an airborne assault of Nadzab, some 30 miles inland. The paratroopers were to link up with an Australian force sent overland prior to the drop. Seizure of Nadzab offered several strategic benefits. It would provide a potential air base for future operations, cut off the Japanese escape route from Lae, and give the Allies control of an important river valley in the immediate area.[156] The combined attack took place on 4 and 5 September 1943. By 0630 on the 4th, the first troops of the Australian 9 Division went ashore, and within four hours, 7,800 men executed the amphibious assault. At 0825 on the 5th, the first of 84 C-47s, loaded with the US 503d Parachute Regiment and some associated Australian units, departed Port Moresby for its 200-mile flight to Nadzab and the first American airborne operation in the Pacific. The associated Australian units were artillerymen who jumped from five of the C-47s, which also carried their dismantled 75-mm howitzers.[157] At 1022 the first trooper jumped. Generals Kenney and MacArthur were present for the drop. Kenney wrote to Arnold:

> You already know by this time the news on the preliminary moves to take out Lae but I will tell you about the show on 5 September, when we took Nadzab with 1,700 paratroops and with General MacArthur in a B-17 over the area watching the show and jumping up and down like a kid. I was flying number two in the same flight with him and the operation really was a magnificent spectacle. I truly don't believe that another air force in the world today could have put this over as perfectly as the 5th Air Force did. Three hundred and two airplanes in all, taking off from eight different fields in the Moresby and Dobodura areas, made a rendezvous right on the nose over Marilinan, flying through clouds, passes in the mountains, and over the top. Not a single squadron did any circling or stalling around but all slid into place like clockwork and proceeded on the final flight down the Watut Valley, turned to the right down the Markham and went directly to the target. Going north down the valley of the Watut from Marilinan, this was the picture: heading the parade at one thousand feet were six squadrons of B-25 strafers with the eight .50 cal. guns in the nose and sixty frag bombs in each bomb bay; immediately behind and about five hundred feet above were six A-20s flying in pairs—three pairs abreast—to lay smoke as the last frag bomb exploded. At about two thousand feet and directly behind the A-20s came ninety-six C-47s carrying paratroops, supplies, and some artillery. The C-47s flew in three columns of three plane elements, each column carrying a battalion set up for a particular battalion dropping ground. On each side along the column of transports and about one thousand feet above them were the close cover fighters. Another group of fighters sat at seven thousand feet and, up in the sun, staggered from fifteen to twenty thousand, was another group of [P-47s]. Following the transports came five B-17s, racks

loaded with three hundred pound packages with parachutes, to be dropped to the paratroopers on call by panel signals as they needed them. This mobile supply unit stayed over Nadzab practically all day serving the paratroops below, dropping a total of fifteen tons of supplies in this manner. Following the echelon to the right and just behind the five supply B-17s was a group of twenty-four B-24s and four B-17s which left the column just before the junction of the Watut and the Markham to take out the Jap defensive position of Heath's Plantation, about half way between Nadzab and Lae. Five weather ships were used prior to and during the show along the route and over the passes, to keep the units straight on weather to be encountered during their flights to the rendezvous. The brass hats flight of three B-17s above the centre of the transport column completed the set up.[158]

There were no troop carrier losses and the unopposed landing secured the area within 24 hours. The drops were 95 percent accurate. There were 11 gliders at Port Moresby loaded with engineers and equipment to reinforce the 503d, but the complete success of the drop meant they were not needed. By daybreak of the 6th, the troop carriers started airlanding infantry of the Australian 7 Division that had been prepositioned at Tsili Tsili (35 miles southeast of Nadzab). By the 14th Nadzab had two parallel 6,000-foot runways and a dispersal area capable of handling 36 C-47s simultaneously. The quick development of an effective ground handling system allowed 27 troop carriers to land and unload within 45 minutes. On the 16th all Allied objectives were in hand. The Nadzab assault had excellent operational results:

Notwithstanding the absence of heavy fighting in the Nadzab jump, the operation against Lae was a masterful employment of all available sources of firepower and mobility. It was the first tactical parachute jump in the Pacific, and the first major tactical airlift of combat troops in the theater. The coordination with the overland feint against Salamaua and the amphibious assault on Lae, with the well-timed support of air and naval forces, was an excellent example of joint planning and operations.[159]

By mid-1943 the theme for successful warfare in the SWPA was clear:

The strategic objective of cutting off Japan from the resources of the Malaya-Netherlands East Indies area would be attained through a scheme of maneuver that gave the chief offensive role to land-based air power. The "land-based bomber line" would be advanced westward along the land mass of New Guinea toward the Philippines, with hostile forces by-passed and neutralized through air action wherever practicable in order to avoid costly and time-consuming operations. The "offensive fighter line" would move forward with the aid of air transport to extend the "destructive effort of bombers." Ground forces carried forward by air and water would seize and make secure an advancing line of air bases. Flank protection would be provided "essentially by air operations." Necessary naval bases would be established under the protection of land-based aviation, with carrier borne planes making their own special contribution by close support of landings undertaken beyond the reach of previously established land bases. Thus might the length of forward movements be increased with a consequent saving of valuable time. This, in brief, was the doctrine taught by a year of successful warfare in the Southwest Pacific, and its acceptance by MacArthur gave new occasion for General Kenney to look to his planes.[160]

The next major operation that the troop carriers participated in was the capture of the Hollandia area in Netherlands New Guinea. The Japanese had occupied Hollandia in April 1942 and eventually wanted to develop it into a final base and last strategic point on New Guinea. The area contained five airfields—Tami, Pim, Cyclops, Santani, and Hollandia. It was 448 air miles from the massive Fifth Air Force center in the Nadzab region. After an intensive series of air attacks, both land- and sea-based, Allied forces launched an amphibious landing on 22 April 1944. The landing forces met very light resistance from the Japanese, whose forces had dispersed to guard other areas, but they did find significant physical troubles. The area was swampy and the few existing roads were muddy tracks. They had to rely on airborne resupply for food and ammunition, using B-24s and B-25s to drop rations at the Hollandia drome. Two squadrons of P-40s occupied the strip on 3 May and were supplied almost entirely by airlanded materiel.[161]

It did not take the Allies long to realize that they had captured a lemon. The bays along the coast did not provide suitable anchorages and the general swampiness precluded major establishments. The planners elected to develop neither a services of supply depot nor an air depot at Hollandia, but rather to concentrate on airfield development. By 3 May the engineers had the Tami strip ready for troop carrier operation, which flew in almost 500 C-47 loads during May. At the same time the 54th TCW ferried nearly 4,000 loads into Hollandia airdrome. Concurrent with the landings near Hollandia, the Allies also assaulted the Aitape coast of Papua New Guinea, rapidly pushing the Japanese out and seizing the Tadji air strip which was pronounced usable on 24 April. The field immediately became a forward base for fighters supporting operations in both areas. It served as interim base, with most forces moving to Hollandia as that strip opened up. Allied forces moved inland to clean up Japanese resistance and relied extensively upon aerial resupply. By late July, for example, 4,500 troops engaged in aggressive patrolling were supplied by air. Indeed, in July the 54th TCW dropped 671 tons of supplies to these patrol activities. By 10 August organized Japanese resistance ceased.[162]

The victory at Hollandia permitted the SWPA to accelerate its plans for the reduction of the remaining portions of New Guinea still under Japanese control. General MacArthur's planners intended to invade Wakde Island, Biak, Vogelkop, and the Halmaheras successively. General Kenney wanted to add to this list an airborne invasion of Selaroe Island and construction there of a fighter field that was to be air supplied for 14 days. This would test the practicality of an airborne invasion of Mindinao. However, GHQ SWPA declined to divert its planned efforts:

> SWPA thus committed its entire effort to an advance up the New Guinea coast along an exceedingly narrow front. Its four remaining operations in New Guinea would advance the land-based bombers by successive occupations of minimum air-base areas, selected in positions lightly held by the Japanese. Air power would prepare the way for each invasion and would protect SWPA's flanks, increasingly vulnerable as the attack moved northward. SWPA experience had demonstrated that air power could perform such a

mission. The only question was whether the execution of four operations in as many months with the limited amount of amphibious shipping and engineering forces available would allow SWPA to reach the point of departure for the Philippines within time alloted.[163]

After seizing Biak Island in late June 1944, the Allied forces planned an extensive airfield development program. A massive shipping backlog, caused by lack of an adequate harbor and an intense Japanese air campaign, stymied the program. Despite this tangle, the Fifth Air Force was able to get air units into Biak using C-47s and bomber units. In fact, between 11 and 20 July the 22d and 345th Bomber Groups almost ceased combat operations to carry cargoes out of Nadzab.[164]

The original plans for the progression up the New Guinea coast did not call for any objectives in Geelvink Bay except Biak, but air planners wanted Noemfoor Island captured. The rationale was that

> an air garrison on Noemfoor would facilitate fighter escort for bomber strikes on the Halmaheras, could maintain the neutralization of Vogelkop airfields, could break up Japanese efforts to reinforce Biak from Manokwari, and would also be of value in case the Japanese navy, observed to be effecting a concentration around Tawi-Tawi, attempted to raid Biak.[165]

The amphibious forces landed on 2 July 1944, meeting a Japanese defense force badly stunned by bomber and naval gunfire. Initially misled by prisoner of war reports that between 3,500 and 4,500 troops were on the island, the commander called for reinforcements. The planners had foreseen this eventuality and dispatched the 503d Parachute Infantry Regiment.

> The 317th Troop Carrier Group had been concentrated at Hollandia, and on the mornings of 3 and 4 July its C-47s dropped 1,424 parachutists on Kamiri strip. Both missions were marred by high inquiry rates—9.74 percent on the 3d and 8.17 percent on the 4th. On the former day, a smoke screen laid by A-20s and B-25s to mask the drop zone from sniper fire drifted over the strip, with the result that many of the parachutists, missing the strip, landed among debris and parked vehicles on either side of it. On the second day the C-47s released the jumpers properly and most of them landed in the drop area, but by this time the engineers had begun compacting the strip and there were more fractures than on the previous morning.[166]

The Philippine Campaign

Following consolidation of their positions in New Guinea, the Allies were ready for the drive to recapture the Philippines. The sequential capture of Morotai, Leyte, and Mindoro placed them in their desired position for a landing in Luzon and a thrust to Manila.

The fighting on Leyte in November of 1944 was tough, and what little air transportation was available was invaluable:

AIRLIFT DOCTRINE

Figure 26

Field congestion limited the commitment of cargo planes to eight C-47s of the 317th Troop Carrier Group. In the month following the arrival of this detachment the C-47s dropped 221.5 tons of quarter-master items, 70.6 of ordnance, 7.2 of medical supplies, and 1.5 of signal equipment to front-line detachments, with the loss of two aircraft and three crewmen to ground fire. Using a Fifth Air Force rescue plane and six L-5s to supplement his eleven L-4s, Major General J. M. Swing, commanding the 11th Airborne Division in its fights through the mountains west of Burauen, claimed to have "supplied the whole division for a month" and to have "learned something that even Hap doesn't know about aerial resupply." The 25th Liaison Squadron dropped an entire 300-bed field hospital, with cots, tents, instruments, and medical personnel, to the division—a feat which the squadron proudly described as "the most audacious, outstanding, and sensational light plane mission in the history of the SWPA."[167]

The island of Mindoro offered an excellent advanced air base for the attack on Luzon. SWPA's final staff study for the Mindoro campaign called for the 503d Parachute Regiment to fly from Leyte and seize an area around San Jose (on the southwestern end of the island) in an airborne assault. The purpose was to spearhead a drive to build fighter and light bomber strips. That portion of the plan was soon revised to reflect an amphibious landing of the 503d. The Fifth Air Force continued to demand a Mindoro airfield in order to neutralize Luzon. The operation was successfully executed on 15 December and airfield construction began on 20 December. Even given violent Japanese air attacks, the Fifth Air Force moved its air units forward as quickly as the engineers could expand facilities, all with a heavy demand on air transportation. Next in line was Luzon.[168]

The basic SWPA instructions for the invasion of Luzon charged the Sixth Army with occupying the beachheads in the Lingayen-Damortis-San Fernando area and driving southward to Manila. The 6th and 43d Divisions were to land in the Dagupan-Mabilao vicinity with responsibility for the right flank. The 11th Airborne Division was to prepare to parachute into the central plains. Early on, the engineers were to build fighter and medium bomber strips. By the end of the first week after 9 January 1945 the Sixth Army had a firm beachhead—30 miles wide and 30 miles deep and the airstrips were ahead of schedule.[169]

On 31 January the 11th Airborne Division landed at Nasugbu (south of Manila) via amphibious ships, with minimum opposition. On 3 February the 511th Parachute Regiment departed their concentration areas at Mindoro on 48 C-47s of the 317th T G, reaching their drop zones at 0820. Their purpose was to seize the commanding terrain at Tagaytay on the critical road northward to Manila. The jump was planned for three waves delivered across two days. The first 18 planeloads landed right on DZs marked by smoke pots set out by advanced scouts. The next interval dropped six miles short when its lead plane accidentally released a parapak and all troopers immediately "hit the silk." The second wave, under explicit orders to ignore the scattered parachutes on the ground persisted in jumping short. The last wave arrived the next morning and landed on the DZ. Only 38.4 percent of the total drop of 2,055 men landed where they were supposed to. However, within three hours of the last drop, the force had captured the Tagaytay Ridge and associated highways and junctions. By the evening of 4 February the linkup with the 11th Airborne Division was complete.[170]

When an early withdrawal of the supporting amphibious shipping left the entire force critically short of supplies, C-47s flew in supplies both to an emergency strip at Nasugbu and in aerial resupply for the paratroopers. These missions were followed quickly by 31 missions that dropped 78 tons of supplies and equipment to the I Corps in the Zambales foothills. The combined air and ground attacks reduced Manila to semirubble and the assault phase on Luzon officially ended on 5 February 1945. Ironically, the Japanese retreated to Bataan. To clean out this concentration, the Sixth Army landed a force at the tip of the peninsula on 15 February. The next day it launched an airborne assault on Corregidor, to cover and then link up with another amphibious attack. The commander of the 503d talked of jump casualties of up to 20 percent because the DZs, a tiny golf course and former parade ground, were studded with broken trees, heavy undergrowth, and damaged buildings.[171]

> At 0759 on 16 February twenty-four B-24s winged away from Corregidor after dropping frag bombs in the island's gun positions. Between 0800 and 0829 eleven B-25s bombed AA positions and the south coast of the island, while thirty-one A-20s bombed and strafed both Corregidor and nearby Caballo Island, where a few AA batteries were operating. Precisely at 0830 the lead C-47 of the 317th Troop Carrier Group passed over the drop zone at 300 feet, observing no activity; at that moment the 3d Battalion, 34th Infantry, pushed off at Mariveles in LCMs. Very quickly, before the Japanese could recover, fifty-one C-47s of the first mission, wheeling over the two small drop areas in counterrotating orbits, deposited their eight man "sticks" from 500 feet. By 0932 all of the transports had made at least three precise runs over their zones. As the paratroopers landed, seventy A-20s strafed and bombed targets on Corregidor and Caballo, and at 0930 naval vessels commenced fire against San Jose beach preparatory to the amphibious landing at 1028. Support aircraft controllers, dropped by parachute or airborne in a hovering B-25, directed close support missions throughout the morning, and shortly after noon the C-47s were back with more paratroops and parabundles. This drop, like the one in the morning, was marred only by a strong and tricky surface wind which blew some of the men over the cliffs or into obstacles outside the drop zones. Enemy machine gun fire caused a few casualties and damaged a few planes, but casualties for the day were only 10.7 percent, or 222 men out of the 2,065 dropped.[172]

That this operation was successful was astounding. The two drop zones were not large—1,500 feet by 450 feet and 1,500 feet by 200 feet. Because of the short zones, only six to eight men could jump on each pass, which meant up to three runs over the target by the C-47s. Six seconds over a drop zone, assuming outstanding pilot judgment, is quite a challenge. It is little wonder that Maj Gen Joseph M. Swing, commander of the 11th Airborne Division, initially believed that the jump might turn out to be a costly mistake.[173]

The cleanup of the rest of Luzon was no easy task, with the Japanese digging in for some bitter fighting; but by the middle of May, southern Luzon was firmly in American hands. The drive to the north was equally tough. Maj Gen Walter

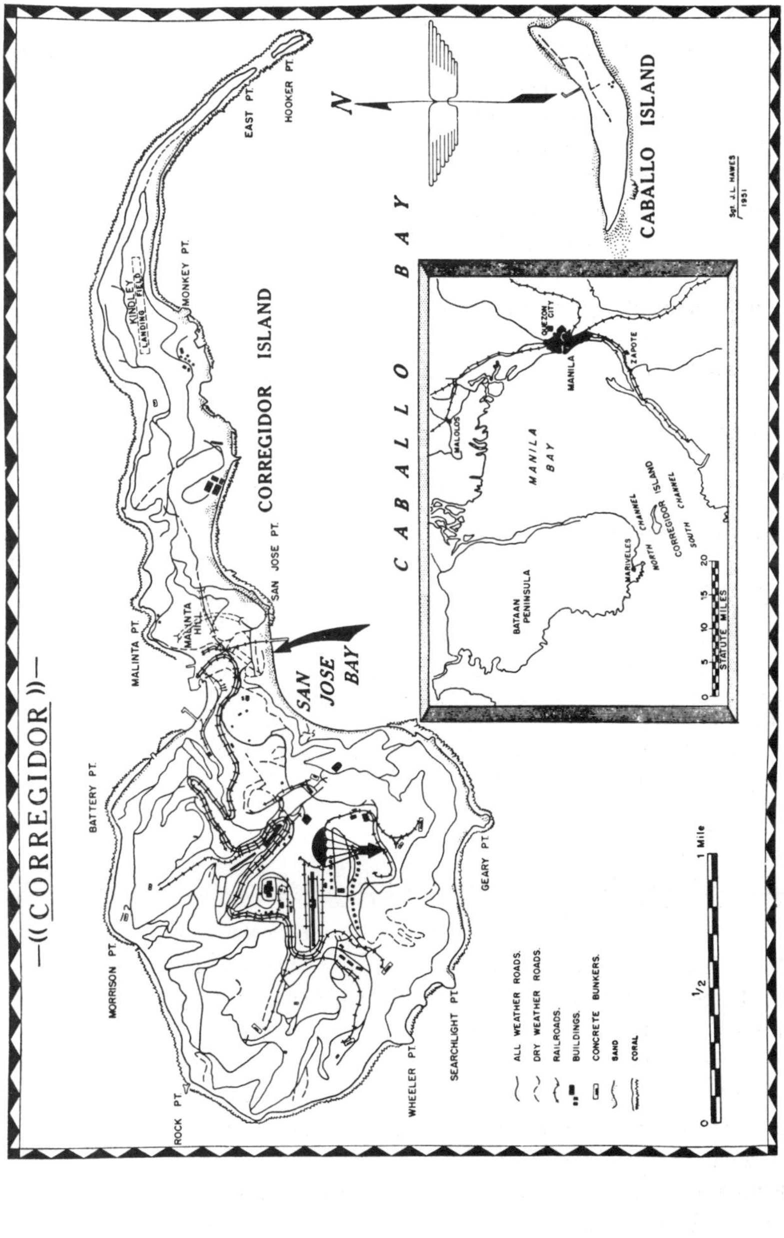

TROOP CARRIER AND THEATER AIRLIFT

Figure 27

Krueger, commander of the Sixth Army forces involved with this effort, was already using aerial resupply for his troops as they fought through mountainous terrain. His forces captured Aparri on the northern tip of Luzon on 21 June 1945 after working their way up the western coast but needed reinforcement to block this Japanese escape route. There followed the only use of gliders in the Pacific theater.[174]

On 23 June the 317th TCG, along with seven C-46s from the 433d TCG for towing the gliders, dropped 994 men on the abandoned Japanese airstrip five miles from Aparri. American rangers and Philippine forces arrived at the field overland and set out smoke signals to mark the drop zone. The gliders carried 19 trucks, 6 jeeps, a trailer, and some supplies. There was no Japanese resistance. Within three days the airdropped force linked up with other US ground forces.[175]

The plan for the ultimate invasion of Japan, Olympic (1 November 1945) and Coronet (1 March 1946), did not include an initial airborne assault. Instead, the 11th Airborne Division would serve as a reserve. The early surrender of Japan in August 1945, however, did not catch General MacArthur's staff unprepared—they had two plans for this contingency, Blacklist and Baker-sixty. FEAF was in operational control of the eventual operation, with the 54th TCW supervising. On 28 August 15 ATC C-54s and 30 troop carrier C-47s carried aviation fuel and communications men to Atsugi airport, 16 miles southwest of Tokyo. The main operation started 30 August, and in 13 days airlifted the 11,300-man 11th Airborne Division and 9,500 troops of the 1st Cavalry Division. They also returned over 7,500 liberated Allied prisoners of war. The Military Analysis Division of the US Strategic Bombing Survey concluded that "no more spectacular transport missions had ever been flown by any military organization anywhere."[176]

A Doctrinal Perspective for the Pacific

The strategy in SWPA called for a measured advance through New Guinea and the Philippines to Japan. An essential element of that strategy was land-based air power, both for air cover against the Japanese air forces and for bombing of tactical and strategic targets. Troop carrier aviation played many roles in this approach. It moved men and equipment directly into battle, both by airdropping and airlanding operations. It resupplied large and small logistically isolated units. It made the fighter and bomber forces truly mobile as units. And it performed the tedious, routine logistical airlift chores of the widely dispersed theater. No wonder its overwhelming orientation was toward logistics.

The SWPA drew its troop carrier doctrine from Field Manual 100-5, *Operations*, and War Department Training Circular 113, *Employment of Airborne and Troop Carrier Forces*. Both of these documents and the popularized experiences in Europe made the prime mission of troop carrier units to be transportation of airborne forces into combat. In SWPA the official secondary mission—logistics—predominated because of the theater's strategy. Had the troop carriers attempted to emphasize the airdrop mission, the entire strategy would have required revision.[177]

What the SWPA operations illustrated doctrinally was the great flexibility of airlift. When troop carriers did execute airborne missions they did very well, even lacking the great organizational entity that evolved in Europe. Given the approach of achieving at least some degree of air superiority, the daylight paratroop drops reinforced experiences in other theaters of the feasibility of daylight operations. The cargo system management that the SWPA developed also made great doctrinal contributions. The 54th TCW organized air freight forwarding units—forerunners of a modern aerial port system—and DAT created its cargo regulating officer program to influence efficiency and combat effectiveness.

Troop Carrier Aviation in the China-Burma-India Theater

The AAF Evaluation Board for the China-Burma-India (CBI) theater put troop carrier operations in the CBI in their proper context in October of 1944: "Supply from the air has been successful because of two outstanding characteristics of air power, namely, speed and flexibility."[178] Experiences in the other combat theaters throughout the war demonstrated that air supply of ground forces was a critical contribution of troop carrier forces. In the CBI, air supply was the "chief and often the only means of supplying Allied ground forces in action against the enemy."[179]

American strategy for the CBI was aimed at keeping the Chinese in the war against the Japanese, thus tying up significant Japanese forces that might turn the tide elsewhere. Allied planners also had a long-range vision of using Chinese airfields as bases for American bombers in the final attacks on the enemy. The best the Allies could do to achieve this end was to provide war materials to the Chinese. A key assumption in this equation, at least early on, was that the Burma Road would serve as the primary supply route into China. The complete fall of Burma to the Japanese in May of 1942 ended the land lines of communication without eliminating need to continue the supply effort. Since the value of air transportation—much less its absolute necessity—were not yet evident, the Allies undertook to build another road from Ledo, in northern Assam, through Myitkyina and into China. Later, Generalissimo Chiang Kai-Shek arranged with the British to construct a road from Imphal, near central Burma, into China. Thus the Allied strategy became one of opening a new land route from India to China across northern Burma in addition to defeating the Japanese in Burma.[180]

The organization of the theater to execute this strategy was something to behold. In reality, the CBI was not a whole unit; rather it had a subtheater for each ally. Adm Lord Louis Mountbatten was warlord for the Southeast Asia Command

AIRLIFT DOCTRINE

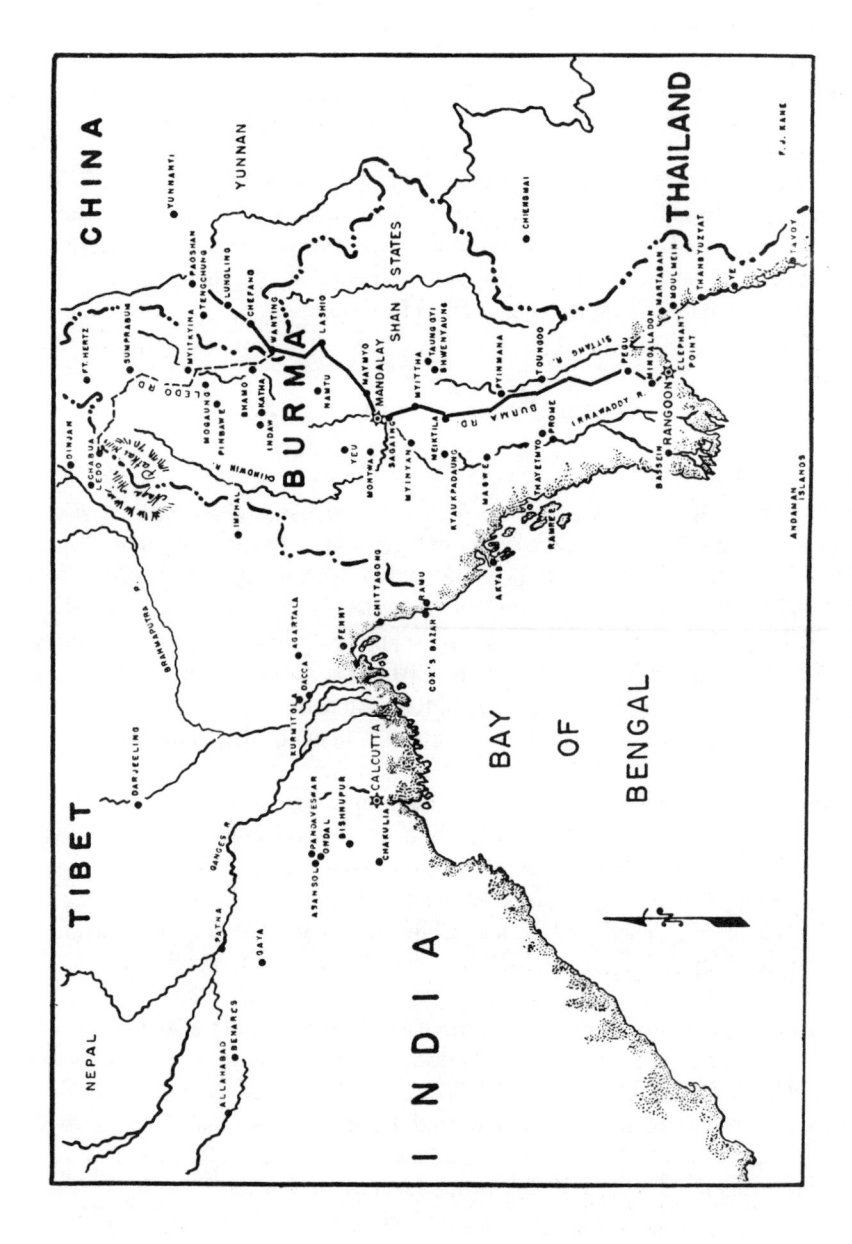

Figure 28. India-Burma sector.

(SEAC), which included India, Burma, Ceylon, Thailand, the Malay Peninsula, and some parts of East Indies. The Generalissimo commanded China and Indochina. The American CBI theater included American forces in both of these areas. It was very much like an interlocking board of directors arrangement that sometimes led to confusion and harsh feelings (as well as words). The command of air forces was even more complex. Troop carrier forces bounced from organization to organization as the whims of the senior chart makers determined. The 443d Troop Carrier Group (with four squadrons) was the American contribution to the Troop Carrier Command of the Eastern Air Command under the administrative control of the Tenth Air Force. This arrangement lasted until May of 1944, when part of the TCC fell to the Third Tactical Air Force, with some elements staying with the Tenth. Later, some parts of the original TCC became the air transportation forces for the Combat Cargo Task Force supporting American and British forces in the Arakan area.[181]

Early Operations

There were numerous small-scale air transport operations throughout 1942 that airlifted retreating Allied forces and refugees, supplied trapped Chinese ground forces in Burma with food, and kept isolated outposts alive. The first Allied ground offensive against the Japanese started in December of 1942 with an overland attack on the port city of Akyab. The Japanese along the route outflanked the two Indian divisions, forcing them to retreat in order to maintain their lines of communication. The Indian troops outnumbered the Japanese but had to withdraw or starve. This first campaign demonstrated the clear need for a new way of supplying troops engaged in jungle warfare.[182]

An official history of aerial resupply efforts in Burma attributes the adoption of that technique at least partially to experiences in the Pacific theater:

> Information concerning the use of transport aircraft for supply of American and Australian troops in Papua filtered into Allied headquarters in Southeast Asia, however, and when combined with the earlier experience in Burma, this information did make an impression. As a result there was a growing desire to see what could be accomplished in Burma by using air transport to supply ground troops operating against the enemy in the jungle.[183]

This interesting reminder of the importance of cross talk between theaters is confirmed by a history of the Services of Supply in the CBI:

> Based upon information received from other theaters, principally the Southwest Pacific where troops under conditions comparable to those in the Ledo area had been successfully supplied by air dropping, it was authoritatively decided to adopt the air supply method. On 4 March 1943 arrangements commenced for experimental dropping of food and supplies to troops in the forward area.[184]

The experimental detail initially consisted of the 60th Laundry Company and the 3477th Ordnance Company, who both packed and kicked out the baskets and parachute bundles. The first airdrop mission occurred on 6 March 1943, flown by C-47s of the AAF Air Transport Command from Chabua. Their efforts proved so successful—and certainly more successful than relying on native bearers who consumed more than they delivered—that the theater organized a formal dropping unit. That unit originally used personnel from the 3841st Quartermaster Truck Regiment as the packers and kickers, and others from the 3304th Quartermaster Truck Company as the receiving units. ATC continued to provide up to 4 aircraft per day (diverted from their primary mission of flying the Hump) until June 1943, when the 2d Troop Carrier Squadron of the Tenth Air Force picked up the mission, increasing available aircraft from 4 to 10.[185]

Brigadier Charles Orde Wingate's first expedition, which began on 18 February 1943, tested the infant concept of airdropping in combat. His Chindit force of British garrison troops, Ghurkas, and a battalion of battle-seasoned Burmese veterans proceeded into Burma to disrupt Japanese communications and propagandize the Burmese people. Altogether, this first Wingate expedition received 303 tons of food and supplies from 178 sorties of Royal Air Force (RAF) transport aircraft.[186]

Strategically and tactically, these operations were not decisive, but they went a long way in refining thinking and tactics for aerial resupply. The effects of these initial efforts, as unsophisticated as they were by later standards, cannot be underestimated.

> Partly as a result of Wingate's effort in 1943, the military gained greater respect for air supply. Lieutenant General Joseph W. Stilwell planned for air supply in his offensive from Ledo, in northern Assam, to Myitkyina in Burma, beginning in December 1943. Lieutenant General Sir William Slim, commander of the British Fourteenth Army, counted on air supply for his 1944 offensives from Imphal in the north and along the coast through Arakan in the south. In September 1943, Major General George E. Stratemeyer, future commander of Eastern Air Command (EAC), stated that "the only way we can supply any force that advances into Burma is by air." When he assumed command of EAC, 15 December 1943, Stratemeyer brought together all the AAF and RAF air supply activities within the Troop Carrier Command under Brigadier General William D. Old. By this time, all of the forces in the area had come under the Supreme Allied Commander, Southeast Asia Command, Admiral Lord Louis Mountbatten.[187]

The Drive to Myitkyina

The coming of the monsoon rains in June 1943 ended the possibility of any more Allied offensives until the autumn. Planning, however, went on apace. General Stilwell wanted to begin construction of the Ledo Road in the fall, counting on aerial resupply for his troops and engineers as they moved forward. His concept included building operating strips for the transports so as to airland as many supplies as possible. One physical objective of the plan was Myitkyina, the use of which not only would improve supply for the combat operations but also would make for a much more efficient route for the AAF Air Transport Command, which was by then operating the Hump airlift to China. General Stilwell would have to drive the Japanese out of the Hukawng and Mogaung areas before he could retake Myitkyina.[188]

General Stilwell's forces began their drive in mid-October 1943 and faced stiff resistance throughout the campaign. The effort in northern Burma lasted until the capture of Myitkyina in May of 1944, and was heavily dependent on aerial resupply. Tonnages increased from 638 in October to 1,669 in December and to 7,309 in April. These figures do not include the 15 tons per day delivered to Brig Gen Frank Merrill's Marauders or supplies delivered to AAF forward operating fields. All told, some 20 percent of the tonnage was airlanded, 42 percent dropped, and the remaining 38 percent parachuted in.[189]

The process of allocating troop carrier capability to these tasks went through an important evolution as the operators gained experience. Initially, monthly operational programs were set in advance, with the Eastern Air Command setting priorities in consultation with higher headquarters. Movement of urgent and emergency requirements was at the discretion of the Troop Carrier Command, if these requirements were not in conflict with primary commitments. The system was ill conceived and too inflexible for the theater needs. Often, much-needed supplies waited for delivery while scheduled missions of overinflated routine requirements flew. Eventually the G-4 of the supported forces ended up working directly with the troop carrier units to prioritize the airlift requests properly.[190]

At the end of March 1944, the Japanese made a major stand. The 22d and 38th Chinese Divisions facing the Japanese had already been in combat for six months and were decimated by casualties and disease. Generalissimo Chiang agreed to send in his 50th Division as reinforcements. The Air Transport Command flew the division from China to Sookerating, Burma, on the backhaul legs of their Hump missions. The 1st Troop Carrier Squadron moved them forward to Maingkwan between 5 and 12 April. During this seven-day period, the 1st Troop Carrier Squadron, with some augmentation from other troop carrier units, flew 280 resupply sorties to the forces in northern Burma and made 203 trips moving the 7,221 troops of the Chinese division.[191]

By late April 1944 the Allied drive for Myitkyina faced the threat of delay from the approaching monsoon season. General Stilwell made the decision for a determined, bold thrust to capture the airfield. Merrill's Marauders executed a seven-day flanking movement through terrible country to put them within 40 miles of the objective. On 17 May a Marauder team, after pushing directly southward, took the field by surprise and radioed to send in occupying forces. The already alerted troop carriers dispatched four aircraft to drop supplies and panels for a follow-on landing of nine gliders.[192]

The Troop Carrier Command placed all of its efforts behind the reinforcement of Myitkyina. On the night of 17-18 May somewhere between 40 and 50 troop carriers carried supplies and reinforcements into the field. On the morning of the 18th, 24 C-47s flew in an antiaircraft battery. By the 19th the troop carriers, with some help from ATC aircraft, had flown in almost 4,000 troops and 500 tons of supplies. These forces were sufficient to hold the airfield but not enough to take the nearby town. The Japanese reinforced their garrison and held out for 76 days, with the Allies finally occupying the village on 3 August 1944.[193]

Even while the siege went on, the airport became a hub for ATC flights over the Hump and for air activities in support of the rest of the north Burma campaign. From May to October there were over 14,000 landings there, delivering more than 40,000 tons of supplies and troops. The air transport traffic became so heavy that, at times, airplanes had to circle for several hours to make their landings. At one point there was a landing or takeoff every 45 seconds during daylight hours.

The C-47s and more capable C-46s flew in every conceivable type of equipment to Myitkyina, including 155-mm guns and heavy engineering equipment. Given this outstanding aerial resupply line, the Allied forces in northern Burma had the confidence to complete their drive south against the Japanese, a campaign that was successfully completed in May 1945.[194]

Organizational Issues

The administrative organization and chain of command for troop carrier activities after the capture of Myitkyina became unnecessarily complicated by other organizational changes in the theater. Troop Carrier Command disbanded in June, replaced by the 3d Combat Cargo Group, which in turn was divided between the Third Tactical Air Force (TAF) and the Tenth Air Force. The combat cargo organization, conceived at Headquarters AAF, had 25 C-47s and 13 to 16 aircrews (a normal troop carrier squadron), but only one-half the maintenance and other support troops usually assigned.

When it became clear that the theater needed an organization dedicated to air transportation issues rather than distracted by tactical concerns, the air planners settled on the Combat Cargo Task Force (CCTF). Its mission, upon activation on 15 September 1944, was aerial delivery of supplies, troop transport, and evacuation, all primarily in support of the Fourteenth Army. It did not have to concern itself with support of ground forces in northern Burma. To protect the new organization from unrealistic and ever-growing demands, all taskings had to be approved by the air commander, Eastern Air Command, prior to execution. Numerous groups and squadrons came and went during the life of the CCTF, with most of the AAF units eventually transferring to the ATC Hump operations. At its height in May 1945, the CCTF had 16 AAF and RAF transport squadrons active under its command.[195]

TROOP CARRIER AND THEATER AIRLIFT

The Tenth Air Force likewise activated its own Air Cargo Headquarters with operational control of its portion of the 3d Combat Cargo Group, four airdrome squadrons, and the 443d Troop Carrier Group. That organization had many of the duties associated with the modern commander of airlift forces (COMALF).

> The responsibilities of the headquarters were: (1) Allocation of loads to subordinate units in conformity with priorities set up by G-4 NCAC; (2) Scheduling of aircraft to airfields where loads were available and delivery to airfields as indicated by allocation of loads and in conformity with established priorities; (3) Liaison with supply packing and shipping agencies (Air Service Command, SOS, Air Cargo Resupply Squadrons, 36 Division, OSS, Air Warning, etc.) to insure availability of loads at airfields where aircraft were based, to expedite loading, unloading, turnaround, and reconsignment of transports, and to insure accuracy of manifests; (4) Keeping the maximum number of aircraft in commission and continuously utilized; (5) Setting up safe flying procedures to include routes and altitude regulations, navigational aids, alert procedures, liaison with fighter organizations, briefing on escape procedure, and inspection of newly-opened airstrips; (6) Seeing after the welfare of flying personnel by providing for feeding transient crews, limiting the number of hours flown, and providing rest and recreation; (7) Establishing airdropping procedures to include training of aircrews and kickers, communications with ground forces by radio and visual means, and liaison with the ground forces with respect to proper selection of DZ's.[196]

Throughout this entire period there were extensive efforts to improve the efficiency of the air transport system. As noted earlier, significant changes in the prioritization process eventually led the G-4 of the supported forces to determine the real priorities of the supplies moved. Planners also worked to improve communications among the forces supplied, the troop carriers, the services of supplies organizations that gathered, packed, and loaded the material, and the senior controlling agencies for airlift. Taken together these many efforts combined to provide a more efficient support of the combat forces. Tonnages increased from 13,000 in May 1944 to 20,000 in July, without any increase in airlift resources—this during the wettest part of the monsoon season.[197]

It is ironic that the entire function of the Allied drive in northern Burma was to open a new road to supply China. Air transport made the entire operation possible and air transportation also made it unnecessary. By early 1945 the air route to China was delivering materiel at a better rate than possible on the newly opened road. Instead the real value of the campaign was that it captured the field at Myitkyina, making the airlift into China more effective. Additionally, any successful offensive based at Myitkyina against the Japanese in Burma had to be counted as a major plus.

Along with the activities in northern Burma, the Allies also planned to take the war to the Japanese in the central coastal area. The Japanese, as usual, were uncooperative, launching their own offensive in early 1944 with Imphal, India, as their main goal. The initial British thrust down the Mayu Peninsula met little resistance, but by 5 February, Japanese forces halted the advance. Suspecting an

AIRLIFT DOCTRINE

enemy counterattack but confident in their aerial lines of supply, the Allies resolved to hold fast. The outnumbered Japanese managed by skillful maneuver to surround the Allied division. The ground troops then concentrated within an "administrative box" to battle the Japanese, a configuration that made them ultimately much easier to supply by air.

Troop carriers sent in resupply missions on 8 February had dropped only half their loads when attacked by Japanese fighters, which damaged one transport and shot down another. The Third TAF provided air cover, but most of the subsequent supply operations were at night until the Allies regained air superiority. During those seven days, over 325 missions (900 sorties) dropped 1,100 tons. Thus supported, the trapped British ground forces turned the tables on the Japanese and began offensive operations. By 15 February day flights were reinstituted and the possibility of a Japanese victory evaporated. In fact, the Allies decimated the Japanese division involved. From February 1944 onward, Allied planners could concentrate more on combat operations and less on worrying about land lines of communication.[198]

The Japanese attacks and resultant Allied need for airlift created a tense situation for the troop carriers. Preparation for an upcoming second Wingate expedition had led to withdrawal of two troop carrier squadrons for glider towing and night formation flying training. The tentative air schedule, even before the Japanese attack, had shown the TCC to be 500 sorties short of what the British ground forces demanded. The British believed that the obvious answer was to borrow airplanes from the ATC Hump operation. Brig Gen William Old, TCC commander, thought that the British requests were inflated to justify calling on these additional resources, but had to indicate his inability to meet them. Nonetheless, he privately expressed his reservations to General Stratemeyer. Subsequently, a proposed British paratroop drop elsewhere was cancelled, and freeing those airlift resources involved in the drop forestalled calling on ATC assets. The rise of the emergency at the "administrative box," however, coupled with the prospective Wingate operation and increased demands to support General Merrill's forces in the north (all of which needs were real enough), led Lord Mountbatten to request the US Joint Chiefs of Staff (JCS) to lend 38 C-47s from the ATC operations. ATC provided 25 C-46s, the equivalent of 38 C-47s.[199]

The ATC C-46s arrived but began operations after they were needed. Flying from 26 February until 4 March, they delivered 520 tons of supplies. There were always at least 20 C-46s available per day, but the average number of flights came out to less than 12. Also, they often delivered less than full loads. During their tenure, the requirement for aerial deliveries actually declined. The C-46s flew instead of, not in addition to, the regularly assigned C-47s. Whatever they could have contributed to the Hump effort, a much greater strategic issue, was at stake.

<blockquote>The explanation of this bungling is more difficult than a description. Some American officers believed that the key factor in explanation was the British desire to establish a</blockquote>

146

precedent for withdrawing transports from the Hump. When a situation arose which might develop to the point where there might be genuine need for the diversion of ATC aircraft, SEAC Headquarters was not content to wait until the need was definite. Rather than asking for the diversion when and if the need developed, Mountbatten asked for the transports immediately. As a result, even though a week's time was consumed in getting JCS approval of the request, the diverted transports arrived at TCC stations nine days before the anticipated emergency. When it was evident that the anticipated crisis would be avoided, the C-46s were already on hand, and a face-saving attempt to use them was necessary.[200]

Operation Thursday

There was enough favorable publicity for General Wingate's first expedition to interest General Arnold in the idea of forming a small air task force to support a second operation. By October 1943 the 1st Air Commando Group completed a rapid training program and was on its way to India. The group included P-51s and B-25Gs for striking power, plus 13 C-47s and 10 C-64s, a light-plane force of 100 L-1s and L-5s, and 225 gliders for transportation. The TCC would augment this transport force by flying in bulk supplies once air fields were ready and would tow in the gliders. General Wingate's ground echelon consisted of five brigades.[201]

Plans called for the second operation (code named Thursday) to begin with 80 gliders landing at two different clearings known as Broadway and Picadilly. The spearhead forces were to convert these clearings to landing strips for C-47s as well as prepare another C-47 landing area. On 5 March 1944, 30 minutes before takeoff, photography revealed that logs obstructed Picadilly; all of the gliders would have to land on Broadway. The C-47s double-towed the gliders, with the predictable number of broken ropes and overstrained engines. A total of 54 gliders made the launch successfully, but of that number, only 35 made it to the night landing at Broadway. Despite these problems, however, the three light bulldozers included in the gliders that made it were able to clear the strip. On the night of 6 March there were 62 C-47 landings at Broadway. That same night 12 C-47s delivered an equal number of gliders to another prospective landing site, but the craft with the bulldozer crashed, delaying availability of that field until the next night. By the 12th all operations moved to Broadway, which proved to be a most capable operating location. In those six days of operations, the TCC and 1st Air Commando Group moved slightly over 9,000 troops, 1,300 pack animals, 245.5 tons of supplies, an antiaircraft battery, and an artillery battery. They continued supplying the columns of the expedition until May 1944, when the operation wound down.[202]

The majority of the resupply missions for the columns occurred at night when Japanese fighters were not a concern. The daylight missions flown with the approach of the monsoons were more susceptible to the fighters, but by this time the Allies had sufficient air superiority to protect the transports, and the Japanese air effort was generally directed elsewhere. The threat from ground fire was worse during the day, of course, but did not affect the volume of air resupply.

Lack of supplies was never a problem for the second Wingate expedition, and the aerial insertion of the initial forces as well as the airlanding of the entire force in enemy territory made the operation possible. There were problems, and the assignment of the commando group to the exclusive support of Wingate appears to have been a doctrinal step backward, unless the expedition is viewed in the modern sense as a task force with its own air component.

Imphal Operations

The Imphal Plain of India, on the border with Burma, is roughly 50 miles long from north to south and 25 miles wide and surrounded by mountains. Imphal town is on the northern end of the plain. The British planned to base an offensive against central and southern Burma there. They had built up substantial stores at the town and had several subdepots throughout the region. These supported the 170,000 troops, civilian specialists, and laborers concentrated in the area. The Japanese began their thrust to capture Imphal on 10 March 1944, just five days after the second Wingate expedition set out. They managed to cut the land lines of communication into the plain and captured the minor supply dump at Tiddim, south of Imphal. The Japanese also isolated the British forces at Dimapur, north of Imphal. The Allies' response was to concentrate a British corps at Dimapur and fly in reinforcements and supplies to Imphal.[203]

These needs, combined with the other commitments already discussed, were too much for the troop carrier forces to support. Lord Mountbatten, having already been to the well once, decided to call again on ATC Hump forces for assistance. This time, however, he felt that the seven days it took to get the last approval was too long and wired the British chiefs of staff that he would divert 30 C-47s or their equivalent from ATC unless he heard otherwise within three days. The American JCS approved the diversion but also made clear that Lord Mountbatten had no permission to make such moves on his own authority. They sent him 20 C-46s, which flew loads into Imphal until 25 April, when 10 returned to the Hump. The remaining 10 returned to ATC control about 1 June.[204]

The additional airlift forces allowed the TCC to move the 5 and 7 Indian Divisions into the Imphal Plain and to shuffle various brigades about the theater. These unit moves were all vital to British successes both in holding towns and beginning their counteroffensives. By late March the Allies were ready to begin a sustained resupply of their forces throughout the plain, but their airlift was too scarce to meet all the demands placed upon it. Lord Mountbatten again asked for ATC assistance. This time the JCS turned him down, but the Combined Chiefs of Staff offered the 64th Troop Carrier Group from the European theater of operations, along with RAF 216 Transport Squadron. This total of five squadrons, originally scheduled to return to Europe in early May, stayed until early June. They allowed the Troop Carrier Command to move over 20,000 tons of Army supplies into Imphal, bring out nearly 30,000 nonessential personnel (thus reducing resupply requirements), and airlift in over 12,000 reinforcements. At the same time, these hard-pressed transporters provided the entire resupply needs of 58,000 Allied troops in northern Burma and supported Wingate's dispersed forces. Even the Japanese admitted the importance of the aerial supply effort. Said a Tokyo radio broadcast, "Our difficulties in operating on the (Imphal) front lie in lack of supplies and air supremacy. The enemy received food supplies through the air route, while our men continued in battle eating a handful of barley or grain." The siege of Imphal ended 22 June 1944.[205]

> Imphal was the final testing ground for air supply. The experience gained in the NCAC area, in the Arakan, in 3 Indian Division operations, and at Imphal convinced air and ground commanders that air supply could sustain an offensive of great enough magnitude to drive the Japanese from Burma. The pursuit of the remnants of the Japanese Fifteenth Army began immediately, and with the end of the rains Fourteenth Army lunged forward to finish the war in Burma.[206]

Pointing out that the resupply and reinforcement of the Imphal units was an effective use of air power almost without precedent, an AAF evaluation board nonetheless noted several factors that precluded achievement of even higher tonnages:

(1) Delays of two to four hours at on-load fields because of nonavailability of supplies or transport between depots and the fields.
(2) Inadequate refueling facilities (pits or trucks) at off-load fields.
(3) Lack of a sufficient number of off-load fields.
(4) Lack of flying discipline at congested off-load fields.
(5) Unnecessary damage to aircraft caused by inexperienced truck drivers.

In addition, the board noted that the failure of some pilots to land at the designated field caused an interruption in the planned supply schedule. Pilots were not familiar with the six strips on the Imphal Plain; apparently they were sometimes poorly briefed and lacked an air-ground communication system.[207]

The pattern for the rest of the war in Burma was set. Between October 1944 and May 1945, the Allies drove eastward and southward, capturing Rangoon on 3 May and for all practical purposes ending the Burma campaign. That campaign relied heavily on air transport for preoffensive buildup and resupply. During this period the Combat Cargo Task Force carried over 332,000 tons of supplies. The troop carrier units assigned to the Tenth Air Force, with something like one-third of the number of aircraft assigned, airlifted nearly 155,000 tons.[208]

Troop carrier aircraft were also responsible for the last parachute assault in Burma in that final drive for Rangoon. On 30 April, 38 C-47s dropped 800 paratroops 30 miles from the city, and delivered additional troops and equipment the following day, all against very little Japanese resistance. The simultaneous amphibious operation aimed at Rangoon arrived to discover that the Japanese had abandoned the city.[209]

Evaluation

The official evaluation of air supply in Burma offered an interesting mixture of doctrinal and practical conclusions. Because the contemporary doctrine did not consider the regular sustained supply of ground troops as a normal function of troop carrier operations, the AAF board felt constrained to say only that air supply of ground units as a temporary or emergency expedient could be effective—this in a theater that disproved the doctrinal emphasis on airborne operations as the primary mission of troop carrier units. The board could well have applied its own conclusion that troop carrier operations in Burma were made possible by the inherent speed and flexibility of air power to draw the more important conclusion that the primary mission of troop carriers ought to be determined by the air transport needs of the combat theater. On the other hand, the evaluation offered a far-ranging set of suggestions that hinged on the point that an effective air supply campaign was dependent on centralized control. It posited the idea that a control board located at the senior air and ground headquarters have the authority to adjust priorities, direct the main operations from one field to another, set schedules, plan and inspect loading arrangements and facilities, and maintain a balance between airdropping and airlanding. Although not exactly on the mark, that suggestion at least recognized many of the important elements of a successful airlift as well as the importance of centralized, high-level visibility and control over operations.[210]

The official evaluation also mentioned what every analyst must conclude concerning air resupply efforts in Burma—that air superiority was essential to a successful effort. The Japanese never extended their air superiority into eastern India and after mid-1943 were severely challenged even in northern Burma. By early 1944 Allied control of the air over Burma was clearly the rule rather than the exception. Superiority, however, does not mean unchallenged control. Fortunately, the Japanese concentrated their forces against the Allies' ground targets rather than transports, for the most part, and made no concerted efforts to disrupt the air transport operations. Had they attempted otherwise, the outcome would have been very much in doubt for the Allies.

> The conclusion that working air superiority is an essential condition for successful air supply operations is axiomatic. Contemplation of what the Japanese Air Force might have accomplished against Allied transports in Burma, even after having lost control of the air, suggests that superiority in the area of air supply operations must be of an extreme degree. Otherwise a well-husbanded and well-directed inferior force may inflict losses out of all proportion to its strength, and it may be able to reduce air supply to a fraction of what could be accomplished unopposed.[211]

In spite of tough flying weather, congested and poor-quality forward operating fields, a command structure that never seemed to stand pat for very long, and a general shortage of just about everything needed to keep airplanes flying, the aerial supply function in the CBI made the entire Allied ground campaign against the Japanese possible and to a large extent successful.

> The Allied ground campaign in Burma from mid-1943 to the end of the war was made possible by air supply. Without goods delivered by air the Wingate expeditions could not have been launched, the second Arakan campaign would have been an Allied disaster. Imphal would have fallen to the Japanese, Stilwell would not have taken Myitkyina, and the final Allied conquest of Burma would not have taken place until amphibious resources had been provided for a major amphibious assault in the south.[212]

The Troop Carrier Heritage of World War II

Troop carrier units throughout the world made major contributions to the war effort, and they did so in many different ways. They were the mechanism by which airborne troops influenced battles; they were the air lines of communication that kept major thrusts moving, surrounded forces supplied, and dispersed units equipped; and they were the forces that made Allied air and ground units truly mobile. Because the troop carriers played so many roles and made so many varied contributions, it is both difficult and, in fact, imprudent to be overly specific in characterizing them. The doctrine that emerged retained the official primary mission of delivery of airborne troops, followed by air resupply of those forces, and included the undramatic aerial logistic mission as third. Troop carriers remained theater of operations forces, assigned for operational control to the theater air forces or an equivalent air organization. The AAF recognized the importance of air superiority for the most efficient air transport operations but was willing to take significant risks if the objective so warranted. Above all, troop carrier forces were tactical forces, listed as combat units, that had some special quality that set them apart from strategic airlift forces. They could be counted on to enter dangerous conditions, perform their missions admirably, and return the next day if necessary.

At the operational level, contemporary doctrine called for highly flexible units prepared to operate from poor facilities into even poorer ones. Airborne operations called for as much extensive training and planning as time allowed, with the best possible application of technology to accurate location of LZs and DZs. Massive vertical envelopment appeared to be the best application of the tactical air transport—and that in daylight.

Hindsight offers the ability to detect flaws in that doctrine. Probably the greatest error made was the persistent belief that airborne insertion of extremely large forces would continue to play an important role in warfare. The specter of the high-intensity battlefield was not yet clear, and the implications of atomic warfare were

AIRLIFT DOCTRINE

AIRBORNE

Figure 29

Figure 30

Figure 31

Figure 32

certainly unexplored for some time to come. It is surprising that the aerial supply line concept did not receive much more consideration, given the experiences in all three major theaters. It may be that the dramatic, publicized, and rich potential of airborne paratroop operations played too big a role in the doctrinal thinking. On the other side of the coin was the great plus that the planners and operators all realized the importance of some level of centralized control over air transport operations. Whether for prioritization of requirements, allocation among types of missions, or just for efficient use of scarce resources, the establishment in every theater of an authoritative agent that could make such decisions was a vital step forward. It would be another 30 years before that principle evolved into a consolidated airlift force.

NOTES

1. John Galvin, *Air Assault: The Development of Airmobile Warfare* (New York: Hawthorn Books, 1969), 2–3.
2. Maj Ronald Boston, "Doctrine By Default: The Historical Origins of Tactical Airlift," *Air University Review*, vol. 34, no. 4 (May–June 1983): 2–3.
3. Brig Gen F. L. Martin, commanding general, Headquarters Third Wing, GHQ Air Force, to commanding general, GHQ Air Force, letter, subject: Airplanes for Use in Parachute Troop Experiments, ca. 1940.
4. John Warren, *Airborne Missions in the Mediterranean 1942–1945* USAF Historical Study No. 74 (Maxwell AFB, Ala.: Research Studies Institute, September 1955), 1.
5. Ibid., 2.
6. Ibid., 3.
7. Warren, *Airborne Missions in the Mediterranean*, 1.
8. Ibid., 1–2.
9. Otto Johnson, adjutant general, War Department, to commanding generals, Army Air Forces et al., letter, subject: Establishment of the Air Transport Command, 30 April 1942.
10. Ibid.
11. Michael Hickey, *Out of the Sky: A History of Airborne Warfare* (New York: Charles Scribners' Sons, 1979), 90; Outline of History, I Troop Carrier Command, 20 June 1942–24 September 1943, n.d., 2.
12. Outline of History, I Troop Carrier Command, 20 June 1942-24 September 1943, n.d., 7–9; see also I Troop Carrier Command Historical Information, historical study, based on an interview with Brig Gen Fred Borum, first commanding general of the I Troop Carrier Command, n.d.
13. W. F. Craven and J. L. Cate, eds., *The Army Air Forces in World War II*, vol. 2, *Europe: Torch to Pointblank August 1942 to December 1943* (Chicago: University of Chicago Press, 1949), 41.
14. Col Samuel Moore, *Tactical Employment in the US Army of Transport Aircraft and Gliders in World War II*, historical study, ca. 1946, chap. 1, 5–6; Craven and Cate, *The Army Air Forces in World War II*, 2:72.
15. Lee Bowen et al., *USAF Airborne Operations: World War II and Korean War*, historical study (Maxwell AFB, Ala.: USAF Historical Division Liaison Office, March 1962), 1–8; Warren, *Airborne Missions in the Mediterranean*, 6–9; Craven and Cate, *The Army Air Forces in World War II*, 2:71–72.

16. Craven and Cate, *The Army Air Forces in World War II*, 2:71–72, 79–81, and 87.
17. Moore, *Transport Aircraft and Gliders,* chap. 3, 18–20; Craven and Cate, *The Army Air Forces in World War II*, 2:167.
18. Warren, *Airborne Missions in the Mediterranean*, 13–14; Bowen, *USAF Airborne Operations*, 4–5.
19. Craven and Cate, *The Army Air Forces in World War II*, 2:442.
20. Ibid., 446; see also Headquarters XII Troop Carrier Command (Prov.), "A Report of TCC Activities Including the Italian Invasion" (1 August–30 September 1943), 1 October 1943.
21. Maj Gen James M. Gavin, *Airborne Warfare* (Washington, D.C.: Infantry Journal Press, 1947), 1.
22. Bowen, *USAF Airborne Operations,* 10; Headquarters VIII Air Support Command, "The Airborne Assault Phase of the Sicilian Campaign," transcript of remarks by Brig Gen Paul Williams, 17 August 1943.
23. Gavin, *Airborne Warfare,* 4–5.
24. Warren, *Airborne Missions in the Mediterranean,* 41–47; Craven and Crate, *The Army Air Forces in World War II,* 2:446–47; transcript of Williams's remarks, 17 August 1943.
25. Warren, *Airborne Missions in the Mediterranean,* 27–36; Craven and Cate, *The Army Air Forces in World War II*, 2:449.
26. Ibid.
27. Warren, *Airborne Missions in the Mediterranean,* 37–41; Craven and Cate, *The Army Air Forces in World War II,* 2:453–54; transcript of Williams's remarks, 17 August 1943.
28. Warren, *Airborne Missions in the Mediterranean,* 47–57; Craven and Cate, *The Army Air Forces in World War II*, 2:454.
29. Craven and Cate, *The Army Air Forces in World War II*, 2:455.
30. Ibid.
31. Transcript of Williams's remarks, 17 August 1943.
32. Ibid.
33. Lt Col Charles Billingslea, observer, Headquarters Fifth Army Airborne Training Center, to chief of staff, War Department, through commander in chief, Allied Forces, letter, subject: Report of Airborne Operations, Husky and Bigot, 15 August 1943.
34. Warren, *Airborne Missions in the Mediterranean,* 54.
35. Ibid., 56–57; Craven and Cate, *The Army Air Forces in World War II,* 2:488–93.
36. Warren, *Airborne Missions in the Mediterranean,* 56–57.
37. Brig Gen Paul Williams, commanding general, XII Troop Carrier Command (Prov.), to commanding general, XII Air Force, letter, subject: Report of Troop Carrier Command in Operation Avalanche, 18 September 1943. See also Maj Patrick Mulcahy, observer, Allied Forces Headquarters, Final Report on the Avalanche Airborne Drop, 10 October 1943.
38. Ibid.
39. Ibid.
40. Craven and Cate, *The Army Air Forces in World War II,* 2:519–20.
41. Williams, Report of Troop Carrier Command, 18 September 1943.
42. Galvin, *Air Assault,* 110.
43. Williams, Report of Troop Carrier Command, 18 September 1943; Warren, *Airborne Missions in the Mediterranean,* 61–62.
44. Warren, *Airborne Missions in the Mediterranean,* 68–69.
45. Ibid., 65–66.
46. Ibid., 58–59. See also Maj Gen Matthew Ridgway, commanding general, 82d Airborne Division, to commander in chief, Allied Forces, letter, subject: Lessons of Airborne Operations in Italy, 25 October 1943; and draft, Allied Forces Headquarters Training Memorandum No. 43, *Employment of Airborne Forces.* October 1943.
47. Warren, *Airborne Missions in the Mediterranean,* 59.

AIRLIFT DOCTRINE

48. Craven and Cate, *The Army Air Forces in World War II*, 2:455.
49. Galvin, *Air Assault*, 109.
50. Ibid.; Craven and Cate, *The Army Air Forces in World War II*, 2:455.
51. Galvin, *Air Assault*, 116–17.
52. Ibid., 117.
53. War Department Training Circular No. 113, *Employment of Airborne and Troop Carrier Forces*, 9 October 1943.
54. Ibid.
55. Galvin, *Air Assault*, 139.
56. Ibid., 140.
57. Ibid.
58. John Warren, *Airborne Operations in World War II, European Theater*, USAF Historical Study No. 97 (Maxwell AFB, Ala.: Research Studies Institute, 3 September 1956), 8.
59. Gen Omar Bradley, *A Soldier's Story* (New York: Henry Holt and Company, 1951), 236.
60. Gen Dwight Eisenhower, *Crusade in Europe* (New York: Doubleday and Company, 1948), 246–47.
61. Warren, *Airborne Operations in World War II*, 13–14.
62. Ibid., 15–16.
63. Ibid., 20–26.
64. Ibid., 26.
65. Ibid., 58–59.
66. Ibid., 16–20.
67. Ibid., 60–61.
68. Ibid., 64–65.
69. Ibid., 66.
70. Ibid., 67.
71. Ibid., 65–69.
72. Ibid., 72.
73. Ibid., 74–76.
74. Ibid., 78.
75. Galvin, *Air Assault*, 155. See also Brig Gen Paul Williams, commanding general, IX Troop Carrier Command, to chief, Army Air Forces, through commanding general, Ninth Air Force, letter, subject: Report of Operation (Neptune), 13 June 1944; and Col John Hilger, assistant chief, Policy Division, Army Air Forces Board, to president, Army Air Forces Board, letter, subject: Evaluation of Neptune-Bigot Report, 5 July 1944.
76. W. F. Craven and J. L. Cate, eds., *The Army Air Forces in World War II*, vol. 3, *Europe: Argument to V-E Day January 1944 to May 1945* (Chicago: University of Chicago Press, 1951), 557.
77. Allied Expeditionary Air Forces Operation Memorandum no. 29, *Supply by Air*, 29 April 1944; Brig Gen Edmund Hill, director, posthostilities planning, to deputy chief of staff, Operations, United States Strategic Air Forces, carrier sheet, subject: CATOR, 31 August 1944; Air Vice-Marshal E. P. Wigglesworth, senior air staff officer, Allied Expeditionary Air Forces, to distribution list, letter, subject: Supply by Air—Organization and Functions of CATOR, 2 June 1944.
78. Warren, *Airborne Operations in World War II*, 81.
79. Information booklet entitled *Headquarters First Allied Airborne Army*, ca. 1944; see also Col E. C. Boehnke, adjutant general, Supreme Headquarters Allied Expeditionary Forces, to War Office et al., letter, subject: Combined Airborne Headquarters, 8 August 1944.
80. Galvin, *Airborne Assault*, 173, 247–48.
81. Warren, *Airborne Operations in World War II*, 95.
82. Eisenhower, *Crusade in Europe*, 303.
83. Warren, *Airborne Operations in World War II*, 86.

84. Maj Gen Paul Williams, commanding general, IX Troop Carrier Command, to commanding general, Army Air Forces, through commanding general, First Allied Airborne Army, and commanding general, United States Strategic Air Forces in Europe, letter, subject: Supply and Resupply by Air, 20 November 1944, 18–19.

85. Gen Omar Bradley, Headquarters Central Group of Armies, to Supreme Headquarters Allied Expeditionary Forces (Main), message, 3 September 1944.

86. Forward Echelon Communications Zone, to Supreme Headquarters Allied Expeditionary Forces (Main), message, 8 September 1944.

87. Maj Gen Hugh Knerr, deputy commanding general for administration, Air Service Command, to assistant chief of staff G-4, Supreme Headquarters Allied Expeditionary Forces, letter, subject: Airlift, 30 September 1944.

88. Ibid.

89. Maj Gen Hugh Knerr, deputy commanding general for administration, Air Service Command, to Brig Gen J. H. Stratton, assistant chief of staff, G-4, Communications Zone, letter, subject: Airlift, 10 October 1944.

90. Lt Gen John C. H. Lee, commanding general, Communications Zone, to Maj Gen Hugh Knerr, deputy commanding general for administration, Air Service Command, letter, subject: 1st Indorsement Airlift, 10 October 1944.

91. Col E. C. Boehnke, adjutant general, Supreme Headquarters Allied Expeditionary Forces, to air commander in chief, Allied Expeditionary Forces, letter, subject: Assignment of Units, 10 August 1944.

92. Col Millard Lewis, director of plans, to deputy chief of staff, Operations, carrier sheet, 26 August 1944.

93. Williams, Supply and Resupply by Air, 20 November 1944, 17.

94. Warren, *Airborne Operations in World War II*, 77–82.

95. Warren, *Airborne Missions in the Mediterranean*, 82–83; Maj Gen F. L. Anderson, deputy commander, Operations, United States Strategic Air Forces, to Maj Gen Laurence Kuter, Headquarters Army Air Forces, letter, 24 July 1944.

96. Warren, *Airborne Operations in World War II*, 83–84.

97. Ibid., 80–86.

98. Ibid., 86–89.

99. Ibid., 92.

100. Ibid., 93–95.

101. Ibid., 94.

102. Ibid.

103. Ibid., 95–100.

104. Ibid., 100–8.

105. Ibid., 110.

106. Galvin, *Air Assault*, 168–69; see also Maj Gen Paul Williams, commanding general, Provisional Troop Carrier Air Division, to commanding general; Army Air Forces, through commanding general, Mediterranean Allied Tactical Air Force, letter, subject: Report of Operation Dragoon, 22 August 1944, and Headquarters Twelfth Air Force, *Troop Carrier Operations 1944*, historical study, ca. 1944.

107. Bradley, *A Soldier's Story*, 416.

108. Warren, *Airborne Operations in World War II*, 88–89.

109. Ibid., 89–90.

110. Bowen, *USAF Airborne Operations*, 68; First Allied Airborne Army, *Allied Airborne Operations in Holland*, historical study, September–October 1944.

111. First *Allied Airborne Army, Allied Airborne Operations in Holland*, 20.

112. Memorandum, Gen H. H. Arnold, commanding general, Army Air Forces, to Maj Gen Edwin House, commanding general, Air Force Tactical Center, subject: Narrative of Market Operation, 4 November 1944.

113. Warren, *Airborne Operations in World War II*, 149–50.

114. Ibid., 91-93.
115. First Allied Airborne Army, *Allied Airborne Operations in Holland.*
116. Warren, *Airborne Operations in World War II,* 149.
117. Bradley, *A Soldier's Story,* 415.
118. Warren, *Airborne Operations in World War II,* 153-54.
119. Headquarters IX Troop Carrier Command, *Air Invasion of Holland,* historical study, September 1945; Warren, *Airborne Operations in World War II,* 154.
120. Warren, *Airborne Operations in World War II,* 123-25, 127-33.
121. Lt Gen Lewis Brereton, commanding general, First Allied Airborne Army, to Supreme Commander Allied Expeditionary Forces (Main), letter, subject: Airborne Operations in Holland September-November 1944 (Market), 22 December 1944.
122. Warren, *Airborne Operations in World War II,* 159-61; Bowen, *USAF Airborne Operations,* 79-80.
123. Ibid.
124. Warren, *Airborne Operations in World War II,* 158-64.
125. Ibid., 165.
126. Lt Gen Lewis Brereton, commanding general, First Allied Airborne Army, to Supreme Commander Allied Expeditionary Forces, letter, subject: Report of Operation Varsity, 19 May 1945.
127. Eisenhower, *Crusade in Europe,* 390.
128. Maj William Carleton, assistant chief of staff, A-2, 322d Troop Carrier Wing, *History of the Directorate of Air Transport, Allied Air Force, Southwest Pacific Area, and the 322d Troop Carrier Wing,* historical study, Calif., 1945, part 1, 1-2.
129. Carleton, *History of the Directorate of Air Transport,* 1-2.
130. Ibid., 5.
131. Ibid.
132. Historical Branch, Intelligence and Security Division, Headquarters Air Transport Command, *The Air Transport Command in the Southwest Pacific December 7, 1941-August 1, 1944,* historical study, May 1946, 256.
133. Col George Cressey, director, Air Evaluation Board SWPA, Report No. 11, Troop Carrier Aviation in SWPA, 22 April 1946, 12-13.
134. Ibid., 14-17.
135. Headquarters ATC, *Air Transport Command in the Southwest Pacific,* 259.
136. Ibid., 260.
137. Ibid., 262-63.
138. Ibid., 261.
139. Carleton, *History of the Directorate of Air Transport,* 6; Cressey, Report No. 11, 8.
140. Cressey, Report No. 11, 18-19.
141. Ibid., 32-34.
142. Ibid., 50-51.
143. Ibid., v.
144. Headquarters ATC, *Air Transport Command in the Southwest Pacific,* note 15, 262.
145. W. F. Craven and J. L. Cate, eds., *The Army Air Forces in World War II,* vol. 4, *The Pacific: Guadalcanal to Saipan August 1942 to July 1944* (Chicago: University of Chicago Press, 1950), 21-26.
146. Intelligence summary relating to Buna operation, source: memorandum, Col C. P. Bixel, to Maj R. J. Riddell, subject: Draft Copy of Report by Col Harry Knight, Army ground force observer, 5 March 1943.
147. Craven and Cate, *The Army Air Forces in World War II,* 4:98.
148. Intelligence summary relating to Buna operations, source: Report of Col H. F. Handy, military observer in Southwest Pacific theater of operations, 23 December 1942.
149. Craven and Cate, *The Army Air Forces in World War II,* 4:116-17.
150. Ibid., 126.

151. Ibid., 135–36; Intelligence summary, 5 March 1943.
152. Craven and Cate, *The Army Air Forces in World War II*, 4:156–58.
153. Ibid.
154. Ibid., 173.
155. Ibid., 175–77.
156. Ibid., 181–85.
157. Galvin, *Air Assault*, 114.
158. Craven and Cate, *The Army Air Forces in World War II*, 4:185.
159. Galvin, *Air Assault*, 116.
160. Craven and Cate, *The Army Air Forces in World War II*, 4:195–96.
161. Ibid., 575–608.
162. Ibid., 608–9, 613–14.
163. Ibid., 616.
164. Ibid., 645.
165. Ibid., 652.
166. Ibid., 659.
167. W. F. Craven and J. L. Cate, eds., *The Army Air Forces in World War II*, vol. 5, *The Pacific: Matterhorn to Nagasaki June 1944 to August 1945* (Chicago: University of Chicago Press, 1953), 385.
168. Ibid., 393–97, 401.
169. Ibid., 404, 406.
170. Ibid., 426–27.
171. Bowen, *USAF Airborne Operations*, 73–74; Craven and Cate, *The Army Air Forces in World War II*, 5:427–29.
172. Craven and Cate, *The Army Air Forces in World War II*, 5:433–34.
173. Galvin, Air Assault, 217–28.
174. Craven and Cate, *The Army Air Forces in World War II*, 5:439–41.
175. Ibid., 441; Galvin, *Air Assault*, 250–53.
176. Military Analysis Division, The United States Strategic Bombing Survey (USSBS), *The Air Transport Command in the War Against Japan*, December 1946, 10; W. F. Craven and J. L. Cate, eds., *The Army Air Forces in World War II*, vol. 7, *Services Around the War* (Chicago: University of Chicago Press, 1958), 201–3.
177. For a discussion of the potential use of airborne armies in the invasion of Japan see the following: Brig Gen F. H. Smith, deputy chief of the Air Staff, Plans, to chief of Air Staff, letter, subject: Staff Study, Air Staff Concept of the Status and Employment of Airborne Armies, 3 January 1945; Memorandum, Col John Stone, chief, Pacific Branch, to Lt Col A. C. Carlson, European Branch, assistant chief of the Air Staff, Plans, subject: Conception of the Status and Employment of Airborne Armies including Command Function and Air Force Relationship in Regard to the Pacific War, 11 January 1945; Brig Gen R. C. Lindsay, chief, Combined and Joint Staff Division, Headquarters Army Air Forces, to Gen Joe L. Loutzenheiser and Col Reuben C. Moffat, routing and record sheet, subject: Airborne Co. ...and and Operations, 5 January 1945.
178. Report of the Army Air Forces—China-Burma-India Evaluation Board, report no. 2, subject: The Effectiveness of Supply of Ground Units by Air in the China-Burma-India Theater, 15 October 1944, 1.
179. Joe Taylor, *Air Supply in the China-Burma Campaigns*, USAF Historical Study No. 75 (Maxwell AFB, Ala.: Research Studies Institute, April 1957); see also Air Command South East Asia, *A Review of Air Transport Operations in the Burma Front to June 1944*, historical study, ca. 1944.
180. Ibid., 4–6.
181. Ibid., 6–8.
182. Ibid., 11–12.
183. Ibid., 12–13.

184. Headquarters Advance Section Three, Air Supply Service, Services of Supply, United States Air Forces in China-Burma-India, *History of Air Dropping,* historical study, ca. 1944, 1–2. See also Edwin Mintz, assistant historical officer, Headquarters Tenth Air Force, historical study, *Air Dropping Northern Burma,* 25 February 1945; Maj John McCaren, intelligence officer, Air Cargo Headquarters, Tenth Air Force, *History of Air Supply in CBI,* historical study, 13 December 1944.
185. Ibid.
186. Bowen, *USAF Airborne Operations,* 29.
187. Ibid., 30.
188. Taylor, *Air Supply,* 17–18.
189. Ibid., 19–20.
190. Ibid., 20.
191. Ibid., 23–24.
192. Ibid., 25; Brig Gen William Old, commanding general, Headquarters Troop Carrier Command, to Maj Gen George Stratemeyer, commanding general, Eastern Air Command, 21 May 1944.
193. Taylor, *Air Supply,* 27–29.
194. Ibid., 32–33.
195. Ibid., 96–99. See also Lt Col Williard West, adjutant, Headquarters Troop Carrier Command, to commanding general, Tenth Air Force, letter, subject: History of Organization, 1 February 1944; Brig Gen William Old, commanding general, Tenth Air Force, letter, subject: Report of Troop Carrier Command Participation in "Thursday Operation," 16 March 1944.
196. Ibid., 35.
197. Ibid., 38–42.
198. Ibid., 60–64.
199. Ibid., 58–62.
200. Ibid., 64.
201. Ibid., 65–66. See also Lt Col Williard West, adjutant, Headquarters Troop Carrier Command, to commanding general, Tenth Air Force, letter, subject: Monthly Historical Report, 24 April 1944.
202. Ibid., 67–72.
203. Craven and Cate, *The Army Air Forces in World War II,* 5:502–3, 508.
204. Taylor, *Air Supply,* 76–77.
205. Craven and Cate, *The Army Air Forces in World War II,* 5:509–10.
206. Taylor, *Air Supply,* 89.
207. AAF-CBI Evaluation Board, Effectiveness of Supply, 19–20.
208. Craven and Cate, *The Army Air Forces in World War II,* 5:244–45.
209. Taylor, *Air Supply,* 120.
210. AAF-CBI Evaluation Board, Effectiveness of Supply, 29–30.
211. Taylor, *Air Supply,* 132.
212. Ibid., 141.

CHAPTER 4

Airlift in the Postwar Era

This chapter aims at drawing together several of the doctrinal points of view that emerged during the postwar era. The section on *Fiscal Content* offers a view of the battles for resources and the force structure decisions that followed World War II. The next section discusses a 1946 effort to consolidate long-range and troop carrier airlift into one organization much like what was finally achieved in 1976. Following the failure of that initiative, the Air Transport Command (ATC) sought to preserve a strategic airlift mission with strong arguments concerning the value of logistic support provided by air transports. The creation of Military Air Transport Service (MATS) in 1948 is covered in the section on *Airlift Unification,* an event immediately followed by the Berlin Airlift—where MATS provided the crews, airplanes, and expertise, but was not the organization in charge.

Following the Berlin Airlift, Maj Gen Laurence Kuter argued for viewing strategic airlift forces in a force deployment and support context, rather than just from the logistics point of view. Exercise Swarmer in the spring of 1950 attempted to blend this perspective and the lessons of Berlin into a new concept of airlift operations. The Korean War erupted very soon thereafter and these new ideas about airlift were replaced by another set of concepts that put all theater airlift—both logistics and airborne operations—under one command subordinate to the air component commander in Korea.

The last one-third of this chapter traces the troop carrier efforts to sustain themselves as a viable force. It also explores the "debate" that erupted between Generals Tunner and Cannon about whether strategic airlift and troop carrier airlift could be merged into one organization and still remain effective fighting forces. The section on *Official Doctrine* reviews the attempts to formally codify airlift doctrine—an attempt successful for theater airlift forces and a failure for strategic airlift.

One must look back into the war years to understand the fiscal and resource constraints all airlift forces faced in the postwar period. Both the War Department and the Army Air Forces (AAF) began to plan for postwar force requirements in the midst of the fighting. Based on a War Department proposal for an Army of 1,700,000 men, the AAF planners proposed an Air Force of 105 groups, which included 11 troop carrier groups. An important assumption underlying the original estimate was that the Air Force would be an "M-day force," maintained at wartime strengths and immediately ready for combat.[1]

The Fiscal Context

There were no fiscal restraints on the force-sizing effort, but General Marshall rejected the Army and Air Force packages as too expensive. The War Department then changed its planning assumptions to include 12 months of mobilization and warning time, and the AAF consequently requested a 78-group postwar Air Force. In August of 1945 that, too, was rejected as financially impractical, forcing Lt Gen Ira Eaker, deputy commander of the AAF, to accept a 70-group force as his bottom line. Of the 35 groups that disappeared into the planning process, only one was a troop carrier unit. Even under the 70-group plan there were to be 10 troop carrier groups, with all tactical groups understrength. Air Transport Command (ATC) was to have a strength of about 20,000 people, regardless of the force size, with no number of aircraft mentioned.[2]

The demobilization of the entire armed forces had a particularly dangerous meaning for the AAF, in that they could not procure new aircraft at a rate that would keep aircraft producers solvent. It was extremely difficult for the AAF to accept even the full level of orders placed during the war. Planning in the spring of 1946 called for troop carrier units to have large helicopters to replace gliders and large transport aircraft capable of direct delivery of fully equipped combat units to the battle zone. All of these, plus many new jet fighters and long-range bombers, were required for a modernized 70-group Air Force. The Bureau of the Budget slashed the Air Force requests, deleting procurement of new transports on the basis that contractors would not be able to meet the proposed schedules. For fiscal 1948, the Air Force put in requests for enough new aircraft to modernize 55 groups and outfit 15 skeleton groups. The House of Representatives cut the request in half, but the Air Force was able to order 27 C-97s and 36 C-119s.[3]

The fiscal 1949 program was a study in number juggling and frustration. Originally, the 55-group interim Air Force was to include 13 very heavy bombardment, 3 light bombardment, 24 fighter, 7 reconnaissance, and 8 troop carrier groups, plus an assortment of long-range transports for ATC. The troop carriers were parceled out to the Far East Air Forces (FEAF), the United States Air Forces in Europe, the Alaskan Air Command, the Pacific Air Command and the Caribbean Air Command, with only three going to the Tactical Air Command. Even though Congress had not acted on a supplemental request for fiscal 1949, Gen Hoyt Vandenberg, the new chief of staff of the Air Force, believed that it had given the go-ahead to expand to the 70-group objective by appropriating the first increment of funds. Consequently, he elected to pursue an aggressive procurement program, including 147 troop carrier and transport aircraft, that would reach a 60-group Air Force by the end of 1948.[4]

The summer of 1948 also saw President Harry S. Truman establish a $14.4-billion cap on the fiscal 1950 defense budget. The outcome of this decision was to force the Air Force to cut back to 48 combat groups. Gen Hoyt Vandenberg appointed a USAF Senior Officer Board, with Gen Joseph T. McNarney, commander of the Air Materiel Command (AMC), presiding as acting chairman, to make recommendations concerning force structure. Meeting through late 1948 and early 1949, the board recommended, and Secretary of the Air Force Stewart Symington accepted, cancelling orders for B-45s, F-93s, and C-125Bs and applying that money to B-36 purchases. In the spring of 1949, the board also recommended purchase of a few light cargo aircraft, concluding that all transport orders ought to be for those designed to meet "emergency and wartime military cargo airlift requirements of the Army and Air Force." This meant continued production of the C-97 until the C-124 could begin its initial operations in May of 1950. It also allowed for continued production of the C-119 for troop carrier aviation.[5]

The pressures of the Korean War, along with the realization that Soviet military strength was growing at an astounding rate, while prior defense budgets had stripped the US armed forces to the bone, finally forced the senior decision makers to admit that the entire military capability of the United States must be built up. In the initial planning process, the Air Force figured it would need a total program of 138 combat wings and 25 troop carrier wings but realized that figure would be rejected as extreme. In August of 1950, General Vandenberg told the Joint Chiefs of Staff the Air Force needed 114 combat and 16 troop carrier wings. The JCS approved a buildup to 95 wings—80 combat and 15 troop carrier—with a target of 30 June 1954. The National Security Council directed a speedup of the timetable to June of 1952. The final program for the 95-wing Air Force included 15 troop carrier wings and 30 Military Air Transport Service (MATS) squadrons. The Air Force met the 1952 deadline, including placing orders for 244 new C-123 assault airlifters.[6]

New Secretary of Defense Robert A. Lovett directed the Joint Chiefs of Staff (JCS) to look to fiscal 1953 and beyond to determine military force needs. The JCS concluded that the Air Force needed to expand to 143 wings—126 combat and 17 troop carrier. The fiscal 1953 aircraft procurement program included 418 cargo aircraft. President Truman had approved the 143-wing program but limited funds so that the program would not be attained until 30 June 1955. The JCS wanted to be ready by 1 July 1954. Newly elected President Eisenhower said that instead of trying to meet the enemy by a particular date, the United States should "get ourselves ready and stay ready." Secretary of Defense Charles Wilson worked to reduce military expenditures and submitted a budget that represented a $5.3-billion cut in Air Force funds for fiscal 1954, with 110 to 114 wings expected to be activated out of a new interim force goal of 120 wings.[7] All of these numbers, of course, were subject to change. Responding to the 143-wing concept, MATS drew up plans to have a modest 30 strategic air transport squadrons by the end of fiscal 1954; in January of 1953, this figure moved upward to 51, and then dropped back to 44 under congressional budgetary limitations in the summer of 1953. A utilization rate of 10 hours per aircraft per day had to be scaled back to 4 hours, and a plan to phase out C-54s and acquire C-124s had to be delayed.[8]

On 7 January 1954, President Eisenhower announced a new defense policy that would emphasize air power and mobile forces that could be held in strategic reserve and readily deployed to meet sudden aggression. Gen Nathan Twining, the Air Force chief of staff, reported to the Senate that the Air Force would seek its ultimate goal of 143 wings and that he had directed a thorough examination of Air Force requirements in light of new weapons. The Air Staff study concluded that some strategic air forces could be reduced due to the more powerful weapons available and that substantial cuts could be made in medium troop carrier forces due to many Army units being returned to the strategic reserve in the United States. This would yield a 137-wing Air Force by the end of fiscal 1957. That force level meant a cut of 6 medium troop carrier wings from the 143-wing program.[9]

Postwar Airlift Consolidation Efforts

The unrelenting pressures to demobilize as quickly as possible were clear even before V-E Day. In April of 1945, Gen Barney Giles issued a letter to all AAF commanding generals, entitled *Reorientation of Army Air Force,* that forecast demobilizing 20 groups (including 8 troop carrier units) prior to the defeat of Japan and anticipated further reductions. These combined factors forced General Eaker to direct, in May of 1945, that "air power which can be applied to the accomplishment of more than one of its missions must not be duplicated."[10] In response, the Air Staff prepared a joint study concerning the consolidation of ATC and Troop Carrier Command (TCC) into one organization. The study, issued in September, recommended organization of one command for all AAF air transport activities. The proposed Air Transport Command would have a Foreign Strategic Air Transport Division, a continental Air Transport Division, and a Troop Carrier Command. The central ATC headquarters was to supervise, coordinate, and ensure flexibility in use of personnel, equipment, and facilities of all air transport activities. The Troop Carrier Command was to provide tactical air transport units and develop doctrines and techniques for airborne operations. The remaining two divisions had the tasks associated with the in-being ATC and were to provide centralized training for all air transport components. The study recommended a separate structure within the theaters of operations but sustained its theme of unity. Directly under the theater air component commander was to be a Theater Transport Air Force (TTAF), with an Air Transport Division and Troop Carrier Command under its control. The TTAF had the charter to supervise, coordinate, and ensure flexibility in use of personnel, equipment, and facilities of all intratheater air transport activities. The troop carrier organization was to perform duties normally associated with troop carrier units, while the Air Transport Division was to provide all other intratheater airlift. Each was to augment the other as required.[11]

The staff's rationale for this proposed organizational scheme encompassed a number of doctrinal issues. First, it made the argument that the whole program should remain an AAF responsibility for flexibility and unified control, rather than fall to the Army service forces or Army ground forces. Second, it rejected assignment to the War Department as duplicative of the AAF's mission and as particularly difficult to manage during contingencies. Finally, the study rejected centralization of AAF and theater air transport forces under one AAF command, apparently because the strategic airlift function would become entangled in theater control problems. The study was not especially clear on this point and also left open to interpretation how the proposed ATC and TTAF would coordinate their activities. On 31 October Brig Gen William McKee, deputy assistant chief of staff for operations, commitments, and requirements, reported that the chief of the Air Staff had approved the consolidation and called a meeting of the affected commands to develop an implementing plan. That approval was apparently withdrawn, because the meeting was cancelled three days later.[12]

Why this specific decision was made, and by whom, is not absolutely ascertainable. But there was a firm decision. It is easy to see how the decision fit into Gen H. H. Arnold's idea that ATC was a special organization that should be kept totally separate from theater-assigned forces. His long, strongly worded letters to Gen Carl Spaatz along these lines support this hypothesis. Also supporting this idea is the fact that General Arnold left many postwar decisions to General Spaatz, as he was to be the next commanding general of the Army Air Forces; but Arnold did not defer this decision. Since the structure proposed by the Air Staff was so strikingly similar to the airlift structure of the 1980s it is interesting to speculate on how it would have performed in the intervening years.

Search for a Strategic Airlift Mission

A monograph prepared by the Military Airlift Command called the postwar period for ATC one of a search for identity. Generals Harold George and Cyrus Smith, the two men who made ATC work in World War II, had to oversee its dismantlement until mid-1946, when they retired. ATC was to go from 3,088 aircraft in September of 1945 to 511 in July of 1946.[13] With these dwindling forces, ATC was to maintain certain national interests lines of communication, support of occupational forces, and show of the flag when called upon. By March of 1946, ATC had to provide detailed justifications of its troop strengths and worldwide operations to the Air Staff—this at a time when it was contracting civilians, who shortly before had been in uniform, to keep some of its routes open.[14]

> operate air transport services (except transport services specifically assigned to other commands . . . and intra-theater services required by oversea commanders) for all War Department agencies supplementary to United States civil air carriers. . . .[15]

Although the aim of the mission statement was to keep ATC from competing with the emerging civil air carriers, it had the effect of reducing ATC to a secondary role—a role with a distinct, and unpleasant, peacetime flavor. At best, this reflected the great confidence that the senior decision makers had in ATC's ability to surge to a wartime requirement. At worst, it showed a lack of understanding of the real wartime requirements for airlift. Nineteenth on its list of 20 missions was the requirement to "prepare and maintain in current status plans for expansion in case of war."[16]

In early December, Maj Gen Robert Webster, the former commander of the European Division of ATC and ATC's new commander, wrote a prophetic letter to General Spaatz concerning the lack of a wartime mission for ATC:

> It is my firm belief that the Air Transport Command must have a fundamental mission that states clearly its primary responsibility in a war emergency. Its continued existence without such a mission on the basis of providing peacetime air transport service as a convenience for military activities, is questionable since such transportation service can eventually be provided more economically and probably more efficiently by the civil air transport industry. The airline concept of the mission is faulty, since there is practically no justification for its survival as such.[17]

General Webster's rationale took advantage of contemporary AAF concerns about a separate Air Force. He noted that the Army ground forces were obviously preparing to take action to achieve strategic as well as tactical air mobility and that their success would come at the budgetary expense of the AAF. It would also deny the AAF the ability to concentrate its own forces. Webster argued that since air power (including air transport capability) would be the first American force called upon in future military actions, it needed to be instantly available. He made one final argument that appealed to prevalent concerns about economics but also had a distinctively modern ring to it:

> Inherent in such an organization, as an added economy apart from its purely wartime mission and actually in furtherance of the training program, is the ability to maintain aerial lines of communication and provide day-to-day support for our forces.[18]

In other words, training for a wartime mission would produce the by-product of airlift for other purposes. His solution was to change ATC's mission statement to read: "Provision of strategic concentration, deployment, and support, by air, for the Army Air Forces and the War Department."[19]

General Webster was equally concerned about ATC's image throughout the armed forces, including within the Air Transport Command itself. To deal with the first problem, he prepared an article for the *Army Times* that sought to tell its readers

Figure 33. Maj Gen Robert Webster, commander of Air Transport Command from September 1946 through June 1947.

why ATC existed. Arguing that ground lines of communication were slow and vulnerable, he drew the obvious conclusion that ATC would be needed for the speedy movement of cargo and people in a war emergency. In answer to the rhetorical question of why we needed a *military* air transport organization, in view of the greatly expanded civil air transport industry, he noted that although there were plans to use the civilians, it would take time to modify their aircraft for use as cargo carriers.[20] ATC also sent a lecture to the Armed Forces Staff College about the Air Transport Command that sought to create an image of wartime vitality for ATC:

> The vital role which will be played by the Air Transport Command as an integral part of the AAF M-day force is only now becoming apparent. Its current strength of approximately 20,000 military personnel and slightly under 200 C-54 aircraft is intended to remain constant, and through vigorous training in all types of air transport operations, the command must be prepared to provide initial deployment of our striking force to any point on the globe, and to provide the nucleus for expansion coincident with the expansion of air and ground forces. The present air transport mission of the command, under which air support is furnished occupation and garrison forces overseas, is secondary to this mission of the formation and training of an integral M-day force, and actually is but a phase of such training and preparation.[21]

General Webster dealt with the ATC staff in a somewhat less-pristine way. Noting that "we are assumed to be in the airline business" by just about everyone concerned, he directed the ATC staff to correct the false impression. "The Air Transport Command is not an airline," he said. "It engages its scheduled operations because it is vitally concerned with retaining the 'know-how' to operate efficiently and to be able to use effectively its aircraft. . . . That is our job in war and we must practice it in peace."[22]

Webster's campaign continued with a letter to General Spaatz in February, suggesting that "further steps toward overall economy and reorganization within the Air Transport Command cannot be undertaken intelligently without authentic definition of its war mission and the issuance of certain doctrine. . . ."[23] The further steps ATC wanted included a definition of a primary war mission and a policy of equipping ATC with four-engine, long-range cargo aircraft. The suggested policy also called for ATC to carry essential military cargo, with the "continued use of contract air carriers . . . not justified on the basis of government economy."[24] The ATC proposal also carried a unique view, for 1947, of how to integrate air transport into war planning:

> Requirements for air logistics will be included as an integral part of all current and future war planning. M-day forces will have capacity for early offensive action according to the characteristics, condition and number of suitable existing transport aircraft, together with the experienced air transport organization and personnel that can be allocated and effectively employed for the deployment and support of such M-day forces, the aircraft utilization efficiency of the air transport organizations employed and the adequacy and distribution of existing stockages of spares.[25]

The response from Brig Gen Bryant Boatner, deputy chief of Air Staff, was not promising. He first reaffirmed that the tactical and strategic air transport arms would remain separate, although nothing in the ATC correspondence suggested otherwise. Boatner was willing to say that the first mission of the ATC was strategic concentration wherever required (except into combat), but he was unwilling to delete the "supplementary" phrase. He also included in his response an enumeration of the Air Staff's policies toward air transportation, which appear to have been written in an information and experience vacuum:

> a. The Air Transport Command strength will be the maximum consistent with sound military planning, budgetary and manpower limitations and the policy of minimum competition with commercial airlines.
> b. The Troop Carrier Command and Air Transport Command will be equipped basically with tactical type transport aircraft, modified as required to fit the particular role but stressing flexibility of employment.
> c. Army Air Force development of transport aircraft will be limited to tactical types.
> d. Air Transport Command requirements for high-performance long-range personnel carriers will be filled by military modification of commercial aircraft developments only when suitable tactical transport types are not available.[26]

Thus, the doctrine of strategic airlift in early 1947, at least in AAF headquarters, was a strange mixture: perform a strategic airlift mission with tactical and converted civilian airlift aircraft, and plan for war by performing a peacetime-oriented mission.

One of the greatest supporters of General Webster's ideas about a ready-to-go Air Transport Command was Maj Gen William Tunner, commander of ATC's Atlantic Division. He wrote to General Webster in February to express his thoughts about the reorganization of ATC, with a far-ranging proposal—a proposal that time would prove to be extremely accurate:

> 1. It is essential that the Air Transport Command reorganize in such a way as to permit the continuation of its principal mission—air transport. This mission is primarily to have in readiness a trained air transport organization capable of rapid expansion in time of emergency. Fundamental training characteristics of such an organization must include the following:
> a. Round-the-clock, 7-days-per-week transport operations with high utilization of equipment.
> b. The handling of diversified loads and the maintenance of even flows of cargo from sources to destinations.
> c. The ability to operate safely under all weather conditions with maximum loads by individual crews.[27]

Maj Gen Robert Harper replaced General Webster as the commander of ATC in July of 1947. He posited a somewhat different perspective on the relationship between ATC and the civil airlines but, on the whole, fully supported Webster's view that the United States needed a strong, in-being strategic airlift capability. He

AIRLIFT DOCTRINE

prepared a somewhat lengthy exposition of his thoughts that is well worth exploring, as it incorporates several ideas still pursued today.

General Harper's opening shot put the fire concept of airlift in perspective—airlift is valuable only insofar as it contributes to the successful prosecution of the war. "We should not lose sight," he wrote,

> of that fact in peace because there is always the danger of organizing our air transport on the basis of efficiency, economy, and convenience suited to the peacetime situation. . . . Our valiant, well-equipped and thoroughly trained fighting forces will be of little use if we cannot establish them quickly as offensive spearheads in advanced zones from which they can operate effectively against enemy bases.[28]

Arguing for an in-being airlift force, he noted that the aircraft manufacturing industry could produce no more new aircraft in the first 18 months of a war than the anticipated attrition of the force existing on M-day. He also made the argument that the aircraft industry would have to have certain strategic materials in order to surge its production during wartime and those materials would have to be airlifted for want of a more reliable source of transportation. He brushed aside the obvious answer of the Stockpiling Act of 1947 with the observation that stockpiles could not conceivably last long in a real war nor could stockpiling really anticipate critical needs dictated by technological advances.[29]

Because the airlift needs that General Harper's study called for amounted to over 1,200 long-range aircraft, he acknowledged that the economy-minded American public would not agree to such a large in-being military force. He also noted that stockpiling of transporters was impractical. The only answer, he argued, was the civil airline sector. He wanted the civilian airlines ready the day an emergency arose, not at some indefinite time later, and urged subsidy of the civil carriers—including sharing the costs of producing cargo aircraft. Also, manufacturers had to produce *cargo* aircraft as that would be the backbone of the future strategic air transport fleet—not passenger planes. "We cannot count on the time required for the installation of heavy floor structure to carry military loads or to otherwise revamp or remodel these aircraft to do the wartime job." The general also made what has become an axiomatic observation, that subsidizing the civil airlines for airlift is cheaper than buying a like amount of military airlift.[30]

He wanted an "active reserve fleet of cargo aircraft employed in peacetime by commercial operators, and available for instant military employment in case of necessity," not a contract operation ginned up in the face of an emergency. Military and civil operations had to be compatible, which called for a peacetime affiliation program in which the civil airlines would perform their services for the government integrated into the military system as fully as possible. Apparently, Harper wanted a program whereby the civilian airlines would be subsumed into the military structure as much as possible during wartime (without a contracting arrangement), and some type of peacetime arrangement that trained for that wartime system. The objective

Figure 34. Maj Gen Robert W. Harper, commander of Air Transport Command from July 1947 through May 1948.

of this training program would be "to the end that maximum standardization may be accomplished and that the management of operations personnel of the ATC will be able to utilize the capabilities of the civil carriers most effectively in time of war." Harper was more than willing to admit that ATC was running an airline-type operation, but only in the sense of large-scale air transportation, not in the sense of a military airline in competition with civil air carriers. He thought in terms of strategic airlift in wartime, with a peacetime mission of practicing for war. He saw an airlift shortfall so great that not only would the United States have to rely extensively on the civil carriers, it would have to provide peacetime subsidies to those carriers to ensure that they had the right kind of aircraft on hand immediately at the beginning of a war.[31]

General Harper had good reason to address the question of airline-type operations head on: the command was facing accusations from "civilian and governmental agencies that the Air Transport Command is overlapping and duplicating the efforts of the civil American air carriers in various parts of the world."[32] This forum was the President's Air Policy Commission, headed by Thomas K. Finletter, called to investigate the state of preparedness of the American aircraft industry in relation to the mobilization requirements of the nation's armed forces. Col John Davies, ATC's deputy commander, told the ATC division commanders that

> a change in our talking and thinking about the primary transport mission of the Air Transport Command is required. This means that we should curtail expressions in publications and discussions that the primary responsibility of the Air Transport Service is to serve the armed forces in a capacity analogous to a civil airline. This should be avoided in the future. We must commence new thought trends which will serve to emphasize the strategic striking force and strategic support concept usually associated with air transport operations. To assist in preparing for this mission it is necessary to maintain a high state of training to permit the maximum of mobility and flexibility. The operation of scheduled flights within the United States and to all parts of the world permits us to continually train personnel for the strategic transport mission. However, the airlift attendant upon scheduled transport operation is a by-product of the mission rather than the primary reason for its existence.[33]

In late December 1947, the Air Force issued a new mission statement for ATC that still left it supplementary to the civilian carriers and still gave it no clearly defined wartime mission.[34]

Airlift Unification

Even with the creation of the Air Transport Command early in World War II, intertheater airlift was not consolidated. The Navy created the Naval Air Transport Service (NATS) on 12 December 1941 and retained it throughout the war. Through the auspices of the Joint Army-Navy Transport Committee (JANATC), the two services did much to reduce duplication and improve services, but at the end of

1944, ATC had 1,700 transports and NATS had 700. The deputy commander of ATC, Brig Gen Cyrus Smith, told the JCS planners that consolidation of ATC and NATS would yield the greatest economy and efficiency; but he also recognized that the interservice rivalry factor would delay the decision until some time in the future. Postwar pressures to economize brought the future sooner than expected.[35]

Through the first half of 1946, ATC proposed, through the AAF to the Joint Chiefs of Staff (JCS), that ATC operate all scheduled air transport, regardless of the service supported. The Navy counterproposed a joint task force arrangement on common-interest routes. The JCS issued a directive to the JANATC to accept the Navy's position for a period of transition and to devise a plan for the eventual elimination of naval participation over the routes of common interest. The ATC commander, Lt Gen Harold George, wrote to the assistant secretary of war for air that acceptance of the common interest concept, which would have to be studied continually and which could not be defined, would scuttle the entire proposal and violate an emerging principle of centralized responsibility by type of transportation.[36] General George proposed instead that the Navy define its requirements and ATC would meet them. The battle was joined.

The issue was unresolved in July of 1947 when the National Security Act created the National Military Establishment, composed of the Departments of the Army, Navy, and Air Force, with James Forrestal as Secretary of Defense. On the same day, President Truman issued an executive order prescribing the function of the military services, which made the Air Force responsible for airlift and support of airborne operation, as well as air transport for the armed forces, except for certain airlift services the Navy would provide for itself. Those exceptions for the Navy included airlift "necessary for essential internal administration and for air transportation over routes of sole interest to Naval forces" where the requirements could not be met by normal air transport facilities.[37] In December 1947, the secretaries of Defense, Navy, and Air Force began discussions concerning the consolidation of ATC and NATS. On the first of January 1948, they had the benefit of the report of the President's Air Policy Commission, which recommended the "consolidation of ATC and NATS into one Military Air Transport Service to handle all scheduled military transport services for the Army, the Navy, and the Air Force."[38] On 9 January, the secretary of the Navy again proposed a joint task force arrangement, an idea the AAF had already rejected.

Secretary Forrestal also needed little time to reject the Navy position, as it did not meet the terms of President Truman's order. Instead, on 15 January 1948 the Secretary of Defense directed the creation of an Armed Forces Air Transport Service (AFATS) under the United States Air Force. AFATS was to "establish, maintain, and operate all air transport required by the Armed Forces and National Military Establishment" with two exceptions. The Navy, per the executive order, would retain its internal administration airlift, with the additional secretarial stipulation that the Navy's own airlift would be primarily of a nonscheduled

AIRLIFT DOCTRINE

Figure 35. Joint service working group that created the Military Air Transport Service.

character. Secretary Forrestal also allowed the Air Force to maintain an organic air transportation capability that would not operate any regularly scheduled trunk-line service. The new order also created an Armed Forces Air Transportation Board, with one member representing each of the three services, that would advise the commander of AFATS about disputes concerning air transport services, define what constituted trunk routes and scheduled services, and resolve complaints about inadequate services. Three days later Secretary Forrestal told the secretaries of the Navy and Air Force that any issues remaining for implementation were to revolve around "how," not "whether."[39]

Even though there was to follow a great deal of debate, even at the service secretary level, the program was on its way. In late January, Secretary Forrestal designated Maj Gen Laurence Kuter to command the new organization. General Kuter was able to arrange a name change for his new command from AFATS to the Military Air Transport Service (MATS).[40] After an interminable number of meetings and conferences to hammer out details, the Secretary of Defense directed, on 3 May, the creation of MATS effective 1 June 1948. That memorandum specifically excluded the responsibility for tactical air transportation of airborne troops and their equipment as well as the initial supply and resupply of units in forward combat areas.[41]

Air Force historian Dr Frank Futrell called the creation of MATS the first fruits of tangible unification; and the first history of MATS notes that the consolidation of ATC and NATS was possible only through the leadership and authority of the newly created secretary of defense position. The Air Force and the Navy would have never reached such an agreement on their own, as World War II clearly illustrated, and the Navy had to be dragged through the entire process. Doctrinally, the ultimate decision had important implications. The separation of tactical and strategic airlift continued, a point validated at the highest levels of the new defense decision-making process. Great emphasis was placed on economies and efficiencies, using peacetime airline terminology, and little if any discussion seemed to emerge concerning wartime benefits.[42] Before the new command could organize itself, the Berlin crisis arose, a crisis solved by a consolidated airlift organization.

The Berlin Airlift

The Berlin airlift was a massive effort to provide supplies, food, and fuel to the 2,500,000 civilian and military residents of West Berlin during the Soviet blockade of ground lines of communication. The airlift lasted from 26 June 1948 until 1 August 1949. During this time the airlift forces completed 266,600 flights and delivered more than 2,223,000 tons, demonstrating that airlift was a key factor on the international and military scenes.[43]

In the face of Soviet aggression, the United States, Great Britain, and France had to decide on an effective response within their military capabilities. Gen Lucius Clay, military governor of the American zone in Berlin, wanted to test Soviet resolve by employing his forces against the blockages on the roads. Gen A. C. Wedemeyer reports that he argued against such precipitous and hopeless action and, instead, recommended to Assistant Secretary of the Army William Draper that the United States should "create an airlift." Secretary Draper concurred and arranged for General Wedemeyer to open discussion with British authorities to get their participation lined up.[44] From the start, senior decision makers proceeded on the assumption that Berlin would be supplied by an airlift. According to Under Secretary of State Robert Lovett, "We decided to stand firm in Berlin and not be thrown out, confident that we could do the job ultimately by the same techniques that we used in lifting approximately 70,000 tons in one month over the hump from India into China at very high altitude."[45]

The myriad of details concerning the Berlin airlift are available and admirably set down elsewhere.[46] However, several important ideas and concepts that emerged from the execution of that outstanding event deserve special consideration. The organizational resources for the airlift, the systemized approach used, and a review of the fundamental lessons available had long-lasting implications.

AIRLIFT DOCTRINE

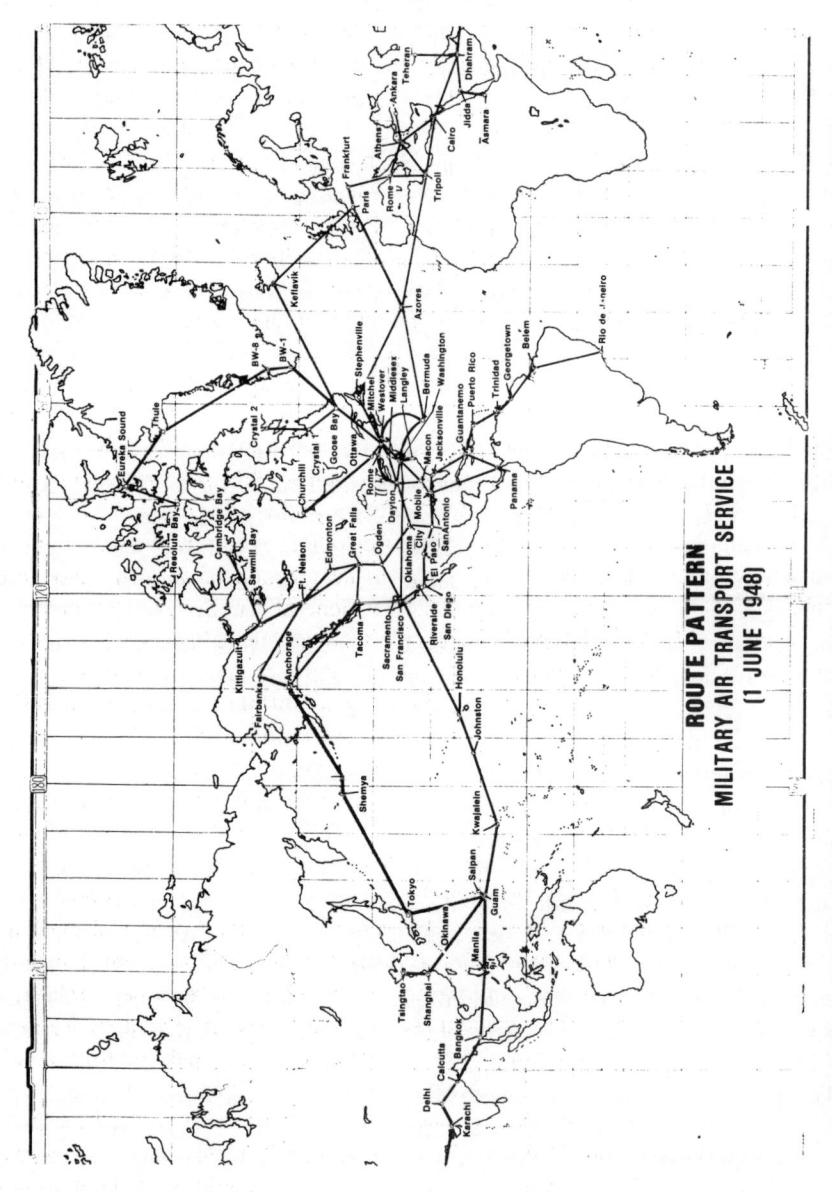

Figure 36. Major worldwide airlift routes in effect when MATS was established.

At the beginning of the airlift, the United States Air Forces in Europe (USAFE) had two troop carrier groups equipped with C-47s, which were controlled by a special branch within the operations division of Headquarters USAFE.[47] Lt Gen Curtis LeMay, USAFE commander, had told General Clay he could airlift 225 tons a day with these and a few additional C-47s from around the command (100 total), but would need an additional 30 C-54s (with two crews apiece) to meet a 500-ton daily requirement for the occupying military forces. On 26 June, General LeMay asked Headquarters USAF for a group of C-54s and requested replacement of his two groups of C-47s with C-54s on an accelerated basis.[48] By 11 July, the Air Force had sent him four troop carrier squadrons with a total of 45 C-54s, one squadron each from Panama, Alaska, Hawaii, and Texas, with one and one-half crews per airplane and orders for 45 days of temporary duty. By 13 July, the arrival of a MATS squadron of nine C-54s added to the three airplanes already in Europe from the Atlantic Division.[49]

Three days after the official starting date of the airlift, General LeMay announced, after conferring with General Clay, that his command would expand the airlift to include the civilian inhabitants of Berlin with a 24-hour-a-day, no-holidays effort. General Tunner had written to General Kuter in early July arguing that since MATS was organized specifically for heavy, sustained airlifts and because its experience included such operations, it was the logical agency for the job. But such was not the case.[50] General LeMay ordered the creation of an airlift task force (provisional), with Tunner as commander. General Tunner was at that time commanding a MATS task force headquarters that was created on 23 July to provide maintenance personnel to perform the 200-hour maintenance checks the C-54s required. His instructions from the USAFE chief of staff included the simple mission of providing airlift to Berlin or elsewhere as directed by USAFE and the right of direct communications with MATS and EUCOM (European Command).[51] His new command of 54 C-54s and 105 C-47s could lift 1,500 tons per day. A parallel British organization had 40 Yorks and 50 C-47s with a capability of about 750 tons.[52] The city needed 3,800 tons per day in the summer and 4,500 tons per day in winter. Generals Clay and LeMay had also asked for 71 additional C-54s along with the maintenance force. The National Security Council pledged full support, and the Air Force directed MATS to send eight squadrons from all over the United States and Hawaii, with nine C-54s each and three crews per airplane, to Germany within 30 days. Thus, General Tunner could expect the additional aircraft within 15 days of assuming command. By 10 August, his and the British force could deliver the 3,800 tons but needed much more capability to meet winter demands. Consequently, on 10 September, the US Air Force ordered the 317th Troop Carrier Group from FEAF to Germany with its 36 C-54s and 72 crews. The Airlift Task Force (ATF) planners calculated that they could meet the 4,500-ton requirement with the 162 C-54s they would have without needing the C-47s of the two troop carrier groups that started the airlift and without counting the British capability. Five C-82s from the 316th Troop Carrier Group would handle any especially bulky cargo. Since the C-47s also took up valuable airspace at less productivity and because managing an airstream with aircraft at different cruising speeds is more difficult, the last one was withdrawn on 1 October 1948.[53]

In mid-October the United States and British airlift organizations merged into the Combined Air Lift Task Force (CALTF), headed by General Tunner. The American component was named the First Airlift Task Force and the British element continued as the No. 46 Group. The directive creating the organization outlined the reason for the merger:

> The purpose of this organization is to merge the heretofore coordinated, but independent, USAF-RAF airlift efforts in order that the resources of each participating service may be utilized in the most advantageous manner. Its primary mission is to deliver to Berlin, in a safe and efficient manner, the maximum tonnage possible, consistent with the combined resources of equipment and personnel made available.[54]

In addition to general efficiency, this new agreement also allowed American planes to fly coal from British zone airfields, greatly enhancing deliveries of that commodity. Additionally it placed the entire system of bases, air traffic control facilities, and services assigned to support the airlift under the operational control of one commander. Noteworthy was the requirement for maximum tonnage rather than a particular target.[55] On 20 October, the Office of Military Government in Berlin decided that the winter minimum had to be raised to 5,600 tons per day instead of the 4,500 originally calculated. The airlifters called for more airplanes.[56]

In addition to 24 Navy C-54s (R5Ds) already ordered to Berlin by the Joint Chiefs of Staff, the Air Force sent 39 more C-54s, including those of the 10th Troop Carrier Squadron—the last left in the Caribbean Command. The new total was 225 C-54s, giving General Tunner an airlift force almost too big for the Berlin airspace.

Not knowing how long the airlift would have to last, or even how much it would eventually have to carry, the task-force approach was a particularly good decision. Given the complexities of several countries having to work together to make the airlift function, plus the multiple United States military agencies that would have to interact smoothly, a task force made up of airlift experts offered the best agent to execute the task. The ATF commander would have to worry about his airlift, and higher headquarters would do what they were used to doing—providing bases and logistical support and coordinating the many players involved.

To make this organization work for him, General Tunner had to integrate the aircraft into a conveyor belt-type airlift flow and needed more aircraft than mathematically appeared necessary. By the beginning of 1949, airlifters were operating from eight into three airfields. Very quickly the narrow corridors into and out of Berlin, combined with the limited airspace over the city and only so much ground space at the three reception fields, placed a premium on filling every "slot" with an airplane every possible time and making every landing available. Ground

Figure 37. The Berlin airlift air corridor system.

control approach (GCA) was the primary controlling agency for all landings at Berlin, as it was the only landing system common to United States and British forces. Initially, the airlifters used six separate altitudes for separation, but found that two altitudes were sufficient with a six-minute separation per altitude. This meant a three-minute takeoff interval at alternating bases. Near the start of the airlift, the planners laid out carefully designed routes, upgraded low-powered navigation beacons to 500 watts, and installed a visual-aerial range at each end of each corridor. British aircraft carried navigators and were less affected by navigation problems.

To make the system work required an extremely standardized flying system that called for strict aircrew discipline. Any variation by an individual aircraft created traffic problems that could take hours to untie. US crews, coming from MATS, troop carrier, and a variety of other sources, required a standardization board to prescribe techniques for each phase of flight, as well as a system of pilot checks every 30 days. The Royal Air Force (RAF) crews were fully qualified Transport Command crews and needed a less-stringent standardization program. All flights were conducted under instrument flight rules, with no variation allowed in approach patterns. Of the three corridors available, the northern and southern were limited to inbound traffic and the central to outbound. The airlifters needed this tight control because of the density of air traffic. All three Berlin terminals were within a six-mile circle; at one point there was an aircraft movement every 30.9 seconds within this highly congested area.[57]

The loading and unloading of the airlifters became an equally important function. European Command (EUCOM) organized an Airlift Support Command for all US Air Force cargo handling, which paralleled the British Army Air Transport organization. These units ensured the maximum payload utilization of each aircraft, to include marrying up as much heavy cargo with light, bulky cargo as possible. EUCOM also devised a system of channeling uniform cargo into specific bases to take advantage of built-up experience. The aircraft operators would call in when about 10 minutes from landing at their departure field, and the cargo specialists started their movement of the next load to the designated parking spot; refueling occurred during reloading by the 12-man cargo team. Much cargo was manhandled through the C-54s' side doors in surprisingly fast time. One test showed that 10 tons of coal in bags could be hand loaded and tied down in 6 minutes, but average time was 15 minutes. Food and industrial loads, which were more difficult to handle, took 28 to 30 minutes. Forklifts worked well in the loading process when on a solid ramp but became hazards to aircraft during winter and spring muddy periods. The cargo handling experts found that a truck carrying the entire load was the best way to approach an aircraft—it reduced the risks of damaging an aircraft and no time was lost during switching trucks. They also service tested the larger airlifters—the C-74s and C-97As—using a portable conveyor belt system that could load 20 tons of coal in 35 minutes, versus 45 to 60 minutes of hand-loading time. The official report of the CALTF said that the trend toward larger transports pointed to a need for further development of mechanical loading aids. By the end of the airlift, total turn-around time at on-load bases was 1 hour and 25 minutes, with 49 minutes the average at off-load points.[58]

All of these actions were developed to maximize the flow of tonnage into Berlin, but they all hinged on the availability of aircraft. The in-commission number of C-

54s grew from 117 in January to 137 in July. It took 319 of the Air Force's 400 C-54s to achieve this rate in Germany. The training program at Great Falls, Montana, absorbed 19. Seventy-five were in the maintenance pipeline, which included airplanes en route to the United States for 1,000-hour checks and replacements en route to Europe to replace those in the United States. MATS was charged with filling the United States-to-Europe portion of the pipeline and with replacing any losses due to accidents.[59] This involved complex scheduling not only for the CALTF but also for MATS, which constantly had to shuffle its remaining C-54s, based both on equity to the affected division and on other worldwide commitments. The planners also had to work for as smooth an input to the 1,000-hour depot maintenance program as possible so as to provide a predictable (and thus efficient) work load for that operation. After starting out with a shortage of maintenance personnel, which was relieved by hiring German nationals, and a spare parts shortage that was solved by airlifting from the United States, maintenance powered up to meet the challenge. Fifty-hour checks took place at air bases in the US zone of West Germany. One-thousand-hour checks started at an air depot in Bavaria but were later shifted to England.[60]

It was an airlift characterized by statistics, for numbers have a way of illustrating, at least in this case, the magnitude of the effort: 2.231 million tons lifted—67 percent was coal; 868 to 886 trips per day; one takeoff or landing every 60 seconds—around the clock; 567,537 flying hours—1,800 hours per day; 35 minute loading average—12 minute unloading average; 31 lives lost in 12 accidents—taxiing errors were the most common mishap; total cost—$181.3 million; 2.5 million people sustained in a round-the-clock, all-weather operation.[61]

The conclusions that may be drawn from the Berlin airlift are myriad, but the fundamental lessons are subject to some debate. The official report of General Tunner's CALTF highlighted three conclusions of special note. It first listed the truly joint and combined nature of the airlift and the spirit of cooperation that marked the entire operation. Its next lesson was the obvious economy of the large aircraft. The C-54 was more efficient and effective than the C-47. Limited experience with the C-54 and C-97s indicated that they, in turn, would prove more economical (and effective) than the C-54. The third lesson, a bit overdrawn but nonetheless doctrinally and strategically important, was that the Berlin airlift—and wartime transport operations—had "proved that cargo and personnel can be carried between any two points in the world, regardless of geography or weather [and] will undoubtedly become a vital factor in any future operation."[62] General Clay provided a grander perspective when he wrote, "We are gaining invaluable experience in the use of Air transport to support military operations and for civil use. The cost of the airlift could well be justified in the contribution to national defense."[63]

Col Jimmy Jay, in his Air War College research report on airlift doctrine argued that the doctrinal legacy of the Berlin airlift was a change in emphasis for tactical air transport from support of airborne assault to routine airlift services within a theater. His thesis was that the Berlin airlift reversed the officially accepted doctrine of tactical combat proficiency with its less-important logistic role. He also argued that the Berlin airlift reinforced the view that differences between strategic and tactical airlift were unnecessarily costly and duplicative.[64] World War II illustrated that, by real usage, the vast majority of troop carrier airlift time and resources were devoted to the logistic role—whether "combat" logistics or mere "routine" logistics. The airborne operations were, to be sure, highly publicized and popular and drew great energies from the tactical airlifters. But, aside from the published doctrine, airborne support was never the troop carriers' primary mission. On the other hand, airdropping supplies to undeveloped facilities, whether to forces just inserted by airborne methods or to any forces in need of such resupply, was a consistent mission for troop carrier aviation. To deal with that mission, the Air Force acquired the C-82 just at the end of World War II and continued to do so after the war. In fact, the C-119, a follow-on to the C-82 and designed to do that job better, was procured after the Berlin airlift. What the tactical airlifters wanted was an airplane that could do all of these missions effectively. Technology was not yet ready to provide the perfect tactical airlifter, one that could deliver large numbers/amounts of people and goods, including large equipment, by both airdrop and airlanding into short, rough fields; but the troop carrier leadership would have jumped at the opportunity for such an airplane.

When General Tunner, and later General Kuter, spoke of large airplanes in a steady stream, they were not preempting the tactical and assault role for troop carrier aviation. Rather they were speaking in the context of ATC- and MATS-type missions. It was a very rare occasion when either of these two generals degraded the importance of tactical airlift. There is no evidence that the Air Force took the argument concerning sustained airlift flows and applied it indiscriminately to the troop carrier forces. If anything, the troop carrier leaders themselves took the steady-stream argument, with the corollary large-airlifter issue and, on their own, argued for tactical airlift missions over strategic distances.

Post-Berlin Military Air Transport Service

Maj Gen Laurence Kuter, the new MATS commander, wanted to dispel any ideas that since MATS had the outward appearance of an airline, it was, in fact, running one. Instead, he stressed the importance of strategic airlift, which he defined as the "sustained mass movement by air of personnel and materiel to any part of the world in support of a military effort, in conformity with overall strategic requirements of that effort, and supervised by the highest echelon of command concerned."[65] It had to be a flexible instrument, he argued, that the commander could apply at the time and place of most value to the overall strategic plan. Drawing on these elements, he called Operation Vittles a strategic airlift—on an endless aerial conveyor belt—that proved the effectiveness of unification.[66]

Using the Berlin Airlift as his example, General Kuter argued that the future of strategic airlift lay, "without question" in the proper type of transport aircraft. He wanted an airplane with "ease of maintenance, high utilization, direct loading and unloading, a maximum useful capacity up to 25 tons, a range of around 3,000 miles, and most important, a low operating cost. Speed is a secondary consideration and should probably be set at about 250 miles per hour." Kuter said the low speed "would not be a problem because strategic airlift would operate into safer rear areas until air superiority was gained over the combat areas per se." He liked the big airplanes because it would take less of them to perform the same mission, thus requiring fewer crews, fewer sorties, fewer flying hours, less maintenance and fuel, and less air congestion—all important considerations. In Berlin, for example, it would have taken one-third the number of C-54s as the C-47s doing the job.[67]

Recognizing that the peacetime Air Force could not afford to have in being the size air fleet needed in an all-out war, General Kuter called for financially strong civil air carriers that could compete successfully with other mass cargo carriers. He was counting on them not only as passenger carriers but also as cargo carriers—an important distinction.[68]

He was not content, however, to think only in terms of strategic airlift. In August 1949, he sent to Headquarters USAF a far-ranging study of the inefficiencies of the air transport arrangements for the National Military Establishment. Even after the 1948 consolidation there were many air transport organizations in the military services that were withheld for administrative use, troop carrier operation, aeromedical evacuation, and various training activities. MATS wanted all of these consolidated under one command.[69]

After positing the "general advantage of consolidation" (economy, flexibility, standardization, and centralized research and development), the study attacked specifics. First came Air Force and Marine troop carrier aviation, which had the most transport airplanes after ATC. What MATS proposed was continued training in assault airlift, support for maneuvers, intratheater logistics airlift for theater commanders, and a more effective integration of the system. Logistics airlift would be better tied into MATS's worldwide traffic routes, while support for maneuvers would be drawn from those units worldwide most capable of lending a hand. Marine airlift would be retained as integral units continuing to work with Marine assault troops and Navy airlift needs but would be assigned other tasks if priorities demanded.[70]

Next in line were the strategic support squadrons assigned to the Strategic Air Command (SAC) for D-day deployment to forward operating bases. Even with the assignment of those three squadrons, SAC would still require considerable ATC augmentation from other sources in the early days of a war. Under the MATS proposal, regular squadrons would be detached to SAC locations and, when not

AIRLIFT DOCTRINE

SUSTAINING BERLIN BY AIRLIFT

Courtesy Air Force Art Collection

Figure 38. "Return for a reload—Berlin Airlift" by Herb Mott.

Figure 39

POSTWAR ERA

Figure 40

Courtesy Air Force Art Collection

Figure 41. "Approach to Templehof" by Robert Lavin.

AIRLIFT DOCTRINE

Figure 42

Figure 43

engaged in SAC maneuvers, would perform other airlift tasks, restricted by time and distance criteria. The advantages of this system, argued MATS, were more units familiar with SAC support procedures and greater ease of transition to other missions after SAC deployed.[71]

Third on MATS's list came the Navy Fleet Logistics Support Wings, which were held over to serve routes of sole Navy interest that MATS could not support. MATS argued that there were no routes of sole interest to the Navy, especially given the joint nature of future warfare. Most of the MATS and Navy routes were in fact parallel on a day-to-day basis. The only likely Navy need that MATS probably could not meet was the actual seaplane support provided to the fleets at sea.[72]

Last on the MATS list was a miscellaneous package of such airlift tasks as executive services for senior officers, individual training, and aeromedical airlift. MATS suggested consolidated pools for administrative airlift, for both equitable distribution and economies of scale. Individual training, argued MATS, should be accomplished on second-line aircraft, not first-line transports. Aeromedical airlift had recently been centralized under MATS by a JCS decision and received little coverage.[73]

The MATS arguments were well balanced and quite reasonable. The command wanted to make the most economic and efficient use of scarce air transport resources for the whole National Military Establishment, organizing in peace for a smooth transition to war. It was more than the reopening of the troop carrier/ATC debate; instead, it had a much broader outlook, concerned with issues that affected all the services. It would be implemented only partially across the next 26 years because of the intricacies of the inter- and intraservice rivalries involved. The Air Staff's response was that the proposal was being studied.[74]

By early July of 1950, General Kuter felt the need to reopen the issue of air transport consolidation with the Air Force chief of staff. Kuter astutely noted that discussions concerning Navy transport elements were not propitious, but he did not hesitate to point out that "current events continue to demonstrate the need for the consolidation of all air transport equipment and activities under one command."[75] The FEAF transport units, ATC and troop carrier, were performing identical logistic and troop movement missions, regardless of cross-training. Operation Vittles showed that the strategic transport mission could easily require tactical augmentation. Exercise Swarmer showed the two transport missions so complementary that a closer relationship should be established. "In the main," said General Kuter, "the original study has been substantiated by the developments and the experiences of the past year."[76] In July, the reality of Korea forced the assignment of 75 troop carrier C-54s to MATS, and General Kuter made it clear to his staff that the vestiges of ATC and troop carrier rivalry would not be allowed to cloud MATS's ability to handle the troop carrier (TC) units assigned to MATS. "TC units are of the strategic type and should be so used, but we must not forget their second priority mission in the tactical or combat field—this must not be

AIRLIFT DOCTRINE

Figure 44. Gen Laurence Kuter, commander of Military Air Transport Service from June through November 1951.

minimized. There must be no suggestion that this headquarters is incapable of handling this tactical aspect."[77]

The ever-tightening budgets of 1949 and 1950 had the net impact on MATS of achieving the mission statement it wanted, but not the resources. The whole MATS program became a "catch-22" of being told to do a job but not being given the resources, with the end result being a grossly unready force. In January of 1950, MATS presented its proposed fiscal 1951 flying-hour program to the secretary of defense's management committee, headed also by Major General McNarney. It was rejected as not in keeping with the administration's economy program. MATS had made the "mistake" of presenting a flying-hour budget based on peacetime transport services to their users. Instead, MATS was to "reorient its current program to obtain, with funds much less than necessary for peacetime requirements, the greatest possible capability for discharge of its D-day mission."[78] The Air Force Budget Advisory Committee took over responsibility for developing a new MATS program, noting that "all concerned have accepted the fact that MATS exists solely for the capability which it represents upon the outbreak of hostilities. . . . MATS should regard peacetime airlift not as a requirement but solely as a by-product of the training needed to give MATS an acceptable D-day capability."[79] Thus, what sound doctrinal argumentation could not achieve, fiscal constraint could produce.

The MATS program, then, was to be based entirely on a training program designed to prepare it for its D-day mission as envisioned in the current joint war plan. That war plan, ironically, was built on capability, not requirements. Since MATS had X number of aircraft, X number were tasked in the war plan. There was as yet no document that said MATS had X, but it needed Y. Surging an airlift system means flying the existing airplanes at a higher utilization rate, usually expressed in flying hours per day per aircraft. Augmenting civil aircraft are prefigured into the calculation at a set utilization rate. The McNarney Plan prescribed the same number of aircrews and airplanes as before with a much lower peacetime flying-hour utilization rate. This was achieved by deleting various services to the airlift customers, reducing frequency of flights over retained routes, outright termination of some routes, and absolute minimum flying (for proficiency) over what was left of the command. It also meant minimal crew ratio per airplane in peacetime, with provisions made for additional crew training at mobilization.[80] Other than in budget documents, this new mission orientation did not show up in any Air Force mission statement or doctrinal documents affecting MATS.

The arrival of the Korean emergency showed the fallacy of such a peacetime, ultra-economy-minded insistence on "cheap" airlift. General Kuter said that the McNarney Plan meant that, prior to 25 June 1951, MATS mission "was being accomplished within a training program ceiling limiting aircraft utilization at 2.5 hours per aircraft per day. Under our peacetime training program we had been conducting transport operations, services and route facilities with skeleton personnel forces, all of which had to be augmented before aircraft utilization could be substantially increased."[81] Airplanes and crews operating at low utilization rates could not become an effective airlift force overnight.

Exercise Swarmer

April and May of 1950 saw a testing of both General Brereton's concept of a strategic airlanding seizure and of the continuous flow so successful in the Berlin Airlift. That test was Exercise Swarmer, held in North Carolina. Its planning involved the airdrop of three regimental combat teams and the airlanding of two others. This was the first maneuver on a corps scale since World War II and uniquely tested several airlift ideas:[82]

> Exercise Swarmer was designed to test the capability of the Air Force and Army to maintain and operate an airhead wholly within enemy held territory. It was to be the first tactical application of the strategic airlift technique to be attempted under simulated combat conditions.[83]

The air component for Swarmer included three coequal subordinates: a tactical air force (TAF), a tactical bomber force (TBF), and an air transport force (ATF). The ATF was divided into a troop carrier division and a strategic air transport division. The troop carrier division had 37 C-82s, 55 C-119s, and 14 Marine Corps R-5Cs (the Navy version of the C-46). The strategic air transport division included 81 MATS C-54s, 7 C-74s, and 12 C-54s of the 8th Troop Carrier Squadron. This force was more than a third of the nation's airlift capability and was larger than the force that supplied Berlin. It also suffered a critical difference from the Berlin Task Force—Swarmer had only one crew per troop carrier airplane and two per the MATS aircraft. General Tunner's Berlin force ultimately had three crews per plane. This massive force was supported by the 7th Transport Medium Port, an Army transportation corps designated to provide logistical support as similar units had done in Operation Vittles. The 7th had 6,000 troops, including five truck companies and six port companies.[84]

The first air assault occurred when 1,900 paratroopers of the 187th Regimental Combat Team (RCT) of the 11th Airborne Division jumped from 69 C-82s and C-119s (in daylight) without any losses attributed to enemy action. Within four hours, the umpires ruled the airhead usable, in spite of claims by the aggressors that they had severely damaged the field prior to departure. Hot on the trail were an additional 7 C-74s and 61 C-54s flying the strategic airlanding mission, all at three-minute intervals. On board were an aerial port commander, the 511th RCT, and one-third of a port company. Umpires ruled that the aggressors shot down two airlifters en route. The enemy in the surrounding hills shelled the transports on the runways, legitimately claiming 37 aircraft. All told, the troop carrier division

POSTWAR ERA

COMMAND STRUCTURE •• EXERCISE SWARMER

HEADQUARTERS
MANEUVER COMMANDER
EXERCISE SWARMER

UMPIRE HEADQUARTERS

US FORCES

TAF (PROV) --- JOC --- THIRD ARMY V CORPS

TAF (PROV):
- 7 TC SQDNS + ADDT'L HV TC LIFT
- 3 FTR GPS
- 2 LT BOMB SQDNS
- 1 RECON SQDN
- TAC ELEMENTS
- SUPPORTING UNITS
- TO INCLUDE 1 ENG AVN BN

THIRD ARMY V CORPS:
- HQ V CORPS
- 82 ABN DIV
- 11th ABN DIV
- 3 INF DIV (STAFF ONLY)
- CORPS TROOPS (COMBAT)
- CORPS TROOPS (SERVICE)

AGGRESSOR FORCES

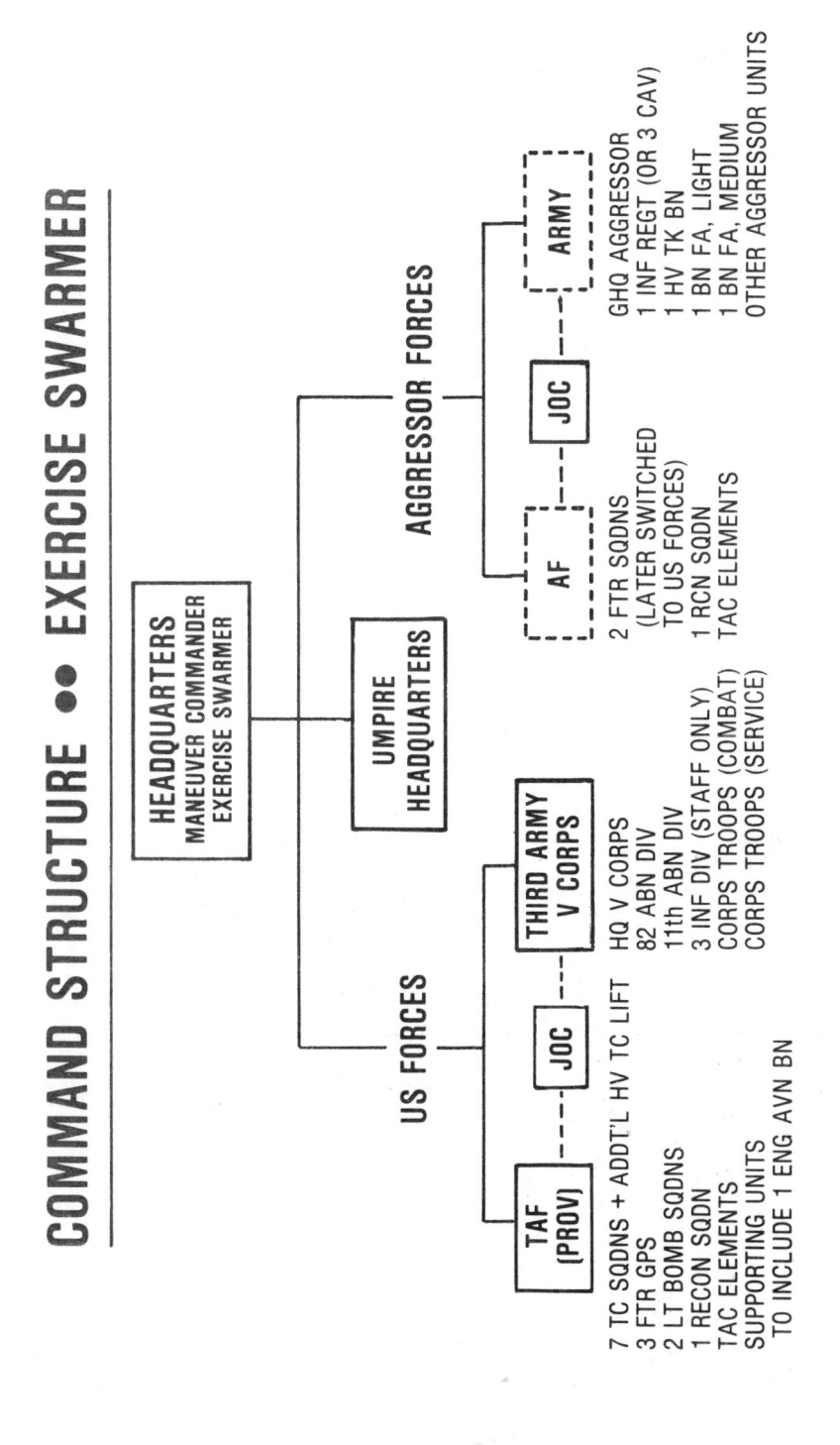

AF --- JOC --- ARMY

AF:
- 2 FTR SQDNS (LATER SWITCHED TO US FORCES)
- 1 RCN SQDN
- TAC ELEMENTS

ARMY:
- GHQ AGGRESSOR
- 1 INF REGT (OR 3 CAV)
- 1 HV TK BN
- 1 BN FA, LIGHT
- 1 BN FA, MEDIUM
- OTHER AGGRESSOR UNITS

Figure 45

dropped 5,606 paratroopers and 365 tons of equipment and supplies, and 8,753 passengers and 2,500 tons landed at the airhead.[85]

Given the size of Swarmer and the many concepts it tested, there were a number of important lessons learned. The C-119 partially passed its first real test for tactical suitability. Its centerline internal monorail salvoed supply bundles quickly and smoothly. It also proved to be an outstanding contributor to the growing capability of the troop carrier forces to airdrop heavy equipment. The C-119s, along with the C-82s, dropped jeeps, trailers, and 105-mm howitzers with 90-foot parachutes. The C-119 also proved very useful in airlanding heavy equipment. It could carry 2½-ton trucks, 55-mm howitzers, 90-mm antitank guns, or a 7½-ton D-4 bulldozer (minus the blade). However, its critical structural weaknesses were equally evident. Despite extensive use of dunnage, trucks damaged the floors. One aircraft sustained a warped fuselage when onloading a D-4, and the C-119 could only land at a prepared airfield—it could not perform an assault landing.[86]

Brig Gen Gerald Higgins, the maneuver chief umpire, noted that although the C-54s and C-74s had performed well enough, their inability to transport bulky tactical equipment limited their use in the early stages of an airhead seizure. The C-119, on the other hand, passed with flying colors, but there was still a "very definite need for assault type transports capable of landing on unprepared fields."[87] General Higgins hoped that the success of the equipment drops might offer a solution to providing long-range, antitank protection for airborne troops.[88]

The Swarmer test of the sustained Berlin-type aircraft yielded mixed results. The plan called for a flow of an airplane every three minutes. Instead, the average interval was five minutes. Even this figure was an amazing accomplishment. Night landings ran at four-minute intervals and bad weather made five-minute intervals mandatory on several days.

The system for managing the airlift was something of a study in inefficiency. The original concept was for the task force headquarters to allocate airlift based on aircraft availability reports from the Air Task Force matched with requirements from the supported forces. This system, however, had no provision for prioritization, and a practice session on D minus 2 got nowhere. The Swarmer Airlift Planning Agency (SAPA) took over, but it was subordinate to the Task Force J-4 and thus lacked final authority. Decisions subject to review and validation were usually late. The communications setup made matters worse. Teletype services between movements control officers and ports of embarkation (POE) were so unsatisfactory that high-priority messages took up to five and one-half hours for delivery. Communications with the airhead were also poor. Due to scarcity of signal personnel, there were no radio teletype connections with the ports of debarkation (POD). Nor were there any liaison officers assigned to the POEs or PODs who could have tracked unit moves, kept the status of aircraft movements, and funneled information between the various elements of the airlift. Intraport communications were hampered by inadequate radios, and the ports lacked advanced information concerning incoming cargoes. Eventually a system of pilot reports helped decrease the unloading times by as much as 25 minutes.[89]

All this added up to the SAPA being ignorant of what had actually been picked up and delivered. The agency resorted to fitting the movement of supplies and units into the airlift pattern rather than vice versa. The net result was congestion at the reception fields. The airlift flow never halted for this reason, but there were long delays and underutilization of airlift resources. Clearly there was much work to be done to assure continuous operation of aerial ports at an airhead.

The overall communications problems were eye opening; Swarmer lacked an organization capable of supporting a joint task force. The ground control approach equipment was not air transportable and thus could not be used at the airhead. None of the Army, Navy, or Air Force units could support its own long-haul communications requirements under tactical conditions. VHF radios were too cumbersome for use of the airhead, and all communications and navigation aids were susceptible to jamming and atmospheric interference. There was no airhead communications organization.[90]

Nor were the MATS airlift forces fully structured for such an operation. MATS was a nontactical organization, not properly equipped for sustained operations at forward locations. "Evidently, if MATS was to participate in tactical operations on short notice it would be necessary to organize MATS units on a T/O&E basis and to provide them with adequate equipment."[91] MATS organization and equipment were intended for long-range, intertheater airlift, not a Berlin-type airlift under combat conditions.[92]

The critical element to the success of the airhead operation was air superiority—Maj Gen Robert Lee, commanding the aggressor forces, stressed *complete mastery* of the air.[93] Bad weather kept the aggressor air force on the ground most of the time, but on the night of D plus 4 (2 May), a Navy night fighter engaged the airlift stream and intercepted 13 transports. Due to the artificialities of the exercise, the umpires could not rule on the number of aircraft destroyed, but the exercise did point out "possibilities which should be carefully studied."[94] The umpires did rule that across the exercise five transports were shot down in the air; worse yet, air attacks on transports at congested airheads claimed 59.[95] Weather precluded an accurate evaluation, but the handwriting was on the wall. Suggested solutions included greater flexibility in the airlift flow, development of a doctrine of night/all-weather fighter protection for the airlift stream, and the early assignment of fighters to the airhead for better protection.[96]

Nonetheless, the air task force commander said that the highlight of the exercise was the "integration of troop carrier and Strategic Air Transport elements into a single Air Transport Force." They were capable, he said, of successful combination and could "logically and successfully complement each other in this type of an operation."[97] But the chief umpire put the results in a bit more terse perspective. A Berlin-type airlift providing logistical support was feasible, he concluded, but there had to be air superiority, a secure airhead, runways in shape for heavy transports, and ample time for arrival of aerial port and command control planners and equipment before the airlift flow really began in earnest.[98] Lt Gen Lauris Norstad, who served as maneuver commander, was more blunt in his final evaluation. He wanted the airlift to be more efficient, increased sorties through an improved allocation process, modification of airborne operations to get more out of available aircraft, and enough improved efficiency to add the equivalent of another group to the exercise. Suggesting that the air transport tactics and techniques were relics of the horse-and-buggy days he said, "There will always be a shortage of transport type aircraft [and] we cannot carry out an expansion of our air transport force until we are sure we have done everything we can to maximize the utilization of what we already have."[99]

Airlift in Support of the Korean War

"As employed in Korea, the FEAF Combat Cargo Command, later renamed the 315th Air Division, represented a new concept in transport aviation—one fleet of cargo planes was to be sufficiently flexible to handle airborne assault and airdropped resupply as well as airlanded movement of cargo and personnel."[100] On the average the air transport force had 210 airplanes. It flew 210,343 sorties, carrying 391,763 tons of cargo, over 2.6 million passengers, and over 307,000 patients. The concept of flexible airlift passed its test with very high marks.[101]

Flexible Airlift

When the North Korean Communist forces invaded South Korea on 25 June 1950, American forces in the Far East were under the control of Gen Douglas MacArthur's Far East Command in Tokyo. The ground arm was the Eighth Army. The air arm, commanded by Lt Gen George Stratemeyer, was the Far East Air Force (FEAF). Maj Gen Earle Partridge commanded the Fifth Air Force, charged with air defense of Japan, and later the tactical air force in Korea. The 374th Troop Carrier Group had two squadrons of C-54s at Tachikawa Air Base (AB), Japan, working for the Fifth Air Force and one at Clark AB in the Philippines serving the Thirteenth Air Force. FEAF also had 13 C-46s and 22 C-47s scattered about Japan, mostly serving as base transports. On 29 June, Fifth Air Force assumed operational control of all air transports and was given authority to receive and control airlift requests.[102]

On the preceding day, the first airlift operations in Korea took place when 7 C-54s, 4 C-46s, and 10 C-47s, protected by 83 fighters, flew 748 people from Korea to Japan. For the next three days the transports flew urgently needed ammunition to

South Korea, losing two C-54s to enemy air action. On 1 July, the troop carriers began deploying part of the 24th Infantry Division from Itazuke, Japan, to Airfield K-1 near Pusan. After 16 C-54s and 1 C-46 had landed at K-1, the Fifth Air Force cancelled further operations because their runway was falling apart. Since the fall of Suwon on 30 June, there was not another field in Korea judged suitable for the C-54s. The only troop carrier group in the theater could not airland forces in the combat zone. They had to rely on the C-46s and C-47s.[103]

By mid-September the Army engineers rehabilitated K-9, also near Pusan, to the point where it could handle all the types of airlift aircraft: K-9 was especially important because other runways in Allied hands were either in too poor a condition or in the wrong location. K-2 at Taegu was crammed with 200 fighters and could be used by transports only in emergencies. Throughout August, the C-46s had been banned from the few available airfields, having been labeled the worst runway killers in Korea. Even the few C-119s temporarily assigned to the 374th in late July were too heavy for the Korean runways. Thus, only the supposedly obsolete C-47 could be regularly used in Korea in the early months of battle. In fact, the C-47s carried some 90 percent of the cargo sorties to Korea through mid-September.[104]

Figure 46. MATS C-54s in Korea.

From the beginning of July, Fifth Air Force Advance at Itazuke was supposed to control and allocate airlift, but that system was more apparent than real. Airlift requests also went to Fifth Air Force Rear, FEAF Operations, the 374th Wing, and sometimes directly to the squadrons. To solve the confusion, a system was devised whereby requests would go to the FEAF transportation office, on to the FEAF director of operations, then to Fifth Air Force Advance. Army requests arrived at FEAF through the Eighth Army's G-4 (Logistics). Fifth Air Force requests went to the division via the A-4 (Logistics). Fifth Air Force Advance soon established its own troop carrier division to "monitor and coordinate all matters pertaining to airlift between GHQ, FEAF, Fifth Air Force, and troop carrier [and] to assign priorities for airlift."[105] This division was part of the FEAF Directorate of Operational Services, which was in charge of noncombat operations. FEAF and GHQ had already agreed that 70 percent of the tonnage carried would go to the ground forces, so the division allocated the remaining capability as it thought best and issued daily fragmentary orders to the 374th Wing. All this added up to Fifth Air Force's judging the priority of its own airlift requirements, with all requests going from Korea to Japan to Korea back to Japan.[106]

At the end of June, Stratemeyer had asked for 330 more airplanes, but this number included only 21 C-54s and 15 C-47s. The Air Force promised 12 C-47s and 4 C-54s. The C-47s arrived, the C-54s did not. In early July, MacArthur wanted one group of C-119s and a paratroop regimental combat team. The Army could not ship the RCT until September and the 314th Troop Carrier Group (Medium), which received a warning order on 13 July, could only manage to deploy a token force of four C-119s to Japan by 3 August. By 16 September, the reinforced 314th had 77 C-119s at Ashiya, Japan. MacArthur had originally planned an attack on Inchon for 15 September, which included an airborne assault on Kimpo Airfield—K-14. Kimpo was important because it was the only airfield in the Inchon area that could handle an extensive airlift, and the limited port facilities at Inchon meant MacArthur's forces would need 700 to 1,000 tons a day by air. He needed the 314th not just for the airdrop but also to make up the air supply shortfall—at the time, all airlift in the theater combined could not provide even 500 tons a day to Kimpo.[107]

Because the RCT could not arrive in time, MacArthur delayed the air assault, and eventually called off a follow-up plan when ground forces captured Kimpo on 18 September and the enemy was in general retreat by the 22nd. On the 20th, the 187th RCT arrived in Japan; on 24, 26, and 30 September, the C-119s and C-54s made 440 trips moving the Army troops from Japan to Kimpo, practically monopolizing the field when airlanded supplies were urgently needed there. The airlift was under the control of FEAF's newly created Combat Cargo Command (CCC).[108]

The growing size of the airlift force demanded a centralized organization. Very much in keeping with the experiences of World War II, the airlift of supplies to Kimpo would be extensive, demanding prioritization of demands, expert judgments on aircraft utilization, and traffic control. FEAF asked Headquarters USAF for a staff to form a provisional cargo command to centralize theater airlift. Gen William Tunner, then deputy commander of MATS, was chosen to be commander. At the same time, a Theater Air Priorities Board was set up to allocate the available tonnage each week on the basis of weekly estimates of tonnage capacity provided by the CCC. The responsibility for establishing priorities within the weekly quotas fell to the Joint Airlift Control Office (JALCO). Even though a theater agency, the JALCO was physically located within the CCC headquarters to make liaison quick and responsive.[109]

The port of Inchon had a maximum capability of 5,000 measurement tons per day. Ground transportation between Pusan and Inchon was not fully satisfactory until December. Airlift had a big job as even the limited capabilities at Inchon's docks were preempted for two weeks while the X Corps reembarked for another landing at Wonsan. At one point, there were 32 ships waiting for a chance to unload. Some were carrying pierced steel planks to build urgently needed runways; they had been waiting since the original invasion 35 days previous. At another time, there were 36 ships in line with an average time of 22 days at Inchon harbor.[110]

On 15 October GHQ decided that an airborne operation in the Sukchon-Sunchon area 30 miles north of Pyongyang would cut off retreating North Koreans and possibly liberate United Nations (UN) forces held as Prisoners of War (POWs). It was flat open country. An air control party rather than pathfinders directed and coordinated the daylight drop on the 20th. In all, nearly 4,000 paratroopers and 570 tons of supplies and equipment were dropped. By the end of the first day's fighting, the paratroops had secured the drop zones, taken key positions and blocked highways and railroads. They killed about 2,700 North Koreans and rescued about 15 POWs. Linkup with UN forces occurred on the 21st.[111]

On 3 October, Tunner was told the Eighth Army would put seven divisions in the field but that of these Inchon port could only support two. Combat Cargo Command could not support five divisions in combat, but the opposition turned out to be weak and four of the five divisions were Korean and needed much less supply. Also, the offensive started later than expected. Fortunately, the Kimpo runway was 6,200 feet long, 150 feet wide, and strong enough to handle C-54s. It also had 160,000 square feet of aprons and 750,000 square feet of concrete parking space—three times as much as any field in Korea. Tunner concentrated his C-54s and C-119s at Ashiya AB, Japan, and planned to deliver to his airlift terminal at Kimpo. For a short time, the CCC delivered some goods to the poor facilities at Suwon, but the heavy C-54 and C-119 traffic soon made it unusable except for fighters. Tunner originally had his transports fly an elongated route around rather than across Korea to avoid enemy problems or interference with combat operations. On 17 September, the first flights into Kimpo (9 C-54s and 24 C-119s) carried 208 tons in base operating supplies and for an airlift support unit set up to run the airlift.[112]

Taking the long route meant an average of one and one-half trips per day, at seven hours of flying time per sortie and one and one-half to two and one-half hours of ground time. Tunner turned it into another Berlin airlift. The original 10-minute interval often was reduced to five minutes. All flights were under instrument flying rules. If there had been sufficient crews, Tunner likely would have used the lights and ground controlled approach (GCA) equipment set up on 23 September for round-the-clock operations. Even with all its ramp space, refueling facilities were inadequate at K-14 and transports were often delayed by the operations of the 75 Marine fighters using the field. Nonetheless, airlift forces moved 800 to 900 tons per day into Kimpo after 30 September, when the airlift route changed to overland flights, reflecting combat successes south of Pusan.[113]

The capture of the Pyongyang airfield (K-23) on 19 October repeated the Kimpo pattern. The nearest waterport (Chanampo) was 30 miles away, did not open until 10 November, and even then could only handle 1,500 tons a day. A railroad and truck shuttle did not begin operating until 9 November. In the interim, airlift had to supply the Eighth Army, which wanted 1,000 tons a day. The Fifth Air Force originally asked for an additional 450 tons, but that was cut back to 60 tons with the realization that air support was not at that time essential. Combat Cargo Command was able to meet its tonnage goals through an in-country shuttle, getting the most from its limited resources. The command flew partially loaded C-119s in to K-23, unloaded, picked up another load from Kimpo and delivered it to Pyongyang, and returned to Ashiya. Thus, the C-119s, with only one crew apiece made two deliveries per day. Meanwhile, 24 crews and 12 C-54s on temporary assignment to Kimpo ran a 24-hour-a-day shuttle to K-23 as well. Tunner's outfit moved 9,434 tons into Pyongyang in the 10 days between 24 October and 2 November. During all of November they flew in 13,618 tons of cargo. They also flew 705 tons into Pusan (K-9), 510 tons into Taegu (K-2), and 3,331 tons into Kimpo.[114]

On 24 November 1950, MacArthur started an all-out effort to occupy all of Korea before bitter winter set in. On the 26th the Eighth Army ran into hordes of Chinese, part of two field armies secretly massed in North Korea. On the 29th, the Eighth Army gave orders for a retreat to the Sukchon-Sunchon area. On 1 December, the Allied forces began evacuating Pyongyang, with the CCC responsible for a great deal of air movement to Kimpo. Indeed, there was even a partial evacuation of Kimpo itself on 9 December.[115]

At the same time, the CCC's C-47s and C-119s were employed in supplying the 1st Marine Division at Choshin Reservoir, which was cut off from other allied forces. Because there were no airfields to support the resupply, airdropping would have to do. The first aid to reach the encircled troops was 25 tons of ammunition dropped on 28 November in 10 C-47 sorties. The next day 16 C-47 sorties dropped 35 tons, but 15 C-119s dropped 80 tons. On 30 November, 113 tons were delivered to a total of five different drop zones (DZs). On 1 December FEAF allocated all its C-119s to supporting the Choshin operation. The C-47s were relieved of airdrop duty and assigned to evacuation of marines from Hagaru-ri—a rough, narrow, dirt strip 2,300 feet long. The C-47s made 221 landings there until its evacuation on 6

Figure 47. Korea: Resupply via airdrop.

December. By using that strip and a worse one at Koto-ri, the air transports brought in 273 tons (mostly ammunition) and took out over 4,600 sick and wounded. Since 29 November, the 314th Troop Carrier Group (TCG) dropped 1,483 tons of supplies to the Marines. The troop carriers even airdropped an 8-span treadway bridge— each span measuring 5 by 16 feet and weighing 2,350 pounds. The Marines needed the bridge to cross a deep gorge where the Communists had destroyed the regular bridge. Fighting their way south, the Marines ended their encirclement on 9 December by making contact with a relief column sent from Hungnam.[116]

The withdrawal of the 1st Marine Division merely signaled the larger effort to move the X Corps. Even though most went by ship, the entire capacity of the Combat Cargo Command, except for C-47s, was placed in support of the additional withdrawal. They used Yonpo (K-27), as it was the only available airfield, with the C-54s and C-119s lifting out 3,891 passengers, 228 sick and wounded, and 2,089 tons of cargo in six days. Yonpo was abandoned on 17 December. It was relatively quiet for two weeks. A Communist offensive launched on 31 December forced the Eighth Army to evacuate Seoul on 4 January 1951. During these actions the CCC airlifted 4,757 tons, evacuated 2,297 patients, and sent 114 C-119s on airdrop missions for allied troops—all in the first five days of January. Kimpo, Seoul Municipal, and Suwon were lost in succession.[117]

AIRLIFT DOCTRINE

By early January of 1951 it was clear that the term "quick and decisive" could not be applied to the Korean War. Makeshift arrangements were changed to more permanent ones. Stratemeyer recommended CCC be replaced by a fully developed assigned organization. As of 25 January 1951, the 315th Air Division (Combat Cargo) replaced the Combat Cargo Command. On 2 February, the 315th moved from Ashiya to Fuchū, near Tachikawa. This put it in better contact with FEAF and helped solve crowding and communications problems. Brig Gen John Henebry replaced General Tunner on 8 February. Along with his new command, General Henebry also inherited responsibility for running his own aerial port system, which General Tunner had fought for since his arrival in Korea. The 6127th Air Terminal group, under the 315th, was created for the task.[118]

The fall of Suwon put additional pressures on the 315th because only one good water port—Pusan—was left and it was 150 miles, over bad roads and railroads, from the front. Many poorly constructed and dangerous airfields compounded the problems. Through January the 315th controlled airdrops of over 3,000 tons—most of the missions classed as routine rather than emergency. American troops retook Suwon on 26 January, and after a few days to rehabilitate it, C-54s immediately went to work. They took in at least 3,500 tons in February. Even with this, C-119s airdropped 3,210 tons to combat troops. All in all, however, the lack of reception fields in the forward areas caused an underutilization of airlift capacity throughout the first quarter of 1951. Combat Cargo had 50 percent greater capacity than in October or November, but tonnage dropped 30 percent. The volume to Korea held up, but the in-country numbers dropped 70 percent, partially because airfields were within distance of Japan and partially because there were no adequate airfields for forward delivery.[119]

Between March and June 1951, the 315th oversaw an airborne drop of the 187th RCT into Munsan-ni (without any spectacular incidents or results), directed a surge in emergency airdrops to support the Allied offensive (followed by a general decline in such supply drops as the combat situation stabilized), and worked to improve the forward airfield situation by operating into Hoengsong, Kimpo, and Chunchon as soon as they were opened/captured. On 1 July 1951, the Communists opened armistice negotiations. Thereafter, troop carrier operations, though large, became more routine in nature.[120]

One apparent exception to this "routineness" was the introduction of the C-124 into service in Korea. This was in response to General Henebry's argument that if he had more modern aircraft with greater load capacities, he could do the same job with fewer planes and aircrews and less airfield congestion. The September test had a single C-124 make 26 flights to Korea, averaging 34,400 pounds of cargo, twice that of a C-54. Henebry asked for an accelerated conversion from C-54s to C-124s, which he got in the autumn of 1952.[121]

C-124 could lift huge amounts of cargo but could operate from only Kimpo, Taegu, Suwon, Osan and Seoul Municipal in Korea on a routine basis. Generally

Figure 48. Aerial resupply: C-119s in Korea.

the airplane needed a 7,800-foot airstrip, which did nothing for tactical needs. In fact, by replacing C-54s that could operate into shorter fields, the C-124 put additional pressure on the C-46s and C-47s to pick up the difference, which in turn increased pressures on the redistribution system. Nonetheless, even when operating at a limited operating weight (80 tons) and at five hours per day utilization, the aircraft marked improved gross tonnage deliveries.[122]

Maj Gen Chester McCarty, the 315th Air Division (AD) commander as of 10 April 1952, said that the concept of flexible air transport would have been best served if the air transport had consisted of a specially designed "all-purpose theater-airlift type" aircraft that could have performed any theater airlift task and be shunted from one type of mission to another as needed.[123]

FEAF's *Report on the Korean War* listed four major conclusions concerning airlift in Korea:

    1. Airlift missions and priorities should be established by the theater commander.

    2. Airlift cannot be allocated exclusively for the use of any service except for special one-time requirements.

    3. All theater airlift should be concentrated to the maximum degree in one command for flexibility and best utilization.

    4. Airlift efficiency can be greatly increased if manning tables are based on twenty-four-hour maintenance and high daily aircraft utilization rates.[124]

It is a masterful summary of airlift doctrine.

Paratroop operations played an insignificant part in the Korean War. They were generally well conducted, but did not have a significant effect on the course of the war. But, they provided excellent field tests that proved the C-119 was adequate for paratroop operations and that heavy equipment drops were capable of replacing gliders.

Beyond any doubt, airlift support for combat units was the greatest contribution troop carriers made to the Korean War. Tactical airlift was indispensable to MacArthur's advances in 1950 and saved many lives by providing supplies when surface transportation was either not available or inadequate. The meat-ax economy drive of 1949, coupled with some poor planning in the theater, meant there were not enough air transports to meet the initial emergency.[125]

Even more airplanes would not necessarily have solved this problem. Tunner wanted to set up a tightly scheduled airlift into and within Korea, with round-the-clock, all-weather, high-utilization operations; but he lacked navigation and ATC facilities for night operations, did not have the numbers of crews needed, and lacked sufficient terminals in the combat zone. Very few forward airfields in Korea could handle a sustained heavy airlift flow. They lacked a sufficient number of airplanes that could deliver the goods forward. Thus, airdrop often became a normal means of supply. Tunner argued that with better planning and support, he could have delivered 8,000 tons a day to North Korea during MacArthur's offensive, perhaps allowing UN troops to reach the Yalu before the Chinese were prepared to intervene.[126]

Strategic Airlift

The first American aircraft lost in the Korean War was a MATS C-54 strafed at Kimpo airfield near Seoul on 25 June 1950.[127] The peacetime airlift to Japan was about 70 tons per month, but expanded to over 100 tons daily—an increase of 3,000 percent in three months.[128] MATS started the airlift with an average utilization rate of 2.5 hours per day and ended up at over 6 hours per day. They achieved this great, but slow, airlift growth by doing what they had done in World War II, operating a good route structure, increasing the airplanes available, and managing the system efficently.

MATS used three major routes to Japan: (1) the Great Circle route (McChord-Anchorage-Shemya-Japan), (2) Mid-Pacific-Southern (Travis-Hickam-Johnston Island-Kwajalein-Japan), and (3) Mid-Pacific (Hickam to Japan via Wake Island and Midway). The Great Pacific route was almost exclusively devoted to passenger service. The Great Circle route took 30 hours, the Mid-Pacific Southern took 34 hours, and the Mid-Pacific took 40 hours. At the beginning of the Korean War there were no personnel at Wake and operations at Kwajalein were minor. MATS had to "beef up" those locations in particular and all en route stops in general with

Figure 49. MATS C-54 Kimpo, 25 June 1950.

maintenance people, general facilities improvements overall, forward supply of parts, and better weather and communication services.[129]

MATS and the Air Force also took several steps to put more resources against the airlift requirements. Starting with less than 60 MATS-assigned airlifters in the Pacific, 40 more C-54s were assigned to the Pacific Division from other divisions, two troop carrier groups of C-54s (about 75 airplanes) were assigned to augment MATS, and over 60 four-engine commercial transports were chartered to fly into Japan.[130]

By early 1951, requirements eased and by March 1952, MATS was managing a long-distance airlift to Japan of 60 military airplanes, 60 charter aircraft and 15 United Nations transports—down from a high of 250 aircraft in 1950. Between July 1951 and June 1952, MATS Pacific Division moved 16,766 tons of cargo and mail, and 53,904 passengers to Japan, returning with 17,968 medical evacuees. Civil airlines carried 67 percent of the passengers, 56 percent of the cargo, and 70 percent of the mail to Japan.[131]

Compared to the Hump and Berlin airlifts, it was an uninspiring operation. It was not dramatic, except that it proved a poorly manned MATS would take more time than desired to surge. It was an airlift made for the civil carriers—they had three crews per plane available and could respond immediately. Since the lift was into Japan, not Korea—the combat zone—the civil airlines had all the advantages. As the war "wound down" to a stalemate, sealift could and did carry the greatest percentage of cargo. There were two overwhelming strategic airlift lessons out of this unemotional performance; do not count on a rapid response from MATS without giving it a peacetime base from which to respond, and do count on civil airlines to be responsive for routine, but large, lifts into noncombat zones.[132]

By January 1951, six months after the start of the Korean War, MATS, like the rest of the Air Force, had turned its outlook around and reported to the Secretary of Defense that it was in phase with the expansion goals of the Air Force.[133] In response to ongoing debates involving the Air Force, Army, Navy, and Department of Defense, concerning airlift consolidation under the 1948 directive, the Air Force Council issued an Air Force position on MATS's mission that presented a balanced view of MATS. For example, the Air Force directed MATS to "provide airlift required in support of approved joint war plans, and to provide scheduled airlift for the Department of Defense . . . subject to priorities and policies established by the Joint Chiefs of Staff."[134] All of this also would, of course, be subject to the authority and direction of the chief of staff Air Force (CSAF). Airlift provided for the Department of Defense would be on a nonreimbursable basis.[135]

MATS took a different view and urged an Air Force position that would prevent the continued dissipation of "airlift power" throughout the Department of Defense. General Kuter wrote to the Air Force chief of staff recommending the following position:

> There should be one, and only one, military air transport system which will include all operations now carried out by MATS, troop carriers, SAC AMC, and eventually the Navy's Fleet Logistics Air Wings and the Marine Corps' Air Transport Groups. The development of any air transport force, helicopter or otherwise, by the Army will be strongly resisted.[136]

Perhaps as a way to overcome resistance to the idea of the Air Force budget having to absorb the costs of providing airlift to the other military services at Air Force expense, MATS also suggested that the Air Force take the position that it would bear only a pro rata share of any personnel and monetary ceilings that would affect the Air Force via MATS.[137]

In an apparent negative answer to MATS's representatives, the heavy troop carrier squadrons assigned to MATS early in the Korean conflict were withdrawn in October of 1951 and returned to the Tactical Air Command. However, the US Air Force vice chief of staff wrote to General Kuter that this reassignment was "not intended to infer that a solution has been reached on the problem of the consolidation of MATS and troop carrier units into one command."[138]

MATS was really fighting two battles. First, it had to convince the Air Force to get its own house in order as "the air transportation organization within the USAF could hardly serve as an inspiration or model to the DOD or to other services." It had to overcome SAC, Air Materiel Command (AMC), and troop carrier concerns before it could expect the Air Force to lead the fight for real airlift unification across the Department of Defense. Command histories noted that the Air Force "was in no position to level a critical finger" and that the "USAF was indeed exceedingly vulnerable to counter charges" of doing the same as the Navy and Marines. Only after solving its internal discrepancies could the Air Force make reasonable advances to the other services concerning consolidation.[139]

Somehow, in the midst of all the bombast and genuine debate, the Department of Defense issued new terms of reference in the summer of 1952 that updated the 1948 directive creating MATS. The new terms made technical revision to procedures but continued the separation of strategic and tactical airlift as well as the separate Navy transport system. The terms for working with civilian carriers continued the practice of having other Department of Defense agencies coordinate with MATS before negotiating or finalizing contracts with such carriers. MATS was also to continue planning for the maximum use possible of civil carriers and was authorized direct contact with the civil and governmental entities required.[140] Absent from the Department of Defense directive, and the ensuing Air Force implementing mission statement, was any suggestion that MATS was supplementary to the civil carriers. Instead, MATS was to provide air transport in support of the Department of Defense (minus the exception discussed).

Troop Carrier Issues

Throughout 1944, the advocates of airborne operations and, consequently, of troop carrier aviation had been busy investigating and publicizing this new form of warfare. In February, Brig Gen H. A. Craig, assistant chief of the Air Staff for operations, commitments, and requirements, reported that General Arnold believed the AAF had only begun to touch the possibilities of airborne operations.[141] At the end of April the Army Air Force Board argued that, in spite of doctrinal and technical weaknesses, the inherent possibilities of vertical warfare were great.[142] In the same month, Brig Gen F. W. Williams, then commander of the 1st Troop Carrier Command, wrote directly to General Arnold, suggesting that the postwar troop carrier force consist of 12 groups, deployed worldwide, with the mission not only of transporting airborne units, but also of training most of the Air Force in how to participate in and contribute to airborne operations.[143] In May, the Air Staff Requirements Division urged the chief of the Air Staff to broaden Air Force views of airborne activities to include all manner of aircraft and ground units in "airphibious" operations.[144]

Wartime Planning Efforts

In September the new commander of the 1st Troop Carrier Command, Brig Gen William Old, began what might be viewed as a letter-writing campaign that kept the potential values of troop carriers in the fore. For example, he wrote to Maj Gen Laurence Kuter, then assistant chief of the Air Staff for plans, extolling the tremendous possibilities of vertical development and offering a scenario for an airborne invasion of Japan. He also sought the latest information concerning the postwar plans for troop carriers.[145] Shortly thereafter he wrote to Lt Gen Barney Giles, deputy commander of the AAF, requesting similar information and suggesting that airborne operations would play a major role in the postwar strategy of the Army ground forces. He also recommended that the Troop Carrier Command assume responsibility, in the United States, for cargo movement between air depots and airfields, including the use of gliders, to provide training to the troop carrier forces.[146] In October, General Kuter, responding for himself and General Giles, was noncommittal as to the exact postwar mission for troop carrier aviation but did let General Old know that the postwar mobilization concepts for troop carriers ranged from 22 to 35 groups, depending on the circumstances of the emergencies confronted.[147] Old followed up with another letter to Kuter in November, providing his thoughts on the detailed basing structure and crew ratios troop carriers would need after the war. He also made an interesting argument concerning rumors he had heard that ATC was to absorb Troop Carrier Command. His position revolved around the point that airborne operations would play an important part in future strategies. Left unsaid was his apparent belief that absorption would negate such strategies. He did go on to say, however, in much more meaningful display of understanding of what airlift consolidation was really about, that it was logical to place both commands under one headquarters "to simplify supply, maintenance, equipment, and personnel problems, and to give the maximum degree of flexibility."[148] General Kuter's response said that he knew of no plans for ATC to absorb Troop Carrier Command but that the AAF Board would be undertaking a study of troop carrier aviation and that General Old's letter would be made available to them.[149]

A New Airborne Concept

In October of 1946 Maj Gen Paul Williams, then commander of the Tactical Air Command (TAC) and a former troop carrier commander, proposed a major change in how the AAF should think about air transportation. He based his idea on the position that airlift moved three kinds of things: (1) individuals, (2) cargo, and (3) integral combat units with their equipment. Arguing that long-range troop carrier aircraft were capable of "transporting entire ground force units over thousands of miles of distance into combat," he said that the whole premise of the Air Transport Command's responsibility for intertheater airlift was no longer valid. Distances involved and equipment utilized could no longer be the criteria for distinguishing between troop carriers and strategic airlift missions. Instead, General Williams wanted troop carriers to be responsible for air transportation of units into combat regardless of the distance involved. Air Transport Command, on the other hand, would be in charge of moving individuals and miscellaneous cargo, again regardless of distance. It was ultimately an argument for consolidation. To the extent that airlift could deliver integral combat forces across long distances directly into combat, it should have that mission. It saved time and had great strategic potential. Organizational distinctions between ATC and troop carriers were rapidly blurring.[150]

The assistant chief of the Air Staff for logistics, Maj Gen E. M. Powers, responded that the proposal was logical, but pending decisions concerning reorganization of the War Department and unification of the military services, a decision would have to wait.[151] On 17 February 1947, Lt Gen Ira Eaker, deputy commander of the AAF, did not favorably consider General Williams' concept because it would detract from the troop carrier's primary mission and result in needless duplication of transport services.[152] He was, of course, absolutely correct. Duplication, overlap, and inefficiency had no place in the air transport organization. This, too, was an argument for consolidation.

General Eaker's letter also served to outline the current AAF policies concerning air transportation. ATC, he said, would have the maximum strength consistent with sound military planning, budgetary limitations, and minimum competition with commercial airlines. The policy did not address how to implement these contradictory notions. Both ATC and Troop Carrier Command were to have tactical-type transports, modified as necessary to stress flexibility. High-performance, long-range personnel carriers for ATC would come from modified civil aircraft only when suitable AAF aircraft were not available. The AAF would also limit itself to development of tactical transport aircraft, which had the marked proclivity to force ATC to the civilian marketplace for its airplanes, especially since the tactical transporters in development had ranges of only about 1,000 miles.[153]

Economics overcame common sense and military judgment in November of 1946 when the AAF disbanded the Third Air Force (Troop Carrier), leaving TAC's three troop carrier groups to be assigned to the tactical air forces. In December of 1948, the Air Force reduced Headquarters TAC to an operating and planning headquarters subordinate to the newly created Continental Air Command (CONAC). Even though earlier decisions seemed to preclude the effort, the troop carrier units airlifted infantry companies from the continental United States to Alaska and back for maneuvers during the winter of 1947-48. In May of 1948, they also airlifted an Army Regimental Combat Team about 500 miles. The new idea of a strategic troop carrier mission just would not go away.[154]

AIRLIFT DOCTRINE

During these difficult economic times TAC submitted a plan to the Air Staff concerning the operation and organization of the Third Air Force (Troop Carrier). The TAC official history for the period says that "although the document containing this plan is no longer extant, its content may be gleaned in part from the Air Staff's reply . . . ," which opens up an interesting array of speculative possibilities.[155] The Air Staff reply directed that the troop carrier mission would be confined to two roles; a tactical one for delivering airborne forces by parachute, glider, or assault transport; and a strategic one to deliver troops and combat equipment in an airlanding operation. The Air Staff also admonished TAC that "no portion of the Troop Carrier mission should encroach upon the function and mission of the Air Transport Command." Most interesting was the Air Staff's point that they had no information concerning future contracts for C-97 aircraft but that the "possibility of assignment of these aircraft to the Third Air Force in the immediate future is slight."[156] In light of subsequent troop carrier initiatives to assume portions of the strategic deployment mission, we might conclude that this May 1946 effort was simply a precursor to General Williams' efforts a few months later.

In February of 1947, Lt Gen Lewis Brereton, the former commander of the First Allied Airborne Army and certainly the foremost American expert on airborne operations, addressed the Air War College. He proposed that airborne warfare was, indeed, much more than a tactical issue—that it was a "*strategic* factor of the greatest importance."[157] He began with a warning that every military planner must take to heart: "It would be a grave error to project previous experience in airborne operations into the future with the intention of establishing principles and methods based *solely* on past operations."[158] Graciously proposing that many of the failures to recognize the ultimate value of airborne concepts were based on the newness of the approach, General Brereton suggested that military operations should take advantage of the dispersion, mobility, range, and speedy concentration of mass that very-large-scale airborne attacks offered. He wanted to build up to a corps-size organization that would seize or build an airhead and control 100 miles of territory. He saw an integrated airlift system to make this concept work: "These may be of a variety of classes, from small, high-speed carriers, to heavy cargo lifters, with all the improvements now foreseen to enable quick take-off and slow short landings."[159] The general rejected technological limits as problems of design and production, not of research. "There seems to be no technological reason," he said, "which will not allow the immediate development of an air carrier for the M-26 or larger tank."[160]

The purpose of the airhead seizure was threefold: first, to provide a location for force buildup; second, to provide an operating location for a tactical air force to defend the operation from enemy ground and air attack; and third, ultimately to provide a field from which air power could operate in an offensive role. Although all of this is very reminiscent of how the war in the Pacific was fought, Brereton certainly stated it on a grander scale, seeking to take advantage of, or to prod, developments in aircraft capability and to offer a modern combined arms approach to warfare. General Brereton saw an integrated battlefield of sorts. Airborne forces would seize the airhead. Air transports would fly in additional ground forces (but not necessarily paratroopers), expand the airhead, fly in tactical air power, and eventually bring in strategic air power. His ideas certainly supported the thinking that airlift should be consolidated into a unified war-fighting organization.

The C-124 as a Source of Controversy

Even if they were enthusiastic and creative, the troop carrier planners were not wild-eyed dreamers. In 1948, for example, they told the Army's Command and General Staff College that the "feasibility of operating, say, 100 transports per hour into and out of ten (10) hastily prepared strips in a deep penetration airhead is a problem requiring *extensive* and *expensive* tests and analysis prior to solution."[161] They were, nonetheless, willing to accept the C-124 aircraft as an interim solution to their desire for a "heavy" troop carrier transporter capable of carrying a 25-ton payload. They also had accepted C-54 aircraft into troop carrier units to "explore the ramifications of utilizing large aircraft in a tactical role." Acceptance of the C-124 was a "stopgap" position, but Headquarters USAF subsequently decided to procure the C-124 as a standard heavy cargo aircraft for troop carriers. Eventually Air Force planners foresaw four troop carrier groups equipped with the big airplane. The Tactical Air Command (TAC) tried to save the situation by arranging for modifications that would make the C-124 usable in the airborne role. Col William Momyer, TAC chief of special projects, attempted to sway the Air Force's decision with a personal call to the Air Staff but was told that

> the C-124 is to be employed primarily in the role of supporting our strategic airlift and a secondary role as a troop carrier aircraft. . . . It is essential that the Air Force not incumber the delivery of the C-124 in view of the acute shortage of transport aircraft for the lifting of our strategic striking force in the event of hostilities. . . .factors that could be accomplished to make the airplane suitable for drop carrier operations should certainly be incorporated, but they must be evaluated in terms of delays to be encountered.[162]

Even though the C-124s were not exactly its choice, TAC did not want to lose any of them to MATS. When General Lee attended a troop carrier conference at the Pentagon in November 1949, he carried with him background papers that outlined the tremendous demands by the Army for air transportability training as part of its strategic deployment concept and the widespread disruption that assignment to MATS with augmentation to TAC would cause. It is interesting that TAC focused its arguments on MATS, as C-124s were also scheduled to go to SAC and the Air Materiel Command.[163]

Figure 50. Loading heavy equipment into a C-124.

By June of 1951, MATS and TAC were battling for possession of the new C-124s the Air Force was buying General Kuter, MATS's commander, wrote to the Air Force director of operations arguing that "because of the critical shortage of strategic airlift, better utilization can be made of the C-124 aircraft" that were programmed for the troop carriers. He noted that the C-124 was unsuitable for airborne operations and for feeder-type intratheater airlift. Airplanes like the C-54 and C-119, with much lighter footprints, caused considerable damage to Korean airfields, he said, and MATS could handle the Army's requirements for airlift of large and heavy items as they came along. The C-124 was a "long-range strategic type transport aircraft," General Kuter argued, "to be operated from first class airfields."[164] The newly formed Eighteenth Air Force (Troop Carrier) of Lt Gen John Cannon's revitalized Tactical Air Command objected vehemently to the MATS position. Eighteenth Air Force offered a number of reasons why MATS should not get the C-124s, which may be summarized as follows:

- The airborne weapon system (with ground and air segments) must maintain its integrity to be an effective weapon.
- MATS could expand its capability by focusing on development of a global route pattern that could be expanded for use by US civil flag carriers.

- Troop carriers are the only organic Air Force air transport that the CSAF could commit on his own, and the Air Force needed that flexibility.
- The Navy should provide more to MATS.
- The Army is already pressing the Air Force to meet its airlift requirements.
- There should be no division of responsibility within the Air Force in its support of the Army's operational needs and TAC is already designated as the only point of contact.
- Loss of the C-124 would delay development of the strategic deployment concept.
- The C-124 has already shown its potential for tactical airdrop and landings and suitability tests in Korea should provide more data.[165]

Each argument offers insight into the events outside the Air Force that played in the airlift debate.

Concerning the "airborne weapon system" argument, hindsight allows us to conclude that the troop carrier leaders, by virtue of their continuing contract with the Army, were years ahead of MATS's and the rest of the Air Force's thinking concerning the concept of strategically deploying Army forces by airlift. MATS's thinking was generally limited to two airlift missions: (1) deployment and support of SAC bombers in an atomic contingency, and (2) routine, but massive, logistics air flows on a global basis. The troop carrier planners, however, were not necessarily correct that, by implication, a force dedicated to the Army was necessary. Nor were they and the Army fully correct in their belief that long-range parachute operations, which appeared to require large chunks of training time, were the ultimate conventional weapon.

The Eighteenth Air Force argument concerning MATS's focusing on route development for civil airlines to use in wartime showed a fundamental lack of understanding of what MATS was already doing. Concentration on that rather hazy proposal obviously would have been unsatisfactory—it would have been a disservice to the nation's multifaceted military airlift needs. The argument was gratuitous, but when another command is trying to "steal" your airplanes you are liable to say almost anything.

The point that troop carriers were the only organic Air Force air transport the CSAF could control was in error at several levels. First, MATS was asking for C-124s, not all troop carrier aircraft. The Eighteenth Air Force was mixing in the larger issue of consolidation. At that level the argument was irrelevant. Second, the argument was grossly parochial. The troop carrier position was that "the decision as to when an emergency necessitates an overriding priority which would take troop carrier units from their basic Air Force mission should be a responsibility of the Chief of Staff, USAF."[166] More reasonable, that is a decision to be undertaken by the Joint Chiefs of Staff, who would certainly have a broader view.

The idea that the Navy should contribute more to MATS was a very good one. It was also politically unrealistic. The Air Force had been fighting that battle since 1948 and reality militated against much more success.

The next three arguments were really related to the first and were the strongest troop carrier position. The Air Force owed the Army air transportation in keeping with the Key West Agreements of 1948. An essential reason for the creation of TAC was to work with the Army. The Air Force was rapidly approaching the point of reserving MATS for support of SAC, and the Korean conflict showed MATS could also be tied up extensively in logistics airlift, although their aircraft were also heavily used early on to move Army forces to the conflict. Eighteenth Air Force was only partially correct, however, that there "should be no division of responsibility within the Air Force in its support of the Army's operational need."[167] As ideas change there is no reason for structures and arrangements to remain static. If there was a valid reason for airlift consolidation, then there was no reason that TAC could not be the point of contact for all issues except airlift, with the new consolidated agency performing the same function just for airlift. There is no overwhelming logic for the "single point of contact" concept if other advantages can offset bureaucratic losses.

Concern over whether the C-124 could perform "tactical" missions soon became bogged down in technical debates about footprint pressures on runways, paratroop concentration capabilities, and runway operating lengths. TAC eventually concluded that the C-124 could operate into and out of the same bases that the troop carrier C-54s did and was willing to live with the lack of meaningful paratroop capability. Troop carrier leaders were willing to accept those shortcomings because they were so dedicated to the idea of strategic deployment of the Army from the United States all the way to combat and because C-124s so enhanced their capabilities to deliver Army heavy equipment and large numbers of combat troops over long distances.

Both commands plus SAC and AMC had C-124s and kept them until 1957 when they were all assigned to MATS. The point is not so much the C-124 itself, but rather the doctrinal issues that surrounded debate over the airplane. MATS was not especially pleased with the airplane because of its relatively short flying distance—1,800 or so miles—but ended up with hundreds of them. TAC did not like several of the tactical limitations of the airplane but fought to get what it could in order to test out strategic deployment concepts.

The Tunner-Cannon Connection

In November of 1950, General Tunner wrote to Lt Gen Lauris Norstad about the anticipated purchase of additional C-119s. Acknowledging that the C-119 was fundamentally sound and could well become the medium transport workhorse for the Air Force, General Tunner nonetheless noted that some two tons of cargo weight could be made available if specialized equipment for airborne missions — presumably both personnel and cargo—could be deleted. He cited the vast majority of time spent in airlanding operations in Korea as proof. "This simply means that twelve thousand tons of vitally needed cargo is still in Japan, which might have been in Korea." He was not drawing an absolute line: "I also believe that, by careful design on the part of the aircraft manufacturer and by a realistic attitude on the part of those individuals dictating troop carrier requirements, we could have a workable compromise satisfactory to everyone."[168] Perhaps he realized that aerial resupply offered so many benefits that the mission could not just be written off in the name of tonnage.

In a letter written in late December of 1950 to Maj Gen William McKee, the assistant vice chief of staff, General Tunner raised the question of airlift consolidation. His experiences in command of the Far East Air Forces Combat Cargo Command gave new credence to his position:

> I have not heard anything in some time about the proposal to consolidate MATS and Troop Carrier. However, my experience as a Troop Carrier Commander in combat in this theatre has served to strengthen my belief in the wisdom of such a consolidation. There is practically no connection between Troop Carrier and Tactical aviation, while there is a very valid connection with other types of transport aviation. The Troop Carrier and MATS jobs in this theatre have been interchangeable almost throughout the whole war to date. We have found here that we are able to effect complete coordination with the tactical people whenever it is required, by the use of liaison officers. As you know, we have dropped paratroopers and we have dropped supplies in large quantities. At these times, we have requested and received the fighter support which we needed. In no case have we suffered from the fact that we are parallel to, and independent of, the Tactical Air Force. From the point of view of economy, as well as the interest of efficiency of operation, I recommend most strongly the unification of all air transport organizations in the Air Force.[169]

In May of 1951, Lt Gen John Cannon, commander of the Tactical Air Command, had the opportunity to comment on both of General Tunner's letters. He said that the additional weight was really 350 pounds, not two tons, but it is difficult to determine which apples and oranges the generals were comparing. More to the point was General Cannon's argument that the airborne and supply-dropping missions were more than important enough for a weight trade-off. Essentially he was right. Experience in World War II and subsequent events in Korea proved him so, at least concerning aerial resupply via parachute. He was more than willing to concede that "it is desirable, however, that aircraft be designed so that the heaviest team of troop carrier equipment may be quickly installed and removed."[170] It was an entirely reasonable position and closer to General Tunner's point than initial reading might reveal.

Given the magnificent advantage of hindsight, General Cannon's arguments concerning consolidation were less reasonable but certainly persuasive. He emphatically believed that troop carrier aviation was an integral part of tactical aviation and offered the following proof for his point:

> (1) Airborne operations of division and larger size are extremely complex, difficult to perform, require a great amount of joint Army and Air Force training and coordination,

AIRLIFT DOCTRINE

Illustrations from Early 1950s
Troop Carrier Doctrine Text

214

and are based upon joint Army and Tactical Air Force staff planning and SOPs of a complexity comparable to that required for close support aviation.

(2) Forward airfields are used by both troop carrier and close support aircraft. Operations of both must be adjusted to fit the other depending upon the urgency of the situation, and, therefore, must be under the same command.

(3) In the face of air opposition, the necessity for air defense of bases, fighter escort, and close control of all air operations, not only requires troop carrier type of operation but precludes the airline concept of cargo operation. Supply and resupply of troops in the combat theater of operations, regardless of method of performance, are a function of tactical aviation. This is but one of the jobs of troop carrier which is an integral part of tactical aviation.

(4) It is vital that the ground force commander in the field have but one air commander to deal with.[171]

The question of whether troop carrier aviation was tactical or not was, in the last analysis, irrelevant. Coordination and liaison could solve many of the problems General Cannon discussed. The ground force commander in the field would still have only one air commander to deal with. This debate centered on the fallacy of composition: troop carriers had a *tactical* mission, therefore they must belong to the *tactical* air command. General Cannon's belief that "any proposal to merge troop carrier and all air transport units into one air transport organization is basically in error in that it combines combat functions with service functions" was a gross misstatement of what airlift consolidation aimed at, and General Tunner had himself to blame for opening that door.[172] The question was whether the airlift mission could be better served by consolidation. Unfortunately, the debate degenerated into questions of definition. Tunner overemphasized tonnage questions and thus created an understandable concern that the tactical mission, which by inference was inefficient, would be degraded.

Meanwhile, in February of 1951, General Tunner responded to FEAF's commander, Gen George Stratemeyer, for a review and evaluation of the FEAF Combat Cargo Command's operations. The report was far ranging and thorough. General Tunner was concerned that air transport continue as a theater issue, with priorities and allocation decided outside service channels. He also raised the issue of the relative importance of airborne and air supply missions. He would not let go of his argument concerning design of tactical airlifters primarily for an airlanding role, although he did modify his numbers somewhat.

> Experience over the last ten years shows that a relatively small percentage of the tactical air transportation effort has been in support of airborne operations while airlanded supply operation consumed the great bulk of the total workload. I believe we must overcome this misconception and more clearly and accurately establish the true role of tactical air transportation. By doing this we may put more emphasis on organizing, training, and equipping for air supply operations and thereby increase the overall tactical air transportation capability many fold. This reevaluation of the tactical air transportation mission would allow us to consider seriously the reduction of specialized equipment in the aircraft which is to be used only periodically for airborne operations. The Korean

> operation alone bears out the importance of this problem when we realize that each C-119 has approximately one ton of specialized equipment and structural strength to support it which is used primarily for airborne missions. If the equipment had not been on the C-119s during the 9,128 sorties flow, an additional 9,128 tons of urgently required supplies could have been delivered at no additional cost. I am not advocating the elimination of all of this equipment but I do want to point out the tremendous expense. I believe much of this loss in airlift capacity can be eliminated by the modification or redesign of some of this specialized paradropping and other equipment.[173]

Airlanding is the preferred method of aerial resupply, as the goods get where they are going with minimum damage and loss. But the lessons from Burma, New Guinea, and a bit later than General Tunner's report, from Korea all validated the vital contribution that airdrop of supplies could make to a campaign. On the other hand, General Tunner was correct that classic airborne operations were certainly not the norm for troop carrier missions. Perhaps he was right that some modification and compromise could be reached. His point was that what the Air Force needed, at least for some interim period, was a long-range, heavy-lift aircraft for worldwide operation; a medium-range, heavy-lift airplane for moving large heavy equipment and airborne operations; and an assault transport for operations into small, marginal airstrips. His call for fewer types of aircraft designed for more flexibility was equally well thought out. Tunner, for all his "routine" logistics experience, was struggling with the recurring question of how to provide as few aircraft types as possible to meet the many different kinds of airlift missions. He wanted to create a philosophy in that direction and drive technology to a solution. It was a reasonable and balanced approach.

After all the emotion had been wrung out of the argument, his position on air transport consolidation was also reasonable:

> Since 1943 there has been considerable discussion of the feasibility of integrating all air transportation in one organization. I believe the whole question must be considered from the standpoint of worldwide requirements for air transportation as well as the United States capability to produce transport aircraft and organize units. During the past several years there have not been sufficient transport aircraft available to handle our total airlift requirements throughout the world. Planned production and procurement programs indicate that this condition will exist well into the future. If this is true, we must prepare to use all available air transportation to the maximum extent possible on the highest priority missions, whether the missions are strategic or tactical. The only way this can be satisfactorily accomplished is by integrating all air transportation into one organization which will have the mission of standardizing the equipment, units and technique insofar as possible. Of course there will be limitations in the standardization of equipment but a great deal can be done to improve the versatility of transport aircraft. My experience commanding Troop Carrier, Military Air Transport Service, and the Marine and Navy units on the Berlin Airlift, Operation Swarmer and here, certainly indicates that much can be done to standardize procedures and techniques. On each of these operations where it was necessary to bring both Troop Carrier and the Military Air Transport Service units and personnel together, I found, although the mission was identical, considerable variation in organization, equipment and training. Because of this, a time-consuming standardization

> program was necessary before the operation could be put on a maximum effort basis. I believe that much greater airlift capability can be developed with available resources by placing all air transportation in one organization and making it available to theater commanders as required by them.[174]

None of the advocates of airlift consolidation proposed to do away with the tactical mission. Rather, they were seeking to provide the most airlift possible and the most appropriate to the needs of the supported combat commander. On the other hand, the "separate" tactical airlift supporters were equally reasonable men who were sincerely disturbed that the unique portions of their missions would be overshadowed by concerns for economy and efficiency, to the detriment of national security. Given the great differences in mission execution at the operational level, the meat-ax economies being exercised periodically by higher authorities, and the natural esprit de corps found in a combat organization, it is little wonder that troop carrier and tactical leaders resisted consolidation.

General Tunner's report also provided an interesting blending of airlift and air power doctrine concerning air superiority and, by inference, the confidence that supported commanders could place in air transport operations.

> Since there has been very limited enemy air opposition in Korea, some questions will probably be raised as to the effect active enemy air operations would have had on air transport operations. I believe these questions can best be answered by reconsidering past experience. In the Pacific and European theaters of operations it was found that air transport operations could be carried out even though the enemy was capable of mounting large-scale air opposition. It is true that air superiority is essential, but since . . . air superiority will be established in any operational area before any type of large scale operations can be started, there is little question of the ability of air transportation to play its normal role even in a theater where air opposition exists.[175]

It is possible to draw from this syllogistic argument that airlift would operate in the face of enemy air opposition, because that is the nature of war.

"Official" Doctrine

Early in the 1950s, the Air University (AU) engaged in a frustrating series of efforts to publish Air Force doctrine. Air University found itself engaged in a running debate with Headquarters USAF and the major operating commands over who should write such documents and what should be in them. Lt Gen Thomas White, then Air Force deputy chief of staff for operations, noted in early 1951 that there was a compelling need for "clear-cut and succinct statements of operational doctrine"; and that although Air University was the "best qualified Air Force agency to prepare such manuals," Headquarters USAF was the "only agency in the Air Force which was always conversant with Department of Defense policies and interservice negotiations." Consequently, Air University would write these manuals, and headquarters would review all such publications. The Air Force Council approved Air Force Manual (AFM) 1–2, *United States Air Force Doctrine*, on 12 March 1953, after five years of tedious work by all concerned. It was a short, tract-size document of sweeping generalities concerning air power and the principles of war that should have offended no one.[176]

Concurrent with the Air University effort to produce a basic doctrine manual, the Air War College Evaluation Staff began work on four manuals designed to expand on the basic doctrine. These included theater air operations, air defense operations, strategic air operations, and air transport operations. Air University planned to produce these manuals by working in close coordination with the responsible Air Force commands. The Strategic Air Command and the Air Defense Command were enthusiastic. MATS was pleased enough with the draft of its manual that it did not even want a review committee. Col William Momyer, the AU head of the evaluation staff, was so surprised at this cooperativeness that he said MATS might not have given "the detailed review necessary for expressing sound doctrinal matters."[177] MATS saw the draft in May of 1952 and apparently submitted final comments on 30 January 1953, after some prodding from the Air University project officer to "obtain a less casual critique." The final draft went to the Air Staff the following March. It was never published.[178]

The tentative manual had much to say for itself but was extremely limited in scope, focusing on a "general concept of the role of air transport forces in a worldwide system of airborne logistics" and excluding "operations conducted by tactical air forces in intratheater operations, feeder or special mission operations [and] the support to be rendered the strategic air forces in the initial stage of war."[179] Having thus deleted several vital elements of air transportation, the manual was partially true to General Arnold's belief in the specialness of strategic airlift but missed the opportunity to offer a comprehensive airlift doctrine. No doubt, the AU writers were influenced by the then prevalent belief that troop carrier and strategic airlift were to be separate organizational entities. They certainly had to be aware of the uproar a more comprehensive document would have caused in Cannon's Tactical Air Command headquarters. Above all, the doctrine experts wanted to get the manual published, and such limitations ensured a minimum number of coordinating agencies. It is ironic that Lt Gen Laurence Kuter, fresh from his assignment as the commander of MATS where he had led a strong battle for airlift consolidation, was the Air University commander during the development and forwarding of the air transportation manual.

Perhaps the most startling statement in the draft manual had to do with the resources allocated to military air transport:

> The requirements for military air transport in time of war will greatly exceed the air transport resources of the nation. This is an inadequacy which is not peculiar to air transport alone, but is shared in varying degrees by all military and civil activities in periods of total mobilization. The deficits which will face air transport can be attributed

chiefly to the higher priorities which are allocated to combat forces and restrict the manpower, materials, and dollars available for the air transport forces.[180]

It is true that there likely will never be enough airlift to satisfy demands. It is quite another thing to doctrinally relegate air transport to permanent second- or third-class status in the resource allocation process. A much more meaningful statement would have sought a balance among Air Force forces rather than to automatically and officially bless the notion that air transport was not important enough to merit an honest budget review. How MATS signed off on that statement is a mystery.

The proposed doctrine did provide some historically interesting statements as to what the characteristics, operational features, and limitations of airlift are. It said that an effective air transport system had speed, range, freedom of movement, flexibility, and mobility. By freedom of movement, the only unusual term, it meant the ability to use routes unhindered by geographic or other obstacles, to execute evasive maneuvers, and to select alternate landing sites based on the tactical situation. The operational features of a global air transport system included dependability, high-payload factors, high-utilization rates, and a highly emphasized air and ground safety program.[181] There were three limitations that air transports suffered. They were vulnerable to enemy air and ground actions, but since the main routes were probably well outside areas of enemy interdiction, there was little chance of meeting enemy firepower there. Transports could not be armed because it meant too great a compromise of payload and would be ineffective anyway due to slow speed and lack of maneuverability. Air transport was also limited in that it could carry cargo only so big before having to either break it down or divert it to surface transportation. Cargoes such as petroleum, oil and lubricants (POL) and coal faced a prohibitive haulage cost per ton mile and would be airlifted only in emergency conditions.[182]

There were some clear-cut pluses in the proposed doctrine. It did continue, and in fact thoroughly justified, the point that strategic airlift was exempt from theater controls.[183] Air transport was a "vital element in the support of the United States military forces." And, the complexity of a global airlift system received official recognition. Civilian airlines could make an important contribution, but nowhere was there a notion of subservience to them—apparently that idea was in its rightful "file 13." Perhaps the most doctrinally durable statement in the entire manual was the paragraph concerning training:

> In peacetime the primary objective of a global air transport command is training; its aim is to make ready, "a military airlift force that can rapidly and efficiently be expanded to meet mobilization requirements." Under this concept any air transport which may be generated is but a by-product of the training effort. In wartime, however, transport is the end product, the primary objective of the command, and training must be so planned and programmed as to present a minimum of interference with the operational mission. The principle concern is the qualification and perfection of personnel in the operational, technical, and administrative functions peculiar to transport conducted on a global scale.[184]

AIRLIFT DOCTRINE

The training arena also offered an out concerning airlift consolidation, although it was overwhelmed by the rest of the manual. Drawing on 12 years of operational experiences, the new doctrine did call for joint training:

> The requirement for joint training between the global air transport forces and other airlift agencies must receive particular emphasis. Experience indicates that there is a continuing requirement for standardization of procedures and techniques of the various military and civil air reserve fleet air transport agencies. Emergency operations in support of joint war plans or critical strategic or tactical situations may arise from time to time and require the participation of all segments of the nation's air transport resources. Therefore, joint and cross training of these forces must be effected if interchangeable or complimentary operations are to be carried out efficiently and effectively. This training applies not only to flight activities, but equally as well to maintenance, traffic, and other airborne logistic practices and procedures.[185]

The door was still open a crack.

Along with the *Air Transport Operations* tentative doctrine manual, Air University also forwarded a parallel text on theater air operations—published as AFM 1-3, *Theater Air Operations*, in September 1953. Its section on theater airlift said that such forces are "employed on behalf of the theater objective rather than any specific component force of the theater. It is this inclusive characteristic that requires centralized direction of the troop carrier forces. . . . It is only through centralized direction that the operations of the forces can be kept sufficiently flexible. . . ."[186] Its order of tasks was movement of personnel and cargo, aeromedical evaluation, and then airborne operations. Personnel and cargo movement included regularly scheduled intratheater airlines with one of the "major airlift functions . . . the delivery of equipment and supplies to the combatant forces."[187]

As a follow-on to the publication of AFM 1-3, TAC's Eighteenth Air Force (the Troop Carrier Command) prepared a draft that the Air Force published as AFM 1-9, *Theater Airlift Operations*, in July of 1954. It too stressed that "maximum advantage of airlift capabilities is realized by employing the basic principles of centralized control and decentralized execution."[188] In theater airlift, this meant that troop carriers and any theater airlift augmentation would be under the control of the theater air commander. Reflecting both the lessons of Korea and the emphasis on flexibility, the newest manual noted that the airlift mission would encompass logistical airlift (to include unit deployment, airdrop and airland supply, and scheduled and nonscheduled airlift); aeromedical operations; airborne operations; and special airlift. "No one task," said the doctrine, "is considered to have an overall priority."[189] There was also new stress on troop carrier capabilities to perform intertheater airlift, especially of combat air forces. In all cases, troop carriers required a very high degree of friendly control of the air due to their high vulnerability to enemy air and ground fire.

Jet Transport Aircraft

Throughout the early 1950s, MATS pushed for an Air Force decision to investigate an all-jet transport. The airlift fleet was aging and needed a modern replacement. In 1953, the Rand Corporation reviewed over 1,000 future aircraft designs, narrowed the field to 216, and compared those against an air transport system similar to MATS's. Rand's conclusions at least helped MATS and the Air Force by providing a set of decision-making criteria:

> 1. Airplanes powered by turbo-prop engines provide lower direct operating cost per ton-mile than do airplanes powered by compound-reciprocating or turbo-jet engines for any combination of design speed, payload in the following area:
>
>> Range—1,500 to 3,500 nautical miles
>> Payload—25,000 to 150,000 pounds
>> Speed—130 to 490 knots
>
> 2. Large airplanes (large payload at long design range) have lower direct operating cost per ton-mile than do small airplanes.
> 3. Large airplanes are less sensitive to variations of operations from the design range, both from the cost per ton-mile and airlift capability standpoints.
> 4. Selection of an aircraft should be based upon the cost to perform the mission by a fleet of the airplanes rather than on the ability of one airplane to fulfill some single payload range requirement.
> 5. The cost of air transportation can be considerably lower in the future than it is today if a well integrated plan for airplane and engine development is aggressively pursued.[190]

Rand also indicated that the payload cost reduction trade-off point was achieved somewhere around the 35-ton limit, thus gaining no additional ton-mile cost advantage above that point. Analyzing all the data, MATS concluded that, for the foreseeable future, this meant that the airlifter would have a 35-ton payload, a 50-ton gross takeoff weight, and a range of 2,500 miles. Because the ton-mile cost system factors in most operating costs, the limiting factor (at least in terms of other than a marginal advantage) must have been in powerplant efficiency. A MATS Aircraft Characteristics and Configuration Board studied the issue and concluded that even under the Air Force's 143-wing expansion program, and counting in civil capability, airlift in wartime was not sufficient to meet needs. The board said MATS needed two types of airplanes, one that could carry 50 tons 3,500 miles and another that could carry 15 tons or 100 passengers the same distance. The 3,500-mile distance requirement reflected the realization that many en route bases, the essence of the current airlift system, would not be available in wartime. MATS was concerned also about long-range aircraft because it had undertaken a program to locate all strategic airlift squadrons within the United States and Hawaii. In addition, the transport service also very much needed a fleet compatible with the Strategic Air Command bombers.[191]

AIRLIFT DOCTRINE

Figure 51. Lt Gen Joseph Smith, commander of Military Air Transport Service from November 1951 through June 1958.

Lt Gen Joseph Smith, who succeeded General Kuter as the MATS commander, urged the Air Force to "announce a firm position in favor of the development of a turbojet transport for military use . . . to meet the needs of MATS."[192] General Smith was so dedicated to the idea of jet transports, and to getting the Air Force to commit itself, that he was willing for anyone to have them, just as long as the Air Force moved:

> I feel that it is timely and necessary for the USAF to get into a jet transport program and that a major command of the Air Force initiate use of jet transports. This doesn't have to be MATS. Appropriate action now could produce jet transports as early as 1958. I propose that procurement action be initiated to provide one 12-plane jet transport squadron on the West Coast and two 12-plane jet transport squadrons on the East Coast as an interim program.[193]

The USAF Directorate of Requirements had already studied the issue and was ready to start more serious efforts. The Air Materiel Command already had six turboprop test-bed aircraft, two YC-97s, two YC-121Fs, and two YC-131Cs that it was ready to turn over to MATS for engine-hour accumulation, establishment of maintenance procedures, and general operating and experience.[194]

In August of 1954, General Smith presented a paper to the Institute of Aeronautical Sciences that not only supported the development of jet-powered transports, but also demonstrated that MATS had apparently abandoned its quest for airlift consolidation with troop carrier aviation.[195] He called for the development of two different, highly capable jet transports. One was to lift critical cargoes that needed to go by fast air express, cargoes such as "high-cost items, scarce materials, nuclear components, whole blood, controlled critical supplies and electronic equipment." The same aircraft would be specialized personnel carriers over high-density, overseas routes. They would need to be pressurized to 8,000 feet for habitability and to avoid passenger fatigue. The general wanted an airplane that would fly at 500 knots, with a range of 3,500 miles, and land on a runway 5,000 to 6,000 feet long with thrust reversers, not "such gimmicks as drag chute braking." The airplanes had to be simple to fly and maintain, with engines on pods rather than embedded in the wings. They also needed to be as compatible as possible with civil aircraft but without compromising the military mission. Such an airplane would be a turbojet.

The all-cargo carrier was the other type of airlifter General Smith proposed. It would be a turboprop capable of carrying 25 tons a distance of 3,500 miles, also into 5,000- to 6,000-foot runways. General Smith suggested wide doors and truck-bed-height loading but said he could cope with higher cargo floors due to innovations in high-lift loading equipment. The cargo carrier had to be as easy to fly and maintain as the proposed passenger airlifter.

The evidence that General Smith had at least shelved the consolidation urge came early in his speech:

AIRLIFT DOCTRINE

> In past years, it has been accepted without challenge that military transport aircraft should be multipurpose with the same type of aircraft being used interchangeably for passengers, evacuation of sick and wounded, hauling cargo and mounting troop carrier operations. We have learned by experience that such a concept is no longer sound or efficient. We must now have one type of aircraft for the express purpose of transporting personnel and wounded and another type exclusively for hauling freight.[196]

This focus on strategic airlift requirements was a clear signal that MATS was entering the jet transport debate looking out for its primary mission and would be unwilling to modify its requirements to accommodate troop carrier concerns. General Smith was clearly a man who put his money where his desires were. In January of 1955 he recommended to the Air Force chief of staff, the early procurement of the C-133 cargo aircraft. The previous July he had recommended the DC-7 as his choice as an interim passenger and cargo aircraft, but in December 1954, he requested the DC-8 or B-707 for long-term jet transport (passenger) needs.[197]

New Tactical Airlifts

During World War II the glider was the standard method of delivering heavy equipment and reinforcements after a paratroop assault. The glider, however, had some significant drawbacks. In combination with its required tow plane, it was twice as vulnerable, took twice the number of pilots, and required about twice the amount of airspace. In darkness and bad weather, gliders were especially hard to handle, and abandoning them was expensive.[198]

The CG-4A standard glider from the war could not carry more than a 205-mm howitzer *or* a tow vehicle. The CG-15A replacement glider was better but still unacceptable to the airborne forces. The CG-13A, which could carry 42 troops or a 10,000-pound payload, was a vast improvement but landed too fast to allow use on small fields or rough ground. In March of 1945 the Air Force declared all existing gliders obsolescent, but it was not until December of 1945 that the AAF decided to undertake a five-glider development program.

In May 1946, the Air Materiel Command, Engineering Division, issued a technical instruction calling for the development of a "single but sturdy powered transport, with low wing and low wheel loadings and with low landing speeds as an interim assault airplane." It specifically noted that the gliders under development be redesigned to meet these requirements.[199] The year 1948 saw the issuance of a contract for a powered version of the XCG-20, to be known as the XC-123. It could land in a space of 800 feet. By September of 1950, TAC said that "both Army and Air Force personnel agree that the requirement for gliders in troop carrier operations no longer exists."[200]

In February of 1951, in pursuance of TAC's goal of an assault-type aircraft capable of operating from unprepared strips, the Air Force informed Air Materiel Command that the C-123 was to be considered part of the Air Force's 95-group program with a goal of 398 aircraft.[201]

The first appearance of the C-123 in tactical operations was the large-scale Army-Air Force Sagebrush maneuver in November and December of 1955. Testing atomic war concepts for the Army, it showed that highly mobile, self-sustaining Army forces, dispersed to strategic locations near such a combat zone, were preferable to concentration of such forces. The C-123, then, was designed to be TAC's assault airlifter.[202]

Another element of TAC's airlift force was the medium troop carrier wing. During the Korean conflict, this meant the C-119 aircraft. However, by November of 1952 Headquarters TAC had decided it wanted a follow-on aircraft, the Lockheed C-130, built to 1951 TAC specifications.[203] The Eighteenth Air Force envisioned the C-130 as being able to meet theater logistics needs at high payloads and speeds, contributing to the assault mission with high-performance landing, takeoff and climb characteristics, and also providing an excellent parachute delivery system.[204] The first flight of the YC-130 took place at Burbank, California, in August of 1954, with the Air Force taking beginning deliveries in April 1955. The YC-120 could carry 90 troops with full equipment or 18 tons of cargo.[205]

The Airlift Heritage of the Postwar Era

The 10 years following the Second World War were, at once, frustrating, exciting, and demanding for airlift forces. Airlift consolidation, in terms of strategic and troop carrier airlift, was rejected at the official doctrinal level and accepted, at least in part, at both the conceptual and operational levels. Airlift consolidation, in terms of the primary mission of troop carrier aviation, was strongly headed in the direction of one theater airlift organization for both airborne paratroop operations and aerial logistics functions. Airlift consolidation, in terms of Department of Defense strategic airlift resources, was generally validated with the creation of the Military Air Transport Service in 1948.

The Berlin airlift proved, among many other things, that airlift could rise to incredible challenges and that it was a fundamental tool of diplomacy in the new political order of the war. In the Korean War, strategic airlift operations proved the folly of low-priority, underfunded, ill-prepared forces. Troop carrier aviation rose to the demands of the Korean War and showed its great flexibility and responsiveness. Paratroop operations in Korea were not important, but aerial resupply activities were critical.

Both MATS and troop carrier planners saw the need for aircraft better suited for their airlift missions. At the end of the period, MATS concentrated on the strategic mission and looked to the potential offered by jet aircraft. The command was very much influenced by its mission of supporting the deployment of the Strategic Air Command. Troop Carrier leaders had to split their efforts between an assault airlifter aircraft to replace the glider—the C-123—and a replacement for the C-119 medium troop carrier aircraft—the C-130. Troop carrier units also vied for ownership of the C-124 to meet their new concept, driven by emerging Army ideas for an aircraft that could deploy comparatively large amounts of Army forces and equipment across long distances into objective areas.

Airlift doctrine for this postwar period may be summarized as follows:

- Troop carrier aviation performs assault airlift; aerial delivery of forces, equipment, and supplies; and long-range deployments of Army personnel and equipment into battle areas.
- It best meets those many missions through one organization for theater airlift.
- Strategic airlift provides for this long-range deployment of Strategic Air Command support forces and the logistic support of Department of Defense forces throughout the world.
- The Berlin airlift proves that the concept of an aerial bridge is an important military and diplomatic tool. It also illustrates the importance of a sustained flow of aircraft as an airlift operational concept.
- Strategic and troop carrier airlift forces are so fundamentally different in mission and outlook as to preclude organizational consolidation.
- Strategic airlift requires consolidation of as many assets as possible under one airlift command in order to gain maximum efficiency.

NOTES

1. Robert Frank Futrell, *Ideas, Concepts, Doctrine: A History of Basic Thinking in the United States Air Force, 1907–1964* (Maxwell AFB, Ala.: Air University, 1974), 102; Memorandum by Brig Gen W. F. Tompkins, director, Special Planning Division, War Department, to commanding general, Army Air Forces, subject: Post-War Permanent Air Force, 11 February 1944.
2. Futrell, *Ideas, Concepts, Doctrine*, 102–3; Outline of the Post-War Air Force, Plan No. 2, a study prepared by Post-War Division, assistant chief of Air Staff, Plans, 11 August 1944.
3. Futrell, *Ideas, Concepts, Doctrine*, 112–13.
4. Ibid., 113–24.
5. Ibid., 125.
6. Ibid., 160–62.
7. Ibid., 164–65, 209.
8. History, Military Air Transport Service, January–June 1953, vol. 1, narrative, 77.
9. Futrell, *Ideas, Concepts, Doctrine*, 211.
10. Ibid., 103.
11. Col Jasper N. Bell, representative of Assistant Chief of Air Staff-3 (AC/AS-3); Capt Everett G. Ratter, representative of AC/AS-4; Col Arthur C. Carlson, Jr., representative of AC/AS-5, staff study,

subject: Supply By Air, a staff study prepared jointly by representatives of AC/AS-3, AC/AS-4, and AC/AS-5, 5 September 1945.

12. Brig Gen William McKee, deputy assistant chief of Air Staff-3, to AC/AS-5, routing and record sheet, subject: Air Transport Organization Plan, 31 October 1945; Lt Col John Ruse, executive, assistant chief of Air Staff-3, to AC/AS-5, routing and record sheet, subject: Air Transport Organization Plan, 5 November 1945; Lt Gen Ira Eaker, deputy commander, Army Air Forces, to AC/AS-5 and AC/AS-3, subject: Future Plans for Air Transport Command, 10 December 1945.

13. Col James Douglas, Jr., deputy chief of staff, Air Transport Command, to commanding general, Army Air Forces, letter, subject: Reduction in Operation of the Air Transport Command, 26 September 1945.

14. Brig Gen Frank Everest, chief, Strategy and Policy Division, AC/AS-5, to Special Planning Division, AC/AS-5 letter, subject: Justification of Air Transport Command Deployment, ca. July 1946; Brig Gen William McKee, chief of staff, Air Transport Command, to commanding general, Army Air Forces, letter, subject: Justification of Air Transport Command Deployment, 21 March 1946; Brig Gen Bob Nowland, commanding general, Pacific Division, Air Transport Command, to S. V. Hall, regional vice president, United Airlines, Pacific Operations, letter, subject: Proposed Agreement for Civilian Augmentation of ATC, ACS, and Weather Service in the Pacific Area by UAL, 18 April 1946; Brig Gen William McKee, chief of staff, Air Transport Command, to acting chief, Organization Division, A-3, Headquarters Army Air Forces, letter, subject: ATC Personnel Requirements, Peacetime Air Force, 3 June 1946.

15. Army Air Forces (AAF) Regulation 20–44, *Air Transport Command,* 18 October 1946.

16. Ibid.

17. Maj Gen Robert Webster, commanding general, Air Transport Command, to commanding general, Army Air Forces, letter, subject: Mission of the Air Transport Command, 12 December 1946.

18. Ibid.

19. Ibid.

20. Maj Gen Robert Webster, commanding general, Air Transport Command, "ATC Geared to Supply of New Triphibious Army," an article presumably submitted to the *Army Times* in 1947, in *A Summary of the Activities of the Headquarters Air Transport Service, 1947,* a collection of documents that took the place of the command history for 1947.

21. Maj Thomas Saunders, acting assistant adjutant general, Air Transport Command, to commanding general, Army Air Forces, attention AC/AS-4, letter, subject: Lecture on Air Transport Command for Armed Forces Staff College, 3 January 1947.

22. Memorandum by Maj Gen Robert Webster, commanding general, Air Transport Command, to chiefs of all divisions, Headquarters ATC, subject: Role of the Air Transport Command, 17 January 1947.

23. Maj Gen Robert Webster, commanding general, Air Transport Command, to commanding general, Army Air Forces, letter, subject: Suggested Army Air Forces Policy Affecting Air Transport, 3 February 1947.

24. Ibid.

25. Ibid.

26. Brig Gen Bryant Boatner, deputy chief of staff, Headquarters Army Air Forces, to commanding general, Air Transport Command, letter, subject: Suggested Army Air Forces Policy Affecting Air Transport, 3 March 1947. For ATC's reaction to this letter see memorandum by Col Jack Hickman, chief, Long-Range Plans, Headquarters Air Transport Command, to chief of staff, subject: Suggested Army Air Forces Policy Affecting Air Transport, 17 March 1947.

27. Maj Gen William Tunner, commanding general, Atlantic Division, Air Transport Command, to commanding general, Air Transport Command, letter, subject: Reorganization of Air Transport Command, 22 February 1947.

AIRLIFT DOCTRINE

28. Maj Gen Robert Harper, commanding general, Air Transport Command, "The Air Transport Command and its Relationship with United States Civil Aviation, Strategic Air Transportation" (unpublished study, ca. 1946), in *A Summary of the Activities of the Headquarters Air Transport Service 1947*.
29. Ibid.
30. Ibid.
31. Ibid.
32. Col John Davies, deputy commander, Air Transport Command, to Maj Gen William Tunner, commanding general, Atlantic Division, Air Transport Command, and Brig Gen Bob Nowland, commanding general, Pacific Division, Air Transport Command, letter, 27 October 1947.
33. Ibid.
34. Air Force Regulation (AFR) 20-44, *Air Transport Command*, 19 December 1947.
35. History, Military Air Transport Service, 1948, 1-5.
36. Memorandum by Lt Gen Harold George, commanding general, Air Transport Command, to assistant secretary of war for air, subject: Consolidation of Services of Army Air Forces Transport Command and Naval Air Transport Service, 6 June 1946.
37. Executive Order 877, Functions of the Armed Forces, 26 July 1947, in Alice Cole et al., eds., *The Department of Defense Documents on Establishment and Organization, 1944-1978* (Washington, D.C.: Office of the Secretary of Defense, 1968), 269; for a discussion of the events surrounding the postwar organization of the armed services see Futrell, *Ideas, Concepts, Doctrine*, 95-100.
38. History, Military Air Transport Service, 1948, 10.
39. Memorandum by Secretary of Defense James Forrestal, to the secretaries of the Army, Navy, Air Force, and the Joint Chiefs of Staff, 15 January 1948; memorandum by Secretary of Defense James Forrestal, the secretaries of the Navy and Air Force, 17 January 1948; memorandum by Secretary of Defense James Forrestal, to the secretaries of the Army, Navy, Air Force, and the Joint Chiefs of Staff, 4 February 1948.
40. History, Military Air Transport Service, 1948, 18-19.
41. Memorandum by Secretary of Defense James Forrestal, to the secretaries of the Army, Navy, Air Force, and the Joint Chiefs of Staff, subject: Organization and Mission of Military Air Transport Service (MATS), 3 May 1946.
42. Futrell, *Ideas, Concepts, Doctrine*, 100; History, Military Air Transport Service, 1948, 37-38; memorandum by Maj Gen Robert Harper, commanding general, Military Air Transport Service, to Mr Symington, 28 January 1948.
43. Maj Gen William Tunner, commander in chief, Combined Airlift Task Force, *A Report on the Airlift Berlin Mission: The Operational and Internal Aspects of the Advance Elements*, 30 August 1949.
44. Gen A. C. Wedemeyer, to Col Nicholas Pasti, letter, 21 January 1974.
45. Futrell, *Ideas, Concepts, Doctrine*, 121.
46. For example, see W. Phillips Davison, *The Berlin Blockade: A Study in Cold War Politics* (Santa Monica: The Rand Corporation, 1958); "A Special Study of Operations Vittles," *Aviation Operations*, vol. 11, no. 5 (April 1949); Lt Gen William Tunner, *Over the Hump* (New York: Duell, Sloan, and Pearce, 1964); and Mark W. Magnan, "The Berlin Blockades—A Discussion of the Factors in Influencing the Decisions to Use the Berlin Airlift" (MA thesis, George Washington University, 1959).
47. Tunner, *Berlin Mission*.
48. Elizabeth Lay, Historical Division, Headquarters European Command, historical study, *The Berlin Airlift*, 1952, 10.
49. John Warren, draft, USAF Historical Study 134, *Troop Carrier Aviation in USAF, 1945-1955* (Maxwell AFB, Ala.: Research Studies Institute, 1957), 45-46.
50. History, Military Air Transport Service, 1948, 164-66.
51. Lay, *The Berlin Airlift*, 57.
52. History, Military Air Transport Service, 1948, 155.
53. Warren, *Troop Carrier Aviation*, 48-49.

54. Tunner, *Berlin Mission*.
55. Ibid.
56. Warren, *Troop Carrier Aviation*, 45–50.
57. Tunner, *Berlin Mission*.
58. Ibid.; Alfred Goldberg, ed., *A History of the United States Air Force, 1907–1957* (Princeton: D. Van Nostrand Company, Inc., 1958), 239.
59. Tunner, *Berlin Mission;* Goldberg, *History of the USAF*, 236.
60. Goldberg, *History of the USAF*, 236.
61. Tunner, *Berlin Mission;* Goldberg, *History of the USAF*, 241.
62. Tunner, *Berlin Mission*.
63. Lay, *The Berlin Airlift*, 11.
64. Lt Col Jimmie Jay, "Evolution of Airlift Doctrine," Air War College Research Report No. 93, Maxwell AFB, Ala., March 1977, 19–20.
65. Maj Gen Laurence Kuter, "Strategic Air Transport and National Security," *Aero Digest*, ca. 1949, 4.
66. Ibid., 1–3.
67. Ibid., 5–7.
68. Ibid., 9–10.
69. Maj Gen William McKee, assistant vice chief of staff, Headquarters USAF, to commander, Military Air Transport Service, letter, subject: Consolidation of the Military Air Transport of the Armed Services, 23 September 1949, with referenced study by Maj Gen Laurence Kuter attached.
70. Ibid.
71. Ibid.
72. Ibid.
73. Ibid.
74. Ibid.
75. Maj Gen Laurence Kuter, commanding general, Military Air Transport Service, to chief of staff, US Air Force, letter, subject: Consolidation of the Military Air Transport of the Armed Services, 10 July 1950.
76. Ibid.
77. History, Military Air Transport Service, July–December 1950, 4–5.
78. History, Military Air Transport Service, January–June 1950, 10.
79. Ibid., 11.
80. Ibid., 11–13.
81. History, Military Air Transport Service, July–December 1950, 2.
82. Warren, *Troop Carrier Aviation*, 83; Ralph Bald, Jr., USAF Historical Study: 80, *Air Force Participation in Joint Army-Air Force Training Exercises, 1947–1950* (Maxwell AFB, Ala.: Research Studies Institute, 1955), 16.
83. History, Military Air Transport Service, January–June 1950, 86.
84. Warren, *Troop Carrier Aviation*, 83–84; History, Military Air Transport Service, January–June 1950, 89–90.
85. Warren, *Troop Carrier Aviation*, 90–91.
86. Bald, *Training Exercises*, 21; Warren, *Troop Carrier Aviation*, 92–95.
87. Headquarters, Maneuver Command, Exercise Swarmer, "Critique Exercise Swarmer," 5 May 1950, comments by Brig Gen Gerald Higgins, chief umpire, 8.
88. Ibid., 5.
89. Warren, *Troop Carrier Aviation*, 96–99.
90. History, Military Air Transport Service, January–June 1950, 106–07.
91. Warren, *Troop Carrier Aviation*, 87.
92. History, Military Air Transport Service, January–June 1950, 104.

93. "Critique Exercise Swarmer," comments by Maj Gen Robert Lee, commander, Aggressor Forces, 12.
94. Ibid.; comments of Brigadier General Higgins, 7.
95. Warren, *Troop Carrier Aviation*, 100.
96. Bald, *Training Exercises*, 24.
97. "Critique Exercise Swarmer," comments by Brig Gen W. F. Wolfinbarger, commander, Air Task Force Swarmer, 20.
98. Ibid.; comments by Brigadier General Higgins, 7–8.
99. Ibid.; comments of Lt Gen Lauris Norstad, maneuver commander, 25.
100. Robert Frank Futrell, *The United States Air Force in Korea, 1950–1953*, rev. ed. (Washington, D.C.: Office of Air Force History, 1983), 556. See this source 713–17 for an outstanding bibliography concerning the air war in Korea.
101. Ibid., 557.
102. Warren, *Troop Carrier Aviation*, 108.
103. Ibid., 109.
104. Ibid., 110–13.
105. Ibid., 114.
106. Ibid., 114–15.
107. Ibid., 116–18.
108. Ibid.
109. Ibid., 119–22.
110. Ibid., 139.
111. Ibid., 125–37.
112. Ibid., 140–42.
113. Ibid., 143–45.
114. Ibid., 146–59.
115. Ibid., 160–64.
116. Ibid., 171–75.
117. Ibid., 175–79.
118. Ibid., 180–82.
119. Ibid., 182–87.
120. Ibid., 188–204.
121. Futrell, *USAF in Korea*, 563, 566–69.
122. Warren, *Troop Carrier Aviation*, 204.
123. Futrell, *USAF in Korea*, 562.
124. Far East Air Forces, *Report on the Korean War*, vol. 1, 26 March 1954, 30.
125. Warren, *Troop Carrier Aviation*, 205–7.
126. Ibid., 208–9.
127. Goldberg, *History of USAF*, 153.
128. Historical Branch, Intelligence Division, Plans Directorate, Headquarters Military Air Transport Service, *Military Air Transport Service Participation in the Korean Emergency: Pacific Airlift (June–December 1950)*, 1 December 1950, 12.
129. Ibid., 1.
130. Ibid., 12.
131. Goldberg, *History of USAF*, 153.
132. House, Committee on Armed Services, Hearings on National Military Airlift, (1960), statement of Lt Gen William Tunner, commander, Military Air Transport Service.
133. History, Military Air Transport Service, January–June 1951, 1.
134. Ibid., 6.
135. Ibid., 7.
136. Ibid., 825.

137. Ibid.
138. History, Military Air Transport Service, July–December 1951, vol. 1, 5.
139. History, Military Air Transport Service, January–June 1951, vol. 1, 28–37.
140. AFR No. 23–17, *Military Air Transport Service (MATS)*, 26 August 1953, attachment 1.
141. Brig Gen H. A. Craig, assistant chief of staff, operations, commitments, and requirements, Headquarters Army Air Forces, to executive director, Army Air Force Board, letter, subject: Long-Range Study on Airborne Operations, 22 February 1944.
142. Report of the Army Air Forces Board, Long-Range Study of Airborne Operations, Project No. (T)27, 29 April 1944.
143. Brig Gen F. W. Evans, commanding general, I Troop Carrier Command, to commanding general, Army Air Forces, letter, subject: Initial Post-War Air Force, 30 April 1944.
144. Brig Gen H. A. Craig, assistant chief of staff, operations, commitments, and requirements, Headquarters Army Air Forces, to chief of Air Staff, subject: Full-Scale Airphibious Operations, n.d. (annotated as written 13 May 1944). See also History, Headquarters IX Troop Carrier Command, March–April 1945, especially chap. 8: Post-War Troop Carrier Aviation.
145. Brig Gen William Old, commanding general, I Troop Carrier Command, to Maj Gen Laurence Kuter, assistant chief of Air Staff, Plans, letter, 12 September 1944.
146. Brig Gen William Old, commanding general, I Troop Carrier Command, to Lt Gen Barney Giles, chief of Air Staff, letter, 22 September 1944.
147. Maj Gen Laurence Kuter, assistant chief of Air Staff, Plans, to Brig Gen William Old, commanding general, I Troop Carrier Command, letter, 14 October 1944.
148. Brig Gen William Old, commanding general, I Troop Carrier Command to Maj Gen Laurence Kuter, assistant chief of Air Staff, Plans, letter, 7 November 1944.
149. Maj Gen Laurence Kuter, assistant chief of Air Staff, Plans, to Brig Gen William Old, commanding general, I Troop Carrier Command, 20 November 1944.
150. Maj Gen Paul Williams, commanding general, Tactical Air Command, to commanding general, Army Air Forces, letter, subject: Policy on the Responsibilities for Air Transportation, 14 October 1946.
151. Maj Gen E. M. Powers, assistant chief of Air Staff-4, to commanding general, Tactical Air Command, letter, subject: Policy on the Responsibilities for Air Transportation, 28 October 1946.
152. Lt Gen Ira Eaker, deputy commander, Army Air Forces, to commanding general, Tactical Air Command, letter, subject: Policy on the Responsibilities for Air Transportation, 17 February 1947.
153. Ibid.
154. Goldberg, *History of USAF*, 139–40.
155. History, Tactical Air Command, March–December 1946, vol. 1, 17; Maj Gen Elwood Quesada, commanding general, Tactical Air Command; Lt Gen Ira Eaker, deputy commander, Army Air Forces, letter, 31 July 1946.
156. Brig Gen Reuben Hood, Jr., deputy chief of Air Staff, to commanding general, Tactical Air Command, letter, subject: Proposed Plan for Third Air Force (Troop Carrier), 6 August 1946.
157. Lt Gen Lewis Brereton, "The Airborne Army" (Paper delivered to the Air War College, Maxwell AFB, Ala., 19 February 1947), 8.
158. Ibid., 2.
159. Ibid., 11.
160. Ibid.
161. Lt Col Neil Matzger, assistant adjutant general, Headquarters Tactical Air Command, to commanding general, Ninth Air Force, letter, subject: Troop Carrier Prognosis, 25 February 1948.
162. Col William Momyer, chief, Special Projects, Headquarters Tactical Air Command, record and routing sheet, 14 October 1948.
163. Troop Carrier Conference, Pentagon, 22 November 1948, a collection of unsigned and undated staff papers and some official letters, apparently for use by Maj Gen Robert Lee, commander, Tactical Air Command, at a Headquarters USAF conference.

164. Lt Gen Laurence Kuter, commander, Military Air Transport Service, to director of operations, Headquarters USAF, letter, subject: Heavy Troop Carrier Program, 29 June 1951.

165. Maj Gen Robert Douglass, Jr., commanding general, Eighteenth Air Force, to commanding general, Tactical Air Command, letter, subject: Heavy Troop Carrier Program, 28 July 1951; for a discussion of the Tactical Air Command's analysis of the C-124 as a potential troop carrier aircraft, see Col Richard Jones, commander, 62d Troop Carrier Group (Heavy), study, subject: The Requirement for Heavy Troop Carrier Organization in Tactical Aviation, 31 August 1951.

166. Ibid.

167. Ibid.

168. Maj Gen William Tunner, commanding general, Far East Air Forces Combat Cargo Command (Provisional), to Lt Gen Lauris Norstad, vice chief of staff, Headquarters USAF, letter, 28 November 1950.

169. Maj Gen William Tunner, commanding general, Far East Air Forces Combat Cargo Command, to Maj Gen William McKee, assistant vice chief of staff, Headquarters USAF, letter, 26 December 1950.

170. Lt Gen John Cannon, commanding general, Tactical Air Command, to director of Requirements, Headquarters USAF, letter, subject: Troop Carrier Critique, 15 May 1951.

171. Ibid.

172. Ibid.

173. Maj Gen William Tunner, commanding general, 315th Air Division (Combat Cargo), to Lt Gen George Stratemeyer, commanding general, Far East Air Forces, letter, 7 February 1951.

174. Ibid.

175. Ibid.

176. Futrell, *Ideas, Concepts, Doctrine*, 198–99.

177. Ibid., 196–97.

178. Ibid., 199; Col R. I. Goewey, Project Status Sheet, subject: AU Manual—Air Transport Operations, n.d.

179. Evaluation staff, Air War College, Air University, draft Air Force Manual, subject: Air Transport Operation, March 1953, iii.

180. Ibid., 1–2.

181. Ibid., 20.

182. Ibid., 4–6.

183. Ibid., 7–13.

184. Ibid., 23–24.

185. Ibid., 25.

186. AFM 1–3, *Theater Air Operations*, 1 September 1953, 26.

187. Ibid., 26–27.

188. AFM 1–9, *Theater Airlift Operations*, 1 July 1954, 1.

189. Ibid., 2.

190. History, Military Air Transport Service, July–December 1953, vol. 1, narrative, 55.

191. Ibid., 54–57.

192. History, Military Air Transport Service, January–June 1954, vol. 1, narrative, 51.

193. Lt Gen Joseph Smith, commander, Military Air Transport Service, through commander, Strategic Air Command, to chief of staff, US Air Force, letter, subject: Modernization of Air Transportation, 20 December 1954.

194. History, Military Air Transport Service, January–June 1954, 52–53.

195. Lt Gen Joseph Smith, commander, Military Air Transport Service, "Turbine Powered Transports" (Paper presented at the Institute of Aeronautical Sciences, 9 August 1954).

196. Ibid.

197. Smith, through commander, Strategic Air Command, to chief of staff, US Air Force, 20 December 1954.

198. Warren, *Troop Carrier Aviation,* 26–27.
199. History Office, Air Materiel Command, Case History of the C-123 Airplane (26 April 1945–1 September 1951), 5.
200. Warren, *Troop Carrier Aviation,* 30–32.
201. Warren, *Troop Carrier Aviation,* chap. 3 working notes.
202. Goldberg, History of USAF, 145.
203. Headquarters, Tactical Air Command, to director of requirements, Headquarters USAF, letter, subject: Procurement of Medium Troop Carrier Aircraft, 7 November 1952.
204. History, Eighteenth Air Force, January–June 1954, vol. 1, 254–58.
205. Ibid.

CHAPTER 5

The Turbulent Years

In early 1952 Gen Hoyt Vandenberg, Air Force vice chief of staff, told the Air War College class that the Air Force was forced to preposition vital stocks overseas, thus not only engaging in an expensive practice but also committing itself to bases that might not be available when needed. He proposed to solve this dilemma with airlift.

> Airlift on the scale we visualize would make it possible to move logistic support with and as the bombers move. If the bombers are forced to divert to alternate bases, the logistic support would likewise be diverted. Without this type support, the strategic bombing force is neither truly strategic nor potent. To have truly strategic striking forces, logistics must be strategically mobile and flexible as the forces it supports.[1]

Military Air Transport Service (MATS) was to live with this concept for the next eight years.

The Airlift Policy Context

In September of 1953, President Eisenhower directed Robert Murray, Jr., under secretary of commerce for transportation and chairman of the Air Coordinating Committee, to

> undertake a comprehensive review of our aviation policy and prepare a statement of present United States policies in the primary areas of aviation interest, for my consideration and approval. This should be done in consultation with appropriate industry, local government and private aviation groups.[2]

Murray transmitted his report to the president in May of 1954 with the observation that "issues of a strictly military nature have been excluded." The president responded to the report, saying that he would use it as a "guide in future consideration" of air policy issues.[3]

The Air Coordinating Committee Report

The most oft-quoted portion of that report, the one most used by those seeking more government business for the airlines, said "the government should, to the greatest extent practicable, adjust its use of air transportation so as to use existing unutilized capacity of United States air carriers."[4] What the advocates who quoted this passage often ignored was that the military and the post office were singled out in the same report for already making extensive use of commercial air service. They also ignored a sentence from the same paragraph they were quoting which recognized that "a government agency must often base its decision on factors in addition to business economies."[5] These factors, plus the point that the quoted policy statement was in and of itself hazy, got lost in the quest for business.

Dr Frederick Thayer, Jr., offers a particularly lucid critique of the quoted passage:

> The phrase "unutilized capacity" was somewhat ambiguous. Outside groups could interpret it as a call for increased military purchases of charter airlift, and it became a limitless proposition when applied to the supplementals. They stood ready to buy or lease as many transports as possible and, no matter how much business they secured, the next aircraft in line was "unutilized." Even had the term been more explicitly limited to the scheduled companies, moreover, it also would have had limitless connotations. . . . Had the military filled one airplane, another would have been added to the schedule and this one, in turn, merely would add still more "unutilized" capacity.[6]

The Hoover Commission

The advocates of increased business for the civil carriers also relied heavily on the 1955 *Report on Transportation* of the Hoover Commission on Organization of the Executive Branch of the Government. That report was a dual-edged sword for MATS. On one side, the committee fully supported the long-held MATS argument that almost all military airlift should belong to it:

> The Committee recommends that MATS should become, in fact, the real logistics air arm of the Department of Defense by the elimination of separate transport type air activities by other commands, with complete responsibility to all of the services being integrated into the one organization.[7]

The committee was specifically referring to the Navy's Fleet Logistic Air Wings and "Quicktrans," the Air Materiel Command's (AMC) "Log-air" operation, and "all the semi-independent transport type operations now uncorrelated and under the various air commands."[8] On the other side of the sword lay two paragraphs that, when taken together, caused confusion. The first was clear:

> There must be a strong, basic backbone structure of military air transportation, operated and manned by military personnel. Once this basic requirement is provided for within the military establishment by MATS, the additional requirements can then be contracted to civilian organizations.[9]

Unfortunately, for policymakers at least, the very next paragraph—a separately numbered recommendation—was apparently in direct contradiction:

> The Committee recommends that the level of MATS' peacetime operations be limited to that necessary to maintain the minimum war readiness of the command. The peacetime operations of the integrated service should be restricted, and realistically limited, to air transportation of persons and cargo carefully evaluated as to necessity for such transportation, and only after all forms of commercial carriers have handled traffic appropriate and properly assignable to their service. Failure to accomplish this means a continuing and expanding military socialism over all air transportation and extending down into the other forms of commercial transportation.[10]

The DOD's response to the Hoover Commission *Report on Transportation* was a well-reasoned "no":

> The size of nucleus fleets of ships and airplanes which it is desirable to maintain is admittedly a difficult problem. It is further a problem on which the present world situation makes past experience of little help. The far-flung dispersal of our forces, the possibility of a sudden outbreak of limited actions, such as Korea, and the probability that if a major war comes it will come with a lightening-like suddenness, argue in favor of maintaining larger nucleus fleets than have been thought necessary in the past. The Department of Defense knows of no other way of solving this problem than to rely on the judgment of the government officials charged with making the decision on the basis of the advice of our best military leaders. It therefore finds it is unable to go along with recommendations which advocate substantially smaller fleets than the judgment of these officials currently in effect has set.[11]

It took five years of congressional hearings and actions by two presidents to determine both the desirability and reasonableness of this beclouded recommendation.

In a related document, another committee of the Hoover Commission recommended that MATS be operated and organized like a business. MATS should have, it said, a revolving fund; the DOD would set it up with an initial cash grant, after which the airlift customers would pay for the services received. Up until this recommendation went into effect in 1957, MATS had operated with normally appropriated Air Force funds, offering its by-product services free.[12]

Although the Air Force wanted to emphasize the development of and apparently the support of the Strategic Air Command (SAC), the Department of Defense showed a marked interest in tactical air and air defense missions. Project Vista, a study by the California Institute of Technology sponsored by all three service secretaries, looked at problems of ground, not air, warfare, especially as related to western Europe. It recommended, among other things, that the United States have two airborne Army corps by 1954. One would be in the continental United States and the other in Europe. This force would require 400 C-124s and 850 C-123s for transport and support.[13]

President Eisenhower wanted, in its most simplified form, a strong national defense at the least cost. That translated to a heavy reliance on nuclear weapons—at the strategic and tactical levels. This led to extensive debates on whether a true nuclear stalemate with the Soviets could exist and whether a limited war could occur. In May of 1954, Gen Otto P. Weyland, commander of the Tactical Air Command (TAC), suggested that the Communists would not start a brushfire-style war in any area where the United States was prepared to fight effectively. Because tactical air forces were already committed to Europe and the Far East, he recommended formation of a highly mobile tactical air force, stationed in the United States, that could be deployed to meet needs anywhere in the world. It became a reality in July of 1955 as the Nineteenth Air Force.[14]

By 1955, the Army, according to its chief of staff, Gen Matthew Ridgway, had a "paper" strength with very little airlift or sealift mobility to meet President Eisenhower's strategic reserve concept. The Army, he said, had "no adequate mobile-ready force now in being and the actual creation of such a force must compete with increasingly emphasized nuclear-air requirements."[15]

In 1956, Congressman Daniel Flood, concerned about the Army's needs for airlift and the Hoover Commission's observation about MATS, conducted hearings on airlift. During these hearings, he was particularly critical of MATS's use of the C-118s and C-121s. These aircraft were militarized versions of civil aircraft, with reinforced floors and wide doors. Congressman Flood expressed concern that these aircraft were not designated for Army use, had several civil characteristics (galleys and stewardesses), and often carried passengers the civil air carriers could have handled. He wanted, instead, an airplane capable of carrying heavy cargo and Army troops together—presumably for the timely arrival of cohesive fighting units. The resulting Appropriations Committee 1956 report became the first formal expression of congressional interest in the airlift business. The final report ignored the Army question but, nonetheless, addressed the MATS/civil air question:

> The committee recognizes the strategic importance and necessity of a strong MATS type of operation. At the same time, the committee notes that it is apparent that commercial air facilities, including scheduled and nonscheduled airlines, are an essential part of the overall mobilization transport strength of the United States, and as it has been stated by Air Force representatives, will provide a major part of the ability of the Nation to meet the huge demands for transport in the event of a sudden war emergency.
>
> Because of the significant role that the Military Air Transport Service plays in our mobilization, the committee does not desire to set an arbitrary limit on the size of the MATS operation. However, it is the opinion of the committee that the Air Force should give attention to handling its air transport business in such a way as to assist in keeping the nonscheduled and other airlines in a reasonably sound financial and operating position.[16]

The Senate Committee on Appropriations issued a parallel report saying that

> the committee wishes to make it clear that the Department of Defense should, in the future, utilize the services of commercial transportation to the fullest extent possible when it is more economical, and that in evaluating relative costs of transportation, the department should recognize the element of time saved as an important factor.[17]

To emphasize their concerns, the conference committee on the fiscal 1957 DOD appropriations bill, represented by Senator Dennis Chavez and Congressman George Mahon, sent a letter to Secretary of Defense Charles Wilson, reaffirming that the House report represented a "joint expression of the intent and desires of the two Committees on Appropriations."[18] The letter also quoted the 1954 President's Air Coordinating Committee report calling for DOD use of the unutilized capacity of the United States air carriers.

In 1957 the Senate Committee on Appropriations held hearings on the civil airline question and heard an apparently effective series of presentations by the Air Transport Association, a representative of the supplemental airlines; and another airline executive, Senator Stuart Symington, former secretary of the Air Force, led the questioning as the ex officio representative of the Armed Services Committee. The language of the final report elevated the issue to a dispute between the DOD and the Congress:

> In summary we do not feel that sufficient effort has been made by the Department of Defense in the international and overseas field to "adjust its use of air transportation so as to use existing unutilized capacity of United States air carriers." It is the wish of the committee, therefore, that within the 1958 appropriations for operations and maintenance and for military personnel the Defense Department reprogram expenditures for operating MATS and other government-owned transport activities sufficiently to permit the funds so reprogrammed to be applied toward procuring the services of United States civil air carriers to meet as nearly as possible 40 percent of the passenger requirements and 20 percent of the cargo requirements of the Military Air Transport Service.[19]

The House, on the other hand, elected not to enter into the controversy. Part of the reason for this may have been a report prepared by the staff of the House Appropriations Subcommittee on the Department of Defense (DOD), that actually put the issue in fairly good perspective. That staff report spoke of a conviction for the need for a substantial amount of *military* airlift and narrowed the problem "to finding ways to measure and methods to balance the conflicting pressures of minimum-cost economy on one hand versus the maximum use of commercial facilities for military needs on the other hand, while maintaining military power for possible war."[20]

The Single Manager Concept

In August of 1956, in response to the Flood subcommittee hearing, MATS sent a letter to Headquarters USAF suggesting that one of the factors contributing to the rough-going was that "the mission of MATS, as stated, is subject to misinterpretation and misunderstanding."[21] A look at the mission statement reveals the correctness of MATS's position. Air Force Regulation 23-17, *Military Air Transport Service (MATS)*, 26 August 1953, and a December 1955 amendment, were the referenced documents. Attached was a copy of DOD Directive 5160.2, also titled *The Military Air Transport Service (MATS)*, dated 25 June 1952. In these seven pages of dense text there was not one mention of a wartime mission for MATS.[22]

The change MATS proposed was simple enough—it wanted a statement to the effect that MATS's mission was to "meet the approved requirements of the Department of Defense as established by the Joint Chiefs of Staff."[23] The Air Force replied that the whole issue was under study as part of the DOD's decision to supply the single manager concept to airlift. James Douglas, then under secretary of the Air Force, led the Air Force reorganization effort. After some typical bureaucratic wranglings, the DOD did publish a new version of its directive number 5160.2 on 7 December 1956, entitled *Single Manager Assignment for Airlift Service*. The directive designated the secretary of the Air Force as the single manager for airlift service of the entire DOD. It integrated into a "single military agency of the Department of Defense all transport type aircraft engaged in scheduled point-to-point service or aircraft whose operations are susceptible to such scheduling."[24] The overriding purpose of the new organization was to ensure that wartime and D-day airlift requirements were met, giving due regard to commercial airlift and economic peacetime operations. All of MATS's airlift transport aircraft (as well as its technical services), along with all but 20 of the Navy's four-engine Fleet Logistic Air Wings transports, and all heavy troop carrier aircraft were to belong to the single manager organization.[25] In September 1957, final arrangements were completed and approved by DOD for MATS to serve as the Single Manager Operating Agency for Airlift Service, with the commander of MATS designated the executive director. MATS continued as a major command of the Air Force as well.[26]

The Department of Defense settled on the single manager concept because of the "diffusion within the military departments and the reliance placed by the services in wartime on a single source . . . the old MATS . . . for airlift service."[27] The senior decision makers, thanks in part to the airlift controversy, saw the wisdom of earlier MATS arguments that the scattering of many air transport functions throughout the services was both uneconomical *and* strategically unwise. This concentration of authority, however, also gave the civil carriers an easily identified target.

Air Force Transportation Policy

The Air Force responded to the melee with the issuance of its own *Statement of Policies in USAF Transport Resources* in July of 1957. The overriding policy objective was to "acquire and maintain in-being military air transport forces which, when augmented by civil air transport resources, are qualitatively and quantitatively capable of providing the airlift support required for successful implementation of war plans approved by the Joint Chiefs of Staff."[28]

At the most fundamental level, the policy statement said that the primary responsibility of the Air Force was to ensure its own combat effectiveness, including the provision of airlift essential to its combat mobility. At the same time, the Air Force accepted the role as the most proper and appropriate agency for operating the air transport services for the DOD. But, it would discharge the airlift mission *in consonance with* its combat mission and within manpower and budget ceilings. That statement reflected the ambivalent position that airlift existed first to serve the Air Force's needs and that meeting greater DOD requirements would be met as *budgetarily possible*. That, of course, was a recognition of reality. It was also a violation of the basic purpose for the creation of airlift forces, especially considering the potential of airlift to impact favorably on military and political successes. This is not to say that the Air Force does not need a degree of organic airlift, or at least a fair apportionment of the national asset. But to say officially in writing, certainly by implication, that when push comes to shove, the Air Force will take care of its own airlift needs first and others on a catch-as-catch-can basis was imprudent and doctrinally unsound. Air power exists to serve the greater national need, not as an end in itself. If a particular portion of air power meets the needs of a number of different military services, then the question of prioritization among forces, as well as among different weapon systems, is legitimate. A parochial expression, on the other hand, encourages other military services to argue justifiably for organic capability and ultimately opens the door to violation of the concept of the unity of air power.

The Air Force was also willing to stand up to the question of how to use civil airlines in peacetime in an equally assertive manner:

> Peacetime rates of operation, routes flown, and basic aircraft configuration generally will be those required to assume immediate readiness for the war mission. This readiness training for D-day generates, as a by-product an important airlift capability. . . .
>
> In peacetime, the Air Force will use civilian transport resources for those needs which exceed the by-product airlift capability generated by training and exercise of military air transport forces.[29]

The Air Force also committed itself to modernizing its air transport forces, to include inventory reduction as new aircraft were introduced. The battle lines were drawn.

MATS's suggestions concerning a change in mission statement were essentially incorporated in the DOD directive in 1957. Subsequently, the official Air Force mission statement for MATS caught up with reality in early 1958 echoing the DOD position.

The Congressional Context

The January and February 1958 hearings of the House Subcommittee on Military Operations, chaired by Congressman Chet Holifield, were called to review the policies, procedures, and operations of the Department of Defense concerning the transportation of military air cargo and passengers. Congressman Holifield's introductory remarks also noted that "organizations and individuals who represent the commercial air carriers have petitioned this subcommittee to make an inquiry into the MATS operations."[30] Additionally, the House subcommittee was interested in the controversy surrounding the Senate Appropriations Committee directive that MATS should contract to commercial carriers 40 percent of its passenger and 20 percent of its cargo business.

The Holifield Subcommittee: 1958

There are many ways to view this series of hearings, but the most productive mechanism is to view them as a doctrinal debate. The civil air carriers proposed a new way of thinking about airlift—regardless of their motives. The Department of Defense essentially, but not completely, defended the status quo approach to airlift. The status quo was itself in a state of flux. The Air Force had only recently been designated the DOD's single manager for airlift, with MATS as the executive agent. The airlift industrial fund was in the process of implementation; MATS had just received TAC's C-124s, the C-133s were just coming on board, and the C-54s were being retired. The civil air carriers were in the midst of converting all their passenger fleets to jets and were experiencing severe economic troubles.

In a very real sense this was a debate between conflicting doctrinal systems. The ultimate criteria for determining who won was agreed upon by all involved—what was best for national defense. The congressional committee served as the judge in this debate. It was, after all is said and done, fairly good at this particular job. The Holifield subcommittee let the airlines open the debate with the testimony of Stuart G. Tipton, president of the Air Transport Association of America, commonly called the ATA.

The ATA Position. Tipton presented a well-structured concept for a "national airlift program."[31] It had three objectives. First, the ATA suggested an in-being national airlift (combined military and civil) capable of meeting the needs of the critical days after D-day. Second, Tipton suggested a greater reliance on the civil air industry in order to assure an expanded airlift capability at a reduced cost. Finally, believing that airlift requirements would continue to grow, he argued for a constant addition to and modernization of the national air fleet. Here his position was particularly important: "One certain way of further expanding the civil airlines capability to support military operations in wartime would be for the Department of Defense to make greater use of the civil carriers in peacetime."[32] The consequence of such a system, he observed, was that as the

> carriers are used more in peacetime, they become ready to do a larger part of the D-day job ... MATS can be phased down in size as greater reliance is placed upon the civil carriers. This will result in decreased requirements for capital investment by the government in transport aircraft.[33]

There was, then, a proposal that placed great reliance on civil sector aircraft in both peace and war, and that, by preference and policy, would take advantage of the economies involved to build a powerful fleet of commercially owned and operated transport aircraft that would carry the majority of cargo and passengers the DOD needed moved by air. This commercial fleet, spurred by the peacetime demands for airlift, would be trained to meet its wartime mission and would consist of the most modern aircraft possible. To execute this doctrine, the airlines proposed a coordinated national program implemented in an eight-step plan, subject to review every six months.[34]

Step one required the DOD to determine military wartime requirements with some unspecified safeguard to preclude inflation of military needs. It would also break the cargo down into light, heavy, outsize (very large or exceptionally heavy), and passenger categories. The outsize cargo was, by definition, the only cargo civil carriers were not equipped to carry.

Step two called for the Civil Aeronautics Board (CAB), in consultation with the Department of State, to determine the wartime requirements for civil commercial operations, both domestic and international.

In step three, the two requirements would be added together and the civil-carrier capability subtracted. This yielded that portion of the deficit the civil carriers could not produce.

In step four, the proposal said that military aircraft to meet the deficit from step three would be retained by the Air Force.

Step five asked the DOD to determine its peacetime airlift requirements as far into the future as practical.

For step six, the commercial carriers would be invited to move the traffic in step five.

Step seven called for the MATS transport fleet (from step four) to be held in a state of constant readiness if all the peacetime airlift could be accommodated by the civil airlines.

AIRLIFT DOCTRINE

On the other hand, step eight would have the Air Force lease its MATS aircraft to civil operators if it could not otherwise meet the demands of step five.

During elaborating testimony, the proposal's inner workings, and thus doctrinal implications, became clearer. The proposal suggested limiting the military planes to carrying only the cargo that specifically required military aircraft. If anything could go on Civil Reserve Air Fleet (CRAF) aircraft, it should go there first because (according to Tipton) there were in 1958 twice as many CRAF-eligible airplanes available as the DOD actually called for under the CRAF plan. Also, because the ATA predicted that by 1961 the $2.5 billion worth of additional equipment on order would provide four times the current CRAF capacity, huge portions of the wartime airlift requirements would presumably be met by CRAF aircraft.[35]

The theoretical result of this numerical exercise could reach a point where there would be no overall tonnage or passenger deficit in step four, hence, "theoretically no need for any MATS fleet."[36] The ATA, however, noted that

> the most efficient and effective way to build up the strongest possible total national airlift capability is for MATS transport operations to be concentrated in those fields which require specialized transport aircraft for the outsize and exceptionally heavy pieces, unusual security precautions, a direct close working relationship with tactical combat units which, for economic reasons, cannot be handled by civil carriers.[37]

This provision would allow for a nucleus MATS airlift force capable of expanding during wartime.

The Military Response. Presentations by DOD, Air Force, and MATS witnesses to Congressman Chet Holifield's subcommittee were not as fully structured as the ATA presentation, but a doctrine of sorts is ascertainable nonetheless. The DOD designated Dudley Sharp, assistant secretary of the Air Force, Materiel, as its lead representative. He presented four objectives for the military air transport force, which actually served as a doctrinal statement of sorts:

> (a) To acquire and maintain in being, military air transport forces which, when augmented by civil air transport resources, are qualitatively and quantitatively capable of providing the airlift support required for successful implementation of war plans approved by the Joint Chiefs of Staff.
>
> (b) To achieve, in those military air transport forces, a state of trained readiness and a peacetime rate of operation which will insure their ability to respond instantly to an emergency and will enable them to carry out their missions at the higher operating rate required by wartime needs.
>
> (c) To utilize military air transport resources in peacetime to defray Department of Defense peacetime airlift requirements—this must be done in the most effective manner compatible with the foregoing objectives.
>
> (d) To utilize augmenting civil air transport resources and services—
>
> > (1) In peacetime to the maximum practicable extent, consistent with requirements and the efficient employment of military resources; and,

> (2) In emergency to the extent that they are available and needed in support of military operations.[38]

As he proceeded through his prepared statement, and in response to follow-up questions, it soon became evident from Sharp's public statements that MATS's primary wartime mission was to support the immediate deployment of SAC forces at either M-day, or (secretly) earlier. MATS forces had to be available almost instantaneously for this mission, and they had to be thoroughly trained for worldwide deployment operations. In order to prepare for these immediate wartime needs, MATS flew on a day-to-day basis, both to achieve individual pilot proficiency and to keep the airlift "system" ready. By this the Air Force leaders meant that the MATS planes needed to fly at a peacetime daily utilization rate as close to forecast wartime needs as economically possible. MATS cited historical evidence to support this principle. "At the beginning of the Berlin airlift," said Brig Gen Albert Wilson, MATS deputy chief of staff for operations, "MATS was operating at approximately 4 hours per day. With priority support, our best effort produced only a 5.5-hour utilization rate at the end of 30 days."[39] The Korean War was equally eye-opening. "At the beginning of the Korean airlift, MATS was manned at 4 hours per day and operating at a utilization rate of only 2.5 hours. At the end of the first 30 days of this operation we attained a utilization rate of only 4.3 hours."[40] It was little wonder, then, that the Air Force wanted MATS operating at a high peacetime rate.

The Air Force also took pains to explain the fundamental underpinning of its peacetime airlift activity—if the airplane would fly anyway, even if empty, then it only made sense to use the cargo and passenger-lift available as a by-product of this training. To do otherwise would likely be the most uneconomic and inefficient course available. The point they were making was that peacetime airlift was performed to train for wartime, not to meet peacetime airlift needs. However, carrying cargo and people in peacetime made more sense than flying aircraft empty and purchasing airlift from the civil carriers.

The military was not at all unmindful of the peacetime needs and wartime contributions that the civil carriers would make. Secretary Sharp made the point emphatically:

> Let me make it very clear that the Air Force must rely on augmentation by the civil air transport industry both in peace and war. I have no doubt that this kind of augmentation will continue to be required in the future. The Air Force favors a sound air transport industry which, operating from a position of economic strength and self-sufficiency, can make a rapid, orderly transition from the peacetime development of trade and commerce, to the rigorous demands of a national emergency.
>
> The Air Force has a clear interest in encouraging the development of the civil air transport industry as a whole, and in continuing the working relationships which now exist between the military and the industry....[41]

Secretary Sharp also pointed out that the Air Force had no doubts that the civil airlines and aircrews would respond in wartime. The Air Force, he said, would reject as unfounded any challenge to the loyalty, patriotism, courage, or professional skill of the civil air industry or its members. Nonetheless, there was a continuing need for an in-being military air transport capability that would handle unique military airlift requirements. The secretary's choice of words on this point was particularly strong:

> There are certain minimum needs ... which, as the basis of timing, experience, availability, readiness and types of equipment, must positively be met by military airlift forces. These are hard-core airlift needs of such crucial importance at the outset of war that reliance for their fulfillment upon anything but a seasoned, properly equipped, disciplined military force such as MATS would be the height of national folly.[42]

Sharp also responded directly to the ATA's proposed "national airlift system." He agreed with the general provisions of steps one, two and five, as these were essentially the mechanisms followed in the status quo to quantify wartime airlift requirements. Steps three, four, six, and eight, which were "based on an idea that any amount and kind of emergency military airlift can be traded off for an equivalent amount of civil airlift," was another matter.[43] Sharp got to the heart of the matter—the ATA proposal would reduce the nation's wartime airlift capability.

> In order for the carriers to run an economic operation on commercial or military business, they must maintain a high utilization rate. A lower utilization rate would mean increased costs. Therefore, carrier aircraft in peacetime uses might replace MATS aircraft, in the total force, at a ratio of 2 for 3, or perhaps 3 for 5. This is because, at the higher utilization rates, fewer aircraft will carry more traffic.
>
> So if we say, for example, that the carriers and MATS start out with 100 aircraft each, or a total of 200, then at some point in time the carriers would have 145 aircraft, and MATS would have 25, or a total of 170. This would represent an unacceptable reduction in the total D-day force. In this connection, I would ask the committee to recall that for an emergency, in addition to the ton-mile requirements per time period, there is a very critical need for aircraft on a trip-by-trip unit basis. It is not likely that Mr Tipton's plan would accommodate this requirement.[44]

The efficiency argument, then, could be turned around against the air carrier. Increasing civil air capability, the secretary argued, was desirable but by no means interchangeable with the type of military airlift provided by MATS. He made a three-part argument to support this critical point. First, uniquely military airlift requirements would not decline in the future. Second, the Joint Chiefs of Staff (JCS) had validated the military forces, augmented by civil aircraft as generally adequate for current needs. Third, the Congress would be kept fully apprised of future changes in Air Force needs.[45]

The Results. There were many other issues discussed in the course of these hearings and eventually many harsh judgments made. The Holifield subcommittee heard nearly 800 pages of testimony and their report noted the toughness of the task at hand:

> Complex questions are posed by this inquiry. The subcommittee will attempt to deal with them on the basis of its best judgment and the available information.
>
> To those military critics who say that the civil air carriers are pursuing a selfish economic interest, and to those civilian critics who say that MATS is engaging in "empire building," the subcommittee rejoins that the issues cannot be so simply disposed. There is an element of truth in both of these aspects, but the larger truth concerns the national defense and the public good. To this larger consideration, the subcommittee report is addressed.[46]

In fact, Congressman Holifield telegraphed his decision-making criteria early in the hearings:

> I think the committee would say that any program that is decided upon should, first, be in the national interest, and, certainly, in deciding upon the program and its implementation, there should be no program adopted that would deter the overall capability on D-day to meet that requirement.
>
> I think we would say no program should be adopted that would deter the military capability on D-day.
>
> And I think we should say that there has to be some type of adjustment in relation to the overall requirement that would not weaken the response of the civilian area on D-day.[47]

The application of that judgment resulted in 22 specific recommendations in the subcommittee's final report. Five were of particular importance.

Recommendation number one called for vigorous steps to modernize the MATS fleet by acquiring "new, large, long-range aircraft of the most modern types as a nucleus for defense capability."[48] The discussion under this item said that MATS was running a scheduled airline for overseas transportation, in effect preempting a "field which should be occupied by the commercial air carriers."[49] The MATS argument that it needed such operations to train for wartime elicited the response that MATS could achieve such training by use of the "transport fleet for handling nonscheduled and emergency traffic, for special requirements beyond the capability of civil carriers and for various technical missions."[50] Testimony by Sharp and several MATS officials that some 83 percent of their peacetime flying hours were for system training and readiness did not ring true. The report's explanatory language was withering:

> If MATS operates a system, it is a system for moving peacetime traffic, not for wartime deployment. MATS has become so preoccupied with peacetime traffic that special exercises in support of SAC or other maneuvers are regarded as interruptions to the "normal flow of training."
>
> Although MATS represents itself as the supporting arm of SAC in war action, and regards its peacetime operations as subserving this end, only about 12 percent of its total flying hours, on the average, is devoted to SAC support. For the most part, MATS "trains" according to traffic routines....
>
> The subcommittee agrees with the comment of the Air Transportation Association that "the testimony of the military leaves a very confused record as to whether MATS flies to train or flies to move traffic."[51]

Air Force arguments to the contrary were brutally turned against them. Sharp's otherwise articulate and effective testimony clinched the congressional attitude: Sharp went further. Even if, for the sake of argument, MATS's training and exercise required only half its present flying time, he believed that the crews and aircraft should still be working to the maximum. In his words:

> I am sure it would be very hard to state that the exact number of hours, the exact minimum hours of training you can have with the MATS fleet and still have it ready—we do know that if we find we can train the MATS fleet in half the number of hours it presently operates—I say if we should find that—it would seem very ridiculous, since we have the fleets and the crews, and the taxpayers have paid for both of them, that we don't use that fleet and those crews to the best advantage of the taxpayer. And we can certainly use those aircraft and their crews much cheaper than we can contract at that level.[52]

The report concluded that the "useful work," in theory a by-product, had become a major end in itself.

Another subcommittee recommendation suggested that MATS "concentrate on outsize and special cargo traffic and technical missions, leaving to the civilian carriers the primary responsibility for the transportation of passengers and the more conventional kinds of military cargo."[53] The DOD concurred in principle with the reservation that it would call on the civil air carriers in peacetime to perform those tasks it likely would perform in wartime, and that the use of the civil carriers did not result in the uneconomic use of the airlift by-product. The DOD also noted that the MATS fleet would be designed primarily to carry cargo but would have built-in capability for conversion to troop carriage when required, in order to provide flexibility.

The Department of Defense and Joint Chiefs of Staff reportedly concurred with the modernization issue, citing plans to retire the C-54 and C-97 and introduce the C-133 to support their position. Both, however, were concerned that a MATS modernization program not be undertaken independent of other military needs. MATS and the Air Force jointly undertook a study to determine airlift needs and settled on the C-130B, plus a substantial number of "swing-tail" jet cargo planes, and continued use of the C-133. MATS also supported an Air Force general operational requirement for a cargo jet to be developed for the 1966–70 time period.[54]

The subcommittee next made three recommendations that revolved around increasing use of civil aircraft in both peace and war. Those recommendations were:

- Establish a full partnership role for CRAF.
- Encourage CRAF to purchase cargo aircraft by giving them a larger share of peacetime business.
- Plan to use the CRAF promptly, rather than the 48 hours then envisioned.[55]

The DOD and MATS stuck to their position that the peacetime operation yielded wartime readiness and that it would be wasteful not to use the by-product airlift. The DOD, nonetheless, noted its intent "consistent with efficient operation of military resources," whatever that really meant, "to improve the present partnership role with civil carriers in moving peacetime traffic, and to contribute to improved war readiness by giving preference to those carriers participating in the CRAF over other civil aircraft."[56] The DOD, however, said that "there is no assurance that cargo traffic diverted from military to commercial aircraft would result in a net increase in total national air cargo capability."[57] None of the military players took issue with the idea of expanding CRAF cargo capability, but they also made clear their position, to varying degrees, that the best way to do so was through a sound civilian market.

The recommendation concerning changing the 48-hour planning factor found no major obstacles. DOD's, JCS's, and MATS's positions all reflected a willingness to use the CRAF airplanes as they became available, with 48 hours being a maximum response time, rather than a minimum. What came through loudly in these responses was the realization that "even with the Civil Reserve Air Fleet assumed to be immediately available on D-day, there would still be a substantial deficit in the combined military-civil capability when compared to the JCS approved airlift requirements for the first 48 hours."[58]

An Evaluation. The constant references in the testimony by military officials, combined with the classified briefings the subcommittee received, convinced the members there was a significant shortfall of cargo airlift for wartime. Their recommendation to modernize MATS was well founded. Their recommendation to improve the CRAF cargo capability was equally well founded. Striking some balance of peacetime spending on civil airlift to stimulate wartime readiness was an eminently reasonable approach. Figuring out how much purely military airlift the nation needed was obviously either a problem the planners had not yet figured out or one the leaders had not yet determined how to articulate. Nor had the military figured out how to explain effectively to an uninitiated audience what comprised an airlift *system*. Their explanations were too readily reduced to questions about how often a pilot needed to land in Paris in peacetime to be ready to do so in wartime. The overwhelming emphasis MATS placed on instant readiness to deploy SAC probably hurt their argument concerning flying airplanes worldwide in peacetime, because it decreased their "instant" availability.

It is clear that the military airlift side of the debate was not well structured or well explained, but there was a clear and present danger in the civil air carrier's position to the continuation of MATS as a viable command. Adoption of the ATA proposal would have meant a significant shrinking of MATS's peacetime size and activity level, with a subsequent decline in wartime capability. As poorly as they defended their positions, the Air Force and MATS officials were correct. They needed an in-being, highly ready military airlift force. Given the absolute choice of which to develop or to continue in-being, the correct answer was MATS. Under a military system, there is absolute control and direction of such a force, in secret if necessary, and therefore no doubts about responsiveness. There are no concerns with disrupting the civil sector of the economy or with strikes and vacation seasons. Airplanes designed to military needs have built-in required capabilities, and crews are fully trained for a variety of missions. Air power does include a strong industrial base and it does include the civil air sector, but it is founded first on a military baseline. It is only after that military baseline is defined, articulated, and secured that air power doctrine should address itself to the military applications of civilian airlines and the like.

The MATS planners apparently knew what they had in mind, but they do not articulate it especially well. They had the opportunity but perhaps had not thought through the implications of their peacetime operations for the context they were facing. They were correct in stating that the CRAF was a vital element in meeting wartime airlift needs. Given the apparent choices, they were equally correct in pointing to its inherent shortfalls. Their arguments should have been much more pointed and self-assured. They needed to prove to the subcommittee, or at least get on the record, that a six-hour-per-day utilization rate was required to meet and *sustain* wartime surge requirements, whether instant SAC deployment was the goal or not. They needed to explain their concept of operating tempo to illustrate why the whole *system* of crews, cargo personnel, mechanics, depots, aerial ports, and command post management structures needed to be in existence and operating at a certain level to meet wartime needs. And, they needed to articulate the uniquely *military* airlift needs that justified a given size of military airlift fleet for wartime needs. It is apparent from reading the recommendations that they succeeded, at least partially, in getting across this last item during the secret executive session.

The Lebanon-Taiwan Crises

In July of 1958, airlift proved itself an important part of US military capabilities. Turmoil in Iraq led Lebanon to seek military assistance from America, and Jordan to ask for similar help from Great Britain. Within 24 hours a battalion of Marines from the Sixth Fleet landed near Beirut. United States Air Forces in Europe (USAFE) and MATS C-124s airlifted Army Task Force Alpha from Rhein-Main Air Base, Germany, to Lebanon, via Turkey, and began providing air logistics support to both US and British forces. On 15 July, the Air Force dispatched elements of its composite air strike force (CASF) to Turkey. The Army forces used 110 C-130s and C-124s to move 3,103 troops and 5,078 tons of cargo. The CASF movement entailed transporting 860 Air Force personnel and 202 tons of cargo into an already established base.[59]

As the Middle East crisis began to resolve itself in mid-August, the Chinese Communists intensified their threats to liberate Taiwan and began a buildup of their air forces opposite the island and initiated an artillery bombardment. One of the Air Force's responses was to send another element of the CASF to Taiwan. The force departed on 29 August and completed the move on 12 September. In addition, MATS moved 12 F-104 Starfighters aboard C-124s. Altogether, 134 MATS and TAC airlifters moved 1,718 people and 1,088 tons of cargo.[60]

Many lessons could be and were drawn from these deployments, but the most obvious one was that responsiveness to global problems required a highly mobile Air Force and an in-being military airlift capability. No civil aircraft were needed for the Lebanon action, but cargo bound for the Pacific backed up at Travis AFB, California, during the Taiwan crisis. MATS sought civil airline bids to assist in the movement of this routine cargo, but this was the height of the vacation business for the airlines and they either bid too high or refused to participate.[61]

The Rivers Special Subcommittee: 1958

In March of 1958 a special subcommittee of the House Committee on Armed Services, under the chairmanship of Congressman L. Mendel Rivers, met to study the Military Air Transport Service. Their study was part of a larger congressional effort to review military basing adequacy. The subcommittee's report was a stinging rebuke to the civil airline industry, other House and Senate committees, and MATS detractors in general. Instead of concluding that MATS was competing with the civil carriers, the report supported the "policy and practice of the military in obtaining the most beneficial use of the airlift generated by MATS's peacetime operation and meeting essential requirements."[62] Nor could military airlift be "expected to subsidize any carrier or class of carrier by the procurement of airlift or other services merely to keep air carriers solvent."[63] Responding to the labeling of

Figure 52. MATS C-124 on the ramp, Beirut, Lebanon, 1958.

MATS as the single largest airline operation in the world, the Armed Services Committee reported itself "astonished and deeply concerned at how few persons with responsible areas [i.e., other congressional committees] are aware of the clear and extensive military need for MATS."[64] These few lines set the slashing tone of the report.

Concerning the alleged ability of the airlines to perform MATS's military missions, for example, the report concluded that "it could as logically be said that bomb bays could be installed in commercial aircraft for delivery of weapons to the target, or commercial trucks be equipped as missile-launching equipment." If anything, the committee appeared ready to reduce the amount of money the DOD spent for commercial airlift.[65]

The report also went to some effort to show that much of what was being called national transportation policy was not. The Hoover Commission Report of 1955—which said that "only after commercial carriers have been utilized to maximum practicable extent, should transportation or service carriers be authorized"—was noted as only one of many recommendations of that commission on which no action was taken.[66] The subcommittee suggested that because this recommendation was not based on full and complete knowledge on the part of the commission's staff of the critical emergency needs for airlift forces, "there was good reason for such lack of action."[67] Nor could many of the reports from both houses of Congress be interpreted as the intent of Congress. "The intent of Congress is normally expressed by legislative means. Congressional will and intent in relation to MATS has been set forth in unmistakably clear terms by means of the legislative action of this committee, as well as by the annual appropriations processes . . . an absolutely incontestable endorsement of MATS by the Congress."[68]

The report, however, was not a blanket endorsement of MATS and the Air Force. For example, it expressed displeasure with the rate and scope of the modernization of MATS:

> Although the Air Force has a program for the replacement of some of those aircraft with more modern turboprop cargo carriers, the rate of replacement appears too slow. Furthermore, there is no plan in existence for the purchase of any modern turbojet transports which appear essential if MATS is to keep pace with the strike forces which it is expected to support in an emergency. The procurement of such aircraft should be given high priority within the Air Force.[69]

The committee had in mind the DC-8, B-707, C-133, and/or C-130B. And, it had in mind 20 to 40 of these within a year as a minimum requirement.[70]

The report did not directly address the Senate-imposed requirement for MATS to contract out 40 percent of its passenger traffic and 20 percent of its contract traffic; but it did note the

> very considerable sums of money which the military services and the Department of Defense expend annually for all forms of commercial airlift. . . . It is impractical for this committee or for any other committee to select an arbitrary percentage of MATS traffic and to direct that it be carried by civil airlines. To do so could force MATS . . . on occasion, to fly its transports empty or with dummy loads in order that the airlines may carry the percentage of traffic specified. Such a procedure would be wasteful of public funds.[71]

The Rivers subcommittee was obviously more susceptible to the arguments and information presented by the military. The members' natural orientation, and subsequently, better understanding of the military issues involved, no doubt played in the decision-making process. More to the point, however, was the fact that they knew a good argument when they heard one.

Maj Gen H. C. Donnelly, assistant deputy chief of staff, Plans and Programs, Headquarters USAF, presented an especially thorough description of the many missions that MATS would be called upon to execute in wartime:

> The justification for the Military Air Transport Service is the same as the justification for any military force and that is to be prepared for war. Similarly, the size of MATS, as is the size of any military force, is determined on the basis of the task to be performed in wartime. . . . The Air Force total wartime airlift requirement represents the airlift which would be required to support the Strategic Air Command, airlift for the deployment of tactical forces and airlift for the support of our worldwide air logistic system. . . . You might find you would be moving some TAC, SAC, Army forces, whatever way war came

about . . . we do have flexible plans. . . . The airlift which will be required to support the strategic offensive is, and will be for some time, the most critical airlift requirement from the standpoint of the time in which the airlift must be provided. . . . Without air transportation, the tactical forces maintained in the United States could only serve as a training base for the tactical forces deployed overseas. With air transportation, these tactical forces constitute a reserve which could be deployed in time to decide the outcome of the air battle in some particular theater of war. . . . We recognize the need for quick reaction and mobility if, with a relatively small force, we are to be able to handle situations short of general war. To avoid expensive multiple deployment of forces and supplies in many potential danger areas, we must provide for air transport of critical men and material in advance of bulk surface shipments. . . . During recent years air transportation has become recognized as a normal part of our air logistic system in both peace and war. . . . The existence of MATS with its worldwide system of bases and routes gives a war planner a framework on which to build both his plans for a major conflict and his contingency plans for military operations in possible situations short of general war.[72]

This may well have been the most comprehensive statement of how the Joint Chiefs of Staff, the Air Force, and MATS viewed the real functions of the airlift system. It reflected a sophisticated concept of operations and visualized a far-ranging mission.

Gen Curtis LeMay, then deputy chief of staff, Headquarters USAF, a military leader highly respected by Congress, also appeared before the Rivers subcommittee. His testimony was particularly timely as it offered him the chance to address the implications of the recent airlift of American forces into Lebanon. His testimony was not only timely, it was also probably the most to-the-point statement Congress heard in 1958:

Our present efforts to preserve peace in the Middle East w... .o not be possible without full military control over the necessary means of transport. Military aircraft [airlift] is an indispensable element of the military establishment in taking these actions. . . . This action was directed prior to a public announcement of United States intentions. Without an effective in-being military air transport force, the Air Force could not have responded in this manner. Rapid deployments such as this one must rely on forces under military control for guaranteed performance. Where the security of the free world is suddenly threatened, we cannot wait for the acquisition of commercial airlift for the most urgent actions. . . . MATS is a vital element of that team. Its tasks and responsibilities cannot be assumed by commercial airlines. There is a primary and overriding requirement for an effective military.[73]

General LeMay also dealt with the "competition" issue, arguing that MATS was in-being to support military forces in an emergency. To prepare for that mission, he said "they must do, in peacetime, daily, the things that they are going to do in an emergency, or they won't be able to do them when the whistle blows."[74] It made little sense, he added, "in flying these planes around empty to get that training. We try to do a little useful work with them, so we haul some cargo and some people that the military establishment requires. . . . I don't think it is fair to the taxpayer to have MATS fly these routes empty to give business to the airlines."[75] It was a short, but powerful, session with General LeMay.

The Holifield Subcommittee: 1959

Congressman Holifield reconvened his subcommittee in May of 1959 to hear testimony on executive action in response to the 1958 recommendations. Testimony by Department of Defense officials, which included no representatives from MATS, indicated a shift on several key points.

This time Perkins McGuire, the assistant secretary of defense for supply and logistics, was the senior representative for the DOD. He took a firm stand in favor of retaining the military airlift capabilities of MATS, including the peacetime movement of people and cargo for wartime readiness and peacetime economies. He also stopped relying on the notion that the support of SAC was a primary consideration in military airlift force sizing. Instead, he argued for a broader approach than previously applied in this forum:

> We must be ready to meet both those requirements that are compressed into the first few days following D-day as well as the continuing need for sustained airlift support in the following days of a general war. In addition we must be prepared to meet the requirements for airlift in a limited war and in the emergencies and crises of a cold war.[76]

This was a much more sophisticated view of the role of the MATS airlift in war and one that put the justification for MATS on a firmer footing. Since the DOD had previously committed itself to also improving relations with and utilization of civil air assets in peace and war, Secretary McGuire was correct in pointing out that the "controversial point is how much of the peacetime load shall MATS move with its own equipment."[77]

The DOD elected to "not seek maximum utilization of military airlift in peacetime."[78] Instead of seeking a six-hour utilization rate, the Air Force would settle for a goal of five hours, the difference being reflected in peacetime civil airlift procurement. Phillip B. Taylor, assistant secretary of the Air Force, Materiel, clarified why the five-hour rate was selected. Noting that the MATS workhorse airplane, the C-124, was obsolescent, he reported that the Air Force was evaluating a replacement aircraft that had to be "capable of carrying both general cargo and vehicles, as well as troops; it must have good loading, takeoff, and landing characteristics and it must operate intercontinentally at a lower ton-mile cost than currently available transports."[79] This, plus the planned acquisition of 50 C-133s, met the modernization goals set forth by the 1958 Holifield subcommittee. It also meant that MATS would have to retire older aircraft or operate at lower utilization rates (or some combination thereof) if additional business were to be available for the civil carriers. The senior decision makers chose modern "rubber-on-the-ramp" at lower utilization rate goals. The utilization rate could be adjusted by retiring additional aircraft; the point was that the capability of MATS (measured in ton-miles) would remain approximately the same. Secretary Taylor, after explaining that the planned MATS capability for wartime was at the acceptable level, made clear that in peacetime "the new policy is to take definite steps to limit the capability of MATS so that in exercising MATS we won't absorb all the military traffic there is."[80]

During the course of the discussions, Secretary McGuire made an important point concerning the number and type of airplanes MATS would eventually have. His testimony reveals that although the DOD was working to meet congressional desires for increased use of civil aircraft, there was a limit:

> I think it is a fallacy to consider . . . that all the planes currently in MATS are going to be wiped out completely and taken over by jets in the immediate future. We are going to have certain types of military missions where conceivably the areas you would have to go into could not handle the biggest jets. We will continue to require different types of aircraft in the military transport fleet. . . . There are a number of factors to be considered. The mission, the conditions under which you carry them out, including airfields and the like. These and other factors influence certainly, the composition of the fleet. If I may demonstrate, in the Lebanon area we had one airfield for practical purposes, to use and we had various types of planes. We may have to come finally to a solution that will be comparable to a long-haul operation, with short-haul distribution in certain types of tactical areas that we come into.[81]

Congressman Holifield followed up on this point later in the hearings to question why the Air Force was buying cargo jets in light of the advertised advantages of turboprop aircraft. His point was that some turboprop manufacturers were claiming low ton-mile operating costs *and* the ability to deliver 32.5 to 37.5 tons of cargo into a 2,500-foot field—which represented 85 percent of the airfields in the free world. Secretary Taylor admitted that

> there is a limit to the number of jet airplanes which MATS could use because the large fields are not always where you want them. There is also a requirement for jets due to their high speed . . . but they must be confined to where you have completely adequate landing facilities. So, there is a balance there, and I would say that no single type would do the complete job.[82]

The administrator for the newly created Federal Aviation Agency, Elwood R. Quesada, also testified at the 1959 hearings. He was a retired Air Force general who had a long and distinguished career in air power. Following his retirement he had been a director for the Lockheed Aircraft Corporation and later the special assistant to the president for aviation. He introduced a conceptual proposal to build an air merchant marine with government-guaranteed loans. Here was yet another doctrinal competitor. He argued that a pure cargo aircraft usable in the civil airlines would stimulate the air cargo market and provide a strong foundation to meet wartime needs. The military basis of his argument was that airlift aircraft would always be low-priority budget items in the Air Force, thus precluding development of truly efficient airplanes. From there, he argued that his concept would allow cargo aircraft development outside this competitive budget arena and still meet both civil and military cargo needs. By this he meant that the vast majority of routine military and civil cargoes had the same characteristics; thus, one airplane type would serve both needs. He then suggested that the

> military cargo fleet should be limited to the so-called "hard-core" requirements, that is, military cargo aircraft used in direct support of the execution of military emergency war plans. It follows that routine cargo support would be provided from outside the military in both peace and war.
>
> This presumes that the military would have guarantees that the national cargo potential, when achieved, would be instantly and wholly responsive to the military needs, on a timely basis.[83]

Because General Quesada was operating under the assumption that some 95 percent of military cargo could routinely be accommodated by a commercially designed aircraft, he was apparently suggesting a substantial cut in the standing MATS fleet.[84] At the conceptual level, at least, the proposal ignored other multiple military factors. It ultimately failed in Congress due to numerous political ramifications.[85]

Fiscal Year 1960 Appropriations Cycle

For fiscal year 1960 the Air Force requested monies to purchase an initial ten jet transports, either the DC-8 or Boeing 707, in military swing-tail configuration. The advantages of such aircraft, the Air Force argued, were many. They were long-range and would thus be less reliant on en route bases in supporting SAC poststrike needs. Their swing tails allowed straight-in cargo loading and unloading for faster cycle time. They also could carry some of the missiles in the military inventory. And, they could deliver Army troops. The proposal ran into a storm of controversy. Some congressmen saw it as an attempt to start an expensive fleet modernization program to the detriment of the airlines. Others criticized the Air Force for not spending funds already allocated and would not listen to Air Force arguments that it delayed purchases to study the alternative aircraft available. The ATA naturally opposed the initiative. Still others wanted money spent on purchasing civil airlift as a way of encouraging aircraft manufacturers and airlines to develop a cheaper alternative to military airlift. Having thus failed in this initial effort, the Air Force requested $50 million in supplemental funds, of which $30 million was for jet engine development. That, too, got bogged down in misunderstanding. Representative Albert Thomas said they needed a new study of airlift needs.[86] The House Report on the Supplemental Appropriations Bill of 1960 drew an unkind, but truthful, picture of the situation, and foreshadowed the future outcome of the debate:

It appears that the Air Transport Association of America is opposed to anything affecting the modernization or strengthening of the Military Air Transport Service. It also appears the Air Force is not ready to purchase new planes, but wants funds instead for further development of the turboprop T-61 engine which it has supported for several years and says requires about $30 million in 1960. To confuse the matter more, the Administrator of the Federal Aviation Agency, who is supporting a program of government-insured loans for commercial carriers, states that these requested funds should be denied; that private industry should develop its own cargo plane, and intimates that the Military Air Transport Service should be on its way out.

It is suggested that any step which weakens or tends to weaken the Military Air Transport Service would be a serious matter. MATS has an important national defense function and must be preserved. It must be modernized, and its costs of operation reduced to a minimum through efficient and economical operation. To be caught in a national emergency without a working unit of MATS would be like not having guns or planes or ammunition under the same circumstances.

It is disturbing that the Air Transport Association actively enters into the MATS picture every year, and on every other phase of aviation that even remotely affects its interests. Civilian aviation has grown by virtue of the generous subsidy it has received from the government. It is now a giant grown fat by government subsidies and high rate charges.[87]

The 1960 Rivers Airlift Subcommittee

When Secretary of the Army Wilber M. Brucker said that Army Chief of Staff Gen Lyman Lemnitzer "was not getting all the cooperation he ought to get from the JCS" for Army airlift needs, Chairman Carl Vinson of the House Committee on Armed Services, appointed a seven-member Airlift Subcommittee the next day.[88] Congressman Rivers headed the special subcommittee. He was directed to

> undertake as promptly as possible a complete inquiry into all aspects of the national airlift including MATS, the CRAF program, other elements of military and civilian aviation pertinent to the subject, the type, number, availability, and adequacy of both aircraft, personnel, and required items of support for a national airlift in support of national defense.[89]

It was a broad charter, and the hearings brought together the many players in the airlift debate. Congressman Rivers began the hearings by noting that both the executive and legislative branches deserved criticism for delay in finding a solution to the important subject of airlift, blaming this situation on previous piecemeal approaches.

The Military Testimony. The special subcommittee covered a variety of issues and discovered a wealth of information in 900 pages of printed testimony. But the core of the hearings, for our purposes, revolved around the presentations by the Army, the Air Force, and the civil airlines. We start with the Army because its testimony reflected the culmination of a long series of arguments the Army made concerning the role of ground forces in the national military strategy. As noted in the previous chapter, the postwar Army developed the concept of strategic deployment by airlift, an incremental step in its air mobility doctrine. The preeminent thinkers in this process were Generals Maxwell Taylor and James Gavin. They were interested in far more than airborne missions originated and executed in the same battlefield area, although that, too, was an important part of their concept. General Gavin said that as early as 1951, the Army asked the Air Force to provide enough airlift for a tactical airborne assault by two and two-thirds divisions *and* also enough to move one division anywhere in the world. In 1956, General Gavin and Maj Gen Earle Wheeler told Senator Symington's Air Power Hearings that the Army needed enough strategic airlift to move simultaneously two divisions (at 5,000 tons per division) to an area with established facilities and 11,000 tons per division to undeveloped areas, plus enough also to move a division within each theater. Indeed, the Army used the 1956 Air Power Hearings as a forum to advocate a flexible response strategy—at direct odds with the administration's general nuclear war orientation. General Wheeler, director of Army plans, and Gen Hamilton Howze, director of Army aviation, said that future land warfare would be characterized by wide dispersal of units, air and ground mobile forces, lethal firepower, and good communications. The Army intended to develop an organic air transport capability on the battlefield but was keenly interested in such Air Force issues as control of the air over the battlefield, strategic deployment, intratheater airlift, and aircraft firepower. General Wheeler reported that Air Force tactical airlift was sufficient for one total division and that the combined MATS/CRAF fleet would not meet requirements for all services during the first 30 days of a general war. Secretary of Defense Charles Wilson told Congress in 1957 that the administration's budget had little money for conventional weapons; "we are depending on atomic weapons for the defense of the nation."[90]

Congressman Daniel Flood said in DOD appropriations hearings in 1956 that the Air Force should have the airlift to move three divisions in 15 days, none in the same direction. Adm Arthur Radford, chairman of the Joint Chiefs of Staff, provided the House Committee on Appropriations a briefing that showed it would take 1,800 C-124s to move one Army division and 30 days' supplies in a 24-hour period. He accused the Army of not understanding the magnitude of moving such a force by air.[91] Army Secretary Wilber M. Brucker told Congress in 1958 that what the Army needed was enough airlift to move the spearhead elements of a two-division force of 5,840 troops and 7,438 tons of equipment. The Army conceded that both sealift and airlift would be required, based on time factors and port availability. It also apparently suggested stockpiling some equipment at overseas locations.[92]

By 1960 the Army's position on flexible response was part of an increasingly influential body of strategic writings that rejected all-out nuclear response as the only or primary response to a worldwide variety of threats. The Rivers subcommittee offered a particularly powerful and appropriate forum to refine the arguments in relation to airlift. Secretary Brucker opened his testimony with the observation that

> Army airlift is not an end in itself. Rather, it is simply a means to an end, the end being the projection of our national military power promptly at the proper time and place anywhere in the world. ... The national policy for the deterrence of war has been fundamental in shaping the philosophy and actions of the Army. It is the Army's view that deterrence must take place at two integrated and concurrent levels of effort. These are the deterrence of general atomic war and the deterrence of limited war.[93]

The Army put its readiness where its philosophy was by creating a Strategic Army Corps (STRAC) of one infantry and two airborne divisions, prepared to move out to any part of the world. But, STRAC needed airlift to be effective.

General Lemnitzer spent a significant portion of his initial testimony illustrating, in as gentlemanly a way as possible, why the JCS's classified presentation on limited war airlift requirements was in error. His basic argument was that the planning scenario, apparently a war in Korea, was a special case where US forces were already deployed, a logistics system already established, and reliable allies already present. But,

> the requirements—even in this special situation—exceed our airlift capabilities during certain periods. Even so, these requirements are far less than those for other possible contingencies which might occur in other areas of the world and so this study is not by itself sufficiently comprehensive to determine the total magnitude of our airlift requirements.[94]

General Lemnitzer's testimony revealed a fully structured concept. He drew attention to the tendency to "regard the requirements of airlift solely from the viewpoint of transporting men, equipment, and supplies to the objective area."[95] He reminded all concerned that this whole movement was to support combat with an enemy. Consequently, he argued, the sequence and arrival rate of the Army forces were equally important. This meant that airlift forces had to be fast, flexible, and of sufficient numbers to move enough Army troops and their supplies and equipment, to deter, respond to, and defeat the enemy. He also pointed out that a given number of aircraft in the inventory did not necessarily mean a fixed level of capability. Such variables as size and tonnage of the forces to be lifted, distances to the objective, required rate of delivery, availability of crews and en route facilities, and utilization rates were factors in determining capabilities. Taking all these factors into consideration, he called for sufficient air transportation to "fly one or two reinforced battle groups with essential combat equipment to any trouble spot in the world, beginning our departure within an hour of the time that the order has been given to move." This initial ground force would need to grow to two divisions within four weeks.[96]

In order to make this system work as effectively as possible, the Army wanted extensive "preallocation" or "predesignation" of airlift. This meant that appropriate Army and Air Force commanders involved would know what specific Army forces required lift, as well as what number and type of aircraft would be needed at what fields. "Experience has proven beyond any doubt that the necessary detailed preplanning can be accomplished satisfactorily only if based on such prior knowledge."[97] The airlift units involved would not be labeled "for Army use only," but rather would be available for other purposes as well. General Lemnitzer also called for additional joint Army-Air Force mobility exercises to refine techniques and plans and to provide the basis for the most effective and timely deployments possible.[98]

Lemnitzer saw the need for airlift as being so great that he recommended the procurement of less than "perfect" airlifter aircraft as an interim measure:

> Ideally, we would like to see new types of aircraft developed and procured which are better tailored to meet our needs than the types now available. However, we cannot afford the delay which this would involve. Consequently, as an immediate measure, we advocate the expedited procurement of additional aircraft from among those types now available. I stress that this is an immediate measure and does not reflect any diminution of Army interest in improved versions of transport and cargo aircraft.[99]

The Air Force also presented evidence of the need for airlift support in a limited war situation. Air Force Maj Gen Hewitt Wheless discussed Air Force movement concepts and requirements, providing details on airlifting the Air Force's composite air strike force (CASF), a "ready-mobile force for rapid deployment to any worldwide objective area," and Army forces to various parts of the war.[100] The thrust of his briefing was that the Air Force needed strategic airlift for the CASF even though it had organic support from TAC-assigned C-130 squadrons, that the Joint Chiefs had considered the strategic airlift needs for deployment of Army forces to Turkey or South Vietnam, and that even with a combined MAC, TAC, and CRAF capability there was still an airlift shortfall for moving just Army forces into an objective area within the desired time. Principal limiting factors of the fleet included flying hours capability and the limits of aircraft handling and servicing capacity at on-load, en route, and off-load airfields. Simultaneous deployments faced the same limitations. The solution to many of these problems, General Wheless said, would be a fleet of modern cargo-type aircraft. Congressman Rivers reviewed the evidence of shortfalls and concluded "this thing is terrible."[101]

The Rivers hearings also reflected a new level of cooperation between the Air Force and the Army. In November 1959, the Tactical Air Command became the sole point of contact for the Air Force with Department of the Army units for all airlift matters related to joint airborne training. In December this concept expanded to include the development and testing of plans for the deployment of Continental Army Command (CONARC) forces. In March of 1960, Air Force Chief of Staff

AIRLIFT DOCTRINE

Gen Thomas White and General Lemnitzer signed an agreement in which the Army would specify the forces and training for a limited-war scenario (over long distances into an austere logistical environment) and the Air Force would attempt to obtain sufficient airlift to meet that scenario. Apparently, the Air Force had sufficient capability to move the forces but, critically, not in the time frame required.[102]

The Rivers hearings gave MATS extensive opportunity to testify, and the command took full advantage to tell its side of the story. Presenting over 200 pages of testimony, MATS told the story of its organization, aircraft, wartime taskings, peacetime training operations, CRAF plans and problems, and modernization needs. A critical resource issue centered around the need for a modern, austere, workhorse cargo aircraft.

> The workhorse airplane will be the backbone of the strategic force. It will fill a requirement in which there exists today a void in both the military and civil inventory. Such an airplane, primarily cargo but with convertible troop seats, can be developed jointly with FAA for both civil and military use. However, the military requirements should be overriding since they are dictated by national security.
>
> The workhorse airplane should be designed as an efficient transport with truck bed height loading and capable of carrying a reasonable payload over intercontinental range. It should have a direct operating cost of approximately 4 cents per ton-mile. Speed is important, but secondary, to utility, range, and productivity.[103]

Furthermore, MATS was willing to "compromise" its needs to the extent that it saw the airlift shortfall as so great as to justify immediate purchase of some off-the-shelf aircraft:

> Past experience indicates that development and production of this type weapon system in operational numbers will require approximately 5 years. This is too long. It goes without saying that all else being equal, we would prefer the full development of a complete weapon system. We need a modern aircraft now and a compromise may be necessary. Such a compromise might be a split buy.
>
> One course of action may be to begin the initial modernization of MATS with modified off-the-shelf procurement which would dovetail with the beginning production of the new aircraft to be developed. . . . When we consider the age and condition of the strategic airlift force, and the job that must be done, we feel immediate action is necessary.[104]

The compromise was built, it is important to note, on the assumption that the workhorse would indeed be developed and procured.

Lt Gen William Tunner, the MATS commander, had figured out even the numbers of aircraft required in the future fleet: 50 C-133s for outsize cargo, 94 off-the-shelf, swing-tail aircraft to support SAC needs, and 188 workhorse aircraft, not counting 5 percent more for annual loss computations, phased in over eight years. The program would replace 447 aircraft and move an Army division and a four-

Figure 53. Lt Gen William Tunner, commander of Military Air Transport Service from July 1958 through May 1960.

wing CASF 300 percent faster than current forces. CRAF would still be required to backfill more routine traffic elsewhere.[105]

The Air Force, represented by Maj Gen Bruce Holloway, director of operational requirements, briefed the subcommittee on the Air Force's position concerning modernizing the MATS fleet. The essence of the program, he said, was that "with the active participation of the FAA [Federal Aviation Administration] and the Army in the establishment of the specifications for this modern cargo aircraft, we hope to enhance the Nation's military and commercial posture through improvement of the overall airlift capability."[106] Because funding limits made it unlikely that more than one such cargo aircraft could be developed, the Air Force was making every effort to meet military requirements and assure an aircraft with a high degree of commercial compatibility. It also would be a state-of-the-art aircraft, in that its development would require no technological breakthrough for production. The Air Force faced three possible courses of action in the development of the modern airlifter:

> (1) Off-the-shelf procurement of either existing cargo aircraft or cargo modified versions of the jet transport aircraft now in operation by both military and civil agencies.
> (2) The procurement of certain projected turboprop aircraft which required a relatively high degree of development funding.
> (3) The pure development of an optimum cargo aircraft.[107]

The Air Force wanted an airplane with a structural payload of between 70,000 to 80,000 pounds, with a minimum payload of 40,000 pounds for nonstop flight across the Atlantic and 20,000 pounds for nonstop across the Pacific. A cruising speed of 440 knots and a 5,000-foot runway capability were also established. The loadability features included truck-bed height and straight-in rear entry, with a minimum cargo envelope 60 feet long, 9 feet high, and 10 feet wide. Finally, the aircraft needed an airdrop capability. The airplane the Air Force was talking about became the C-141.[108]

The Army and Air Force also discussed tactical airlift requirements. The net result of their presentation was that the Army wanted to use C-130s, C-123s, and C-119s in airborne and airlanding operations on a worldwide basis. For strategic deployments, their concept relied on MATS for delivery of forces to some forward location, with tactical airlift units supplying the actual insertion and resupply in combat areas. The Air Force lacked sufficient numbers of the right types of aircraft and counted on using C-124s to fulfill part of the Army's needs. The special subcommittee noted the multiple uses assigned to the C-124 and also raised the question of whether the Air Force was truly being responsive to Army needs. In fact, the specific question of whether tactical airlift ought not to belong to the Army for added responsiveness actually came up. Army officials were quick to point out that the Air Force had been exceptionally responsive to Army needs and that the airplanes belonged with the Air Force, not the Army.[109]

Exercise Big Slam/Puerto Pine. In November of 1958, General Tunner proposed to test MATS's surge and sustain wartime ability *and* to determine if MATS could move a large Army force from the United States to meet some overseas contingency. After intensive negotiations for money, Army forces of sufficient size to test the concepts, and locations for the exercise, Big Slam/Puerto Pine eventually occurred between 14 and 28 March 1960.[110]

The statistics of the operation were, for the times, staggering. It cost $10.6 million, flew 50,496 hours, and moved 29,095 troops and 10,949 tons of cargo in 1,263 sorties. At its peak, there were more than 100 aircraft airborne in the airlift stream at one time. They used 25 million gallons of fuel and involved 32,000 MATS personnel. The operation took half of the MATS transport fleet to support the Army airlift.[111]

The exercise picked up Army forces and equipment at 14 on-load bases and unloaded at Ramey AFB and Roosevelt Roads Naval Station, Puerto Rico. The airlift flow was designed to surge the utilization rate from a peacetime five hours to a proposed seven hours. At the same time, the entire MATS worldwide fleet surged to the same operational tempo. The MATS fleet found that it could surge to the desired rate and desired on-time departure and operational readiness goals but that the system started to grind down at the end of 15 days. MATS accomplished Big Slam/Puerto Pine at a cost of 84-hour work weeks for ground crews; 8 months of detailed planning; massive prepositioning of spares, equipment, and personnel; and crew duty days that ran from 24 (basic) to 35 (augmented) hours. There were no major aircraft accidents, but the aircrews faced some of the worst flying weather ever encountered by MATS's most experienced pilots.[112]

General Tunner used his briefing of the exercise to the Rivers subcommittee to answer MATS's critics. Concerning those who called for a MATS peacetime utilization rate of one to one and one-half hours per day, he noted that MATS needed the ability not only to *surge* but to *sustain* its operations. There is also "no substitute for the training and development of crew coordination," he argued.[113] "This can only be gained by actual extended overwater operations." General Tunner also noted that many critics had neither the knowledge of classified JCS-approved war plans nor the military experience to make these judgments.[114]

MATS and CONARC reached several *joint* conclusions that apparently had significant impact on the subcommittee. They are summarized below:

- The obsolescence of the majority of the MATS fleet seriously limits the size of the Army forces which can be deployed and the timeliness of the deployment.
- The success of the exercise was largely attributable to the close and direct working relationship between the CONARC and MATS forces.
- Similar large-scale mass airlift exercises should be conducted to more distant destinations on a yearly basis.
- Civil airlines should not be directly involved in such exercises.[115]

Figure 54

The essence of the MATS position concerning the exercise was that MATS and the Army did a superb job—they worked hard and long. But, the exercise was really proof of the inadequacy of MATS. As usual, General Tunner was terse: "It took so many airplanes and so much effort to do such a small job."[116]

MATS had one conclusion of its own that reflected both a change in airlift thinking and a critical shortfall in MATS capabilities:

> There is a requirement for MATS to develop within its materiel resources a greater mobility to respond to any emergency airlift requirement. Cellular support elements of varying size and composition to meet varying needs can now be identified, and action has been initiated to improve our mobility.[117]

The Results. The recommendations of the Rivers subcommittee had a far-ranging impact on both military and CRAF airlift. The report began by taking to task the way the Joint Chiefs of Staff arrived at airlift requirements, providing a unique insight into the highly classified process:

> In reaching its position, the Joint Chiefs of Staff had under consideration three assumed military situations:

1. Six months of mobilization followed by 60 days of general war;
2. General war, without warning or prior mobilization, D-day and M-day coinciding; and
3. The resumption of hostilities in Korea under a limited war situation.[118]

The subcommittee rejected the six-month warning scenario as luxurious. Recent experiences in Lebanon and Formosa warned them "to seriously question the validity of this assumption."[119] Using that as a departure point, the final report also noted that the

> only reason that MATS was able to meet the timetable of the strategic airlift requirements of the Joint Chiefs of Staff in support of the Lebanon crisis was because a number of MATS aircraft were airborne in the vicinity of the European theater at the time of need and were thereby able to be immediately diverted from a peacetime mission to the JCS requirement.[120]

The scenario concerning a general war without warning also elicited several critical comments. First, the DOD considered current airlift capability (including assuming the CRAF to be almost immediately effective) as marginally effective, but some segments of the Air Force disagreed. The chief of staff of the Army disagreed; the Navy representative disagreed; and the Marine Corps representative called strategic airlift capability seriously inadequate. Furthermore, the report concluded that the CRAF would not be immediately effective and the JCS plans assumed no airlift attrition. Under the current plans, the subcommittee called strategic airlift capability seriously inadequate. Second, the report reasoned that because some 75 percent of MATS's capability was allocated to SAC and TAC during the first 20 days of the scenario, the Army, Navy, and Marine Corps were almost totally excluded from military airlift, having to rely on the CRAF. The presidentially approved courses of action included tactical deployments as a hard-core requirement for MATS to perform. The report reasoned that the next iteration of JCS plans would show a significant increase in the need for strategic airlift. The subcommittee also raised an eyebrow, after due consideration for the vital importance of the mission, at the almost exclusive preallocation of airlift to Air Force forces to the exclusion of the other services' requirements.[121]

The limited war in the Korea scenario, in addition to being a best-case illustration, had two additional failings according to the report. First, in spite of all the favorable elements and the application of total MATS and CRAF capabilities, the cargo shortages for the Korea scenario were greater than the cargo shortages of general war without warning. Second, this scenario assumed no other limited-war requirements simultaneously elsewhere in the world. The conclusion: "the subcommittee can see no good purpose in further belaboring this point. The facts speak for themselves."[122]

Like just about everyone else who entered the debate, the Rivers subcommittee could not quite get a handle on the right level for MATS's peacetime utilization rate. Even General White, the Air Force chief of staff, did not want to be pinned down too tightly:

> To say exactly five hours is cutting it pretty fine. But it has to be somewhere on the order of a half or somewhat more of the utilization rate we expect of the fleet in an emergency. ... Certainly, to say exactly five hours—it might be five and one-half or it might be four and one-half, but the experience and judgment of the responsible people must be considered. I think there is no substitute for that. ....[123]

The special subcommittee wrestled with the issue, placing great emphasis on the importance of exercising the entire airlift system to prepare for a wartime surge. The suggestion by some civil air carriers that MATS reduce to something like one hour per day was not so subtly dismissed as a quest for more business. Ultimately the committee could arrive at no firm number and relied on General White's formula of not less than half the wartime surge rate.[124]

The subcommittee report reviewed tactical airlift needs. It concluded that there were "serious deficiencies both as to the availability and positioning of tactical aircraft" and recommended the acquisition of additional assault-type modern airlifters to replace the aging C-123.[125] What appeared to concern the subcommittee was that the primary general and limited-war mission of TAC's active duty troop carrier units, as viewed by the Air Force, was to support the movement of fighter and reconnaissance units, and only after completing that deployment would these units be committed to the traditional troop carrier theater missions. There was also concern about the need to physically collocate tactical airlift units in the European and Pacific theaters for immediate availability. The report further noted, as a subtle note of warning perhaps, that the Army did not want organic tactical airlift assuming that the Air Force lived up to its role of providing a pool of adequate size for the Army to perform its mission.[126]

The far-ranging hearings and final report also considered what Congressman Rivers called the "private airlift" of SAC strategic support squadrons, AMC logistic support squadrons, Navy organic airlift, and Marine Corps organic airlift. The subcommittee recommended that the next annual review of such organizations give full consideration to "bringing these operations under centralized control."[127]

The report made some very specific suggestions concerning the CRAF and commercial airlift procurement practices. It wanted legislative authority to call up the CRAF in periods short of general war, contractual arrangements between the companies and workers calling for no strikes during periods so designated by the president, and commitments to produce modern, long-range cargo aircraft. In short, the subcommittee wanted a viable CRAF program that military planners could count on. After hearing a great deal of sometimes conflicting testimony, the subcommittee came to the conclusion that one of the prime, but perhaps unspoken, reasons that the carriers wanted more MATS business was because the competitive bidding process in effect created extremely low rates and thus discouraged many good business practices and voluntary expansion of the cargo fleet. It, therefore, moved to deal incrementally with the problem by making the following recommendations:

> (1) That, to the extent of the congressional set-aside in annual appropriation bills, the procurement of civil augmentation airlift be initially restricted to the participants of CRAF.
> (2) That civil augmentation airlift be procured on an advertised competitive basis.
> (3) That in the event advertised bidding does not result in a rate which is deemed by the procuring agency to be fair and reasonable, both to the government and the bidder, that civil augmentation airlift be procured from CRAF participants on a negotiated basis under the terms of existing law.
> (4) That competitive or negotiated contracts under (2) or (3) above, for such procurement shall be for periods not to exceed 3 years and include standard clauses for termination, etc., as provided in the Armed Services Procurement Regulations and other pertinent directives.
> (5) That any contract negotiated under the foregoing provisions include an option on the part of the government for annual reviews during the full term of the contract, with authority to extend the contract for increments of 1 year throughout the contract term, based on the government's evaluation of the performance of the contractor.
> (6) That the reasonableness of the negotiated rate of each negotiated contract shall be subject to annual review and, at the option of the government, shall be subject to renegotiation.
> (7) In the procurement of civil augmentation airlift from the participants of CRAF, the Commander of MATS, in order to insure maximum CRAF participation and an equitable consideration of all CRAF participants, shall exercise discretion in the award of contracts.
> (8) That civil augmentation airlift requirements which cannot be met under any of the foregoing provisions, shall be procured on an advertised competitive basis from among any bidders who qualify with the bid specifications, without regard to participation in CRAF.[128]

The fact that the promilitary subcommittee made this recommendation signaled a quantum change in thinking about how to encourage and use civil airlift.

The testimony by General White led to a fascinating interchange between the general and Congressman Rivers. Throughout the hearings, the Congressman had made several references to his belief that MATS had been ignored or intentionally treated as a second-class citizen in the resource allocation process of both the DOD and the Air Force. Apparently, he had a specific fix in mind:

> **Mr. Rivers.** Why shouldn't MATS, or whatever it is called in the future, be set up by legislation?
>
> **General White.** Be set up by legislation?
>
> **Mr. Rivers.** As a command.
>
> **General White.** You mean as a specified command or something of that order?
>
> **Mr. Rivers.** Yes.

AIRLIFT DOCTRINE

General White. Well, I can only say that—I don't think it would solve any of the problems. MATS's real problem—and I think it is pretty well established—is that we need modern equipment.

And that is a question of dollars. I don't think it is a question of organization.

Mr. Rivers. Oh, no. No, sir. You don't think if we write an act to say MATS is hereby a command, we are going to stop there, do you?

General White. Well—

Mr. Rivers. We will try to put the responsibility on somebody and stop some of this lip service, you see?

General White. Well, MATS is presently a creature of the Joint Chiefs of Staff.

Mr. Rivers. That is right.

General White. And if you created legislation that took them out of the Joint Chiefs of Staff—I don't know where you would put them, but you get into all sorts of problems.

Mr. Rivers. Now we might require the Chief of the Joint Chiefs of Staff, whomever he may be, to make a report, at such and such a time, on the condition of MATS.

General White. Of course that can be done now.

Mr. Rivers. Well, that isn't done now, though, you see.

General White. Well—

Mr. Rivers. We want to make a man have a little responsibility. I think—I don't know what it would contain, but I believe it would be an improvement on what is going on now.

General White. Well, I can only say, Mr. Chairman, I don't think that is your purpose. It doesn't needle me at all, because MATS is not a creature of the Air Force.

Mr. Rivers. No. That is exactly what I am talking about.

General White. It belongs to the Joint Chiefs of Staff right now.

Mr. Rivers. That is right. MATS is not a creature of the Air Force. And therefore the responsibility for MATS—the people have felt it wasn't their baby.

Mr. Smart hit the nail on its head. He said, "It is the outstanding orphan in the Department of Defense." And I am positive of that. Nobody felt like they ought to— "MATS hauls everybody, so let's let somebody else look out for them."

Now, General, I believe you have heard that statement before.

General White. I have heard it before, Mr. Chairman, but I don't subscribe to it.

Mr. Rivers. You don't subscribe to it.

Well, it might be a good thing if you would. And as future events may point out—

General White. Sir—

Mr. Rivers. If we set up an air command now with the capacities to give us what we need to provide the airlift, maybe we ought to pinpoint some of these things a little better than they have been in the past.

General White. I think you would find difficulty finding any organization that is more interested in flying, more capable of doing the job, or more responsive under present circumstances to the Army's aspirations and requirements, than the Air Force.

Now you can make many changes. But after all, it was the Air Force and the Army that made these agreements and not anybody else.

Mr. Rivers. This is the first time since the MATS has been created, to my knowledge, that the Chief of Staff of the Air Force and the Chief of Staff of the Army have really gotten together on what the Air Force could do for the Army in time of trouble. And I think it is because the two fellows that are at the head of those two jobs happen to be such good friends and can get together and talk things out. But that is because of the character and the makeup of these two individuals. It is not because of the Joint Chiefs of Staff. I think that is the reason for it.[129]

Perhaps Congressman Rivers was not totally off base. The final report called MATS a weapon system that should have a designation more consistent with its mission. MATS, it said, should be redesignated the Military Airlift Command.[130]

In January of 1960, the Department of Defense submitted a budget request for fiscal year 1961 that included $120.4 million for airlift, $70.4 million for 25 C-130Bs, and $50 million for an uncompromised cargo airlifter that could perform either tactical or strategic functions. In the midst of his hearing, Congressman Rivers proposed to the House Appropriations Subcommittee to recommend $50 million for the uncompromised cargo carrier and $335 million for 50 swing-tail C-135s and 50 long-range C-130s (the E model). The House eventually voted the Air Force its originally requested $120.4 million plus $250 million for 50 long-range C-130s and some number of C-135s. Deputy Secretary of Defense Donald A. Quarles asked the Senate to reduce the $250 million to $150 million. The Senate partially complied by cutting back to $190 million, directing that 50 C-130Es come from that sum. In its final version, Congress appropriated $310.8 million and directed the money could not be diverted to other purposes and that the airlifter aircraft procured could not be used for scheduled passenger services. This final figure actually left few funds for the C-135s as the 50 C-130Es would cost $170 million.[131]

The Presidential Context

In the midst of the many attacks on MATS, Assistant Secretary of Defense and former Secretary of the Air Force James Douglas suggested that a special study group of prominent citizens examine the issue. General Tunner reported that he fully supported their effort and personally presented it to new Secretary of the Air Force Dudley Sharp. General Tunner even proposed a list of candidates. In January of 1966, Secretary Sharp asked Gordon Reed, a civilian industrialist with a long record of government service, to head up the study committee. The task the secretary set for the Reed Committee included investigating the best way to contract for commercial airlift, the number of peacetime flying hours required to achieve wartime rates, the dependability of the Air Force Reserves and Air National Guard for backup airlift, the best modernization program for MATS, and any related items the committee wanted to cover. With the issuance of the Presidentially Approved Courses of Action in February, the Reed Committee charter expanded to review those as well.

The Role of MATS in Peace and War: February 1960

The 1958 Holifield subcommittee had buried near the end of its long list of recommendations one that called on the president to direct a new study of civilian policy, using the 1954 Air Coordinating Committee report as a base.[132] In July, President Eisenhower directed the secretary of defense to study the role of MATS in peace and war. The study took a year and a half in the Office of the Assistant Secretary of Defense for Supply and Logistics. General Twining said the JCS made 18 airlift studies during 1958, three of which were "about the size of the New York telephone book." Airlift, he said "has been studied and restudied more than any other single problem we have."[133]

In July of 1958, President Eisenhower directed the secretary of defense to undertake such a study to include a review of possible MATS duplication of commerical enterprises, keeping in mind the military's need for worldwide combat mobility and realistic training, as well as the economic use of the peacetime airlift by-product.[134] In January of 1960, the National Security Council reviewed and approved a draft report, with some modification, submitted by the secretary of defense. The final report, entitled "The Role of Military Air Transport Service in Peace and War," was issued in February 1960.

That report reflected several critical doctrinal issues that showed a great change in thinking about military airlift in only five years. It noted that the size and scope of MATS's peacetime operations were keyed to approved, hard-core military airlift requirements for wartime. Hard-core requirements could be for either general *or* limited war. Included in the definition of hard-core requirements were "nuclear retaliatory forces, the SAC poststrike recovery mission, tactical deployments, movement of missiles, special munitions, etc."[135] The addition of tactical deployments, which meant both Army and Air Force missions, was a fundamental change, serving not only to build up the justification for MATS aircraft, but also recognizing the importance of the Army to national strategy.

Included in the report were nine Presidentially Approved Courses of Action that would shape MATS for the next 20 years. They, in their entirety, were:

> 1. That MATS be equipped and operated in peacetime to insure its capability to meet approved military hard-core requirements in a general war and in situations short of general war, and such other military requirements as cannot be met adequately by commercial carriers on an effective and timely basis.
>
> 2. That the modernization of MATS's hard-core military airlift capability be undertaken in an orderly manner consistent with other military requirements and in keeping with the objectives of paragraph 1 above.
>
> 3. That MATS's routine channel traffic (regularly scheduled, fixed routes) operations be reduced on an orderly basis, consistent with assured commercial airlift capability at reasonable cost, and consistent with economical and efficient use, including realistic training, of the MATS capacity resulting from the provisions of paragraph 1 above.
>
> 4. That as commercial carriers make available modern, economical long-range cargo aircraft and as further orientation of MATS to the hard-core function is effected, increased use should be made of the services of such commercial carriers.
>
> 5. That, with respect to services overseas and to foreign countries, commercial augmentation airlift procurement policies and practices be better adapted to the long-range Department of Defense requirements, so as to encourage and assist in sound economic growth, development, and maintenance of an increased air cargo capability; that there be explored the feasibility of:
>
> (1) Expanding the provisions of paragraph 3 above to apply to other MATS operations in addition to routine channel traffic;
>
> (2) (a) Procuring commercial cargo airlift only from air carriers, as defined in Section 101 (3) of the Federal Aviation Act of 1958, and increasing the amount of such airlift obtained at tariff rates filed with the Civil Aeronautics Board as distinguished from airlift obtained through the practice of advertising for bids;
>
> (b) Requiring that all cargo carried by commercial carriers be so moved;
>
> (3) Entering into longer term contracts for MATS traffic; and
>
> (4) Giving preference in the movement of MATS traffic to those commercial carriers:
>
> (a) Who are effectively committed to the Civil Reserve Air Fleet (CRAF) program;
>
> (b) Whose facilities and equipment are most advantageous to the emergency needs of the Department of Defense; or

(c) Who are demonstrating a willingness and ability to acquire uncompromised cargo aircraft; and that legislation be sought if necessary to permit accomplishment of any of the foregoing considered desirable.

6. That since the development of long-range, economical turbine-powered cargo aircraft is essential to MATS modernization and to long-range evolution of a modern civil cargo fleet, suitable arrangements should be made for Defense and industry participation in the costs of such development.

7. That purchase loan guarantee legislation, if proposed, contain provisions to insure the immediate availability of cargo aircraft covered thereby to meet military and mobilization requirements.

8. That consideration be given to equipping certain Air Force Reserve and Air National Guard units with transport aircraft that might be available from MATS excesses as augmentation forces for MATS in time of emergency.

9. That the role of CRAF be re-examined with the objective of insuring optimum effectiveness and responsiveness of commercial airlift services to the Department of Defense under all conditions.[136]

The rationale supporting each approved action was the same presented by the many witnesses discussed earlier. What is important is that there was now a presidential seal on how to develop and employ strategic airlift forces. Some elements of previous doctrine were validated, others were changed. The airlines would get some level of business but not what they wanted by any means. MATS would henceforth officially have a wartime flavor. Strategic airlift would be modernized and significantly consolidated under a single manager. The Army's flexible response strategy was indirectly validated.

The Reed Committee Report: April 1960

In April 1960 the Reed Committee made eight recommendations, five of which are particularly germane to this study. Number one suggested procuring civil air transportation at tariff rates approved by the CAB (to give them more financial incentives and to get MATS out of the middle of the issue) and also recommended allocating business to civil carriers based on their contributions to CRAF, modernization plans, and financial status.[137]

Recommendation two was that the hard-core requirements of MATS needed reevaluation prior to any permanent size revisions. In particular, "a greater portion of MATS peacetime capacity should be employed in training exercises with the Department of the Army and other tactical units which MATS must deploy in time of emergency." This certainly made more sense than flying around empty, opened up some level of routine lift to the commercials, and provided much needed training to both the Air Force and the Army.[138]

The third major point related to the ever-perplexing problem of MATS's peacetime utilization rate. The Reed Committee recommended one-half of the projected sustained wartime rate. Its analysis noted that MATS needed to be prepared to meet both sortie intensive, quick response missions and a minimum 30-day, worldwide surge requirement. Civil carriers could satisfy passenger requirements; but even when finally capable of carrying a large amount of cargo, the Reed Committee still called for a high state of readiness for MATS.[139]

In terms of the Reserve/Guard question, the Reed Committee said that these factors were generally reliable and could be counted on for four hours per day in an emergency if properly manned and allowed to fly one-half of that rate in peacetime. "Additional excess transport aircraft can be absorbed," said the report, and "the equipping of the National Guard with strategic transports helps to satisfy MATS's wartime missions."[140]

The final Reed Committee recommendation of special note was that MATS should be modernized through procurement of off-the-shelf jet cargo aircraft and the immediate approval of a development program for future airlifters.[141] At the time, MATS had 31 C-133s (total of 50 forecast), 107 C-118s, 56 C-121s, and 256 C-124s—450 large four-engine transports in all. The Reed Committee recommended 50 C-133s, 50 swing-tail jets, and 232 new design (workhorse or otherwise) cargo jets—a total of 332 transport aircraft.[142]

Worldwide Mobility for MATS

Based on its experiences in Big Slam/Puerto Pine and other contingencies, MATS requested an addition to its mission statement to the effect that MATS would "establish and maintain equipment, manpower, and supplies to provide its own worldwide mobility."[143] Lacking an affirmative response in 1960, MATS published its own mobility manual for "planning and conducting contingency operations."[144]

The manual summarized 20 years of airlift experience and represented the institutional shedding of the last vestiges of the airline mentality:

> The Military Air Transport Service is an essential element of the United States military instrument of national power. Therefore, within its functional area it must be capable of supporting the strategy that military or other government agencies evolve to achieve national objectives. All elements of MATS must be prepared to operate in unity with and/or in support of other elements of the Air Force, other military services, other agencies of the government and the forces of the allied nations.
>
> The uncertainty of the time and location of military and associated actions makes it axiomatic that the strategic airlift force and services have worldwide mobility. Experience has forcefully demonstrated this necessity. Mobility allows the force to move from an established base to a new base and operate with minimum delay. Mobility also provides the ability to move essential supporting elements of off-line bases and establish airlift

> operations in a minimum time and with minimum resources. The mobility of the strategic airlift force in turn translates to the mobility for other military forces.
>
> When emergencies develop within the boundaries of the free world, a capability for the swift movement of personnel, supplies, evacuation of United States citizens, and the sick and wounded is required. Airlift forces provide the means by which these functions are accomplished. This often requires the airlift service to operate into bases which may or may not be prepared to support the MATS force.
>
> The airlift and service forces of MATS must maintain a mobile capability to accomplish any task or combination of tasks within the purview of their mission, and within the resources available or made available.[145]

By this point, the MATS mission was universally recognized as supporting SAC, providing airlift for the fighters and bombers of TAC's composite air strike force (CASF), deploying Army and Navy combined forces worldwide, and operating aerial logistics missions to theaters where combat existed or was expected.[146] It was very much the influence of the campaign and election of President John F. Kennedy that hastened and publicized MATS's new mission orientation, but as illustrated, MATS was already headed in this direction.

During his campaign for the presidency, Senator Kennedy attacked the Eisenhower administration for both a missile gap and for unrealistic preparations for limited war.[147] In a book review of B. H. Liddell Hart's *Deterrence or Defense*, Kennedy wrote that "we should take steps to give greater mobility—by air and by sea—to our conventional forces in the Army and Marines."[148] In his first State of the Union address on 30 January 1961, President Kennedy said:

> I have directed prompt attention to increase our airlift capacity. Obtaining additional air transport mobility—and obtaining it now—will better assure the ability of our conventional forces to respond, with discrimination and speed, to any problem at any spot on the globe at any moment's notice. In particular, it will enable us to meet any deliberate effort to avoid our forces by starting limited wars in widely scattered parts of the globe.[149]

In March, President Kennedy announced a new approach to US defense policies that fundamentally aimed at deterring "all wars, general or limited, nuclear or conventional, large or small."[150] In particular, the potential for response to limited wars—especially guerrilla wars—had to be improved. Because of the "great likelihood and seriousness of this threat," President Kennedy emphasized, "we must be prepared to make a substantial contribution in the form of strong, highly mobile forces trained in this type of warfare, some of which must be deployed in forward areas, with a substantial airlift and sealift capacity and prestocked overseas bases."[151] That conventional war strategy essentially survives to this day.

In order to put the new strategy into effect, the DOD requested several changes in the airlift program. It increased procurement of the longer range C-130Es from 50 to 99 (which reflected a deletion of 26 shorter range C-130Bs from the troop carrier program). The DOD also diverted 17 KC-135s on the production line to transport configuration and ordered 13 more—for a total of 30 C-135s (but not swing tail)—for MATS. In defending the new program and answering the question of why there were only small troop strength increases for the Army, new Secretary of Defense Robert McNamara noted that the administration was increasing antiguerrilla forces and that "a major factor affecting the effectiveness of a military force in limited war is mobility. We are proposing a very sizable increase in modern, long-range transport cargo aircraft."[152] The C-130s and C-135s were an interim measure. The C-141 (to be) was the ultimate goal.[153] The MATS history for 1961 reflected MATS's support for this approach. "From the MATS point of view the C-130E could buy the time needed to develop the C-141, and meanwhile fill the gap between capability and requirement for Army airlift."[154]

The official mission statement for the C-141 fully reflected the new flexible response strategy, as well as the great flexibility of the aircraft:

> This aircraft was to provide long-range airlift capability in support of Department of Defense worldwide airlift requirements, to include the global airlift of cargo, troops, military equipment, the aerial delivery of cargo, the paradrop of troops and equipment, and the evacuation of patients. It would also be employed on a worldwide basis to provide airlift for DOD combat forces in connection with war readiness training, cold war, contingency, limited war, and general war requirements in accordance with the priorities established by the Joint Chiefs of Staff.[155]

Secretary McNamara looked at strategic mobility not as an entity in and of itself, but rather as part of the entire defense program. His scheme for rapidly responding to emerging threats was an enduring one:

> 1. Military forces can be deployed in advance to potential trouble spots.
> 2. Equipment and supplies can be pre-positioned in those areas and military personnel moved by airlift when required.
> 3. Equipment and supplies can be stored aboard ships deployed near potential trouble spots and the men airlifted when needed.
> 4. Both men and equipment can be held in a central reserve in the United States and deployed by airlift and sealift as required.[156]

Secretary McNamara recognized the strengths and weaknesses of each element and wanted an appropriate blend of each. In fact, he wanted a balanced defense program; in particular, he said that both airlift and sealift "must be brought into balance with the forces, equipment, and supplies to be deployed."[157] Prepositioning of forces, he noted, provided the fastest response capability and reduced the need for airlift and sealift, but it also introduced a great degree of rigidity in the United States military posture. Central reserves of mobile general purpose forces, ready for immediate deployment, provided maximum flexibility, but required very large airlift and sealift forces. A compromise position, he suggested, was prepositioning equipment and supplies either in land-based or sea-based depots overseas. This still required airlift to move troops to join up with their materiel. Some of the factors to be taken into consideration in a prepositioning decision included loading facility limitations, political restrictions by the host country, and the need to climatize certain types of equipment. "Thus," concluded Secretary McNamara, "we are using a combination of all the methods available to increase our quick reaction capability." Airlift was no longer a second-class citizen; it was part of the DOD mobility strategy.[158]

Lt Gen Joe Kelly, the new MATS commander, put the new role for MATS into clear perspective when he said that the

> increased emphasis on limited war capability, the Presidentially Approved Courses of Action, and the language of MATS modernization legislation all point to a reorientation of MATS activity from a predominately scheduled operation to a posture responsive to the requirement for rapid global deployment of limited war forces as well as the requirements of general war.[159]

Part of this maturation process included a testing of General LeMay's "Clearwater" concept. That idea envisioned a dual forward/rear basing for tactical air wings in which fighter squadrons would main base in the United States and rotate periodically to dispersed bases in Europe. MATS's capabilities played a key role in that concept. The test occurred in October of 1963, when MATS moved 15,000 troops of the 2d Armored Division from Texas to West Germany in 63 hours. The concept was for the troops to "marry up" with equipment already prepositioned in West Germany. Three-fourths of the 440 tons of cargo carried belonged to the TAC CASF that was also involved in the exercise.[160]

The DOD and Air Force were sufficiently convinced of the workability of the concept to transfer three C-130 squadrons from Europe to Ohio in June of 1964.

The eventual Clearwater directive called for consolidating the 1602d Air Transport Wing with the 322d Air Division (AD) (both in Europe) and to place the 322d AD under MATS by 1 April 1964. The commander, 322d AD (MATS) would be dual-hatted, working for both MATS and the commander in chief, United States Air Forces in Europe (CINCUSAFE). The report of the MATS, USAFE, TAC study group, minus the TAC imprimatur, concluded that the consolidation had been smooth and efficient with no indication that it would not continue to work well in the future.[161] The report readily admitted a short trial period—the last quarter of fiscal 1964—but nonetheless suggested that the variety of airlift experiences in this period supported its optimism. For example, during the transition period there was an unusually heavy intratheater period with a 25-percent overfly of programmed flying hours. The 322d planned and executed the airlift phases of two major exercises that included airlanding and airdrop activities.

One observation offered by the report reflecting concern over potential conflicts of interest for a "dual-hatted" 322d AD commander is of particular interest. The

Figure 55. Gen Joe Kelly, commander of Military Air Transport Service from June 1960 through July 1964.

AIRLIFT DOCTRINE

evaluation conference, in rejecting such concerns, offered a singularly pragmatic view of the consolidation concept:

> There is frequently no clearcut demarcation between intertheater and intratheater airlift. Many airlift tasks are, in varying degrees, a mixture of both. The significance of this fact is that the single airlift commander in the theater, because of his dual responsibilities, maintains a dual interest; and, therefore, as a result of his day-to-day management of both inter/intratheater airlift forces, has a more complete picture of the airlift situation. This provides the capability to respond more quickly in some cases to short notice emergency requirements than would be possible under a two commander/split responsibility concept. This overall knowledge also supports greater economy in the employment of resources in instances where duplication can be eliminated by such actions as consolidating airlift requirements, rescheduling missions to permit more effective use of opportune capability, or combining support elements at stations where both MATS and theater aircraft are operating.[162]

The report also made the critical point that because the 322d AD would have to rely on pipeline replenishment for its people in the future, "special care must be exercised by USAF in filling personnel requisitions." In other words, the tactical expertise needed as part of the 322d's management function would have to be met by the personnel system being especially careful to assign experts to the division.

Col Louis Lindsay, TAC's chief airlift expert, nonconcurred with the evaluation group's overall conclusions. His most cogent reasons are noted here:

> The short period of time in which the airlift consolidation has been operating has failed to produce sufficient data or experience upon which to formulate a valid evaluation of the system.

> Adoption of this system could result in serious degradation and misuse in time of war of one of the most essential assets available to the theater commander. The consolidation of strategic and tactical airlift as outlined by the USAFE-MATS agreement (JUNCTION RUN) is fundamentally in opposition to USAF approved doctrine and procedures governing the command and control of military airlift.

> Tactical Air Command is fundamentally opposed to the consolidation of tactical and strategic airlift functions under MATS in the overseas commands because such consolidations will not insure the continuous in-place availability of essential, current tactical air and assault airlift command and staff capabilities. In the past, theater airlift organizations have always been tactically oriented with TAC providing the augmentation for smooth and rapid expansion in emergencies. The assault airlift command, staff, and operating skills, developed in the Tactical Air Command, have regularly rotated into the theater airlift organizations. Similarly, personnel returning from overseas theaters to the Tactical Air Command have provided a continuous flow of data on current assault airlift developments, problems, and special needs worldwide. Without this interchange, the continuous updating of assault airlift tactics, techniques, and procedures will be impaired. The absence of skilled assault airlift personnel in overseas airlift commands will severely limit, if not completely compromise, the capability for rapid expansion in emergencies.

> Since assault airlift, tactical fighter, reconnaissance and Army units are integrated into the basic air/ground fighting team, mutual confidence and common understanding among all of these elements are essential. Therefore, all Air Force forces involved in the combat and combat support roles have been properly grouped in Tactical Air and in the overseas Air Force component commands. Command of these tactical forces has been, and should continue to be, vested in a single tactical command whose first and full-time obligation is to the tactical mission.[163]

The user's opinion—that of USAFE—prevailed, at least in Europe. The experiment continued, notwithstanding Colonel Lindsay's well-articulated position.

Army Aviation

The Army did not stand rhetorically still in its quest not only for a meaningful role for Army forces but also for what it rightly considered a modification to the national military strategy. In so doing, the Army raised considerable concern in the tactical airlift community.

The essence of the debate actually went back to an agreement between the Air Force and the Army, signed in May of 1949, that recognized the Army's need for some organic aviation. That agreement allowed Army fixed-wing aircraft up to 2,500 pounds in weight and helicopters of up to 4,000 pounds. Both services were buying helicopters; the Army had plans to use them to airlift infantry rifle companies; the Air Force planned to use them to support air assaults and battlefield transportation. As the concepts evolved, the Army wanted bigger airframes, but the Air Force objected that this would obviously duplicate an Air Force mission. In October of 1951, Secretary of the Army Frank Pace and Secretary of the Air Force Thomas Finletter attempted to resolve the issue by signing another agreement that omitted weight references but provided for organic Army aviation for combat and logistical functions within an area 60 to 75 miles deep behind the battle line.[164]

Gen Matthew Ridgway, then commander in chief of the United Nations Command in Korea, recommended the Army establish 10 helicopter battalions, each with three companies, for a typical field army. The Army approved four battalions per field army. The Air Force again objected, and the battle resulted in another interservice agreement in November 1952. That agreement limited fixed-wing aircraft to 5,000 pounds but set no weight limit for helicopters. The aircraft were for aerial observation, command control, aeromedical evacuation within the combat zone, miscellaneous other tasks, and "transportation of Army supplies, equipment, personnel and small units within the combat zone."[165] The Air Forces would be responsible for:

a. Airlift of Army supplies, equipment, personnel and units from exterior points to points within the combat zone.

b. Airlift for the evacuation of personnel and materiel from the combat zone.

c. Airlift for the air movement of troops, supplies and equipment in the assault and subsequent phases of airborne operations.

d. Aeromedical evacuation for casualties from the initial point of treatment or point of subsequent hospitalization within the combat zone to points outside of the combat zone; and in airborne operations, the evacuation of all casualties from the objective area until such time as ground link-up is attained.[166]

The combat zone would normally be 50 to 100 miles in depth. This agreement remained in effect until the Vietnam War.

MATS's Future Contribution

The acquisition of the C-130E, and its assignment to MATS, was a compromise position—a "hold-the-fort" effort to meet emerging Army needs for both strategic and tactical mobility, until the C-141 came on line. MATS specifically noted that the C-130E was primarily designed as a troop carrier aircraft but could perform the "entire spectrum of intertheater as well as intratheater airlift missions."[167] MATS emphasized, however, that the C-130E normally could not be considered a long-range, troop-carrying airlift because of its austere design. The C-130 airframe was originally designed and developed for TAC as an assault short-range airlifter to support the Army airdrop mission. It was extremely noisy in the cargo department, was marginally heated, had a disconcerting tendency to irritating vibrations, and lacked latrine and galley arrangements for long flights. On the other hand, it was rugged and, with the pylon-mounted fuel tanks, had sufficient range for unrefueled crossing of the Atlantic and one-stop crossing of the Pacific.[168]

In May of 1962, Headquarters USAF directed MATS to develop day and night airdrop capability for all its C-124 units. In March of 1963, the new MATS mission statement called for all of its units to be trained and equipped in all airlift tasks consistent with aircraft capabilities. "Mobility and flexibility will be inherent in these forces."[169] Formation airdrop entered MATS in a big way. Secretary McNamara extended this concept into a powerful vision of future airlift:

> The distinction between troop carrier and strategic airlift operations based upon differences in equipment will no longer be significant once the C-130Es and C-141s are acquired. Both of these aircraft are suitable for either mission.
>
> Admittedly, the two missions require different training, but there does not seem to be any serious obstacles to cross training the MATS crews. It may also prove desirable to increase the rate of utilization of the troop carrier forces. The measures would greatly increase the flexibility of our transport forces for both missions.

TURBULENT YEARS

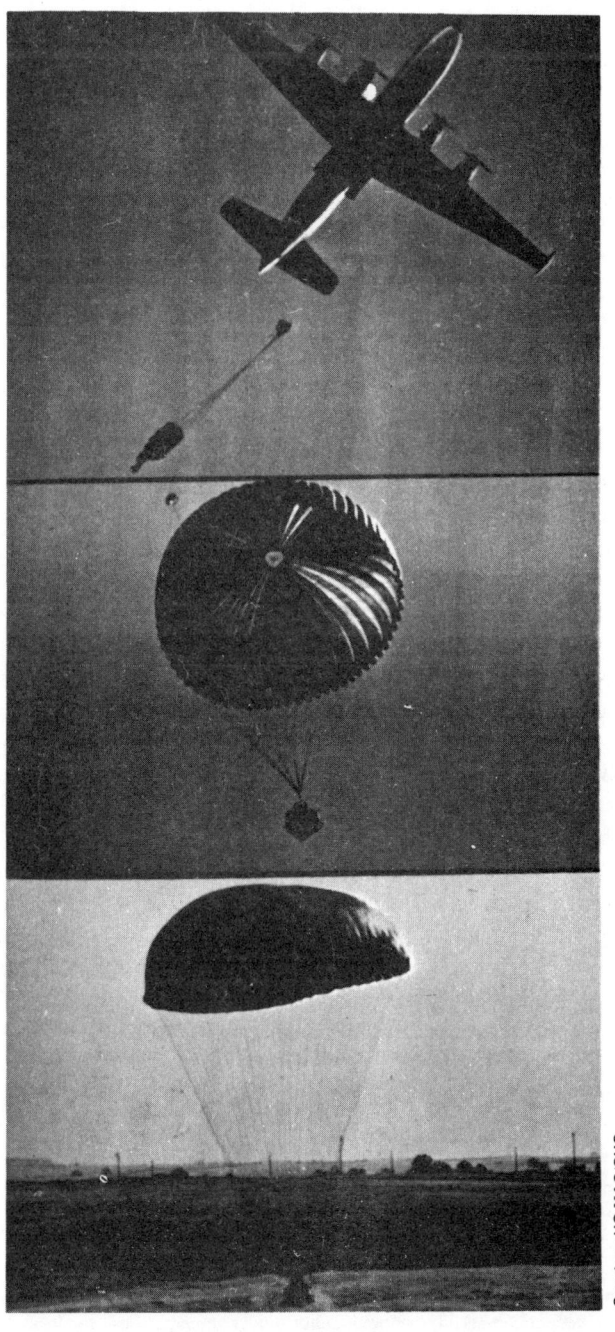

Figure 56. Heavy airdrop.

> Indeed, the C-141 may open up entirely new vistas in troop carrier operations. For example, it might prove to be entirely feasible to load troops and their equipment in the United States and fly them directly to the battle area overseas, instead of moving them by strategic airlift to an overseas assembly point and then loading them and their equipment on troop carriers. Thus, the line of demarcation between the strategic airlift mission and the troop carrier or assault mission may, in time, become less important. This type of operation might require certain improvements in global communications and control and also possibly some changes in organization.[170]

The secretary went on to note that the DOD and Air Force were both studying the issue of how to best organize their force. To complete the single manager concept, the Air Force had moved the Air Force Logistics Command's logistic support squadrons and SAC's strategic support squadrons to MATS. Congressman Rivers submitted legislation in both 1962 and 1963 to rename MATS the Military Airlift Command and make it a specified command under the JCS. The consolidation of all the C-124s into MATS showed Air Staff support for the general concept, but it opposed establishing a specified command as unnecessary.[171]

General LeMay, by then Air Force chief of staff, told the Rivers Special Subcommittee on National Military Airlift in 1963 that "airlift is an essential and invaluable national resource. It will be increasingly important that airlift forces be effectively organized. Their cost and their value to the entire military establishment demand our best management effort."[172] He reported that he had reviewed the airlift organizational question and saw "no compelling reasons to change our present arrangements."[173] His rationale was that the strategic and tactical airlift forces performed clearly different missions. Strategic airlift lent itself to centralized control, whereas assault airlift (the current label for tactical airlift) did not "lend itself to centralized control of the United States, but rather must be capable of complete integration into the command structure exercising control of the battle area."[174] Nonetheless, the Air Force was continuing its study of the issue.

General Kelly, testifying at the same hearing, articulated a different view of airlift. He characterized it as having three phases: deployment, resupply, and assault. He suggested that there was already a central airlift force in that it was neither strategic nor tactical. Theater commanders did need, he admitted, some amount of airlift capability under their operational control; but there was still a need for a central airlift force for training and "all of the things that make for economy of effort under a single airlift command."[175] In a letter to Headquarters USAF, General Kelly drew a somewhat clearer picture of his arguments for centralization of command:

> The consolidation of all long-range deployment aircraft, including the C-130E, under a centralized airlift command would increase responsiveness, produce economies of force and eliminate duplication. Centralization of command would have an additional benefit in permitting the airlift resource to be shifted rapidly to those areas where the need was most apparent. Thus JCS unified/specified commanders would, in reality be afforded a greater assurance of meeting pressing commitments under emergencies in their areas.

> Furthermore, the JCS could commit aircraft capability to joint commanders to satisfy theater requirements under normal operations.[176]

As indicated, the DOD and Air Force were studying the organizational questions about airlift. In April of 1964, Secretary of the Air Force Eugene M. Zuckert proposed a better statement of MATS's mission to make it clearly responsible for all intertheater airlift including both initial deployment and subsequent resupply and logistics mission. TAC airlift would provide augmentation as required, under MATS control for that particular effort. He wanted TAC, on the other hand, to be clearly required to provide short-haul intratheater logistics and assault airlift for the unified commanders. MATS airplanes would be equally available to augment theater forces under the operational control of the theater air commander. The C-130Es would, under this scheme, transfer to TAC as the C-141 came into the Air Force inventory.[177]

The essence of his rejection of the reorganization of airlift forces rested on the assumption that the interchangeability of airlift aircraft and their missions was a temporary phenomenon. The future airlifters would be more specialized for particular missions. He reportedly envisioned high-speed passenger aircraft and outsize cargo haulers in MATS, with tactical airlift relying on vertical takeoff and landing (VTOL) aircraft. Mission and aircraft compatibility were transitory.[178]

In essence, he believed that since MATS was already responsive to the JCS, there remained only the need to make the status quo better, but not necessarily different. He suggested improving movement control procedures, command and control responsiveness, and better support of the Army's training needs.

Both Secretary Zuckert's and General LeMay's positions were opposite that presented by the Concepts Division of the Research Studies Institute (RSI), prepared in late 1961. Maj Gen David Burchinal, director of Air Force plans, tasked RSI to perform this special study noting that future troop carrier and MATS squadrons would have common aircraft that could be used interchangeably for global deployments, aerial logistics, and intratheater airlift missions. He wanted a review undertaken to recommend a future airlift organization that would "establish practices in peacetime which enhance the wartime airlift capability, provide for an appropriate degree of flexibility and centralized control," and assured survival in a general war.[179] Lt Col Edward Wiley's final report recommended a unified airlift command, using a logic exactly opposite the secretary's:

> It has become increasingly apparent through repeated demonstrations that both long-range deployment of combat forces and maneuver of forces during battle can be accomplished by one type of aircraft. As the aeronautical state-of-the-art progresses, greater versatility in aircraft can be expected. One fact emerges clearly, *this airlift resource is clearly a combat force,* it must be constituted, trained, maintained, and operated for employment by and support of the JCS and its combatant commands. It must be completely responsive to the desires of the JCS. . . . The requirement for intratheater tactical airlift must be

recognized. The prerogatives of the theater commander have to be considered; however, since long-range large hold aircraft represent a critical national resource, no part of it can be reserved for the exclusive use of any one command. In the past, it has not been practical to divert heavy or medium four-engine transports from one theater to another. As the speed and range of aircraft are improved, such reassignments during emergencies become feasible. The inherent flexibility of aircraft enhanced by longer range and faster speeds makes it reasonable to divert resources from one theater to another in response to national rather than local priorities. Therefore, it is concluded that combat airlift forces possessing sufficient range and speed for such maneuvers should be centrally controlled. These forces should be operated, maintained, and trained for the employment by and support of theater commanders but they should be subject to recall by the JCS as required for use elsewhere. When such recall is effected, these forces should be capable of complete integration with other elements of the combat airlift force. Such integration can only be insured by central control of training and complete standardization of support and operational functions. . . . In order to establish universal and non-exclusive access to these critical airlift forces for all combat commands, we conclude that a unified combat airlift command headed by a military commander and under the direct control of the JCS should be established. Only in such a command can all of the experience and combat airlift resources be brought together to achieve the most effective utilization of this critical resource.[180]

To solve the obvious theater problem, the unified command would have permanently assigned liaison officers with other unified commands and major airlift users for planning purposes and to serve as part of a combat command headquarters for airlift forces made available to them during contingencies. The report was not absolutely on the mark, but it had the ring of a future organization to it.[181]

Gold Fire I

The election of President Kennedy not only provided a favorable climate for airlift development per se, but also offered the Army the opportunity to test its mobility concepts. Secretary McNamara said he would not place weight limits on the development of Army aviation and in 1962, asked the Army to provide him with an "imaginative study on the future role of Army aviation without regard to traditional military doctrine."[182] The Army appointed Lt Gen Hamilton Howze, commander of the XVIII Airborne Corps, to direct the study, which was completed in August of 1962. Air Force historian Dr Robert Futrell summarized the results of that comprehensive study:

> The Howze Board recommended the organization of two new types of completely airmobile Army units. These would be air assault divisions, each with 459 organic aircraft, and air cavalry combat brigades, each with 316 aircraft. It also stated a requirement for two new types of special purpose Army air units: air transport brigades, each with 134 aircraft, and corps aviation brigades, each with 207 aircraft. The Board visualized that the air assault division would employ air-transportable weapons together with armed helicopters and fixed-wing aircraft as a substitute for conventional ground artillery. The

Figure 57. Low altitude parachute extraction system being tested in Exercise Goldfire I in 1964.

air assault division would also be allotted 24 Mohawk aircraft in order that it might perform a "very close" support mission for its own troops. Possessing a very high degree of tactical mobility, the air assault division would be able to make deep penetrations into enemy territory, to outflank an enemy by moving over inaccessible terrain and executing quick strike delaying actions, or to serve as a highly mobile combat reserve for other more conventional divisions. While the air assault division would probably be able to perform most of the missions expected of airborne divisions, it would be particularly valuable for conflicts outside of Europe. The air cavalry brigade would be equipped with a large number of helicopters, and the brigade would be useful for attacks against an enemy's flanks and rear areas and for attacks against hostile armored penetrations, since it would have large numbers of anti-tank weapons—including missiles—mounted on its helicopters. Each air assault division would be supported by an air transport brigade, which would have 54 helicopters and 80 AC-1 Caribou light transport aircraft. The brigade would pick up cargo delivered by Air Force aircraft and carry it forward to the ground troops. Under this concept the Air Force would provide "wholesale" distribution of cargo and the Army air transport brigade would "retail" the cargo to frontline units.[183]

The Joint Chiefs of Staff recommended in January of 1963 that the recently created US Strike Command (STRICOM) test the Army concepts in conjunction with Air Force airlift capabilities. Secretary McNamara concurred.[184] Gold Fire I, conducted at Fort Leonard Wood, Missouri, in October and November of 1964, was the STRICOM test exercise. The Air Force provided the aircraft for this exercise. The Army held parallel testing of its organic aircraft in a separate test.[185]

The MATS role was to strategically deploy Army forces to centralized locations from which the joint task force's C-130s redeployed the troops and equipment to forward operating strips. Assault airlift liaison officers provided coordination and assistance to Army planners down to battalion level. C-130s used standard assault landings and tested the low-altitude parachute extraction system (LAPES), the parachute low-altitude delivery system (PLADS), and the ground proximity extraction system (GPES). For mobility and aerial resupply, the Army made extensive use of the C-130 as well as Air Force CH-3C and UH-lF helicopters.[186]

The heart of the command control system for airlift was the Airlift Task Force, with its key agency being the Movement Control Center (MCC). When an Army unit wanted resupply or transportation, the request went to the MCC which centrally directed the C-130 and transport helicopters. In emergencies the liaison officers communicated directly to the MCC, with the officially approved request arriving later through Army channels. During the heads-up period, the MCC planners could determine the best vehicle and method for delivery, based on their own experiences and the inputs from the liaison officer.[187]

After reviewing all the "evidence" from the various exercises, Secretary McNamara concluded that the Army should not have its own combat area air forces. The Caribou lost the cost-effectiveness contest with the C-130, and proposed purchases were severely reduced in the 1965 budget.[188] Nonetheless, under the advice of the JCS, McNamara did eventually allow the Army to form the 1st Cavalry Division (Airmobile) in 1965, with some 15,700 men and 434 organic aircraft, including 283 UM-1 Iroquois utility helicopters and 50 CH-47 Chinook transport helicopters. The 1st Cavalry soon left for Vietnam.[189]

New Airlift Aircraft

MATS received the first C-133 in August of 1957. It was originally designed for airlifting such big missiles as the Atlas and Minuteman. Its turboprop restricted airspeed to under 300 knots. At high gross weights it was limited to medium altitudes, had limited range, and needed long runways. On top of that, it had a long record of maintenance and materiel support problems. "As MATS participated more and more with the Army in joint airborne exercises, a need developed to airlift bulky Army equipment."[190] The C-141 would be able to make substantial contributions to the emerging airlift requirements, but it could not lift outsize cargo. MATS was looking for another airlifter, as was the Air Force.

Headquarters USAF issued a specific operational requirement (SOR) in June 1962. MATS coordinated closely with the Army, which wanted rough field landing and takeoff capability and airdrop capability built into the SOR airplane—called the

TURBULENT YEARS

Courtesy HQ MAC/CHO

Figure 58. C-141 rollout.

CX-4. Major aircraft manufacturers—Douglas, Lockheed, and Boeing—were all involved at the time in researching the feasibility of a giant cargo airplane. The Boeing CX-4 study apparently greatly influenced MATS thinking about heavy airlift. The Boeing report argued that the possibility of air transporting "heavy" Army (armored, infantry, and mechanized units) was realistic.[191]

The revised SOR, issued in June 1963, called for a structural capacity of 130,000 to 150,000 pounds (up from an original 100,000) to include carrying wheeled and tracked vehicles. It was to be capable of airdropping cargo and taking off at maximum gross weight from an 8,000-foot runway. At no payload, but with sufficient fuel for a 4,000-mile flight, it was to be capable of takeoff within 4,000 feet. With a payload of 100,000 pounds plus fuel reserves, it was also supposed to be able to land in not more than 4,000 feet. The 4,000 feet would have to include minimally prepared airstrips, thus bringing "MATS transports closer to battle areas than had been the case theretofore."[192] MATS saw this as a way to reduce "support aircraft requirements and eliminate 'middleman' handling both in deployment and resupply."[193] It would reduce maintenance on tracked vehicles by lifting them directly to the objective area. It would reduce the requirement for a complex logistics network to the rear of any combat zone, eliminate dependence on surface ships and railroads to deploy heavy equipment (that is, main battle tanks, bridge units, and the like), reduce the vulnerability of large forces, and cut the requirement for smaller intratheater aircraft. Because of its ability to use support area airfields, it would in effect quadruple the number of usable, existing airfields in the free and contested areas of the world.[194]

On 22 December 1964, Secretary McNamara, after conferring with President Lyndon B. Johnson, announced over nationwide television that the C-5A would be developed. His announcement said that the envisioned 50 airplanes, when combined with the C-141 force, would increase airlift capability by 600 percent by 1970.[195]

The Airlift Heritage of the Turbulent Years

The period 1955–65 was an extremely turbulent one for airlift. The national military strategy evolved from use of massive retaliation to one of flexible response. This evolution greatly changed how senior leaders thought about airlift. By the end of the period, air transportation had become an integral element in devising responses to a complex set of international events.

MATS began, after all is said, as a peacetime airline with a unique wartime mission to support SAC. As the importance of conventional (versus nuclear) responses to military and political threats became the norm, MATS became a combat-oriented organization epitomizing air power—fast, flexible, and centrally controlled. Troop carrier aviators progressed as well. They saw very early the strategic deployment needs of the Army, in addition to its tactical mobility requirements, and attempted to meet those issues head on.

The relationship between civil and military airlift also evolved. After the dust settled from the acrimonious debate over the proper role of the civilian carriers both in peace and war, a more realistic and balanced approach emerged. The uniquely military requirements for MATS overshadowed many of the self-serving civil air arguments and, in a very real sense, made many of their concepts obsolete. There can be no doubt that the CRAF airlift force would have made a genuine contribution in a large war, as it did later in Vietnam. Nor is there doubt that the government needed to develop policies to encourage the sustainment of long-range civil cargo and passenger capabilities. Nonetheless, at bottom, the 1958 ATA proposal would have done the nation a grave disservice.

The doctrine that emerged from the period may be summarized as follows:

1. Airlift is a critical element of the national military strategy. It provides speed and flexibility in a complex world.
2. The distinctions between strategic and tactical airlift are blurring. A revolutionary approach to testing consolidation is desirable.
3. Military airlift has several unique roles to perform in contingencies and wartime that absolutely demand an in-being, properly trained, highly responsive system that civil air carriers cannot provide.
4. Military airlift aircraft will be designed to perform a variety of missions but will not be primarily designed as passenger aircraft.

5. Civil air carriers make a vital contribution to airlift needs in that they can fill in on routine missions for MATS forces diverted to other activities, they provide a large portion of wartime passenger capability, and they make a significant impact on bulk cargo-carrying wartime missions.

Courtesy HQ MAC/CHO

Figure 59. MATS C-118, C-124, and C-97 (front to rear).

AIRLIFT DOCTRINE

Courtesy HQMAC/CHO

Figure 60. MATS C-133.

Courtesy HQMAC/CHO

Figure 61. MATS C-130.

Figure 62. MATS C-135.

NOTES

1. Robert Frank Futrell, *Ideas, Concepts, Doctrine: A History of Basi Thinking in the United States Air Force 1907–1964* (Maxwell AFB, Ala.: Air University, 1974), 151.
2. Air Coordinating Committee, *Civil Air Policy* (Washington, D.C.: Government Printing Office, May 1954), II.
3. Ibid., III.
4. Ibid., 17.
5. Ibid.
6. Frederick C. Thayer, Jr., *Air Transport Policy and National Security: A Political, Economic, and Military Analysis* (Chapel Hill, N.C.: University of North Carolina Press, 1965), 130.
7. Commission on Organization of the Executive Branch of Government (Hoover Commission), Committee on Business Organization for the Department of Defense, Subcommittee on Transportation, *Report on Transportation* (Washington, D.C.: Government Printing Office, March 1955), 295.
8. Ibid.
9. Ibid.
10. Ibid.
11. House, Committee on Government Operations, Subcommittee on Military Operations, *Military Air Transportation*, 85th Cong., 2d sess., 1958, statement of Earl B. Smith, director for transportation, communications, and petroleum policy, Office of the Assistant Secretary of Defense (Supply and Logistics), 363.
12. Thayer, *Air Transport Policy*, 130–31.

AIRLIFT DOCTRINE

13. Futrell, *Ideas, Concepts, Doctrine*, 167.
14. Ibid., 225–26.
15. Ibid., 228.
16. House, Committee on Government Operations, House Report No. 2011: *Military Air Transportation*, 85th Cong., 2d sess. (Washington, D.C.: Government Printing Office, 1958), 38–39, quoting *House Report No. 2104*, 84th Cong., 3 May 1956.
17. Ibid., 39, quoting *Senate Report No. 2260*, 84th Cong., 18 June 1956.
18. Ibid., 39–40, quoting Senator Dennis Chavez, chairman, Subcommittee on Department of Defense Appropriations, and Congressman George Mahon, chairman, Subcommittee on Department of Defense Appropriations, letter, to Secretary of Defense Charles Wilson, ca. 1956.
19. Ibid., 41–42, quoting *Senate Report No. 543*, 85th Cong., 28 June 1957.
20. Ibid., 40–41, quoting report of the the House Appropriations Subcommittee on the Department of Defense staff inquiry into Military Air Transport Service (MATS) activities, January 1957.
21. History, Military Air Transport Service, July–December 1956, 1:1.
22. Air Force Regulation (AFR) 23–17, *Military Air Transport Service (MATS)*, 26 August 1953.
23. History, Military Air Transport Service, July–December 1956, 1.
24. Department of Defense Directive No. 5160.2, *Single Manager Assignment for Airlift Service*, 7 December 1956; see History, Military Air Transport Service, January–June 1958, 1:166–69, for discussion of the Airlift Service Industrial Fund; see History, Military Air Transport Service, January–June 1957, 1:90–100, for a thorough history of the single manager concept for airlift.
25. Ibid.
26. Ibid.
27. Air Transportation Division, Director for Transportation Policy, assistant secretary of defense (Supply and Logistics), report, subject: The Role of Military Air Transport Service [MATS] in Peace and War, February 1960, 7.
28. AFR 76–19, *Air Transportation: Statement of Policies in USAF Transport Resources*, 24 July 1957.
29. Ibid.
30. House, Committee on Government Operations, *Military Air Transportation*, 1958, 1, statement of Congressman Chet Holifield, chairman.
31. Ibid., 3–11, statement of Stuart Tipton, president, Air Transport Association of America.
32. Ibid., 5.
33. Ibid.
34. Ibid., 5–6.
35. Ibid., 9–10.
36. Ibid., 10.
37. Ibid.
38. Ibid., 497, statement of Dudley Sharp, assistant secretary of the Air Force (Materiel).
39. Ibid., 512, statement of Brig Gen Albert Wilson, deputy chief of staff, Operations, Headquarters Military Air Transport Service.
40. Ibid.
41. Ibid., 501, Dudley Sharp.
42. Ibid., 503.
43. Ibid., 506.
44. Ibid., 507.
45. Ibid.
46. House, Committee on Government Operations, *House Report No. 2011*, 1950, 4.
47. House, Committee on Government Operations, *Military Air Transportation*, 1958, 388–89, Holifield.
48. House, Committee on Government Operations, *House Report No. 2011*, 1958, 5.
49. Ibid.
50. Ibid.
51. Ibid., 90.
52. Ibid., 92.
53. Ibid., 5–6.

54. Col Andrew Lerche, assistant deputy chief of staff, Plans, Headquarters Military Air Transport Service, disposition form, subject: Status of Actions Taken on Congressional Recommendations, 9 March 1959.
55. House, Committee on Government Operations, *House Report No. 2011*, 1958, 5–6.
56. Lerche, Status of Actions.
57. Ibid.
58. Ibid.
59. Futrell, *Ideas, Concepts, Doctrine*, 305.
60. Ibid., 306.
61. Ibid., 326.
62. House, Committee on Armed Services, Report of Special Subcommittee No. 4, *Investigation of National Defense: Phase II*, 85th Cong., 2d sess. (Washington, D.C.: Government Printing Office, 1958), 2–3.
63. Ibid., 3.
64. Ibid., 4.
65. Ibid., 5
66. Ibid., 7.
67. Ibid., 7.
68. Ibid.
69. Ibid., 9.
70. Ibid., 9–10.
71. Ibid., 10.
72. House, Committee on Armed Services, Special Subcommittee No. 4, *Investigation of National Defense: Phase II*, 85th Cong., 2d sess., 1958, 95–97, testimony of Maj Gen H. C. Donnelly, assistant deputy chief of staff, Plans and Programs, Headquarters USAF.
73. Ibid., 206, testimony of Gen Curtis LeMay, vice chief of staff, Headquarters USAF.
74. Ibid., 212.
75. Ibid.
76. House, Committee on Government Operations, Subcommittee on Military Operations, *Military Air Transportation (Executive Action in Response to Committee Recommendations)*, 86th Cong., 1st sess., 1959, 2, statement of Perkins McGuire, assistant secretary of defense (Supply and Logistics).
77. Ibid.
78. Ibid.
79. Ibid., 15.
80. Ibid., 34, statement of Philip Taylor, assistant secretary of the Air Force (Materiel).
81. Ibid., 2, Perkins McGuire.
82. Ibid., 65, Philip Taylor.
83. Ibid., 202, statement of Elwood R. Quesada, administrator, Federal Aviation Agency.
84. Ibid., 213.
85. Thayer, Air Transport Policy, 173–95.
86. Ibid.
87. Ibid., 179.
88. Ibid., 198.
89. House, Committee on Armed Services, Special Subcommittee on National Military Airlift, *Hearings before Special Subcommittee on National Military Airlift*, 86th Cong., 2d sess., 1960, 4056, statement of Congressman L. Mendel Rivers, chairman.
90. Thayer, *Air Transport Policy*, 136–44.
91. Futrell, *Ideas, Concepts, Doctrine*, 232.
92. Thayer, *Air Transport Policy*, 136.
93. House, Committee on Armed Services, *Hearings on National Military Airlift*, 1960, 4062–63, statement of Wilber Brucker, secretary of the Army.

AIRLIFT DOCTRINE

94. Ibid., 4071–72, statement of Gen Lyman Lemnitzer, chief of staff, US Army.
95. Ibid., 4074.
96. Ibid., 4073–76.
97. Ibid., 4077.
98. Ibid.
99. Ibid.
100. Ibid., 4113–20, statement of Maj Gen Hewitt Wheless, deputy chief of staff, Plans, Headquarters USAF.
101. Ibid., 4130, Congressman Rivers.
102. Futrell, *Ideas, Concepts, Doctrine*, 327.
103. House, Committee on Armed Services, *Hearings on National Military Airlift*, 1960, 4184, statement of Col Herbert Ogleby, chief of traffic, deputy chief of staff, operations, Headquarters Military Air Transport Service.
104. Ibid., 4184–85.
105. Ibid., 4190, statement of Lt Gen William Tunner, commander, Military Air Transport Service.
106. Ibid., 4303, statement of Maj Gen Bruce Holloway, director of operational requirements, deputy chief of staff, Operations, Headquarters USAF.
107. Ibid., 4305.
108. Ibid., 4309–10; see also Walter Krause et al., *C-141 Starlifter: Narrative* (Scott AFB, Ill.: Office of Military Airlift Command [MAC] History, 15 January 1973), for a detailed description of the early steps in the acquisition of the C-141.
109. Ibid., 4219–77.
110. Rebecca Noell, Military Air Transport Service, historical study, *Exercise Big Slam/Puerto Pine 14-28 March 1960* (Scott AFB, Ill.: Office of Information, March 1961), 1–14.
111. House, Committee on Armed Services, *Hearings on National Military Airlift*, 1960, 4790–91, 4805, statement of Maj Gen Ben Harrell, Headquarters United States Continental Army Command.
112. Ibid., 4792–94, 4804; Noell, *Big Slam/Puerto Pine*, 12–13.
113. House, Committee on Armed Services, *Hearings on National Military Airlift*, 1960, 4796, testimony of Lt Gen William Tunner.
114. Ibid., 4794.
115. Ibid., 4801–3, General Harrell.
116. Ibid., 4807, Lt Gen William Tunner.
117. Ibid., 4798, General Harrell.
118. House, Committee on Armed Services, Special Subcommittee on National Military Airlift, *Report of Special Subcommittee on National Military Airlift*, 86th Cong., 2d sess. (Washington, D.C.: Government Printing Office, 1960), 4030.
119. Ibid.
120. Ibid.
121. Ibid., 4033.
122. Ibid., 4034.
123. House, Committee on Armed Services, *Hearings on National Military Airlift*, 1960, 4892, statement of Gen Thomas White, chief of staff, US Air Force.
124. House, Committee on Armed Services, *Report on National Military Airlift*, 1960, 4040–41, 4052.
125. Ibid., 4052.
126. Ibid., 4034–35.
127. Ibid., 4052.
128. Ibid., 4053–54.
129. House, Committee on Armed Services, *Hearings on National Military Airlift*, 1960, 4894–95, exchange between Congressman Rivers and General White.
130. House, Committee on Armed Services, *Report on National Military Airlift*, 1960, 4055.
131. Futrell, *Ideas, Concepts, Doctrine*, 328–29.

132. House, Committee on Armed Services, *House Report 2011*, 1958, 10.
133. Futrell, *Ideas, Concepts, Doctrine*, 325.
134. The Role of MATS in Peace and War, appendix 1.
135. Ibid., 2.
136. Ibid., 5–6.
137. Gordon Reed, chairman, Reed Committee, to Dudley Sharp, secretary of the Air Force, report, subject: Reed Committee Report on MATS, 4 April 1960, 1.
138. Ibid., annex E.
139. Ibid., 8.
140. Ibid., 9.
141. Ibid., 3.
142. Ibid., annex B.
143. History, Military Air Transport Service, January–June 1961, 1:3–4.
144. MM 2-2, *MATS Mobility Manual*, 7 April 1961.
145. Ibid., 2–1.
146. History, Military Air Transport Service, January–June 1961, 4–5.
147. Futrell, *Ideas, Concepts, Doctrine*, 329.
148. Ralph Sanders, *The Politics of Defense Analysis* (New York: Dunellen, 1973), 191.
149. Ibid., 193.
150. Futrell, *Ideas, Concepts, Doctrine*, 331.
151. Ibid.
152. Ibid., 334.
153. Ibid.
154. History, Military Air Transport Service, 1 January–30 June 1961, 1:242–43.
155. Ibid., 249.
156. House, Committee on Armed Services, Special Subcommittee on National Military Airlift, *Hearings before Special Subcommittee on National Military Airlift*, 88th Cong., 1st sess., 1963, 5965, statement of Secretary of Defense Robert McNamara.
157. Ibid.
158. Ibid., 5966–67.
159. History, Military Air Transport Service, 1 January–30 June 1962, 1:6.
160. Gen Howell Estes, Jr., "Modern Combat Airlift," *Air University Review*, vol. 20 (September–October 1969): 22.
161. Maj Gen H. G. Thorne, Jr., deputy chief of staff, Operations, Headquarters United States Air Forces in Europe, to Headquarters USAF, letter, subject: USAF Response to DOD Airlift Study and Required Follow-on Actions, 17 July 1964, with Report of USAFE-MATS-TAC Conference on Evaluation of Airlift Consolidation in Europe attached. See also History, Military Air Transport Service, 1 January–30 June 1964, 1–14, for a detailed discussion of the airlift studies of this era.
162. Ibid.
163. Ibid.
164. Futrell, *Ideas, Concepts, Doctrine*, 179.
165. Air Force Letter No. 55–5, *Memorandum of Understanding Relating to Army Organic Aviation*, 19 November 1952.
166. Ibid.
167. History, Military Air Transport Service, January–June 1962, 50.
168. Ibid., 52-57.
169. History, Military Air Transport Service, 1 July 1962–30 June 1963, 1–2.
170. House, Committee on Armed Services, *National Military Airlift*, 1963, 5968, Secretary McNamara.
171. History, Military Air Transport Service, July–June 1963, 7–11.
172. House, Committee on Armed Services, *National Military Airlift*, 1963, 6062, General LeMay.

173. Ibid.
174. Ibid.
175. Ibid., 6163–70, statement of Gen Joe Kelly, commander, Military Air Transport Service.
176. History, Military Air Transport Service, July–31 December 1963, 1:7.
177. History, Military Air Transport Service, 1 January–30 June 1964, vol. 1, pt. 1: 5–8.
178. Ibid., 11.
179. Maj Gen David Burchinal, director of plans, deputy chief of staff, Plans and Programs, Headquarters USAF, to Research Studies Institute, letter, subject: Study of Airlift Organization, 6 October 1961.
180. Lt Col Edward Wiley, project officer, Research Studies Institute, report, subject: Airlift Organization Study, December 1961, 63–66.
181. Ibid., 91.
182. Futrell, *Ideas, Concepts, Doctrine*, 410.
183. Ibid., 410–11.
184. Ibid., 415.
185. Ibid.
186. Maj Robert G. Sparkman, "Exercise Gold Fire I," *Air University Review*, no. 3 (March–April 1965): 16:25–30.
187. Ibid., 31–38.
188. Futrell, *Ideas, Concepts, Doctrine*, 415.
189. Ibid.
190. History, Military Air Transport Service, 1 July 1962–30 June 1963, 1:247.
191. Ibid., 247–49.
192. Ibid., 256–58.
193. Ibid., 258.
194. Ibid.
195. History, Military Air Transport Service, 1 July 1964–30 June 1965, 1:172.

CHAPTER 6

The Vietnam Era

This chapter is about an era, not a war. To be sure, there is coverage of airlift in the Vietnam War but only on a limited scale. Instead of a detailed treatment, the chapter focuses on doctrinal lessons and results; its endnotes refer the reader to more definitive treatments of particular areas and events. Others have already written, or will someday write, the thorough studies of combat, rich with human quality. The point of this chapter is not to degrade in any way the valiant efforts of the airlifters nor their many vital contributions, but to put their toils in the perspective of grand-scale contributions to the national security.

Clearly, airlift was an important factor in Southeast Asia (SEA) before 1964, but it was in that year the US military began its heavy involvement there. That was the year the public policymakers made commitments—both physical and psychological—that would demand the nation's attention for 10 years and weigh on its conscience even longer. Although important events occurred elsewhere during this period—specifically, in the Middle East—it is neither arbitrary nor inconvenient to talk about 1964 to 1975 as the Vietnam era.

The Doctrinal Context

The August 1964 version of the Air Force's basic doctrine manual, Air Force Manual (AFM) 1–1, *United States Air Force Basic Doctrine*, carried (for the first time) a discussion of several Air Force missions, including airlift. It said that

> in conventional warfare, airlift contributes to rapid concentration of air and ground forces and resupply of tactical units in the field. In addition, long-range or strategic airlift participates in the support of heavy theater logistics requirements. Air superiority is required for effective airlift, and close control is necessary for the efficient utilization of tactical airlift.[1]

It is interesting to note that airlift is treated first as an entity, then as a sum of its parts.

The manual left it to each major command to develop a supplement that would provide the details of its specific mission. Thus, in September of 1965, the Military Air Transport Service (MATS) submitted a draft AFM 2–21, *Airlift Doctrine*. In preparing that draft, the MATS staff placed great credence in Secretary McNamara's statement that "the line of demarkation between the strategic airlift mission and the troop carrier or assault mission may, in time, become less important."[2] The MATS Doctrinal Development Committee was told that "the time to eliminate the 'line of demarkation' is now. . . . With the present and future capacity of MATS to perform all phases of the airlift mission, the concept of airlift need no longer be fragmented, but can now become an entity. Therefore, the terms [strategic and troop carrier] no longer accurately describe airlift."[3]

Gen Howell Estes, Jr., the commander of MATS since July of 1964, forwarded the draft to Headquarters USAF with a discussion of airlift unity that summarized 25 years of evolution in airlift thinking and capability. It is well worth reading in its entirety:

> Air Force directives assigned to TAC and MATS the task of writing separate manuals on "assault" and "strategic" airlift operations respectively. I feel that this "two-manual" approach perpetuates post World War II thinking and fails to acknowledge and exploit the full capability of the modern transport aircraft in its primary role. To write a doctrine which addresses itself only to certain airlift tasks ignores the wisdom and foresight which has today provided us such multipurpose aircraft as the C-130, C-141, and soon the C-5A.
>
> Accordingly, you will note the word "strategic" is not used in the proposed doctrine. This terminology is not adequately descriptive of the current airlift task. Airlift is an instrument of national and military power in its own right, as well as an essential supporting element to strategic and tactical combat forces. Unfortunately, this is not very well understood or appreciated within our own Air Force. It is my opinion that the full functional capability of airlift must be addressed as an entity in order to exploit the flexibility of airlift forces. Such capability cannot in any way be considered divisible.
>
> In furtherance of this position, the current mission statement for the Military Air Transport Service directs the maintenance of a military airlift system necessary to perform all airlift tasks. MATS activities include operating across the entire spectrum of airlift from airdrop missions to intercontinental logistic support. Its daily tasks go far beyond the strategic and tactical roles. Therefore, I have directed the drafters of this manual to evaluate all aspects of airlift operations in order to project airlift doctrine as an entity.[4]

The proposed manual called airlift a "specialized increment of military power" that "must be considered in terms of airlift systems' capabilities, not in terms of strategic or tactical tasks."[5] The great flexibility of airlift allowed it to simultaneously deploy to and execute within a theater. "Designations which imply peculiar capabilities of certain transport aircraft and their crews are now largely invalid."[6] Instead, the airlift user should think of airlift in terms of phases of an operation—deployment, assault, resupply, and redeployment.

The draft was the first comprehensive statement of modern airlift thinking. The suggested concept of organization was that

> capability is considered an entity which is divisible only by intent in specific operational situations. Permanent organizational fragmentation of this resource in any manner decreases its optimum efficiency and effectiveness. The organization of airlift forces includes a centrally directed command and control system with decentralized operational

Figure 63. Gen Howell Estes, Jr., commander of Military Airlift Command from July 1964 through July 1969.

AIRLIFT DOCTRINE

command to insure orderly and timely application of airlift resources in all methods of employment.[7]

Airlift could be employed in deployment/redeployment missions, combat airlift operations, logistical support operations, and aeromedical evacuation operations, which left room for forces assigned to MATS and directly to the theater commanders; but all airlift forces could and would participate in each type of mission as required.[8]

Aerial ports became, more clearly than before, an integral part of the airlift system. The draft drew a sophisticated role for the aerial ports and, at the same time, articulated the direct delivery concept:

> Adequate aerial port support is essential to logistical airlift operations to insure effective utilization of airlift aircraft and to provide timely handling of air shipments to the user. An effective port operation increases airlift capability by reducing aircraft ground/turnaround time, and reduces the intransit time of critical high-value items. The flexibility and increased range of airlift aircraft enables the rendering of point-to-point service from the place of origination to ultimate user. This reduces sole dependency upon large, fixed coastal ports of aerial embarkation. Since the value of logistical support operations is largely measured by savings in intransit times of user requirements, the operation must be supported by an efficient aerial port function.[9]

The MATS submission also addressed the question of vulnerability of all airlift forces. It admitted the obvious: airlift forces are vulnerable to air and ground attack. The answer to this problem, at least in part, lay in solving the question of exposure to these attacks:

> With greater range, speed, and carrying capacity, fewer sorties are required to deliver a particular force. Faster on/offload capabilities further reduce the rate of exposure in the forward area. New types of landing gear will permit greater dispersion of operations, and rear operating base requirements are reduced. With current airlift capabilities, dangerous areas can be circumnavigated; escort is practical while in the combat area and, using aerial delivery techniques, the airlift force can offload and return to safety without landing and without exposure on the ground in the forward area.[10]

In January 1966, the Headquarters USAF assistant deputy chief of staff, Plans and Operations, Maj Gen Arthur Agan, Jr., wrote to the Military Airlift Command (MAC) noting that "based on previous guidance expressed by the Secretary of the Air Force (SAF memo to the deputy secretary of defense, 8 April 1964), by Gen John McConnell, and advice of the Air Staff, it has been decided that there should be separate airlift manuals."[11] The Tactical Air Command (TAC) was to continue its work on AFM 2–4 (assault airlift) and MAC was to resubmit AFM 2–21 (strategic airlift), working together to avoid duplication.

Consequently, AFM 2–21, *Strategic Airlift*, published in September 1966, focused on the intertheater airlift mission of logistical support, aeromedical evacuation, deployment/redeployment, and limited airborne assault operations. The "oneness" of airlift disappeared from the manual, but the chapter on introductory material did allow for strategic airlift to "be applied and employed to discharge tactical airlift functions" by augmenting tactical airlift forces.[12] The chapter concerning employment of the strategic airlift forces contained numerous references to missions that would normally have a tactical flavor. In limited wars, for example, MAC's forces could directly introduce combat forces into battle areas and deliver supplies to deployed forces. Overall, the primary mission was the "support of and participation in combat operations."[13] Considering that AFM 2-21 had to be approved by Headquarters TAC and Headquarters USAF, it was a fairly successful statement of new airlift concepts. Official recognition of the multiple capabilities of strategic airlift represented acceptance of fact. The Air Force and perhaps higher authorities were not yet convinced of the "unity of airlift." The Vietnam experience would ultimately change their minds.

AFM 2-21 was preceded, by one month, by the new AFM 2-4, *Tactical Airlift*. It, too, was a balanced approach to the airlift facts of life, allowing for the augmentation role to work in either direction until the requirement was appropriately reduced. Critically, "when this occurs, an operational interlock of strategic and tactical airlift force will insure optimum effectiveness."[14] The term *interlock* became known popularly as *interface*. Strategic airlift would, generally, deliver goods and people to some rear base; tactical airlift would then deliver them, on a sustained basis, to the Army brigade level (battalion/company level if required) where the Army would further redistribute the goods with organic assets. This became known as the wholesale/retail approach to air lines of communications, with MAC and TAC delivering goods in wholesale quantities and the Army redelivering in quantities closer to retail.[15]

AFM 2-4 also said that none of the four basic tasks of tactical airlift—logistics, airborne, aeromedical, and special operations—had an overall priority, "for priority may vary widely as the joint force area (theater) situation changes daily."[16] The essence of this concept was flexibility and responsiveness to theater commander needs. It was a logical follow-on to the fundamental doctrinal justification for organizationally including tactical airlift as an integral part of the joint air-ground combat team, that is, the theater air force. The supporting rationale not only addressed the airlift consolidation question, it also provided an argument against the Army's having very much organic airlift capability:

> Through this command arrangement, the essential joint force experience and highly specialized tactical airlift skills are available to meet the fluctuating demands of military operations within the narrow limits of time and space allowed by the everchanging combat situation. This integration of tactical airlift with other Air Force tactical air elements provides the joint force command with a complete, responsive air resource package capable of functioning in a wide range of combat intensities, thereby obviating the need for costly duplication of capabilities by the other services. In the management of tactical airlift, maximum advantage of capabilities and maximum effectiveness in a combat

environment are realized by employing the basic principles of centralized control and decentralized execution.[17]

The "debate" concerning airlift consolidation was on temporary hold, and the statement alluding to Army airlift had been settled in April of 1966. That agreement signed by the chiefs of staff of the Air Force and Army established that the Army would "relinquish all claims for CV-2 and CV-7 aircraft and for future fixed wing aircraft designed for tactical airlift."[18] The Air Force agreed to "relinquish all claims for helicopters and follow-on rotary-wing aircraft which are designed and operated for intra-theater movement, fire support, supply and resupply of Army Forces."[19] The two chiefs, however, looked to future aircraft when they also decided that the "Army and Air Force jointly will continue to develop vertical takeoff and landing (VTOL) aircraft. Dependent upon evaluation of this type of aircraft, methods of employment and control will be matters for continuing joint consideration by Army and Air Force."[20]

The new doctrinal thinking was publicly discussed in the 1965-66 Special Subcommittee on Military Airlift hearings. Congressman L. Mendel Rivers reestablished the special group to review the status of military airlift in terms of modernization, responsiveness to worldwide needs, and tactical airlift needs. Secretary of the Air Force Harold Brown led off the testimony with a far-ranging review of airlift matters, in effect reporting the doctrinal positions of the DOD at the beginning of the US buildup in Vietnam.

After reviewing the DOD responses to the 1960 Presidentially Approved Courses of Action and the first Rivers subcommittee recommendations in 1960, Secretary Brown began a presentation of contemporary actions concerning airlift. First, he noted that MAC would have movement control of all airlift aircraft engaged in long-range deployments, regardless of command assignment, to prevent station saturation and permit an orderly airlift flow from on-load to off-load bases. Concomitantly, MAC airlifters would be under operational control of the assault airlift commander when augmenting tactical airlift forces. It appears that, at this level of concern, airlift consolidation was a fait accompli.[21]

Secretary Brown echoed Secretary Robert McNamara's 1961 concerns about mobility assets in general when he pointed to the need for a quick reaction capability "based on a judicious mix of airlift, sealift, and prepositioning."[22] The update of McNamara's concern was that even with fast deployment cargo ships and sea-based prepositioning (which required airlift for forward movement of cargo), "no matter how you do it, what our analysis indicates is that there is a very large airlift component of strategic deployment in the most economical and most expeditious plans."[23]

Brown was, of course, supporting President Johnson's initiative to improve mobility forces, albeit with an Air Force flavor. Johnson's message to Congress on the state of American defenses in 1965 foreshadowed a program still pursued in 1984:

> We must further improve our ability to concentrate our power rapidly in a threatened area so as to halt aggression early and swiftly. We plan expansion of our airlift, improvement of our sealift, and more prepositioned equipment to enable us to move our troops overseas in a matter of days, rather than weeks.
>
> To this end, we will—
>
> Start development of the C-5A cargo transport. This extraordinary aircraft capable of carrying 750 passengers will bring a new era of air transportation. It will represent a dramatic step forward in the worldwide mobility of our forces and in American leadership in the field of aviation.
>
> Build fast deployment cargo ships, capable of delivering military equipment quickly to any theater. This represents a new concept in the rapid deployment of military forces. These ships will have a gas turbine engine propulsion system, a major advance in marine engineering for ships of this size. Such vessels will be deployed around the globe, able to begin deliveries of heavy combat-ready equipment into battle zones within days or even hours.
>
> Increase our forward floating depot ships stationed close to areas of potential crisis.[24]

Concerning the C-5A, Brown focused on its ability to deploy quickly relatively large, fully equipped forces, thus possibly reducing the length of an emerging confrontation by solving the problem early on. This ability, combined with what the C-141 would provide, along with a healthy Civil Reserve Air Fleet (CRAF), allowed Brown to claim that "this dramatic increase in our capability to project our power rapidly . . . will have far-reaching effects. . . . It will be a major deterrent to nonnuclear aggression, just as our Strategic Air Command is the major deterrent to nuclear attack."[25] This was a heady elevation of airlift and reflected yet another recognition of the vital contribution airlift could make to national security.

At the operational level, Brown also discussed the assault airlift air lines of communication concept. Its goal, he said, was to deliver goods to the user with minimum, or no, aerial transshipments, to achieve a one-step delivery from the main logistics base to the consumer. He also observed that the current aircraft limitations made interface with helicopters and land delivery modes necessary. But he looked forward to a time when the Air Force could "develop aircraft that can economically deliver further and further forward" perhaps with vertical/short takeoff and landing (VSTOL) aircraft.[26] He was, however, willing to commit publicly to the idea of having both the C-141 and C-5 deliver directly to forward logistics bases rather than main ones in the rear if the landing zones could handle them.[27]

When queried about airlift consolidation, Brown provided one link in the thinking of why the Air Force had decided not to pursue that course of action. His reasoning revolved around the interface concept, which was very much a logistics-oriented approach to the question:

> It is a very different thing to carry, on the one hand, equipment from Travis to Bien Hoa than it is to deliver it in an assault landing zone. It is not obvious to me, in fact I don't think it is so, that these should both be done by the same organization. I do think that strategic airlift should be under one organization, and it is. I think that MATS, as executive director for the single manager of airlift, does perform this function except for a few odds and ends, which I admit exist.
>
> But this business of moving aircraft from TAC to MATS or from MATS to TAC, I think is a good way to handle a load change that can occur from one kind of mission, strategic lift over long distances, to another kind, lift within a theater or assault airlift in another situation.[28]

He also suggested, in keeping with the concept of putting long-range aircraft in MAC and training for all airlift missions, that crews could not be expected to be proficient in both strategic and assault tactics without detracting from their assault skills.

Deputy Secretary of Defense Cyrus Vance took a somewhat different tack, covering questions concerning making MAC a specified command. He focused on whether organizational arrangements were responsive to the Joint Chiefs of Staff (JCS) and the unified and specified commands; and he concluded they were, with a few improvements needed and implemented. Status quo improvements included:

- Improved information for the JCS on the status of MAC and TAC strategic airlift assets.
- Movement control by MAC of strategic deployments.
- Increased utilization rates for MAC and TAC airlifters through increased crew/aircraft ratios.
- Earlier inclusion of MAC planners in the deployment planning cycle.
- Establishing a joint transportation board within the JCS to constantly monitor mobility forces for trouble spots and to work priority and reallocation of lift resources.[29]

These actions answered the immediate concerns about responsiveness of airlift assets and systems, all of which ultimately admitted the logic of the argument to make MAC a specified command. Tied into this argument, but actually distinct from it, was the question of consolidation. Congressman Rivers wanted a strong airlift program and apparently believed that both consolidation and specification were the best way to sustain it. A minor twitch of the status quo here and there would be a normal adjustment to changing requirements, but a response as large as the program Deputy Secretary Vance described spoke volumes in favor of Congressman Rivers's hypothesis. Strong pressures from Rivers in the form of support of presidential DOD airlift programs uniquely shaped airlift doctrine, if indirectly.

Other factors obviously played in this process. Gen Paul Adams, commander of the US Strike Command (STRICOM), offered a much more conservative approach to airlift, one based on the concept that "aircraft capabilities should not be the overriding determinant" of airlift organization, command, management, and operations.[30] Instead, he argued that these functions should be driven by the mission requirement of supporting combat. His point was that strategic and tactical airlift forces had missions of such a different nature that similar aircraft were not the issue; rather, the different missions called for different organizations. These two highly specialized forces, made so by intensive training, should not be thought of, or organized as, interchangeable. "Strategic airlift," he said, "was a national resource that must be controlled at the highest echelons, while control of the resources of tactical airlift must be vested in that CINC who is given the task of prosecuting the particular effort that is limited in scope and geography."[31]

Congressman Rivers and his special subcommittee apparently were satisfied with the DOD's efforts to recognize the importance of strategic airlift. The committee report noted the improvements Secretary Brown listed and dropped the question. The subcommittee, however, warned the DOD and services "not to rest on their recent and projected accomplishments of increasing our strategic airlift capability, but make an equal effort to improve our tactical airlift capability by the continued modernization of the assault airlift fleet."[32] The report built a strong foundation for their position.

First, it rejected the C-141 and C-5A as appropriate answers to assault airlift needs:

> It has been stated that the C-141 and the C-5A will have a tactical airlift capability. The subcommittee is of the opinion that neither of these aircraft are the optimum, or even desirable aircraft for the assault mission of tactical airlift. While both aircraft will have excellent heavy drop capability and can carry large payloads, neither will be efficient at airdropping a full load of paratroopers, and neither will have the assault landing or takeoff capability of the present C-130 aircraft. Neither aircraft qualifies as STOL aircraft. The C-5A, the better of the two, requires 4,000 feet of semi-improved runway to land its full load. Therefore, the subcommittee does not consider these aircraft as replacements for the C-130 assault aircraft. Both aircraft will have the capability to operate as tactical aircraft up to forward staging areas where protected and improved runways exist. However, it will require aircraft with good STOL or VTOL capability to airlift the forces, equipment, and supplies to the forward battle areas where forces of battalion size are located.[33]

Yet, TAC had told the hearings that there was a clear tendency toward reduction of assault airlift capability. Secretary Brown's testimony that "modernization of the Tactical Air Command was completed in September 1965" only added fuel to the fire.[34] Although there was no approved study in the DOD, JCS, or Air Force on tactical airlift requirements, TAC briefers provided the hearings with a clear rationale for concern:

> Conditions in Southeast Asia, in the Dominican Republic, . . .and, indeed, in most of the areas of the world where a limited war potential exists, confront us with certain common problems. At the heart of the matter is the fact that our total military resource does have limits. Most of these areas share transportation problems not unlike those of Vietnam: underdeveloped road and rail networks, rugged terrain, jungle, or conversely, desert, frequent heavy rainfall, natural water barriers, or island geography.

AIRLIFT DOCTRINE

> A spectre which looms high is the possibility of multiple contingencies and requirement for assault airlift in quantities which could tax or overtax present capabilities....
>
> In looking ahead, it appears unlikely that there will be a lessening of the need for assault airlift. To the contrary, every improvement in the modernization and updating of combat forces embodies the rapid reaction and increased mobility concept.[35]

The final report accepted TAC's initiative to modify the C-130E or procure a so-called C-130J, which would require only 1,800 feet for takeoff (and 1,400 feet for landing) with a gross weight of 120,000 pounds.

A slide General Adams used in his briefing of the subcommittee summarized quite effectively the general airlift doctrine that finally emerged in the 1965-66 period (fig. 64). Although the chart reflects only C-130s in the operation and tactical airlift phases, the C-123s and C-7s could, and would, serve in those roles as well. This doctrine was tested in Vietnam and, paradoxically, found both sound and wanting in some fundamental ways.

Overwater Airlift

The 315th Air Division, originally the theater airlift headquarters for the Far East Air Forces (FEAF), retained the same designation when FEAF merged into the Pacific Air Forces (PACAF) in 1957. The division flew airlift under priorities set by the Western Pacific Transportation Office (WTO). It had operational control of 24 C-124s stationed at Tachikawa AB, Japan, plus four squadrons of C-130s at Clark AB and Ashiya AB. Clark was the principal gateway to Southeast Asia (SEA) for both MATS and 315th aircraft; overlap and duplication were inevitable. "During the summer of 1962, the 315th furnished seven scheduled flights weekly from Clark to Tan Son Nhut, while MATS provided twenty-one."[36] The commander in chief, Pacific Command (CINCPAC), proposed exclusive dependence on MATS, but PACAF resisted strongly, saying it needed C-130s for unique in-country missions. MATS and the 315th consolidated their aerial ports at Clark and traffic was allocated to each command based on decisions by a single air traffic coordinating office.[37]

The overwater missions of the 315th "supplemented surface shipping, helped overcome severe seaport bottlenecks during the American buildup, and cut down delivery and handling time for essential parts and equipment."[38] None of this fine service could overcome the fact of two separate Air Force tactical airlift systems for support of SEA. The 315th Air Division (AD) worked for CINCPAC; the 834th AD worked for Military Assistance Command, Vietnam (MACV). They both relied on the same force of C-130s. By 1967, PACAF planners recommended inactivating the 315th, creating a directorate of airlift and an ALCC at PACAF headquarters in Hawaii, and assigning the C-130 wings to PACAF's numbered air forces. The 834th

VIETNAM ERA

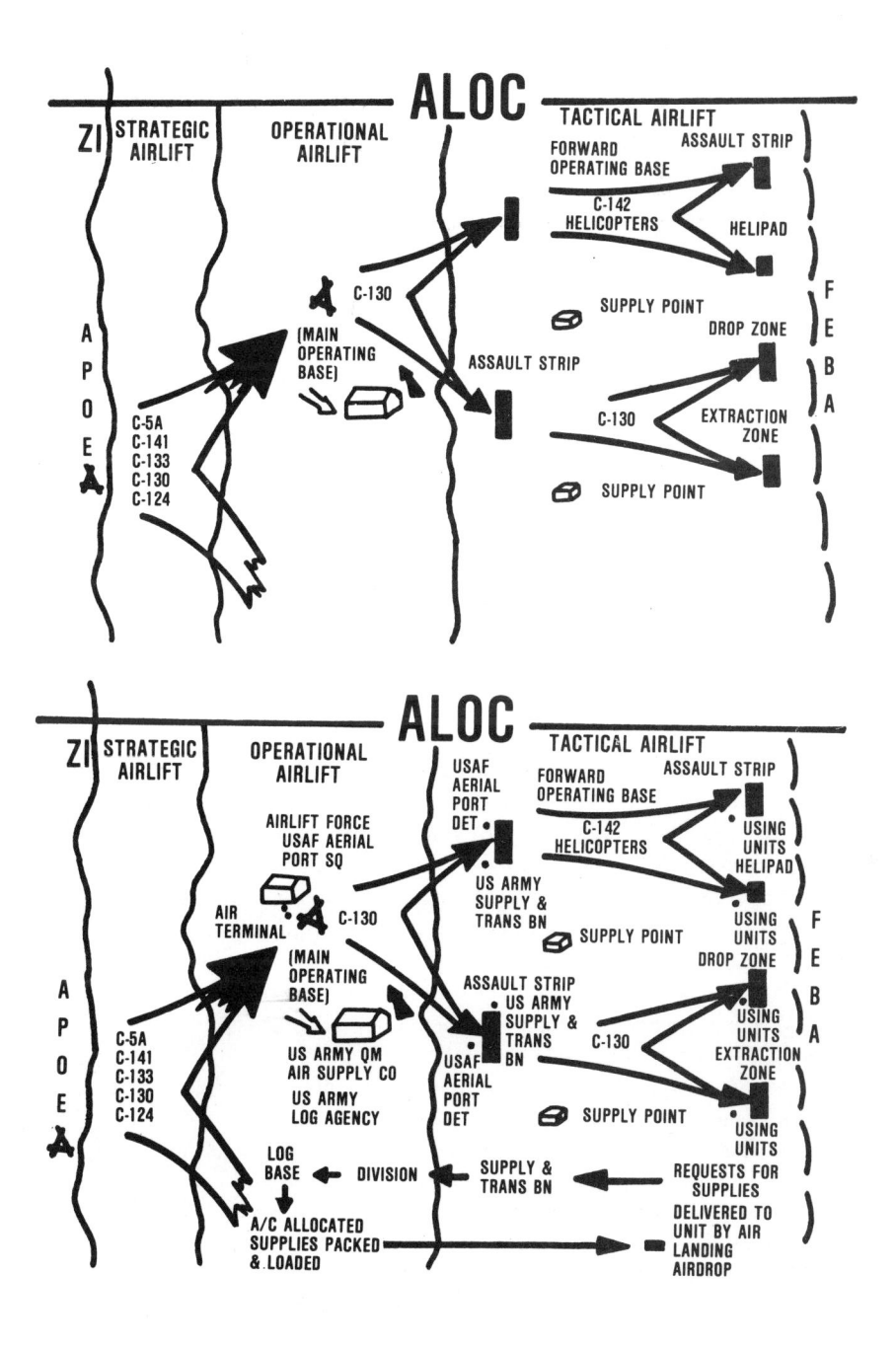

Figure 64

Air Division (AD) would continue its in-country management role. After some delay caused by uncertainties in Korea, the main structure proposed by PACAF was approved. The 315th was inactivated in April 1969.[39]

MAC's intratheater logistics airlift mission grew massively between 1965 and 1969, as shown in the following chart:

	1965	1966	1967	1968
Cargo Tons	53,198	117,465	141,113	155,005
Passengers	175,539	254,080	343,027	398,671

By 1968 this translated to 150,000 passengers and 45,000 tons of cargo monthly to and from SEA. At first, Tan Son Nhut was the only regular in-country off-load point, but this eventually grew to include Da Nang, Cam Ranh Bay, Pleiku, Bien Hoa, and Phu Cat, thus greatly reducing the pressures on the redistribution system. Lt Gen Glen Martin, the Air Force inspector general, viewed the overlap of MAC and 315th AD routes as complementary rather than duplicative, and CINCPAC told its subordinate commands to forward airlift requests (intratheater) to the WTO instead of MAC, for apportionment of requirements between MAC and organic airlift.[40]

The surging demands for C-130 capabilities in Vietnam in 1968 finally led the deputy secretary of defense to direct the discontinuance of overwater flights for those airplanes. The transfer of the overwater mission to MAC was unexpected at all levels throughout PACAF, leaving a tremendous requirements information gap. MAC elected to use C-141s and contract for B-727s. Outsize cargo was carried by the 22d Military Airlift Squadron (MAS) at Tachikawa AB, dedicated to operating for the 315th AD.[41]

The C-124s of the 22d MAS had been staging operations out of Tan Son Nhut AB since 1965 but were phased out in March of 1969. At that point, the 50th MAG C-124s at Hickam picked up the responsibility for on-call outsized airlift in the Pacific area, including into Vietnam. When that unit deactivated in November of 1969, Twenty-Second Air Force, through its Southeast Asia Area Command Post at Clark AB, took over the task of selecting and operating MAC aircraft already in the Pacific to support CINCPAC's outsize requirements. Active duty C-133s, plus some Air National Guard and Air Force Reserve C-124s, became the only outsize carriers available until the introduction of the C-5. The typical mission profile for the C-133s in this role was to fly from Travis AFB to an on-load station, thence to an off-load base in SEA. On the return trip, the C-133s often carried repairable helicopters.[42]

Tactical Airlift in Vietnam

The bulk of the tactical airlift job in Southeast Asia during the Vietnam era was done with C-130s and C-7s, supplementing the C-123s in place before the end of 1964. The system that handled the tactical airlift mission, typical of most American combat airlift organizations at the beginning of hostilities, was perhaps not well founded in existing doctrine. Also typically, however, it grew and changed to meet the demands of the situation.

The Airlift System

General Curtis LeMay, after a visit to Vietnam in April of 1962, said "there is no effective airlift system."[43] The nonsystem reportedly had two problems: not enough aerial port facilities and poor command, control, and communications. Provisional units set up as a fix were replaced by the 315th Troop Carrier Group (Combat Cargo) and the 8th Aerial Port Squadron, both C-123 units, in December of 1962. A third C-123 squadron bedded down at Da Nang AB in April of 1963 and the fourth was activated in October 1964 at Tan Son Nhut AB.[44]

The introduction of the C-130 shuttle system into Vietnam in 1965 gave rise to the idea of an in-country air division under the Southeast Asia Airlift System (SEAAS) and was given impetus by the secretary of defense's decision to transfer C-7s to the Air Force. Gen William Momyer, Seventh Air Force commander, fully supported a mid-1966 plan for the air division to absorb the airlift control center; own the C-7s, the C-123 wing, and an aerial port group; and exercise operational control of the C-130s. The new 834th Air Division opened business at Tan Son Nhut on 15 October 1966 under the command of Brig Gen William Moore with Col Louis Lindsey as director of operations.[45]

The creation of the new division paralleled the reorganization of the aerial port system. From the first half of 1965 to the middle of 1966, the aerial port workload in Vietnam increased from 30,000 to 140,000 tons per month, almost overwhelming the system's efficiency. In 1965 the system grew from 8 to 35 detachments working for 3 squadrons, but shortages in raw numbers and skills limited effectiveness. Equipment was unreliable too. In November of 1966, these units had 437 forklifts authorized, 236 assigned, and 134 in commission. Throughout 1965 there was also a chronic shortage of pallets. Rough handling ruined some, and their value in bunker construction caused many more to disappear. Thanks to PACAF ministrations, 1,800 new pallets appeared late in 1965.[46]

By mid-1967, the number of aerial port detachments and operating locations leveled off at 40. Cargo tonnage peaked at 209,000 in March 1968 and then stabilized at 180,000 tons per month. The units were still undermanned and needed strong emphasis from Momyer to deal with equipment shortfalls and maintenance problems. Nonetheless, the aerial porters persevered and made vital contributions. They did not go unrecognized:

> The indispensable aerial port contribution in Vietnam was accomplished with little guidance from prewar doctrine. Those who served in these units were forced to overcome the exigencies of their inexperience, insufficient manning, inadequate equipment, and low priorities in acquiring better facilities. The National Defense Transportation Association bestowed its annual award, both in 1967 and 1968, upon the squadrons of the 2d Group thus rendering them much-needed recognition. For the future the demonstrated need for greater preparedness brought an expansion of the aerial port function in the Air Force Reserve forces. Reserve aerial port units provided much of the manpower for the 1968 expansion in Korea following the Pueblo incident, and over the next four years the units expanded from twelve squadrons to a strength of thirty-nine squadrons and twenty-nine flights. It thus appeared that the Air Force had taken note of the troubles in aerial port mobilization in Vietnam.[47]

The 834th Air Division's airlift control center (ALCC) was the hub of daily force management. It received emergency requests through MACV's combat operations center, unit move and special mission requests from the traffic management agency, and reports from aerial ports concerning cargo levels, changing the numbers into daily schedules. Balancing these and many more factors, the ALCC became an important element for flexibility in the system. To coordinate an array of transport detachments, aerial ports, airlift control elements, combat control teams, and aircrews, the 834th needed an effective communications system. The uniqueness of this emerging airlift system justified a separate airlift control communications net, which in turn was a reflection of a broader independence from the tactical air control system. The ALCC had been physically separated from the Seventh Air Force Tactical Air Control Center (TACC) at Tan Son Nhut since 1965. The ALCC was formally subordinate to the TACC, but the new AFM 2-4 only required the ALCC be located "adjacent to" or be "operationally connected" to the TACC, which still allowed for integration of airlift operations into the overall air war.[48]

Although ALCC was nominally subordinate to the Seventh Air Force Tactical Air Control Center, requests for airlift went to the ALCC on the Military Assistance Command, Vietnam (MACV), Traffic Management Authority (TMA), rather than to the TACC. The 823d AD, through its ALCC, scheduled missions, cut frag orders, monitored airlift status, and coordinated with the MACV Combat Operations Center on emergency requests. "In short, the 834th AD operated the tactical airlift resource, and the MACV TMA provided effective operational control."[49] The Seventh Air Force TACC lacked the staff and organization to handle the volume of airlift business. The Tactical Air Control System (TACS) radio net similarly lacked the ability to handle airlift communications, and a dedicated airlift request network was established. The ALCC was aligned to be responsive to MACV more than to the Air Force component commander.

In 1968, President Nixon's strategy for American withdrawal combined with an increasing Vietnamization of combat roles became clear. The decline in American ground forces led to a concomitant decline in airlift activities. In-country work loads dropped from a peak of 82,500 tons in 1969, to 38,000 in 1970, to 20,000 in 1971. In March of 1969, there were 18 fixed airlift control element detachments countrywide—their highest number. Beginning in late summer 1970, many were consolidated with aerial port detachments. Four were deactivated in 1970. The 2d Aerial Port Group started 1969 with 42 detachments and operating locations and ended 1971 with a total of 7.[50]

The ceasefire that became effective on 28 January 1973 foretold several changes for airlift, with the American presence in SEA tied to what was diplomatically possible. Some Americans remained in Thailand, others were in the Philippines. "The role of Air Force air transport in this strategy was crucial, linking the widespread forces in peacetime and affording a flexible capability in crisis for augmentation, lateral shipments, or withdrawal."[51]

MACV closed on 29 March 1973, replaced by the United States Support Activities Group (USSAG) in Nakhon Phanom, Thailand. The Seventh Air Force also moved to Nakhon Phanom. The former Saigon airlift control center merged with the control center at U-Tapao, Thailand, controlling, scheduling, and mission following all C-130s in SEA.

The C-130

With the decision to increase the American presence in Vietnam in 1965, requirements for airlift, within the country and into it, grew. Those requirements were to be met in large measure with the C-130 Hercules. Early in the year there were six C-130 squadrons in the Pacific—four permanently assigned in Japan, one rotational squadron in Japan, and one rotational squadron in the Philippines. By mid-1965, this increased to eight squadrons—four permanent and four rotational. Beginning the previous summer, the offshore-based C-130s had flown missions in Vietnam under varying command arrangements. The 315th AD at Tachikawa AB, Japan, had occasionally given daily scheduling authority for its C-130s to the 315th Troop Carrier Group (Combat Cargo) airlift control center at Tan Son Nhut, maintaining ultimate control through its mission commander.[52]

The Military Assistance Command, Vietnam (MACV), J-3 and Gen William Westmoreland (MACV commander) wanted a partial squadron of eight C-130s assigned in-country to handle growing demands. The 315th AD had been opposing similar initiatives since 1962 and continued to argue that in-being arrangements allowed them both to deal with in-country needs and to be available for operations elsewhere. The Pacific Command (PACOM) opted to send four C-130s to Tan Son Nhut for an indefinite period, joining three already there on temporary duty. The movement included the stipulation that crews and planes would rotate from offshore bases and the entire program would be adjusted according to operational requirements.[53]

The in-country C-130 force was a part of the Southeast Asia Airlift System (SEAAS), under MACV operational direction via the 315th Group's airlift control center. MACV established the SEAAS in October of 1962 with the 315th Group exercising control of Vietnam-based air transports. By the end of 1965, 32 C-130s were operating from Tan Son Nhut (14 Bs), Vung Tan (5 Es), Nha Trang (8 Es), and the newly opened Cam Ranh Bay (5 Es). Shortages of ramp space and base facilities plus aerial port inadequacies limited faster expansion.[54]

The high-load capacity of the C-130s greatly aided the SEAAS, as did their 24-hour-a-day capability. The on-board navigation radar helped to overcome problems with air traffic control and navigation aids in South Vietnam. "The C-130 thus evolved into a high-volume, 24-hour, air logistics service linking the main airfields."[55] Marginal forward strips remained the province of the four squadrons of C-123s stationed in-country. In mid-1965, the 315th AD limited C-130 operations to airfields over 3,500 feet in length. Although this policy was safety conscious and made maximum use of tonnage capacity, it did not take advantage of the proven C-130 assault capabilities so carefully developed and nutured over the years. This limitation caused pressures from TAC and Headquarters USAF to exploit these tactical capacities, and in November the 315th AD relented. Its new directive allowed operations into all airfields within the performance characteristics of the C-130. An intense training program followed. "The decision to use the C-130 for short field work, coupled with efforts to improve selected forward strips to meet the minimum Hercules landing-takeoff capability, paved the way for the application of this aircraft to battles of the future."[56]

The expanded role for the C-130s was linked to General Westmoreland's planned offensive and mobile tactics against Communist forces. MACV requested four additional squadrons based on calculations showing one air movement and 20 days of air supply per month per airborne brigade, 10 Vietnamese battalion movements per month, and 8 highland battalions requiring continuous air supply. MACV got what it wanted and TAC converted the rotation program into a permanent beddown.[57]

In 1968 the permanently assigned airlift force for the support of SEA was 13 C-130 squadrons, 6 C-7 squadrons, and 4 C-123 squadrons. Unit inactivation of C-130As and C-130Bs began in late 1969, with those aircraft going to the Air National Guard and Air Force Reserve. This left four squadrons of C-130s offshore in March 1972. These declines were based on MACV estimates of airlift needs. Both the JCS and CINCPAC made plans under the assumption that MAC C-141s would be used either to directly assist in operations or to backfill for C-130s.[58]

Brig Gen John Herring, the 834th AD's commander (since June of 1969), recommended in 1971 that the in-country C-130 detachments revert to their home wings for maintenance and materiel management responsibility. This, combined with the declining work load, led to the merger of the 834th into Seventh Air Force headquarters on 1 December 1971. The airlift control center maintained its separation from the TACC, becoming instead a division of the newly created Seventh Air Force directorate of airlift under the operations deputate.[59]

When MACV closed in 1973 and the Seventh Air Force moved to Thailand, two C-130 squadrons went to Clark AB and one to Kadena AB—these being the total offshore C-130 force after 1973. Four TAC rotational C-130s plus 10 from a detachment at Nakhon Phanom, Thailand, ended up at U-Tapao. The Vietnamese got two squadrons of C-130As pulled back from the Reserves and Guard.[60] (Two years later those airplanes became the property of the People's Republic of Vietnam.)

The C-7 Ownership Problem

The US Army had first tested the CV-2 Caribou in Vietnam in 1961 and judged it "extremely valuable and useful."[61] Late in the same year CINCPAC rejected Army plans to deploy a company of the airplanes into Vietnam in 1962 because C-123s and Army U-1 Otters already requested would serve the purpose. The Air Force was against the Caribous going to Vietnam (let alone to the Army), and argued that if

Every C-7 flight is different, except the last one...

deployed the aircraft should be under centralized aircraft system control. MACV promised to integrate the CV-2s into the airlift system. Consequently 18 left Fort Benning, Georgia, for Korat, Thailand, arriving in June and July of 1962. Eight moved to Vietnam in July for test purposes. The remaining 10 arrived in December after the test proved the Caribous could make effective airlift contributions operating into strips too short for the C-123. The unit—the 1st Aviation Company—was headquartered at Vung Tau. There was much talk of, but no action toward, placing the CV-2s within the airlift system.

MACV wanted a second Caribou company, but the Air Force resisted, arguing that such corps-level airlift programs would be detrimental to overall airlift efficiency. In January 1963, CINCPAC concurred that all Caribous should "be included in the established airlift system."[62] In March, the JCS agreed with CINCPAC. Nonetheless, in July 1963, a second Caribou company (the 61st Aviation Company) arrived at Vung Tau. The 61st worked for corps commanders, while the 1st strove to operate within the SEAAS. However, the 1st departed Vietnam in December 1963 as part of a token force reduction and the 61st continued primarily working directly for Army commanders.[63]

By mid-1964 the JCS had approved return of a second aviation company of Caribous to Vietnam; but General LeMay disagreed, arguing that the CV-2s should be part of the airlift system. They returned, nonetheless, and outside the SEAAS. In April 1965, Maj Gen Joseph Moore, Seventh Air Force commander, revived the issue of controlling the Caribous within the airlift system. He recommended scheduling them through the ALCC using MACV priorities. General Westmoreland, who had already requested additional Caribou companies to raise the total to six, rejected the Moore proposal. By the end of 1965 there were 88 CV-2s in Vietnam.[64]

Gens John McConnell and Harold Johnson, chiefs of staff of the Air Force and Army, met during this time to resolve the constant problems of the CV-2, the new CV-7 (the Buffalo), and the helicopter supply role. As noted earlier, their discussions resulted in the Army's relinquishing claims to future fixed-wing aircraft, transfer of the CV-2s and -7s to the Air Force, and the Air Force's renouncing the helicopter airlift role.[65]

The transfer raised the question of how to integrate the Air Force-designated C-7s. General Momyer wanted to integrate them fully into the SEAAS. The Army commanders wanted the airplanes under their mission control, otherwise helicopters might have to be diverted from combat missions and the airlift system would be reduced to near constant tactical emergency. The April transfer agreement allowed for attachment of the C-7s to the tactical commanders, and General Westmoreland apparently supported such an approach. General McConnell was willing to compromise. In October 1966, Momyer said that any change from dedicated services would occur only gradually. He reportedly envisioned that at some point the C-7s would be nominally integrated into the renamed Common Service Airlift

System (CSAS), but assigned daily to regional direct air support centers, actually outside the CSAS command, control, and priority systems.[66]

Airlift Support of Ground Operations

The major thrust of all aircraft in Vietnam was to support operations by the troops on the ground. This was true of fighters and bombers as well as of helicopters and the cargo planes—C-123s, C-130s, and C-7s. Some examples of the airlifters' support of these troops are illustrative.

Search and Destroy

"The allied war situation in February 1965 was in serious disarray."[67] The Vietcong had "virtual control" of large areas in the central provinces, and many overland routes were under Communist control. C-123s repeatedly had to provide lift of supplies and reinforcements along routes normally served by roads. For example, in late spring, the C-123s had to fly in relief forces to Phuoc Binh, Dong Xoai, and Quang Ngai to overcome enemy attacks. Four C-130s had to be called in early June to augment the in-country airlift force. It took over 200 C-130 sorties into Pleiku to keep that post supplied in June—Highway 29 from the coast was closed. The late spring-summer tactical airlift was characterized by American troop carriers air landing Vietnamese units.[68]

On 28 June President Johnson approved a movement of the 1st Cavalry Division (Airmobile) to Vietnam, signaling an offensive in the offing.

> The structure of the new airmobile division reflected the latest technical and doctrinal developments within the Army. The division initially had eight infantry battalions, three with a parachute capability. It was authorized 434 aircraft, nearly all of which were helicopters and were to be used primarily for troop mobility. Most of the aircraft were placed within two assault helicopter battalions, a cavalry squadron, and a thirty-nine-ship aerial rocket battalion. Within the division, but organized separately for general support, were several dozen heavier CH-47 Chinook helicopters. The Caribous were not an integral part of the division but had been attached since 1964.[69]

The 1st Cavalry set up its base camp at An Khe, 30 miles inland from Qui Nhon via Highway 19—by then open. Communist pressure at a civilian irregular defense camp at Pleiku prompted movement of a battalion task force there in October. The battalions moved in using Caribous and division helicopters, which also served as the aerial supply link to An Khe and elsewhere. On 18 October the Army decided to seek out the enemy, putting additional pressure on the already strained Army air system. Additional battalions moved in from An Khe made the situation more

AIRLIFT DOCTRINE

demanding. American Army officers saw what was called the Ia Drang Valley campaign as the combat test of airmobile tactics.[70]

These tactics relied on helicopters, which in turn had to have fuel. Fuel supplies at Pleiku had already begun to fall and, by the 29th, had reached the zero level. C-130s started a lift of 500-gallon fuel bladders (10 to 15 per airplane) as well as considerable amounts of ammunition. At first these supplies were delivered to the Pleiku new airfield and redistributed by Army resources. Later, the C-130s and C-123s used a 4,000-foot strip at Catecka Tea Plantation which had become the principal refueling point for the helicopters. The airlift system delivered an average 186 tons per day to the campaign, of which 58 percent was petroleum. The Air Force came to better accept the airmobile concept during the campaign, and the Army came to better understand the Air Force's capabilities to support them.[71]

Junction City

> The search-and-destroy ventures typically centered around one or more C-130 airstrips which became the focal points for buildup and resupply. Allied helicopters and infantry combed the surrounding region, sought out the enemy, and exposed him to the killing effects of air and artillery firepower. The C-130s played a central role in Operation Junction City, the largest of the search-and-destroy operations to date. This operation opened in February 1967 with the war's first and only American battalion-size parachute assault and featured substantial use of airdrop resupply.[72]

Operation Junction City was envisioned as a way to entrap massive numbers of the enemy. In January and February of 1967, the Americans deployed forces and established logistics bases on three sides of the objective area. The C-130 assault force operated from Bien Hoa, with the drop zone (DZ) near Katasm. The force consisted of 26 C-130s—all to drop the 2d Battalion, 503d Infantry, of the 173d Brigade on 22 February 1967. An airborne forward air controller communicated with the formation by radio and set off colored smoke bombs to confirm the DZ. The 780 men who jumped from 16 C-130s landed exactly where they were supposed to. There was no enemy fire.[73]

The Air Force combat control team that had jumped with the Army marked the impact point for the equipment drop. Eight C-130s dropped equipment, and two executed container delivery system (CDS) drops—over 80 tons altogether. Five aircraft received hits but all 10 returned to Bien Hoa for reloading for another container drop. Load recovery in the DZ was somewhat troublesome. The initial CDS loads were heavily damaged and some loads landed in a nearby swampy area. The Air Force Combat Control Team (CCT) had to borrow a radio from a forward air controller to improve their ground-to-air communications. Follow-up supplies during the next six days started with many inaccurate drops but generally improved with time.[74]

Allied troops, often maneuvering by helicopter lift, roved through the area and linked up with the 173d at Katum, often relying solely on helicopters, Caribous, C-123s and C-130s for supply and movement. This floating-brigade experiment ended on 8 April, having proved that a mobile unit could deny the enemy freedom of action. The CCTs assured flexibility, and the main limiting factor for airdrop resupply appeared to be the ability of the receiving unit to absorb large deliveries. Helicopter delivery was obviously preferable to parachutes, but aerial drops were an expedient well worth keeping.[75]

Khe Sanh

> Airlift made possible the allied victory of Khe Sanh in 1968. For eleven weeks early in the year, the defenders of this post were exclusively resupplied by air and withstood the attacks of four North Vietnamese regiments. The campaign bore comparison with the classic combat airlifts of Stalingrad, Burma, and Dien Bien Phu. The success at Khe Sanh reflected the application of lessons drawn from past campaigns, the improved technology for tactical airlift now at hand, and the absolute allied air superiority. The outcome of the struggle was a triumph of tactical defense used in intelligent combination with heavy firepower and air lines of communication.[76]

United States intelligence became aware of growing enemy forces around Khe Sanh in mid-December 1967. North Vietnamese units that heretofore had moved around the allied position on their way south began taking up positions north and southwest of the airstrip. There may have been 15,000 combat troops in the vicinity, and they began probing the Khe Sanh perimeter in January 1968. Because it essentially was cut off from ground resupply, Khe Sanh would have to rely on an air bridge until relieved.

United States forces in Khe Sanh included two infantry battalions and an artillery battalion—all part of the 26th Marine Regiment. On the 16th of January, Air Force C-130s airlifted in another infantry battalion. At that time, the defenders had enough food, fuel, and ammunition to last 30 days. Consideration of an additional infantry battalion led to review of the supply situation and the conclusion that the daily requirements could be met by the current 15-per-day C-130 missions, but that an additional 75 sorties would be needed to build up to a 35-day supply.[77]

The Communists then began to increase the volume and frequency of their mortar, rocket, and artillery fire into the base. On the 21st of January, the main ammunition dump was hit, prompting a request for a tactical emergency aerial resupply. C-123s started an immediate resupply and C-130s resumed landings on the 23d. For the next eight days, Air Force deliveries averaged 250 tons per day, with C-130s carrying most of the loads to take advantage of their larger payloads.[78]

In response to the obvious American reliance on, and success with, the air bridge, the North Vietnamese, well dug in and hidden in the hills surrounding the base, set

AIRLIFT DOCTRINE

Figure 65. C-130 low-altitude, parachute extraction system: Khe Sanh.

up automatic weapons and antiaircraft fire to greet the incoming transports. The enemy also intensely bombarded the airfield, creating direct hit hazards, tearing up the air strip on several occasions, and littering the field with fragments. Air crews responded by staying in the clouds as long as possible, flying steep, tight approach patterns, and minimizing their time on the ground by speedy off-loading. The Marine ground controlled approach (GCA) unit that made landings possible in low ceilings and poor visibility was damaged on 7 February, which slowed the resupply effort for a few days until it was repaired.[79]

C-130 landings decreased on 12 February and C-123 landings increased. Large tonnage deliveries of ammunition, food, and construction materials were to be accomplished primarily by the C-130 container delivery system (CDS) and the low-altitude parachute extraction system (LAPES). The CDS deliveries started on 13 February on a small drop zone (300 square yards) to the west and just outside the main camp perimeter. The system worked well and had the extra advantage of allowing the C-130s to take advantage of cloud cover. Bad weather often prohibited actual aircraft landing, but the CDS program allowed deliveries in spite of the weather. When the Marine GCA unit was again hit on the 19th, the airlifters switched to another radar system that, after some practice, also provided for accurate drops.[80]

VIETNAM ERA

In March the weather began to clear up significantly, which allowed strike aircraft to pound enemy emplacements surrounding the base. It also meant the loss of the protective overcast for the airlifters. Due to a shortage of LAPES rigging items, such missions were seldom more than two a day. Instead, the 834th AD proposed using the ground proximity extraction system (GPES), which used an arresting cable to hook and pull loads from extremely low-flying C-130s. All told, there were 52 LAPES missions and 15 GPES deliveries (which did not start until the latter part of March). For the month, the Air Force delivered 5,100 tons, and the course of the battle shifted in favor of the allies.[81]

"Airlift made possible the allied victory in Khe Sanh in 1968. . . . The defenders of this post were exclusively resupplied by air and withstood the attacks of four North Vietnamese regiments."[82] Using an average of less than 10 percent of the in-country airlift force, the Air Force (between the end of January and early April) delivered 12,430 tons of cargo in 1,128 sorties. Three C-123s were destroyed, and at least 18 C-130s and 8 C-123s sustained battle damage.[83]

Tet Offensive: 1968

The sustained aerial resupply of Khe Sanh was accomplished in the face of the countrywide Tet offensive. The Communist attacks, some of which apparently had been launched 24 hours early, were in full swing by the night of 30–31 January at literally hundreds of locations. Attacks on airfields throughout the country cut into airlift mission rates significantly—down from a 1,100-per-day average to 625 sorties on the 31st for example. The increased tempo of fighting was already putting strains on allied stocks, a situation made worse by the fact that inland road movements had been blocked or interrupted by the Vietcong.[84]

Routine requests were overshadowed for several days by the emergency airlift requirements, with the entire airlift system executing a full range of missions. Two C-123s airdropped five tons of supplies to Kontum on the night of 2 February. On the same day, 17 C-130 sorties moved 500 troops and over 100 tons of equipment of the 101st Division from Song Be to Tan Son Nhut. There was a shuttle between Tan Son Nhut and Bien Hoa to carry aircraft spares for the Vietnamese air force. In the delta region, C-130s and C-123s carried 30,000 tons of cargo in 15 days to support an area normally heavily dependent on road networks. By 4 February, the airlift system was carrying only priority cargo but even then did not have enough assets. General Westmoreland ordered that the restoration of surface transportation have equal priority with defeating the enemy. The airlift system was overtaxed.[85]

The *Pueblo* crisis in January had already drawn off out-of-country C-130s and, at CINCPAC's request, two more TAC squadrons arrived at Tachikawa AB, Japan, 7-9 February. Sixteen C-130s and 25 crews were sent to Cam Ranh Bay, beginning their in-country missions on 11 February. On 25 February, an eight-plane detachment began flying from Nha Trang, raising the C-130 fleet in Vietnam to 96.[86]

Demands on the C-123s were also increasing, and 16 Ranch Hand C-123 spray aircraft were converted to airlift work beginning on 8 February and not returning to normal duties until 20 March. To ease a growing airfield congestion problem, the C-130s flew at night when possible, and aerial ports received additional equipment and people. Through the surge, airlift aircraft suffered only modest losses. Forty-two C-130s, 33 C-123s, and 9 C-7s were hit by ground fire; but only 1 aircraft, a C-130, was shot down. The airlift system's flexibility and responsiveness fully proved their worth in the Tet offensive. Airlift tonnage in January averaged 3,780 tons per day and climbed to 3,880 in February and 4,420 in March. Efficiency was down as measured, for example, by sorties per airplane; but this was explained by the general chaos of the period, bad weather, and overuse of facilities. All in all, it was an excellent response. General Westmoreland was pleased to note the special contributions the airlifters made through troop movements and maintenance of airlines of communications when surface lines were disrupted. "The classical role of tactical airlift," he said, "has been admirably performed in its truest sense."[87]

Kham Duc

The US Army Special Forces camp at Kham Duc was 10 miles from the Laotian border and served as a reconnaissance and training site. It was in a mile-wide bowl, surrounded by hills 2,000 feet high. As at Khe Sanh, Communist preparations for an attack became obvious, and in May, airlifters started carrying in American infantry and artillery reinforcements. By the evening of the 11th, despite Communist harassing fire, C-130s, C-123s, and C-7s had taken in 1,500 troops, including 900 Americans. That evening, however, General Westmoreland decided the camp was not so defensible as Khe Sanh and ordered its evacuation. "The ensuing air evacuation in the presence of a strong enemy was without plan and without precedent in American experience."[88]

Intense ground fire drove away some Chinooks, and the camp was soon encircled by the North Vietnamese. Lt Col Daryl Cole flew in a C-130 that was immediately swamped by civilians trying to get out. On his takeoff roll, mortar bursts flattened a tire. After two hours of intense work stripping away the tire, and with fuel flowing from holes in the wings, Cole managed a takeoff, with a three-man CCT team as his only passengers. He landed safely on the foamed runway at Cam Ranh Bay and earned the Mackay Trophy for 1968.[89]

At 1100 Maj Ray Shelton landed a C-123 at Kham Duc and took off safely with 70 passengers. At 1230 another C-130 could not land because of ground fire. At 1525 Maj Bernard Bucher managed to land his C-130 and pick up more than 100 civilians. The aircraft took off to the north and was shot down with no survivors.

Next came a C-130 flown by Lt Col William Boyd, Jr., that successfully landed, picked up another 100 or so passengers, and safely made a departure to the south. He made it to Chu Lai, with dense smoke and bullet holes throughout the aircraft. Boyd received the Air Force Cross. The next C-130 in was piloted by Lt Col John Delmore. It took heavy ground fire, lost its hydraulics, and crashed, coming to rest beside the strip. The five-man crew made it out unhurt.[90]

Shortly after 1600, three C-130s made it in and out of Kham Duc, carrying out full passenger loads, including the last defenders. The ALCC then inexplicably ordered the three-man CCT back on the ground and the C-130 they were on brought them in. Maj John Gallagher, Jr., and two other controllers were the only Americans on the ground and took shelter in a culvert near the runway. Lt Col Alfred Jeannotte, Jr., landed his C-123 in the face of fire from all directions but, not seeing the controllers, took off. He spotted the small group after takeoff but could not reland due to low fuel. He received the Air Force Cross for heroic effort. Next a C-123, piloted by Lt Col Joe Jackson and Maj Jessie Campbell, managed to drop like a rock from 8,000 feet, land, pick up the controllers, and take off safely. Lt Col Jackson received the only Congressional Medal of Honor awarded to an airlifter in SEA, Maj Campbell the Air Force Cross, and the rest of the crew Silver Stars. The ALCC ordered another plane to land and look for the already saved CCT but rescinded the order as the aircraft was approaching the runway.[91]

Four helicopters and two C-130s were destroyed, but over 500 people were saved, "nearly all in the final minutes when speed was essential and only the indispensable C-130 could do the job."[92] The fog of war created an unbelievable situation with the CCT team, but the dedication of the airlifters saved them.

American reappraisal of its role in South Vietnam saw MACV, under the new leadership of Gen Creighton W. Abrams, Jr., deemphasize major search-and-destroy operations. Airlift remained important, but the missions were generally less urgent. The monthly airlift work load reached its peak in March of 1968 at 138,000 tons. C-130 sorties also peaked in March (14,300), whereas the top C-123 month was October (9,500). The eight-ship Nha Trang C-130 task force closed in April, one of three C-130 temporary squadrons in Vietnam left in the spring, and a second departed in August. At the end of the year there were 72 C-130s in Vietnam.[93]

The period 1969 through 1971 was typified by a general reduction in tempo and intensity, although there were emergency and forward area operations. During the 1970 incursion into Cambodia the heaviest airlift contribution was in support of the 1st Cavalry, primarily delivering petroleum and ammunition. Most of the goods were redistributed by CH-47 and CH-54 helicopters. In the two months of that operation the 834th AD's air transports moved 75,000 passengers (including 3,100 Cambodian refugees moved by C-7s) and 49,600 tons of cargo.[94]

The following year saw the American support of Vietnamese operations in Laos. The order for Lam Son 719 Operation envisioned airlifters moving forces and equipment to the northern provinces in the preparatory phase, airlanding supplies at

AIRLIFT DOCTRINE

Khe Sanh, and airdropping in Laos if needed. Requirements seemed to grow daily and the airlift forces had to be increased. On 30 January 1971, in-country C-130s went from 48 to 57 airplanes, crew ratios increased from 1.4 to 1.7, and the maintenance force expanded. It was an around-the-clock operation. In all, the movement of the contingency force of 9,250 troops and 1,700 tons of cargo took 592 C-130 and 12 C-123 sorties—all this between 26 January and 6 February. Nearly all went into Quang Tri and Dong Ha. Khe Sanh was to be the logistics hub, but the poor condition of its runway delayed availability until 19 February. By mid-March, under heavy Communist pressures, some 17,000 South Vietnamese troops fighting in Laos began to withdraw. For the rest of 1971, fighting in Vietnam remained comparatively light.[95]

An Loc

In early April of 1972, the Communists began a major drive from Cambodia to seize Loc Ninh, block Highway 13 into An Loc, capture An Loc to be the center of government for the Communist-liberated provinces, and open the way to Saigon. The defenders at An Loc were Vietnamese. Sustained helicopter resupply was precluded by an enemy antiaircraft regiment, and Communist capture of Quan Loi airstrip eliminated fixed-wing landings. The Vietnamese air force (VNAF) began airdrops into the small perimeter (1,094 by 766 yards) on 12 April, with very poor results. On 15 April, a VNAF C-123 was shot down and another was blown up on 19 April. These ineffective results brought requests for US Air Force C-130s from MACV.[96]

The DZ for the first American drop at An Loc was 219 yards square. On its initial run-in, the C-130, piloted by Maj Robert Wallace, took ground fire damage to its rudder but dropped its load. The second airplane came from a different direction but was also hit by ground fire that killed the flight engineer and wounded the navigator and copilot. Capt William Caldwell and SSgt Charles Shaub each received the Air Force Cross for getting the burning aircraft back to Tan Son Nhut. Apparently, of the 26 tons dropped by the two C-130s, none were recovered in An Loc. A change in tactics (high-speed, low-level entry, pop up to 600 feet for the drop, and return to low level for egress) on the 16th kept two aircraft from being hit; but on the 18th a C-130 flown by Capt Don Jensen—flying what turned out to be the last daylight low-level mission—was hit and crashed (the crew survived).[97]

To avoid the barrage methods of ground fire the Communists were using over the DZ, the Americans turned to the ground radar air delivery system (GRADS) to be able to release from altitudes above the threat. On the night of 19–20 April, the crews released at 8,000 feet, using the MSQ-77 mobile search radar at Bien Hoa for guidance, with six more GRADS drops over the next four days. There were many problems with recovery because of smashed or broken loads—the Vietnamese

324

packers and their American advisors were unfamiliar with the methods for high-altitude, low-opening (HALO) drops, which stopped after 23 April. The airlifters turned to container delivery system (CDS) drops for three nights, but a C-130 was lost on 25–26 April after entering a "wall of fire." For the next seven nights, they continued their efforts. On the night of 3-4 May, another C-130 was shot down by the increasingly intense enemy fire. That signaled the end of the CDS and return to the HALO system.[98]

The HALO drops continued to face problems of parachutes only partially opening or failing to open altogether. There was also a growing shortage of devices that opened the chutes after they had fallen the appropriate distance. Because the Communists had used an SA-7 surface-to-air missile in Quang Tri Province on 29 April, a return to low-level operations could be potentially a disaster. The best solution turned out to be GRADS-directed, high-velocity drops, begun on 8 May. This system used 1,000- to 2,000-pound loads, heavily layered with honeycombed cardboard and stabilized with slotted parachutes. Accuracy was high, which not only got the goods there but made it easier to retrieve them. HALO missions continued on a reduced scale, but the success of the high-velocity method made it clear that the resupply campaign would be won. On 20 June, 10 C-130Es from the United States arrived with the adverse weather aerial delivery system (AWADS), but the GRADS method remained predominant. Pressures subsided somewhat at An Loc, but the Communists still attacked movements on Highway 13 and held the Quan Loi airport at year's end.[99]

Kontum

While the desperate efforts to keep An Loc were taking place, airlift was needed elsewhere to respond to Communist incursions. United States airlifters helped haul troops and equipment from Tan Son Nhut to Kontum. MAC C-141s began carrying passengers and cargo from Tan Son Nhut to such places as Da Nang, Bien Hoa, and Pleiku. With an average of four and a high of eight aircraft in-country in late April, the C-141s could account for 25 percent of the total Air Force airlift work load. This small force allowed the C-130s to concentrate on airdrops and forward deliveries. Two TAC C-130 squadrons were sent from the states in May to improve airlift capability and to help in a critical effort on Kontum, which had been isolated on 24 April.[100]

The Communists got very good at hitting aircraft on the ground at Kontum. A C-130 was damaged on takeoff on 26 April and had to be parked and repaired there. Another C-130 that had just landed was damaged, and a Vietnamese C-123 took a direct hit and burned. On 2 May, a C-130 lost several feet of a wingtip colliding with a helicopter on the crowded airhead but survived to execute an emergency

AIRLIFT DOCTRINE

landing at Pleiku. Another C-130 delivering fuel was hit by rocket fire on 3 May, and US Air Force daylight operations at Kontum ceased.[101]

Nighttime C-130 landings relied heavily on suppression by AC-130 gunships. On 25 May the North Vietnamese captured the east end of the runway and the threat of ground fire ended C-130 landings. Using the GRADS system, the C-130s sustained the surrounded forces until they reclaimed much of the city, allowing landings to start again on the night of 8–9 June. Reports of SA-7 missiles were met with allied artillery fire into enemy sectors and flare shells set off near the runway to distract SA-7s. There was an SA-7 fired at a transport on 13 June, but it was avoided. The last airdrop took place 14 June, capping a 48-drop surge since 7 June.[102]

A special note for the Kontum effort was the use of adverse weather aerial delivery system (AWADS). The first AWADS drop in Vietnam took place on 1 June at Dray Rieng in Cambodia, and 16 such deliveries supplied Kontum in June.

> Assessments of AWADS operations were generally favorable. AWADS was less accurate than the GRADS and more costly in terms of equipment, training, and necessary support. On the other hand, AWADS could be used in regions that could not be supplied by GRADS and was independent of enemy action against ground radar sites. AWADS also allowed evasive maneuvers not possible when under GRADS guidance. Aircrews of the 61st were ingenious in adapting the AWADS computer for high-altitude work and in overcoming weaknesses in intelligence and charting materials. It appeared that both the AWADS and its associated stationkeeping equipment had proven their reliability, and that both added valuable tactical capabilities.[103]

By the end of June, the Communist spring offensive was clearly a failure. Air transport made a decisive contribution to the allied victory but soon returned to the pre-Easter offensive drawdown. In accordance with the Paris peace agreements, a cease-fire became effective on 28 January 1973. American POWs were to be released and the last American troops withdrawn within 60 days. American C-130s provided support for the joint military commission that made arrangements for the POW release, and MAC C-141s brought the prisoners out. The airlift force continued to provide support to American efforts in Cambodia but ended with the fall of Phnom Penh in mid-April 1975. It also helped evacuate Americans and Vietnamese from Vietnam.

Tactical airlifters in SEA proved what similar forces had proved in World War II and the Korean War—they could and would deliver the goods when and where needed. They flew in harm's way and, through a combination of ingenuity, grit, and individual bravery, made the best of a tough situation.

Strategic Airlift Support of SEA

The growing war in SEA placed extreme pressures on the MAC airlift system due to shortages in personnel and resources. Commitments were increasing significantly while MAC was phasing out several old aircraft and phasing in its C-141s.[104]

Figure 66. MAC C-141 in South Vietnam.

MAC began the period with 21 squadrons of C-124s, 3 of C-133s, 7 of C-130s, and 3 squadrons of C-135s. The C-124s, rapidly approaching obsolescence, took 95 hours to make a trip from Travis AFB to Saigon and return. At a mission utilization rate of 6.7 hours per day, that came out to just over 13 days for one trip. The C-133 had greater cargo capacity and range, but its turboprop speeds made it marginal for strategic airlift. The C-130s and C-135s in MAC's inventory were interim measures, each having its own shortcomings. All paled in comparison to the C-141 destined to begin flying into SEA in August of 1965. By 1968, the last C-141—number 284—entered MAC. The command received its first C-5 on 17 December 1969—on the 66th anniversary of the Wright brothers' first flight. Seventeen of the C-5s would have replaced the 308 planes used daily in the Berlin airlift. The first C-5 mission into Vietnam was in August of 1971.[105]

Building a System

To meet the needs of US activity in Vietnam, MAC took two steps that formed the basis for its response throughout the war. First, the command placed priority on moving its aircraft through the system as quickly as possible. This not only would provide the obvious advantage of more goods and people delivered per time period, but it also meant better maintenance at the home station and more responsiveness to other possible contingencies. The other action MAC pursued was to make the route system work properly—to deal with the problems of parking, loading, and unloading congestion. The planners and operators increased and improved crew staging, determined optimum ground times at en route stations, and increased emphasis on work load forecasting.[106]

There was excruciating attention to detail in every facet of the entire system. By placing the bulk of en route staging crews at Hickam AFB and Wake Island, ground times dropped from 15 to 5 hours and 15 to 4 hours respectively. Every possible flight by the Air Force Reserves was used to carry opportune cargo from MAC aerial ports, to generally improve worldwide system productivity, to lower backlogs, and to reduce requirements for commercial augmentation. Flights were also routed away from the most congested stations. Communications and coordination between the primary aerial ports at Travis AFB and Hickam AFB were singled out for improvements, so that aircraft departing Travis without a full utilization of allowable cabin load were identified at takeoff for possible additional loads out in the system. To reduce a near saturation condition at Clark AB, Mactan AB became a primary point for C-124s intertheater through flights bound for SEA.[107]

At the beginning of 1965, all passengers and cargo destined for SEA went through the Travis aerial port. At the same time, there was only one port in Vietnam (Saigon) and one in Thailand (Bangkok) routinely handling MAC channel traffic. Extensive review of the aerial port/route structure interaction yielded dramatic results. Optimizing C-141 payload and range characteristics led to establishment of East Coast aerial ports of embarkation (APOEs) using a Northern Pacific route and also reducing through traffic at West Coast APOEs from 183 to 84 per month. Delivery times dropped from 95 to 38 hours. Establishing routine channels from Dover to Saigon, Dover to Clark, and Charleston to Bangkok was not only operationally important, it was a significant departure from SOP and showed the inherent flexibility in the system. Also, three additional APOEs opened in 1965, designated to support specific destinations in the SEA area, as illustrated below:

New APOE	*Destinations Supported*
Kelly AFB	Clark AB, RP
	Tan Son Nhut AB, Vietnam
	Kadena AB, Japan
	Kimpo AB, Korea
Norton AFB	Kadena AB, Japan
	Da Nang AB, Vietnam
	Okinawa, Japan

VIETNAM ERA

McChord AFB   Tachikawa AB, Japan
               Seoul, Korea

Later a McGuire-to-Bien Hoa channel was added for troop movement, with an extremely high (98 percent) utilization rate.[108]

The aerial port system, at the beginning of the surge of MAC support for SEA, began with the premise of coastal APOEs serving only selected destinations in adjacent ocean areas. This concept evolved earlier when there were few airlifters of relatively short range; they were saved for the overwater routes where they could be most productive. The limited number of on-load ports on the West Coast, combined with only two major off-load ports in SEA, soon congested the airlift system. Lack of effective user forecasts did not help. Thus, the opening of East Coast APOEs for SEA support radically changed the system's outlook to what MAC called multidirectional ports and also reinforced the source-to-user concept. The C-141 drove the ideas to fruition, providing more efficient services.

To make sure that truly high-priority items moved quickly, the Red Ball Express system, which was aimed especially at Army vehicles, aircraft parts, and aircraft, came into being in 1965. MAC guaranteed movement within 24 hours of receipt in an APOE. A year later similar procedures were applied (with the 999 program) to all services.[109]

Also vital to the successful movement of cargo through the aerial port system was the 463L cargo handling system. Originally conceived in 1957, specific operational requirement (SOR) 157 called for the 463L system to have four major parts:

> (1) *Terminal*—the intermediate point at which all cargo must pass through the 463L system. Terminals could vary in size and configuration, but all would have to maintain the capability to receive, ship, process, document, label, and sort cargo.
> (2) *Cargo Preparation*—essentially, all equipment associated with the palletization and restraint of cargo, to include pallets, nets, coupling devices, and containers.
> (3) *Cargo Terminal Handling*—the K-loaders, forklifts, trailers, and similar vehicles used to load and unload cargo aircraft.
> (4) *Aircraft Systems*—all component items installed in the aircraft which were related to the cargo process, such as rail, roller, and lock systems.[110]

The C-141 was the first airlift aircraft designed with an integral system for rapid cargo handling built into it from the start.

Initial procurement of the ground handling equipment, pallets, and nets was conservative and placed the entire system "behind the power curve." Only through increased and continuous procurement, improving maintenance, and intensive daily management were shortfalls overcome. Maintenance reliability problems with ground equipment plagued the system throughout the war.

To improve aircraft utilization, MAC instituted the Fast Fly program. One step in this program was to extend the workweek from 40 to 48 hours. Another step was to increase logistical support by expanding the forward supply system from 45 to 57 forward supply points.[111]

AIRLIFT DOCTRINE

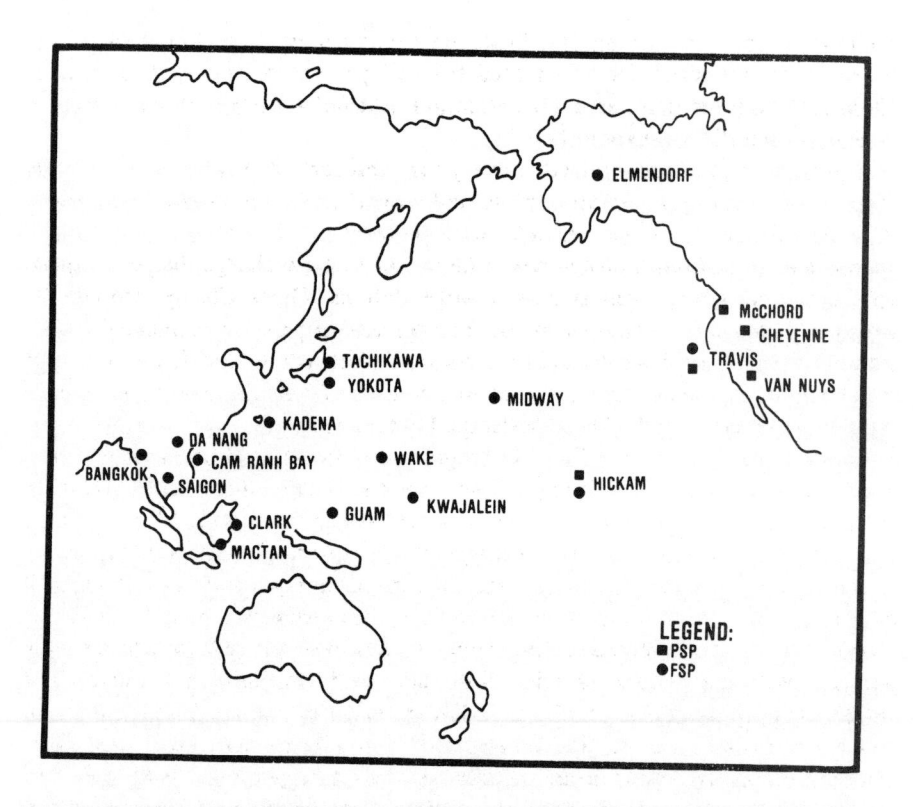

Figure 67. The MAC self-support system for Southeast Asia operations.

The forward supply support (FSS) system offers a way of supplying peculiar spares in support of the worldwide airlift route structure. A primary supply point (PSP), generally a MAC base, provides a carefully selected range of spare parts to forward support points (FSP). There is a whole management system built around maintaining the airlift force throughout its structure, and the FSS is only a part of the grander concerns. Stock levels and material actually carried are the result of a carefully calculated process that includes such items as what support can the host base system provide, what skilled maintenance personnel can and should be assigned to a particular location for the most payback, what physical facilities are available, what tools are needed and available, and what is the nature of the maintenance problems likely to develop. To oversee and manage this process, MAC created centralized reporting and monitoring programs and devised ways of moving critical parts through the airlift system—on a dedicated basis if needed. MAC also established central repair points (CRP) at Yokota AB and Clark AB for centralized repair and testing of delicate electronic components. Supply departure reliability for the airlift force increased from 93 percent in 1965 to 98 percent in 1968. It is only through meticulous attention to detail—brought on by a sense of system—that airlift works at its best.[112]

Ground times were scrutinized at every turn and early departures were strongly encouraged. Returning aircraft were routed around choke points and high-density stations whenever possible. Quick Stop procedures, a one-hour "ops stop" approach to all stations transited where there was no crew change, helped to speed up the aircraft flow. Even at crew change stations, Quick Change procedures, which included crew swap-out at the airplane and paperwork completed before landing, led to a one-hour ground time standard. The idea was to do en route-type maintenance at regular bases, not at locations in Vietnam. This both reduced saturation in-country and allowed better quality maintenance.[113]

Another vital point of the Fast Fly program was switching from a maintenance inspection system based on flying hours to one based on regular intervals (number of days). Col Benjamin Foreman, chief of maintenance for the 60th Military Airlift Wing at Travis, originated this isochronal (ISO) system. The old program made aircraft due inspections at irregular intervals, resulting in no work on one day and three to five aircraft awaiting inspection the next. Maintenance complexes could not schedule work effectively, and the supply system was not fast enough for peak periods. With the increased utilization rate, problems only got worse. The isochronal program, based on a 70-day, 35-day, and 7-day home station inspection, was a resounding success. The 35-day and 70-day inspection docks (one each) could be scheduled a year ahead of time for work load purposes. With only two aircraft tied up at a time, more were available for operations. Mission planning based on days rather than anticipated flying hours was much simpler and predictable. It is far easier to plan a particular mission, or series of missions, against specific tail numbers based on the ISO system than on predicted flying hours that are subject to numerous changes. The full impact of quality maintenance was a logical outcome, and the supply system could respond much more rapidly to the new approach.[114]

All of these actions resulted in a superb airlift response. MAC was able to effect its many changes because it owned and operated its own system. MAC called this "Airlift System Integrity." By 1969 MAC could claim that "the current MAC command post system is organized whereby the MAC Air Forces, area, and base command posts, with their separate and distinct functions, form an integral chain of command from Headquarters MAC to the lowest and most distinct echelon of command to exercise command control of the airlift force."[115] This was not totally true in 1965 and part of 1966. The airlift command post system, very much like the rest of airlift, was designed and manned for peacetime. To initially meet growing special missions to SEA (as there were few channels to SEA), MAC deployed airlift control forces (ACF) that later were renamed airlift control elements (ALCE).

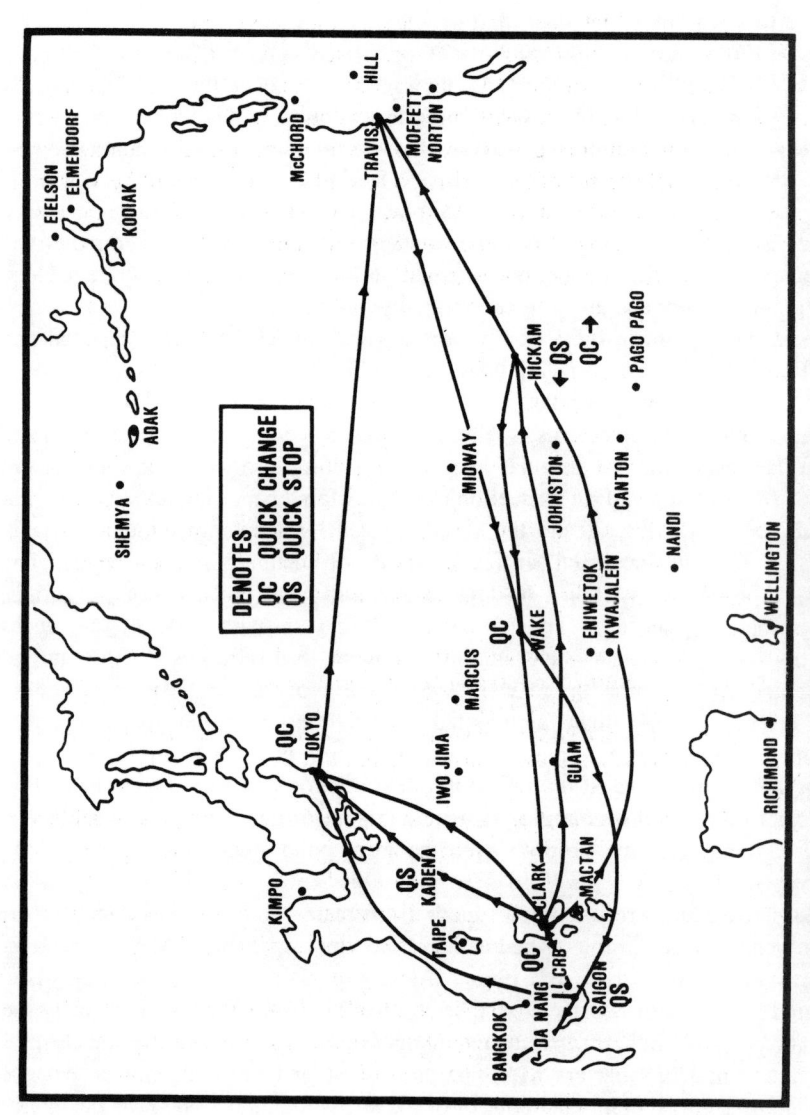

Figure 68. The MAC Quick Stop/Quick Change aircraft maintenance system for Southeast Asia operations.

These operated in the place of area airlift command posts, as there were none for Vietnam. MAC's Far East Airlift Command Post (FEACP) located in Tachikawa AB, Japan, responded by creating an operating location at Clark AB. The Fast Fly program, a modernized jet fleet, and a generally mounting volume of movements called for faster and faster response. General Estes said he was "convinced that positive command control of the MAC airlift force is the key to achievement of the higher utilization rates and successful mission accomplishment."[116] He directed the ACPs to cease being monitoring agencies and to begin functioning as central control points. "Operational control of the Airlift Command Post system will be a clear-cut line from MAC Command Post to the MAC Air Force Command Post to the area to the base. . . ."[117] He demanded a near-perfect functioning of the ACP and placed the whole system directly under the control of individual commanders.

Blue Light

Operation Blue Light carried 2,952 troops and 4,749 tons of equipment of the 3d Infantry Brigade, 25th Infantry Division, from Hickam AFB, Hawaii, direct to Pleiku, Vietnam, between 23 December 1965 and 23 January 1966. A mixture of 88 C-141s, 126 C-133s, and 11 C-124s flew 231 missions and finished the deployment eight days early. It was the "most massive airlift of US troops and equipment into a combat zone."[118] Apparently, everyone was pleased:

> This movement by air, said Secretary of Defense Robert S. McNamara, was a striking demonstration of the Air Force's increased airlift capability as well as the professional skills of the Military Airlift Command. General Westmoreland, Commander of the US forces in Vietnam, said in appraising Operation Blue Light, "This was the most professional airlift I've seen in all my airborne experience."[119]

Not bad for an operation that was originally planned in five days. Several factors contributed to the success, but the most important was the joint training the 25th ID had been conducting with the 1502d Air Transport Wing (renamed the 61st Military Airlift Wing—MAW) since 1962. Each organization was then familiar with the needs and procedures of the other. General Estes even said that "this airlift has been carried out many times."[120] The earlier training used C-124s and some C-130s, so load plans and selection procedures had to be adjusted for the C-141s and C-133s and airlift expertise called in from Twenty-Second Air Force and the 60th MAW. C-141s were new to the fleet and SOPs were still being developed. Nonetheless, the on-scene workers persevered and succeeded.

This was the first operational test for the C-141, as well as the first deployment of combat-ready troops from home station to an offshore combat location. The decision to use a mix of C-141s for everything they could haul, plus the C-133s for outsize cargo, was a good one (the C-124s were used as replacements for prime aircraft only). The operation got the MAC planners thinking about force mix and gave them a leg up for when the C-5A would come into the inventory. This decision was complicated by the question of safe operation into Pleiku AB. The 6,000-foot strip barely met C-141 operational standards, and its load-bearing capability for a sustained period was questionable. The decision to use the air base proved right—there were 240 landings without damage. There was no question about using the C-133. There was plenty of real world experience with it, and its short-field capabilities were also well proven.

For all its specialness, Blue Light was in many ways a routine airlift. It flew scheduled flights over predetermined routes. There were stage crews available along the routes. "There was nothing to prevent a normal logistics lift. There was no en route threat, staging bases were not being bombed, and the destination airport was relatively secure."[121] But it was a first, pulled off with aplomb. It was so smooth, almost so easy, that it reflected the ultimate in airlift doctrine—fast and flexible. The C-141 proved its combat airlift capability, and the recovery base concept was validated. The C-141 took over the role of some of the C-124s and all C-130s with a fourfold increase in airlift capability, taking approximately one-third the time it took a C-124 or C-133.[122]

Eagle Thrust

By November of 1967 the strategic airlift system had matured sufficiently for a movement twice the size of Blue Light to succeed. In Eagle Thrust, MAC moved 10,024 troops and 5,357 tons of the 101st Airborne Division direct from Fort Campbell, Kentucky, to Bien Hoa AB, Vietnam. The 391 airlift missions, moving in eight noncontinuous increments, from 17 November until 18 December 1967, completed the move 53 hours ahead of schedule.[123]

The deployment aircraft flew over and through the existing airlift structure, with departures from Kentucky keyed to time slots in the route structure. This took into account stage crew posture and en route station capabilities, routine missions already in the system, and retrograde needs. Twenty-two C-133 missions flew the outsized equipment over one route, and the 369 C-141 missions flew two other routes to SEA. Using engine-running off-load procedures developed in Blue Light, the C-141 average off-load time at Bien Hoa was 7.4 minutes, reducing ramp saturation potential and exposure to ground fire. The C-133s were on the ground an average of about two hours. The recovery base concept was used to great effect.[124]

At US Air Force request MAC figured closure time under varying surge conditions as well as a comparable deployment to Rhein-Main, Germany. The figures are instructive as to the capabilities of the airlift system:

	Bien Hoa	Rhein-Main
Maximum continuous effort without degrading normal traffic worldwide	18.7 days	18.0 days
Minimum closure time, some TAC/Reserve augmentation, normal worldwide traffic	6.7 days	3.3 days
Contingency conditions, TAC/Reserves cover JCS withhold, normal passenger traffic only	4.2 days	1.9 days
National emergency, CRAF call-up, voluntary reserves	2.2 days	23.5 hours

The implications must have been staggering for any planner concerned with prompt response to an emerging problem anywhere in the world.[125]

Combat Fox

Although in the midst of great expansion in support of US operations in SEA in general, and the Tet offensive in particular, MAC engaged in yet another "largest single strategic airlift in history" in 1968. Following the seizure of the USS *Pueblo* by the North Koreans, MAC C-124s, C-130s, C-133s, and C-141s flew more than 800 missions to Korea from the United States, SEA, and Japan in support of tactical air forces. Five Air Force Reserve airlift units were called to active duty primarily to backfill regular channel airlift requirements. MAC created ALCEs at Osan, Kimpo, Kusan, and Suwon, Korea; and at Misawa, Japan. Between 29 January and 17 February, these stations handled 1,036 aircraft, 13,683 tons of cargo, and 7,996 troops. The Combat Fox airlift more than doubled Eagle Thrust, while maintaining the logistics airlift into SEA.[126]

The Combat Fox deployments and redeployments required 37.7 million ton-miles of capability. Twenty of these came from normal MAC channels. After being alerted on 25 January 1968, MAC commenced deployment operations on the 28th from seven on-load stations in the United States to three stations in Korea and one in Vietnam. Immediately following the completion of the Combat Fox operation on 12 February, MAC was alerted by the Joint Chiefs of Staff to begin deployment of forces to Vietnam within 48 hours to help counter the Tet offensive. The requirement was to airlift an Army brigade from Fort Bragg to Chu Lai and a reinforced Marine regiment from El Toro to Da Nang. MAC considered activating Stage I of the CRAF; but after a special appeal for maximum augmentation, voluntary commercial response was sufficient to keep MAC port levels within acceptable management levels. These two operations combined to increase forecast

MAC cargo requirements by 48 percent and passenger forecasts by 13 percent. The airlift response was outstanding.[127]

An Interim Report on Southeast Asia Airlift Doctrine

In 1970, when it appeared that US involvement in Vietnam was clearly ending, the House Subcommittee on Military Airlift held hearings to review how the airlift picture had changed over the four years since the last hearings. A presentation by the Military Airlift Command summed up strategic airlift experiences and doctrine from Vietnam. Noting that strategic airlift in 1970 bore little resemblance to airlift in the 1940s and 1950s, the briefing officer put 30 years of change in a nutshell: "What was a transportation agency in the 1950s is rapidly becoming a strategic combat airlift force for the 1970s."[128] The distinction between tactical and strategic airlift was kept clear, with the urging not to confuse MAC's "evolving combat airlift capabilities" or consider them as a replacement for the "extremely essential tactical airlift forces."[129]

In 1970 the first and fundamental mission and the reason for the existence of strategic airlift was deployment—deployment to rear forward area airfields. With careful preplanning, the deploying units would be introduced into the theater as integrated fighting forces ready to move forward by theater airlift and surface transportation. A division could move to Europe or the Pacific in just a few days. The second major MAC mission was employment of forces in the combat zone. This mission was keyed to augmenting tactical airlift forces in emergency and unusual circumstances or when the magnitude of the airlift task was great. Such missions included repositioning within the forward area, especially of outsize equipment.[130]

The third and "most demanding role of strategic airlift" was continuing or preplanned resupply of deployed forces. "The C-5/C-141 force," said MAC, "will perform an increasing amount of preplanned logistic resupply between established CONUS multidirectional aerial ports and dispersed overseas destinations. As today, this will consist mainly of channel traffic airlift."[131] In spite of stringent JCS restrictions on the use of airlift, demands for airlift services increased 264 percent between 1965 and 1970. Upwards of 80 percent of MAC's airlift effort had been dedicated to supporting SEA, an amazing figure that reflected a high degree of confidence in airlift flexibility.[132]

The MAC briefing also highlighted the need for multiple offload points in a theater of operations as a lesson of airlift activities in SEA. Altogether, MAC operated into 26 bases, thus reducing theater system work load and speeding up distribution to the user. During the heaviest periods of resupply, MAC averaged 44 military and 29 commercial contract flights per day into SEA with an average ground time of 1.8 hours. The use of recovery bases outside of Vietnam meant shorter ground times, fewer demands on theater resources, and less time susceptible to enemy interdiction. The soon to be C-5/C-141 team was viewed as complementary, making a wide choice of delivery options available to the user. All of this reduced congestion, increased utilization, and permitted a smoother flow of aircraft.[133]

The command also said that a basic concept of strategic airlift was to move forces directly from the United States to the desired off-load points, "be they aerial ports, depots, bare bases, or when necessary, the forward area."[134] It was a forward-looking doctrine.

> This source-to-user concept is becoming more feasible because modern airlift aircraft have improved strategic capabilities as well as the ability to perform in a variety of combat missions. When direct delivery by strategic airlift is feasible, transshipment is minimized, thus reducing the work load of theater air- and surface-transportation. In a remote presence posture there may be very little theater transportation available in the early stages of a deployment. The source-to-user concept is fundamental to and dependent on all of our other operating procedures.[135]

Vitally linked to this source-to-user idea was the availability of as many off-load points as possible. The MAC analysis of Europe and the Pacific regions focused on four types of runways, with runway and ramp dimensions and weight-bearing capabilities being the major variables. Even though all 2,400 airfields surveyed were over 4,000 feet long, three of four categories were not suitable for sustained heavy operations because of weight-bearing limitations. This meant 1,169 airfields required at least a 50-percent overload factor for runway usage and/or engineering support to keep the fields in shape for even reduced levels of airlift operations. There were 60 airfields in Europe and 53 in the Pacific judged capable of supporting sustained, heavy C-5/C-141 airlift operations.[136]

Experiences in SEA showed that sophisticated aerial ports were not an absolute necessity. Even during high-volume, sustained resupply operations, the new MAC doctrine said, only minimal facilities would be needed for off-load in the forward area. This, however, put a high premium on effective interface with the airlift user. This translated into an ongoing affiliation program between specific airlift units and Army, Air Force, and Marine strike forces, which entailed a great deal of preplanning and training for unit deployments. It also called for airlift control elements and associated equipment, involvement in the affiliation training, and preparation for independent deployment as well. This interface relationship, the MAC presentation claimed, was relatively manageable with the principal limitation for rapid deployments being the "speed with which forces can be prepared and marshalled."[137]

Resupply interface was more difficult to define and control. During unit deployments, off-load was primarily of troops and rolling stock—easily handled. Resupply missions delivered pallets and containers, which have to be handled—a more difficult procedure. Lack of ramp space and use of taxiways become more problematic for efficient use of the destination airfield by other aircraft, as well as slowing down airlift frequency. Some space could be freed up through the use of matting, similar to improvements at Da Nang, Bien Hoa, and Tan Son Nhut. Another way to improve handling of resupply cargo, especially the large volumes associated with C-5 deliveries, was the C-5 air transportable loading dock. It was a modular dock that could be transported along with required power, accessories, and 75 personnel in two C-5s and assembled in eight hours. Off-load time for 36 pallets was 15 minutes.[138]

The 1970 doctrine also admitted that large-scale deployments would be out of the question without the Civil Reserve Air Fleet (CRAF). Nonetheless, CRAF limitations were recognized. Civil airplanes had no outsize capability and required a sophisticated ground environment. The doctrinal result was that civil aircraft would be used to carry "large numbers of people and bulk cargo between major air terminals."[139]

The question of vulnerabilities of the airlift system also received attention. At home station, vulnerabilities would be reduced by the fact that about half the fleet was always away and that there were dispersal plans for the other aircraft. The flexibility offered by the new generation of C-141s and C-5s would avoid concentration at en route bases, and multiple flow patterns would allow circumvention of threatened routes and bases. Vulnerability in objective areas was the most serious threat; and multiple off-load bases, flow control, and very short ground times were thought to partially reduce the problem. The assistant secretary of the Air Force for installations and logistics, Phillip Whittaker, addressed the question of whether C-5s would carry cargo into hostile areas, such as Khe Sanh:

> There is frankly a difference of opinion. There is a feeling on the one hand that the C-5 is configured to go in as you know to secondary airfields to provide this very rapid offload to go in and make air drops of supplies. Therefore, it does have the physical capability of carrying the freight right into the forward areas.
>
> On the other hand, you are talking about a big and pretty vulnerable piece of hardware that you don't want to subject to hostile action unless you absolutely have to.
>
> So I can't really give you a firm answer. The intention would be to protect the C-5 to the maximum extent, subject of course to getting the necessary cargo moved to the forward area.[140]

Lt Gen George Baylon, deputy chief of staff for plans and resources, Headquarters USAF, also spoke to that issue, noting that in a Khe Sanh type of situation

> the tactical air forces would most appropriately assume that responsibility, and further, it ought to be understood, I believe, that should any particular situation demand it, the military airlift force [MAC], based on an appropriate decision, would undertake that task, whatever it might be.[141]

The 1972 Easter Offensive

The demonstrated flexibility of the global airlift system was tested again in the Easter offensive in Vietnam in 1972. On 5 April 1972, Gen Creighton Abrams, Jr., commander of MACV, urgently requested additional forces from the JCS. Consequently, TAC started a series of major deployments known as Constant Guard I through IV. Under Constant Guard I a squadron of F-105Gs from McConnell AFB, Kansas, two F-4 squadrons from Seymour-Johnson AFB, North Carolina, and several EB-66s from Shaw AFB, South Carolina, departed for Thailand. Thirty-eight C-141s lifted 854 troops and 400 tons of cargo in this movement, while four TAC C-130s moved en route maintenance teams and equipment to their locations. Constant Guard II saw similar movement of two F-4 squadrons, one each from Homestead AFB and Eglin AFB, Florida, to Thailand.[142]

Constant Guard III was the largest single move in the history of TAC. Four squadrons of F-4s of the 49th Tactical Fighter Wing at Holloman AFB, New Mexico, moved to Takhli, Thailand. MAC C-5s, C-141s, and commercial carriers moved 3,195 personnel and 1,600 tons of cargo in nine days. By way of comparison, it took 56 days to get the first ground troop forces to Korea from the United States in 1951. Twenty-four hours after arrival in Thailand, F-4s were flying missions in support of South Vietnamese forces near An Loc.[143]

Constant Guard IV saw the deployment of two C-130E squadrons to join tactical airlift forces at Ching Chuan Kang AB in Taiwan. MAC augmented these and other SEA intratheater airlift forces in an operation code-named Cold Map, freeing up the C-130s for in-country work. In the last three months of the fiscal year, MAC's airlift forces moved 18,521 tons of cargo and 19,226 passengers within the Pacific area.[144] In May alone, MAC operated 100 of these missions. As usual, every effort was made to get the most from each mission. For example, one C-141 mission moved Army ammunition from Kadena to Da Nang, and then carried Air Force ammunition from Da Nang to Takhli.[145] During this period MAC also provided airlift support to Strategic Air Command B-52s and tanker forces deploying to Guam and Thailand, to include movement of cargo, personnel, and ordnance.[146]

Prior to this surge, the C-5 had not operated in what MAC considered a combat environment, but in May its airland capability was tested. On 3 May MACV requested the emergency airlift of six MK-48 tanks from Yokota AB, Japan, to Da Nang. Each tank weighed 49 tons. Off-load procedures were planned to minimize exposure to rocket fire. After touchdown and during taxi, all tie-down chains except one were removed. As the C-5 cargo doors were being opened and the drive-off ramps positioned, the tank driver started his engine. The tank then was able to drive off and start directly toward the battle area. The off-loading sequence took 7 minutes and ground times were 30 minutes or less.[147] Immediately following on the heels of this aviation first, MAC C-5s moved 42 M-41 tanks (24 tons each) and 8 M-548 tracked recovery vehicles (7.5 tons each) in 15 missions to Da Nang and

AIRLIFT DOCTRINE

Figure 69. MAC C-5A departing South Vietnam.

Cam Ranh Bay.[148] Average off-load time was 32 minutes. Altogether, C-5s flew 201 missions in SEA during the last quarter of fiscal 1972, compared to 102 missions in the first nine months of the year.[149] The C-5 arrived at off-load stations with sufficient fuel to recover to an offshore base for refueling, maintenance, and crew change.

The Israeli Airlift: 1973

Deputy Secretary of Defense William Clements, Jr., said that if the United States could have found any other way to transport material to Israel, it would not have used MAC—but there was no effective alternative.[150] American support of Israel in its 1973 confrontation with Egypt and Syria could not count on sealift for immediate needs. It would have taken approximately 30 days to generate sufficient lift, and the en route time would have been an additional 12 to 14 days. Jet transports could deliver the goods in 18 hours. The small fleet of Israeli commercial airliners could not provide the volume needed, and American civil airlines apparently wanted no part of the operations. President Richard M. Nixon ordered an immediate airlift to

VIETNAM ERA

Israel. Initial plans called for the use of the Azores as a meeting point for American and Israeli planes, but that was quickly shelved because it would not get enough material to Israel in time. On 13 October the decision was made to fly into Lod Airport at Tel Aviv.[151]

Because of the fear of losing their oil supplies, no European country except Portugal would allow the airlifters to use their facilities. Lajes Field (Portuguese Base Number 4) became the one and only en route stop. It took careful planning to avoid total saturation there, for Lajes could handle only 25 C-141 and 5 C-5 aircraft on the ground at one time. Because the mission called for a round-trip of nearly 13,000 miles, stage crews were positioned at Lajes and three US bases. Additional fuel, maintenance personnel, and aircraft spares were also sent to Lajes Field. The airlift flow, based on a complex calculus, was limited to 36 C-141s and 6 C-5s eastbound daily; this meant enough people at Lajes Field to handle a combined flow of 72 C-141 and 12 C-5 east/west flights per day. The facilities in the Azores and at Lod could not handle this flow, so MAC established airlift control elements at both locations to control the aircraft and aerial port activities.[152]

The first C-5 landed at Lod on 14 October, but its 113,000 pounds of cargo had to be unloaded by hand (in three and one-half hours) because the C-5 with the ground-handling equipment had aborted at Lajes Field. Within the three days, MAC was averaging 700 tons of daily delivery, including ammunition, medical supplies, parts

Figure 70. MAC C-5A departing Lajes AB, Azores, in support of Israeli resupply operation.

AIRLIFT DOCTRINE

Figure 71. First MAC aircraft (a C-5A) to land at Lod Airport, Israel.

for damaged aircraft, 175-mm cannon, 155-mm howitzers, and M-60 and M-48 tanks. By 20 October, deliveries reached 4,500 tons per day. The US airlift ended on 14 November, after 32 days, when shipping began to arrive in sufficient amounts to end the need for further airlift. Altogether, 145 C-5 and 422 C-141 missions moved 22,395 tons of military equipment and supplies. Because a good portion of MAC's efforts were directed toward the Israeli airlift, the command increased commercial augmentation, particularly in the Pacific, to ensure that worldwide commitments were met.[153]

Several lessons were immediately obvious from the Israeli airlift, but four are of particular importance. The first was that airlifters needed to be capable of air refueling (AR). Earlier arguments that an all-jet force decreased dependence on island bases were generally true, but the extra flexibility from AR would have paid high dividends.

The C-5s used in the Israeli airlift did not use their AR capability because of concerns over the impact of such maneuvers on the questionable wing on the aircraft. Later, it was found that AR would have put less stress on the wing than the extra takeoffs and landings. The C-141s were not air refuelable. With aerial refueling, both aircraft could have carried more cargo, thus delivering more, faster, with fewer missions flown (fig. 72).

Refueling	Payload (Tons)		Missions Required	
	C-5	C-141	C-5	C-141
Lajes and LOD	74.3	27.6	145	421
With no en route bases	33.5	0	659	0
In-flight and LOD (No en route landing)	107.4	32	101	364
Missions avoided as result of IFR			44	57

*House Committee on Armed Services, *Research and Development Subcommittee Hearings on the Posture of Military Airlift* (1975), 77, statement of Gen Paul Carlton, commander, Military Airlift Command.

Figure 72. Air refueling potential saving in the Israeli airlift.*

The second lesson was that the C-5, under attack for numerous design and cost problems, proved the value of having an airlifter that could carry heavy cargo loads and heavy military equipment and deliver them across long distances quickly (fig. 73). Third, the airlift fleet was put at risk. The US Navy's Sixth Fleet provided air cover and radar coverage to keep the peace in the Mediterranean. But there was a concern about terrorist attacks at Lajes, where the field was not secure, and about attacks from missiles stationed in Egypt. Fourth, the years of developing a highly mobile command, control, maintenance, and aerial port system for support of an airlift effort paid off.[154]

Estes on Airlift

In the March–April 1966 issue of the *Air University Review*, MAC's new commander, Gen Howell Estes, Jr., explained "The Revolution in Airlift."[155] Drawing on the premise that no other principle of war had more significance in the present age than flexibility, he argued that "global military airlift has been shown, throughout the era of the cold war, to be a principal medium of achieving maximum military flexibility."[156] The airlift revolution had two phases: (1) acceptance and use of military airlift and (2) removal of technical limitations. The proof he offered for this argument provides both a review of past airlift and a flavor for what the Air Force was thinking about airlift.

Concerning the past, he noted that the June 1948 creation of MATS related to the air movement of people and things in a logistical context. "No actual military mission was mentioned, nor was there any hint of any such concept as combat

AIRLIFT DOCTRINE

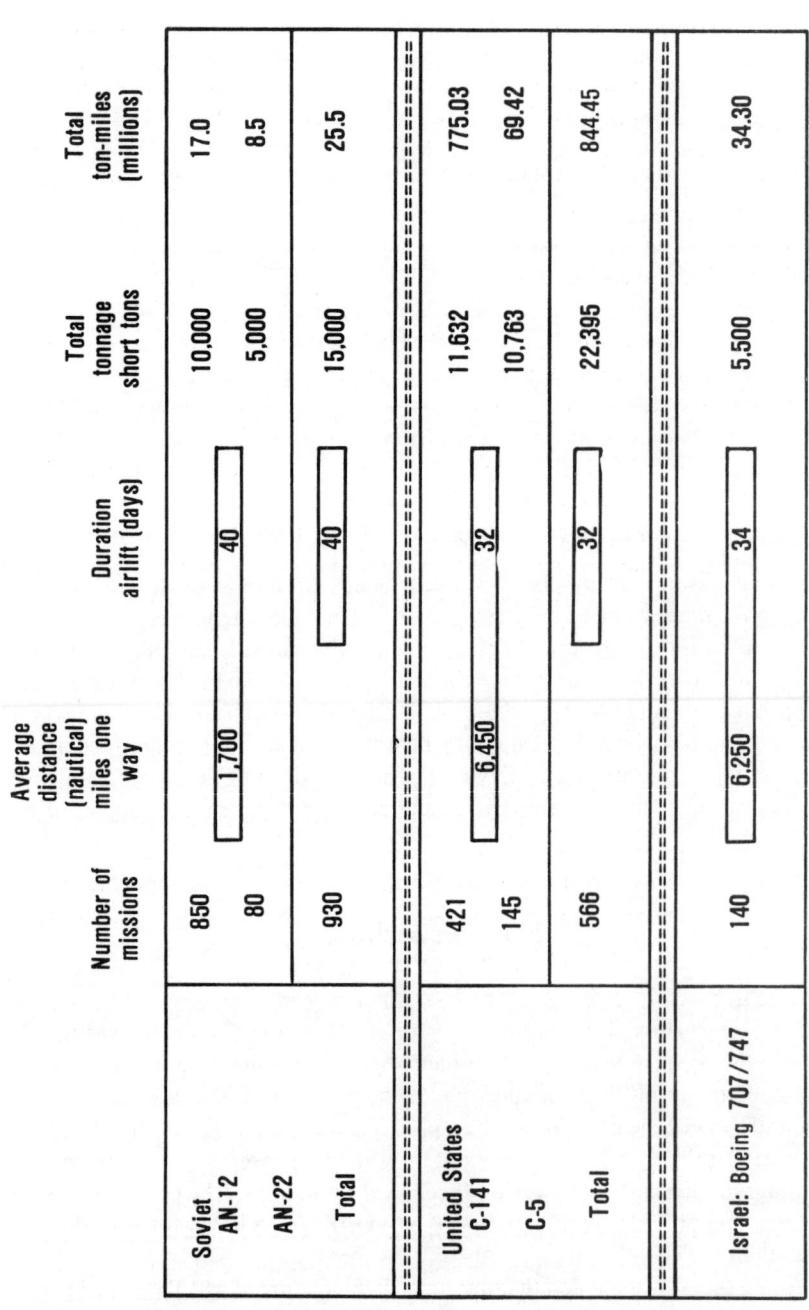

	Number of missions	Average distance (nautical miles) one way	Duration airlift (days)	Total tonnage short tons	Total ton-miles (millions)
Soviet					
AN-12	850	1,700	40	10,000	17.0
AN-22	80			5,000	8.5
Total	930		40	15,000	25.5
United States					
C-141	421	6,450	32	11,632	775.03
C-5	145			10,763	69.42
Total	566		32	22,395	844.45
Israel: Boeing 707/747	140	6,250	34	5,500	34.30

Figure 73. Comparison of USAF, Israeli, and Soviet airlift efforts during the Israeli airlift.

airlift."[157] The Berlin Airlift demonstrated, he argued, the enormous potential of airlift and the lack of aircraft designed for the airlift purpose. The five years following Korea revealed the Air Force is using MATS "with increasing intensity as a means of tightening its own logistics management," with overseas depots shutdown, reduced members of domestic depots, and tremendous reductions in inventories and high-value supply pipelines.[158] The beginning of MATS' potential combat mission was the specified ton-mileage requirements in the emergency war plans for support of SAC, TAC nuclear-capable forces, and the remainder, if any, to the Army. "And of course, there was no formal provision for limited war situations requiring massive ground force deployments."[159] The Big Slam/Puerto Pine exercise, discussed in chapter 5, is what helped to shift emphasis from the "logistical mission of MATS to its total airlift potential."[160]

By the beginning of the buildup in Vietnam, Estes said, MAC had become "the key element in a far-ranging change in national policy: to a strategy of multiple options for flexible, measured response to any situation in the spectrum of war."[161] This he termed linear progress, with the obvious advantages of airlift outweighing its limitations. The second phase of the airlift revolution "will have been achieved when the limitations have been essentially eliminated."[162] Here we find a remarkable discussion of the interrelationship of technology and airlift. The historically validated constraints on airlift consisted, in Estes's assessment, of at least nine overlapping factors: speed; range/payload trade-off; flexibility of employment; cubic capacity; loadability; self-sufficiency; terminal base requirements; fuel dependency; and direct operating costs.[163]

No single aircraft up to 1966 had overcome these constraints. The C-124 had a significantly improved cube and load capacity, but its slow speed and short range limited its strategic benefits. The C-135 jets had great range, speed, and payload but had loading problems, needed long runways, and had no airdrop capability. The C-130s, on the other hand, had excellent loading qualities, could operate into primitive strips, and had excellent airdrop characteristics. However, their relatively slow speed and low payload limited the most flexible airlifter built to date in terms of rapid response. The C-133 could carry huge, outsize missile loads over short distances, but it was slow and maintenance-intensive, and it could not carry many of the Army's outsize requirements. "Even with the full mix of C-124's, C-130's, C-135's, and C-133's, however, the overriding requirement—the moving of sizeable forces, with equipment, to distant areas within weeks—could not be met in its entirety."[164] The advent of the C-141, Estes argued, obviated many of the historic airlift constraints due to its high speed, range/payload options, flexible runway requirements, good loading characteristics, and its airdrop capability. Limited to carrying only 60 to 65 percent of the current Army divisional equipment, the C-141 was the transitional airplane in the airlift revolution. The real revolution was attendant on the C-5A. "It will for the first time permit the MAC force to respond without qualification to total airlift requirements, including the maximum demand—the division-force move."[165]

To support his position, Estes relied on several projected capabilities of the C-5A, coupled with forward-looking operations concepts. The aircraft, of course, would have great speed and range/payload and cubic capacity. Its kneeling feature and visor nose would provide drive-through capability. This was a great loadability feature. Maintenance factors, Estes said, would improve with time and would be reduced by the fewer takeoffs and landings required by the range and speed factors. Even though it was the world's largest aircraft, its ability to routinely operate from 8,000-foot runways, and even into 4,000-foot ones, provided great flexibility.

> In Southeast Asia, the C-5 will be able to use 600 percent more airfields than are available to present cargo jets. The same order of increase will obtain in other less developed areas of the world, which are always the most fertile seedbeds for limited war.[166]

The bottom line was that if the airplane lived up to its expectations "global military airlift will be completely revolutionized. Gigantic combat loads or vast tonnages of supply and resupply will be deliverable in hours or days from any small originating fields in the United States to any area in the world up to and including the edge of battle."[167] General Estes was clearly a man of intellect and vision. His 1966 article spoke of the great promise of the C-5A, but it was his follow-on article, "Modern Combat Airlift," in the September–October 1969 issue of the *Air University Review* that made his most lasting contribution to airlift thinking.[168]

His theme in that 1969 piece revolved around the idea of combat airlift:

> The role of modern combat airlift, then, is to airlift combat forces and all their battle equipment, in the size and mix required—with the greatest speed—to any point in the world, no matter how remote or primitive, where a threat arises or is likely to erupt.[169]

Airlift forces had to be ready to go in opposite directions simultaneously. Such an airlift force can work in concert with other mobility assets like fast sealift and prepositioning, he said, "but the basic requirement is invariant: to rush integral, combat-ready fighting forces anywhere, including the battle area itself, without a preliminary massing of logistics."[170]

From Estes's perspective, there was still not a complete understanding of the airlift revolution.

> Many think of the strategic airlift capability of the near and more distant future as being precisely what it has always been, except that there is more of it: in effect, merely a "brute force" quantitative expansion of something we had in World War II. What they do not realize is that the jet age and the technology that makes an aircraft like the C-5 possible have also engendered a radical qualitative alteration in airlift . . . the important point is that we have at the same time achieved a new kind of airlift.[171]

Estes could well have also underscored "aircraft like the C-5," for the essence of his point was not the C-5 per se, but rather a technology that allowed large loads to be moved across long distances into or very close to the battlefield, in a very short time. This is what provided a whole new kind of airlift. Such a capability, if used, could possibly help avoid the long, drawn-out, Vietnam-style wars. The "irresistible rationale" for modern combat airlift was "that a strategic concept of gradual buildup has always—an invariant under transformation—exacted a very high price."[172] On this point, in an article that had to pass an Air Force security and policy review, Estes quoted Sun Tzu: "There has never been a protracted war from which a country has benefited."[173] He could reach no other conclusion except that future wars must be fought with quick, large applications of force—via combat airlift.

Estes also drew an important distinction between airlift and national defense transportation. Airlift, to be sure, could complement massive sealift (for example) but "this is a derivative capability and a secondary role."[174] The general's point makes a particularly important distinction.

"Numerous studies," he readily admitted, "have concluded what appears almost self-evident: the MAC C-141/C-5 force would make its maximum contribution to the national effort, under a wide variety of circumstances, in conjunction with sealift and prepositioned equipment."[175] However, to deter war anywhere in the world "or to contain aggression with maximum force in minimum time, ton-mile efficiency per se is far less relevant than fast, effective force deployment. And that is the one dominant capability of the MAC combat airlift force."[176]

Airlift Consolidation

Col Louis P. Lindsay chaired a special committee that reviewed the airlift system in SEA for 1965 to 1968. In June of 1976 the report of that special committee cited "duplications in control, aerial port, and support elements in Southeast Asia" and recommended a single airlift command.[177] TAC objected that this would "diminish the 'tactical' orientation of the force"—an argument heard often before.

In fact, General Momyer's end-of-tour report as Seventh Air Force commander addressed the issue in some detail:

> There is one major lesson which stands out above all others with respect to airlift and that is that tactical airlift is distinctly different than strategic airlift. It operates in an environment which demands association and integration with other tactical forces and it must be directed and controlled by the theater air commander as are the other forces under his jurisdiction. Whereas the strategic airlift task can, in an ultimate sense, be handled by a commercial carrier, the theater airlift task is rooted in combat which requires emphasis on entirely different factors such as short, relatively unprepared fields, exposure to ground fire, coordination with escorting fighters and integration into the tactical control system for direction, assistance and redirection. The tactical air control center and the airlift control

centers are the means by which the Air Component Commander harmonizes his forces to support the operations and needs of all forces in the theater. It would indeed be a grievous error to create a single airlift force. All of the experience and facts which have emerged from the Vietnam War again point up the validity of the separate entities of strategic and tactical airlift. Whereas, one could not tell the difference between a 707 and a C-141 cargo coming to a protected and secure base such as Cam Ranh Bay, there was never any doubt of the kind of airlift going into Khe Sanh, Lai Khe, Kham Duc and the many other bases where the tactical airlift was in a real sense a combat force under enemy fire. The lesson of Vietnam on airlift further enforces the same lessons of World War II and Korea on the separation of strategic and tactical airlift forces as combat demands have dictated the separation of strategic and tactical air forces. Theater war demands the assignment of tactical forces which had been designed, nurtured and led by commands devoted to this highly specialized form of warfare.[178]

His arguments, however, did not suffice to stop the consolidation.

Nonetheless, both Gen David Jones (the Air Force chief of staff) and Gen Paul Carlton (MAC's commander) saw the need to "recognize and preserve the image and spirit" of the tactical airlift force after consolidation.[179] The command wanted to enhance the airlift/user relationship, retain and enhance mobility of its forces, and enhance the tactical capabilities of its C-5/C-141 forces, as well as preserve the tactical image of the forces it was gaining. To this end, MAC proposed several steps that eventually came to fruition in one form or another:

- Completely integrate C-130 operations into the existing MAC structure by assigning command and control to the MAC numbered air forces.
- Retain "tactical" in the name of C-130 units.
- Establish air divisions to retain the original identity and numerical designation of tactical airlift managers in the theaters.
- Require the commander/chief or vice/deputy of any agency with tactical responsibility to have tactical experience.
- Establish two mobile airlift control centers (ALCCs) developed but not yet organized by TAC.
- Establish four mobile airlift control elements (ALCEs) developed but not yet organized by TAC.
- Establish a tactical airlift development center at Pope AFB.[180]

What is especially important about these suggestions, other than the obviously sincere desire to retain the "tacticalness" of the units coming to MAC, was the equally clear desire to improve the tactical orientation of the strategic forces. The "two-way street" nature of consolidation was a fallout of considerable importance.

After much Air Force and DOD internal discussion, Secretary of Defense James R. Schlesinger issued a program decision memorandum on 19 July 1974 to the secretary of the Air Force, directing the consolidation of all airlift forces in the DOD under a single manager by the end of FY 1977 and specified command status for MAC.[181]

On 29 August 1974, General Jones, the chief of staff, informed every major Air Force activity of the decision, providing the ultimate rationale for consolidation:

Figure 74. Gen Paul K. Carlton, commander in chief of Military Airlift Command from September 1972 through March 1977.

AIRLIFT DOCTRINE

"To achieve better integration of overall airlift, strategic and tactical airlift assets will be consolidated under MAC. . . . All Air Force tactical airlift C-130 aircraft and associated support in TAC, [Alaskan Air Command] AAC, [United States Air Force Southern Air Division] USAFSO, USAFE, and PACAF will be transferred in place to MAC."[182]

Following the decision to consolidate, two important issues remained—how to organize to support the theaters and whether to make MAC a specified command. MAC and USAFE met in October 1974 to develop a plan for the "as is/where is" transfer of the tactical airlift system to MAC. MAC argued that there should be one central point of management for current operations, scheduling, and command control. Under this proposal, European Command (EUCOM) and USAFE would validate and provide consolidated theater airlift requirements to the air division, which would in turn schedule and operate the missions. USAFE, on the other hand, wanted tasking authority directly to the individual airlift flying units and aircrews. This authority was to be exercised through an ALCC collocated with Headquarters USAFE at Ramstein AB, Germany. MAC could not accept the level of detailed control USAFE wanted, as it violated the principle of centralized direction and decentralized execution.[183] The MAC history of these discussions puts the arguments in a more positive perspective:

> While the Secretary of Defense decision to designate MAC as single manager for all strategic and tactical airlift would create one airlift system in place of independent strategic and tactical systems, it tended to conflict with the "unity of command" doctrine in overseas theaters. Now, it appeared, there would be two commanders with overlapping airlift mission responsibilities. On the one hand, MAC had to retain operational control of all airlift forces to achieve the full benefits of a single manager. Yet, the Air Force Component Commander (AFCC) needed to have operational control of aircraft forces when they required integration with other USAF forces, to insure unity of Air Force effort—especially when airlift was in direct support of combat operations or tactical employment exercises.[184]

Out of this debate came the theater airlift manager (TAM) concept. The ultimate desire was for an airlift system most responsive to the theater commander. Thus, in the TAM system, the designated senior officer would exercise operational control of theater airlift for the Air Force component commander (AFCC) and manage intertheater airlift for MAC. There would be one voice for airlift in a theater. This would make total airlift resources potentially available to theater needs in a streamlined way. The AFCC would task the TAM, who would accomplish the tasks with the most effective and efficient mix of resources available. Visibility over all resources, direct communications to MAC's numbered air forces, and the general flexibility of a single manager would combine to provide better overall service. Full coordination with the tactical air control system would be maintained. The concept was ultimately accepted and applied worldwide.

The Air Staff agreed with consolidation but was against making MAC a specified command. On 13 March 1975, the secretary of the Air Force formally recommended that the Air Force, instead, retain MAC as a major command.[185] The Air Force argued that specified command status would centralize functional responsibilities at too high an organizational level, open the door to making Navy sealift and Army transportation units specified, involve the JCS in day-to-day airlift business, and violate the combatant nature of the unified and specified concept. The Air Force was also concerned that a specified MAC would require reorganization of the JCS "leading to headquarters layering and coordination difficulties that might reduce airlift responsiveness."[186] The Air Force doctrine experts were particularly concerned that a specified command structure would preempt the Air Force's mission to provide close combat and logistical support for the Army; take airlift away from the Air Force component commander; set a precedent for splintering Air Force tactical forces by function (reconnaissance, close air support, interdiction, for example); and allow the Army to vie for more organic airlift if the consolidated/specified system was less responsive to Army needs than the current system. Others voting against specification felt that the JCS, through the Joint Transportation Board, could already assure equitable application of airlift resources; that confusion would result from not specifying other transportation agencies; and that there were no apparent advantages to be gained by creating another specified command.[187]

The Joint Chiefs of Staff, less the chairman, concurred with the Air Force's recommendation not to establish the new specified command. Gen George Brown wrote a separate memorandum to the SECDEF strongly supporting specification:

> a. Airlift resources are major assets for furtherance of our security policy, and importance of airlift as a factor in planning for combat operations will be heightened by the consolidation of tactical and strategic systems. Under these circumstances, the MAC commander should receive his strategic direction directly from the Joint Chiefs of Staff, who are charged with this responsibility under the law.
>
> b. The establishment of MAC as a specified command would further unification as a principle and increase the stature of the commander, Military Airlift Command, in his relationship with the commanders in chief worldwide.
>
> c. It is acknowledged that the present system, through the use of the Joint Transportation Board, already provides the Joint Chiefs of Staff with sufficient authority over MAC to set priorities and allocate resources. Nonetheless, I am persuaded that the establishment of MAC as a specific command would clarify the chain of command by making the commander of the Military Airlift Command as well as the commanders in chief of the unified commands directly responsible to the Joint Chiefs of Staff.
>
> d. While the present command arrangement has worked well in peacetime when airlift assets are generally adequate to satisfy requirements, it will face increased demands in wartime, when we can expect competition not only among unified and specified commanders for worldwide resources, but also among conflicting demands within a theater and between US requirements and those of our allies. Under these circumstances,

AIRLIFT DOCTRINE

> the Joint Chiefs of Staff will have the responsibility for setting priorities and allocating resources. They can accomplish this task best under a command arrangement in which the commander, Military Airlift Command, reports directly to the Joint Chiefs of Staff along with the commanders of unified and specified commands.[188]

MAC saw several additional advantages. The command thought that additional Air Force representation in the joint structure was, a priori, an advantage and that specification would enhance the Air Force's ability to influence decisions on the airlift role in national security matters. MAC also said that specification would recognize the broad continuing mission of MAC, a particularly relevant point in view of increased responsibilities to operate a worldwide airlift force supporting all services and the unified and specified commands. The command thought that specification would additionally smooth airlift consolidation due to its elevated status. To solve the question of specified command versus major command, MAC proposed that it be both a specified command for airlift matters and a major command for Air Force unique or nonairlift matters. No changes in normal day-to-day functions would be required. Budgeting, programming, and administration would equally remain unchanged.[189]

The question of making MAC a combatant command was a particularly sensitive one. A study by Lt Col Anthony Ptacek of the MAC legal staff pulled together MAC's position. Ptacek's arguments, summarized below, were powerful:

- Combatant means taking part in or being prepared to take part in active fighting. Historical examples, official mission statements, training practices, and airlift consolidation all illustrate that MAC forces meet either definition.
- MAC performs, among many other missions, a logistical function. "The addition of the logistical function no more converted MAC to a logistical command than did the addition of training functions to SAC convert it to a training command."
- Congressional language concerning combatant unified or specified command intended that commands with strategic or tactical importance could be unified or specified.[190]

On 9 June 1976, Deputy Secretary of Defense William Clements, Jr., reaffirmed the decision to make MAC a specified command. On 2 July 1976, General Brown forwarded a memorandum to the SECDEF with a proposed change to the unified command plan (UCP) designating MAC a specified command. On 21 January 1977, the Joint Chiefs of Staff announced that the president had approved the UCP change on 16 December 1976 and that SECDEF directed implementation as of 1 February 1977.[191]

The Doctrinal Context at the End

In March of 1973 General Carlton opened the MAC commander's conference with comments challenging his people to streamline the airlift force in the post-Vietnam era in line with the new emphasis on economics, and yet do a better airlift job:

> As we enter the post-SEA environment, the budget constraints relative to Defense spending are obvious. Presently, we are realigning our combat airlift forces, reducing the six qualified airlift wings to two qualified airlift wings. Due to these fiscal constraints, certain priorities must be established—all agencies within the command must tighten their belts, optimize their resources, institute procedures whereby we can get the job done more efficiently and effectively for less—in essence, we must become better managers.[192]

This philosophy was very much in keeping with how aircraft operated; post-Vietnam pressures would merely mean doing better.

In November of 1975 Department of Defense representatives testified at a House Research and Development Subcommittee hearing on the posture of military airlift concerning the future of airlift at the end of the Vietnam War. The DOD witnesses presented a unified theme concerning the need to improve airlift capabilities incrementally to support a NATO contingency. Maj Gen John McWhorter, Jr., director of strategic mobility for the organization of the Joint Chiefs of Staff, warned that "should our deployment capability be inadequate, the United States is then faced with the dilemma of choosing between the use of nuclear weapons or backing down on our commitment."[193] He concluded that "only airlift can respond in the critical first two weeks—the time we either deter the war or prove our ability to contain the [Warsaw] Pact with conventional arms."[194]

Maj Gen Benjamin Starr, Jr., director of transportation for the Air Force, outlined the Air Force's plan to enhance the ability of airlift to deal with this mission. The program included increased utilization rates for the C-5 and C-141 (by increased ratios and improved spares postures), aerial refueling for both aircraft, stretching the C-141, using tactical aircraft to augment strategic forces, and modifying wide-body civil aircraft for oversize capability.[195] In addition to the enhancement program, the Air Force continued to support the advanced tanker cargo aircraft (ATCA), a derivative of a commercial wide-bodied aircraft configured to carry cargo and provide air refueling capability. The primary argument advanced for the ATCA was that it would enhance airlift capability by making it possible to exploit the air refueling capacity of the C-5 (also proposed for the C-141) to the fullest. The ATCA would carry cargo "only during contingencies to augment the strategic airlift force when the situation so dictates and the aircraft is not otherwise dedicated to other missions."[196] The big payoff was to be the ATCA's ability to deliver large quantities of fuel over great distances. The modification of

AIRLIFT DOCTRINE

MODERN AIRLIFT

Courtesy HQ MAC/CHO

Figure 75

Courtesy HQ MAC/CHO

Figure 76

VIETNAM ERA

Courtesy HQ MAC/CHO

Figure 77

Courtesy HQ MAC/CHO

Figure 78

the C-5 wing to ensure a 30,000-hour service life was the final element of the airlift initiatives.

Brig Gen Jasper Welch, Jr., the Air Force assistant chief of staff for studies and analysis, described the 10-year, $2-billion airlift enhancement program as designed to meet the most demanding task for airlift—reinforcement of NATO. The enhancement program was based on increased effectiveness of existing forces and modification of existing aircraft (both civil and military). Seeking to deploy 180,000 tons in 30 days in a balanced fashion, the proposed program concentrated on the "long pole in the tent"—oversize cargo—and was calculated to solve the oversize deficiency and cut deployment times in half.[197]

Gen Paul Carlton, commander of the Military Airlift Command, said he thought it extremely important to determine how present assets could be more efficiently managed and effectively utilized.[198] Calling the crucial strength of modern strategic airlift its flexibility and responsiveness, he noted that "until relatively recent times, the basic mission of airlift was founded in resupply operations." However, "the concept of flexible response required a rapid, long-range air deployment capability, and when the C-141 entered the inventory in 1965, the credibility of this strategy was greatly enhanced."[199] Concerning tactical airlift and the decision to consolidate airlift resources under MAC, General Carlton was clearly a supporter of keeping the tactical nature of the theater airlift forces intact. "Tactical airlift forces," he said, "currently have a command and control system which is essential to mobility, flexibility, and responsiveness demanded of these forces."[200] And, he supported development of the advanced medium/short takeoff and landing transport (AMST) aircraft. He also suggested that the government and industry seek ways to jointly develop the next generation of outsize civil cargo aircraft.[201]

In answer to the question of how far forward in the combat environment the C-5 and C-141 would operate, General Carlton called on the recent Vietnam experience to make a doctrinal statement as valid today as it was in 1975:

> It depends on how much carrying the freight to that point is worth to the JCS or the operation that is going on. We have already used the [C-5] both in Saigon and Da Nang, in Vietnam, in very high risk zones. We have operated under the threat of the SAM, of the surface-to-air, as well as air-to-air, under very unusual circumstances such as the second Tet offensive when we hauled tanks into Da Nang. We don't expose it unless the risk is worth it. We treat it very carefully and conservatively, but to answer your question, if the risk is worth taking to win the battle, we will take it. Just like we will with any airplane.
>
> It is not quite as well equipped to survive, nor is the 141, but they are not a lot different, particularly the 141, and the 130. There is a little more survivability in the 130 due to foam in the tank. Both of those airplanes are equipped and operated in Saigon in the recent evacuation with antiradiation devices to warn it against surface-to-air missiles. The answer to your question is, how much is it worth to us to do it? The JCS makes the decision on the use of the C-5 under almost all circumstances of risks.[202]

The 1975 hearings revealed that MAC, constrained by the realities of a postwar drawdown, was forced into the very traditional doctrinal mode, at least for airlift, of squeezing every ounce out of existing assets. The C-5 wing modification program was a preservation effort, while the CRAF modification C-141 initiatives were enhancements of "current" aircraft. The AMST program was inherited from TAC, whereas the ATCA initiative was an Air Force-sponsored program that had airlift implications. The civil airlines also testified at the November hearings, this time complaining that MAC was competing with the commercial carriers in terms of cargo carriage. The civilian industry was receiving an ever-decreasing share of the cargo dollar as DOD requirements dropped drastically following Vietnam.[203]

The Airlift Doctrinal Heritage of the Vietnam Era

Characterizing the airlift doctrine of the Vietnam era is perhaps the most difficult task in this study. As ever, the doctrine evolved, as did the technology available. Ingenuity and perseverance were never lacking. There was a vast potential number of lessons learned, but they do not necessarily reflect the fundamental issues. One cannot help but be impressed by the intellectual and physical courage of the era. In many ways, airlift performance in the Vietnam era reaffirmed what had been learned many times before: airlift can be counted on, even in the face of tremendous obstacles. Here, then, is one possible list of doctrinal conclusions to be drawn from this time period.

- Intertheater airlift—with the introduction of highly capable jet cargo planes—is a vital element of military strategy at both the national and theater levels.
- Intratheater airlift is highly capable and reliable, even in the face of significant ground-to-air threats.
- Relatively high-volume tactical airlift aircraft are the mainstay of intratheater airlift operations. Assault airlift aircraft are required for specialized missions.
- Intratheater airlift makes a critical contribution to ground force employment and sustainment.
- Fixed-wing intratheater airlift aircraft ought to be Air Force assets. Rotary-wing transport aircraft ought to be Army assets. Assignment of tilt-wing transport aircraft will be decided later.
- Airlift forces should be combined under one high-level organization to increase responsiveness to military needs and to provide economies.
- The one airlift organization is so important to national concerns that it should be a specified command. This greatly improves airlift responsiveness.

AIRLIFT DOCTRINE

NOTES

1. Air Force Manual (AFM) 1-1, *United States Air Force Basic Doctrine*, 14 August 1964, 4-3.
2. Timetable and agenda, Doctrinal Development Committee, Headquarters Military Air Transport Service, 30 November 1964.
3. Ibid.
4. Gen Howell Estes, Jr., commander, Military Air Transport Service, to deputy chief of staff, Plans and Operations, Headquarters USAF, letter, subject: Operational Doctrine, 23 September 1965.
5. Ibid., with draft AFM 2-21, *United States Air Force Airlift Doctrine*, n.d., chap. 1, 8, attached.
6. Ibid.
7. Ibid., chap. 2, 2.
8. Ibid.
9. Ibid., chap. 2, 14.
10. Ibid., chap. 2, 9.
11. Maj Gen Arthur Agan, Jr., assistant deputy chief of staff, Plans and Operations, Headquarters USAF, to Military Airlift Command, letter, subject: Operational Aerospace Doctrine and Aerospace Tactics, 7 January 1966.
12. AFM 2-21, *Strategic Airlift*, 26 September 1966, 1.
13. Ibid., 2.
14. AFM 2-4, *Tactical Airlift*, 10 August 1966, 2.
15. Ibid., 3.
16. Ibid.
17. Ibid., 2.
18. Chief of staff Air Force, to Tactical Air Command, commander in chief Pacific Air Forces, commander in chief, United States Air Force in Europe, Air University, Air Force Logistics Command, message, subject: Navy/Air Force Agreement on Airlift, 201737Z, April 1966.
19. Ibid.
20. Ibid.
21. House Committee on Armed Services, Special Subcommittee on Military Airlift, *Military Airlift*, 89th Cong., 1st and 2d sess., 1965 and 1966, 6615-16, statement of Secretary of the Air Force Harold Brown.
22. Ibid., 6616.
23. Ibid.
24. Ibid., 6784, statement of Deputy Secretary of Defense Cyrus Vance.
25. Ibid., 6616-17, Secretary Brown.
26. Ibid., 6618.
27. Ibid., 3.
28. Ibid., 6923-24.
29. Ibid., 6788-90, Secretary Vance.
30. Ibid., 6986, statement of Gen Paul Adams, commander in chief, United States Strike Command.
31. Ibid.
32. House Committee on Armed Services, *Report on Military Airlift by Special Subcommittee on Military Airlift of the House Committee on Armed Services*, 89th Cong., 2d sess., 1966, 7204.
33. Ibid., 7203.
34. Ibid., 7190.
35. Ibid., 7191.
36. Ray Bowers, *Tactical Airlift* (Washington, D.C.: Government Printing Office, 1983), 114.
37. Ibid.
38. Ibid., 378.
39. Ibid.
40. Ibid., 380-83.
41. Ibid., 383-84.
42. Ibid., 384-85.
43. Ibid., 105.
44. Ibid.

45. Ibid., 190–91.
46. Ibid., 191–94.
47. Ibid., 258.
48. AFM 2-4, *Tactical Airlift*, 10 August 1966. See also Roy Chapman, "Tactical Airlift Management in Vietnam," *Signal* 24 (August 1970): 35–37.
49. Lt Col John Lane, Jr., *The Air War in Indochina*, vol. 1, monograph 1, *Command and Control and Communications Structures in Southeast Asia* (Maxwell AFB, Ala.: Airpower Research Institute, 1981), 78.
50. Bowers, *Tactical Airlift*, 467–69, 487.
51. Ibid., 615.
52. Ibid., 169–74.
53. Ibid., 174. See, for example, Airlift/Logistics Division, Operations Analysis, Headquarters USAF, "C-130 Shuttles vs C-130 PCS Operation in Southeast Asia," December 1966.
54. Bowers, *Tactical Airlift*, 174–76. See also Irvin Lee, "Controlling the Lifeline," *Airman* 12 (April 1968): 16–17. To compare the development of the airlift system with the US Army's system, see Lt Gen Joseph Heiser, Jr., Vietnam Studies Series, *Logistics Support* (Washington, D.C.: Department of the Army, 1974).
55. Bowers, *Tactical Airlift*, 179.
56. Ibid., 179–80.
57. Ibid., 181–83.
58. Ibid., 472–73.
59. Ibid., 471–72.
60. Ibid., 601.
61. Ibid., 45.
62. Ibid., 109–11.
63. Ibid., 121–22.
64. Ibid., 122.
65. Ibid., 233.
66. Ibid., 358.
67. Ibid., 203.
68. Ibid., 203–4.
69. Ibid., 208–9.
70. Ibid., 209–13. See also Harry Kinard, "Battlefield Mobility of the New U.S. 1st Air Cavalry Division," *NATO's Fifteen Nations* 2 (April–May 1966): 38–41; Harry Kinard, "A Victory in the Ia Drang: The Triumph of a Concept," *Army* 17 (September 1967): 71–91; John Albright, John Cash, and Allan Sandstrum, *Seven Firefights in Vietnam* (Washington, D.C.: Office of the Chief of Military History, United States Army, 1970).
71. Bowers, *Tactical Airlift*, 209–15.
72. Ibid., 270. See also Lt Gen Bernard Rogers, Vietnam Studies series, *Cedar Falls-Junction City: A Turning Point* (Washington, D.C.: Department of the Army, 1974); "The Airborne: Obsolete," *Journal of the Armed Forces* 106 (9 November 1968): 12–13; Curtis Messex, "Air Drop Mission to Katum," *Air Force Magazine* 54 (September 1971): 46–51; Robert Sigholtz, "Jump into War Zone C," *Infantry* 57 (September–October 1967): 38–40.
73. Bowers, *Tactical Airlift*, 270–76.
74. Ibid., 276–78.
75. Ibid., 278–82.
76. Ibid., 298. See also Maj Claudius Watts, "Aerial Resupply for Khe Sanh," *Military Review* 52 (December 1972): 79–88; Maj Gen Burl McLaughlin, "Khe Sanh: Keeping an Outpost Alive," *Air University Review* 20, no. 1 (November–December 1968): 57–77; John Galvin, *Air Assault: The Development of Airmobile Warfare* (New York: Hawthorn Books, 1969), 306–11; William Greenhalgh, Jr., "'A-OK': Airpower Over Khe Sanh," *Aerospace Historian* 19 (March 1972): 2–9; Bernard Nalty, *Air Power and the Fight for Khe Sanh* (Washington, D.C.: Office of Air Force History, 1973); Mayers Shore, 2d, *The Battle for Khe Sanh* (Washington, D.C.: United States Marine Corps, 1969).
77. Bowers, *Tactical Airlift*, 196–97.
78. Ibid., 297–99.
79. Ibid., 299–302.

80. Ibid., 302–4.
81. Ibid., 307.
82. Ibid., 295.
83. Ibid., 315.
84. Ibid., 318–22. See also Donald Oberdorfer, *Tet!* (Garden City, N.J.: Doubleday, 1971); Carl Berger, ed., *The United States Air Force in Southeast Asia* (Washington, D.C.: Office of Air Force History, 1977), 52–61.
85. Bowers, *Tactical Airlift*, 322–28.
86. Ibid., 329.
87. Ibid., 329–30.
88. Ibid., 343–44. See also Lt Col Alan Gropman, USAF Southeast Asia Monograph Series, vol. 5, monograph 7, *Airpower and the Airlift Evacuation of Kham Duc* (Maxwell AFB, Ala.: Airpower Research Institute, 1979); Joseph Browning, "Co-ordinated Effort Saves Force: The Evacuation of the Kham Duc Special Forces Camp," *Aviation Week and Space Technology* 89 (9 September 1968): 92–93; Flint DuPre, "Rescue at a Place called Kham Duc," *Air Force and Space Digest* 52 (March 1968): 98–100.
89. Bowers, *Tactical Airlift*, 344.
90. Ibid., 344–45.
91. Ibid., 346–47.
92. Ibid., 347.
93. Ibid., 347–50.
94. Ibid., 493–502.
95. Ibid., 508–9.
96. Ibid., 539–42. See also John Frisbee, "Air Drop at An Loc," *Air Force Magazine* 55 (November 1972): 40–42.
97. Bowers, *Tactical Airlift*, 542–44.
98. Ibid., 542–48.
99. Ibid., 548–56.
100. Ibid., 559–66.
101. Ibid., 566–68.
102. Ibid., 568–70.
103. Ibid., 574.
104. Kenneth Patchin, Office of MAC History, historical study, *Strategic Airlift to SEA (1964–1973)*, 12 September 1973; History, Military Airlift Command, 1 July 1965–30 June 1966, 497–98.
105. Patchin, *Airlift to SEA*, 1–4; Warren Delker, study project officer, A Military Airlift Command Input to Project Corona Harvest on Strategic Airlift in SEA, 1 January 1965–31 March 1968, 31 December 1969, I-I-9.
106. Delker, *Strategic Airlift in SEA*, I-I-4 to I-I-5.
107. Ibid., I-I-4 to I-I-6, I-I-16 to I-I-19.
108. Ibid., III-I-6 to III-I-7; History, Military Airlift Command, 1 July 1963–30 June 1966, 499–508.
109. Delker, *Strategic Airlift in SEA*, III-I-16. See also "Red Ball, 1966," *National Defense Transportation Journal* 22 (July–August 1966): 28–30; Thomas Scott, "The 'Red Ball' Flies and Rolls Again," *Army Digest* 22 (February 1967): 8–12.
110. Lt Col Gary May, *The Impact of Materials Handling Equipment on Airlift Capabilities*, Airpower Research Institute Research Report No. 83-7 (Maxwell AFB, Ala.: Air University Press, August 1983), 21.
111. Delker, *Strategic Airlift in SEA*, I-I-33; History, Military Airlift Command, 1 July 1965-30 June 1966, 2:1033.
112. Delker, *Strategic Airlift in SEA*, I-IV-2 to I-IV-7.
113. Ibid., I-I-33 to I-I-39; History, Military Airlift Command, 1 July 1965-30 June 1966, 508–9; Twenty-Second Air Force Regulation 66–4, *Depot, Field and Organizational Maintenance, Quick Servicing of Aircraft*, 4 March 1966.
114. Delker, *Strategic Airlift in SEA*, I-II-4 to I-II-9.
115. "Airlift System Integrity," 14 July 1969 (white paper prepared by Military Airlift Command, Directorate of Plans and Programs); Delker, *Strategic Airlift in SEA*, I-V-6 to I-V-9.
116. Delker, *Strategic Airlift in SEA*, I-V-12.

117. Ibid., I-V-14.

118. Twenty-Second Air Force Report on Operation Blue Light, 23 December 1965-23 January 1966, 1: Delker, *Strategic Airlift in SEA*, II-I-1 to II-I-2. See also History, Military Airlift Command, 1 July 1965–30 June 1966, 430–38.

119. Twenty-Second Air Force, Operation Blue Light, 1.

120. Ibid., 2.

121. Lt Col Neil Sorenson, "Airlift Doctrine: Is it Adequate for a High Threat, High Intensity War?" *Airlift Operations Review* (July 1981).

122. History, Military Airlift Command, 1 July 1965–30 June 1966, 429–38.

123. Delker, *Strategic Airlift in SEA*, II-I-2.

124. Ibid., II-I-3; Mary Whittington, Historical Services and Research Division, Headquarters Military Airlift Command, historical study, *Eagle Thrust (17 November–30 December 1967)*, January 1969, 5–6. See also Twenty-Second Air Force, *Final Report Operation Eagle Thrust*, 17 November–18 December 1967.

125. Whittington, *Eagle Thrust*, 63–66.

126. Delker, *Strategic Airlift in SEA*, II-I-3 to II-I-5.

127. House Committee on Armed Services, Subcommittee on Military Airlift, *Hearings on Military Airlift*, 91st Cong., 2d sess., 1970, 6339–41, statement of Maj Thomas Simmons.

128. Ibid., 6350, statement of Capt Earl Van Inevegen.

129. Ibid.

130. Ibid.

131. Ibid.

132. Ibid.

133. Ibid., 6355–58.

134. Ibid., 6358.

135. Ibid.

136. Ibid., 6358–59.

137. Ibid., 6360.

138. Ibid., 6360–62.

139. Ibid., 6363.

140. Ibid., 6681, statement by Phillip Whittaker, assistant secretary of Air Force for installations and logistics.

141. Ibid., 6683, statement by Lt Gen George Boylan, deputy chief of staff, Plans and Resources, Headquarters USAF.

142. Maj A. J. C. Lavalle, ed., USAF Southeast Asia Monograph Series, vol. 2, monograph 3, *Airpower and the 1972 Spring Invasion* (Maxwell AFB, Ala.: Airpower Research Institute, n.d.), 17–27.

143. Ibid., 25.

144. History, Twenty-Second Air Force (Fiscal Year 1972), 125–26.

145. Ibid., 132.

146. Ibid., 125.

147. Lavalle, *Airpower and the 1972 Spring Invasion*, 56–57; History, Military Airlift Command (Fiscal Year 1972), 1:123–25.

148. History, Twenty–Second Air Force (FY 1972), 128-29.

149. Patchin, *Strategic Airlift to SEA*, 19. For more details concerning early C-5 missions, see History, Military Airlift Command (Fiscal Year 1972), 1:257–60, and Gen Jack Catton, commander, Military Airlift Command, "Ask the Man who Owns One," *Commanders Digest* 12, no. 6 (15 June 1972).

150. Office of History, Military Airlift Command, historical study, *Flight to Israel*, 1974, 7–8. See also History, Military Airlift Command (Fiscal Year 1974), 1:136–56.

151. *Flight to Israel*, 6–7.

152. Ibid., 9–11.

153. Ibid., 13–15.

154. *Flight to Israel*, 12–13.

155. Gen Howell Estes, Jr., "The Revolution in Airlift," *Air University Review* 17, no. 3 (March–April 1966): 2–15.

156. Ibid., 4.

157. Ibid., 5.
158. Ibid.
159. Ibid., 6.
160. Ibid.
161. Ibid.
162. Ibid.
163. Ibid.
164. Ibid., 9.
165. Ibid.
166. Ibid., 13.
167. Ibid., 15.
168. Gen Howell Estes, Jr., "Modern Combat Airlift," *Air University Review* 20, no. 6 (September–October 1969): 12-25.
169. Ibid., 18.
170. Ibid.
171. Ibid., 19.
172. Ibid., 18.
173. Ibid.
174. Ibid., 19.
175. Ibid., 25.
176. Ibid.
177. Bowers, *Tactical Airlift*, 650.
178. Lt Col Jimmie Jay, "Evolution of Airlift Doctrine," Air War College Research Report No. 93, Maxwell AFB, Ala., 1977, 59–60.
179. Gen Paul Carlton, commander, Military Airlift Command, to Gen David Jones, chief of staff, United States Air Force, letter, 16 November 1964.
180. Ibid.
181. History, Military Airlift Command, July 1974-December 1975, 1:308. See the same source, 44–48, for a discussion of consolidation during this era.
182. Chief of staff, United States Air Force, to commander, Military Airlift Command et al., message, subject: Consolidation of Airlift Forces, 27 August 1974.
183. History, Military Airlift Command, 1974–1975, 320–22.
184. Ibid., 321–22. Maj Gen Thomas Aldridge, deputy chief of staff, Plans, Headquarters Military Airlift Command, informal talking paper, subject: Division of Responsibility Between a Theater Air Force Component Commander (AFCC) and the Theater Airlift Manager (TAM), 25 June 1975.
185. Working paper entitled "Point Paper for the Chairman," JCS, subject: Airlift Consolidation, no author, 25 June 1975; Military Airlift Command, briefing script and slides, subject: Airlift Consolidation CINC's Briefing, ca. 1975; Maj J. W. Bushey, Directorate of Tactical Airlift Forces, Headquarters USAF, background paper, subject: Single Manager vs Specified Command, 16 May 1975; John Shea, assistant deputy chief of staff, Plans, Headquarters Military Airlift Command, background paper, subject: Specified Command Status for MAC—Pros and Cons, 26 November 1976.
186. History, Directorate of Doctrine, Concepts, and Objectives, 1 July 1974–31 December 1974, 53–54.
187. Point paper for chairman, Joint Chiefs of Staff, 25 June 1975; memorandum, E. C. Aldridge, Jr., acting assistant secretary of defense (program analysis and evaluation), to Deputy Secretary of Defense Clements, subject: Airlift Consolidation, 25 March 1976.
188. Draft memorandum, Gen George Brown, chairman, Joint Chiefs of Staff, to secretary of defense, subject: Airlift Consolidation, ca. 1975.
189. Brig Gen John W. Collens, deputy chief of staff, Plans, Headquarters Military Airlift Command, point paper, subject: Airlift Consolidation and Specified Command Status, 27 May 1976; John F. Shea, assistant deputy chief of staff, Plans, Headquarters Military Airlift Command, point paper, subject: MAC as a Specified Command—CINCMAC/COMAC Relationships, 6 September 1977.
190. Lt Col Anthony Ptacek, to command section, Military Airlift Command, staff summary sheet, subject: Authority to Establish MAC as a Specified Command, 19 October 1976. See also memorandum, Maj William Bennett, Policy and Doctrine Division, to Director of Programming and Policy,

Headquarters Military Airlift Command, subject: How Far Forward Will Airlift Be Flown, 2 March 1977.

191. Memorandum, William Clements, Jr., deputy secretary of defense, to secretaries of the military departments et al., subject: Airlift Consolidation, 9 June 1976; memorandum, Gen George Brown, chairman, Joint Chiefs of Staff, to secretary of defense, subject: Amendment of the Unified Command Plan, 2 July 1976; Joint Chiefs of Staff to commanders of unified and specified commands, message, subject: UPC change—MAC Specified, 212117Z January 1977.

192. History, Military Airlift Command, Fiscal Year 1973, 1:153.

193. House Committee on Armed Services, *Research and Development Subcommittee Hearings on the Posture of Military Airlift*, 94th Cong., 1st sess., 1975, 179–80, statement of Maj Gen John McWhorter, Jr. For a detailed discussion of the legislative history of these initiatives see History, Military Airlift Command, Calendar Year 1976, 1:192–205.

194. Ibid., 193.

195. Ibid., 201–3, statement of Maj Gen Benjamin Starr, Jr.

196. Ibid., 206.

197. Ibid., 230–41, statement of Brig Gen Jasper Welch, Jr.

198. Ibid., 9, statement of Gen Paul Carlton.

199. Ibid., 10.

200. Ibid., 71.

201. Ibid., 502.

202. Ibid., 88–89.

203. Ibid., 164–66.

CHAPTER 7

The Modern Airlift Era

This chapter traces some of the more recent developments in airlift doctrine and concepts. The section on the mobility triad addresses the strategy-level questions of how best to develop forces to project combat power. The discussions of the Congressionally Mandated Mobility Study (CMMS) show the results of a comprehensive analysis of mobility force structure needs, applying various assumptions about elements of the mobility triad, to arrive at airlift requirements. The section entitled *A View from the Top* seeks to provide both a programmatic and national military strategy context for the airlift decisions that were made in the period. To aid in understanding the internal decision-making process involved in shaping airlift forces and doctrine, the section on *A View from Inside* is included. In short, what these first sections provide is an overview of the process of decision making.

The second half of the chapter looks at the doctrinal implications of the four weapon systems considered in these decision processes. The advanced medium short takeoff and landing (STOL) transport (AMST) was the precursor to the airlift debate of the 1980s. It provided the technological and conceptual base for many of the arguments that later developed. Following the rejection of the AMST, the Air Force immediately formed the C-X Task Force to reanalyze and redefine airlift needs. How the Task Force thought about and articulated those needs was a doctrinal watershed. The question of whether a commercially designed cargo airlift aircraft—the Boeing 747—was a reasonable alternative toward solving airlift needs is also investigated, especially as it relates to comparisons to the C-5. The separate section on the ramifications of selecting the C-5B aircraft as an interim airlift solution concludes that the decision not only was a doctrinal step backward but also was a recognition of airlift's importance to the national military strategy. The implications of the C-17 aircraft, both in terms of the direct delivery concept and of what it may mean in future warfare, are treated in the last section of this chapter.

The Mobility Triad

Throughout most of the 1980s, senior decision makers talked of a mobility triad of airlift, sealift, and prepositioning. Each leg of this triad made contributions to the question of how to project forces to a threatened area. Each element was recognized as having strengths and weaknesses that, when balanced against each other, provided a logical trail of capabilities to meet the various stages of conflict.

AIRLIFT DOCTRINE

Gen James Allen addressed the mobility triad in terms of military force projection. His concern was directed toward articulating the concept as it related to responding to crises and winning wars:

> Force projection dictates the need for a balanced mobility force of airlift, sealift, and prepositioning programs that will permit a rapid, independent response to a crisis at any location in the world. These mobility programs should be capable of sustaining independent operations in the crisis area until the conflict can be terminated on terms favorable to the United States.
>
> Airlift mobility forces must provide a rapid deployment and employment capability of combat units to and in the battle area. Rapid establishment of sea and air lines of communication is required to insure a favorable termination of hostilities.[1]

General Allen was echoing Gen Howell Estes's thoughts from 1969: think of airlift as a warfighting issue, not as a part of a transportation system.

This approach to the mobility question was graphically summarized in a presentation by Brig Gen Donald Brown, MAC deputy chief of staff for plans, in testimony before the House Research and Development Subcommittee in April 1981. Figure 79 illustrates General Brown's approach to achieving force projection through balanced mobility.

AIRLIFT
- FAST
- FLEXIBLE
- LIMITED CAPACITY
- AIRFIELD DEPENDENT

FORCE PROJECTION

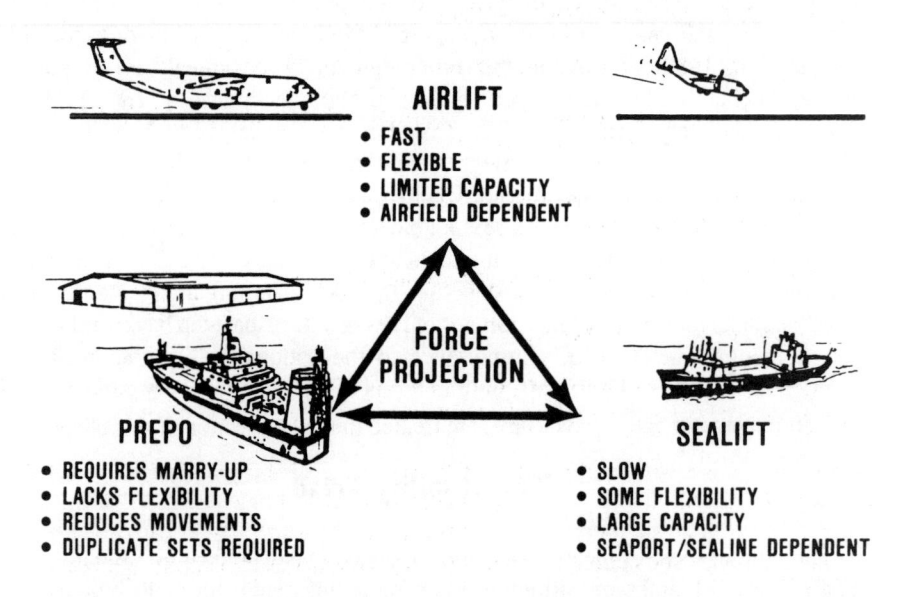

PREPO
- REQUIRES MARRY-UP
- LACKS FLEXIBILITY
- REDUCES MOVEMENTS
- DUPLICATE SETS REQUIRED

SEALIFT
- SLOW
- SOME FLEXIBILITY
- LARGE CAPACITY
- SEAPORT/SEALINE DEPENDENT

Figure 79. Balanced mobility.

Lt Gen Paul Gorman, director for plans and policy for the JCS, provided a thorough review of how airlift, sealift, and prepositioning can interact to provide a balanced force projection capability.

> If the time required to transport an item is not the critical consideration, sealift is more cost-effective than airlift. If time is of the essence and a unit or piece of equipment is needed immediately, sealift is less cost effective than airlift. Any cost benefit comparison of airlift to sealift encompasses opportunity costs. We would deploy forces to the Persian Gulf to protect access to oil. Early arrival of even a few forces could be determinant in deterring an attack on oil producers in the first place, or in dissuading an attacker from pressing his aggression. While well-conceived maritime prepositioning programs can reduce some airlift and sealift requirements, they do not necessarily provide for early arrival and could detract from tactical flexibility if the conflict occurs where the marriage of troops and equipment is difficult. The US needs a balanced program of airlift, sealift and prepositioning to have an assurance of success in deterring or defeating a potential adversary be it in the Persian Gulf region, Europe, Korea, South America, or elsewhere.
>
> One might conceive of a future scenario in which such would be the case. But that scenario would be dependent on very early warning and deployment of a more formidable amphibious armada than we now could mount out, plus fortuitously situated maritime prepositioned equipment, arrival ports, and airfields. Such scenarios seem relatively few, and relatively improbable. Given the uncertainties against which US strategy must provide, we need capabilities:
>
> To employ a sea-based airpower at all times.
>
> To deploy land-based airpower quickly, prepared for immediate employment.
>
> To enter any portion of the gulf littoral forcibly, either by amphibious assault or by airborne assault, or by both in conjunction.
>
> To airland promptly both complete land force units and the manpower for prepositioned unit materiel.
>
> To unload and prepare for action the prepositioned equipment.
>
> To sustain any force we deploy.
>
> There is no foreseeable circumstance when we can dispense with either airlift, or sealift, or prepositioning. For speed, we will need all three.[2]

Testifying at the same hearings, Gen Robert E. Huyser noted that sealift "provides the volume, but not the timeliness so critical in the first, early days of conflict."[3] Slowness, of course, is a relative term; but when compared with airlift, movement of goods and people via sealift is measured in days, via airlift in hours.

> Sealift's contribution to rapid deployment is sustainment/resupply of forward deployment forces or forces rapidly airlifted during the early critical days of a conflict. Sealift cannot meet the critical 15-day deployment period identified in the CMMS. Sealift requires weeks to deploy forces.[4]

This deployment begins only after loads requiring sealift have been moved from their original locations to the departure ports. Once the loads arrive at the destination port, they must be unloaded and transshipped. This transportation mode, then, best serves to carry large volumes of materiel and especially bulky items—late-arriving units and goods needed to sustain and replenish a force over a longer period of time.[5]

Land-based prepositioning is another facet of the mobility triad. Its primary advantage is that it is in place, if planners have correctly assessed where the battle will take place. This reduces intertheater movement requirements, but the method suffers from a number of limitations. First, it reduces flexibility. Although prepositioning signals an American commitment to friend and foe alike, removal of those supplies and equipment for use in a contingency elsewhere could have the unintended opposite effect and an obvious negative impact on readiness in that theater. Prepositioning also relies on a favorable political climate in the host nation to allow the stockpiling. A government may be under internal political constraints to not allow such practices but still be an ally. On the whole, a region may hold our national interests but not be politically suitable for prepositioning. Prepositioning of ammunition, petroleum, oil, and lubricants (POL), and similar stocks is a difficult enough process, but placing unit equipment in storage presents a separate set of problems. Sophisticated and sensitive items like helicopters and avionics equipment cannot be readily stored, both because of environmental control problems and because of their expense. Duplicate sets of equipment prepositioned mean either less training for forces in the United States or added expense. In some cases, equipment and arms would not be stocked because there is not enough to begin with. Also, prepositioned materiel is a lucrative target for terrorists and conventional forces alike.

Prepositioning relies on effective airlift. Carrying up to 10 percent of materiel not prepositioned for a division, the forces to use the equipment and stores must still arrive in the theater in a timely manner, move to the prepositioned stocks, open and prepare them for use, and then proceed to the battle. The premium is on getting there in the first place—via airlift. In some cases, prepositioned materiel will be far from where the battle is, often in regions with poor or delicate transportation nets and/or in climates or seasons of the year not conducive to surface travel—again placing demands on airlift to put the goods where needed, when needed.

Seaborne prepositioning is a unique blend of mobility capabilities. It is flexible in that materiel can be more easily moved about and diverted and, if properly positioned, is clearly faster to reach if it started from the United States. It is also less vulnerable than land-based stocking if properly operated. Susceptibilities to

MODERN AIRLIFT ERA

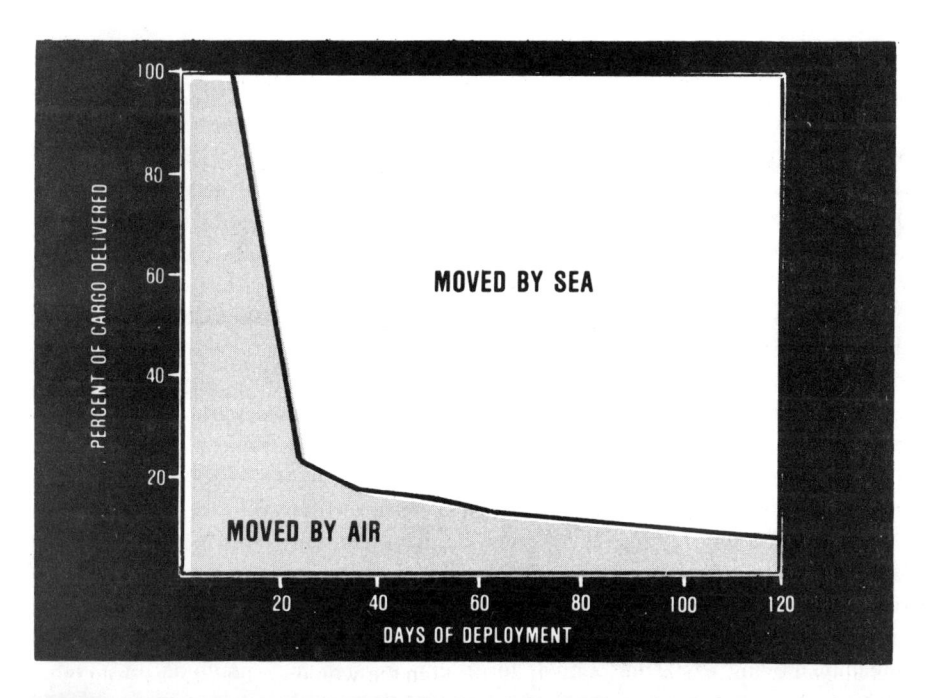

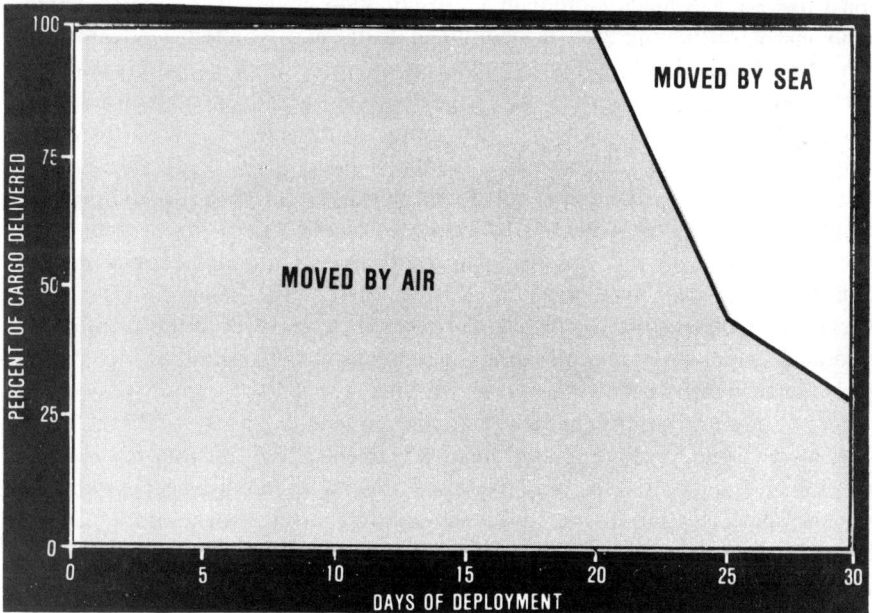

Figure 80. Airlift and sealift contributions in a 30- and 120-day deployment.

political sensitivities are almost nil. But, goods still must be redistributed, often by airlift; there must still be a marry-up between forces arriving by airlift and the shipborne items; and operations through seaports are required as well. Alton Keel, assistant secretary of the Air Force for research, development, and logistics, illustrated the point in the FY 1983 budget hearings by noting that "to fill out the near-term prepositioned ships (NTPS) brigade stationed at Diego Garcia requires 31 C-5, 115 C-141, and 31 CRAF [Civil Reserve Air Fleet] B-747 sorties to move 11,000 troops and 3,500 short tons of residual cargo."[6] What airlift lacks in capability (especially small, austere airfield capability) the United States pays for in the time it takes to bring forces into battle.

Deputy Secretary of Defense Frank Carlucci, an enthusiastic advocate of rapid sealift and prepositioning, viewed the three parts of the mobility triad as mutually reinforcing. Without the equipment that cannot be prepositioned, he said, "the units may well not be able to operate." Rapid sealift, he had to observe, still does not meet the full requirement, and we need strategic airlift to fill that gap.[7]

Airlift is fast and flexible. It is limited by the amount of goods it can carry and it is dependent on airfields. Its greatest contributions come early in conflicts requiring rapid deployments, any time during a conflict when combat conditions call for emergency or high-priority movement or resupply, and before a conflict when the threat of moving a sizable combat force into an area may preclude undesirable developments. It is much more than a transportation mode—it is an instrument of policy and a warfighting tool. It readily and just as easily provides movement for international peacekeeping bodies, removes refugees from danger, and moves disaster relief goods and services. Its appearance at airfields throughout the world signals interest and commitment. The ability to airland or airdrop forces and equipment across long distances in a matter of hours gives civilian leaders and military planners a flexibility not found elsewhere. These capabilities also complicate planning by potential adversaries and can give them serious pause. When properly sized and equipped, an airlift force—in conjunction with other combat forces—can overcome, at least partially, the volume and airfield dependency problems that airlift faces. A tactical fighter wing and elements of an airborne division (for example), put in the right place at the right time, are a potent combat force in many parts of the world. The mere capability to rapidly project such a force is a powerful deterrent to adventurism. Assistant Secretary Keel said "airlift is the most visible, responsive, and flexible element of our mobility resources. In many situations, airlift is the only means of responding rapidly, because of either the geographic location or the speed with which the threat develops."[8] General Huyser put it succinctly: "There is no substitute for the rapid responsiveness of airlift."[9]

The Congressionally Mandated Mobility Study

Maj James Crumley, Jr., writing in the winter 1983 *Airlift Operations Review*, sought to describe the unanswerable: "What's the Requirement?" His opening paragraph is a classic illustration of a critical problem faced by airlift advocates:

> One of the difficult aspects of discussing airlift needs, shortfalls, and problem areas is obtaining consensus on what the airlift requirement really is during wartime. More than 150 studies in the last 15 years have proclaimed shortfalls in both intertheater and intratheater airlift and most people now recognize that we don't have enough airlift capability to deploy, employ, and resupply the combat forces this country possesses. Yet, the original C-141 buy was cut from 350 to 280 aircraft; the original C-5 buy was cut from 120 to 81; the advanced medium STOL transport (AMST) was cancelled; the C-17 has been delayed; CRAF enhancement has had a checkered funding history with minimal program results (one aircraft modified since 1974); and the C-5/Boeing 747 controversy in the Congress reconfirmed a lack of accord on either airlift capabilities or requirements.[10]

Section 203 of the Department of Defense Authorization Act of 1981 said that no funds for the full-scale engineering development or procurement of the C-X (or any other new transport aircraft) could be obligated or expended until the secretary of defense made four certifications. Secretary Weinberger made those certifications on 7 December 1981:

> 1. That the national security requirements of the United States for additional military airlift capability merit initiation of the C-X program.
> 2. That the magnitude and nature of the military cargo and materiel to be airlifted to the Indian Ocean area and other areas of potential conflict are sufficiently well defined to permit identification of a deficiency in military airlift capability.
> 3. That the magnitude and characteristics of military cargo and materiel to be transported by air to such areas are sufficiently well defined to provide clear justification and design parameters for such aircraft.
> 4. That plans for such aircraft are sufficiently well developed to make such full-scale engineering development both economical and technically feasible.[11]

He based those certifications on an evaluation of many airlift alternatives and a study of overall US military mobility requirements—called the Congressionally Mandated Mobility Study (CMMS)—submitted to Congress on 21 May 1981. That study examined four airlift scenarios: a regional conflict in the Persian Gulf, a Soviet invasion of Iran, a NATO-Warsaw Pact conflict, and a conflict in the Persian Gulf accompanied by a precautionary reinforcement in Europe.[12]

The CMMS evaluated the airlift needs in all four scenarios against an assumed 1986 baseline force structure that included an ongoing airlift enhancement program of modification of the C-5 wing, additional C-141/C-5 wartime spare parts, and a CRAF enhancement program that provided the equivalent of 32 B-747s.[13] The study also assumed that eight SL-7 fast sealift ships would be available, that six full Army divisions of prepositioned materiel configured for unit sets (POMCUS) would be

AIRLIFT DOCTRINE

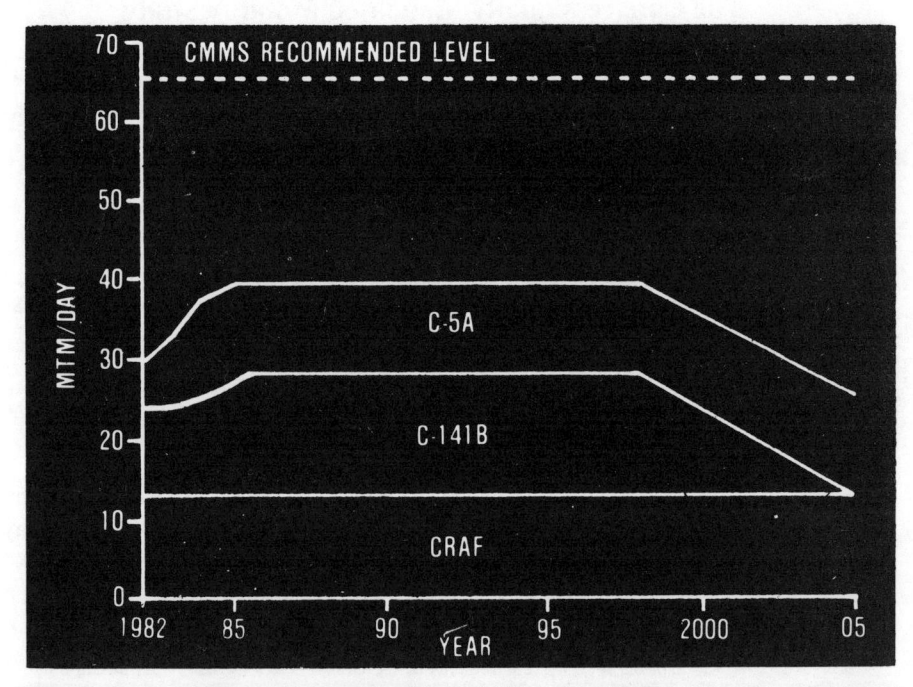

Figure 81. CMMS recommended airlift capability versus projected status quo capabilities.

available in NATO, that there would be additional Air Force and Marine prepositioning in NATO, and that there would be maritime prepositioning ships for a two-brigade-size Marine air-ground task force (MAGTF).

The CMMS evaluated two primary alternative solutions against this baseline and the requirements of the various scenarios:

Program A

- 130 tons of prepositioned munitions and resupply in Southwest Asia.
- Maritime prepositioning of a third brigade-size MAGTF [Marine air-ground task force].
- 20 million ton-miles per day of additional outsize/oversize airlift capability.
- Dedicated RO/RO [roll-on, roll-off] shipping with a capacity for 100,000 tons.
- Provisions of adequate support to the Army's D-day force in Europe through some combination of prepositioning, host nation support, or other mobility means to be developed after further negotiations with European allies.

Program B (Additions to Program A)

- 15 million ton-miles per day of additional outsize/oversize airlift capability.
- Dedicated RO/RO shipping with a capacity for 170,000 tons.

The study concluded that neither program is able to satisfy all unit closure requirements. Program A is recommended as the preferred program. Although it has somewhat less capability than Program B, the cost is significantly less.[14]

This recommendation meant that the minimum goal for airlift capability, constrained by fiscal pressures, should be at least 66 million ton-miles per day (MTM/D). In addition, analysis of the CMMS showed that at least half of the recommended increase should be in outsize cargo capability. The CMMS did not provide any detailed analysis of intratheater requirements.

The 66 MTM/D airlift requirement documented by the CMMS is not the "real" airlift requirement and defining such is, as Crumley pointed out, probably nearly impossible. Scenario assumptions can readily drive that number in any direction. Nonetheless, the CMMS figure has become accepted as the minimum airlift capability improvement goal. The least demanding scenario in the CMMS needed 83 MTM/D of airlift capability to meet required delivery dates of needed combat forces.[15] The CMMS recommended level was an affordable one, not one that solved the problem:

> The CMMS recommended program of airlift, sealift, and prepositioning does not satisfy the unit closure requirements of any of the four scenarios. The program was preferred over larger programs because it provides the greatest improvement for a reasonable amount of investment. . . . The CMMS recommendation does not meet the requirements of any of the CMMS scenarios, nor does it meet the requirements of the Defense Guidance.[16]

How best to fill the gap became an item of considerable debate—a debate of fundamental importance to airlift doctrine.

A View from the Top

In his 1980 annual report, Secretary of Defense Harold Brown noted that given a schedule of forces required in a deployment, "the mobility forces required for initial deployment can be determined relatively easily."[17] Tactical mobility forces were judged harder to determine. Airlift and sealift were considered force multipliers because they precluded the need to position forces and supplies in every potential location. Sealift, however, was not fast enough, and airlift, beyond that available from the civil sector, was considered expensive. Prepositioning was the attractive mobility option when the location of conflict could be predicted and the consequences judged sufficiently serious. Key improvement areas noted were the ability to deploy additional forces to NATO and to deploy forces in limited contingencies without reliance on intermediate bases or overflight rights. Programs to put these views into action included enhancement of the Civil Reserve Air Fleet, the C-141 stretch and refueling modification (a near-term increase of 30 percent in capability), C-5 and C-141 utilization rate increases, prepositioning increases in Europe, and the KC-10 advanced tanker/cargo aircraft (whose primary purpose was to improve deployments in limited contingencies).[18] The 1980 report also announced the cancellation of the AMST program, based on the assumptions of a European conflict where a sophisticated transportation network competed favorably with the "speed and responsiveness of tactical airlift."[19] In a rather hazy look to the future, Secretary Brown did suggest a potential opening for tactical airlift improvements:

> Future work on limited contingencies—where distances are greater and road and rail lines are minimal or nonexistent—may show a more significant value and need for intratheater airlift. Moreover, it may prove feasible to use a single basic aircraft design for tactical airlift and other purposes. The resulting reduced unit cost could make modernization of tactical airlift economically attractive.[20]

By the time Secretary Brown submitted his 1981 report, mobility objectives had shifted to recognition that conflicts in the Middle East, Persian Gulf, or Korea were more likely than one in NATO, thus "warranting additional considerations in our mobility planning."[21] In order to improve early deployment requirements of simultaneous scenarios, Secretary Brown had taken steps to have commercial ships and aircraft of NATO members available for US use in reinforcement of Europe. A CRAF program to encourage airlines to convert passenger aircraft to potential cargo carriers was initiated. The C-141 and C-5 improvement programs continued, as did both prepositioning of Army equipment in Europe and the KC-10 program. There was also an initiative to build maritime prepositioning ships (MPS), load them with supplies and equipment for an armor-heavy Marine division-sized force, and station them in the vicinity of potential crises.[22] In addition to the maritime prepositioning, Secretary Brown also discussed a new airlift aircraft—the C-X.

> We have also programmed funds to develop a new airlift aircraft designated the C-X, which will improve significantly our ability to deliver the full range of military equipment, including the "outsize" materiel that, at present, can be airlifted only by the C-5. Procurement of the C-X will add to our ability to meet demands of a NATO/Warsaw Pact war, and when complemented by the maritime prepositioning program, will enhance our ability to respond to contingencies outside of Europe. The design of this aircraft may be a derivative of the technology developed in advanced medium short take-off and landing (AMST) prototypes, though substantially larger than the aircraft in that now terminated program. Or it may be based on relatively small modifications of other existing designs such as the C-5A or the 747. The aircraft will be optimized for intertheater, not intratheater missions. After initial deployment and resupply it could be used for intratheater purposes (if surface transportation cannot do the job), perhaps at some sacrifice in payload and with some airfield operations problems.[23]

Secretary Brown's FY 1982 report showed a significant reorientation concerning mobility forces. The long-term goal became being able to simultaneously support "full-scale deployments to Europe and to other potential trouble spots. We would wish to meet both the intertheater and intratheater demands of such a dual contingency."[24] For NATO reinforcement, "both airlift enhancement and prepositioning would reduce existing mobility shortfalls at about the same costs (for articles delivered within the first 10 days) and could be implemented by about the same date."[25] Movement of the new Rapid Deployment Force (RDF) to worldwide trouble spots was a more difficult problem to solve. Selecting the right mix of airlift, fast sealift, and maritime prepositioning was viewed as a matter of costs which, in the RDF context, meant responsiveness:

> Fast sealift, the least costly option, could deliver division-size forces from the CONUS, prepositioning ships could deliver the same elements in about one to two weeks and airlift, the most expensive option, could respond within a few days. However, rapid response is the key to successful employment of the RDF in most scenarios. Therefore, it is clear that we must have more airlift, complemented by fast sealift, to meet the global challenges to our national interests.[26]

The FY 1982 sealift improvement package included acquisition and conversion of eight SL-7 high-speed (33-knot) ships to be able to deliver a mechanized division to the Persian Gulf in 20 to 26 days, or to the front line in Europe in 15 days. The program also sought military break bulk, roll-on/roll-off, and tanker ships for positioning in the Indian Ocean. This was called the near-term prepositioning ships program. The MPS program, begun in FY 1981, was continued, as was the CRAF enhancement, C-5/C-141 improvements, and (on a lesser scale) the KC-10 initiatives from earlier years.[27] C-X development also received continuing support, and its concept of operations expanded.

> The evolution of modernized heavier weapon systems and the recent crises in Southwest Asia have brought more clearly into focus the need for a new airlift aircraft that will help meet the demands of simultaneity. This aircraft has become known as the C-X. When operational, the C-X is expected to carry, over intercontinental distances, the full range of military equipment, including the new XM-1 tank and other outsize cargo that now can be airlifted only by the C-5. The C-X will also be capable of operating into austere airfields, greatly improving our ability to respond to global contingencies.[28]

The mobility program presented by Secretary of Defense Caspar Weinberger was the most demanding yet seen. Its long-term goal was to be able to concurrently reinforce Europe, deploy forces to Southwest Asia, and provide support to other potential conflict areas. As a result of the need for additional airlift, documented in the Congressionally Mandated Mobility Study, Secretary Weinberger reported a program to procure 50 new C-5s and 44 additional KC-10s. Calling the C-5 "our most flexible mobility resource," Secretary Weinberger said that acquisition of more C-5s would provide "17 more aircraft during the program period [FY 1983-

87] than would be possible with a new design [the C-17]."[29] Ground- and sea-based prepositioning remained an important element of the mobility concept, as did fast sealift, C-5/C-141 modification programs, and CRAF enhancements. All of this still left an airlift shortfall; so the DOD would continue to evaluate new designs, including the C-17 initiatives. Secretary Weinberger also reported on new programs to improve sealift unloading capabilities.[30]

Secretary Weinberger's 1984 annual report was a ringing endorsement of the importance of mobility forces, particularly the role airlift played. "Mobility forces," he said, "are an indispensable component of our global response capability. They allow us to project power worldwide—even to austere regions— and sustain that power over long periods."[31] Mobility objectives expanded as well, with the long-term goal calling for the ability to meet the "demands of a worldwide war, including concurrent reinforcement of Europe, deployments to Southwest Asia and the Pacific, and support for other areas."[32] All previous mobility programs were continued, including the C-17:

> Intended to contribute to our intertheater airlift needs as well as provide intratheater capability, the C-17 will be able to carry the full range of military equipment, including the M-1 tank and most other outsize cargo that only the C-5 can carry now. It will also be able to operate from austere airfields, thus greatly improving our ability to respond to global contingencies.[33]

In his 1985 annual report, Secretary Weinberger no longer talked about mobility forces; instead, he discussed force projection. The linkage of national strategy to force projection capability was stronger than ever.

> Our strategy of deterrence through forward defense with limited peacetime presence requires a rapid deployment capability. For deterrence to be effective, we must be capable—and be seen as being capable—of responding promptly to aggression, with forces of sufficient size and strength to limit the extent of a conflict and protect the security of friends and allies. A credible deterrent, then, hinges to a large extent on our ability to deliver forces rapidly to distant trouble spots and to sustain them once employed. Projection forces give us that capability.[34]

The secretary's report essentially continued to support the programs responsible for the upward trend in force projection capabilities seen over the past several years. Of particular importance to airlift was a commitment to begin full-scale engineering development of the C-17.

> Though smaller than the C-5, the C-17 will be able to carry the full range of military equipment, including all armored vehicles and most outsize cargo. Unlike most other intertheater aircraft, it will be able to operate into austere airfields, thereby increasing the amount of cargo that can be delivered directly to operating locations. After its intertheater mission is completed, it could be used to augment the C-130 force in moving troops and materiel within the theater.[35]

A View from Inside

The programmatic tale of the C-17 is a primer in the politico-military affairs of airlift. In late 1979 the Department of Defense reoriented its airlift thinking. The AMST airlift program was cancelled and a C-X Task Force formed to determine the parameters for a new airlifter to meet intertheater airlift needs. The C-X Task Force recommended an airplane that could carry outsize cargo across intercontinental distances into small, austere destination airfields. On 10 December 1979, a Headquarters USAF program management directive called for just such an airplane and directed a request for proposal (RFP) to contractors on 15 April 1980. The new airlift aircraft was to achieve initial operational capability (IOC)—16 operational aircraft delivered—by 1987. On 22 January 1980 the Air Force issued the C-X preliminary system operational concept calling for the long-range austere field capability. Secretary Brown suggested advancing the IOC to 1985 and increasing aircraft range.[36]

In March of 1981 the administration submitted an $80-million FY 1981 funding request for the C-X. The Research and Development Subcommittee of the House Committee on Armed Services was not receptive to arguments for the new airplane and deleted its funding. The rationale the subcommittee used to deny funding is as good a summary as any of the debate to come.

> The committee strongly supports the requirement to enhance our strategic mobility capability. The committee is cognizant of our present deficiencies but is not convinced that the C-X is a good approach to enhancing our airlift capability over the near and intermediate term. Many of the functions defined for the C-X can readily be performed by the C-5A aircraft. The significant modification program currently scheduled for the C-5A will extend its operational lifetime many years into the future.
>
> The C-X does nothing to address our near term lift deficiencies. The Department of Defense was unable to present adequate justification for the need for the C-X. Consequently, the committee recommends termination of the C-X effort for fiscal year 1981. The committee requests that the Office of the Secretary of Defense review our current strategic mobility capabilities, delineate a plan to correct the deficiencies through prepositioning of equipment and the procurement of readily available assets, that is, ships and aircraft, and review the alternatives that are available for the transportation of oversized and outsized cargo that are necessary to solve our longer-term strategic requirements.[37]

On 28 November 1980, Deputy Secretary of Defense W. Graham Claytor, Jr., approved the C-X mission element need statement with the amendment that the secretary of defense would have final approval of the choice for a new C-X or selection of a derivative of an existing transport. On 17 January 1981, the airplane companies submitted their proposals. Lockheed proposed the C-5 as an alternative to the C-X. On 24 April, Secretary of the Air Force Verne Orr advised Congress that the C-5 did not meet the minimum requirements of the C-X RFP. He also informed

Lockheed that the C-5 would remain in consideration as an alternative to the C-X. On 28 August 1981, Secretary Orr announced that the McDonnell-Douglas C-X entry—to be later called the C-17—had been chosen as the C-X source selection team's choice. The number of aircraft to be built was to be announced when the DOD awarded the production contract.[38]

After the selection of the McDonnell-Douglas C-X design, the Air Force announced that a mix of airlift aircraft was still an option under consideration to satisfy requirements. Consequently, in mid-September 1981 Boeing submitted a proposal for the Air Force to use B-747 freighters to solve the airlift problem and Lockheed likewise submitted a proposal to fill the gap with C-5Ns (new). The Air Force reviewed the submissions but concluded that the best program would be a combination of the C-17s and an expanded CRAF enhancement program. On 22 September Under Secretary of the Air Force Edward C. Aldridge, Jr., advised Dr R. E. DeLauer, under secretary of defense for research and engineering, that the C-X was ready for full-scale engineering and development. Dr DeLauer waited more than two months to forward the mandatory Air Force C-X certifications to Secretary Weinberger.[39]

DeLauer's rationale for delay was that "we should consider whether there is sufficient chance of the C-X program failing Congress and thus not redressing the airlift shortfall to justify the risk of proceeding with this new development."[40] He contended that the C-5N and B-747 options had lower initial acquisition costs, congressional support, and earlier IOCs. The C-17 admittedly had better military utility and potentially lower life-cycle costs. Secretary Weinberger, on 7 December 1981, finally certified to Congress that "the national security requirements of the United States for additional military airlift capability merit initiation of the C-X program."[41] Meanwhile, both houses of Congress denied Air Force requests for C-X research and development funds, instead providing $50 million in procurement funds for existing wide-bodied aircraft.

On 22 December 1981, Deputy Secretary of Defense Carlucci told Secretary Orr that he had decided to postpone selection of an airlift aircraft pending further study. He directed the Air Force to prepare a system-analysis study of alternate proposals and the C-17 and provide a ranking of each in terms of military utility, acquisition costs, life-cycle costs, and production schedules.[42] The Air Force analysis endorsed the C-17. The briefing given to Deputy Secretary Carlucci in January of 1982 recommended a short-term program that procured KC-10s and pursued additional CRAF enhancements. For the long term the Air Force wanted C-17s with an IOC of 1988—all this based on funding profiles then available for the C-17. The C-5N option was rejected because it provided far less airlift than needed, did nothing for the aging C-130 and C-141 fleet, and was a 1960s design aircraft whose favorable price assumed few modifications.[43] One slide from that briefing summarized the Air Force's position on the overall comparisons.

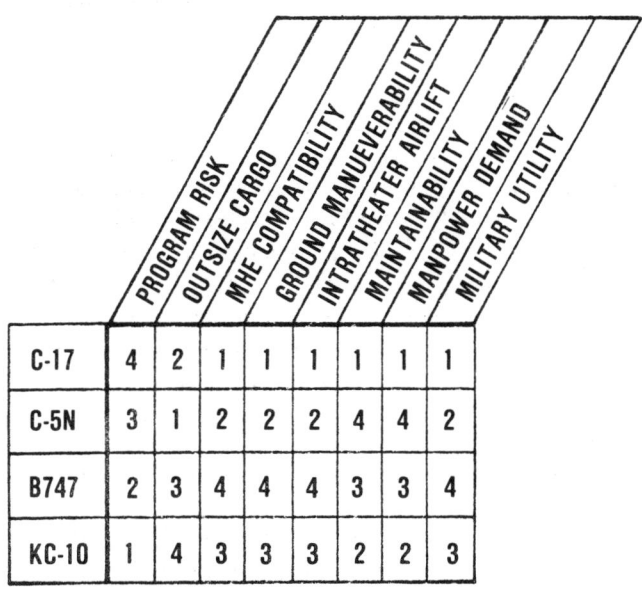

	PROGRAM RISK	OUTSIZE CARGO	MHE COMPATIBILITY	GROUND MANUEVERABILITY	INTRATHEATER AIRLIFT	MAINTAINABILITY	MANPOWER DEMAND	MILITARY UTILITY
C-17	4	2	1	1	1	1	1	1
C-5N	3	1	2	2	2	4	4	2
B747	2	3	4	4	4	3	3	4
KC-10	1	4	3	3	3	2	2	3

RANK: 1 - BEST
THROUGH
4 - WORST

Figure 82. Airlift candidate comparison.

The KC-10 was to operate in any of three modes: all airlift, all refueling, or a mixed mission of carrying cargo for the aircraft being refueled on a deployment. After three weeks of independent analysis, and under the pressures of formulation of the president's budget for FY 1983, Secretary Weinberger asked the Air Force to consider the C-5N and C-17 under the assumption that either aircraft could be funded at the fastest prudent pace. Secretary Orr then concluded that the C-5N could be operationally ready three years earlier than the C-17. On 26 January 1982, Lt Gen Kelly Burke, Air Force deputy chief of staff for research, development, and acquisition, announced that the Air Force, under the revised financial posture, recommended the procurement of 50 C-5Ns and 44 KC-10s.[44]

Secretary Orr wrote of his decision in early February 1982 that

> I decided on a near term airlift enhancement program which provides for the acquisition of 44 KC-10s (to be considered mobility assets) and 50 C-5s. I felt compelled to choose the C-5 as the better *near term* solution for several reasons, but most significantly, with the increased near-term funding, 17 more C-5s than C-17s will be delivered by FY 87, providing 3.8 million ton-miles more airlift than the C-17 alternative.[45]

However, he also supported a modest research and development program for the C-17 to preserve the option of initiating a C-17 development program in FY 84 "if we later deem it appropriate as part of our long-term airlift acquisition plan."[46] Secretary Orr said that his

> overriding consideration in the choice between the C-5 and C-17 is the conclusion—documented in the CMMS and numerous other studies over many years—that a significant airlift shortfall exists *now!* Consequently, the objective is to increase airlift capability as quickly as possible. Hence, a good program soon was chosen over a somewhat better program later. This choice is also consistent with an apparent signal from Congress which eliminated RDT&E [research, development, test and evaluation] funds for airlift in FY 82.[47]

Gen James Allen, commander in chief of the Military Airlift Command (CINCMAC), noted that the decision represented an important recognition of the critical role of airlift in the overall defense posture, but he still wanted the C-17. "The capabilities represented by the C-17," he told Secretary Weinberger, "are needed in order to alleviate the remainder of the intertheater shortfall and to satisfy critical intratheater airlift requirements." And, the C-17 would "make an excellent replacement for the aging C-141s and C-130s, beginning in the decade of the 1990s."[48] The new C-5s would add to outsize airlift capability by nearly 60 percent and the KC-10s would add flexibility. Together, they could deliver 1,870 tons of cargo per day to main operating bases in Southwest Asia, but this created an additional intratheater requirement of 1,235 tons per day for an already hard-pressed C-130 force that could airlift no outsize cargo.[49]

On 17 March 1982, the Boeing Airplane Company proposed to Secretary Weinberger four different 747-200F (freighter) aircraft procurement options to meet airlift requirements faster and more cheaply than the C-5N/KC-10 decision. Instead of the Air Force's program, Boeing proposed a solution that would provide equal ton-mile airlift capability up to four years sooner and save $6.9 billion. The Air Force had earlier rejected the B-747 in comparison to the C-5, C-17, and KC-10, but Air Force Chief of Staff Gen Lew Allen, Jr., believed the proposal merited consideration as a potential replacement for the CRAF freighter program. The Air Force restudied the question and, on 6 May 1982, Deputy Secretary Carlucci rejected the offer, essentially on the basis that a balanced program of C-5Bs, KC-10s, and a viable CRAF program would be the best solution. Commercial freighters could best serve in the CRAF rather than in the Air Force's organic fleet. But the commercial option was kept very much alive in the Senate.[50]

On 13 May the Senate amended the FY 1983 Defense Authorization Bill to prohibit restarting the C-5 production line and moved $520 million from the airlift budget for C-5 procurement to purchase of surplus commercial wide-body cargo aircraft owned by domestic companies. Senators Thomas Eagleton and John Danforth argued that the 747s would serve only as stopgaps until the C-17 became

Figure 83. Gen James Allen, commander in chief of Military Airlift Command from June 1981 through June 1983.

available. Senator Ted Stevens said he would propose an amendment earmarking $200 million for C-17 research and development. Eventually, after much more maneuvering, the Congress approved $847 million for the C-5B, $144.8 million for the procurement of three wide-body commercial aircraft (747s), and $1 million for C-17 research and development. Given that the C-5s were by then known to cost $1.2 billion more and were to be delivered one year later than originally claimed, it was a significant victory. The $1 million for the C-17 was "a drop in the bucket" in terms of the program, but it at least kept the option alive.[51]

Following more than a year of intense and sophisticated analysis of the C-17's capabilities, combined with strong presentation by defense officials, the FY 1984 defense budget had a somewhat more realistic $60 million for C-17 research and development.

On 29 September 1983, Secretary of the Air Force Verne Orr and Air Force Chief of Staff Gen Charles A. Gabriel jointly released the *US Air Force Airlift Master Plan* noting that "the ability of the United States to successfully deter aggression, limit conflict, or wage war depends on our ability to rapidly deploy and sustain fighting units. Airlift provides the capability to deliver forces where they are needed in time to make a difference."[52] The plan committed the Air Force to modernizing the military airlift force using the C-17 as a mainstay aircraft. It is primarily a long-term look at airlift force structure needs both in terms of operating capabilities and raw tonnage requirements. What is doctrinally important about the plan is that it formalized the C-17 as both an inter- and intratheater aircraft. It is the nearest thing to an official statement of modern airlift doctrine. The force structure recommended by the plan is summarized here:

- Retire 180 older C-130s between 1991 and 1998.
- Retire 54 C-141s as they reach the end of their useful service life by 1998.
- Transfer C-141Bs to the air reserve forces [ARF] between 1991 and 1998.
- Acquire 180 C-17s by 1998.
- Retain 114 C-5s to be manned by active duty and ARF personnel.
- Retain a minimum of 11.3 MTM/D in the CRAF program.
- Retain a minimum of 144.9 MPM/D (million passenger miles per day), an equivalent measure of passenger capability in the CRAF program.[53]

The overall constraining factor in this force was the CMMS recommendation that airlift capability should be at least 66 MTM/D. Under the plan, in keeping with very traditional airlift doctrine, the least productive aircraft are retired as late as possible, some aircraft are transferred to the air reserve forces to preserve as much airlift capability as possible (and modernize these forces), C-5s with their unique capabilities are retained, and CRAF capability is also retained, at least at current levels. The C-17 is acquired to fulfill both intertheater and intratheater airlift needs. The plan is flexible enough to allow for either active duty or reserve forces to operate the C-5 fleet, and to allow expansion with additional C-17s as other portions of the fleet age out.

Calculations used to arrive at the force mix are based on using the C-17 in its direct delivery mode *and* performing an intratheater shuttle. Increasing the use of the C-17 in an intratheater mode to take advantage of its inherent flexibility has the ultimate impact of requiring additional C-17 aircraft, either to provide additional intertheater/shuttle service or to be dedicated to intratheater activities. Other combinations of aircraft buys were considered but rejected on the grounds of operating costs, manpower requirements, or lack of flexibility. The C-17 has to be included to meet *both* inter- and intratheater outsize cargo needs and to take advantage of its improved characteristics in any scenario.[54]

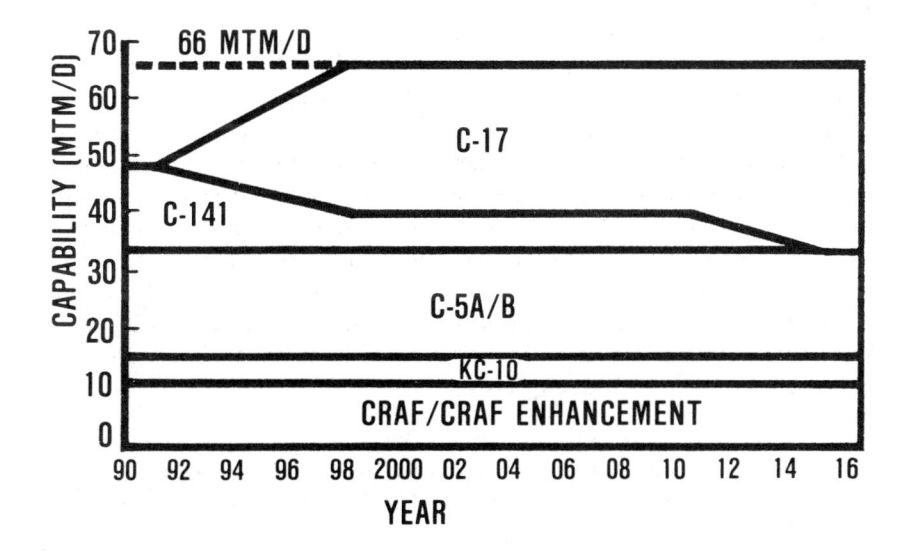

Figure 84. Airlift master plan intertheater airlift contribution.

The Doctrine Debate

This brief summary gives the outline of the events leading to the decision to procure C-5Bs and KC-10s as a near-term solution to airlift needs. That decision process was filled with economic and political factors, with military questions often peppered in only to support a particular argument. As with the major airlift debates of the late 1950s, there were significant doctrinal implications for each of the recommended alternatives. Rather than becoming bogged in the overwhelming morass of cost and scenario-dependent details, it is more fruitful to review the individual airlift systems advocated and the doctrinal ramifications of each.

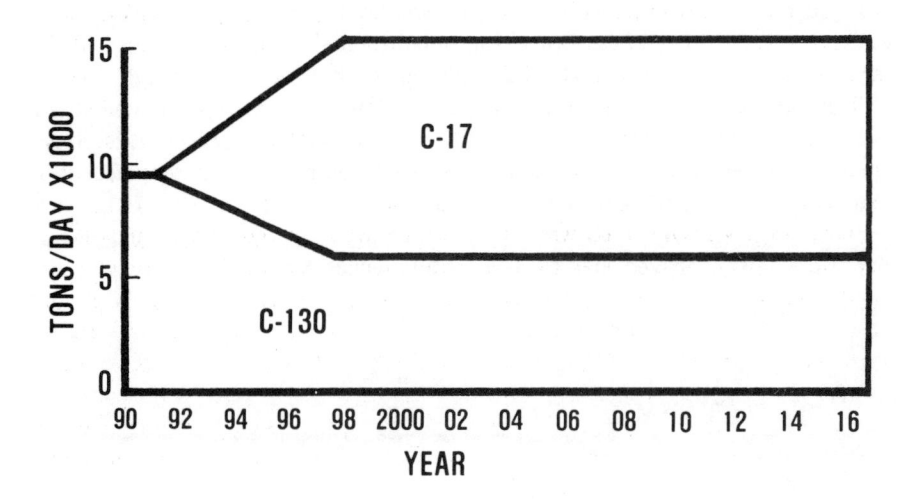

Figure 85. Airlift master plan intratheater airlift contribution.

The AMST

In March of 1963 Air Force Chief of Staff Gen Curtis E. LeMay directed Gen Bernard A. Schriever, commander of Air Force Systems Command, to make "a comprehensive study and analysis of the Air Force structure projected into the 1965-1975 time period."[55] The effort, deemed Project Forecast, included recommendations concerning both the C-X heavy logistics support aircraft and encouragement of an operationally effective vertical/short takeoff and landing (VSTOL) aircraft.[56]

The 1966 report of the Military Airlift Subcommittee of the House Committee on Armed Services recommended that the Air Force give favorable consideration to the C-130J aircraft as a replacement for the C-130As and Bs, because of its projected assault capability. The Tactical Air Command (TAC) elected to purchase C-130Es. By 1970, TAC officials were telling the same subcommittee that experiences in Southeast Asia (SEA) led to the conclusion that there was a "positive need for the replacement for the C-130, and there is no such aircraft in sight."[57] Planners from TAC argued that the lack of a rapidly deployable short takeoff and landing aircraft, the short C-7/C-123 ranges, and C-130E runway requirements all supported this requirement. Two additional factors made a medium STOL aircraft TAC's first priority. First, the command could not see an early availability of a VSTOL aircraft "competitive with the STOL in cost or in capability to perform the total mission—including deployment and the wide variety of missions which are assigned to theater airlift resources."[58] Second, the thousands of Army helicopters had "reduced the operational requirement [for a VSTOL] by moving the interface point slightly more rearward. "The ability of the Army to support forward positions in contact with the enemy with helicopters," admitted the TAC planners, "is an established fact."[59] That almost stunning admission immediately preceded an equally surprising statement that "we take a realistic view and admit the C-130 and its replacement should be operated more rearward to avoid heavy enemy fire, and that aircraft of lesser cost must be handled by the far-forward equipment."[60]

Instead of a VSTOL, TAC wanted an airlifter with a cargo compartment larger than the C-130 but smaller than the C-141. It would be the backbone of the tactical airlift force, providing the interface between major air and sea ports and the ground force transportation systems in the forward area. Routine operations at a 2,000-foot strip, with a 35,000- to 60,000-pound payload in-theater, or a 25,000-pound payload for longer deployments, were to be some of the general parameters that TAC would seek in a required operational capability (ROC) statement to be submitted to Headquarters USAF in the near future. In the interim, TAC supported an off-the-shelf buy of either C-8s (Buffalos) or MD-188s to augment the aging and diminishing fleet of C-7s and C-123s.[61]

The subcommittee report took the Air Force to task for not supporting modernization of the tactical airlift force in the post-Vietnam era. It pointed out that the Air Force was inconsistently arguing that airlift capability would improve between 1966 and 1974—in ton-miles—even though sortie generation capability dropped 35 percent. Additionally, the report showed a sophisticated understanding of the relationship between strategic airlift and tactical airlift.

> The ability for the strategic airlift element to rapidly deploy military forces under the various contingency plans is of little value if the military does not have the tactical airlift capability to rapidly distribute the military equipment and supplies down to the user units within a theater of operation.[62]

Calling an approved program for tactical airlift modernization nonexistent, the subcommittee report called for off-the-shelf procurement of STOL aircraft to deal with the immediate C-7 and C-123 problem, continued research and development into a VSTOL aircraft, and support for the urgent requirement to develop the STOL aircraft TAC wanted.[63]

In May of 1970 TAC submitted ROC No. 52-69 calling for the AMST. The introduction of the C-5A had generated a requirement for an immediate and massive theater distribution system; and TAC planners also knew that the speeds, ranges, cargo-lift capability, and STOL capabilities of current aircraft were limited. The TAC ROC called for an airplane with a 3,600-nautical mile unrefueled range with the capability of sustained operations carrying a 14-ton payload from a 2,000-foot runway midway through the mission profile. It had to be weight, not cube, limited, be compatible with the 463L cargo handling system, and have airdrop features. Requests for proposals were released in January 1972 and included a design-to-cost goal of $5 million for the 300th production article in fiscal year 1972 dollars. By 31 March 1972, the Air Force had received AMST proposals from Boeing, McDonnell-Douglas, Fairchild, and Bell and a joint proposal from Lockheed and North American Rockwell. In August the Air Force formally set forth the AMST Program Development Memorandum—*Advanced Medium STOL Transport Prototype*.[64]

The AMST became embroiled in questions of cost advantages/disadvantages when compared to the C-5A, Lockheed proposals regarding modified C-130s, and actual performance. In 1975 the Air Force told the General Accounting Office of eight specific advantages the AMST would have over the C-130:

   1. Delivery of two and one-half times the payload of the C-130 onto 3,500-foot runways.
   2. Delivery of sizable payloads onto runways not accessible to the C-130.
   3. Delivery of mixed loads of cargo and troops routinely and safely.
   4. Accommodation of most Army equipment and other items unable to fit in the C-130, such as the Army's 155-millimeter self-propelled howitzer.
   5. Utilization of turbofan speeds of about 465 miles per hour.
   6. Utilization of more efficient vehicular loading and unloading procedures to reduce exposure to hostile fire.
   7. Utilization of steeper landing approaches for increased survivability.
   8. Improved reliability and maintainability.[65]

The Army's Combined Arms Combat Developments Activity at Fort Leavenworth, Kansas, published the results of its study of the AMST in August of 1977, concluding that a tank-carrying AMST offered the Army the "most flexible and efficient tactical airlift system."[66] It argued that the ability to carry a main battle tank was an essential feature for tactical airlift and that "STOL is a highly desirable capability during the combat phase of operations in developed countries and in all phases, to include the buildup, in underdeveloped countries."[67]

The Military Airlift Command (MAC) was a strong supporter of the AMST, seeking to make it as responsive as possible to all theater needs. The MAC concept of operations foresaw the airplane as a tactical transport that would augment the strategic portion of the airlift force as circumstances dictated. The command planned to use the airplane in six different missions: intratheater tactical airlift, tactical aeromedical evacuations, deployment, intertheater strategic airlift augmentation, national objective missions (humanitarian, civilian evacuation, civil disturbances, natural disasters, and transport of peacekeeping forces), and training.[68]

Admitting a lack of certainty in predicting enemy capabilities or willingness of a particular commander to commit an AMST in a given set of operational circumstances, MAC nonetheless said that historically "mobility and resupply of forces engaged at or near the FEBA [forward edge of battle area] have been supported by tactical airlift. It can be expected that the AMST will continue to provide this support."[69] The airplane was to operate in an environment characterized by a variety of small arms fire and light to medium antiaircraft fire, with the possibility of radar-controlled and/or low-intensity surface-to-air missiles being deployed by the enemy. Hostile aircraft attack was possible, the planners said, but friendly forces were presumed to have air superiority. Low-level air maneuverability, steep-approach angles, small turn radius, and ground maneuverability were to contribute to survivability.[70]

MAC's goal was an integrated airlift force to meet the entire spectrum of requirements and the command felt the AMST was the best candidate to provide such a force. A study by the Braddock-Dunn-McDonnell Corporation provided the conclusion that air mobility was required for sufficient battlefield responsiveness and that the AMST was the only means of mobility to contain a major Soviet breakthrough in a NATO conflict. The projected number of outsize vehicles in NATO needing airlift required the AMST's ability to move an Army brigade in 24 hours.[71]

In the future Army units could double and there was a need to triple ammunition resupply missions. The AMST, MAC argued, was the best airplane to meet this variety of needs. It was designed to accommodate 100 percent of the firepower and 97 percent of the combat support vehicles. It was three times as productive as the C-130 for ammunition delivery and its STOL capability provided an excellent hedge against interdiction by decreasing reliance on main operating bases. It could place cargo closer to the user (making helicopter resupply more effective) and was much more maneuverable on the ground than the C-5. The STOL capability also meant the enemy would have to target more runways and cut those hit into much shorter segments to stop AMST operations. The projected ability to carry 37 tons over a 2,600-mile range and land at a 2,600-foot runway also gave it a well-balanced strategic airlift capability. The STOL capability meant that priority delivery direct from on-load bases to destination could occur without time-consuming and sometimes risky strategic-tactical interfaces. An added benefit was the same concept used by the C-130 units that earlier supported the composite air strike forces—move priority goods and people over strategic distances, then stay in the theater to provide tactical airlift.[72]

The Air Force fully supported the broad range of uses for the AMST, adding its own set of arguments for the airplane.

> The tactical airlift force must be able to interface with strategic mobility forces to provide sustained resupply as well as the movement of troops and materiel within the combat zone by means of airland and airdrop operations. Direct delivery is a basic objective in order to minimize costly transshipment operations. The range, speed, runway requirements, and cargo bay dimensions of a new tactical airlift aircraft should allow a broad range of on-call capabilities, thus substantially reducing the need for forward area inventory stockpiles. The ability to respond rapidly and reliably to various locations within the theater of operations can increase overall system efficiency by permitting fewer committed forces,

that is, the personnel, supporting firepower, and combat vehicles, to influence and defend larger areas.[73]

Gen Robert Huyser, CINCMAC since 1979, prophetically argued, "I believe state-of-the-art technology has us at a point where we should not define such an aircraft as tactical or strategic—we just discuss it as an airlifter capable of dual roles."[74]

The McDonnell-Douglas YC-15 prototype airplane made its first flight in August 1975. The Boeing YC-14's first flight was in August 1976. By August 1977 the flight test program was complete, and the Air Force issued the proposals instruction package in September 1977 in anticipation of a contract award in April 1978. In December 1977, the AMST was dropped from the president's fiscal year 1979 budget. Source selection went on hold.[75] Secretary of Defense Harold Brown ordered a study to evaluate alternative programs to meet tactical airlift requirements. The study—loosely called the tactical airlift modernization study (TAMS)—showed the AMST to be the most cost-effective method for moving the intratheater airlift needs the services had stated. On the other hand, it also said that the AMST had not been fully justified in terms of alternate intratheater transportation modes. After several more attempts to gain support for the aircraft, the AMST was lain to rest in October 1979 with a decision to pursue the C-X, an aircraft larger than the C-141, smaller than the C-5A, and capable of strategic and tactical missions.[76]

The C-X Task Force

In November 1979, the Air Force, Army, and Marine Corps formed a task force to define the nature and magnitude of future airlift requirements for worldwide force projection. In March 1980, Maj Gen Emil Block, Jr., the director of the C-X Task Force, reported to Congress on the task force's extremely thorough analysis.[77] His report used the task force's matrix for airlift requirements analysis (fig. 86).

Potential areas of conflict for the 1985-90 time frame included a rapid reinforcement of NATO, a Persian Gulf scenario, a Korean conflict, deployments to Zaire, and similar actions in Venezuela. The objective in selecting these scenarios was to test a variety of threats and airlift tasks across different distances, environments, and ground lines of communication. It was a far-ranging, demanding look at a multitude of potential areas where airlift might have to operate—truly a global perspective.[78]

The forces needed to counter the threats were covered in classified portions of the study, but the presence of representatives of all three services worked to provide a realistic picture of the airlift requirements for each scenario. Using a representative requirement for both inter- and intratheater airlift, General Block also presented a series of charts showing relative capabilities and shortfalls. (Note: The

Figure 86. Gen Robert Huyser, commander in chief of Military Airlift Command from July 1979 through June 1981.

AIRLIFT DOCTRINE

Figure 87. The McDonnell-Douglas YC-15.

representative intertheater outsize requirement was 25 percent.)[79] What is important about this part of the process is that the task force was reviewing a whole range of airlift missions with an eye to *one* airplane's solving the majority of the airlift equation.

On-load bases for the scenarios were those where appropriate forces or supply centers existed. Range/payload calculations showed a minimum essential range for worldwide to be about 2,400 nautical miles (NM), key contingency ranges from 2,400 to 3,200 NM, and peacetime ranges from 3,200 to 5,000 NM. Critically, the C-X had to be able to carry a minimum of 130,000 pounds (three infantry-fighting vehicles or one combat-configured XM-1 tank) at least 2,400 miles and land on a 3,000-foot-long runway.[80]

The C-X Task Force considerations of potential off-load airfields were the most comprehensive undertaken and reflected a new step in airlift thinking—the search for true direct delivery. The basic philosophy was that operating into small, austere airfields improved force deployment and employment flexibility, enhanced the aircraft flow by decreasing ground lines of communication requirements, closed combat force on time and at the right place, and complicated enemy interdiction efforts. Such a concept also sought to solve the long-standing problem of competition for airfield space. The ability to operate at austere locations meant that

Figure 88. The Boeing YC-14.

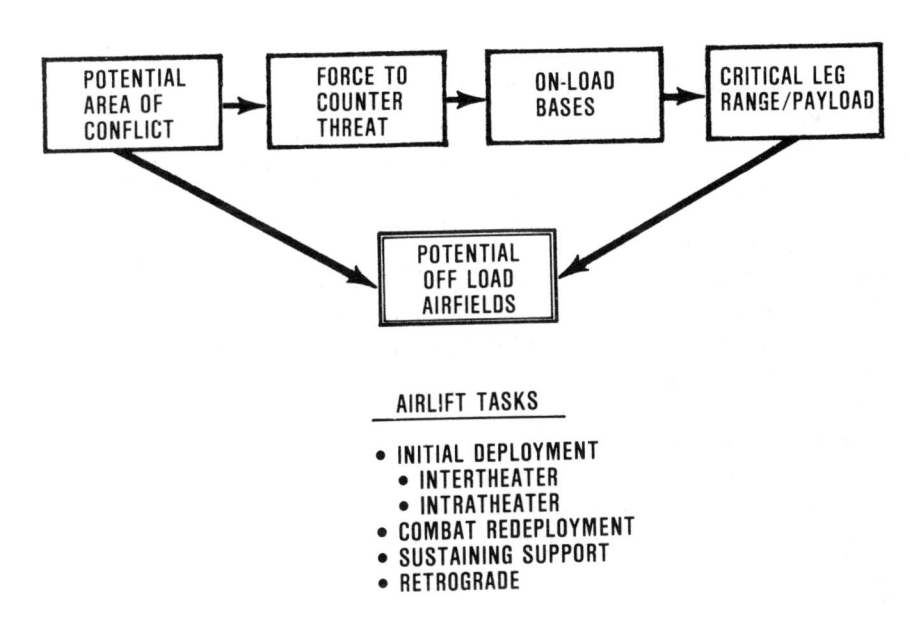

AIRLIFT TASKS

- INITIAL DEPLOYMENT
  - INTERTHEATER
  - INTRATHEATER
- COMBAT REDEPLOYMENT
- SUSTAINING SUPPORT
- RETROGRADE

Figure 89. C-X task force airlift requirements matrix.

AIRLIFT DOCTRINE

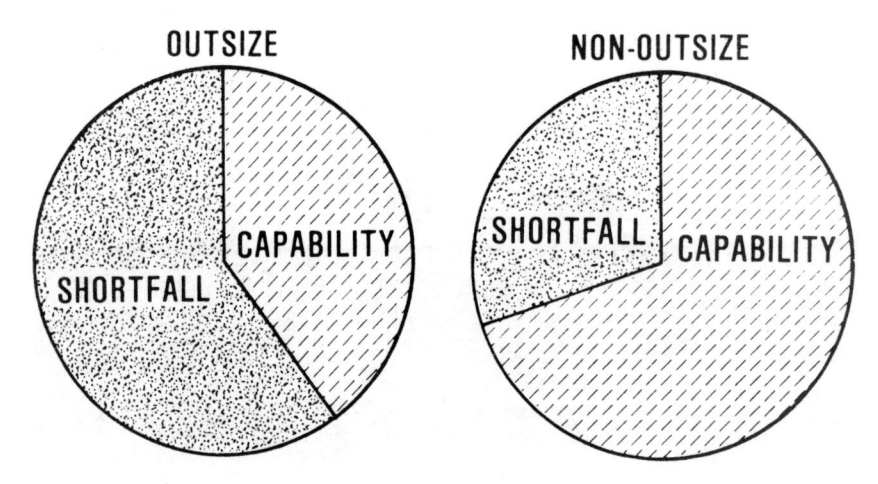

Figure 90. Representative intertheater capability.

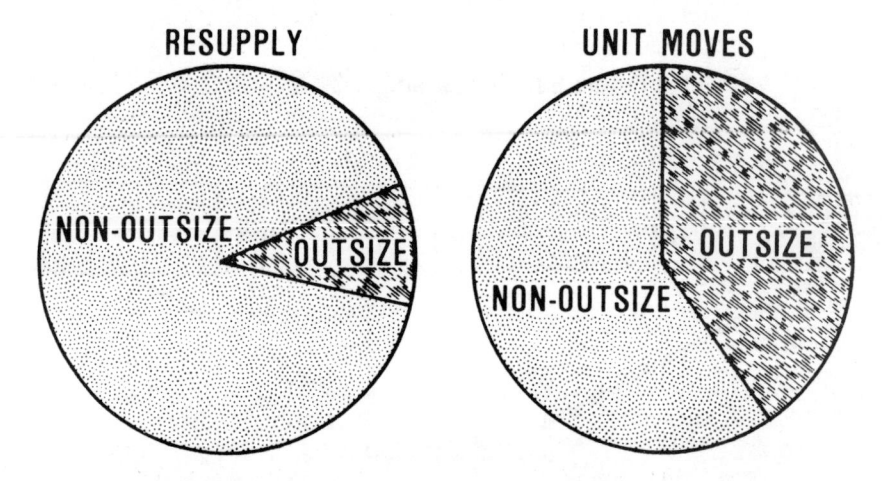

Figure 91. Representative intratheater requirements.

bedding-down airlift forces in-theater would face much less competition for space from host-nation and deployed forces. "The bottom line," said General Block, "is that we need inter- as well as an intratheater airlift aircraft with an outsize capability that can operate into a small, austere field. Those two things are common to inter- and intratheater requirements."[81]

The airfield environment included not just runway length and width but also temperature and elevation, composition and load-bearing capacity, taxiway width

392

MODERN AIRLIFT ERA

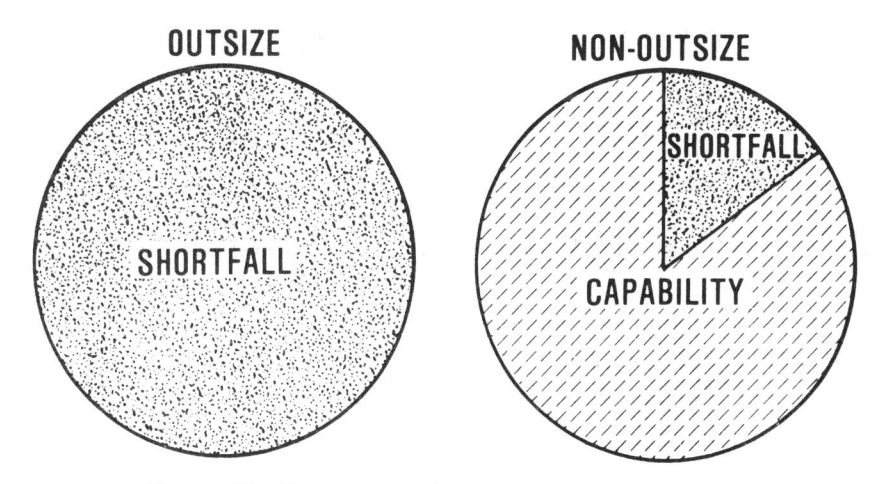

Figure 92. Representative intratheater capability.

and location, size access, and other users of parking areas. Typical small, austere airfields in the objective areas looked like this:

- West Germany—3,000 to 4,000 feet long (paved), 98 feet wide, narrow taxiway (40-50 feet), and limited parking area (50,000 feet^2).
- Saudi Arabia—3,000 to 5,000 feet long (unpaved/semiprepared), 80-150 feet wide, no taxiways, and no formal ramp.
- Korea—2,500 to 5,000 feet long (paved), 80-110 feet wide, no parallel taxiway or turnaround area, and limited parking area (110,000 feet^2).
- Zaire—2,500 to 3,500 feet long (unpaved/semiprepared), 90-100 feet wide, no taxiway or turnaround area, and limited parking area (50,000 feet^2).
- Venezuela—2,600 to 5,000 feet long (unpaved/semiprepared), 80-110 feet wide, no taxiway or turnaround area, and limited parking area (less than 100,000 feet^2).

By way of reference, two C-130s needed slightly less than 100,000 square feet of ramp space, two C-141s needed 300,000, and two C-5s needed 500,000.[82]

Overall, there was a 330-percent increase in the availability of free-world destination runways when the required width dropped from 150 feet to 90 feet, and there was a 70-percent increase in available runways (width greater than 90 feet) when length decreased from 4,000 to 3,000 feet.[83] All told, moving from a 10,000 × 150-foot runway to a 3,000 × 90-foot runway made for an almost tenfold increase in the number of airfields available worldwide.[84]

Because shorter, narrower austere airfields generally also have little ramp space, comparisons of C-X and C-5 in terms of their ability to operate in such poor facilities also favored the C-X. A typical ramp for two C-5s (1,000 × 500 feet with

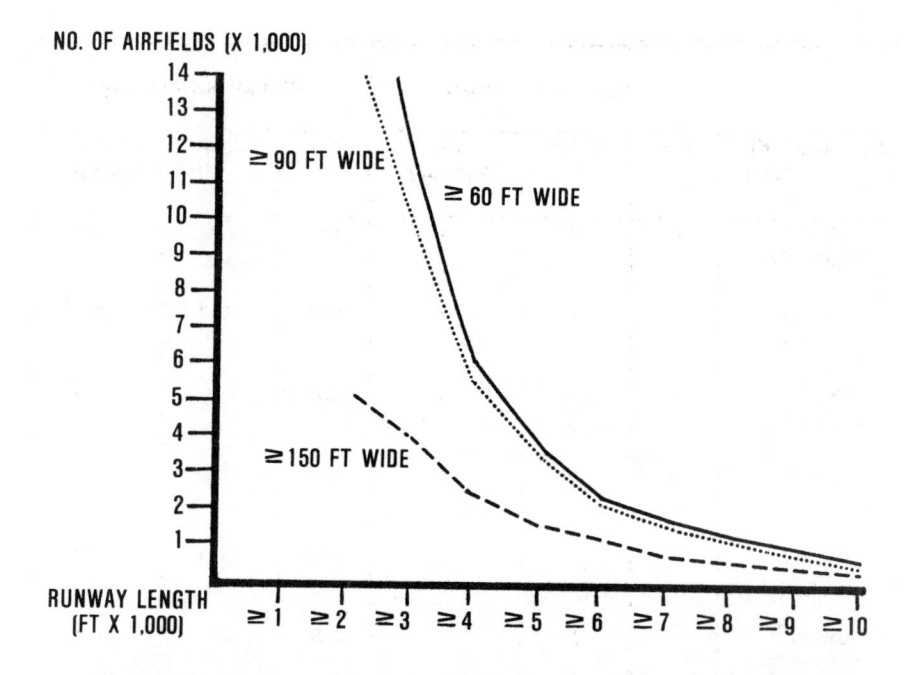

Figure 93. Free-world runway distribution (less United States).

a single entrance) could hold eight C-Xs. Depending on ramp dimensions, the ratio of C-Xs to C-5s varied from 6:1 to 3:1. In the five scenarios the C-X Task Force examined, 55 percent of the ramps greater than 100,000 square feet were too small or too narrow to hold a C-5.[85] Even after adding the ability to back up easily to a notional C-5, the C-X still showed a plus.

The C-5s and C-141s were essentially limited to operating to and from runways equal to or greater than 5,000 feet by 150 feet (by 90 feet if parallel taxiways or turnaround areas were available). Only one-third of the airfields in the 3,000 by 90-foot range were usable in the objective areas, thus severely restricting system flexibility and delivery rate. Larger airfields also generally meant additional movement time over ground lines of communication to the objective area. Increasing the number of aircraft into the larger fields merely speeded up the chance of saturating those fields.[86]

The C-X Task Force concluded that expanding CRAF capability would be a cost-effective way of reducing nonoutsized cargo shortfalls, but would not reduce the large outsize shortfall. Nor would CRAF improvements deal with intratheater requirements. Neither an improved C-5 nor a modified B-747 would provide an effective solution:

MODERN AIRLIFT ERA

	Maximum on Ground			Throughput (Tons/Day)		
Ramp Area (Ft²) (Length × Width)	C-X	C-5A	C-5 W/Backup	C-X	C-5A	C-5 W/Back
500,000 (1000 × 500)	8	2	4	5760	1728	3456
400,000 (800 × 500)	7	2	3	5040	1728	2592
400,000 (1000 × 400)	6	1	2	4320	864	1728
300,000 (750 × 400)	4	1	2	2880	864	1728
300,000 (1000 × 300)	6	1	2	4320	864	1728
200,000 (500 × 400)	3	1	1	2160	864	864
200,000 (1000 × 200)	2	0	1	1440	0	864
100,000 (500 × 200)	2	0	1	1440	0	864
100,000 (333 × 300)	1	0	1	720	0	864

Figure 94. Ramp space comparisons.

Based on operational experience, the Air Force believes that the C-5 does not have the capability to operate into small, austere airfields (physical size: 223-foot wing span, 248-foot fuselage length). The C-5 requires a runway width of 148 feet to turn 180°, requires taxiways 60 feet wide; it cannot back up and does not have adequate clearances for the obstacles normally associated with smaller, austere airfields. The Boeing 747 also has limitations because of its physical size and would require a considerable development effort to adapt it for outsize cargo. The cockpit must be raised, the nose door enlarged, the cargo floor strengthened and the landing gear made to kneel to facilitate loading. Even with kneeling, the cargo floor would be about 9 feet above ground, and the aircraft would still have loading restrictions. A derivative of the Boeing 747 is not nearly as capable as a modernized C-5 and does not offer any cost or schedule benefits.[87]

AIRLIFT DOCTRINE

The final conclusion was obvious. The Air Force needed the C-X in order to best meet modern combat needs. The C-X request for proposal required an aircraft that could deliver a full range of combat equipment over intercontinental distances; operate through a 3,000-foot runway environment; airdrop troops and equipment; have ground maneuverability characteristics that would permit routine operations through small, austere airfields; be designed for survivability; have excellent reliability, maintainability, and availability; and have a low life-cycle cost.[88]

This conclusion was a doctrinal watershed, completing 40 years of evolution in both thinking and technology. The Air Force wanted a single airplane that could perform numerous airlift tasks in a wide variety of environments, in both peace and war. Intellectually gone were the days when there would be two kinds of airlift—two airlift organizations—two airlift concepts. Concentration on user needs and projected operating locations yielded a different mind-set. Long-range airlift was simply a part of a single airlift mission—delivery of the goods where needed and when needed.

The B-747

Acquisition of B-747 as a mainstay of the airlift fleet, even if only as an interim measure, would be reminiscent of purchasing C-135s in the early 1960s and of much earlier decisions to rely on commercially designed airlifters to perform military airlift missions. Advocates of such systems viewed MATS/MAC airlift as "strategic airlift" operating from large, well-established bases into other large, well-established bases. Such a viewpoint sees airlift primarily as a logistics and passenger operation, a very routine, albeit surging, extension of peacetime airline-type operations.

The general arguments have fundamental implications as to how airlift is viewed in the context of its contribution to warfare. What is particularly important in the long view is that ultimately there was a strong weight given to warfighting, even in the face of the economic attractiveness of a commercial buy.

Deputy Secretary of Defense Carlucci rhetorically asked if the cost question did not, in fact, outweigh performance issues, but answered in the negative.

> Is the C-5's added cost justified by its performance? One of the strongest advantages of airlift is its ability to deliver initial defensive forces and their critical support before even the fastest sealift can arrive. If we compare the performance of the DOD program with a commercial freighter alternative during this initial period in each of the CMMS scenarios, we find that the DOD program is considerably better at deploying Army and Marine Corps forces. This result is particularly striking should we need to reinforce Europe subsequent to a Persian Gulf deployment. In that case, we find that the DOD program provides at least a third more capability to deliver Army or Marine units than the commercial alternative.[89]

To take advantage of the speed and flexibility of airlift, Carlucci wanted a military airlifter.

At issue was not just the question of delivering outsize cargo per se, as a properly designed military aircraft (a C-5 or a C-17) clearly could do what the B-747 could not. Gen Paul X. Kelley, then commander of the Rapid Deployment Joint Task Force, provided a most graphic illustration of this point:

> To me as an infantry man, and as a combat commander, the analogy is fairly simple. If I want to move people, I hire a Greyhound bus. If I want to move my grand piano, I hire a moving van. That is unless I want to strip the grand piano piece-by-piece in order to fit in a Greyhound bus, and then have divisions of people at the other end working conceivably under combat conditions putting it together piece-by-piece.[90]

Lt Gen Kelly Burke, chief of Air Force research and development, put the whole military versus commercial question in clear perspective:

> By that we mean the ability to operate these aircraft in and out of airfields where we had not prepositioned equipment and that we didn't even know that we were going to quickly need to go into, to get them in and offloaded quickly with the equipment in the right condition and be on their way.
>
> To talk first about the flexibility and responsiveness, the ways to operate airplanes into places that you haven't planned ahead for and to do things that you haven't necessarily anticipated. There is a fundamentally different design philosophy in the way commercial airlifters are built and the way military airlifters are built, and that is because it is assumed that a commercial airlifter is going to operate from major terminal to major terminal and that it will have whatever equipment is there and whatever trained people are necessary for that purpose.[91]

The Air Force had also provided an important point about flexibility, noting that the lack of airdrop capability in civil aircraft would "result in military operations (of all services) that are restricted to areas with guaranteed surface resupply. Airdrop capability must be maintained to provide the military commander with the required degree of planning flexibility."[92] Remember, the doctrinal question is one of a military airlifter with airdrop capability designed in, versus a civil airlifter lacking this capacity in any meaningful sense.

Movement of outsize equipment and cargo is an integral consideration in making an airlift decision. Approximately 41 percent of a mechanized Army division's equipment is outsize (by weight) and a modernized mechanized division will show a growth to 55-percent outsize needs. Even infantry divisions are showing a similar trend; comparable figures show a change from 26 percent today to 33 percent (by weight) in the future. Even as the Army changes its future force structure to lighter divisions, outsize requirements will remain, if only at a higher organizational level.[93]

To overcome this deficit, some suggested that if MAC more carefully scheduled its existing fleet of C-5s, outsize requirements for the representative CMMS scenarios could be delivered by their latest required delivery dates, and B-747s could be used to fill bulk and oversize cargo shortfalls. It is an alluring but erroneous argument. Outsize requirements are not evenly distributed across a deployment period, and a deployment is not necessarily satisfactory if all outsized equipment and cargo arrives by the end of the development period. At the detailed analytical level, the concept failed the test of delivering the goods:

> In recent weeks, questions have been raised about the validity of the outsize cargo requirement. Those questions are based on the contention that the existing C-5 fleet could meet our outsized cargo movement requirements. We do not accept that contention. Our calculations show that, *even if it were dedicated to the movement of outsized cargo,* the existing C-5 fleet could not meet requirements in any of the CMMS scenarios. Totally committing the C-5 force to carrying outsize cargo would still leave us well over 50 percent short of the aggregate outsize cargo demand over the first 20 days in the four CMMS scenarios.[94]

Lloyd Mosemann, deputy assistant secretary of the Air Force for logistics, offered a comparison of the C-5 and B-747 in terms of the preparation for shipment and delivery of the helicopters of an air assault division, which he characterized as a division very likely to be air transported in a contingency: "The required assembly and disassembly times for the Boeing 747 vice the C-5A are six times more man-hours (8,322 man-hours). More than half of these hours must be performed at destination prior to employing these helicopters in combat."[95] The point is not so much the comparison of the C-5 with the B-747 as the comparison of an aircraft *designed* for a military mission versus one *adapted* to a military mission.

Mosemann also took on the questions of using the C-5 only for outsized cargo. He argued that individual load characteristics, the necessity to maintain unit integrity, and inherent flexibility gave the military airlifter the edge over a commercial aircraft in the critical early days of a deployment:

> The units moved in the first five days are Air Force, Army airborne, air cavalry, and air mobile; and prepositioned units. These units have little outsize equipment. Delivering these units as soon as possible requires all available airlift resources, including the use of outsize capable aircraft in an oversize role. The outsize equipment in these units tends to be low-density equipment (for example, helicopters). When this requirement and the capability to move it are measured in tons, or in millions of ton-miles per day, the results may be misleading. The C-5 missions carrying outsize helicopters will have lower payloads than they would if carrying outsize equipment or outsize armour. These factors combine to give the impression that little of the C-5 capability is being utilized in the first five days.[96]

Equally important, integral fighting units delivered in the order and on a schedule set by the theater commander is the goal of airlift. Military fighting power needs to move as units. Some outsize equipment and cargo are bulky but not heavy. Units need to arrive in the operating area as integral fighting units, prepared to fight when they hit the ground.

Lt Gen R. H. Thompson, the US Army deputy chief of staff for logistics, testified in June 1982 to the importance of unit integrity in combat:

> Airlift is absolutely essential to the rapid transport of critical supplies, replacements, and forward deployment of major combat units in the area of operations. Although force composition and equipment requirements vary with the scenario, there are several important principles associated with deployments. The first is the need for a balanced force, one that contains an appropriate percentage of combat and support forces. An improper force mix makes no tactical sense, and reduces the operational flexibility of commanders.
>
> Another is the need to maintain a high degree of unit integrity in order to facilitate employment in the combat zone. I believe that the airlift shortfall has been clearly and accurately articulated. Its impact on closure times in the various scenarios is of concern to our Army. The need for outsized airlift is particularly acute and limits our responsiveness and flexibility.[97]

Consequently, military airlifters capable of carrying outsized cargo are not used exclusively for that purpose. Instead, they carry a mix of cargo types, large volumes of bulk and oversized cargo, or are elevated to exclusively outsize cargo as the situation demands. Only the outsize-capable military airlifter offers this flexibility, not only in terms of cargo types but also in terms of where it can operate to and from. Gen James Allen best summarized the question by stepping outside the CMMS scenario limitations to suggest that the C-5 should be selected over the B-747 because that choice would provide the "flexibility needed to meet a wide range of contingencies which might confront us."[98]

The Air Force position that the military airlifter was preferable to the civil airlifter was a natural outgrowth of emerging airlift doctrine. Commercially designed air transport aircraft, even relatively inexpensive ones available fairly quickly, are no longer considered sufficient for military airlift. They are less flexible and generally less effective. This does not mean, however, that civil cargo and passenger airlift are not important to the airlift scheme. Air Force policy and programming realities, and consequently its doctrine, rely extensively on the CRAF. The Air Force's ultimate reaction to the B-747 offer was to claim that the "best way to obtain cargo capability, therefore, would be to modify all or part of the 113 CRAF B-747s to fully capable cargo (compatible) aircraft with strengthened floors and cargo doors."[99] The nation relies on CRAF for slightly over 50 percent of its airlift capability, a figure that includes 98 percent of total passenger-lift capability.[100] This full force of over 300 long-range aircraft can be called into service within 48 hours. The unique capabilities and requirements of the CRAF aircraft are taken advantage of and planned for in the operational concept for the CRAF. Doctrine calls for generally using that force for operations between well-developed main operating bases—or at least built-up facilities.

The use of CRAF as augmentation to long-range military airlift, both as a replacement for military airlifters withdrawn from routine operation to support a contingency and as a direct contributor in major deployments, has a long history.[101] The program was conceived after World War II and formalized in 1952. In 1963 the concept of activating the CRAF in three incremental stages (rather than operating on an all-or-nothing principle) was finalized. Beginning in 1961 the Air Force has followed a program of interrelating its peacetime procurement practices for commercial airlift with wartime requirements for augmentation.[102] Since the mid-1970s MAC has consistently followed a path of seeking funds to enhance the capability of the CRAF to carry more cargo. These enhancements are economically attractive when compared to actually owning comparable airlift capability; they allow the civil aircraft to continue their peacetime role and add a degree of flexibility to the civil fleet.

In 1970 Capt William Bennett summed up the relationship between civil and military airlifters, a doctrinal relationship that remains today:

> Significant changes have occurred in airlift over the last 20 years. Probably most significant is the divergent paths the military and civilian organizations have followed in development of aircraft. Although this is the case, we feel that the military airlift system and commercial airlines are complementary and strengthen the overall national airlift posture. We believe that civil augmentation of military capability will be necessary in the future to satisfy both peacetime and wartime requirements.[103]

It is ironic that the same committee that Captain Bennett addressed in 1970 concluded that the strategic airlift shortfall projected for the mid-1970s was cause for grave concern. "If the decision not to buy additional C-5 aircraft stands," said the committee report, "other solutions to this cargo deficit must be found."[104] Speaking directly to the lack of outsize cargo capability in civil aircraft, the report said:

> The largest commercial aircraft now in production, the Boeing 747, when offered as a cargo aircraft, will accommodate only 34 percent of an armored division's equipment by weight and only 37 percent of the equipment weight of a mechanized division. Without this outsize airlift capability, the rapid deployment of certain types of Army divisions will be severely restrained; and the time required to close the necessary force in times of emergency will be dangerously extended. The reduced C-5 force has been described as "a calculated risk." In the opinion of this committee, extending the time required to close the necessary military force is a risky calculation and endangers the success of a NATO contingency operation and the contingency plans for Asia.[105]

The C-5

In July of 1968, the chief of staff of the Air Force approved a mission statement for the C-5 that overwhelmingly emphasized its strategic airlift mission. In the main, this meant operations into rearward bases.

> The C-5 will be used to airlift combat and support forces, supplies, and equipment directly from the CONUS and overseas rear area logistics bases into airfields in the overseas forward area where it will interface as appropriate with tactical airlift or other transportation modes. The high flotation characteristics and short take-off and landing ability being built into the C-5 will enable it to operate into airstrips previously denied large jet transport aircraft. This would include the capability to operate into semiprepared airstrips in the 4,000 ft range which have a bearing capacity equivalent to California Bearing Ratio 4 soil overlaid with M-8 matting. However, tactical airlift forces normally will be utilized in active forward combat areas because of the risks involved and because of the responsive nature of such airlift forces to the changing tactical situation. The C-5 will be used predominately in deployment and logistics lift to the more rearward areas. However, when tonnage requirements justify and the risk is acceptable the C-5 may also be employed for lift to forward areas.[106]

In September of 1980, Secretary of the Air Force Hans Mark appeared before Senator William Proxmire's Subcommittee on Priorities and Economy in Government to discuss the C-5A. He called the 77 C-5 airplanes in the Air Force inventory a unique capability, "the only aircraft that our nation possesses which can carry the largest equipment that the US Army has in its inventory."[107] Without it, the United States could move only light infantry and airborne forces. The C-5s, he said, "are crucial to our ability to deploy our armed forces around the world . . . the judgments we make on this matter must be made with the greatest of care. We must be certain that we preserve the capability to move our forces with all of their equipment overseas quickly."[108] To preserve that unique capability, the Air Force elected to modify the wing of the C-5A to permit operation of these aircraft at full capacity and obtain an additional 30,000 flying hours per aircraft.

An exchange of letters between Secretary Mark and Russell Murray, assistant secretary of defense for program analysis and evaluation, illustrated the arguments to come about the C-5 and C-X. Very soon after a briefing from General Block, Murray wrote Mark to suggest several shortfalls in the C-X Task Force analysis. He characterized the Air Force's position as supporting the C-X because it would have "access to a vastly greater number of fields," and suggested that the C-5 "may not have been accorded even-handed justice in the comparison (yet)."[109] Secretary Mark's response to this letter was an even-handed answer to the real question of why the government should choose the C-X over the C-5. It was ultimately a rejection of the C-5 as an airlifter that could routinely operate into small, austere air fields:

> The C-5s in our inventory are a vital, necessary part of our integrated airlift force, but additional C-5 aircraft would not reduce the dependency of our airlift force on major airfields. The C-5 tests on unprepared surfaces at Harper Dry Lake and on matting at Dyess Air Force Base were terminated before completion because of runway and aircraft damage. The results of these tests plus the operational experience we have gained over the past 12 years have shown that the C-5 is not compatible with the small, austere airfield environment because of aircraft size and operating characteristics. I know that originally we thought C-5s should be able to do that, but we were wrong.[110]

AIRLIFT DOCTRINE

The ideas of pouring more concrete or layering matting also drew attention. Pouring concrete posed workability problems—where to put it, local resistance, its being limited to certain countries. It could also make target selection for an interdiction plan very easy. The concept also admitted a reliance on substantial air facilities for operation of the C-5. Using matting to provide additional ramp space, which presumed appropriate runways and taxiways, suffered from its own set of limitations. To make enough ramp space to hold two C-5s (500,000 square feet) would mean 1,575 tons of AM-2 aluminum matting that could be flown in on 17 C-5 sorties or prepositioned.[111] None of this sounds especially flexible or conducive to rapid deployment.

The off-runway question has some particularly important doctrinal implications. The C-5, after wing modification, would routinely be allowed to operate on paved runways not less than 5,000 by 90 feet if prepared taxiways or turnaround areas were available, Mark said. These safety margins could be changed to increase the risk to the aircraft, but only up to a point. The C-X could perform with less risk-taking, as it was designed for the more demanding runways without resort to off-runway/taxiway operations, which can be exacerbated by adverse weather conditions. It was not a question of whether a C-5 could operate in a given set of circumstances but, rather, if a sustained airlift operation in those same circumstances would be better served with a C-X. "Airlift capability," Secretary Mark said, "should not depend on operations that 'bang up' airplanes and reduce effectiveness for sustained operations. The use of emergency procedures is not a sound basis for planning sustained operations."[112] The C-X was designed to the same off-runway features of the C-5; so any advantage to such capabilities was not unique, and avoiding reliance on them was a bonus. In 1982, the ability of the C-5 to maneuver off-pavement in wet, soft soil with ruts 10 to 12 inches deep (or snow up to 14 inches deep), was considered advantageous when compared to the B-747.[113] It is an advantage, but it is not a capability one wants to *have-to* take advantage of.

In 1981 General Burke said the C-5A was the mainstay of the strategic airlift force, reflecting the newly recognized importance of moving outsized equipment and cargo. He was, however, concerned that there were not enough C-5As. If there were more, they would provide the assurance of being able to go into large international-type airports, "but typically countries will only have one of those, and if that is not available, or if the Army or Marine Corps are operating in areas distant from there, you would be well advised to have more flexibility and be able to get into the smaller, more austere airfields which are found in much larger numbers."[114] General Brown was more specific. Yes, he said, a C-5 could deliver an XM-1 tank into a 3,000-foot runway, over a 50-foot obstacle, take off, and fly another 500 miles. But, "if you take a series of aircraft with average crews randomly selected and operate continuously through such an airfield environment, you would not be able to. The planned wartime use of the C-5 would call for us to use airfields that are available for continuous operation."[115]

MODERN AIRLIFT ERA

Selecting the C-5 as a cornerstone for increasing airlift capability also selects an airlift doctrine that places most emphasis on operating from main bases to main bases, albeit fairly efficiently. It accepts reliance on intratheater airlift and other transportation modes *after* rapid delivery to main bases. In fact, it places additional pressures on an intratheater airlift system that is already incapable of distributing outsize combat equipment. It trades time and combat effectiveness for volume. It is a doctrine from the 1960s. It is a doctrine that confuses delivery of goods and people with combat usefulness.

Improved airlift capability through the acquisition of additional C-5s is certainly better than no additional capability, and it is better than acquisition of airlift aircraft primarily designed for civil use. It is not better than an acquisition of an aircraft such as the C-17.

The C-17

The timely delivery of troops, equipment, and supplies where needed is the airlift mission. Airlift aircraft have to be able to operate in restrictive environments without relying on extraordinary procedures. Risking damage to themselves, other

Figure 95. The McDonnell-Douglas C-17.

aircraft, their cargoes, or other military facilities is the sign of a poorly conceived and designed airlift aircraft. The airlift system must consist of aircraft with intertheater range, large cargo capabilities, and operating characteristics that routinely allow safe operations through restrictive airfields. Airlift aircraft must be designed to carry all the types of equipment and cargoes a supported combat force can reasonably expect. If properly designed, an airlifter will be air refuelable and able to deliver its cargo or troops by airdrop, extraction, or airlanding modes.[116] These attributes, of course, describe the C-17.

When the secretary of the Air Force signed and forwarded the Airlift Master Plan to Congress, he was supporting not just the C-17, but the articulation of a new airlift doctrine. That doctrine is based on the well-founded tenets of all air power: speed and flexibility. The new airlift doctrine is the combination of many features into one aircraft concept.

- The aircraft should be capable of carrying all of the kinds of equipment and supplies required to project and sustain combat forces during the early days of a conflict.
- The aircraft should be able to deliver substantial loads over intercontinental ranges and be air refuelable.
- The aircraft should be able to deliver its cargo by airlanding, airdropping, and/or extraction.
- The aircraft should be designed to survive in a hostile environment.
- The aircraft should be compatible with the airfields that best support combat forces in the objective area.[117]

Although some of these requirements are met by individual airlift aircraft, no single aircraft can currently meet the total doctrine criteria. The technology under which current aircraft were designed would not allow it, nor, in the past, would doctrine.

The C-X Task Force and the Military Airlift Command developed the C-X to meet shortfalls in *total* airlift capability. The current intertheater aircraft have been used almost exclusively in the intertheater mode; they lack the operating characteristics necessary for tactical airlift. Current intratheater aircraft are designed for tactical work in forward areas but lack long-range capability with any reasonable size load and cannot deliver a full range of combat equipment. Additionally, MAC looked to a system perspective to design the C-17. There are numerous aircraft designs that produce the MTM/D necessary to meet intertheater shortfalls, but if those aircraft fail to consider the whole airlift, this failure has only compounded other airlift missions. Solving only the first half of the equation means additional pressures on an already overtaxed and undercapable second half.

To deal with this total system question requires a direct delivery philosophy. Direct delivery "addresses the most basic airlift requirement: timely delivery of combat forces to a point as close as possible to the battle."[118] Such an approach moves cargo and troops directly to a forward-operating location served by today's tactical airlift force or by surface transportation. This bypasses the transshipments required of operation through main bases. The benefit of direct delivery is the "reduction in the time required to deliver the combat soldier and his equipment to the battle."[119] The CMMS, for example, estimated that direct delivery would provide a 7- to 15-percent improvement in unit closure times in deployment to Southwest Asia.[120]

The direct delivery concept adds the C-17 to the scheme in main operating base (MOB) operations, in direct deliveries to forward operating locations (FOLs), and in intratheater shuttles between MOBs and FOLs and among FOLs. There is no other aircraft designed to be effective in all these modes. System flexibility and responsiveness to combat commander needs are improved quantitatively.

The traditional view of airlift is to use C-141s, KC-10s, and the CRAF to deliver oversize and bulk cargo and passengers from a major airfield in the United States to a major airport overseas, and C-5s to fly outsize, oversize, and bulk cargo in the same structure. C-130s then would deliver high-priority oversize and bulk cargo and equipment from the major overseas airfield to a destination airfield near the objective area. Surface transportation would be needed to move outsize materiel, plus whatever other goods are left that do not qualify for priority movement on the limited intratheater air assets. The C-5s could not be counted on for routine or sustained intratheater airlift to austere airfields.

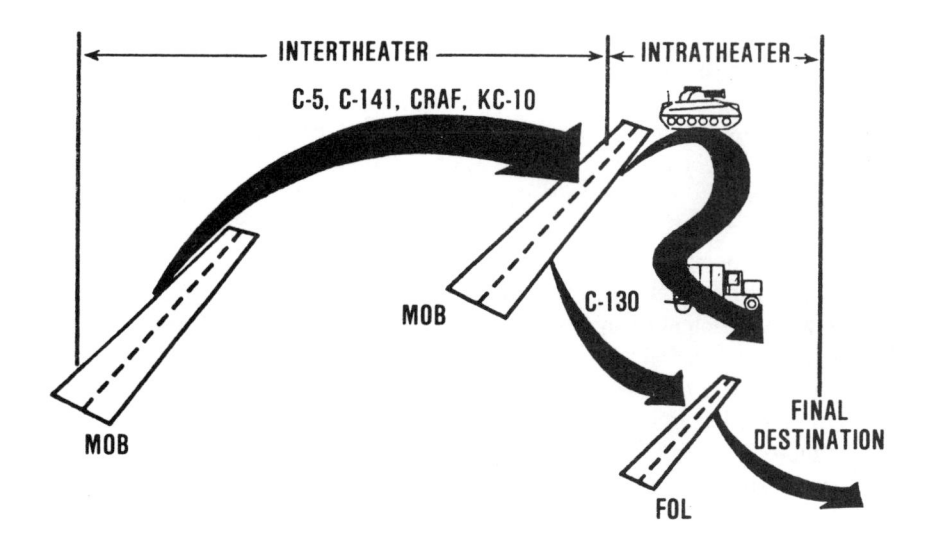

Figure 96. Traditional airlift concept.

AIRLIFT DOCTRINE

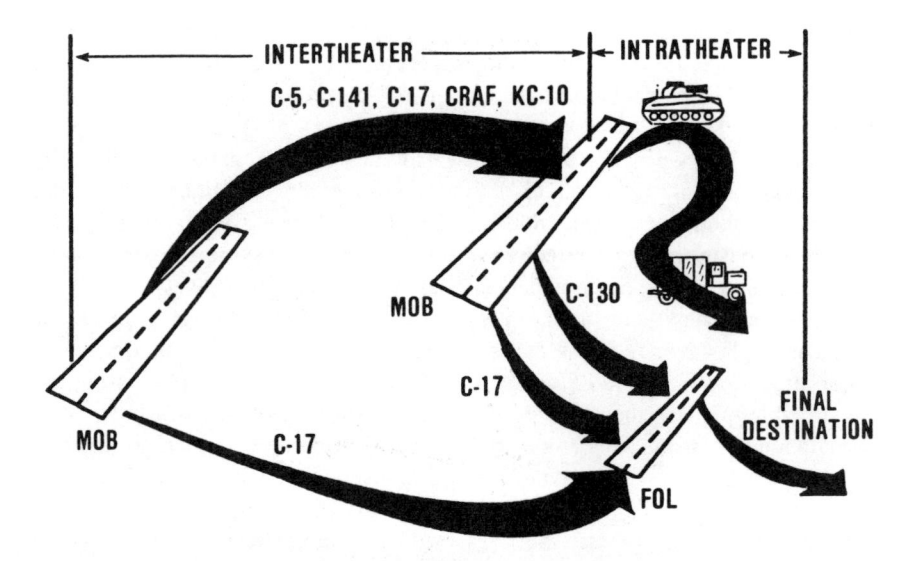

Figure 97. Direct delivery airlift concept.

An Analytical Review

Postulating use of the C-17 aircraft in Exercise Ahaus Tara 83 illustrates the advantages of direct delivery. In that exercise, the destination airfield at Puerto Lempira, Honduras, was unsuitable for C-141 and C-5 operations because of runway length, runway composition, and limited ramp space. As a result, 2 C-5 and 32 C-141 missions had to deploy payloads to La Mesa airport, 240 nautical miles away. Then it took 160 C-130 sorties to complete the deployment. The UH-60 Blackhawk helicopters brought in by the C-5s had to self-deploy from La Mesa to Puerto Lempira. The C-130s also moved 1,803 Honduran troops, including 347 airdropped, and 127.5 tons of cargo from Honduras bases to Puerto Lempira—a total of 232 C-130 sorties for the exercise. The C-130s were split between La Mesa and Tegucigalpa due to ramp congestion at La Mesa. Using C-17s with direct delivery capability would have taken 19 deployment missions direct from the United States to Puerto Lempira. With *one* intratheater shuttle those same C-17s could have delivered all of the Honduran forces, including the airdrop operation. No bed-down of aircraft in theater would have been required and no support operations at La Mesa and Tegucigalpa airfields would have been needed. The economy of force, increased rapidity of operations, and flexibility of direct delivery are indispensable in combat.[121]

MODERN AIRLIFT ERA

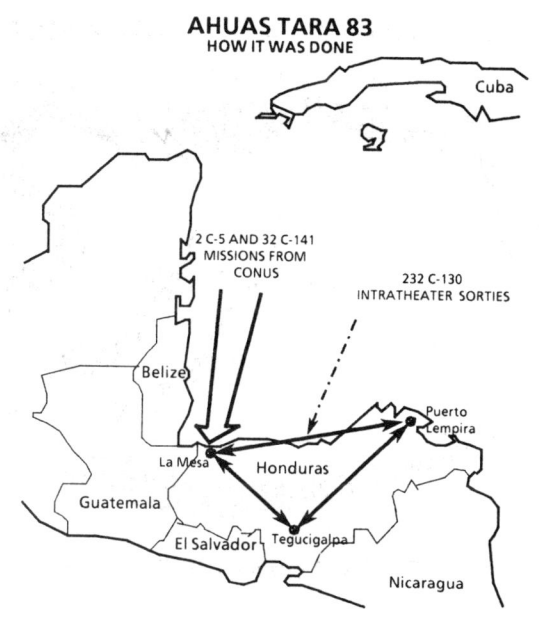

AHUAS TARA 83
HOW IT WAS DONE

Figure 98

AHUAS TARA 83
HOW IT COULD HAVE BEEN DONE

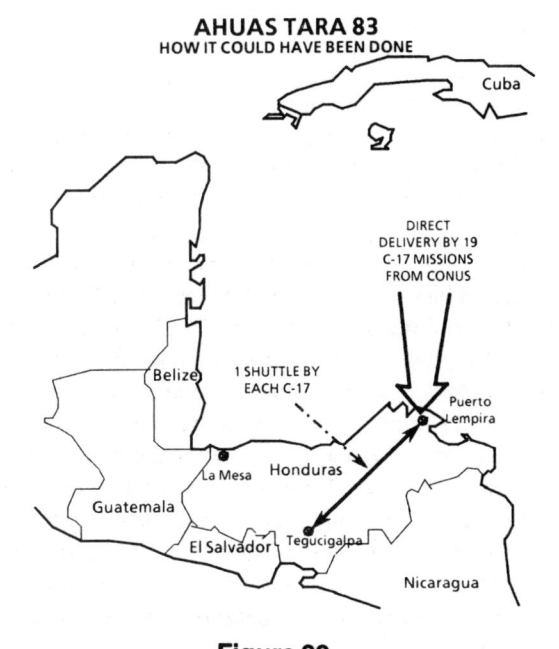

Figure 99

The C-17 is fully designed for direct delivery into small, austere airfields. Such a field is characterized by runways as short as 3,000 feet, narrow taxiways, small ramps, and limited facilities, and is normally operated by a nonairlift unit. The C-17 can carry its maximum load of 86.1 tons over 2,600 miles and has excellent long-range capabilities at ranges between 2,400 and 3,200 miles. It is air refuelable. It has superb ground-handling characteristics. The C-X RFP called for the capability to operate on the small ramps normally associated with austere airfields—ramps averaging 250 by 300 feet or 300 by 400 feet. The C-17, with a 165-foot wingspan and 172.5-foot length, can operate two aircraft on the smaller ramp and three on the larger one. It can routinely operate on 90-foot-wide runways and 50-foot-wide taxiways typical of austere runways. It can operate from unpaved, semiprepared compacted surfaces, such as sandy clay or gravel, even at its heaviest payload. It will routinely be able to back up, using upward-deflected engine exhaust to minimize dust and debris and to eliminate interference with ground personnel and equipment.[122]

The C-X RFP said the "Air Force intends that the C-X system be a rugged, reliable workhorse that is simple to maintain and operate. Undue complexity or technical risk will be regarded as poor design."[123] This is more than a design philosophy or desire for a cheap airplane. The term workhorse is critical as it describes an airplane that can confidently be expected to routinely operate in tough conditions, and it has to be affordable. The C-17 numbers are astonishing:

- C-17 costs per flying hour will be comparable to the C-141B, even though the C-17 can deliver twice the C-141B's payload.
- Maintenance manpower requirements for the C-17 are over 40 percent less than the C-5, despite a higher planned wartime utilization rate for the C-17.
- The C-17 will need 15,000 fewer manpower positions than a comparable C-5/C-130 force while providing the same intertheater capability and 78 percent *more* intratheater capability.
- Across a 30-year life cycle it will yield a savings of $16 billion when compared to the C-5/C-130 force needed to provide a like capability.[124]

All of these factors combine to produce a superior airlift aircraft that exemplifies the most forward-looking airlift doctrine.

Headquarters MAC used its M-14 strategic airlift computer model to test the C-5 and C-17 in a representative Southwest Asia scenario. The model considers real-world constraints that cannot be reflected in MTM/D analysis—constraints such as limited airfield parking spaces and limited numbers of airfields. The M-14 cannot yet determine the advantages of direct delivery per se, but it can quantify the advantages of the C-17's size, maneuverability, and maintainability.

The C-17's maneuverability, backing capability, and smaller dimension, when compared to the C-5 or B-747, allow two to three times as many C-17s to be parked on the same size ramp. At equal ground times, this means more C-17 arrivals per day than C-5s. In fact, the C-17 has shorter ground times. The analysis showed the

MODERN AIRLIFT ERA

C-17 flew 69 percent more sorties than a like number of C-5s. Because of the C-17's better ground characteristics, its use freed up enough ground space to allow more C-141B sorties.[125]

Airlift Force	C-5	C-17	C-141B	CRAF
215 C-141s, CRAF, and 108 C-5s	4,863	—	11,314	10,188
215 C-141s, CRAF, and 108 C-17s	—	8,215	11,980	10,255

Figure 100. Total sorties flown in 30 days.

More sorties meant more tons delivered. It also meant dramatic improvement in on-time delivery. When the C-17 was included instead of the larger aircraft, essentially all available outsize cargo was delivered where needed, when needed. The overall results were instructive.[126]

Aircraft	Total Delivered	Outsize Delivered	Percent of Outsize Cargo Delivered On-Time
C-5	36,349	17,917	42
C-17	46,791	22,362	99

Figure 101. Cargo delivered (tons) by C-5 and C-17 in 30 days.

The C-17 made the whole system work better by reducing overall congestion. It had to divert 65 percent less often than a C-5 flying the same network, and total system diversions were reduced by 47 percent.[127]

AIRLIFT DOCTRINE

Airlift Force	C-5	C-17	C-141	CRAF	Total
215 C-141s, CRAF, and 108 C-5s	361		662	256	1279
215 C-141s, CRAF, and 108 C-17s		125	401	153	679

Figure 102. Diversions (with cargo or passengers).

Multiple computer runs of the scenario through the M-14 system yielded additional information of particular interest:

- The C-17 delivered more cargo and more outsize cargo than the same number of C-5 aircraft. Perhaps of even greater significance is the fact that the C-17 delivered all of the available outsize, on time, to the proper location (99.17 percent overtime evenly 41.9 percent for the C-5).
- The C-17 delivered 30 percent more total tons of cargo than the same number of C-5s in the thirty-day scenario. The C-17 also delivered 25 percent more outsize cargo to the theater.
- Large numbers of diversions are generally caused by aircraft exceeding their scheduled ground time. ... Diverted cargo will invariably arrive late and the C-5 experienced almost three times as many diversions as the C-17.
- The C-17 caused total cargo delivered to be increased by 11 percent while the percentage of on-time cargo increased from 41.0 to 53.5 percent.[128]

These figures *do not* reflect direct delivery, only operation into main bases. Because that concept is at the cutting edge, it will take time for analytical efforts to catch up. We do know, however, that the C-5 cannot routinely operate into small, austere airfields on a sustained basis. The C-17 will. The C-130 cannot forward deliver outsize cargo and equipment or deploy forces across intercontinental ranges. The C-17 will. It does not take a broad inductive leap to see what the analytical results will be.

As the war in Vietnam illustrated, airlift doctrine calls for excruciating attention to detail with an eye ultimately toward efficiency. The fact that even the largest airlift aircraft does not really deliver very much means that planners and operators must wring the last possible ton out of an already small force structure. An airplane that is better in terms of getting people and things where they are needed, when they are needed is, per se, a more desirable airlifter. The changing nature of warfare, national commitments, and user requirements has combined with technological potential *and* vision to redefine "when" and "where."

A Summing Up

In January of 1982 Air Force Secretary Verne Orr briefed Deputy Secretary of Defense Frank Carlucci on airlift needs and recommended an airlift program. That briefing contained this viewgraph:

> The User's Opinion
>
> Chief of Staff—US Army
>
> I believe that it is vital for the Air Force and Army to stand firm on the C-X (C-17) so we can get an airlift aircraft that meets our wartime requirements.
>
> Gen John C. Meyer
>
> CINC Readiness Command
>
> The C-17 is the only aircraft that has been proposed that addresses our total airlift shortfall, the movement of outsize and oversize combat equipment directly to an airfield where it can be quickly brought to bear on the enemy without transshipment.
>
> Gen Donn A. Starry
>
> CINC USAFE
>
> We need an airlifter that can operate routinely into our colocated operating bases during intensive fighter operations. The narrow taxiways, small ramps, and off-pavement obstructions dictate the C-17 as that aircraft.
>
> Gen Charles A. Gabriel
>
> RDJTF Commander
>
> It seems clear that the C-X (C-17) could make the decisive difference in a Southwest Asian conflict. Without the strategic and tactical flexibility this aircraft can provide, our task is monumental.
>
> Lt Gen Robert C. Kingston[129]

In December of 1981, Maj Gen Perry Smith, then director of Air Force Plans, wrote a letter to Dr James Wade, Jr., principal deputy under secretary of defense for research and engineering, to provide some personal observations concerning the C-17/C-5 debate. General Smith's letter, better than any other, summed up the operational commander's point of view about airlift aircraft:

> One of the great problems in trying to choose the best aircraft for this nation to buy to handle the military airlift requirements for the next 30 to 40 years is that national mobility

AIRLIFT DOCTRINE

requirements are terribly dependent on scenario assumptions. Therefore, *any* aircraft can be made to appear as the least expensive acquisition by simply changing the scenario to favor a competing aircraft's capabilities.

Where does this lead us? Since any airlift aircraft will reduce the shortfall and can be made to appear the most attractive by scenario manipulation, the best long-term solution for the nation may become obscured by a deluge of salesmen, brochures, and augmentation.

At this point I feel we should review the original requirements developed by the services—without reference to a specific aircraft. Looking at user demands (Army, Air Force, Navy, and Marines) and current capability, the C-X Task Force developed a Mission Element Needs Statement (MENS) that described the nation's requirements for a new airlift aircraft. The Congressionally Mandated Mobility Study added emphasis and provided guidance for an attainable ton-miles-per-day goal.

As a former commander of a Tactical Fighter Wing in Europe, I can verify the finding of the C-X Task Force for that area. In a warfighting scenario, my airfield at Bitburg would be saturated by fighter operations; my parking areas were too small for outsize capable airlifters or jumbo jets; I could expect regular damage to my runways that would restrict usable length; and, yet, I needed the capability to receive outsize cargo. An outsize cargo capable aircraft that had the performance to land, take off, and maneuver on small, austere airfields would have given me the required capability to plan for and execute resupply and augmentation during contingencies.

Speaking to my Army counterparts in NATO, I found that their requirements for small, austere airfield operations during resupply, augmentation, and employment were similar, but on a much greater scale. Their mobility requirements, including a large proportion of outsize cargo, had to be filled by delivery to an aerial port of delivery (APOD) and then transshipment to their operating location by C-130s or surface means. This ruled out outsize air movement and slowed the responsiveness of the mobility system to the operational commander.

My eight years of operational experience in NATO and review of the other C-X/CMMS scenarios lead me to only one conclusion: The Air Force accurately described the national airlift aircraft requirement in its C-X MENS and RFP. The requirement for a military airlift aircraft that can carry outsize, oversize, or bulk cargo over intercontinental ranges; operate on main operating bases without degrading the launch, recovery, or service of combat aircraft, even while subject to enemy attack; support operational commanders at the small, austere airfields in the battle area; and deliver by all known means (airland, airdrop, extraction) is still valid.

We need an outsize airlifter that can operate when we are at war and the bombs are falling on very busy airfields in overseas areas. During my 2 years at Bitburg, the C-5 landed there once to deliver the F-15 simulator. It could not get off the runway since the taxiways were too narrow. Even if it could get off the runway there was practically no place to park it without seriously interfering with peacetime operations. Needless to say the wing commanders at Hahn, Bitburg, Zweibrucken, Sembach, etc., would not have much trouble choosing between C-17s and C-5s for the outsize airlifter of the future. I would be remiss if I didn't reflect their point of view. Certainly the operational commander's concerns should have some weight in the decision calculus of OSD [the Office of the Secretary of Defense].[130]

General Allen's testimony before the Subcommittee on Sea Power and Force Projection on 24 March 1983 offers a powerful summary of the advantages of the C-17 and its role as the next generation airlifter.

> The importance of acquiring the C-17 as this Nation's next generation airlifter is based on the need to increase capability to the minimum goals set by the DOD, to provide a flexible capability to replace the aging C-130 and C-141 aircraft, and to do so within the fiscal constraint which we can realistically anticipate during the next two decades. The C-17 was designed to accomplish the mission of moving modern, war-fighting equipment at the least life cycle cost. This emphasis on reducing the long-range costs of operating and owning a transport aircraft has resulted in a design which offers efficiency and cost savings not available in alternative aircraft. A C-17 squadron, for example, requires 42 percent fewer people to operate and maintain than a C-5 squadron of the same size. This manpower advantage results from the simplified and modern systems which require, for example, only three C-17 crewmembers compared to seven for the C-5. This simplicity of design also reduces maintenance man-hours per flying hours (MMH/FH) from 43.35 for the C-5 to 18.6 for the C-17—a 57-percent reduction. These reduced manpower requirements, along with other efficiencies in design such as advanced aerodynamics and a modern, state-of-the-art engine, result in a C-17 costing over $68 million less in O&S costs than a C-5 over an expected 30-year life. Cost savings, of course, are only part of the equation—the C-17 will be capable of performing the full-range, combat airlift missions. Operating on either long-range intercontinental missions or short-range missions within the theater, the C-17 will be capable of routinely operating through runways only 3,000 feet long. This short-field capability, along with combat offload, truck bed height loading, and the capability to back up, make the C-17 fully compatible with a C-130 type, intratheater environment. When denied the opportunity to airland, the C-17 offers the field commander the flexibility to airdrop supplies and equipment or deliver with the low-altitude parachute extraction system (LAPES). This military utility within the theater, combined with long-range efficiency and cost effectiveness, make the C-17 a vital element in our long-range force modernization plans.[131]

"The more I study the airlift program," General Allen said, "and the more I study the airlift requirements for the future, the stronger I feel our nation's airlift posture must have the C-17."[132]

Official Airlift Doctrine

Air Force doctrine has five interrelated purposes. It
  (1) Describes aerospace missions and tasks.
  (2) Provides guidance to combat commanders.
  (3) Provides guidance for weapons development programs and force planning.
  (4) Provides guidance on the relationships with other services.
  (5) Provides a point of departure for every activity of the Air Force.[133]

AIRLIFT DOCTRINE

It reflects the "officially sanctioned beliefs and warfighting principles which describe and guide the proper use of aerospace forces in military action."[134] It is not a static statement. It evolves as thinking matures and as judgments become sharper.

The 1979 version of AFM 1-1, *Functions and Basic Doctrine of the United States Air Force,* included a fairly substantial recognition of the combat orientation of the airlift mission:

> Through our strategic and tactical military airlift, we can deploy our forces to any part of the world and support them there. Airlift embodies a key facet of a fundamental Air Force capability—rapid, long-range mobility. Airlift can be used to support joint and combined operations, as well as military assistance and civilian relief programs.
>
> Our ability to resupply allies in a timely manner builds confidence and stability. We must be able to insert our forces directly into a combat area and then resupply them. This capability can also be used for evacuation.
>
> The airlift force—which is made up of both military and civil contract aircraft—performs four primary tasks:
>
> Employment Operations
> Strategic and Tactical Deployment of Combat
>   Forces and Equipment
> Logistics Support
> Aeromedical Evacuation[135]

Even this version of the manual, however, had subtle tinges that separate kinds of airlift forces, even though it did not separate forces and missions as distinctly as previous editions.

The 1984 AFM 1-1, *Basic Aerospace Doctrine of the United States Air Force,* represents yet another step forward in thinking about airlift as the aerial movement of goods and people, rather than as segments of that mission. This version more effectively recognizes the variety of tasks that airlift forces may be called upon to perform and the range of aerospace environments it must be prepared to operate in. The linkage to higher goals and strategies is clear; airlift is not an end in itself, after all:

> Airlift objectives are to deploy, employ, and sustain military forces through the medium of aerospace. The airlift mission is performed under varying conditions, ranging from peace to war. As a combat mission, airlift projects power through airdrop, extraction, and airlanding of ground forces and supplies into combat. Through mobility operations, the joint or combined force commander can maneuver fighting forces to exploit an enemy's weaknesses. As a combat support mission, airlift provides logistics support through the transportation of personnel and equipment. In peacetime, airlift provides the opportunity to enhance national objectives by providing military assistance and civilian relief programs. Airlift, therefore, accomplishes the timely movement, delivery, and recovery of personnel, equipment, and supplies, furthering military and national goals.[136]

The new manual also talks to viewing airlift from strategic or tactical perspectives, which is a clear effort to move away from labeling and separating forces and missions:

> Airlift may be performed from a strategic or tactical perspective. Strategic (intertheater) airlift transcends the boundary of any one theater and is executed under the central direction of higher authority, normally in support of a more pervasive or overall effort. In contrast, tactical (intratheater) airlift is performed within a theater of operations and supports theater objectives through the rapid and responsive movement of personnel and supplies.[137]

This approach is a quantum change from previous efforts to express the airlift mission and a step toward recognizing the unity of airlift.

The Air Force uses its 2-series manuals to express its operational doctrine. In these manuals the basic principles of fundamental doctrine are applied to detailed mission description and methods for preparing and employing aerospace forces.[138] This process of doctrine-writing incrementally provides more specific information and concepts to the development, deployment, and employment forces. AFM 2-4, *Tactical Airlift,* was written in 1966, while AFM 2-21, *Strategic Airlift,* was updated in 1972. The Military Airlift Command is, at this writing, in the process of doing what General Estes suggested in 1965—combining the two manuals to reflect the oneness of airlift and to emphasize how all airlift tasks and capabilities are aimed at its one mission.

The Airlift Doctrinal Heritage of the Modern Era

Even the short period covered in this chapter will have a lasting impact on airlift doctrine. The key elements of that impact are summarized here:

- Airlift forces are the linchpin of conventional national military strategy; as such they are the backbone of deterrence.
- Airlift forces are the key element in the mobility triad of projection capability.
- Airlift forces must be capable and prepared to deliver combat forces as close to their area of operations as possible, as early in the conflict as possible. This ultimately means abandoning the doctrinal view of force projection as a three-step process:
    a. Main operating base to second main operating base.
    b. Second main operating base to forward operating location.
    c. Forward operating location to final destination and instead view it as a two-step process: (1) main operating base to forward operating location and (2) forward operating location to final destination.
- Civil cargo and passenger aircraft augment military airlift aircraft; they are not a replacement for organic military airlift aircraft.

NOTES

1. Senate, Committee on Armed Services, Subcommittee on Sea Power and Force Projection, *Department of Defense Authorization for Appropriations for Fiscal Year 1983: Part 6*, 97th Cong., 2d sess., 1982, 3964, statement of Gen James Allen, commander in chief, Military Airlift Command.

2. Senate, Committee on Armed Services, Subcommittee on Sea Power and Force Projection, *Department of Defense Authorization for Appropriations for Fiscal Year 1982: Part 4*, 97th Cong., 1st sess., 1981, 1755, statement of Lt Gen Paul Gorman, director for plans and policy, Organization of the Joint Chiefs of Staff.

3. House, Committee on Armed Services, Research and Development Subcommittee, *Hearings on Military Posture and H. R. 2970: Part 4*, 97th Cong., 1st sess., 1981, 965, statement of Gen Robert Huyser, commander in chief, Military Airlift Command.

4. House, Committee on Appropriations, Subcommittee on the Department of Defense, *Department of Defense Appropriations for 1983: Part 4*, 97th Cong., 2d sess., 1982, 770, statement of Lloyd Mosemann, deputy assistant secretary of the Air Force (Logistics).

5. For a well-reasoned strongly pro-sealift position, see Advanced Amphibious Study Group, Headquarters United States Marine Corps, Draft Planner's Reference Manual, vol. 1 (of three) August 1983, 2-4-1 to 2-4-7; see also Lt Col Ray Linville, "Maritime Prepositioning: A Logistics Readiness and Sustainability Enhancement," *Air Force Journal of Logistics* 8, no. 1 (Winter 1984): 2–10; and Association of the United States Army, Special Report: *Strategic Mobility: Can We Get There From Here—In Time?* 1984.

6. Senate, Committee on Armed Services, *DOD Authorization for Appropriations for FY 1983: Part 6*, 1982, 3978, statement by Alton Keel, assistant secretary of the Air Force, research, development, and logistics.

7. House, Committee on Appropriations, *Department of Defense Appropriations for 1983: Part 7*, 97th Cong., 2d sess., 1982, 57, statement of Deputy Secretary of Defense Frank Carlucci.

8. Senate Committee on Armed Services, *DOD Authorization for Appropriations for FY 1983: Part 6*, 1982, 3978, Keel.

9. House, Committee on Armed Services, *Military Posture and H. R. 2970: Part 4*, 1981, 963, General Huyser.

10. Maj James Crumley, Jr., "What's the Requirement?" *Airlift* 5 (Winter 1983): 21.

11. Secretary of Defense Caspar Weinberger to Senator John Tower, chairman, Committee on Armed Services, letter, 7 December 1981.

12. Ibid.

13. Memorandum, Gen Charles Gabriel, chief of staff, US Air Force, and Secretary of the Air Force Verne Orr, to secretary of the Army, secretary of the Navy, chief of naval operations, commandant, US Marine Corps, and commanders in chief of the unified and specified commands, subject: US Air Force Airlift Master Plan—Action Memorandum, 29 September 1983, III-3.

14. Ibid., III-4.

15. Senate, Committee on Armed Services, *DOD Authorization for Appropriations for FY 1983: Part 6*, 1982, 3965, General Allen.

16. House, Committee on Appropriations, *Department of Defense Appropriations for 1983: Part 4*, 1982, 798–99, Mosemann.

17. Department of Defense, *Annual Report Fiscal Year 1980* (Washington, D.C.: Government Printing Office, 1979), 195.

18. Ibid., 198–208.

19. Ibid., 210.

20. Ibid.

21. Department of Defense, *Annual Report Fiscal Year 1981* (Washington, D.C.: Government Printing Office, 1980), 205.
22. Ibid., 205–12.
23. Ibid., 212.
24. Department of Defense, *Annual Report Fiscal Year 1982* (Washington, D.C.: Government Printing Office, 1981), 197.
25. Ibid., 198.
26. Ibid.
27. Ibid., 197–206.
28. Ibid., 201.
29. Department of Defense, *Annual Report to the Congress Fiscal Year 1983* (Washington, D.C.: Government Printing Office, 1982), III-94.
30. Ibid., III-91 to III-99.
31. Department of Defense, *Annual Report to the Congress Fiscal Year 1984* (Washington, D.C.: Government Printing Office, 1983), 207.
32. Ibid., 209.
33. Ibid., 212.
34. Department of Defense, *FY 1985 Report of Secretary of Defense Caspar W. Weinberger to the Congress* (Washington, D.C.: Government Printing Office, 1984), 173.
35. Ibid., 179.
36. History, Military Airlift Command, 1980, 74–76.
37. House, Committee on Armed Services, *Department of Defense Authorization Act: Report No. 96-916*, 96th Cong., 2d sess., 1980, 90.
38. History, Military Airlift Command, 1981, 67-68.
39. Ibid., 69–72.
40. Ibid., 71–72.
41. Weinberger to Tower, 7 December 1981.
42. History, Military Airlift Command, 1981, 73–74.
43. House, Committee on Appropriations, *DOD Appropriations for 1983: Part 7*, 1982, 13–40, referenced slide on page 24.
44. History, Military Airlift Command, 1982, 84–86.
45. Memorandum, Secretary of the Air Force Verne Orr to chairman, Joint Chiefs of Staff, subject: Airlift Enhancement Program, 5 February 1982.
46. Ibid.
47. Memorandum, Secretary of the Air Force Verne Orr to deputy secretary of defense, subject: Airlift Enhancement Program, 5 February 1982.
48. Gen James Allen, commander in chief, Military Airlift Command, to Secretary of Defense Caspar Weinberger, 5 April 1982.
49. History, Military Airlift Command, 1982, 86–87.
50. Ibid., 88.
51. Ibid. 88–92.
52. Gabriel and Orr, Airlift Master Plan, 29 September 1983, cover letter.
53. Ibid., V-8.
54. Ibid., V-11.
55. Robert Frank Futrell, *Ideas, Concepts, Doctrine: A History of Basic Thinking in the United States Air Force 1907-1964* (Maxwell AFB, Ala.: Air University, 1974), 438.
56. Ibid.
57. House, Committee on Armed Services, Subcommittee on Military Airlift, *Hearings on Military Airlift*, 91st Cong., 2d sess., 1970, 6393, statement of Col Bill Richardson.
58. Ibid.
59. Ibid.

60. Ibid.
61. Ibid., 6393-97.
62. House, Committee on Armed Services, *Report on Military Airlift*, 91st Cong., 2d sess., 24 June 1970, 9230.
63. Ibid., 9231.
64. George Watson, Jr., Office of History, Headquarters Air Force Systems Command, historical report, *The Advanced Medium Short-Take-Off-and-Landing Transport (AMST) and the Implications of the Minimum Engineering Development (MED) Program*, n.d., 1-8.
65. Ibid., 31.
66. United States Army Combined Arms Center, executive summary, subject: Advanced Medium STOL Study, August, 1977.
67. Ibid.
68. John Shea, assistant deputy chief of staff, Plans, Headquarters Military Airlift Command, to distribution list, letter, subject: Employment Concept for the AMST, 4 January 1977.
69. Ibid.
70. Ibid.
71. Maj Robert Ewart, Directorate of Operational Requirements, Headquarters Military Airlift Command, point paper, subject: AMST: The Missing Link, 17 October 1979.
72. Ibid., Major Evans, Directorate of Operational Requirements, Headquarters Military Airlift Command, point paper, subject: The AMST Requirement in Summary, 25 October 1979.
73. House, Committee on Armed Services, *Research and Development Subcommittee Hearings on the Posture of Military Airlift*, 94th Cong., 1st sess., 1975, 278-79, statement of Maj Gen Benjamin Starr, Jr., director of transportation, Headquarters USAF.
74. Gen Robert Huyser, commander in chief, Military Airlift Command, to General Slay, commander, Air Force Systems Command, message, 222100Z October 1979.
75. Watson, The AMST, 81.
76. Ibid., 81-87. See also Major Ewart, Directorate of Operational Requirements, Headquarters Military Airlift Command, draft, Talking Paper on C-X, 2 November 1979.
77. House, Committee on Armed Services, Research and Development Subcommittee, *Hearings on Military Posture and H. R. 6495: Part 4*, 96th Cong., 2d sess., 1980, 1802, statement of Maj Gen Emil Block, Jr., director, C-X Task Force, and chief of staff, Military Airlift Command.
78. Ibid., 1773.
79. Ibid., 1779-81.
80. Ibid., 1806.
81. Ibid., 1783.
82. Ibid., 1779.
83. Ibid., 1805.
84. House, Committee on Armed Services, *Military Posture and H. R. 2970: Part 4*, 1981, 987, statement of Brig Gen Donald Brown, deputy chief of staff, Plans, Headquarters Military Airlift Command.
85. Memorandum by Secretary of the Air Force Hans Mark to Assistant Secretary of Defense Russell Murray, program analysis and evaluation, subject: C-X Analysis, 17 March 1980.
86. House, Committee on Armed Forces, *Hearings on Military Posture, and H. R. 6495*, 1980, 1806, General Block.
87. Ibid., 1808.
88. Headquarters Military Airlift Command, draft, A Validation of the Requirement, Concepts, and Design for the C-7, ca. 1983. See also memorandum by Gen Charles Gabriel, chief of staff, US Air Force; Gen John Wickham, chief of staff, US Army; Gen Paul X. Kelley, commandant, US Marine Corps; Secretary of the Air Force Verne Orr; and Secretary of the Army John Marsh, Jr., to the secretary of defense, subject: C-17 Validation Report-Action Memorandum, 6 February 1984; and Col Don

Lindbo, briefing, subject: HQ MAC Task Force Report on Validation of C-17 Requirements, Concepts, and Design, n.d.

89. House, Committee on Appropriations, Subcommittee on the Department of Defense, *Department of Defense Appropriations for 1983: Part 7*, 97th Cong., 2d sess., 1982, 7, statement of Deputy Secretary of Defense Frank Carlucci.

90. Ibid., 10, statement of Gen Paul X. Kelley, assistant commandant, US Marine Corps.

91. Senate, Committee on Appropriations, *Department of Defense Appropriations for Fiscal Year 1983: Part 3*, 97th Cong., 2d sess., 1982, 17, statement of Lt Gen Kelly Burke, deputy chief of staff, research, development, and acquisition, Headquarters USAF.

92. Senate, Committee on Armed Services, *Department of Defense Appropriations for Fiscal Year 1983: Part 6*, 97th Cong., 2d sess., 1982, 4000, Headquarters USAF, answer to question submitted by Senator Sam Nunn.

93. Ibid., 4000.

94. House, *DOD Appropriations for 1983: Part 7*, 1982, 7, Carlucci.

95. House, Committee on Appropriations, *Department of Defense Appropriations for 1983: Part 4*, 1982, 786, Mosemann.

96. Ibid., 751–52.

97. House, *DOD Appropriations for 1983: Part 7*, 1982, 11, statement of Lt Gen R. H. Thompson, deputy chief of staff for logistics, Headquarters USAF.

98. Gen James Allen, "The Best 101st Air Mobile Division in the World Isn't Going to Deter a Soul if it Can't Fight Outside the Confines of Ft Campbell, Ky.," interview with L. K. Levens and B. F. Schemmer, *Armed Forces Journal International* 119 (July 1982): 50–56.

99. Secretary of the Air Force Verne Orr to Melvin Price, chairman, House, Committee on Armed Services, letter, 4 June 1982.

100. Gen James Allen, commander in chief, Military Airlift Command, to Secretary of Defense Caspar Weinberger, letter, 2 April 1983.

101. House, Committee on Government Operations, Subcommittee on Military Operations, *Military Air Transportation*, 86th Cong., 2d sess., 1960, 130–31.

102. History, Military Air Transport Service, July–December 1952, 1:325–31; History, Military Air Transport Service, July–December 1954, 1:156–66; History, Military Air Transport Service, January–June 1955, 1:122–32; House, Committee on Armed Services, Special Subcommittee on Military Airlift, *Military Airlift*, 89th Cong., 1st and 2d sess., 1965 and 1966, 6720–69; House, Committee on Armed Services, Subcommittee on Military Airlift, *Military Airlift*, 91st Cong., 2d sess., 1970, 6278–6337; House, Committee on Armed Services, *Posture of Military Airlift* 1975, 16–20, 457–543; Senate, Committee on Armed Services, Subcommittee on Procurement Policy and Reprogramming, *Civil Reserve Air Fleet (CRAF) Enhancement Program*, 96th Cong., 1st sess., 1979, 1–28; House, Committee on Appropriations, Subcommittee on the Department of Defense, *Department of Defense Appropriations for 1981: Part 6*, 96th Cong., 2d sess., 1980, 498–518, 553–608.

103. House, Committee on Armed Services, *Hearings on Military Airlift*, 1970, 6280, statement of Capt William Bennett.

104. House, Committee on Armed Services, *Hearings on Military Airlift*, 1970, 9227.

105. Ibid.

106. Gen John McConnell, chief of staff, US Air Force, to Gen Howell Estes, Jr., commander, Military Airlift Command, letter, subject: C-5 Mission Statement, 19 July 1966.

107. US Congress, Joint Economic Committee, Subcommittee on Priorities and Economy in Government, 94th Cong., 2d sess.; 95th Cong., 1st sess.; 96th Cong., 2d sess., 1981, 560–61, statement of Secretary of the Air Force Hans Mark.

108. Ibid.

109. Memorandum by Russell Murray, assistant secretary of defense, program analysis and evaluation, to the secretary of the Air Force, subject: C-X Analysis, 3 March 1980.

110. Mark to Murray, C-X Analysis, 17 March 1980.
111. Ibid.
112. Ibid.
113. House, Committee on Appropriations, *Department of Defense Appropriations for 1983: Part 4*, 1982, 775, statement of Lloyd Mosemann.
114. House, Committee on Appropriations, Subcommittee on the Department of Defense, *Department of Defense Appropriations for 1981: Part 3*, 96th Cong., 2d sess., 1980, 1009–10, statement of Lt Gen Kelly Burke, deputy chief of staff, research, development, and acquisition, Headquarters USAF.
115. House, Committee on Armed Services, *Hearings on Military Posture and H. R. 2970: Part 4*, 1981, 988, statement of General Brown.
116. Headquarters MAC, *Draft C-17 Validation*, 2-7 to 2-8.
117. Ibid., 3–4.
118. Ibid., 3–11.
119. Ibid., 3–13.
120. Senate, Committee on Armed Services, *DOD Authorization for Appropriation for FY 83: Part 6*, 1982, 4019.
121. Headquarters MAC, Draft C-17 Validation, 3-14 to 3-17.
122. Ibid., 3-18 to 3-23.
123. Lt Gen Lawrence Skantze, commander, Aeronautical Systems Division, Air Force Systems Command, to the Boeing Co., McDonnell Douglas Corp., and Lockheed Corp., letter, subject: C-X Acquisition Program Request for Proposal (RFP): F33657-80-R-0227, 15 October 1980.
124. Headquarters MAC, *Draft C-17 Validation*, 4-1 to 4-8.
125. Ibid., 5–2.
126. Ibid., 5–3.
127. Ibid.
128. Ibid., A 2-7 to A 2-8.
129. House, *DOD Appropriations for 1983: Part 7*, 1982, 27.
130. Maj Gen Perry Smith, director of plans, Headquarters USAF, to James Wade, Jr., principal deputy under secretary of defense for research and engineering, letter, 16 December 1981.
131. Senate, Committee on Armed Services, Subcommittee on Sea Power and Force Projection, *Department of Defense Authorization for Appropriations for Fiscal Year 1984: Part 6*, 98th Cong., 1st sess., 1983, 3173, statement of General Allen.
132. Ibid., 3172.
133. Draft AFR 1–2, *Assignment of Responsibilities for Development of Aerospace Doctrine*, 4 August 1983.
134. Ibid.
135. AFM 1–1, *Functions and Basic Doctrine of the United States Air Force*, 14 February 1979, 2–11.
136. AFM 1–1, *Basic Aerospace Doctrine of the United States Air Force*, 5 January 1984, 3–5.
137. Ibid.
138. Draft AFR 1–2, *Aerospace Doctrine*, 4 August 1983.

CHAPTER 8

Ideas and Concepts

Airlift doctrine has changed significantly over the past 60 years. In the 1920s and 1930s, air transportation was viewed first as a logistics tool for use between air depots, and later as a way to help move air forces about the United States both in maneuvers and in defense of the country's coastlines. In World War II air transportation of high-priority goods and people across long distances emerged as the prime reason for existence of the Air Transport Command (ATC). Because these goods and people were of such strategic importance to the war effort, ATC forces were exempt from control by theater commands, and ATC resources were centrally controlled by the highest level of authority. Troop carrier organizations, on the other hand, were specifically designated to provide airlift for Army paratroop forces and to resupply them as well. The value of air transportation was quickly recognized by theater commanders, who more often used troop carrier resources for logistics missions than for paratroop operations. The troop carrier units offered a flexible, responsive way of providing mobility for a great variety of forces.

Following World War II, several efforts were made to consolidate strategic and troop carrier organizations, but these initiatives were unsuccessful primarily due to the very strength of troop carrier airlift—its flexibility and responsiveness. Senior leaders were convinced that if consolidation occurred, the "tacticalness" of the troop carriers would be overwhelmed by the unrelenting routineness of strategic airlift operations. As the Army developed and refined its concepts of strategic deployment of forces across long distances directly into objective areas by air, the troop carrier planners shifted their focus to include such operations under the tactical umbrella. In a similar manner, the Department of Defense (DOD) sought to put as much strategic airlift under one command as possible, leading to the creation of the Military Air Transport Service (MATS) in 1948. The Berlin airlift served to highlight the point that a combined-airlift organization could achieve the airlift mission better than any other organizational arrangement.

By the mid-1950s, the Army had refined its thinking to the point that it officially called for airlift support of long-range deployments. The Air Force, however, planned to use MATS airlift to support Strategic Air Command deployments and troop carrier airlift to support strike force movements. The Army's airlift needs were not ignored by either the Air Force or the Joint Chiefs of Staff, but emphasis and wartime planning focused on other missions. In peacetime MATS was primarily a logistics tool for the DOD, performing airlift-type operations as a by-product of training. The US civil airlines were highly critical of MATS's peacetime

AIRLIFT DOCTRINE

operations and asked Congress for relief. A change in the national military strategy, brought on by the election of John F. Kennedy, forever changed many of these perspectives.

President Kennedy called for a flexible response strategy that gave great impetus to the development of airlift forces. Emphasis shifted to providing MATS, soon to be renamed the Military Airlift Command (MAC) in recognition of its importance, with the capability to deploy Army units and their equipment very quickly across intercontinental ranges. The C-141 workhorse aircraft was to become the backbone of the MAC fleet. The C-5 aircraft concept also grew from this changing view of the importance of moving Army forces and equipment by air to the battle area. The Army also found favorable hearing for its ideas concerning battlefield maneuver via helicopter and small airlift aircraft. It was also in the early 1960s that the DOD began to think seriously about a proper mix of forward-deployed forces (in peacetime), sealift capabilities, prepositioning of equipment and supplies in likely regions of conflict, and airlift forces.

The gradual and sustained buildup of American involvement in Vietnam served to fully reorient airlift thinking. Tactical airlift performed very few paratroop missions of the type seen in World War II, but it performed heroic aerial resupply of besieged forces. It also executed seemingly endless, unrelentingly routine logistics missions for the theater commander. And it proved that Air Force airlift could be responsive to Army mobility requirements. In 1965, the Army and Air Force agreed that the Army would be responsible for its own helicopter air transportation and that the Air Force would provide fixed-wing air transport. The issue of future technology aircraft was left to the future. In Vietnam the C-130 became the tactical airlift aircraft of choice wherever it would fit into the airfield in question. It carried more people and equipment faster, requiring fewer sorties and providing more support. The strategic airlift forces, likewise, emerged from the Vietnam War with a new outlook. The advent of the fast, long-range C-141, followed later by the C-5, proved that airlift could move large forces over long distances and make a difference. This new airlift system also provided the senior decision makers and planners with an unprecedented degree of confidence in the ability to react quickly and effectively with a military force.

Ultimately, the Vietnam era illustrated that tactical and strategic airlift forces should be consolidated into one force, which officially occurred in 1976. Two kinds of efficiency supported their decision. More important was the point, argued for 20-odd years, that by putting the two forces under one organization there would be a synergistic effect that would yield more airlift responsiveness than the simple sum of the two capabilities. The other, a peacetime economies argument, said that dollars and manpower would be saved. To further enhance the responsiveness of these combined airlift forces, MAC was designated a specified command under the Joint Chiefs of Staff in 1977.

IDEAS AND CONCEPTS

Following the Vietnam War, MAC supported the Tactical Air Command's 1970 initiative to develop the advanced medium short takeoff and landing (STOL) transport (AMST), but to no avail. What was finally important about the AMST was its recognition, in design, of the importance of delivering large pieces of Army combat equipment into austere airfields. Budget problems and an emerging consensus that the military needed more strategic airlift deployment capabilities led to the cancellation of the AMST and the immediate follow-on development of the C-X aircraft.

The C-X development process, with its emphasis on operating environment, dual strategic and tactical capabilities, and outsize cargo demands, combined to produce a unique aircraft concept. The resulting C-17 is to perform a full range of airlift missions and thus represents the most modern example of airlift doctrine. The "battles" in the Pentagon and the Congress that led to the selection of the C-5B as an interim step prior to the acquisition of the C-17 offered a splendid view of history repeating itself. The process may be described as follows: There is a newly articulated shortfall in airlift capability that must be met as soon as possible. Some aircraft companies offer unsolicited alternatives comprised of modified status quo aircraft. The military supports an aircraft that is the best but latest available. Parts of the Congress support an aircraft that is the cheapest, the soonest, and the worst of three alternatives. The senior decision makers direct multiple analytical studies and restudies of alternatives based on various funding profiles and planning assumptions. These decision makers finally select an interim aircraft that is at best a recognition of the importance of airlift, at worst a highly controversial choice, and in the middle a compromise until the best aircraft is available, all depending on one's viewpoint.

There are literally dozens of conclusions that can be drawn from this review of airlift concepts and doctrine. Some are obvious, others are more subtle.

Airlift at Risk

At this writing, a popular question is whether large, expensive airlift aircraft will be placed in harm's way. In other words, will leaders and planners risk having airlifters damaged and/or shot down? The question is much more complex than it appears to be, with a number of ramifications at every level. In its simplest form the answer is that airlift has always been put at risk and will be in the future, but that human lives will not be thrown away wantonly. How important will the mission be? What is the payback? What kind of risk—enemy aircraft? small arms? radar-guided missiles and guns? shoulder-fired weapons? terrorists? extremely hazardous weather? What kinds of countermeasures are available? Is it a one-of-a-kind mission or a sustained operation? What are the other current and anticipated demands on airlift assets? Are the aircraft available the right ones? What does "in harm's way" mean—guaranteed shoot-down? a high percentage of lost crews and aircraft? 10-percent loss rate? 3 percent? less than 1 percent?

Clearly, airlift aircraft must be designed to operate in some degree of risk. Modern warfare will not allow otherwise. Planners and leaders must have the confidence to call on airlift and be assured of success—however that too is defined. Airlift doctrine since, and including, World War II has called for airlift to be a risky business, especially relative to aircraft capabilities. Increasingly, airlift aircraft have been conceived and designed for dangerous operations. There is a whole subset of concepts and operations developed just for this reason. Minimum ground times; great ground maneuverability; the recovery base concept; agility in the air; improved command, control, and communication; austere field capabilities; aerial delivery training and tactics; and special exercises have been developed, tested, and executed to meet the requirements of combat airlift operations.

Airlift Doctrine and National Strategy

There is a critical link between today's military response to the threats the United States faces in the world and airlift doctrine. The current strategy appears to rely on a strong conventional military capacity to deter conflicts from arising, to stop escalation of confrontations, and, should all these fail, to respond to aggression effectively enough to prevent resort to nuclear weapons. All of these options are founded on a responsive, meaningful airlift capability. Lacking the ability to project a useful military force rapidly, the strategy becomes a house of cards.

Every element of airlift doctrine supports this strategy. Airlift forces can and do respond very quickly to taskings, even taskings that seem to change every few hours as a crisis clarifies itself. Crews, maintenance personnel, aerial port units, and a myriad of other support elements train on a daily basis to fight. The affiliation program, joint airborne air transportability training, large-scale exercises, and even routine channel missions are aimed at preparing to respond quickly. The many years of confidence building through real-world execution in the face of combat and the day-in and day-out preparations for execution are what make the current strategy viable. The will of the national command authority to respond is not enough. The means of response are also vital.

A poorly thought out or ineffectively executed airlift doctrine can have far-ranging impacts on national military strategy. For example, if airlift doctrine supports a force that will operate on a sustained basis only into main bases, then the strategy must accommodate this viewpoint. If doctrine says that airlift aircraft will operate only within certain parameters of risk, the strategy likewise must take those limitations into account. If, on the other hand, airlift doctrine offers a highly flexible operational concept, the strategy may likewise be more flexible. Doctrinal emphasis on different force structures can equally affect the military strategy.

Overemphasis on civil capability, for example, might reduce preconflict actions in terms of secrecy, timeliness, or will to act. Too much reliance on reserve forces could equally mean different timetables and response options. Achieving the proper balance between these and active duty airlift forces is a doctrinal effort of great importance.

Just as the strategy depends on airlift, airlift depends on strategy. As we saw in the 1950s, if the strategy focuses on a nuclear response, then airlift has a much different mission. If the strategy relies on conventional forces, airlift becomes more important. Yet, even within the conventional context, the kind of response will greatly affect airlift. For example, the maritime concept that places most emphasis on force projection through sea power, thus ignoring the contributions of air power, would place continuing but scaled-down demands on airlift. Even if there is a more balanced approach that calls on air, land, and sea power, the regions we see as likely conflict centers have strong implications for airlift doctrine. A strategy that focuses on only one region, for example, would call for a different airlift doctrine from a strategy that sees the potential for military actions from a worldwide perspective.

Even varying the details of a worldwide scenario perspective has great meaning for airlift. Estimates of warning time, and the philosophical willingness to rely on those estimates and the warnings themselves, could mean an airlift force oriented primarily to main base operations over relatively long lead times. This in turn means a particular type of aircraft and probably fewer of them. On the other hand, a strategy and orientation that sees the potential threat as relatively unpredictable, that takes into account the fog of prewar circumstances, and that wants to minimize risk-taking with the national security will yield a larger, more flexible airlift force and a different doctrine.

Airlift doctrine—our views on how to develop, employ, and deploy airlift forces—shapes and is shaped by national military strategy. These are not academic questions but rather ones of supreme importance. The national security rests on properly equipped, trained, and prepared airlift forces, which in turn rely on an effective airlift doctrine.

Making Airlift Doctrine

Current Air Force doctrine says to view airlift from the perspective of inter- and intratheater missions. To this must now be added the special operations mission. Ultimately, airlift must be looked at from the perspective of the combat mission. There has been an inexorable drive across the last 60-odd years to make clear that airlift is a warfighting issue. To be sure, it performs humanitarian and foreign policy tasks, but its real reason for being is to deter wars, and failing that, to fight and win them.

Airlift doctrine is made by people—a large variety of people with their own set of interests, world views, and abilities. For the senior decision maker this means a wealth of inputs, often representing diametrical positions, for each decision. Anyone involved on a day-to-day basis with airlift quickly comes to feel that there is not anyone who does not have an idea or an opinion about airlift. Consequently, for there to be progress even in thinking about airlift, there must be a seemingly endless series of conferences, memorandums, point papers, and the like. Once an idea is fairly well articulated and defended, there must follow the very same process in order to make the idea an official position, and even more work to change the doctrine into tactics, training, hardware, and operational plans. For it is only when these are accomplished that doctrine has utility. It is important to visualize, debate, and write about a direct delivery concept, for example. It is equally important to make that concept a reality.

Some doctrinal initiatives are limited by technology. ("Can we build an airplane or communications system that will do what we have in mind?") Others are limited by personalities and ideas. ("Won't troop carrier aviation lose its tactical orientation if we merge it with strategic airlift?") Still others are limited by what we euphemistically call political factors. ("Will Congress support it?") Finally, some ideas are limited by status quo doctrine. ("Doesn't current doctrine preclude putting theater airlift under someone else's control?")

Airlift doctrine is made in a system. For the decision maker and idea originator alike, this doctrine-making system has several implications. New ideas (or even old ones) may be well articulated, thoroughly documented, and eminently logical and still fail to progress. They must also somehow be linked to current doctrinal and strategic concepts, be of proven combat benefit, make the most of existing resources, save money, be less expensive than alternatives, be backed up by volumes of unshakable analytical data, and be fully coordinated before official introduction into the decision-making arena. And they still may fail to gain acceptance. Some things take time.

Expressing Airlift Doctrine

This study has illustrated just some of the myriad of ways airlift doctrine is expressed: formal manuals, budgets, force structure initiatives, testimony to Congress, procurement of aircraft, operational plans, and war. We often have seen several of these different methods operating at once, in different directions, sometimes with undesirable results.

It is tempting to suggest that the experts on airlift—the Military Airlift Command—should be the sole proprietors of airlift doctrinal expression, but several factors combine to make this wrong. First, the more airlift doctrine is discussed and understood, the better it is for airlift. Second, the wide application of airlift in military affairs calls for a wide variety of contributors. Third, the Air Force's formal doctrine development system calls for Headquarters USAF to be the final arbiter in doctrinal affairs so as to be able to integrate efforts and provide a perspective not available elsewhere. It is not an unreasonable idea. Finally, the wide application of airlift to military affairs means that others "force" their way into the process. Airlift, especially from the point of view of the users, is so vital to military success that they will not stand by and let such a critical process occur without their participation.

One other note becomes important in this process. Airlift doctrine, by its very nature, must be expressed by the military system, not the civilian one. Policy questions about how to equip a force to meet the doctrine may rightly lie in the civilian field, but not the determination of the fundamental opinions of how to best develop, employ, and deploy that force. Those are questions involving military expertise. Civilian questions more rightly concern themselves with whether to expend the resources necessary to meet the doctrine and to assess the meaning of the doctrine for national strategy.

Airborne Operations

It is rare to find a major military exercise planned today that will not include a deployment of airborne forces across strategic ranges—forces that will, with their equipment, parachute into an objective area within a matter of seconds of when they were planned to arrive. Extensive resources are expended to train and equip airlift and ground forces for this mission. Some have suggested that such large-scale operations can never be executed in the face of modern weapons. Others question the military payback of such expensive training.

Several factors come into play in answering these doubts. Airborne operations on the scale we are discussing may be preceded by special operations and air-to-ground strikes or bombings to deal with the ground-to-air threat, and they will likely be accompanied by air-to-air and air-to-ground forces, all to increase the likelihood of success. It may also be that such large-scale operations can be planned for execution at locations not as heavily defended as others. The element of surprise may also be used to advantage, both in the sense of executing the operation at all and in the sense of using appropriate tactics and diversions. As the planners learned in World War II, airborne operations are not to be executed just because the capability exists, but the capability does need to exist. Airhead seizure at the appropriate point, flanking maneuvers of the right size force, insertion of forces where an airhead does not exist, and emergency reinforcements are valuable tools for the field commander.

The ability to perform such operations over strategic distances is an added bonus. Enemy forces must be concerned about such attacks and expend resources and forces to prepare for them. The proper amount of doubt about the outcome can deter aggression in the first phase. Allies in less-developed nations can be reassured just as easily by such capabilities. The appearance of a powerful force seemingly overnight can have startling effects. Early on in many scenarios, the forward deployment of a fighting force to seize or defend certain geographical points will have long-lasting effects on enemy capabilities. The battlefields of Europe are not the only potential trouble spots in the world.

Airborne operations are risky, they are expensive to train for, and they are hard on equipment. But the flexibility and potential payback, when applied in proper circumstances, overshadow the disadvantages. This study illustrates that the planning complications and resource implications of a foe are enormous when the United States has airborne resources in-being and well trained. The paybacks of this strategy in underdeveloped areas in surprise response to aggression, in airhead seizure operations, and in giving aid and comfort to our Allies make airborne operations a potent weapon. The strategic airborne operation must be a complicating factor of enormous proportions for potential aggressors around the world and offers an especially flexible tool for our senior planners and leaders. However, airborne operations run the grave risk of failure if they are not trained for and are not well-planned joint endeavors. The airlift force must never be left out of this planning process. The airborne force must also be sustained, and reinforced, as well as withdrawn if necessary. Other Air Force forces must equally be fully prepared to support the initial and follow-on operations.

Large-scale airborne insertion of troops and equipment is not appropriate for every situation, theater, or war. Nonetheless, the contributions such capabilities can make in other circumstances make their development well worth the effort.

The Mobility Triad: Force Projection

There is a DOD mobility doctrine even if it is not articulated as such. It says, in effect, that military forces will be prepared to deploy rapidly and that the mobility forces needed to deploy and sustain them will be developed by the military services. The DOD doctrine says that the mobility triad—airlift, sealift, and prepositioning—will be developed in a balanced fashion, and in balance with the forces to be deployed. This doctrine is fundamentally important to airlift doctrine. It puts emphasis on rapid deployment, which means that airlift will not be primarily oriented to logistics operations. It means that airlift thinking and concepts will be attuned to moving combat units, including their equipment, into combat theaters as close to their objective areas as possible. It also means that intratheater airlift must be prepared to relocate some prepositioned stocks (as needed), to redistribute goods delivered by sealift (again as needed), and to provide high-priority tactical mobility and support to combat forces.

The idea of balance among the mobility triad elements may not be what it appears at first sight. Balance in this context means taking advantage of the strengths of each element and solving the individual weaknesses. Airlift becomes the key element in this process because time is of the essence in the application of military force in the majority of cases. It makes operations feasible where prepositioning is not, and where sealift does not arrive early enough. Almost regardless of the amount of prepositioning and sealift available, airlift is the ingredient that rapidly delivers the troops (and the equipment that cannot be prepositioned) to make use of the prepositioned stocks. Balance, then, will inevitably lead to a high degree of reliance on airlift. This in turn means that airlift doctrine must provide a force that is flexible and responsive.

Special Operations

Air Force special operations forces were reassigned from the Tactical Air Command to the Military Airlift Command in March of 1983. Some MAC airlift forces are trained and equipped to support special operations activities. The most difficult question facing planners is how and when to take advantage of that capability. The difficult question of whether to use scarce airlift resources during a deployment, for example, must be faced the same way the risk calculation (in general) is approached. On the other hand, the question of using airlift forces in situations where those forces are not demanded elsewhere calls for a more subtle, but nonetheless necessary, review of possible future calls on those same airlift forces. The inherent flexibility of the airlift system, with its many capabilities, puts special pressures on the military planner. The fact that airlift forces can engage in such a variety of missions is both a blessing and a curse.

Consolidation and Direct Delivery

Ultimately there is one airlift mission—the delivery of what is needed, where it is needed, when it is needed. All organizational, doctrinal, and resource issues must be answered in relation to that mission.

The organizational consolidation of strategic and tactical airlift not only admitted the logic of increased efficiency but also opened the door to the fuller development of the direct delivery idea. Some 30 years after the Air Staff first considered the idea, the two types of airlift were merged under one command in 1975–76. With the development of a theater organization to monitor, manage, and control all airlift operating in or through a given theater (or areas of operations), the most can be made of a very few assets. As noted in chapter 6, this increased efficiency provides more than just the sum of the two kinds of airlift—there is in fact a synergistic effect

AIRLIFT DOCTRINE

that yields a dividend, a flexibility not possible before. In the long run, the consolidation also set the stage for the maturation of the direct delivery concept. Even before consolidation MATS/MAC was talking about direct delivery, then called the source-to-user concept. The consolidation allowed the concept to develop logically in a much more unfettered atmosphere. It is interesting that one of the prime arguments against consolidation was that the tactical units would lose their tactical orientation and thus be less responsive to the theater commanders. Instead, the strategic force has benefited from the tactical experiences and influences, and the two together have devised a concept that will be more responsive to theater and strategic needs than either one was before.

Prior to consolidation—MAC's becoming a specified command—there were many hands in the pot, each with its own specific concerns. There was not one centralized point that could devote its energies to thinking about, and acting on, how the whole airlift force could be integrated into a unified fighting force. Organizational consolidation went far toward solving many of the problems associated with such a disjointed system. Airlift can now be viewed as a continuum of overlapping tasks and capabilities.

Consolidation meant that two ways of thinking about airlift could eventually become one. The three-step deployment process could more readily evolve into a two-step process. Instead of viewing airlift as a strategic leg to a main operating base, a tactical leg to a forward operating location, and an Army leg to the front, we can now conceptualize it as a deployment (or supply) leg to a forward operating location and an Army leg to the front. None of this, however should cause us to lose sight of the fact that there will still be a requirement for airlift into main operating bases, tactical redistribution of goods and people, and airdrop of supplies and forces in various scenarios. In other words, direct delivery is not a replacement for other airlift missions. Rather, it is one more tool in the airlift mission arsenal. It reorients our thinking on how to execute certain airlift missions, but those missions (capabilities) still have an important role to play in warfare.

Direct delivery, nonetheless, is a radical departure from how we generally conceptualize and plan airlift operations today. Numerous questions need clarification. For example, in a typical deployment now an Army unit and its equipment are loaded aboard C-5s, C-141s, and civil aircraft, and airlifted to a main operating base. The Army units form up and proceed to the battle area either by surface or air lines of communication. As the units arrive and move out, the Army builds up a logistics support structure for those forces. There is a certain amount of time that naturally is available for such a system to grow. With direct delivery, each unit will load onto a direct delivery aircraft and be delivered very close to its battle area. This means less time for the Army logistics structure to build up to support those forces. It means that they will need resupply and support in general much faster than in the current system. Almost immediate resupply will have to be built into the deployment scheme in the beginning. There will also likely be additional

IDEAS AND CONCEPTS

pressures on the intratheater airlift system to be even more responsive to the combat forces than it is now. While all this is going on, the deployment of support forces, follow-on forces, and the whole support structure will be occurring at the main operating bases, probably at a quickened pace.

The direct delivery concept means getting into conflict sooner, which demands a support structure sooner. All combat and support forces involved will have to prepare to deploy faster than they do now. In addition, surface modes of deployment will have to be faster as well. Fast sealift will have to be ready to sail earlier and the forces or goods to be deployed will have to be available at the seaports earlier. At the receiving end, seaports and/or over-the-shore debarkation means will have to be available and ready. In a very real sense, direct delivery faces the same "problems" that an aerial assault faces. The planners and commanders cannot just put a force forward; they must support, resupply, and link up with that force.

This "do it all faster" impact has special meaning for the Air Force. It places additional emphasis on quickly deploying tactical air forces to locations where they can operate effectively and supporting and resupplying them at rates that make them meaningful combat forces. There is already a premium on early arriving air forces in a conflict; their value will only increase in a direct delivery deployment. This challenge will be partially met by the advantages offered by a C-17-type aircraft. Planners must, however, take into account the multiple demands placed on such capability in shaping a force for deployment and in supporting such a force. Because the ground forces will be engaged in battle sooner than currently envisioned, and farther forward geographically, Air Force forces will continue to have to operate from relatively underdeveloped facilities, perhaps even more so than they do now. Main operating bases distant from the battle area will be less valuable, as will aircraft with relatively short range and short effective time over target. Direct delivery also places an additional demand on tactical air forces to protect airlift operations and to protect the locations into which they will be operating.

For the Military Airlift Command direct delivery clearly has many ramifications. Aircraft for this mission must be rugged and highly dependable. Command, control, and communications will likewise have to be tough and reliable. There will be a need for additional combat control teams and airlift control elements, additional and better materiel handling equipment, and an innovative review of loading and unloading techniques and equipment. "Throw-away" pallets and nets may be required. Training for crewmembers and support personnel will also be challenging. A typical direct delivery mission may well include aerial refueling, coordination with tactical aircraft within the area of operations, an "assault-type" landing into an austere environment, taxing ground maneuvers, recovery to a main operating base for fuel, servicing, and carrying a load to be airdropped at some forward location. Crews would also need to be proficient in low-altitude parachute extraction system (LAPES) operations, station-keeping techniques, and low-level activities. In order to get the most from the capabilities inherent in the direct delivery aircraft, many crews will have to be proficient in many tactics and techniques.

Direct delivery also places a premium on deliberate planning and affiliation training. The force likely to be direct delivered needs to be identified "now" so that effective load planning for the direct delivery aircraft and for the concept can be accomplished ahead of time. In essence, the units to be deployed this way should plan exclusively for the aircraft type that will move them. There should be no doubt in anyone's mind about what kind of aircraft will show up to deploy these forces or what kind of resupply and support they can expect within a given time frame during and after deployment. Likewise, the MAC direct delivery force, because of its unique capabilities, should be confident about the units, or at the very least the kinds of units, it can expect to deploy in a conflict. This does not necessarily mean that a particular aircraft will be reserved for a particular unit to be deployed, but rather that the best use of that kind of capability will have been planned already, based on the type of unit to be direct delivered.

As the military gains more experience with the direct delivery operation, it is likely that the concept will be applied to varying degrees to less-capable aircraft. This means that military aircraft types normally thought of in terms of main base operations will be tasked to operate under more stringent conditions depending on the demands of the airlift scenario. For the most part, however, at least as it applies to the current generation of airlift aircraft, the direct delivery concept offers the potential for an extremely well-integrated airlift system. The C-17 will be the direct delivery aircraft of choice, the C-5/141/Civil Reserve Air Fleet (CRAF) team will be the main operating base system, and the C-130 force will be the theater tactical airlift workhorse. After the initial direct delivery portion of the deployment is complete (in a relative sense), the C-17 will be the one aircraft that offers a flexibility not before available to both the theater commander and the worldwide airlift system that, lest we forget, must continue to operate.

None of the above items are problems or roadblocks, nor are they particularly original concerns. Rather they serve to illustrate the point that direct delivery of the scope envisioned with the operation of a C-17 aircraft has more impact than just saying that we get the combat forces there faster. Direct delivery represents a better use of airlift than before. It is an incremental step in military utility. Just as aerial delivery of high-priority goods and passengers in World War II was better than waiting for sealift; just as delivery of forces and equipment into main operating bases is better than waiting for sealift and makes prepositioning a workable alternative; so direct delivery close to a combat area is better than main base delivery and redistribution by surface and air. But this process proves the importance of careful planning, full exploration of what the concept means for other forces, and recognition of the integrated nature of a battle.

The C-17 will make the direct delivery concept work the best of any of the aircraft we have, and more. Because of its many and varied capabilities, the C-17 will also put great emphasis on improved command, control, and communications, and may eventually cause a rethinking of command relations. The AMST/CX/C-17 trail has especially shown the close-working relationship that has evolved between MAC and the Army, a relationship that must continue and expand.

The United States Army generally will be, by volume and weight, the largest airlift customer in a conflict. If the Military Airlift Command can satisfy the deployment and resupply needs of an Army force, the command can meet the requirements of other military forces. This means that Army forces and equipment must be designed to fit on airlift aircraft, and that airlift aircraft must be designed to carry what the Army needs (and operate in appropriate locations). This is a two-way street that seeks to blend the best possible capability for each force. Each strives to accommodate the other, but it is the Army needs that prevail, within the limits of technology and ever-present budgetary constraints. Both, of course, are aimed at executing the military strategy devised by both the national leadership and the theaters to be supported.

In the battlefield doctrine that the Army currently plans with and that it envisions for the future, not enough has been said about airlift. The Army and the Air Force, along with the other services, need to explore more fully the ramifications of the Army doctrine and the realities of the future battlefield.

Very clearly, many future conflicts will be intense. Even in poorly developed countries there are many sophisticated weapons that will threaten US forces. In several potential conflict areas American forces may be outnumbered, while in others the sophisticated weaponry available to the enemy will be cause for grave concern. The Army has developed an aggressive response to these situations, an offensive-oriented response that places great reliance on maneuver and mobility. As part of this doctrine, the Army has continued its battle-proven reliance on organic helicopter assets. As this study has illustrated, there has been a long and sometimes parochial debate between the two services about the proper role of the helicopter and Army aviation in general. That dialogue needs to continue, and it is, in fact, progressing. At the generic doctrine level, it is generally recognized that Army aviation and Air Force airlift will work closely together to deliver the goods wherever and whenever needed. The strengths of each asset will be used and maximum cooperation will be sought. This, however, may not be enough.

Consideration needs to be given to formalizing some issues in both Army and Air Force doctrine. For example, airlift will always be a scarce resource. Within a theater this means that a fast, responsive system for requesting airlift, evaluating airlift requests, prioritizing airlift allocations, and executing airlift missions must be planned for, in existence, and well trained before a conflict. Slow, cumbersome procedures and organizational layering must be removed and/or streamlined. Combat intensity means less decision time, more room for the fog of war, and less room for plodding. Trying to balance the theater's needs in light of direct delivery, main base operations, forces yet to be deployed from the United States, resupply needs, and emergency combat requirements makes none of this easier and places a great premium on a simple, smoothly operating system. A commander of airlift forces (COMALF) with a great deal of flexibility, good communications, and broad authority over airlift forces will go far toward meeting modern needs.

For some 60 years, military and civil airlift have been linked by procurement policies and employment doctrines. Because the civil air transport can greatly aid the military mission, there was for many years a strong notion both in some military circles and in the Congress that we could encourage and rely on civil capability instead of military capability. CRAF capability is, after all, a cheap airlift force for the government and the civil carriers have been responsive to national needs. However, this study points to a change in how we think about the civil-military airlift relationship. The growth of military airlift capability in pursuit of the CMMS goals will play in this process, but that kind of growth is not new, and the command has adapted to such changes in the past. The key factor will be the direct delivery concept. As planners become more knowledgeable about how to apply that concept, we may find less dependence on civil air in the early stages of deployment than we do now. On the other hand, we may find just the opposite. The rapidness of the direct delivery method may very well put added pressures on the CRAF system to respond quickly and effectively. It is an area that requires intensive study.

Some Thoughts on the Future of Airlift Doctrine

It does not take a crystal ball to argue that airlift will continue to be a vital element in the defense of the United States. As the world becomes more complex and the military calculation more difficult, there will be an even greater reliance on airlift capabilities to make good on commitments, signal intentions, and respond rapidly and flexibly to emerging conflicts. These demands will be especially important as American interests are challenged in the less-developed nations where airlift will be the most decisive force projection capability available.

Airlift aircraft of the future will have to be rugged, reliable, and survivable, certainly more so than they are now. They will have to be prepared to operate in very austere locations with tactics and concepts well thought out ahead of time. Well-trained, versatile crews and support personnel; extremely mobile support systems; and multicapable aircraft will be the hallmark of the future airlift system. As technology makes the hardware available, airlift systems will continue to evolve. Airlift doctrine will continue to progress regardless of the technology. And that may be the single most important lesson of this study. People of vision will pursue more responsiveness, more flexibility, and better combat effectiveness with what they have in hand. As they analyze these ideas and see what better equipment would do for them, then they will articulate those needs; but first will come the ideas.

The C-17 is the next generation airlift aircraft, but it is clearly not the end of the road. There is still very much a need today to investigate follow-on aircraft for the C-130. An aircraft designed specifically for the theater airlift mission, and what that mission will be in the future, deserves full examination. Issues of cost, operational efficiencies in the sortie-intensive role, and operational capabilities in the mid- to high-threat environment call for continued research into future airlift aircraft. At some points in history, the airlift system operated with many kinds of aircraft, many of them relatively inefficient. At other points, leaders and planners sought the one great airlifter that could literally do it all. Technology may one day provide that aircraft, but it has not yet done so. It is very easy when advocating a particular aircraft to overclaim its impact. Fighting for limited defense resources very often produces that result.

Thinking about airlift means thinking about combat. It may also include thinking about diplomatic missions, channel missions, peacetime contractual management, passenger services for dependents, humanitarian missions, or special assignment airlift missions. But ultimately it means combat. Any activity that does not contribute to that philosophy, any attitude that does not reflect a preparation for the combat airlift mission, any doctrine that does not serve that end is suspect and dangerous. The mission of airlift is combat airlift—the delivery of what is needed, where it is needed, when it is needed.